BCL - 3rd ed

ECONOMIC DEVELOPMENT OF TAIWAN, 1860–1970

A Publication of the Economic Growth Center, Yale University

ECONOMIC DEVELOPMENT
OF TAIWAN, 1860–1970

SAMUEL P. S. HO

New Haven and London, Yale University Press, 1978

Designed by Sally Sullivan Harris
and set in Monophoto Times Roman type
by Asco Trade Typesetting Limited, Hong Kong.
Printed in the United States of America by
Vail-Ballou Press, Binghamton, New York.

Published in Great Britain, Europe, Africa, and
Asia (except Japan) by Yale University Press,
Ltd., London. Distributed in Latin America by
Kaiman & Polon, Inc., New York City; in
Australia and New Zealand by Book & Film
Services, Artarmon, N.S.W., Australia; and in
Japan by Harper & Row, Publishers, Tokyo Office.

Library of Congress Cataloging in Publication Data

Ho, Samuel P S
  Economic development of Taiwan, 1860–1970.

  (Publication of the Economic Growth Center, Yale
University)
  Bibliography: p.
  Includes index.
  1. Taiwan—Economic conditions. I. Title. II. Series:
Yale University. Economic Growth Center. Publications.
HC430.5.H6   330.9′51′249   77-5555
ISBN 0-300-02087-2

*To my mother
and
to the memory of my father*

Contents

Tables

Foreword

This volume is one in a series of studies supported by the Economic Growth Center, an activity of the Yale Department of Economics since 1961. The Center is a research organization with worldwide activities and interests. Its purpose is to analyze, both theoretically and empirically, the process of economic growth in the developing nations and the economic relations between the developing and the economically advanced countries. The research program emphasizes the search for regularities in the process of growth and changes in economic structure by means of intercountry and intertemporal studies. Current projects include research on technology choice and transfer, income distribution, employment and unemployment, household behavior and demographic processes, agricultural research and productivity, and international economic relations, including monetary and trade policies, as well as a number of individual country studies. The Center research staff hold professorial appointments, mainly in the Department of Economics, and accordingly have teaching as well as research responsibilities.

The Center administers, jointly with the Department of Economics, the Yale master's degree training program in International and Foreign Economic Administration for economists in foreign central banks, finance ministries, and development agencies. It presents a regular series of seminar and workshop meetings and includes among its publications both book-length studies and journal reprints by staff members, the latter circulated as Center Papers.

Hugh Patrick, Director

Preface

The record of Taiwan's economic performance in the twentieth century is an enviable one. The economy, except for the period of World War II, has grown steadily, and indeed in the past two decades it has ranked among the fastest growing economies in the developing world. The rise in per capita income has been accompanied by dramatic changes in the structure of the economy. The evidence further suggests that in the last quarter of a century income distribution has become more equal. Apparently, economic growth in Taiwan, in contrast to what has happened elsewhere in the developing world, has been unusually egalitarian. Because of this performance, there exists considerable interest among development economists and policymakers in the Taiwan experience.

The purpose of this volume is to describe and to explain the economic development of Taiwan from about the 1860s to the 1970s, with particular emphasis on the period since 1900. It is generally recognized that the pace and pattern of economic development are influenced by political and social as well as economic forces, i.e., development has both an economic and a noneconomic dimension. Therefore, a full understanding of any economy would require the examination of both the economic and the noneconomic issues. Although a number of the major noneconomic forces, e.g., the Japanese occupation of the island, are explicitly remarked and taken into account in the analysis, the focus of this volume is primarily on the economic aspect of development. Thus, this study offers only a partial picture of Taiwan's development.

Economic progress in Taiwan during the twentieth century has been attained largely through the growth of peasant agricultural production made possible by the intensive application of modern inputs. In the early part of the century most of the increased agricultural output was exported. Industrialization began gradually in the 1930s and accelerated after World War II, a process that has been facilitated by the continuing growth in agricultural productivity. An important dynamic element in Taiwan's economic development has been the government, which has played a central developmental role in the colonial period as well as during the period since independence. Government investments in material and human capital and the economic policies of the government have affected all aspects of Taiwan's economic development. In crucial periods the government also played a critical entrepreneurial role. This study concentrates on three sectors of supreme importance: peasant agriculture, manufacturing, and government. Fortunately, data are also relatively more accessible and of better quality in these areas. By focusing on these sectors, the study inevitably underplays the other aspects of the economy, in particular the commercial and financial sectors and the other services.

During the course of the preparation of a study such as this, one accumulates a long list of individuals and institutions to whom one is deeply indebted. One of the great pleasures of seeing the study published is the opportunity it provides to express publicly one's gratitude. Most of all, I am grateful to the Economic Growth Center at Yale University for affording me the opportunity to undertake this study and to the Joint Commission on Rural Reconstruction in Taiwan for providing me a base of operations during my period of field research in 1965–66.

In the past decade I approached many individuals and institutions in Taiwan for data and assistance. I am grateful to them for their courtesy and cooperation. I am especially indebted to the following: T. H. Shen, Y. C. Tsui, Y. T. Wang, T. H. Lee, I. G. Chen, Y. E. Chen, Myrna Lee, and Gary Lu of JCRR; M. H. Hsing of the Institute of Economics, Academia Sinica; T. K. Tsui and W. H. Yeh of the Council for International Economic Cooperation and Development; S. C. Pan of the Bank of Taiwan; C. E. Meng of the Central Bank of China; N. T. Lu of the Land Bank of Taiwan; C. C. Lee and C. L. Chang of the Directorate-General of Budgets, Accounts, and Statistics; and the Taiwan Provincial Library.

At one stage or another of my research I received valuable advice and suggestions from Thomas Birnberg, Raymond Goldsmith, Simon Kuznets, Ramon Myers, Hugh Patrick, Gustav Ranis, William Speidel, and Lloyd Reynolds. I am also grateful to the two anonymous referees who read the first draft of this study and made valuable comments upon it.

The main financing for travel and research was provided by the Economic Growth Center. I also received financial support from the University of British Columbia Committee on Research and the UBC–Canada Council Small Grants Committee. The final version of this study was written during 1975–76, when I was on sabbatical leave, which was in part financed by a Canada Council leave fellowship. I would like to express my appreciation to the Canada Council for its generous support.

Portions of chapters 4 and 12 appeared in the *Journal of Economic History* and *Pacific Affairs*, respectively. I am grateful to the editors of these journals for permission to use material that originally appeared in their publications.

A large share of the cost of preparing a book inevitably falls on one's spouse. I cannot begin to speak of what I owe to my wife's affection and good-natured support.

Abbreviations

AID	Agency for International Development (United States)
BOT	Bank of Taiwan
CBC	Central Bank of China
CIECD	Council for International Economic Cooperation and Development (Republic of China)
CUSA	Council on U.S. Aid (Republic of China)
DGBAS	Directorate-General of Budgets, Accounts, and Statistics (Republic of China)
ESB	Economic Stabilization Board (Republic of China)
GDP	gross domestic product
GNP	gross national product
JCRR	Sino-American Joint Commission on Rural Reconstruction
LDC	less developed country
MOEA	Ministry of Economic Affairs (Republic of China)
MOF	Ministry of Finance (Republic of China)
NT$	New Taiwan dollars
OT$/T¥	Old Taiwan dollars/Taiwan yen
PBAS	Provincial Bureau of Accounting and Statistics
PDAF	Provincial Department of Agriculture and Forestry
PDCA	Provincial Department of Civil Affairs
PDOF	Provincial Department of Finance
PDOR	Provincial Department of Reconstruction
PFB	Provincial Food Bureau
ROC	Republic of China

1

Introduction

The island of Taiwan lies astride the Tropic of Cancer, between the Malay Archipelago and Japan, and is separated from mainland China by the Taiwan Strait. Its area of 35,855 square kilometers (13,840 square miles) is slightly larger than the Netherlands or about the combined size of the states of Connecticut, Massachusetts, and Rhode Island.[1] In terms of natural resources, Taiwan is only modestly endowed. Its most important mineral resource is coal, estimated at about 700 million metric tons, but because of the narrowness and the depth of most seams, only one-third of the reserve is economically recoverable.[2]

Taiwan's most important natural resource is its agricultural land, but this too is limited in quantity as well as in quality. Only one-fourth of its total area is arable, and after centuries of continuous intensive use, the natural fertility of its farmland is low and diminishing. Taiwan, which in 1974 had a population of more than 15.8 million, has a population density of around 440 persons per square kilometer, one of the highest in the world. Taiwan's chief agricultural advantage is its subtropical climate, which extends the growing season and allows the cultivation of several crops a year. The semitropical climate also provides Taiwan with the rainfall and humidity necessary for plant growth. However, rainfall varies both seasonally and geographically;

1. DGBAS, *Statistical Abstract of the Republic of China*, 1973, p. 26.
2. Willert Rhynsburger, *Area and Resources Survey: Taiwan*, pp. 152–53. Taiwan, which lies in the same geological belt as the other important oil-producing areas in the Far East, is well endowed with all the essential requisites for the generation, accumulation, and retention of oil and gas. In recent years a small number of petroleum and natural gas reserves have been discovered, and most geologists concur in the belief that the prospect of finding additional oil and gas reserves in Taiwan or off its coast is good.

northern Taiwan suffers from occasional floods and southern Taiwan from frequent droughts.[3]

If natural resources alone determine the rate of economic growth, the possibility of rapid economic development in Taiwan is remote. Fortunately, natural resources are not the sole ingredients required for economic development. This is not to say that they are unimportant. Obviously a country with abundant natural resources, other things being equal, is better off and can develop more easily and rapidly than one which lacks them. But trade, labor, and capital can substitute for natural resources, and Taiwan, like most countries, has the minimum amount of natural resources required for economic development.

Aside from the fact that it is modestly endowed by nature, Taiwan shares a number of other common characteristics with many other less developed countries: (1) It is located in the semitropical region of the world. (2) Its economy, until very recently, was based on the production and export of a small number of primary products (in the case of Taiwan, sugar and rice). (3) For part of its history, it was a colony of a more economically advanced nation. But, as with every economy, Taiwan also has its unique features. (1) Several major migrations brought to Taiwan not only additional manpower but also skills and technology more advanced than those possessed by the indigenous population at the time. (2) Throughout most of the twentieth century, Taiwan's government participated actively in developing the economy. (3) Finally, in several crucial decades, but particularly in the 1950s, Taiwan was the recipient of sizable amounts of external aid.

Its similarities with other less developed countries and its unique features combine to make Taiwan an extremely useful and illuminating case study of economic development. Such a study is all the more interesting because Taiwan has been successful in its development efforts. Its agricultural output increased more than 7-fold in the twentieth century and its industrial output nearly 20-fold from 1952 to 1974, so that Taiwan ranks among the fastest growing economies in the developing world.

---

3. Taiwan lies in the path of the east Asia monsoon system that brings moisture from the Soviet Far East over Japan and Taiwan to points south in the winter months, and moisture from the Indian Ocean over Taiwan to points north in the summer months. In the winter, when the air current comes from the north, the on-shore wind is blocked by Taiwan's rugged mountains, and most of the precipitation occurs in the northeastern parts of the island while the southern section of the island experiences its dry season. In the summer, when the air current changes and southwest wind prevails, south Taiwan has its wet season. The mountains also intensify weather variations, causing at times excessive rainfall and prolonged dry seasons.

To appreciate current economic problems and conditions and to understand the process of economic development, it is necessary to take a long look backward. Fortunately, there exist sufficient data to provide a reasonably accurate documentation of Taiwan's economic conditions from the last quarter of the nineteenth century to the present, a period that saw Taiwan move from a traditional economy toward modern growth. The focus of this book is primarily on this transition. Because of changes in political and economic conditions, the transition period can be logically divided into two sub-periods: transition under colonialism (1895–1945) and transition toward modern growth (1946–70).

Before the twentieth century, Taiwan was a traditional peasant economy. However, this is not to say that Taiwan was stagnant or unchanging. Toward the end of the seventeenth century, Chinese peasants began to migrate to Taiwan in large numbers, providing the manpower to settle the island. In the next two centuries, population, cultivated land, and output increased slowly but steadily. The economy was traditional in the sense that it was based on traditional agriculture, was fragmented, and was not highly commercialized. In the middle of the nineteenth century, Taiwan was opened to foreign traders. However, contacts with the outside world were limited to the treaty ports. For all practical purposes, at the end of the nineteenth century Taiwan remained a closed, self-sufficient economy.

In 1895 Taiwan became a Japanese colony. Under the guidance of the colonial government, the island was developed as an agricultural appendage to Japan. Gradually, a triangular relationship connecting Taiwan's agriculture, its nonagricultural sector, and Japan developed. Taiwan's agriculture exported rice and sugar to Japan, and its nonagricultural sector imported Japanese manufactured goods to sell, along with commercial services, to agriculture. Subsequent chapters will show that, using this triangular relationship, Japan extracted substantial profits from the island colony.

From Japan's viewpoint, first of all a profitable colony required a productive economy and second the economy must remain under direct Japanese control. The job of increasing production and retaining control over the economy was the responsibility of the colonial government. Few aspects of the economy escaped its attention. Through its efforts, a traditional agriculture was made more productive and commercialized. With government encouragement and protection, a small corporate enclave was established, and it provided agriculture with industrial inputs and commercial services (e.g., finance and transportation). By the 1930s Taiwan had an economy that is best described as open and dualistic: a large peasant agriculture existing side by side with a small, modern, nonagricultural sector, both of which relied heavily on trade with Japan.

Because it was the peasant sector that was developed with government assistance, the economic dualism that emerged in the colonial period did not rigidly partition the economy into two isolated parts—a modern enclave and a traditional agricultural sector. Rather, there were considerable interactions between agriculture and the enclave. Indeed, it was largely through these interactions, often initiated by the government, that agriculture received the new inputs and advanced technology that made possible its development. That Taiwan's agriculture began its modernization in the colonial period also made the task of economic transition in the postcolonial period less difficult.

The defeat of Japan in World War II brought colonialism to an end in Taiwan. The termination of the triangular mode of operation and increased population pressure, brought about in part by the flow of mainland refugees to Taiwan, increased the urgency to industrialize. In the 1950s the government on the one hand continued to modernize agriculture and on the other hand attempted to enlarge the modern enclave through import substitution. In this manner the economic center of gravity gradually shifted from agriculture to industry. The continued development of agriculture was important because it made easier the transfer of resources—labor and savings—from agriculture to the nonagricultural sector. Besides an unusually strong agriculture, Taiwan was also able to rely on foreign aid for substantial assistance during this crucial transition period.

For a short period the import substitution approach to industrialization was successful. But, given Taiwan's limited domestic market, the easy phase of substituting domestic production for the import of consumer nondurables passed quickly. As economic growth turned sluggish, the government made the crucial decision to once again pursue a pattern of development that relied heavily on export. However, now it was the export of industrial rather than agricultural goods. Beginning in the late 1950s, the government relaxed some of the controls it had imposed on the economy to implement its import substitution strategy and introduced programs to promote export. The result was a phenomenal growth in industrial exports and outputs in the 1960s.

Industrialization is steadily altering the economy. The relative size of agriculture, measured by its share in either total outputs or in total inputs, declines each year. Manufacturing has clearly emerged as the growth sector. With industry growing rapidly, agriculture and the nonagricultural sector have become fierce competitors for resources, including labor. Finally, Taiwan's development has been financed increasingly since the late 1950s and almost exclusively since the late 1960s by its own savings. As of the mid-1970s, the evidence suggests that if transition growth continues (and there is every reason to believe that it will), Taiwan will emerge fully industrialized before the close of the twentieth century.

The outline of this study is as follows. Chapter 2 describes the traditional economy, concentrating primarily on population growth and the settlement of agricultural land before 1895. Its purpose is to provide the historical background for the more intensive study of how this traditional economy was first transformed to an open, dualistic colonial economy operated for profit by Japan and then to a growing industrial economy in the post-World War II period.

Chapters 3–6 provide an extensive discussion of Taiwan's development during the colonial period. Chapter 3 begins with an analysis of the pattern of development that was to prevail in the colonial period and a review of the colonial government's role in this development. In the case of Taiwan, the colonial pattern of development required a productive agriculture. How this was achieved is the topic of chapter 4. Chapter 5 discusses the emergence of the industrial enclave, and chapter 6 discusses whether colonial development benefited the Taiwanese.

The remaining chapters of the book are devoted to an analysis of the development process in the post-World War II period, particularly the period after 1952. Chapter 7 introduces the reader to the problems of the postwar period. It discusses the development strategies employed to transform the dualistic economy inherited from the colonial period and how foreign aid made it possible for Taiwan to achieve both economic development and a strong military capability. Chapter 8 sketches the main economic trends and structural changes experienced during 1952–72. Transition growth in the postwar period was made possible to a large extent because of the continued strength of Taiwan's agricultural sector. In chapter 9, agricultural development in the postwar period, as well as the changing problems facing agriculture, is analyzed. Chapter 10 deals with the most dramatic economic phenomenon of the postwar period—industrialization—and focuses on how government policies influenced the pace and pattern of industrial growth. Economic development cannot occur if suitable levels of savings and investment are not generated. The allocation of output between consumption and investment and the sources of savings are topics covered in chapter 11. In conclusion, lessons from Taiwan's development experience and its future economic prospects are reviewed in chapter 12.

2

The Traditional Economy

To appreciate fully how Taiwan developed since the 1890s, it is essential to know the initial conditions. The purpose of this chapter is to briefly describe the economic conditions existing at the end of the nineteenth century and to review the economic forces that helped to create these conditions.

EARLY SETTLEMENTS

At the turn of the seventeenth century, when Western merchants began to penetrate China by sea, Taiwan was a frontier territory inhabited by aborigines of presumably Malayo-Polynesian origin and by small bands of Chinese and Japanese pirates. Taiwan's early economic history is therefore a story of migration and land settlement.[1]

In an attempt to gain a foothold in the China market, the Dutch occupied Taiwan from 1624 to 1662. Under the administration of the Dutch East India Company, the island quickly became a meeting ground for Dutch, Chinese, and Japanese merchants. Raw silk, silk

1. For discussion of Taiwan's economic history in the seventeenth century, see James W. Davidson, *The Island of Formosa, Past and Present*; John E. Wills, Jr., "The Dutch Period in Taiwan History: A Preliminary Survey," presented to the Research Conference on Taiwan in Chinese History, Pacific Grove, Calif., Sept. 26–29, 1972; Fu-yuan Wu, "Taiwan Economic Chronology," *Collection of Writings on Taiwan's Economic History, No. 4* (Taipei: BOT, 1956), pp. 89–188; Takashi Nakamura, "Agriculture and Agricultural Encouragement in Taiwan During the Dutch Period," *Collection of Writings on Taiwan's Economic History, No. 1* (Taipei: BOT, 1954), pp. 54–69; Iku Okuda, Atsushi Miura, and Mao-shih Chen, "Taiwan's Agriculture During the Dutch Period," *Collection of Writings on Taiwan's Economic History, No. 1* (Taipei: BOT, 1954), pp. 38–53; Seiichi Iwao, "Sugar and Tea Trade Between Taiwan and Persia During the Dutch and the Cheng Period," *Collection of Writings on Taiwan's Economic History, No. 2* (Taipei: BOT, 1955), pp. 53–60.

7

Table 2.1. Chinese Population and Cultivated Land in Taiwan

	No. of households	No. of persons	Cultivated area (ha)
Ca. 1650	25,000[a]	100,000[a]	7,187[b]
Ca. 1680	30,000[c]	200,000[c]–350,000[a]	17,898[d]
1811	241,217[e]	2,003,861[e]	—
1887	—	3,200,000[f]	350,575[g]
1905	—	2,899,458[h]	624,501[i]

[a] Cheng-hsiang Chen, *Taiwan, An Economic and Social Geography*, pp. 46–48.
[b] Takashi Nakamura, "Agriculture and Agricultural Encouragement in Taiwan During the Dutch Period," in BOT, *Collection of Writings on Taiwan's Economic History, no. 1*, pp. 68–69.
[c] Mei Shi, *Four Hundred Years of Taiwanese History* (Tokyo: Otowa Shobo, 1962), pp. 148–49.
[d] Cheng-hsiang Chen, *Land Utilization in Taiwan*, p. 51.
[e] Hsien-wen Chou, *History of Taiwan's Economy during the Ch'ing Dynasty*, p. 65.
[f] Ping-ti Ho, *Studies on the Population of China, 1368–1953*, p. 164.
[g] Cheng-hsiang Chen, *Taiwan, An Economic and Social Geography*, p. 50.
[h] Census Bureau, *Census of 1905, Statistical Tables*, p. 8.
[i] JCRR, *Taiwan Agricultural Statistics, 1901–1955*, p. 11.

piece goods, and porcelain were imported from China and reexported to Japan and Java. European merchandise also found its way to Japan and China via Taiwan. Trade was brisk and profitable.

Because the Dutch valued Taiwan mostly for its strategic location and as an entrepôt, little attention was paid to developing the island's resources. Agriculture was primitive, but, as we shall see, it was sufficiently productive to create a small surplus, and some rice and sugar were exported. Besides farming, the other major economic activity was hunting, which supported a flourishing trade in deerskins.[2] The most significant development in the Dutch period was the start of the Chinese migration to Taiwan.[3] Quantitative evidence of the early migration is sketchy and its reliability uncertain but the little that is available provides a basis for speculation. Table 2.1 presents estimates of Taiwan's population and cultivated area from circa 1650 to 1905.

2. With the extinction of the deer population in the latter part of the seventeenth century, this colorful trade came to an end. See Takashi Nakamura, "The Production of Deerskins and Trade with Japan in the 17th Century," *Collection of Writings on Taiwan's Economic History, No. 8* (Taipei: BOT, 1959), pp. 24–42.

3. As early as A.D. 605 the Chinese knew of the existence of Taiwan, but large migration to the island is not known to have taken place until the seventeenth century (see Ta Chen, *Chinese Migration with Special Reference to Labor Conditions*, pp. 37–41).

When the Dutch arrived in Taiwan in 1624, they reported a Chinese population (largely concentrated in the vicinity of Tainan) of 25,000.[4] In the 1650s the Chinese population in the Tainan area was about 100,000.[5] Assuming that these figures are usable, the Chinese population in Taiwan quadrupled from 1624 to 1650, indicating that a substantial number of Chinese moved to Taiwan during the Dutch period. This early movement of population to Taiwan is not surprising, because at that time China was in the turmoil of a dynastic change—from the Ming to the Ch'ing—which of course provided impetus to such movements.

In the Dutch period, land was settled mainly around what is now Tainan *hsien*. In 1656 the Dutch reported 5,578 hectares of land under rice, 1,573 hectares under sugar cane, and 36 hectares under other crops. The total figure of 7,187 hectares of cultivated land is probably an underestimation since some cultivated land undoubtedly escaped the Dutch registration. Perhaps, as many as 10,000–12,000 hectares of land were cultivated. The Dutch land record is of some interest because it shows a large area of land planted with sugar cane, much more than required by the island's population. More sugar cane was produced than required by domestic needs because oceangoing vessels extended the market beyond the confines of the island. Thus, even in this early period, some specialization of production was evident.[6]

The nearly forty years of Dutch rule came to an end in 1662, when the Dutch were driven out of Taiwan by the Ming loyalist Cheng Ch'eng-kung (Koxinga) and his army of 25,000 men.[7] With Cheng came not only his army and its dependents but those who shared his

4. Davidson, *Island of Formosa*, p. 13.

5. Both the 1624 and 1650 figures probably underestimate the Chinese population in Taiwan. First of all, they include only those Chinese living under Dutch jurisdiction, i.e., the southwestern part of Taiwan. However, since most of the sizable Chinese settlements were located in this area, the exclusion of Chinese living outside Dutch jurisdiction does not make these figures unusable. There also may be some inherent defects in the information used to derive these early population estimates. We are uncertain how the early population figures were obtained but most likely they were based on the head tax the Dutch imposed on that part of the population over the age of seven. There is every reason to believe that the Chinese would try to evade this tax. Any success on their part would give the Dutch population figures an additional downward bias.

6. A substantial share of Taiwan's sugar production was exported by the Dutch to Persia: 260 metric tons (MT) in 1640, 299 MT in 1652, and 428 MT in 1661 (see Iwao, "Sugar and Tea Trade," p. 56).

7. By 1660 the struggle between the Ming dynasty and the Manchu forces had all but ended in favor of the Manchus. Cheng Ch'eng-kung and his army represented the last major force still loyal to the Ming dynasty. .

political allegiance.[8] Some were also attracted by the inducement of free land and the exemption of land tax for three years.[9] We have no record of the influx, but when Cheng's administration ended in 1683, the Chinese population in Taiwan was estimated at between 200,000 and 350,000. Most of the immigrants probably came to Taiwan either with Cheng in 1661 or immediately after his arrival, because in later years the Manchus ordered the withdrawal of all inhabitants along large stretches of the south China coast toward the interior and emigration to Taiwan was prohibited.

To be self-sufficient in food, Cheng turned his soldiers into farmers, issued orders that work in the fields was obligatory, and encouraged experienced farmers to settle in Taiwan. With the increase in population and the active encouragement to farm, land settlement during Cheng's administration extended from Tainan southward to include the present municipality of Kaohsiung and northward to the present hsien of Yunlin. Total cultivated land registered in 1684, the year after Cheng surrendered to the Manchus, was 17,898 hectares of which 7,307 hectares were paddy fields and 10,591 hectares were dry fields. Again, because of the tendency of farmers to underreport for tax purposes, these figures are probably biased downward. If we assume that 20,000 hectares of land were cultivated in 1684, cultivated area approximately doubled since 1650 or increased by about the same percentage as population.

TAIWAN'S ECONOMY IN THE CH'ING DYNASTY

Population and Land Settlement

After the capitulation of the Ming loyalists to the Manchu (Ch'ing) dynasty in 1683, Taiwan became a prefecture (*fu*) of Fukien Province. In the next two centuries the traditional agricultural mode of production that existed in mainland China was gradually reproduced in Taiwan as thousands and thousands of Chinese migrated, sometimes illegally, to the island.[10] The arrival of these settlers provided Taiwan

8. Yung-ho Ts'ao, "Settlement of Taiwan During the Cheng Period," *Collection of Writings on Taiwan's Economic History, No. 1* (Taipei: BOT, 1954), p. 76.

9. Davidson, *Island of Formosa*, pp. 50–51. Also see T'ing-i Kuo, *A Summary Account of the History of Taiwan* (Taipei: Cheng Chung, 1954), pp. 56–58.

10. Unrest and revolt in Taiwan would sometimes force the Manchus to prohibit migration from mainland China to Taiwan. Until 1760 immigrants were not allowed to bring their families. On occasion they were given permission to send for their families once they became settled. For examples, see Fu-yuan Wu, "Taiwan Economic Chronology," entries under 1684, 1732, 1740, 1745, 1747, and 1760.

with the additional manpower needed to exploit its natural resources.

From the memorials of an official of the Manchu government we learn that Chinese immigrants were either seasonal workers from Kwangtung or permanent settlers from the southern coast of Fukien.[11] It seems that the people from Kwangtung at first came to Taiwan not to settle but to work the land seasonally. Each year they arrived in Taiwan in the spring and, after selling their autumn crops, returned to their families in Kwangtung for the winter. By the nineteenth century, however, most of the Kwangtung immigrants had discontinued their annual trip back to the mainland and had become permanent settlers. In 1811, when each household was required by the *pao-chia* system[12] to register its members, a Chinese population of 2,003,861 was recorded.[13]

In 1887, in response to the French threat to Taiwan, the Manchu government altered its indifferent attitude toward the island and elevated it from a prefecture to a province. Liu Ming-ch'uan, an energetic and experienced official, was appointed its governor. Immigration, instead of being prohibited or passively allowed, was actively encouraged. From 1884 to 1891 the government subsidized immigrants' travel expenses across the Taiwan Strait.[14] A population count in 1887 recorded 3,200,000 Chinese in Taiwan. The first Japanese census conducted in 1905 found a population (excluding Japanese and aborigines) of 2,899,458. According to Davidson, an American correspondent in Taiwan when it was ceded to Japan in 1895, 200,000 or 300,000 Chinese fled Taiwan to escape the disorder that came after the cessation.[15] When this outflow is taken into account, the 1887 population figure becomes more acceptable. The 1905 census also revealed that of the 2,890,485 Chinese who identified themselves as

11. Ping-ti Ho, *Studies on the Population of China, 1368–1953*, p. 164.
12. The *pao-chia* system is a mutual responsibility scheme for holding both the village and the family responsible for the conduct of their members.
13. Ramon Myers rejects the 1811 pao-chia figure because "the regional population distribution as compared to that of 1750 seems most unrealistic," and replaces it with his estimate of between 500,000 and 750,000 (cf. his "Taiwan Under Ch'ing Imperial Rule, 1687–1895: The Traditional Economy," *Journal of The Institute of Chinese Studies of The Chinese University of Hong Kong* 2 [Dec. 1972]: 375). However, he does not tell us why he thinks the earlier population figure and the earlier regional population distribution are more realistic or why regional distribution could not have changed between 1750 and 1811, a period that may have witnessed significant population movements. In any case, even if one doubts the reliability of the 1811 figure, to reduce it from over 2 million to 500,000–750,000 seems too drastic.
14. Ho, *Population of China*, p. 164.
15. Davidson, *Island of Formosa*, p. 561.

"islanders," 2,492,784 came from Fukien, 397,195 from Kwangtung, and only 506 from other parts of mainland China.[16]

The western plains and foothills of Taiwan were settled largely in the eighteenth and nineteenth centuries. As the immigrants came from the mainland, they drove the aborigines from the plains in the south and from the foothills in the north, until the aborigines were isolated in the central mountain range and the rugged east coast. It is difficult to trace quantitatively the process by which land was brought into cultivation because extensive underregistration of land throughout the whole period made the Ch'ing land record unreliable. By not registering their land, many households evaded the land tax.[17] The extent of underregistration became evident only after Liu Ming-ch'uan conducted the 1885 cadastral survey, which uncovered sufficient unregistered land to more than triple the revenue from land tax. However, the 1885 survey was only partially completed so its findings still underestimated the extent of cultivated area during the Ch'ing period. When the Japanese completed their cadastral survey in 1904, they found 625,299 hectares under cultivation, a figure that nearly doubles the 1885 survey figure of 350,575 hectares. If the reasonable assumption is made that 500,000 hectares of land were cultivated in 1890, then over 450,000 hectares of land were brought into cultivation during the two centuries of Ch'ing imperial rule.

Land was settled during the Ch'ing dynasty under several arrangements, which in later years determined the tenure system.[18] Some plots of land were cleared by individual farmers who held the land in private ownership and some were rented from pacified aborigines and cleared by individual settlers who then became the tenants. However, most were settled under the sponsorship of wealthy Chinese or that of the government. Land settlement required labor, capital, and protection from the unfriendly aborigines. The immigrants were able to provide labor, but for capital and protection they had to turn to the wealthy Chinese and the government for help and sponsorship. In return for

16. *Census of 1905, Statistical Tables*, p. 336.
17. Before the tax rate was reduced in 1729, Taiwan was reported to have had a more burdensome land tax than the mainland. This undoubtedly also encouraged settlers to evade the land tax by not registering land. Cf., Hsien-wen Chou, *History of Taiwan's Economy during the Ch'ing Dynasty*, p. 97.
18. The following discussion of land settlement is based on Santaro Okamatsu, *Provisional Report on Investigation of Laws and Customs in the Island of Formosa* (English ed.), (Kobe: Provisional Commission for Research on Customs in Formosa, 1902), pp. 26–75, and Chou, *History of Taiwan's Economy*, pp. 19–25.

the sponsor's capital (tools, draft animals, weapons) and protection (which sometimes meant costly punitive expeditions against the aborigines), the reclaimed land became the property of the sponsor, but the settlers had the perpetual right to work the land at a fixed rent.

Regardless of the details of the initial arrangement, the sponsor of land settlement was called *ta-tsu hu* and the settlers who cleared the land were called *hsiao-tsu hu*. As more immigrants arrived from the mainland, the hsiao-tsu hu leased a part or all of their holdings to the newcomers and also became landlords. In this fashion a three-level tenancy system evolved: the cultivators (the subtenants), the hsiao-tsu hu (the tenant-landlords), and the ta-tsu hu (the great landlords). This complex system remained until it was revised by the Japanese in 1904.

Trade

The paucity of solid economic data makes it necessary to examine Taiwan's economy primarily through its external trade sector, where some data are available. Little is known of the volume or trend of Taiwan's external trade prior to the middle of the nineteenth century. We do know, nevertheless, that until the last half of the nineteenth century, Taiwan's external trade was solely in the hands of Chinese merchants, operating largely from Amoy. The legal exclusion of foreign merchants from Taiwan ended in 1858, when the Treaty of Tientsin designated Anping as a treaty port. In 1860 the Treaty of Peking opened Tamsui as a treaty port, and three years later Keelung was added as a supplementary port to Tamsui and Takao (present day Kaohsiung) as a supplementary port to Anping. With the opening of these ports to foreign ships, much of the Taiwan trade was taken over by British and American merchants. However, the junk trade, which continued at a reduced volume, remained exclusively in Chinese hands.

Shortly after Taiwan was opened to foreign merchants, the Chinese Imperial Maritime Customs was established in Taiwan, and its records provide the most detailed information about nineteenth-century Taiwan.[19] The custom data presented below show the sum of exports or imports of the two custom districts in Taiwan, Tamsui–Keelung in the north and Anping–Takao in the south. These figures essentially represent the island's total external trade carried by clippers and

---

19. For a number of reasons that are elaborated in the Statistical Appendix, the customs data must be used with care. However, despite its many defects, the custom record still provides the most accurate and detailed information about Taiwan's trade and economy in the nineteenth century.

Table 2.2. Value of Major Export Commodities as a Percentage of Value of Total
Export, 1868–94 (Annual averages)

	1868–70	1871–75	1876–80	1881–85	1886–90	1891–96
Camphor	8.4	3.3	2.3	0.8	0.9	9.1
Coal	2.0	2.2	1.7	1.4	1.6	1.1
Brown sugar	51.1	57.3	41.4	31.9	24.1	22.6
White sugar	8.5	3.4	5.5	4.5	2.8	3.0
Tea	9.4	26.6	46.1	58.7	66.6	58.4
Rice	9.8	2.3	0.1	[a]	[a]	0.2
Miscellaneous	10.8	4.8	2.8	2.7	3.8	5.6
Total export	100.0	100.0	100.0	100.0	100.0	100.0

Source: Based on Chinese Imperial Maritime Customs, *Annual Trade Tables for
Various Chinese Ports (Taiwan)*, various issues.
[a] Less than 0.05%.

steamers. Intra-island trade is not completely excluded but is kept
to a minimum by two factors. First, the *likin*[20] on exports kept intra-
island trade to a minimum. Second, the small amount of intra-island
trade that did exist was most probably carried by junks (which are
excluded from the customs data).

The custom data show that Taiwan's export volume, in index form
with 1881 as 100, increased from 26 in 1868 to 133 in 1880 and thereafter
leveled off.[21] As the net barter terms of trade showed only a slight
increase after the 1870s, the income terms of trade, i.e., the real quantity
of imports that could be purchased from the proceeds of Taiwan's
exports, essentially followed the movement of real export. Indeed,
except for the early 1880s during the Sino–French conflict, Taiwan's
import volume followed closely its export volume.

A breakdown of Taiwan's exports (table 2.2) reveals the chief export
items to be sugar and tea. Rice was likely also an important export
item, but after the early 1870s rice was transported primarily by junks
and was therefore not included in the customs data. The facts that in
1868–70 rice export averaged over 100,000 piculs (5,968 metric tons)
a year and that by value it was nearly 10 percent of total exports testify
to its importance. These three export commodities accounted for

20. A relatively small tax on merchants and traders. It was levied either as a transit
tax on goods as they passed *likin* stations or as a sales tax. For a detailed discussion of the
likin see Edwin G. Beal, *The Origin of Likin* (Cambridge: Harvard University Press,
1958).
21. This and the following figures in this paragraph are taken from table A58.

Table 2.3. Value of Major Import Commodities as a Percentage of Value of Total Import, 1868–94 (Annual averages)

	1868–70	1871–75	1876–80	1881–85	1886–90	1891–94
Opium	72.6	74.3	65.2	54.1	49.2	43.5
Cotton goods	10.5	10.1	9.7	10.7	8.4	8.3
Woolen goods	5.7	4.2	5.0	4.2	3.5	3.2
Rice	0.1	0.7	0.5	2.2	0.7	3.9
Bag, hemp, and straw	0.4	0.3	0.6	0.8	0.4	0.4
Tobacco	1.0	0.8	1.0	0.8	0.2	0.4
Metal	0.8	1.4	2.3	2.6	1.8	2.8
Miscellaneous	8.9	8.3	16.6	24.1	35.6	38.6
Total	100.0	100.0	100.0	100.0	100.0	100.0

Source: Based on Chinese Imperial Maritime Customs, *Annual Trade Tables for Various Chinese Ports (Taiwan)*, various issues.

80–90 percent of Taiwan's export. Of these three commodities, rice and sugar were traditional crops and tea the newcomer.

Turning to Taiwan's import (table 2.3), we find its composition in the last half of the nineteenth century to be that of a typical under-developed economy. Almost exclusively, Taiwan imported consumer goods. Opium was the single largest import by value, accounting for 45–75 percent of total imports. When opium smoking was put under strict government control in 1901, smokers numbered 152,044, or over 5 percent of the Taiwanese population.[22] Cotton and woolen goods together accounted for another 12 to 16 percent of total imports. With no manufacturing industry, imports of raw materials were negligible. Small quantities of lead, which was used as lining for tea boxes, accounted for most of the metal imports. Other metal imports went to supply a small government-operated munition factory in Taipei. Finally, imports became increasingly diversified as consumers in Taiwan, perhaps reflecting the increased prosperity brought about by the expanding foreign trade, demanded a wider variety of goods. This is particularly noticeable after 1875. Miscellaneous imports as a share of total imports increased from 8.3 percent in 1871–75 to 24.1 percent in 1881–85, and 38.6 percent in 1891–94.

Nearly all Taiwan's imports and between 70 and 90 percent of its exports were transported to or came from Hong Kong and other

22. *Special Population Census of Formosa, 1905*, p. 108.

Chinese ports.[23] The inclusion of the junk trade would make these percentages even higher. As indicators of the final destination of Taiwan's exports or the origins of its imports, however, these figures are misleading. The lack of suitable port facilities made it impossible for large ocean vessels to dock in Taiwan, so it was necessary for Taiwan to ship its exports and receive its imports at the larger mainland ports. Of the major imports, opium came from the Middle East and India, and the textile goods from Great Britain and later also Japan. Of the major exports, sugar went to north China and Japan, and tea went to America, Europe, and Southeast Asia.

These trade figures suggest that after Taiwan opened its ports to foreign merchants, the volume of trade increased impressively for a decade, from about 1870 to about 1880. Thereafter the rate of growth declined considerably, so that total trade leveled off at a volume about twice that of a decade before. The total volume of trade in the early 1870s was around 2 million custom taels; by the early 1880s it had increased to about 4 million custom taels.[24] From the trend and the composition of Taiwan's external trade in the nineteenth century we can tentatively conclude that (1) the island's general level of economic development was relatively low and (2) the economy was incapable at that time of responding in a sustained manner to the stimulus of external trade. For verifications of these conclusions, as well as to gain some clues as to why the economy failed to respond more positively to the opening of trade, we now turn to a brief discussion of the early development of three of Taiwan's leading produces: rice, sugar, and tea.

Production

Because the art of farming was brought to Taiwan by Chinese immigrants, Taiwanese agriculture in the nineteenth century shared many common characteristics with agriculture in south China. Although the Chinese agricultural techniques were traditional, their introduction to and adoption by Taiwan in the eighteenth and nineteenth centuries were nevertheless a major development in Taiwan's economic history. Each group of immigrants brought to Taiwan new varieties of rice and sugar cane seeds. By the end of the nineteenth

23. Chinese Imperial Maritime Customs, *Annual Trade Tables for Various Chinese Ports* (*Taiwan*), any issue.

24. The custom (*haikwan*) tael is a fictitious currency used by the customs as a unit of account. It was designated to equal 584 grains of silver of 992.3 fineness.

century, nearly 1,700 varieties of rice seeds, most of them early ripening, were planted in Taiwan. Unfortunately, seed selection to eliminate low-yielding varieties was not widely practiced. Some organic fertilizers were applied to the land by most peasants, and in a limited fashion, irrigation facilities were constructed by wealthy landlords or on a cooperative basis. The traditional Chinese approach to agriculture, however, did not stimulate technological change, and productivity increased only slowly in the Ch'ing period.[25] By the end of the nineteenth century, 1 hectare of land yielded perhaps no more than 1.2 metric tons of brown rice.[26] Most probably the increase in agricultural output in the eighteenth and nineteenth centuries had as its primary sources the increase in land and labor inputs. Very limited data on rice production or its export exist before the twentieth century. However, the scanty evidence that is available suggests that Taiwan enjoyed a small surplus of rice during at least some parts of the Ch'ing period.[27] Evidently, the Chinese immigrant farmers, using only the traditional techniques, were able not only to support themselves on the newly settled land but also to generate a small surplus for export.

Sugar, as an export item, was more significant than rice. It is common knowledge that in the Ch'ing period Taiwan supplied north China

25. Recently Ramon Myers estimated that during the Ch'ing period grain yield may have doubled or quadrupled (cf. Myers, "Traditional Economy," pp. 373–75). Undoubtedly yield did increase but I doubt that it increased by so much as Myers's estimates suggest. Using the identity yield (kg/ha) =

$$\frac{\text{per capital grain output (kg/person)} \times \text{population (persons)}}{\text{cultivated area (ha)}},$$

and assuming that per capita grain output is constant, Myers estimated yield directly from population and land statistics. However, estimates of cultivated area and population for Taiwan during the Ch'ing period contain considerable margins of error. He also made arbitrary adjustments to the population figures that are questionable, e.g., the lowering of the 1811 population by more than one-half, from more than 2 million to between 500,000 and 750,000. Consequently, I find it difficult to accept his yield estimates. Given Myers's assumptions, a doubling or quadrupling of yield implies a doubling or quadrupling of population per cultivated area. Given the availability of unsettled land in Taiwan during the Ch'ing period, this is not likely to have occurred. Even in the first half of the twentieth century, unsettled land was still available so that population per cultivated area declined only after 1920, and then very slowly.

26. In 1901–05 the average annual yield of rice in Taiwan was 1.3 MT/ha.

27. Between 1723 and 1744, Taiwan exported an average of 3,733 tons of rice per decade. From 1746 to 1827, Taiwan conducted what was called the *tai-yun*, the supply of rice to military garrisons in Fukien. For more details see Shih-ching Wang, "Taiwan's Rice Production and Export During the Ch'ing Period," *Taiwan Wen-hsien* 4 (March 1958): 27–31, and Chou, *History of Taiwan's Economy*, pp. 35–36.

with sugar and that substantial quantities were also exported to Japan. Again the lack of statistics makes quantitative verification difficult. For the latter part of the nineteenth century, however, export data and some production estimates do exist (table 2.4). Judging by the level of sugar production at the turn of the twentieth century and by the export data, these production estimates seem reasonable.

Except for a possible increase in production in the late 1860s, production and export of sugar remained remarkably stable, with production fluctuating between 40,000 and 50,000 metric tons (MT). The apparent increase in production in the 1860s, as suggested by the rise in export, was probably statistical. The reader is reminded that foreign vessels were not legally allowed in Taiwan until 1858 and the Imperial Customs did not cover all Taiwanese treaty ports until 1864. Conceivably, therefore, the early increase in export was the result of better coverage by the customs and a once-and-for-all shift in the type of carrier used, from junks to steamers. In all probability, Taiwan, before 1870, was already producing 30,000–40,000 MT of sugar annually.

The stability shown by sugar production and sugar export in the last half of the nineteenth century indicates a relatively stagnant industry.[28] Certainly the writings of contemporary observers support this assertion and also provide the reason for the stagnation. According to eyewitness reports of production techniques during the 1880s, both the cultivating method and the crushing processes were primitive. One observer described cane cultivation as follows:

> Through negligence in cultivation, the cane here dwindles to a very small size, the joints only averaging from 1 to 1/2 inches in circumferences, and little or no attention seems to be devoted to the plant beyond putting it in the ground. Even for irrigation, which during the periods of small rainfall or drought, will be of material advantage, no means whatever are provided. Plantings are made from cuttings about one in three years. These are first soaked in water for about 20 days, until the buds begin to sprout. They are then placed obliquely in the ground, more or less in line, with one end protruding, the furrow for their reception being scrapped with the hands. A little manure is placed over them, but beyond this,

28. For an interesting description of how the sugar industry was organized, see Myers, "Traditional Economy," pp. 388–92.

Table 2.4. Production and Export of Sugar, 1865–99 (MT)

	I Production[a]	II Export[b] (excludes junk trade)	III I − II[c]
1856	—	9,652[d]	—
1865	—	8,801	—
1866	—	13,577	—
1867	—	15,307	—
1868	—	16,619	—
1869	—	16,293	—
1870	44,608	36,043	8,565
1871	43,796	35,222	8,573
1872	46,801	37,935	8,866
1873	39,238	30,614	8,623
1874	49,909	41,401	8,508
1875	38,129	29,494	8,635
1876	61,503	53,121	8,382
1877	45,410	36,683	8,727
1878	33,641	24,956	8,684
1879	54,286	46,172	8,114
1880	72,460	64,197	8,263
1881	54,004	45,542	8,462
1882	45,563	37,008	8,555
1883	55,248	46,798	8,450
1884	66,673	58,346	8,326
1885	42,312	33,722	8,590
1886	32,236	23,537	8,699
1887	42,044	33,451	8,593
1888	48,083	39,555	8,527
1889	42,978	34,395	8,583
1890	52,111	43,628	8,484
1891	42,969	34,386	8,583
1892	44,826	36,262	8,563
1893	39,429	30,807	8,621
1894	52,851	44,375	8,476
1895	—	42,735	—
1896	—	43,504	—
1897	—	39,013	—
1898	—	40,223	—
1899	—	31,089	—

[a] Production estimates are from Hsien-wen Chou, *History of Taiwan's Economy during the Ch'ing Dynasty*, p. 41.
[b] Export figures are from Chinese Imperial Maritime Customs, *Annual Trade Tables for Various Chinese Ports (Taiwan)*, various issues.
[c] Because of rounding, these figures may not be the exact difference between columns I and II. They represent the sugar consumed in Taiwan and sugar exported by junks.
[d] Only the exports to north China.

with perhaps an exceptional and occasional weeding by some of the more careful growers, nothing further is done.[29]

The crushing of cane was done by stone rollers in primitive mills, of which 1,400 existed in the late nineteenth century. Even when foreign merchants demonstrated that more juice could be extracted from one passage of cane through an iron roller than three passages through a stone roller, the native merchants and money lenders who controlled the sugar crushing business were not interested in adopting the new machine. The Chinese were apparently afraid that innovation would "interfere with the arrangements which they said were, as far as they were concerned, sufficiently remunerative to themselves."[30] Thus large amounts of sugar were burned as bagasse. The sugar industry remained in this primitive state until the Japanese modernized it with new production techniques and mechanization in the early decades of the twentieth century.

The sugar industry forfeited its leading export position to tea in the 1870s, and indeed for much of the last half of the nineteenth century the level of activity in the tea industry determined the general economic prosperity of the island. Certainly the trade data indicate this. From an obscure position in the 1860s, tea rose to become the leading Taiwanese export in the 1870s and 1880s, accounting for 50–60 percent of total exports by value. During the same period, sugar's share of total export fell from nearly 60 percent in the early 1870s to slightly over 20 percent in the early 1890s. The trend of total export—rapid increase from the 1860s to the 1880s and leveling off after the 1880s—was largely determined by tea.

Unlike sugar and rice, the tea industry developed as a direct consequence of the opening of trade with the West.[31] Tea was of course grown in Taiwan before the arrival of foreign merchants in the 1860s, but the leaves were of inferior quality and were used only as a blend with higher quality tea from the mainland. In 1866 John Dodd, a British trader, by importing plant slips from Fukien and providing

29. From a report written by Dr. W. W. Myers and published as an appendix to United Kingdom, Foreign Office, *Diplomatic and Consular Reports on Trade and Finance, China: Report for the Year 1890 on the Trade of Taiwan* (present day Tainan) (London, 1891), p. 16 (hereafter *Reports* with appropriate port and year).

30. Ibid., p. 18. Also see *Reports*, Taiwan (present day Tainan), 1888, p. 3.

31. The following paragraphs on tea production are based primarily on materials presented in Davidson, *Island of Formosa*, chap. 23, pp. 371–96, and *Reports*, Tamsui, 1887, 1889, and 1890.

working capital to the farmers, was successful in producing oolong tea in Taiwan that was acceptable on the world market. In 1867, skilled workmen were imported from Fukien to fire the tea in Taiwan, a process that had always been done in Amoy. An added innovation took place in 1881, when a Chinese merchant introduced the method of manufacturing pouchong tea (a type of scented tea much favored among overseas Chinese in Southeast Asia) to Taiwan.

The demand for Taiwan's oolong tea in the United States spurred export of tea from 82 MT in 1866 to 8,188 MT in 1888 (table 2.5). The increased production was made possible largely through an increase in land allocated to tea cultivation. The tea trade was initially handled by foreign establishments, but the profits soon attracted many Chinese merchants into the business and the market structure became quite complex.[32] The preference of the Chinese merchants and growers for quick profit and their lack of interest in quality control led to careless picking, selecting, and packing, which resulted in a rapid deterioration of the Taiwan tea. The fraudulent practice of adulterating high quality tea with poor leaves from the mainland became widespread. As its reputation declined, Taiwan's export position became precarious. Attempts to rectify the situation met with little success. The Amoy Chamber of Commerce issued regulations to control the malpractices but with no effect. Later in 1889, Liu Ming-ch'uan, the governor of Taiwan, procured an experienced planter from India to establish a model tea farm to show the farmers the advantages of proper cultivation and manufacture of tea. Unfortunately, the expert found little support or interest among the local tea growers and left in 1890.

While the Taiwan tea industry was floundering, Ceylon, Japan, and India were carefully fostering their tea industry, and soon Taiwan found itself unable to compete in the world market. Export of tea, after its initial rapid growth, leveled off in the 1880s to around 18 to 20 million pounds a year, while the output of tea in Ceylon increased from 1 million pounds in 1880–84 to 419 million pounds in 1895–99.[33] The refusal of the growers to recognize the importance of quality control and the general apathy of peasants toward the adoption of new techniques combined to stunt the growth of the Taiwan tea industry at infancy, and a good opportunity to develop the island was lost.

32. For a description of how the tea trade was organized, see Myers, "Traditional Economy," p. 395.

33. Donald Snodgrass, *Ceylon: An Export Economy in Transition* (Homewood, Ill.: Irwin, 1966), p. 35.

Table 2.5. Tea Export, 1866–98 (MT)

	Export of oolong tea to U.S.	Export of oolong tea to Europe	Total export of all tea
1866	—	—	82
1867	—	—	123
1868	—	—	240
1869	—	—	331
1870	—	—	637
1871	—	—	899
1872	922	34	1,180
1873	572	26	944
1874	1,278	129	1,514
1875	2,221	182	2,514
1876	2,942	500	3,562
1877	3,494	276	4,185
1878	3,697	584	4,854
1879	4,437	479	5,142
1880	4,936	289	5,471
1881	5,433	279	5,830
1882	4,720	341	5,461
1883	5,112	462	5,990
1884	5,342	329	5,966
1885	6,636	422	7,422
1886	6,258	417	7,334
1887	6,587	544	7,627
1888	6,785	430	8,188
1889	6,594	457	7,884
1890	6,446	442	7,759
1891	6,816	338	8,189
1892	6,899	333	8,268
1893	8,381	338	9,936
1894	7,596	342	9,313
1895	7,217	356	8,869
1896	8,766	259	9,739
1897	7,562	311	9,305
1898	7,375	312	9,312

Note and Sources: The export figures of oolong tea to the U.S. and to Europe are from the Amoy Chamber of Commerce returns and are published in James W. Davidson, *The Island of Formosa*, p. 395. The total export figures are those reported by the Chinese Imperial Maritime Customs except for the last three years, which are from the Japanese Customs Reports.

We conclude this chapter by noting what is perhaps already obvious, i.e., in the more than 200 years it governed Taiwan, the Manchu (Ch'ing) government, consistent with its behavior in other parts of China, showed little interest in developing or modernizing Taiwan. The only significant attempt by the government to promote economic development came toward the end of the nineteenth century, when a handful of enlightened officials in China recognized the need to modernize their own regions of authority. Such an official was Liu Ming-ch'uan, who governed Taiwan for a short period before it became a Japanese colony. The seven years of Liu's administration (1884–91)[34] represented the first and only serious effort by a Ch'ing official to modernize the island and to provide it with the bare minimum of infrastructure needed for economic development.

The energetic new governor stirred up a storm of activity.[35] Numerous ambitious economic projects were initiated, of which the most outstanding were the construction of a north–south railroad, the laying of a cable line from Taiwan to Fukien, the dredging of Keelung and Kaohsiung harbors, a cadastral survey of the island, the establishment of a shipping company, and the revival of the coal industry. For all his efforts, results were meager. In seven years of construction only the Taipei–Hsinchu section, a total of 107 kilometers, of the north–south trunk line was completed. Telegraph lines were installed connecting Taipei and Tainan, Tamsui and Foochow in Fukien province, and Anping and Penghu. The dredging of Keelung harbor was initiated in 1889 but was only partially completed. The cadastral survey was never completed. His attempts to establish a shipping company and to revive the coal industry ended in failure. It is ironic that all Liu's projects were eventually concluded successfully by the Japanese. The lack of political and financial support from Peking was probably the main reason for Liu's failure, but a contributory reason was the attitude of the local population, who after centuries of neglect not only did not respond to Liu's efforts but at times viewed them with apathy and hostility.

What emerges from the evidence presented in this chapter is that, within a traditional context and by traditional Chinese standards, Taiwan experienced a significant degree of economic change in the eighteenth and nineteenth centuries. In this period, population grew

34. From 1884 to 1887, Liu, then the governor of Fukien, administered Taiwan as a prefecture of Fukien.
35. Samuel C. Chu, "Liu Ming-ch'uan and the Modernization of Taiwan," pp. 37–53.

steadily and a substantial part of the island was brought under cultivation. But, lacking an overland transport system, Taiwan did not become a well-integrated economy but existed as a collection of relatively isolated communities whose social and economic structure reflected their ancestral villages in Fukien and Kwangtung.[36] Although aggregate production increased, there is little evidence that per capita income rose significantly. The economy, consisting primarily of an agricultural sector, was operated by Chinese immigrants, mostly on a traditional basis, using techniques brought from the mainland. However, because of the more favorable land/labor ratio in Taiwan, the traditional system was able not only to support an expanding population but also to produce a small surplus. Through the ports of Takao–Anping in the south and Keelung–Tamsui in the north, Taiwan exported its surplus sugar, rice, and tea and imported opium and other consumer goods. The opening of these ports in the second half of the nineteenth century to foreign traders provided Taiwan with several opportunities to accelerate its development, but the inertia of a traditional economy was great and these opportunities went largely unanswered. As the nineteenth century came to a close, Taiwan, although in possession of a sophisticated traditional society,[37] was still economically backward, and its modernization would require basic institutional and structural modifications.

36. One reflection of this isolation is the wide disparity in commodity prices within the island (cf. Myers, "Traditional Economy," p. 401).

37. For a general description of social and economic institutions in Taiwan during the Ch'ing period, see Ramon H. Myers, "Taiwan Under Ch'ing Imperial Rule, 1684–1895: The Traditional Order," *Journal of the Institute of Chinese Studies of The Chinese University of Hong Kong* 4 (Dec. 1971): 495–520, and his "Taiwan Under Ch'ing Imperial Rule, 1685–1895: The Traditional Society."

3

Economic Development under Colonialism

A dispute over Korea in 1894 precipitated the first Sino–Japanese war, which ended in the defeat of Imperial China. In the negotiations that ensued at Shimonoseki, one of the concessions made by the Ch'ing government was the cession of Taiwan to Japan. For the next fifty years Taiwan was a Japanese colony and had imposed on it a pattern of growth that relied heavily on the export of primary products to Japan. Operating within this colonial framework, Taiwan achieved a rate of growth that was impressive for a traditional economy in the early stages of transition. This chapter provides an overview of how the economy operated in the colonial period. First, I review Taiwan's overall growth record. I then describe the pattern of development or the mode of operation that was imposed on Taiwan. Finally, I argue that the agent most responsible for Taiwan's pace and pattern of development in the colonial period was the colonial government.

ECONOMIC TRENDS AND MODE OF OPERATION

Colonization brought to Taiwan a number of profound changes that were to have far-reaching economic consequences. They may be summarized as follows: The transition from a neglected Chinese province to a Japanese colony in effect turned Taiwan from an essentially closed to an open economy, and economic development was a consequence of this opening-up process. Once a part of the larger and more dynamic Japanese economy, Taiwan found its market considerably broadened. Subsequent chapters will show that colonization also brought to Taiwan a substantial inflow of material and human capital. When combined with the indigenous resources (labor and land) the productive capacity of the island was markedly enhanced. Equally

25

essential was the influx of advanced technology, which, when properly adapted to local conditions, greatly increased productivity. But most important, the colonial government, with vastly different objectives and preferences than the Imperial Chinese government, was involved actively in developing the island. It was the agent, the entrepreneur, that mobilized the resources and made development possible.

These altered demand and supply conditions were to produce in Taiwan, a few years after its cession to Japan, economic changes and growth that continued steadily until World War II. Table 3.1 summarizes Taiwan's economic performance during the colonial period in the form of selected economic indicators.[1] It clearly shows that under colonialism Taiwan experienced a period of steady if not spectacular growth. From 1903 to 1940, total product in constant prices increased by roughly 45 percent per decade. However, growth was not constant: it was more rapid from the late 1910s to the early 1930s than in the other periods. Output growth was accompanied by a dramatic rise in population, caused primarily by a rapidly declining death rate. Between 1906 and 1943 the death rate was cut by nearly one-half, from 31.3 to 17.6 deaths per 1,000. In the same period, the birth rate remained steady at around 40 births per 1,000. In consequence, between 1905 and 1940, population grew approximately 26 percent per decade, from about 3.04 million to 5.87 million. Therefore, the decadal growth rate of per capita output was approximately 19 percent. The available evidence suggests that this performance far surpassed that achieved by mainland China in the pre-World War II period. In the more growth-oriented post-World War II period, Taiwan's performance in the colonial period seems less unique. But even today, many less developed countries have not been able to sustain a growth rate comparable to

1. Since the growth indicators are based on data of varying quality, they are not equally reliable. In particular, because many of the statistics needed to estimate total product were not gathered during the colonial period, the two estimates of total product presented in table 3.1 must be considered as quite crude. However, they are probably usable for detecting long-term trends. Despite some discrepancies, they suggest growth rates that are reasonably consistent with each other and with that of the less aggregated but probably more reliable production and trade indexes. Furthermore, the differences in the growth rate of agriculture and that of the total product implies a change in the economic structure that seems reasonable for an economy at an early stage of development. Toward the end of the colonial period, the share of agriculture in total product was about 40 percent. If the total product and agricultural production increased at the rate suggested by the data in table 3.1, then three decades earlier in 1910 the share of the agricultural sector was about 50 percent, a proportion that is consistent with what we know about early colonial Taiwan.

Table 3.1. Selected Indicators of Economic Development during the Colonial Period

	Population (millions)	Net domestic product in 1937 prices (1937 = 100)	GNE in 1934–36 prices (1937 = 100)	Index of agricultural production (1935–37 = 100)	Industrial production		Public RR freight distance (million MT·km)	Export volume index (1925 = 100)	Import volume index (1925 = 100)
					General index (1937 = 100)	Sugar production (1000 MT)			
1905	3.04	a	30	39	a	50	26	21	31
1910	3.29	37[b]	43	42	24[c]	204	88	39	49
1915	3.48	36	45	48	30	208	143	49	54
1920	3.66	40	71	48	30	223	220	44	68
1925	3.99	62	74	68	51	480	386	100	100
1930	4.59	79	90	79	70	810	507	122	136
1935	5.21	102	112	98	88	965	639	180	179
1940	5.87	93	99[d]	93	123	1,133	904	196	172

Note and Sources: The net domestic product estimates are by T. H. Lee and the gross national expenditure estimates are by T. Mizoguchi (cf. tables A1 and A2). The index of agricultural production is a revision and extension of work originally done by JCRR (see table A33). The index of industrial production is constructed by the author (see table A49). The sugar production figures are for sugar years and are from the Taiwan Government-General, *Taiwan Sugar Statistics*, various issues. The freight distance data are from PBAS, *Taiwan Province: Statistical Summary of the Past 51 Years*, p. 1166. The import and export volume indexes are constructed by the author (see table A59). Except for 1910, the population figures are from the census (see table A10). The 1910 figure is from the household registration record. ª Not available. ᵇ 1911. ᶜ 1912. ᵈ 1938.

that achieved by colonial Taiwan. Quite clearly, the rate of growth achieved by Taiwan during the colonial period was significant and represented a break from its past development pattern.

It is useful to think of Taiwan's colonial economy as composed of two sectors: agriculture and nonagriculture. Their relative sizes, in terms of their shares of total employment, were approximately agriculture 70 percent and nonagriculture 30 percent. In other words, agriculture was by far the most important employer and producer in the economy, and its importance diminished only slightly during the colonial period. As later chapters shall discuss in greater detail, the most significant and pervasive changes in the colonial period occurred in agriculture. Indeed, it was the development of agriculture that was most responsible for colonial Taiwan's economic growth. Agriculture grew initially at around 2–2.5 percent a year, and, after 1920, at an annual compound rate of 3.8 percent, exceeding by a significant margin Taiwan's rate of population growth. This steady increase in agricultural production generated impressive and growing amounts of marketable surplus, enabling Taiwan's agriculture to become a valuable source of savings.

Taiwan's industry, except for food processing, experienced fewer changes than did agriculture and remained relatively underdeveloped. Largely reflecting the modernization of the sugar industry, industrial production increased by about 6 percent a year between 1912 and 1940. However, growth was more rapid before than after 1930. In the 1930s, as the sugar industry matured and its rate of expansion declined, the growth of industrial production also declined substantially despite a quickened tempo in Japanese efforts to industrialize Taiwan. Because Taiwan's industrial base in the early decades of the twentieth century was extremely small, the 6 percent annual growth rate in industrial production over nearly three decades did not dramatically alter the relative importance of industry in Taiwan.[2]

To support agricultural growth, a number of modern services were developed. To facilitate the commercialization of agriculture, an inexpensive and efficient transport system was developed both within Taiwan and between it and Japan. Railroad and harbor construction was accelerated with enthusiasm almost immediately after the Japanese assumed control. By 1908 the two most important harbors—Keelung in the north and Kaohsiung in the south—were connected by rail.

2. Early industrialization is discussed in greater detail in chap. 5.

Modern banking and financial institutions were established to service production as well as the growing volume of internal and external trade. Whereas not a single modern financial institution existed at the end of the nineteenth century, there were five modern banks with more than 50 branch offices serving Taiwan in the late 1920s.[3] Supporting these in the countryside were about 300–400 credit cooperatives.

The colonial strategy was to develop Taiwan to complement Japan; thus the emphasis was placed on the economic integration of the two regions. Put simply, Taiwan was to become an agricultural appendage of Japan, to help it feed its growing industrial population. In terms of resource flows, this meant a relatively simple relationship between the two domestic sectors and between Taiwan and Japan. The agricultural sector produced and exported its sugar and rice to Japan. Japan, in turn, exported manufactured (consumer and capital) goods to Taiwan's nonagricultural sector. To complete the flow, the agricultural sector purchased industrial goods and commercial services from the nonagricultural sector. The economic objective of this triangular mode of operation was for Japan to extract from Taiwan what Paauw and Fei have termed an "export surplus," defined by them as "the surplus from exports over and above imports required to maintain the existing level of production."[4] This surplus was in part reinvested to increase Taiwan's productive capacity and in part transferred to Japan.

Taiwan's triangular mode of operation as well as its success in generating an "export surplus" is evident from its trade statistics. In the decade before colonization, less than 1 percent of Taiwan's imports came from, and about 10 percent of its exports went to, Japan. Chapter 4. will show that soon after colonization, the growth of agricultural production accelerated, the consequence of capital investment and the introduction of more advanced technology. Increased agricultural productivity, of course, made it possible for Taiwan to meet Japan's growing demand for agricultural products, and Taiwan's export rose dramatically. Between 1900 and 1939 Taiwan's export volume increased more than 18-fold, and by the late 1920s Japan was already absorbing 80–90 percent of this growing trade.[5] Imports increased less rapidly, but a preponderant share of them also came from Japan: 68

3. PBAS, *Taiwan Province: Statistical Summary of the Past 51 Years*, p. 1067.
4. Douglas S. Paauw and John C. H. Fei, *The Transition in Open Dualistic Economies*, p. 5.
5. Tables A59 and A64.

Table 3.2. Composition of Exports and Imports, 1900–39 (Annual averages as
         percentage of total)

	1900–09	*1910–19*	*1920–29*	*1930–39*[a]
Total export	100.0	100.0	100.0	100.0
Food	76.2	77.3	82.9	84.5
Rice	23.2	14.5	19.1	25.9
Sugar	27.8	50.6	50.6	46.8
Other	25.2	12.2	13.2	11.8
Other primary Products	21.1	11.5	9.6	8.6
Mfg. and misc. products	2.6	11.2	7.4	6.8
Total import	100.0	100.0	100.0	100.0
Food and other primary products	29.2	38.2	41.5	34.1
Mfg. and misc. goods	70.8	61.8	58.4	65.9

Source: Taiwan Government-General, *The Annual Taiwan Trade Statistics,* various
issues.
[a] 1937 and 1938 are excluded because trade data for these years are imcomplete.

percent in the 1910s and 1920s and over 80 percent in the 1930s. Nearly
all Taiwan's industrial imports were supplied by Japan.[6]

Table 3.2, which presents Taiwan's trade composition by commodities, shows how the triangular relationship with Japan operated. Nearly
all Taiwan's exports were primary products. Of them, food was the
most important, rising steadily from less than 70 percent of total
export in 1900 (table A63) to over 80 percent after the 1920s. Aside
from food, Taiwan supplied Japan with a limited amount of raw
materials: camphor, camphor oil, coal, and alcohol. Up to 70 percent
of Taiwan's imports were industrial in origin; much of the volume
was consumer goods, and nearly all of it was supplied by Japan. Cotton
textile was imported to clothe the local population, and fertilizer was
imported to meet the production needs of agriculture. Machinery and
transport equipment were also imported, the former to equip the food-
processing industry and the latter to develop a transport system to
carry the agricultural and agricultural processed goods to market. The
large import of food, which for a food surplus country may be baffling,
was also to accommodate the needs of the Japanese. Special foods and
beverages were imported from Japan to satisfy the demand of the

6. Table A65.

several hundred thousands of Japanese living in Taiwan, and some rice was imported from Southeast Asia so that a greater quantity of Taiwanese rice, a variety that the Japanese found more palatable than rice grown outside the empire, could be exported to Japan.

The strength of the economic bond between Taiwan and Japan and the significance of one to the other are best seen by examining Taiwan's two major export items, rice and sugar. By value, these two commodities accounted for 50–70 percent of Taiwan's total exports. In every year, over 90 percent of Taiwan's sugar output was exported, and in the 1930s about half of Taiwan's rice output was also exported. Nearly all Taiwan's rice and sugar exports went to Japan. Before World War II, rice and sugar comprised approximately 15 percent of Japan's total imports, and Taiwan's contribution to this was substantial. It was Japan's major supplier of sugar; in the 1930s it provided nearly 75 percent of the sugar consumed in Japan.[7] Because Taiwan was densely populated and because rice was its staple food, it was in a less favorable position to supply rice to Japan on a large scale. Yet it did remarkably well. Even before the sharp rise in agricultural productivity in the 1920s, approximately 20 percent of Taiwan's rice harvest was exported each year to Japan. Thereafter, as rice production per capita increased in Taiwan, more and more rice was exported. By the 1930s, approximately, 45 percent of Taiwan's annual rice harvest was exported to Japan, accounting for over 30 percent of Japan's import requirements.

Taiwan was an economic asset to Japan not only because it was a source of food and raw materials, but equally important, because Japan was able to obtain Taiwan's primary products without exchanging an equivalent value of manufacturing goods. Except for the first decade of its occupation, Taiwan exported substantially more than it imported.[8] From 1916 to 1944 Taiwan's export surplus (here defined in the conventional manner) as a share of its export averaged 26 percent. Because Taiwan's trade was mostly with Japan, the export surplus

7. William W. Lockwood, *The Economic Development of Japan*, p. 536.
8. The presence of a large export surplus should not be taken as evidence that colonization was the most profitable course Japan could have adopted. To evaluate the profitability of colonization, it is necessary to consider the opportunity costs of the Japanese capital, labor, and technical and entrepreneurial talents sent to develop Taiwan as well as the costs of any economic dislocation within Japan caused by colonization. One example of this latter type of costs is the higher sugar price paid by Japanese consumers as a result of Japan's colonial policy. The question of whether colonization was profitable is, of course, a much different and a more difficult problem than the one being discussed here.

was essentially to Japan's advantage. The very large and persistent export surplus was made possible because in Taiwan the income distribution decision was largely in Japanese hands. The real wage in Taiwan was kept low, so total consumption as well as imports of consumer goods also remained low. Profit, on the other hand, was high. Part of the profit was reinvested in Taiwan, but much of it was transferred to Japan.

THE AGENT OF GROWTH

Taiwan's creditable economic performance and its success as a colony were to a great extent the achievements of the colonial government. It is not an exaggeration to say that economic growth in the colonial period was initiated and sustained through government efforts. Besides maintaining stability and order, intermediate goods so vital to development, the colonial government also introduced and carried through crucial economic programs designed to promote development. Through its fiscal instruments and preferential treatment of Japanese investors, the government also influenced income distribution and ensured that the "export surplus" generated by the economy remained in Japanese control. Because of its importance and prevailing influence on the economy, the colonial government's role in the development of Taiwan requires closer scrutiny.[9]

The colonial government had two principal economic objectives: (1) to promote the production and export of sugar and rice and (2) to keep economic power in Japanese hands. They were basic objectives because the government was committed to develop Taiwan's economy to complement that of Japan and to make colonization "profitable," i.e., to generate a growing "export surplus." In other words, the government was committed to make the triangular mode of operation work and be profitable for Japan. Much of what the colonial government did in Taiwan can be explained in terms of these objectives.

Development

The colonial government participated actively in the development of Taiwan from the beginning of its administration. The extent of its involvement is indicated by the fact that, after 1920, government

9. For a more thorough discussion of the colonial government's activities, see my "The Development Policy of the Japanese Colonial Government in Taiwan, 1895–1945," in Gustav Ranis, ed., *Government and Economic Development*, pp. 287–328.

exhaustive expenditures absorbed 11–16 percent of Taiwan's total product.[10] Total government expenditures as a share of total product were 12–18 percent. For a less developed country, these impressive statistics suggest that the colonial government was an active force in Taiwan's economy from the beginning of the twentieth century and that its level of direct participation remained high throughout the colonial period.[11]

Subsequent chapters shall analyze in greater detail the economic consequences of the government's actions in the area of economic development. For now, we use the government expenditure data to sketch the broad outline of its economic program. The Taiwan Government-General's expenditures by functional distribution for selected years are presented in table 3.3.[12] They show that its development expenditures and fixed investments consistently absorbed over 40 percent of its total expenditures, much of which was used to promote, directly or indirectly, the production and export of agricultural commodities.

One area that received considerable attention was human resources. Government activities in health and education had far-reaching effects. The average life span of Taiwanese increased significantly, and the literacy rate among Taiwanese rose from 1 percent in 1905 to 12 percent in 1930 and 27 percent in 1940.[13] These improvements undoubted-

10. Our attempts to separate the exhaustive from the nonexhaustive expenditures were not entirely successful. We did, however, identify the major nonexhaustive expenditures (interest payments, pension payments, and transfer payments to the private sector on capital account), and when these are excluded from total government expenditures, the residual is a crude but acceptable measure of exhaustive expenditures. The ratios of government expenditures to total output used in this paragraph were obtained by dividing our estimate of government exhaustive expenditures by T. H. Lee's estimates of total product.

11. These expenditure figures give only a partial view of the government's impact on the economy. For one thing, the current expenditures of government enterprises and government monopolies, which in the 1930s fluctuated between 50 and 90 million yen, are excluded from government expenditures. Government monopolies and enterprises dominated not only the modern transport sector but also the production and distribution of important consumer goods such as tobacco and alcoholic beverages. The government also influenced the economy through semiofficial institutions such as the Bank of Taiwan, the Farmers' Association, and the Irrigation Association. Because of both its economic size and autocratic nature, the colonial government was the paramount force in the economy.

12. The Taiwan Government-General was the highest level of government in colonial Taiwan. It had the broadest tax base, the largest budget, and was by far the most important decision-maker in Taiwan.

13. These are census figures. Literacy is the ability to read and/or write Japanese.

Table 3.3. Functional Distribution of Total Expenditures of the Government-General, Selected Years (Percentage of total)

	1900	1905	1910	1915	1920	1925	1930	1935	1939
Total expenditures (million yen)	14.8	10.7	26.6	21.2	51.5	41.8	63.4	65.1	116.5
Percentage distribution:	100.0	100.0	100.0	100.0	100.0	100.0	100.0	100.0	100.0
Current expenditures	47.6	75.7	73.9	81.5	64.9	74.5	65.7	74.4	72.5
General	27.9	43.0	32.5	33.2	38.7	43.3	32.8	32.3	38.8
Development	17.0	17.8	23.5	19.9	16.1	17.9	20.3	18.7	20.1
Transfer payments	0.7	0.9	0.4	a	a	a	a	11.8	4.7
Interest on public debt	2.0	14.0	16.8	23.7	5.4	9.5	8.8	9.2	4.3
Unallocable expenditure	a	a	0.7	4.7	4.7	3.8	3.8	2.4	4.6
Capital expenditures	52.4	24.3	26.1	18.5	35.1	25.5	34.3	25.6	27.5
Fixed capital formation	52.4	25.2	26.5	19.4	34.1	20.5	26.9	24.4	24.4
Transfer to capital account of domestic sectors	—	—	—	—	—	—	6.0	—	4.0
Direct loans and advances	—	—	—	—	2.9	5.9	2.3	2.4	—
Purchase less sales of property	a	-0.9	-0.4	-0.9	-1.9	-0.9	-0.9	-1.2	-0.9

Notes and Sources: These figures were obtained after reclassifying and reorganizing the expenditures of the Taiwan Government-General. The reclassification used as its primary source the Government-General's Final Account of Receipts and Expenditures, which appears annually in Taiwan Government-General, *Taiwan Government-General Statistics Book*. The annual figures for 1898–1939 as well as information giving the basis for the reclassification can be obtained from the Economic Growth Center, Yale University, on request.
a Less than 0.05%.

ly had a positive effect on the population's productivity and its ability to acquire new skills. Thus they indirectly facilitated agricultural development.

Agricultural development and export were also given direct stimulation. Realizing that the successful development and commercialization of agriculture required as a minimum the existence of an inexpensive mode of transportation, the government worked steadily to expand and maintain the island's network of roads and railways. In budgeting its expenditures, the government consistently gave high priority to transport and communication, allocating from 40 to 60 percent of its developmental expenditures and fixed investment to this sector.[14] When it was ceded to Japan, Taiwan had almost no roads or railways. In 1920, it had 637 km of public railways and 3,553 km of roads and in 1940, 907 and 12,076 km, respectively.[15]

The buildup of capital around the periphery of agriculture can only stimulate its growth indirectly. For dramatic results, actions directed at agriculture itself are needed, and here the colonial government was also the main catalytic agent. The available evidence indicates that the government devoted large amounts of its energy and money to transform agriculture. At least one-third of the government's development expenditures, or 10 percent of its total current expenditures, was spent on promoting agriculture through research, extension, and subsidies.[16]

The Government-General was also the island's foremost investor in the colonial period. On the average it allocated to capital formation an amount equivalent to 40 percent of its total current expenditures, or about 20 percent of the exhaustive expenditures of all levels of government. Table 3.4, which presents the Government-General's annual investments in fixed capital distributed by use, shows that the largest share went to transport and communication, which over the years consistently received about 60 percent of the total. Next in importance was its direct investment in agriculture.

In a rice economy such as Taiwan's, water control facilities are the capital stock most required in the production process. Only when this is realized can one fully appreciate the strategic value of public investments in agriculture. Besides its direct investments, the amounts of which are indicated in table 3.4, the government also provided grants

14. Ho, "Development Policy of the Japanese Colonial Government," pp. 313–15.
15. *Taiwan Province: Statistical Summary*, p. 1147.
16. Ho, "Development Policy of the Japanese Colonial Government," table 9.6.

Table 3.4. Fixed Capital Formation of the Government-General Distributed by Use
(Annual averages as percentage of total)

	1898– 1904	1905– 1909	1910– 1914	1915– 1919	1920– 1924	1925– 1929	1930– 1934	1935– 1939
Total (million yen)	4.5	5.2	8.9	8.2	15.9	14.1	15.0	22.0
Percentage distribution:	100	100	100	100	100	100	100	100
A. Agriculture	*4.4*	*11.8*	*15.5*	*16.9*	*15.1*	*12.0*	*25.3*	*19.5*
1. Irrigation	4.4	11.8	8.9	7.2	6.9	1.4	2.7	a
2. Flood control	—	—	4.4	9.6	8.2	10.6	22.6	19.1
3. Other	a	a	2.2	a	—	a	—	0.4
B. Transport and communication	*71.1*	*62.7*	*47.8*	*55.4*	*67.9*	*68.1*	*60.0*	*65.9*
1. Harbor	11.1	17.6	20.0	13.2	15.7	21.3	22.0	20.5
2. Rail	55.6	41.2	18.8	27.7	40.3	29.8	20.7	24.1
3. Road	a	—	2.2	7.2	8.8	10.6	11.3	9.5
4. Other	4.4	3.9	6.7	7.2	3.1	6.4	6.0	11.8
C. Other	*24.5*	*25.5*	*36.7*	*27.7*	*17.0*	*19.9*	*14.7*	*14.6*

Source: See table 3.3.
[a] Less than 0.05%.

and loans to finance the construction of irrigation projects that had its approval but were not under its direct supervision. These forms of aid became particularly important after 1920, when the Irrigation Association, a semiofficial organization, was established throughout the island.

From 1906 to 1942 the total area under irrigation increased from 200,000 to 545,000 hectares, and irrigated land as a percentage of cultivated land increased from 32 to 64 percent.[17] For these years, the combined sum of direct government investments in irrigation and government grants for irrigation construction as a share of total investment in irrigation is presented in table 3.5. It is evident that until 1920 the government directly financed out of its budget practically all irrigation investments. After 1920, through the Irrigation Association, the government was able to supplement its expenditures by mobilizing and channeling a part of rural savings to investment in irrigation facilities. Even during this latter period, however, the government still directly financed between 30 and 50 percent of the total investment in irrigation. For the period 1900–44, 47 percent of the cost of irrigation construction was paid directly by the government

17. *Taiwan Province: Statistical Summary*, p. 594.

Table 3.5. Total Investment in Irrigation Facilities over Five-Year Periods (Million yen)

	Government[a]	%	Irrigation association	%	Total	%
1900–04	0.3	100	—	—	0.3	100
1905–09	2.9	94	0.2	6	3.1	100
1910–14	2.9	100	—	—	2.9	100
1915–19	3.0	79	0.8	21	3.8	100
1920–24	12.9	48	14.0	52	26.9	100
1925–29	16.1	29	39.4	71	55.5	100
1930–34	6.5	36	11.7	64	18.2	100
1935–39	—	—	6.4	100	6.4	100
1940–44	32.7	69	14.9	31	47.6	100
Total						
1900–44	77.3	47	87.4	53	164.7	100

Sources: For the sources of the data on government investment, see table 3.3. The figures on investments of the irrigation associations are taken from BOT, *On The Problems of Taiwan's Irrigation* (Taipei: BOT, 1950), p. 95.
[a]Includes the direct investment in and the grants for irrigation construction provided by the Government-General.

and the rest by the Irrigation Association.[18] Between 1926 and 1930 the Irrigation Association also borrowed 18.7 million yen from the government for irrigation construction. Because World War II interrupted the repayment of these loans, they essentially became government grants. When these loans are included with the other government investments in irrigation, the government met 58.2 percent of the total cost of irrigation development in the colonial period.

Control

Besides promoting agricultural production and export, the colonial government's other prime concern was to keep economic power in Taiwan under Japanese control. In every possible way, either openly or covertly, the government encouraged the concentration of economic power in the corporate sector and tried to ensure that this sector was owned and controlled by Japanese.

The sugar companies that dominated Taiwan's corporate sector

18. For the ten major irrigation projects completed during the colonial period (supplying water to 177,297 hectares of land), the Government-General provided nearly 60 percent of the total construction costs of 65 million yen (see Shigeto Kawano, *A Study of Taiwan's Rice Economy*, p. 40).

were favorites of the government. In 1905, by government decree, the sugar-producing areas in Taiwan were divided into supply regions, with each region assigned to a refinery. In other words this government regulation made the sugar companies monopsonists. Then in 1909 the government encouraged the formation of a sugar cartel, later known as the Taiwan Sugar Association, which was given the power to regulate, with government guidance, such matters as the level of price and export. The government supported this arrangement by restricting the expansion of existing factories and the construction of new refineries. With these privileges, the monopolistic structure of the industry was guaranteed. The cartel arrangement suited both the sugar companies and the government. The sugar companies were able to maximize their profit jointly, and the government, by allowing the cartel to exist, was in a strong position to influence and control the industry. At times, even such internal financial decisions as the magnitude of dividend payments could not be made without government approval.[19] In effect, through the monopolistic industrial structure it helped to create, the government was able to influence the size of the "export surplus" and the savings ratio.

The emergence of an indigenous industrial class was never encouraged; in fact, government policy was to discourage the emergence of such a class. Until 1924 Taiwanese were not allowed to organize or operate corporations unless there was Japanese participation.[20] Even after this restrictive rule against Taiwanese participation was rescinded, Taiwanese were reluctant to seek entry to the modern corporate sector because of its domination by Japanese capitalists. Thus the modern sector remained a monopoly of the Japanese capitalists. Through its power to regulate and license and by granting exclusive privileges to Japanese capitalists, the government successfully kept economic power from the Taiwanese.

The government fiscal system was also used to generate and control the "export surplus." To finance its development programs, the government reorganized the fiscal system inherited from Imperial China and made it a productive source of revenues. From 1898 to 1939, over 95 percent of the Government-General's fixed investment was financed

---

19. U.S. Office of Naval Operations, *Civil Affairs Handbook, Taiwan (Formosa)— Economic Supplement*, OPNAV 50E–13 (Washington, D.C., 1944).

20. Han-yu Chang, "Evolution of Taiwan's Economy During the Period of Japanese Rule," *Collection of Writings on Taiwan's Economic History, No. 2* (Taipei: BOT, 1955), p. 96.

from its current revenues.[21] The tax structure was such that a preponderant share of the burden fell on the Taiwanese consumer and
the rural sector. Indirect taxes (including monopoly profits) and land
taxes accounted for 70–80 percent of the government's current receipts. Even though the corporate sector, because of its ability to pay
taxes and the ease of enforcing tax compliance, was one of the most
obvious sources of government revenue, it was never effectively tapped.
Except in 1918–21 and the late 1930s, when temporary taxes on excess
profits were collected, the burden of the direct taxes on the corporate
sector was insignificant. Although excise taxes were levied on goods
and services produced by the modern corporate sector, it is doubtful
that with its monopolistic power the corporate sector would have
allowed these taxes to be shifted backward. Consequently, a reasonable
assumption is that they were shifted forward to the consumer. Thus
the tax burden shouldered by the Japanese-owned corporate sector in
comparison to its ability to pay was indeed light. This meant that the
corporate sector was able to capture and retain in the form of profits
the bulk of the "export surplus" generated in Taiwan.

To summarize, in the colonial period the economy of Taiwan was
developed to satisfy Japan's economic needs. A triangular mode of
operation relying heavily upon primary product exports was imposed
on the island. By and large, Taiwan was a successful and profitable
colony. Its economy expanded and a growing "export surplus" was
generated. The agent most responsible for Taiwan's development was
the colonial government. Using resources mobilized by its fiscal instruments, it invested in the social and economic infrastructure needed
for economic development. To keep the surplus generated by the expanding economy in Japanese control, it gave Japanese capitalists
preferential treatment and discouraged the emergence of a Taiwanese
entrepreneur class. By allowing economic power in Taiwan to become
concentrated in the hands of a limited number of Japanese capitalists
who were also deeply involved in the government, the colonial government was able to increase its ability to direct the island's economic
development as well as its influence over such key economic variables
as the savings ratio.

In terms of its mode of operation and in terms of the objectives and
actions of the colonial government, Taiwan's colonial experience is
generally similar to that of many other colonies. However, there is one

21. Ho, "Development Policy of the Japanese Colonial Government," table 9.2.

significant difference. A common consequence of economic development under colonialism, traceable to the triangular mode of operation adopted by most colonial economies, is the partitioning of the economy into two insulated parts: a modern, export-oriented enclave and a large backward agricultural sector. This sharp dualism makes postcolonial development difficult. What set the Taiwan experience apart from that of most other colonies is that its economy was not so strictly compartmentalized. The main reason for the difference was that the export commodities (sugar and rice) promoted by Taiwan's colonial government were cultivated by the traditional peasant sector. Furthermore, as chapter 4 will show, the modernization of rice and sugar production was done without the introduction of a plantation system. Consequently, during the colonial period the peasant sector was increasingly brought into contact with the rest of the economy. Indeed, as we shall see, there was a significant degree of sectoral interaction between agriculture and nonagriculture. Because postcolonial Taiwan inherited a more integrated economy, it had a considerable head start, in comparison to the other ex-colonies, in its efforts to industrialize.

4

The Making of Modern Agriculture

When Japan acquired Taiwan, its agriculture was traditional. Although some tea and sugar were exported, the volume traded, as reported earlier, was small, and both tea and sugar production had become stagnant. To support themselves and their families, the bulk of the Taiwanese farmers grew rice and sweet potatoes. Because the basic requirement for the triangular mode of operation and for the generation of an "export surplus" was a productive agriculture, one of the first tasks the colonial government set out to achieve was the modernization of agriculture.

The transformation of traditional agriculture poses numerous complex and difficult problems for the government. For one thing, unlike other areas where the government can act by itself or in conjunction with only a handful of private entrepreneurs, in agriculture it is necessary for the government to obtain the cooperation of hundreds of thousands of individual farm households. The main purpose of this chapter is to study how this difficult transformation was effected. First, I show that Taiwan's agricultural structure in the colonial period was more or less a continuation of the traditional structure. Next, the production records achieved during the colonial period are established, and the quantifiable inputs to agriculture are identified and measured. The sources of agricultural growth are then determined, and the relationships between technology and rural institutions are discussed within the context of Taiwan's agricultural development. Finally, I provide some estimates of the surplus generated by Taiwan's agriculture in the colonial period.

RURAL FRAMEWORK

Colonization did not dramatically disturb Taiwan's rural organization. The unit of cultivation remained the small family farm. In 1922, the first year for which we have consistent official statistics, there were 385,277 farm households in Taiwan. By 1940 the number had increased to almost 430,000. In the colonial period, because unsettled arable land still existed, agriculture was able to expand in part through the clearing of marginal land. In fact, from 1910 to 1940 cultivated land per farm household (average size of farm) remained remarkably stable at around 1.97 hectares (4.87 acres) per farm household.[1] Evidently, land was brought into cultivation at approximately the same rate as new farm families were formed. These farms are small by most non-Asian standards, but they are larger than the farms in Japan and in most parts of China.[2]

Government surveys in 1920, 1932, and 1939 provide information on the distribution of agricultural households by farm size.[3] When the biases in the 1920 survey are taken into account, these surveys indicate that the distribution of agricultural households by the area of land cultivated remained more or less unchanged from 1920 to 1939: approximately 25 percent of the farms had less than 0.5 chia (1.2 acres) of land; 20 percent between 0.5 and 1 chia of land; 39 percent between 1 and 3 chia of land, and 16 percent more than 3 chia of land.[4] The distribution also does not seem to vary very much by regions.

The aforementioned surveys also contain information on the distribution of cultivated land among owners.[5] From these it is readily apparent that although many Taiwanese owned land, most were small holders. Land was unequally distributed. According to the 1920 survey, the lower 42.7 percent of the owners held 5.7 percent of the land while the upper 11.5 percent of the owners held 62.1 percent of the land. But because the 1920 survey considers the landlord's agent to be the landowner if the landlord resides in an enumerating district other than where the land is located, the 1920 figures probably understate the

1. Based on figures in JCRR, *Taiwan Agricultural Statistics, 1901–1955*, pp. 7, 8, and 11.
   2. In the 1930s, the average size of farm (cultivated land per farm household) was 2.69 acres in Japan and 2.47 acres in the double-crop rice region of China.
   3. Table A37.
   4. For a discussion of the shortcomings of these surveys see the note attached to table A36.
   5. Table A36.

inequality of landownership. The 1932 and 1939 surveys are more carefully tabulated, but unfortunately they contain less information, giving only the number of holders by size of holding.[6] The results of these later surveys, however, display similar characteristics, i.e., a large number of families were landowners, but each held small parcels of land. In 1939, 64 percent of the landowners held less than 1 chia of land, and only 655 landowners possessed more than 50 chia (120 acres) of land.

Although many Taiwanese peasants owned their land, it would be a mistake to think of colonial Taiwan as a land of peasant proprietors. According to figures collected by the colonial government, in 1910 33.7 percent of the agricultural population were owner-cultivators, 42.8 percent were tenants, and 23.5 percent were part-owners and part-tenants.[7] By 1941, the respective percentages were 30.4, 37.4, and 32.2. Thus, during the course of the colonial period the number of part-owners increased relatively more than owners and tenants. It would, therefore, appear that some holders were forced to sell part of their land while other more successful ones purchased or rented additional land. Considering those who owned at least a portion of the land they cultivated, between 1910 and 1941 there was a slight relative increase of this category, from 57.2 to 62.6. Owner, part-owner, and tenant do not of course represent a descending order of economic status. In particular the category part-owner is very elastic, including both poor and well-to-do peasants.

Information on the amount of land cultivated by owner-cultivators and by tenants is available from government surveys in 1920–21, 1927, 1930, 1932, and 1939.[8] The coverages of these surveys are not exactly similar, but they are sufficiently close to permit a few cautious statements. First, from 1920 to 1940 land cultivated by tenants as a percentage of total cultivated area remained fairly stable at around 57 percent. Second, until the extensive irrigation projects sponsored by the colonial government began to take effect in the 1930s, a substantially higher percentage of the land cultivated by tenants was paddy land. In 1927, for instance, paddy land accounted for 58 percent of the land

---

6. There is some evidence that, between 1900 and the 1930s, land ownership became more concentrated. See Edgar Wickberg, "The Effect of Japanese Policies on Land Tenure in Taiwan," paper presented to the Twentieth Annual Meeting of the Association for Asian Studies, Philadelphia, March 23, 1968, mimeo.

7. PBAS, *Taiwan Province: Statistical Summary of the Past 51 Years*, pp. 513–14.

8. Table A40.

cultivated by tenants but only 38 percent of the land cultivated by
owner-cultivators; in 1932 the figures are 63 percent for tenants and
36 percent for owner-cultivators, and in 1939 the figures are 68 and
56 percent. Because paddy land embodies substantially more investments than dry fields, this suggests that given the traditional rural
framework landlords were better able to mobilize the resources needed
to improve their land through irrigation.

The major alteration introduced by the Japanese to the traditional
tenure arrangement was to change the three-level tenancy (composed
of ta-tsu-hu, hsiao-tsu-hu, and subtenants) system to a two-level
tenancy (composed of hsiao-tsu-hu and subtenants) system. When the
cadastral survey was completed in 1904, the government introduced
reforms to clear up existing landownership claims so that the new
land tax introduced that year could be properly enforced. As part of
this reform, in 1905 the government bought out the ta-tsu-hu and
made the hsiao-tsu-hu the legal owners of the land and directly responsible for the land tax.[9] The removal of the ta-tsu-hu, however,
was not a change as radical as it may seem, for by the end of the nineteenth century the ta-tsu-hu's power over the land had already diminished considerably.[10]

The changes in the land tenure arrangement and the new land tax
helped to alter the framework within which the Taiwanese peasants
labored. The elimination of the ta-tsu-hu transferred income streams
from those who were neither involved nor interested in agriculture to
those who had a direct stake in agriculture and were therefore more
likely to use the resources productively. With the clarification of
property rights and a more efficient government, the land tax, for the
first time in Taiwan's history, was collected effectively and regularly.
The value of the land was reassessed and of the ten grades of paddy
land used to classify land by the Japanese, seven yielded a tax payment
that was higher than any category of land tax collected during the
Manchu period.[11] The pressure of meeting these tax payments and

9. Under this new arrangement, the subtenant usually paid a share rent to the *hsiao-tsu-hu* that ranged from 40 to 60 percent of the harvest, depending upon the location and quality of land. One government survey suggests the share rent paid in Taiwan to be about 8–10 percent of the land value (see Taiwan Government-General, *The Economics of Renting Farm Land, a Survey, Report of Basic Agricultural Survey no. 39*, 1939).

10. A detailed discussion of the tenancy system at the beginning of the twentieth century is given in Santaro Okamatsu, *Provisional Report on Investigation of Laws and Customs in the Island of Formosa*, pp. 26–75.

11. Wickberg, "Effect of Japanese Policies."

the knowledge that the tax would not be arbitrarily determined each year must have encouraged landowners to produce more and to use their land more productively.

Furthermore, with the ownership question clarified so that "land-owners were guaranteed rights of property security, transfer, and inheritance,"[12] the way was cleared for landowners to make larger and more permanent investments, to lease land more freely, and to exchange land. The 1905 "land reform" did not, however, make any attempt to transfer land to the tillers, consolidate landholdings, or alter the relationship between the hsiao-tsu-hu (now the landlords) and the sub-tenants (now the tenants). Perhaps the colonial government saw no reason or need for a more radical change. More probably, it was aware that any attempt to radically alter the existing tenure arrangement might prove disruptive and thus defeat its objective to increased production.

PRODUCTION AND SOURCES OF GROWTH

Output

Table 4.1 presents the pattern of agricultural growth in the colonial period and the overall picture is clear.[13] Until the onset of World War II, agricultural production increased steadily, with only occasional setbacks caused by unfavorable weather. Between 1901–05 and 1936–40, agricultural production (total output produced on farms) grew at a compound rate of 3.4 percent per annum. If we discount the growth between 1901 and 1906 as partly statistical, the increase in agriculture production is still impressive: from 1906 to 1940, it grew at a compound rate of 3.2 percent a year. When agricultural production is disaggregated and the growth patterns of the various crop groups are examined, the patterns are found to be quite dissimilar. Major food crops, which are dominated by rice and sweet potatoes, showed the slowest growth.[14] This is hardly surprising in view of the fact that rice and sweet potato productions were already at relatively high levels in 1910, making dramatic increases thereafter difficult, particularly when unsettled land

12. Ramon Myers and Adrienne Ching, "Agricultural Development in Taiwan under Japanese Colonial Rule," p. 562.
13. The data used in analyzing output growth are official government statistics. Generally speaking, after 1906, they are reasonably reliable. For an evaluation of these statistics, see the Statistical Appendix.
14. Barley, wheat, sorghum, millet, barnyard millet, Indian corn, and buckwheat are the other crops in this group.

Table 4.1. Fitted Growth Rates of Agricultural Production, Various Periods

	All crops, meat, and dairy products	All crops	Food crops				Fiber crops	Other crops	Meat and dairy products
			Total	Major food	Minor food	Industrial food			
1906–40	3.22	3.20	3.19	2.72	5.50	4.54	3.39	2.17	3.34
1910–19	2.85	2.81	2.72	1.54	3.41	7.22	3.22	1.23	3.80
1920–29	5.12	5.19	5.19	4.23	9.61	7.50	4.92	3.37	3.40
1930–39	3.48	3.40	3.32	2.43	3.03	5.79	15.71	7.45	4.00

Notes and Sources: A fitted growth rate is calculated by fitting the equation $X = X_0 (1 + r)^t$ to the data and estimating r. Thus it is an estimated compound rate of growth taking into account all years within the specified period. These calculations are based on the data in table A33.

was not in great abundance and food crops had to compete with the expanding industrial food crops for land. Furthermore, since the demand for major food crops tends to be relatively inelastic with respect to income growth, one would expect their production to increase at a relatively slower rate. Indeed, without the Japanese market, where a large share of Taiwan's rice output was exported, the growth of major food crops would have been even slower.

Between 1906 and 1940, minor food crops, which includes fruits and vegetables, both easily spoiled cash crops, experienced the most rapid growth. Before the completion of the rail network and the feeder roads, the outlets for these cash crops were limited. But once the transportation bottleneck was eliminated, there were great incentives to increase output, and the farmers responded to the changed conditions. Of the early decisions by the colonial government, the one that affected agriculture most directly was the decision to promote sugar cane production. Cane production increased from less than 1 million MT in 1905 to over 12 million MT in 1939.[15] This dramatic rise explains the rapid growth of industrial food crops. Fiber crops (cotton, jute, and ramie) were produced, but only in small quantities. Their rapid increase in the 1930s was the result of government efforts to shift resources from rice to prevent further declines in rice prices and to make Taiwan more self-sufficient in the raw materials used for bags needed for transporting rice and sugar.

One of the more striking features of Taiwanese farming and one that it shares with prewar Japan and mainland China is the underdevelopment of animal husbandry. Since pasture farming is an extremely inefficient way to produce food energy, it is normally neglected where land is limited relative to population. In the case of Taiwan, pasture farming can be said not to exist. In 1930 fewer than 391,000 head of cattle (mostly oxen and water buffalo) were reported,[16] and they were used chiefly as draft animals. Hogs, which need little land, were the main source of meat, and after crops were the most important output of the Taiwanese farms. But above all, the Taiwanese peasants were cultivators. In 1935–37 the production of meat, poultry, and miscellaneous dairy products came to a little more than 13 percent of total agricultural production by value. In earlier years the share would have been even smaller.

Among the crops cultivated, rice, sugar cane, and to a lesser extent,

15. Table A43.
16. Taiwan Government-General, *Taiwan Agricultural Yearbook*, 1934.

sweet potatoes were dominant. Even though the production of vegetables and fruits grew at rates that were two or three times more rapid than rice, their total production at the end of the colonial period was still small in comparison to that of rice. The production value of rice, sugar cane, and sweet potatoes in constant prices consistently totaled approximately 85 percent of total crop production.[17] In terms of acreage, these three crops also consistently occupied over 80 percent of the total crop area.[18] Thus, the advances made by the minor food crops and by the fiber crops, though important, take on less significance in the light of their relative positions among crops. The one significant shift in output composition is the increasingly dominant position of sugar cane. The enlarged capacity of the modern sugar refineries, the ability of the Japanese market to absorb the sugar produced, and the active encouragement given to the sugar industry by the government all contributed to make sugar cane a more important crop. Between 1910 and 1940 sugar cane's share of total crop production increased from 10.8 to 22.2 percent, and its share of crop area increased from 8.4 to over 15 percent. This happened during a period when both total crop production and crop area were growing rapidly.

To understand how Taiwan's agricultural growth was brought about, we need to consider both the demand and supply conditions in agriculture. When Taiwan became a Japanese colony and the larger Japanese market was opened to it, the market opportunity available to its farmers broadened considerably. Furthermore the completion of a network of railroads and feeder roads shortly after Japan occupied Taiwan eliminated the possibility of economic paralysis that often results in the absence of communication, even when market possibilities exist. Thus, in the colonial period Taiwan's agriculture faced generally favorable market conditions, without which, needless to say, the growth in agricultural production would not have been so great.

The following aggregate supply function is estimated for Taiwan's agriculture with data for 1910–42:

$$\ln Y_t = 2.724 + 0.104 \ln P_t + 0.181 \ln P_{t-1} + 1.097 \ln I_t,$$
$$ (0.134) \qquad (0.125) \qquad\quad (0.062)$$
$$R^2 = 0.953, \tag{4.1}$$

where Y_t is agricultural output, P_t the index of the ratio of prices of agricultural products to the prices of nonagricultural products, and I_t

17. Calculated from ibid., various issues.
18. Table A42.

measures the growth of the productive capacity of agriculture. It is assumed that I_t grew at 2 percent per annum, approximately the growth rate of aggregate agricultural input.[19] The standard errors of the coefficients are given in parentheses. The regression results show that the price coefficients are small and not statistically different from zero at the 10 percent level. The trend variable, I_t, explains most of the variation of Y_t.

The ambiguous relationship between relative prices and agricultural output may be explained by several factors. The price data used in the regression analysis are not of the best quality and may not reflect accurately the prices at the farm level.[20] Perhaps more significant is that over a period of several decades agricultural production is influenced by many complex, long-run forces, of which relative prices is only one. To better understand the development process, we need to consider factors other than prices. One approach is to study the productive capacity of Taiwan's agriculture in order to see how it has expanded and the extent to which its growth can explain the increase in agricultural output.

Inputs

Generally, four types of input to agriculture are identified: land, labor, working capital, and fixed capital. In the case of Taiwan, four inputs can be approximately quantified: land, labor, fertilizer, and irrigation service. For an underdeveloped and capital-poor country such as Taiwan, irrigation facilities represent a large share of the agricultural fixed capital, and fertilizer is the only important current input purchased by the farmers. Thus, it would seem that irrigation services and the consumption of fertilizers can justifiably serve, respectively, as measures of fixed capital input and working capital input. They become all the more acceptable when better alternative measurements do not exist.[21] All four of the quantifiable inputs increased during the colonial period, though at greatly different rates

19. The growth of agricultural inputs shall be discussed in greater detail below.

20. The index of prices received by farmers is estimated by dividing a value index by an output index. The price index of nonagricultural products is based on a relatively small number of price series, and therefore its reliability is questionable.

21. Yhi-min Ho has suggested some other alternatives; see his *Agricultural Development of Taiwan, 1903–1960*, and his "Taiwan's Agricultural Transformation Under Colonialism: A Critique." For my comments on these alternatives, see my "Agricultural Transformation Under Colonialism: The Case of Taiwan," and "Agricultural Transformation Under Colonialism: Reply and Further Observations."

Table 4.2. Agricultural Output and Inputs, 1910–42

	Y_A Gross agric. output (1000 T¥ 1935–37 prices)	X_1 Land (ha)	X_2 Labor (1000 male equiv.)	X_3 Fertilizer (working capital) (1000 T¥ 1935–37 prices)	X_4 Irrigation (fixed capital) (ha)
1910	152,274	750,698	1,078	9,526	226,706
1911	165,380	809,225	1,146	9,212	232,584
1912	147,724	806,487	1,164	11,565	234,180
1913	168,693	822,611	1,205	11,621	232,966
1914	161,670	837,891	1,232	12,726	238,488
1915	174,562	837,939	1,221	16,938	242,455
1916	182,923	849,278	1,200	18,561	246,806
1917	200,423	858,937	1,193	19,730	261,977
1918	189,890	915,532	1,214	18,116	278,197
1919	191,755	894,924	1,208	19,181	301,416
1920	177,963	858,912	1,117	23,386	305,270
1921	187,442	875,458	1,115	23,084	310,918
1922	209,448	917,521	1,161	19,465	315,095
1923	201,766	904,326	1,173	23,086	327,375
1924	237,701	938,531	1,220	24,778	333,067
1925	250,962	965,225	1,247	27,119	350,471
1926	246,448	977,530	1,245	28,427	370,588
1927	260,439	969,802	1,228	30,809	379,012
1928	270,814	979,782	1,232	34,473	388,274
1929	273,005	972,247	1,204	33,926	438,380
1930	293,348	1,012,119	1,267	35,558	441,477
1931	298,514	1,028,718	1,315	39,479	449,649
1932	343,560	1,078,691	1,363	38,146	449,764
1933	310,960	1,074,132	1,387	42,292	457,455
1934	338,042	1,083,120	1,414	46,403	461,244
1935	361,515	1,130,806	1,496	51,832	465,920
1936	374,377	1,144,767	1,515	55,989	485,613
1937	375,313	1,123,585	1,480	59,124	510,868
1938	393,463	1,103,956	1,451	60,767	527,320
1939	399,189	1,146,839	1,503	63,411	532,454
1940	344,711	1,173,973	1,563	73,456	530,113
1941	345,673	1,183,697	1,596	67,189	543,098
1942	349,876	1,154,824	1,591	50,817	545,094

Notes and Sources: Gross agricultural output is gross production minus seeds and feeds. Production data are from Taiwan Government-General, *Taiwan Agricultural Yearbook*, various issues, and PFB, *Taiwan Food Statistics Book*, various issues. Estimates of seeds and feeds are from Yhi-min Ho, *Agricultural Development of Taiwan, 1903–1960*, table A-1. Land is total crop area, and the data were compiled by the Rural Economic Division (RED) of JCRR by adding the area under all crops, except the green manure crops. One minor adjustment of the JCRR data was made. For 1910–18, to account for the unreported crop areas under vegetables, 16,545 hectares (the average for 1919–23) were added to JCRR's estimates. Labor is the "gainfully occupied" persons in agriculture

Table 4.2 (continued)

in male equivalent as estimated by Y. M. Ho adjusted by multiplying it by the multiple cropping index. Ho's estimates are from his *Agricultural Development of Taiwan, 1903–1960*, pp. 43–44. The multiple cropping index is constructed by RED, JCRR (see table A39). Working capital is assumed to be the supply of fertilizers. Estimates of fertilizer supply after 1919 (1924 for farm-produced fertilizers) are from Taiwan Government-General, *Taiwan Agricultural Yearbook*, various issues. The estimates for the years before this date are those of the author (see tables A44 and A45 for a description of the estimating procedures). Fixed capital is approximated by the area under irrigation; the data are from PBAS, *Taiwan Province: Statistical Summary of the Past 51 Years*, p. 594.

(see table 4.2). Of the four, fertilizer experienced the fastest increase, followed in order by irrigation, land, and labor.

When Japan acquired Taiwan, the better and more accessible land was already under cultivation but some unsettled arable land still existed. Thus, during the early part of the twentieth century, agricultural production could still expand by going to the extensive margin. For tax purposes, the Japanese kept careful tabulation of cultivated areas, and these figures show that it increased from 633,647 hectares in 1906 to 859,446 hectares in 1941.[22] With a subtropical climate the cultivation of two and often more crops per year on a single piece of land is feasible in Taiwan. Therefore, an alternative to bringing more land into production is to use the same land more intensively. The multiple cropping index, which measures the intensity of land use, increased in Taiwan from 113 in 1911 to 132 in 1941.[23] Clearly, as unused arable land became more scarce or more difficult to settle, Taiwan farmers resorted more and more to double cropping. It would seem that crop area (cultivated area corrected for multiple cropping) is a better measurement of land as an input to agriculture than cultivated area.[24]

Compared to land, labor as an input to agriculture is conceptually more difficult to define and statistically more difficult to estimate. Agricultural labor statistics were not collected during the colonial period. However, several estimates of labor input to agriculture have been computed, the most acceptable of which is probably Y. M. Ho's estimate of gainfully employed over the age of 12, converted to male

22. Table A39.
23. Ibid.
24. Land, of course, is not a homogeneous input, and quality differences need to be taken into account when estimating land as an input to agriculture. However, the information needed for this type of adjustment is not available.

equivalents.[25] The weakness of this estimate as a measurement of labor input to agriculture is that it assumes that laborers work the same number of days each year. With the adoption of labor-using techniques, e.g., double cropping, chemical fertilizer, a complex irrigation rotation scheme, and better seed preparation, it is difficult to imagine that this assumption holds true. In colonial Taiwan, possibly the most decisive factor determining the number of days farmers spent on farm work is the extent of multiple cropping. Therefore it is believed that a better approximation of labor input to agriculture is obtained if Ho's estimates of gainfully employed are adjusted by the multiple cropping index. When this is done, we find that agricultural labor increased from 1,078,000 male equivalents in 1910 to 1,596,000 male equivalents in 1941. Because of factor substitution, multiple cropping most likely will not cause an exactly proportional increase in labor input. Consequently, the adjusted estimates have built into them an undetermined degree of upward bias.

The largest and most important component of working capital in colonial Taiwanese agriculture was fertilizer. Until chemical fertilizers were introduced in large quantities, farmers used mainly traditional farm-produced fertilizers such as compost, night soil, animal manure, and green manure. Using such data as population, animal population, and area planted with green manure crops, estimates of traditional fertilizer supply are extended back to 1910 and indicate that before 1920, farm-produced fertilizers accounted for about 60–70 percent of the total fertilizer supply. A major development in Taiwanese agriculture, reflecting the growing interaction between agriculture and nonagriculture, was the increasing use of commercial fertilizers by peasants, so that from 1920 to 1940, chemical fertilizers and vegetable (mainly soybean) oilcakes accounted for about two-thirds of the total fertilizer supply available in Taiwan. The combined supply of traditional and commercial fertilizers is assumed to measure working capital used in agriculture.[26]

Data on fixed capital input are lacking in Taiwan. In a rice economy such as Taiwan's, irrigation facilities represent the leading form of fixed

25. While the estimating procedures used are different, all these estimates are based on demographic data and therefore their reliability ultimately rest on the quality of the population censuses and the household registration records. Fortunately for the period under investigation, Taiwan maintained very accurate population statistics.

26. Normally, working capital would also include insecticides and pest control implements. Because insecticides were used sparingly if at all in the colonial period, their absence from our estimates of working capital is a minor defect.

capital in agriculture. Therefore a reasonably good proxy for capital input to agriculture may be the area under irrigation. The data on irrigated area are set forth in table 4.2. Considering the extent of government control over irrigation facilities, the government statistics on the size of irrigated area, especially after the completion of the cadastral survey in 1904, must be judged reliable. Because of the massive government participation in constructing and improving irrigation works, we suspect that irrigation facilities increased faster than agricultural capital as a whole. Consequently, the trend of fixed capital input when measured by the area under irrigation may be biased upward.[27]

Sources of Growth

With the output and input data in table 4.2 we can determine the extent to which the increase in output is explained by the increase in the quantifiable inputs and by the increase of the productivity of these inputs. Various indexes of agricultural productivity are presented in table 4.3. The simple measurements of productivity, i.e., land productivity and labor productivity, show rapid increases. But, as a general rule, the broader the coverage of resources defined as input, the better the productivity measurement. When an aggregate input measurement is used so that the effects of factor substitution are eliminated, the rise in productivity becomes less pronounced.[28] The evidence suggests that before the mid-1920s, overall agricultural productivity remained unchanged, if it did not decline; thereafter total productivity increased rapidly. Using two different sets of weights to aggregate the inputs, I estimate λ, the rate of productivity increase, for various periods, and the results, presented in table 4.4, confirm what is shown in table 4.3.[29]

27. There are bits of evidence which show that some of the nonirrigation capital input increased during the colonial period at rates substantially faster than the growth rate of irrigation facilities. For example, between 1910 and 1940 land under fruit trees (as a proxy for orchard trees) increased sevenfold while irrigated area increased slightly more than twofold. Thus, it is possible, although unlikely, that the index of irrigated area underestimates rather than overestimates the growth of capital input.

28. The aggregate input used is a weighted geometric average of the four quantifiable inputs, i.e., land, labor, working capital and fixed capital. For details see table 4.3.

29. λ is estimated by fitting the following relationship:

$$R = A + \lambda t,$$

where $R = \ln Y_A - (\alpha_1 \ln X_1 + \alpha_2 \ln X_2 + \alpha_3 \ln X_3 + \alpha_4 \ln X_4)$.

Y_A, X_1, X_2, X_3, X_4, and t are, respectively, gross agricultural output, land, labor, working capital, fixed capital, and time. The α's are factor shares. For details see table 4.3.

Table 4.3. Indexes of Agricultural Productivity

	Labor productivity	Land productivity	Aggregate input I	Aggregate input II	Overall productivity Using aggregate input I	Overall productivity Using aggregate input II
1910	100	100	100	100	100	100
1911	102	101	105	103	103	105
1912	90	90	109	107	89	90
1913	99	101	112	109	99	101
1914	93	95	115	113	92	94
1915	101	103	121	118	95	97
1916	108	106	123	119	98	100
1917	119	115	125	122	105	108
1918	111	102	128	125	97	100
1919	112	106	128	125	98	100
1920	113	102	127	124	92	94
1921	119	105	128	125	96	98
1922	128	112	129	126	106	109
1923	122	110	133	129	100	102
1924	138	125	138	135	113	116
1925	142	128	144	140	114	118
1926	140	124	146	142	111	113
1927	150	132	147	143	116	119
1928	156	136	151	147	117	121
1929	160	138	151	147	119	122
1930	164	143	157	153	123	126
1931	161	143	163	158	120	124
1932	178	157	167	163	135	138
1933	159	143	171	166	119	123
1934	169	154	176	170	126	130
1935	171	158	186	180	128	132
1936	175	161	190	184	129	133
1937	179	165	190	184	130	134
1938	192	176	189	182	137	142
1939	188	171	195	189	134	139
1940	156	144	205	197	110	115
1941	153	144	204	197	111	115
1942	156	149	193	187	119	123

Notes and Sources: The aggregate input, $\bar{I}$, is a weighted geometric average of the individual inputs, i.e.,

$$\bar{I} = X_1{}^{\alpha_1} X_2{}^{\alpha_2} X_3{}^{\alpha_3} X_4{}^{\alpha_4}, \quad \sum_{i=1}^{4} \alpha_i = 1,$$

where X_1, X_2, X_3, X_4 are, respectively, land, labor, working capital, and fixed capital. The parameters, α's, are factor shares. Two estimates of α's are used:

	α_1 (Land)	α_2 (Labor)	α_3 (Working capital)	α_4 (Fixed capital)
Alternative I	.4488	.3107	.1655	.0749
Alternative II	.4439	.3085	.1463	.0979

Table 4.3 (continued)

The α's in alternative I are computed from the results of a 1926 government survey of 150 representative rice farms (Taiwan Government-General, *Economic Survey of Major Agricultural Crops, no. 3, Rice, Report of Basic Agricultural Survey, no. 13*, 1928). The α's in alternative II are based on four unpublished cost surveys of rice farming conducted by the Taiwan Provincial Food Bureau during 1947–48. Farmers in Taiwan can be divided into those that grow mainly rice, mainly sugar cane, and mainly sweet potatoes. That rice farming is by far the most common type of farming in Taiwan, that the factor shares of sweet potato and sugar cane farming possibly differ from that of rice in a compensating manner, and that there is no other suitable alternative, combine to argue strongly for the use of the α's from the rice surveys as weights for the inputs. For the sources of the input and output data, see tables 4.1 and 4.2.

Table 4.4. Estimated Annual Rates of Productivity Increase, λ, for Alternative Sets of α's

	λ	Standard error	R^2
Alternative I			
1910–42	0.0106	0.0013	.6711
1910–20	−0.0017	0.0052	.0120
1920–39	0.0174	0.0017	.8489
Alternative II			
1910–42	0.0111	0.0013	.6955
1910–20	−0.0005	0.0052	.0012
1920–39	0.0180	0.0017	.8616

Note: The method for deriving alternative α's is explained in table 4.3.

Since estimates of labor and fixed capital are probably biased upward, the results shown in tables 4.3 and 4.4 are believed to be conservative estimates of productivity increase. Regardless of the weights used to aggregate the inputs, the conclusion that must be drawn from the results is unchanged. Until the 1920s, agricultural output increases can essentially be explained by the increasing use of land, labor, working capital, and fixed capital. In fact, between 1910 and 1920, λ was negative, although not statistically significant.[30] But from the

30. The decline in total productivity in these years can be explained possibly by the fact that the input estimates used (specifically, labor and fixed capital) were upward biased. An alternative and perhaps more likely explanation is that while the state of the arts in Taiwanese agriculture remained approximately stable in the first quarter of the twentieth century, the quality of two of the inputs to agriculture (land and labor) deteriorated. Land brought into cultivation after 1910 was inferior in quality. The flu epidemics during 1915 and 1920 weakened considerably the agricultural workers and increased the number of women in the labor force. Both these developments must have had some negative effects on labor productivity.

1920s until the end of the colonial period, λ was positive and statistically significant. For these years, large portions of the output increases can be explained only by that unknown factor, technological change.

By multiplying the relative factor shares and the percentage increase of each input category, it is possible to obtain a measurement of the contribution of each input as well as that of technological change to the growth of total output.[31] When this is done, with the factor shares of alternative I (table 4.3) as weights, it is found that of the 151 percent increase in output between 1910 and 1939, increase in crop area accounted for 23 percent; increase in labor, 12 percent; increase in working capital, 85 percent; increase in fixed capital, 11 percent; and technological change, 20 percent. When the factor shares of alternative II are used as weights, a generally similar pattern of input contribution to output growth is obtained.[32] That over one-half the output increase can be attributed to increases in working capital emphasizes again the importance of fertilizer to Taiwan's agricultural growth.

TECHNOLOGY AND AGRICULTURAL TRANSFORMATION

There were two distinct phases of agricultural development in the colonial period. The first, lasting until the mid-1920s, was a period of relatively slow agricultural growth whose source can be traced almost entirely to the increases of the quantifiable inputs: land, labor, working capital, and fixed capital. It was also a period when unsettled land was still in sufficient supply to maintain a favorable land/labor ratio in Taiwan's agriculture.[33] The second phase, from approximately the

31. Assume that the production function is a Cobb–Douglas function,

$$Y = AX_1^{\alpha_1}X_2^{\alpha_2}X_3^{\alpha_3}X_4^{\alpha_4}, \qquad \sum_{i=1}^{4}\alpha_i = 1,$$

where Y is the output, the X's are the inputs, the α's are the factor shares, and A is the shift parameter for technological change. Differentiating the function with respect to time, we get the following:

$$\frac{\dot{Y}}{Y} = \frac{\dot{A}}{A} + \alpha_1\frac{\dot{X}_1}{X_1} + \alpha_2\frac{\dot{X}_2}{X_2} + \alpha_3\frac{\dot{X}_3}{X_3} + \alpha_4\frac{\dot{X}_4}{X_4},$$

where the dotted terms are the first derivatives with respect to time.

32. Of the 151 percent increase in output, increase in crop area accounted for 22 percent; increase in labor, 12 percent; increase in working capital, 75 percent; increase in fixed capital, 12 percent, and technological change, 30 percent.

33. The ratios of cultivated land to agricultural population during the colonial period are:

mid-1920s to the 1940s, was a period of rapid growth, even though the land/labor ratio deteriorated. In this latter period, technological change played a vital role in·agricultural growth. One might say that in the second phase, Taiwanese agriculture began to take on characteristics of a modern, scientifically oriented sector. Furthermore, technological change occurred in Taiwan without disrupting the traditional system of peasant cultivation.

Technological change is never altogether absent in traditional agriculture. As population grows, the need to survive often induces farmers to seek ways to increase yields by developing labor-using cultivating techniques. In Taiwan, as in China and Japan, where peasants have perfected this art, agriculture has become extremely labor intensive. These traditional adjustments to changes in resource endowment, which may be considered technological change of a sort, are important because they come from within traditional agriculture and are effective without the adoption of new nonagricultural inputs or the introduction of new rural institutions. Traditional technological change is, however, based primarily on personal experiences, without the assistance of modern agricultural science, and consequently it is relatively ineffective in raising output quickly. But to transform agriculture it is necessary to increase output substantially faster than population increases. For this, a different form of technological change, one based upon modern agricultural science, is needed. In the case of Taiwan it was this second type of technological change that transformed production. We shall therefore be concerned solely with the nontraditional form of technological change.

In Taiwan, technological change came in the form of two types of nonconventional inputs—modern agricultural science and new rural institutions—both coming from outside agriculture. Agricultural science introduced to the farmers better seeds, fertilizers, and more effective cultivating techniques. It was the extension service system, however, that made scientific farming an effective agent of growth. The rural institutions ensured that the findings of agricultural science were widely disseminated, extensively adopted, and correctly applied. One lesson from the Taiwan experience is not that scientific farming is

	ha/person		ha/person
1906–10	.304	1926–30	.304
1911–15	.299	1931–35	.286
1916–20	.300	1936–40	.275
1921–25	.309	1941–45	.242

important but rather that science alone cannot transform agriculture without certain rural institutions being created first or at least concomitantly.

The agent most responsible for putting technology to use in agriculture was the colonial government. It is instructive to see what innovations were introduced by the Japanese, how they were introduced and diffused, and what institutions were created to facilitate agricultural changes.

From the time Taiwan was theirs to govern, the Japanese administrators made strong efforts to apply scientific knowledge and techniques in the development of the island. In no area of the economy is this more evident than in agriculture. Borrowing skilled technicians and agronomists from Japan, the colonial government set about to adapt improvements developed in Japan and elsewhere to the conditions in Taiwan. As early as 1899 the government allocated funds to operate agricultural experiment stations. The Taiwan Agricultural Research Institute was established in Taipei in 1903, followed by district agricultural improvement stations in strategic farming districts. At first these research organizations were only loosely related, but after 1921 they were all brought under the supervision of the Central Research Institute.[34] It was through these research institutes that technology was selectively introduced after controlled experimentation.

The major achievement of these research institutes was the successful adaptation to Taiwan of seeds with higher yields, greater resistance to disease and high wind, and more receptivity to fertilizer and intensive care. The best examples are the development of better cane shoots and rice seeds.[35] Realizing that a modern sugar industry can be created on the island only if the low yield native cane (collectively called bamboo cane) was replaced by better varieties, the government, in 1896, imported new cane varieties (rose bamboo and lahaina) from Hawaii for experimental cultivation.[36] In 1901 Dr. Inazo Nitobe, invited to Taiwan to study ways to improve sugar cane cultivation, suggested increased application of fertilizer and irrigation and the adoption of

---

34. For a description of the structure and organization of the Central Research Institute, see Kiwata Ide, *Record of the Taiwan Administration* (Taipei: Taiwan Cultural Commission, 1956), pp. 771–82.

35. Although the government concentrated its efforts on improving sugar cane and rice, significant advances were also made in other areas. In particular, the introduction of improved varieties of tea, pineapple, and hogs had widespread effects in Taiwan.

36. Shooy-geng Lu, "Research and the Taiwan Sugar Industry," *Taiwan's Sugar* (Taipei: BOT, 1949), p. 3.

improved shoots.[37] The government quickly implemented Nitobe's suggestions, and in 1902 the rose bamboo cane imported earlier for experimentation was officially released for general planting, and regulations encouraging the use of fertilizers, new shoots, and irrigation were promulgated.[38] In terms of yield and sugar content, the rose bamboo cane offered only minor improvements over the native variety. The more important technical breakthroughs were not to come until the 1920s, when cane varieties with average yield more than twice, and sugar content by weight 40 percent higher than, that of rose bamboo were introduced for general planting.[39] After Hawaii, Java, and the Philippines prohibited the export of cane shoots to Taiwan in 1930, technological improvement in sugar cane slowed considerably.

Given the nature of Taiwan's agriculture, the improvements made in rice seeds were probably of even greater significance than those made in sugar cane. Japanese rice varieties were introduced to Taiwan soon after Japan occupied the island. However, it took the Japanese many years before it developed a strain that suited the subtropical climate and the different soil conditions in Taiwan. Meanwhile, the government executed a policy of eliminating inferior native varieties (commonly called *chailai* rice) from planting and of propagating those with high yield. In 1910 more than 1,300 varieties of chailai rice were planted, of which nearly 1,200 were identified.[40] The difference in yield among some varieties of chailai rice was as much as 29 percent.[41] By vigorously restricting the planting of inferior varieties, the number of chailai varieties was reduced to 390 in 1920. Some improvements in yield were made through this selective process, but progress was slow. The breakthrough came with the successful introduction of the higher yielding Japonica varieties of rice (commonly called *ponlai* rice). The first ponlai variety, *nakumura*, was released for general planting in 1924, followed in 1926 by the release of the most popular rice variety ever introduced in Taiwan, the *Taichung* no. 65.[42] The rapid adoption

37. Andrew J. Grajdanzev, *Formosa Today*, p. 58.

38. Peasants with more than 5 acres of land planted with sugar cane were eligible to receive 3.6 T¥ for shoots and 5 T¥ for fertilizers per 0.25 acre. With respect to irrigation, the regulation allowed the government, at its discretion, to subsidize up to one-half the cost of irrigation and drainage projects that cost more than 1,000 T¥.

39. Taiwan Sugar Corporation, *Annual Statistical Report of Taiwan Sugar Industry*, pp. 39–41.

40. Tsay-yan Sung, *Development of Seed Technology in Taiwan*, p. 1.

41. Shigeto Kawano, *A Study of Taiwan's Rice Economy*, p. 15.

42. By the mid-1930s, nearly 40 percent of the rice crop area was planted with Taichung no. 65 (see Kawano, *Taiwan's Rice Economy*, p. 64).

Table 4.5. Per Unit Area Consumption of Fertilizer, Annual Averages (kg/ha)

	Rice[a]	Sugar cane[a]	Total[b]
Soybean cake			
1922–24	72.72	100.23	80.60
1930–32	156.20	47.08	155.80
Ammonium sulfate			
1922–24	.88	59.91	9.91
1930–32	19.66	370.73	67.05
Calcium superphosphate			
1922–24	17.23	34.81	19.33
1930–32	37.06	60.47	41.56
Combined chemical fertilizer			
1922–24	2.57	439.94	74.94
1930–32	13.96	406.31	65.98

Source: Computed from Taiwan Government-General, *Taiwan Agricultural Yearbook*, various issues.
[a] Fertilizer consumed per unit crop area.
[b] Fertilizer consumed per unit cultivated area.

of the new varieties helped to raise the average rice yield in Taiwan from 1,379 kg/ha (hectare) in 1911–20 to 1,594 kg/ha in 1921–30, and 1,935 kg/ha in 1931–40.[43] In retrospect, the introduction of ponlai rice may have been the single most important agricultural innovation made during the colonial period.

Experiments found that, in comparison with chailai rice, ponlai rice not only was more dependent on fertilizer but also reacted more favorably to fertilizer.[44] Such findings may have helped to convince the government to coordinate the introduction of new rice seeds with that of chemical fertilizers. Until the introduction of ponlai rice, commercial fertilizer was used in Taiwan in limited amounts, most of which was applied to sugar cane. Table 4.5 compares the distribution of four major commercial fertilizers by crop for the periods 1922–24 and 1930–32. Except for soybean cake, a fertilizer long familiar to Taiwanese farmers, very little commercial fertilizer was applied to rice before 1924. Fertilizer was applied more intensively on sugar cane,

43. Table A43.
44. The experiments showed that, when fertilizer application was increased from nil to a "normal" amount, the yield of ponlai rice increased by 30 percent compared to an increase of only 12 percent for chailai rice. When this normal amount was doubled, the yield of ponlai rice increased by another 14 percent while that of chailai rice declined by nearly 6 percent. Cf. Kawano, *Taiwan's Rice Economy*, p. 15.

but even here the consumption was not particularly heavy.[45] Yet, less than ten years later and shortly after the introduction of ponlai rice, the per unit area consumption of these four major types of commercial fertilizers in the cultivation of rice increased at least twofold.

The rapid rise in fertilizer consumption can be explained by several factors. First, the introduction of ponlai rice and its rapid adoption increased the demand for fertilizer. As a percentage of the total area under rice cultivation, the area under ponlai rice increased from 4.6 percent in 1924 to 21.4 percent in 1930 and 50.7 percent in 1940. Farmers switched willingly to ponlai rice because with the prevailing prices it was usually more profitable to grow ponlai than chailai rice.[46] Secondly, to be effective, fertilizer needs water, and by the late 1920s several large irrigation projects were completed and were providing water to farmers.[47] Fertilizer, new seeds, and irrigation are complementary inputs, and by design or luck the colonial government made them available to peasants at about the same time and each made the others more effective. Finally, the colonial government created in Taiwan a rural organization that introduced innovations and distributed supplies quickly and efficiently.

Innovation, to be effective, must be adopted and properly employed at the farm level. Therefore, institutional facilities are needed to disseminate information, to convince the farmers of the benefits of the innovation, and to facilitate the adoption of the innovation. A slow response of peasants to technology is often caused by the absence of the necessary institutional facilities in traditional agriculture. Eager to make this type of nonconventional input more accessible to agriculture, the colonial government encouraged, and often directly participated in, the restructuring of existing rural institutions or the creation of new ones.

Much of the colonial government's early attention to agriculture was directed to the cane farmers. Here, the private sugar companies, interested in increasing sugar cane supply, offered a natural channel

45. In the early 1920s, fertilizers were applied more intensively to sugar cane partly because shoots sensitive to fertilizer were already available and partly because sugar companies disseminated information and supplied fertilizer to the sugar cane farmers.
46. Taiwan Government-General, *Economic Survey of Major Agricultural Crops, no. 6, Rice, Report of Basic Agricultural Survey no. 16*, 1928, and *Economic Survey of Major Agricultural Crops, no. 9, Rice, Report of Basic Agricultural Survey no. 19*, 1928.
47. The Taoyuan Irrigation System, after 12 years of construction, was completed in 1928, and the Chianan Irrigation System was completed in 1930. Together they covered 170,000 hectares of land.

of communication. Although the sugar companies leased a large portion of the land they owned to private cultivators, they retained control over or directly cultivated about 40,000 hectares. The latter areas were operated very much like plantations in that the companies through their managers supervised all aspects of cane cultivation and harvest. Even the land leased to private cultivators was usually under the supervision of the companies. Thus a large portion of the cane growers, the hired hands, and the tenants of the sugar companies were in fact wage earners acting under the direction of the sugar companies. Their position in agriculture enabled the sugar companies to be effective extension agents, and it was through them that the cane farmers received the subsidized fertilizers and the high yielding shoots provided by the government.[48]

The sugar companies, however, could not be counted on to bring progress to all of agriculture. A more direct channel of communication between the government and the Taiwanese peasants had to be created.[49] Traditional institutions offered little assistance. At first, the government relied on its administrative organs—the police and the pao-chia system (see chap. 2, n. 12)—to provide extension services. The pao-chia system was used mainly to disseminate information. The police, however, were given a wider variety of tasks to perform, including the promotions of higher yielding rice seeds, new farming techniques, and the planting of windbreakers.[50] The exchange of low

48. More than 4 million yen were used by the government to subsidize fertilizer purchases during the fifteen years (1902–16) the program was in effect. An indication of the effectiveness of the sugar companies as extension agents is that 5 years after the introduction of the rose bamboo cane in 1902, it covered 60 percent of the sugar crop area in Taiwan.

49. The Japanese were very much concerned with this problem and wanted to devise a proper method to introduce innovations to agriculture so as to make sure that they were understood and correctly adopted. See Inazo Nitobe, "How to Lead the Taiwanese Farmers," *Report on Taiwan Agricultural Affairs* 113 (Apr. 1916): 257–63; Minoru Togō, "The Creation of Organizations for Improving Agriculture," *Report on Taiwan Agricultural Affairs* 152 (July 1919): 395–98; and Akira Murakoso, "The Mission of Prefectural Farmers' Associations," *Report on Taiwan Agricultural Affairs* 142 (Sept. 1918): 637–45.

50. For discussions of the role of police in agricultural development, see Shunji Shiomi, "Police and Economic Development in Taiwan During the Japanese Period," *Bank of Taiwan Quarterly* 5 (March 1953): 253–73; Ramon H. Myers and Adrienne Ching, "Agricultural Development in Taiwan"; Hideo Tanaka, "Agricultural Police Administration and Its Relation to the Development of Taiwan's Agriculture," *Report on Taiwan Agricultural Affairs* 152 (July 1919): 401–03; and Minoru Togō, "Essay on Police Supervision in Colonial Agriculture," *Report on Taiwan Agricultural Affairs* 144 (Nov. 1918): 771–74.

yielding native rice seeds for high yielding ones in the early decades of the twentieth century was conducted under such police supervision. This may explain why the exchange was completed so quickly. Even after they were removed from formal extension work, police officers were occasionally called on to persuade reluctant farmers to adopt new farming techniques.

Useful as they were, the police and the pao-chia system served only as stopgap devices. Not until the establishment of the Farmers' Association (*nokai*) on an islandwide basis did the government have an effective extension service system. The Farmers' Association (FA) was first organized near Taipei in 1900, at the initiative of wealthy farmers and landlords. The government quickly realized the potential of this institution as a channel of communication with the farmers and began in the late 1900s to participate actively in its development. In a few years FAs existed in every perfecture, with the colonial government, through its top perfectural officials and the Japanese agricultural technicians, in control. In essence, the FAs became an arm of the government. Memberships and fees were made compulsory for all farm households. FAs eventually took charge of such important functions as the improvement and extension of seeds, the maintenance of a seed multiplication system, the prevention and control of animal and plant diseases, the training of agricultural technicians, the execution of agricultural surveys, the purchase of fertilizers, seeds, and equipment needed by members, and the management of warehouses. By the 1920s the Japanese had in the Farmers' Association exactly the type of institution they needed to bring scientific farming to Taiwan: one that could perform research, disseminate information, offer extension services, and supply the farmers with nonagricultural inputs.

Supporting the FAs were other newly formed organizations such as the Small Agricultural Unit (SAU) and the credit cooperatives. The former was developed to serve as a convenient point of contact between farmers and agricultural experts. All together several thousands of these units were created, each headed by a government-approved leader.[51] Whenever information was to be disseminated, the SAU leader would call his group together for group education. The credit cooperatives were created to ease the shortage of working capital in agriculture. In 1913 there were 13 credit cooperatives in the countryside.

51. These SAUs went by different names such as Agricultural Small Society, Agricultural Practice Society, and Organization for Development of Villages.

This number quickly multiplied to 214 in 1920, 332 in 1930, and 443 in 1940.[52] By extending the organized money market to the countryside, credit became more accessible and its cost considerably lower. By 1940 the organized money market (development bank, commercial banks, and the agricultural credit cooperatives) provided over 50 percent of the rural credit in Taiwan.[53] Interestingly, with credit more accessible, farmers were now more willing to borrow for production purposes. Surveys show that in 1933 about 50 percent of the outstanding rural debts were incurred for production purposes, and in 1940 this share was nearly 64 percent.[54]

Although these rural institutions were separately administered, their efforts to develop agriculture were coordinated through the influence and supervision of the colonial government. Between the FAs and the agricultural cooperatives, the Japanese had created an institution that was second only to the government in size. In the late 1920s and the early 1930s, when they were at their heights, the FAs and the agricultural cooperatives employed approximately 40,000 people. Of these, 13,000 were extension workers, 9,000 of whom were agricultural advisers working with the small agricultural units at the village level.[55] On a per farm household basis, this would amount to approximately one extension worker for every 32 farm households. The size of the operation is perhaps indicative of the magnitude of effort needed to transform traditional agriculture.

The Taiwanese experience seems to support much of what economists have recently learned about the transformation of traditional agriculture.[56] For example, it is now realized that the inputs needed to transform agriculture are highly complementary. Improved-yield seeds,

52. Taiwan Government-General, *Taiwan Agricultural Yearbook*, various issues.
53. Taiwan Government-General, *Agricultural Credit Survey, Report of Basic Agricultural Survey no. 43*, 1941, pp. 4–5.
54. Taiwan Government-General, *Survey of Agricultural Credit, Report of Basic Agricultural Survey no. 33*, 1935, and *Survey of Agricultural Credit, Report of Basic Agricultural Survey no. 43*, 1941.
55. PDAF, *The Reorganization of Farmers' Associations in Taiwan*, 1950, p. 20. It is unclear what constituted an extension worker. One suspects that many who do not normally fit the title (e.g., SAU group leaders and model farmers) are included in this figure. But even taking this into account, colonial Taiwan probably still had more extension workers per farm family than do many less developed countries today.
56. For example, see Bruce F. Johnson and John W. Mellor, "The Role of Agriculture in Economic Development," *American Economic Review*; John W. Mellor, *The Economics of Agricultural Development* (Ithaca, N.Y.: Cornell University Press, 1966); and Yujiro Hayami and Vernon W. Ruttan, *Agricultural Development in International Perspective*.

to be effective, require fertilizer as well as irrigation; their effectiveness in turn depends upon the existing stock of knowledge, research, and extension work. The lack of even one of these factors would make the others less productive. Taiwan's agriculture was able to grow rapidly, particularly during the late 1920s and the 1930s, precisely because all the necessary inputs were available to the peasants as a package. The shortage of some of these inputs before the 1920s also explains the lack of productivity increase during the early period.

The Taiwanese case also demonstrates that given the complementary nature of the inputs needed to transform agriculture and the structure of traditional agriculture, it is impossible for technology to transform agriculture by itself without extensive restructuring of agricultural institutions. In turn, this places a great demand on administrative, organizational, and technical skills, which Taiwan did not possess. They had to be borrowed from Japan. As late as 1940, there were still about 2,500 Japanese agricultural and forestry technicians, representing nearly two-thirds of the total number working in Taiwan.[57] An even larger number of Japanese held administrative posts both in the rural organizations and in government departments that dealt with agriculture. Without this Japanese personnel, agricultural transformation in Taiwan would have been made more difficult. Apparently, not only must technology and the modern inputs come from outside traditional agriculture, the human resources that are needed to make technology effective may also have to be imported.

AGRICULTURAL PRODUCTIVITY AND AGRICULTURAL SURPLUS

Rising productivity in agriculture made its most direct contribution to economic growth by increasing total output. Chapter 5 shall show that it also enabled agriculture to release some of its labor to the nonagricultural sector. In colonial Taiwan, another significant consequence of rising agricultural productivity was the appearance of a growing agricultural surplus (AS), defined as the difference between agricultural output (Y_A) and the consumption of agricultural goods by the agricultural household sector (C_A^A). Of greater importance to development was the concurrent rise in the net flow of material resources from agriculture (NAS), making agriculture a net provider of resources to the other sectors.

57. George W. Barclay, *A Report of Taiwan's Population to the Joint Commission on Rural Reconstruction*, p. 63.

The following identities can be easily verified:

$$AS = Y_A - C_A^A = R_N^A + E_A + C_N^A - M_A^C \tag{4.2}$$

$$NAS = AS - (C_A^N + R_A^N + R_A^W + I_A^N), \tag{4.3}$$

where R_N^A is the flow of agricultural raw material to the nonagricultural sector, E_A is the export of agricultural goods, C_N^A is the consumption of agricultural goods by the nonagricultural household sector, M_A^C is the final consumption of imported agricultural goods, C_A^N is the consumption of manufactured consumption goods by the agricultural household sector, R_A^N and R_A^W are the flows of current inputs from, respectively, the nonagricultural sector and abroad to agricultural production, and I_A^N is the manufactured capital goods purchased by agriculture.

Using agricultural surveys and time series data, T. H. Lee has skillfully put together estimates of the various commodity flows between agriculture and the nonagricultural sector.[58] From these estimates and using equations (4.2) and (4.3), *AS* and *NAS* can be derived, and the results are presented in table 4.6. Although I have doubts about the reliability of some of Lee's estimates, I generally agree with the conclusion implied by his data, i.e., that Taiwan's agriculture produced a substantial surplus in the colonial period.[59]

The impressive growth of Taiwan's agricultural productivity would by itself suggest the existence of an agricultural surplus. And indeed the available evidence does show such a surplus for the period 1911–40. In current prices, Taiwan's agricultural surplus rose from an annual average of 53 million yen in 1911–15 to nearly 360 million yen in 1936–40. Between 1911–15 and 1936–40, the current value of nonagricultural goods allocated to agriculture ($C_A^N + R_A^W + R_A^N + I_A^N$) increased more than eightfold. Nevertheless, in this same period the current value of net agricultural surplus rose from an annual average of 22 million yen in 1911–15 to an annual average of 99 million yen in 1936–40.

Taiwan's agricultural surplus accounted for 54 percent of its total agricultural production in 1911–15 and over 70 percent in 1936–40.

58. Teng-hui Lee, *Intersectoral Capital Flows in the Economic Development of Taiwan, 1895–1960.*

59. For lack of data, many of Lee's estimates are based almost completely on agricultural surveys. These surveys used small samples (50–200 households), usually not randomly selected, and were primarily directed at rice farming families. Because of these characteristics, the reliability of estimates based on these surveys is often questionable.

Table 4.6. Agricultural Surplus, 1911–40 (Annual average in million yen)

	1911–15	1916–20	1921–25	1926–30	1931–35	1936–40
A. Agricultural surplus (AS)						
(1) − (2)	53.0	100.2	146.8	193.5	206.1	359.3
1. $R_A^N + E_A + C_N^A$	54.8	105.5	154.6	204.1	208.5	362.5
2. M_A^C	1.8	5.3	7.8	10.6	2.4	3.2
B. Net agricultural surplus (NAS)	22.4	36.8	42.1	50.2	60.3	98.6
$(A) − (3) − (4) − (5)$						
3. C_A^N	24.3	43.7	67.7	86.6	90.6	168.8
4. $R_A^W + R_A^N$	5.6	17.2	28.7	45.3	47.0	82.4
5. I_A^N	.7	2.5	8.3	11.4	8.2	9.5
C. NAS in 1935–37 prices	50.9	54.4	18.4	53.8	87.9	87.0
(6) − (7)						
6. AS/P_A	93.0	107.7	148.2	193.5	257.6	299.4
7. $(C_A^N + R_A^W + R_A^N + I_A^N)/P_N$	42.1	53.3	129.8	139.7	169.7	212.4
D. AS/agricultural production	54.4%	53.3%	60.5%	65.2%	70.9%	70.8%
E. NAS/agricultural production	23.0%	19.6%	17.4%	16.9%	20.8%	19.4%

Sources: Estimates of R_N^A, E_A, C_N^A, C_A^N $R_A^W + R_N^A$ and I_A^N are from Teng-hui Lee, "Intersectoral Capital Flows in the Economic Development of Taiwan, 1895–1960," table 2.2. M_A^C is from PBAS, Taiwan Trade Statistics For the Last Fifty-three Years (1896–1948). P_A, an index of agricultural prices, is a Paasche index, obtained by dividing the Laspeyres production index in table A33 into a value index with similiar coverage constructed especially for the purpose. P_N, an index of prices of nonagricultural goods, is from Lee, "Intersectoral Capital Flows," and includes the prices of two current inputs, four capital goods, and seven manufactured consumer goods.

This suggests that a substantial share of agricultural output must have been marketed. Sugar cane, by value the second most important crop in Taiwan, was sold almost exclusively to refineries, and rice, the most important crop, was also highly commercialized. One Japanese economist estimated the average rate of commercialization of rice (the sum of urban consumption and net export of rice divided by production) for 1936 to 1938 to be 73.8 percent.[60] In contrast, Buck's survey of China in the early 1930s indicates that the rate of commercialization in China was 36 percent for rice and 33 percent for wheat.[61]

More significant is the finding that agriculture also generated sizable amounts of net surplus in the colonial period. Except for the 1920s, when its share was somewhat less, net agricultural surplus nearly always absorbed one-fifth of the rapidly expanding agricultural production. Numerous mechanisms operated to help transfer the net surplus from agriculture: agricultural taxes, the savings of both individual and corporate landlords,[62] and the strong monoposonistic power of buyers of agricultural goods.[63]

All the data presented so far are expressed in current prices, so to measure the real increase in *AS* and *NAS*, we must eliminate the effects of price changes. In table 4.6, *AS* and *NAS*, measured in 1935–37 prices, show interesting trends. Until 1920 real agricultural surplus increased rather slowly but, thereafter, it increased rapidly. This trend corresponds closely to the behavior of agricultural productivity, and we are once again reminded of the intimate relationship between agricultural productivity and agricultural surplus. Net agricultural surplus in constant prices behaved somewhat differently. Starting in the 1920s, reflecting the extensive introduction of current inputs to agriculture and the increase in agricultural fixed capital, a growing volume of nonagricultural goods flowed into agriculture. However, it was several years before agriculture responded fully to these investments. Consequently, *NAS* declined in the early 1920s before increasing dramatically in the 1930s. Thus, in order to increase agricultural productivity,

60. Kawano, *Taiwan's Rice Economy*, table 118.
61. These figures are obtained by adding the percentage of production sold by the peasants and the percentage paid to landlords (see John L. Buck, *Land Utilization in China*, p. 236).
62. In the 1930s, the sugar companies owned more than one-tenth of the cultivated land in Taiwan.
63. For a more detailed dicussion, see my "Agricultural Transformation under Colonialism: The Case of Taiwan," pp. 337–40.

Taiwan first found it necessary to reduce, for a short time, the size of its net agricultural surplus.

In this chapter we examined in some detail the process by which Taiwan's agriculture was transformed from a backward to a highly productive and commercialized sector. Agricultural production advanced at a slow but steady pace until the 1920s; thereafter, it increased rapidly. Although increases in inputs, especially land before the 1920s and fertilizer and irrigation after the mid-1920s, can explain much of the output increases, a substantial portion of the increased production is attributed to increases in productivity made possible by better seeds, more appropriate techniques of cultivation, improved knowledge, and an islandwide extension system. The rise in agricultural productivity was not only the source of Taiwan's "export surplus," but it also paved the way for Taiwan's eventual industrialization because it permitted agriculture to release labor and savings to the nonagricultural sector.

5

The Industrial Enclave

One significant development in the colonial period was the emergence of an industrial enclave in Taiwan. Because Japan's interest was to develop Taiwan's potential to export agricultural products, the enclave did not expand rapidly. To better understand the relationship that developed between agriculture and the industrial enclave, we need to examine Taiwan's early industrialization more closely. A review of the early records is also useful because it provides us with the necessary background against which post-World War II industrial achievements can be compared and evaluated.

The main purposes of this chapter are to examine the rate and pattern of industrial growth in the colonial period and to trace the sources of industrial labor and capital. We shall show that although industrialization occurred, it was at a fairly slow pace. Power was used more widely and a larger number of workers were employed by modern factories. Production increased, but the most dramatic increases were in industries that processed agricultural goods. By the end of the colonial period, Taiwan had built a small, but not insignificant, industrial base. Certainly, a solid industrial foundation was laid. The evidence also indicates that although there was considerable interaction, in the form of resource flows, between agriculture and industry, the extent of the interaction and its impacts were minimized by Taiwan's subordinate position and close ties with Japan.

EXTENT AND PATTERN OF INDUSTRIALIZATION

The Factory Enclave

Agricultural growth and commercialization cannot easily occur without the support of some industrial infrastructures, at a minimum the services of modern commercial and financial facilities and an efficient transport system. These were created in Taiwan soon after its colonization and their capacity expanded quickly. The freight distance carried by the public rail system increased from 3.8 million MT-km in 1900 to 219.9 million MT-km in 1920, and 904.0 million MT-km in 1940, and the ocean freight handled at Taiwan's harbors increased from 251,000 MT in 1910 to 2,709,000 MT in 1940.[1] Less obvious but no less important to Taiwan's development were the emergence and steady growth of a factory enclave. If we adopt the official definition of a factory as a manufacturing establishment that used power or employed at least five workers, the growth of the factory enclave is described by the following statistics.

From 1915 to 1940 the number of private factories increased sevenfold, from 1,323 to 8,940, and from 1915 to 1935 the number of private factories employing power increased nearly ninefold, from 642 to 5,492. The total horsepower installed in private factories more than quadrupled from 60,000 in 1920 to 256,000 in 1939.[2] From 1914 to 1941 factory employment rose from 21,800 to 127,700 and mining employment from 6,500 to 53,700.[3] The growth of factory as well as mining production is presented in table 5.1, which shows that for nearly three decades (1912 to 1940) factory and mining production expanded at about 6 percent per annum.[4] Indeed, from 1912 to 1929 the compound rate of growth exceeded 9 percent, a performance that compares favorably with many less developed countries of today. Taken together, these statistics indicate that Taiwan's industry (manufacturing and mining) not only increased its capacity in the colonial period but also improved its production technology.

The main source of industrial growth in the colonial period was the food processing industry. Indeed, one might even go so far to say that Taiwan's early industrialization was merely an extension of its agricultural development.[5] As late as 1930, food processing accounted for 64 percent of all registered factories, 55 percent of

1. Table A55, and **PBAS**, *Taiwan Province: Statistical Summary of the Past 51 Years*, pp. 1202–04.
2. All statistics on private factories are from ibid., pp. 767 and 770–71.
3. Ibid., p. 759 and table A23.
4. Construction and handicraft production (output of establishments that employed fewer than five workers and used no power) are excluded from this index, and their omission is a major weakness.
5. Not richly endowed with mineral resources, mining remained relatively unimportant in Taiwan despite substantial Japanese efforts at exploration and excavation.

Table 5.1. Fitted Annual Compound Growth Rate by Industry

	1912–45	*1912–40*	*1912–19*	*1920–29*	*1930–39*
General index	4.70	5.91	9.39	9.42	6.84
Mining	2.90	4.40	2.47	7.75	5.95
Manufacturing	4.64	5.94	11.04	9.64	6.35
Private manufacturing	5.71	7.31	16.06	11.26	6.58
Food	5.23	7.05	15.32	11.47	5.10
Sugar	5.88	7.83	19.80	12.22	5.04
Other	2.12	3.66	2.63	6.80	5.74
Chemicals[a]	6.62	8.08	23.77	11.29	11.08
Nonmetallic					
minerals	5.56	6.44	4.73	5.35	5.36
Textiles	7.11	9.24	1.66	13.76	10.98
Metals	14.79[b]	134.03[c]	—	—	210.26[d]
Production of					
monopoly bureau	−1.83	−2.02	−1.96	−0.80	2.27
Electric power	14.54[e]	16.14[f]	—	14.01	20.92

Notes and Source: A fitted growth rate is calculated by fitting the equation $X = X_0 (1 + r)^t$ to the data and estimating r. Thus it is an estimated compound growth rate taking into account all years within any period. The growth rates are computed from table A49.
[a] Following the classification used by the Japanese, this includes the production of paper.
[b] 1936–45.
[c] 1936–40.
[d] 1936–39.
[e] 1919–45.
[f] 1919–40.

factory employment, and 76 percent of the gross value of factory production.[6] Of the food processing industries, the most important was sugar refining. In 1921 sugar production was 61 percent of the gross value of factory production.[7] Even in the 1930s, after manufacturing had become somewhat more diversified, the share of sugar in the total gross value of factory production was still about 50 percent. Sugar production, with government encouragement and under Japanese management, increased dramatically, rising from an annual average output of 82,000 MT in the 1900s to 251,000 MT in the 1910s, 498,000 MT in the 1920s, and 948,000 MT in the 1930s.[8] More than anything else, the pace of industrialization in colonial Taiwan was set by the growth in the sugar industry.

6. *Taiwan Province: Statistical Summary*, pp. 763–66 and 778–87.
7. Ibid., p. 802.
8. Table A43.

Besides food processing, two other important areas developed in the colonial period: the chemical and ceramic (nonmetallic mineral products) industries. Together in 1930 they accounted for 20 percent of factory employment and about 10 percent of the gross value of factory production.[9] The chemical industry expanded particularly rapidly, with an average growth slightly above 8 percent per annum from 1912 to 1940. Here, as in food processing, the growth and commercialization of agriculture had its impact because Taiwan's chemical industry was linked closely to agriculture—its two most significant products were chemical fertilizers (an input to agriculture) and alcohol (which used molasses, a by-product of sugar production, as raw material). It should be noted that both these minor industries not only used raw materials that were readily available in Taiwan but also employed relatively unsophisticated technology.

Growth in factory manufacturing was most rapid from 1912 to 1919; thereafter the rate of growth steadily declined. With an extremely small industrial base at the beginning of this century, any sizable increment in output would have produced a very rapid rate of growth. However, the quick rise in factory manufacturing from 1912 to 1919 was also a reflection of the strong but temporary stimulus of World War I to industrialization. With Europe engaged in war, Japan took advantage of the decline of Western exports to Asia to expand its industrial exports to China and other Asian countries. Consequently, for the duration of the war, it had less to export to Taiwan,[10] and the shortage of manufactured goods in Taiwan encouraged many local manufacturing establishments to appear. Our industrial production index reflects this development as well as the subsequent contraction at the end of the war, when Japanese manufactured goods were once again exported to Taiwan in large quantities.

The growth of factory production in the 1920s and the 1930s was substantially below that achieved before 1920 (cf. table 5.1). Fixed on the image of Taiwan as an agricultural appendage to Japan, the colonial government and the Japanese capitalists did little to diversify Taiwan's economy. Consequently, as the sugar industry matured and its growth slowed, so did the general rate of industrialization in Taiwan. Because Taiwan was not an efficient producer of sugar, the

9. *Taiwan Province: Statistical Summary*, pp. 763–66 and 778–87.
10. From 1913 to 1918 the total volume of goods imported from Japan declined by 24 percent and that of imported manufactured goods by almost 37 percent.

growth of the industry was confined to the Japanese market, where it received preferential treatment.[11] By the early 1930s, Taiwan was already supplying over 85 percent of the sugar Japan imported. Clearly, without new markets the growth rate of sugar production attained in the earlier decades of the twentieth century could not continue. Indeed, the growth of refined sugar output declined from 19.8 percent in the 1910s to 12.2 percent in the 1920s and to 5.0 percent in the 1930s. This, more than any other factor, explains the decline in the growth of factory production.

Not until Japan began war preparation in the mid-1930s did it alter its strategy of promoting Taiwan as a two-commodity agricultural economy and belatedly begin to broaden the island's industrial base. Specifically, the colonial government and Japanese capitalists took steps to expand Taiwan's capacity to produce selected manufactured goods previously imported from Japan, and to create capacities in industrial raw materials needed by Japan's heavy industry.

To reduce Taiwan's dependence on Japanese imports, fertilizer production was increased and an effort was made to increase textile production by moving to Taiwan used Japanese machineries.[12] However, the most intensive efforts at modernization were reserved for the metal product and industrial chemical industries. The number of prime movers in the metal industry increased from 126 sets in 1933 to nearly 1,400 sets in 1941, and the value of production in the same period increased nearly 10-fold, from 6 million to 59 million yen.[13] In the chemical industry, similar impressive gains were made: the number of prime movers increased from 240 sets in 1933 to over 1,600 sets in 1941 and the value of production nearly quadrupled, from 20 million to 76 million yen.[14] The single most important development in this period was the formation of the Japan Aluminum

11. Summer typhoons and winter frost made much of Taiwan's land marginal for sugar cane production. These natural disadvantages were compounded by Taiwan's backward cultivating techniques. Thus Japan could have obtained sugar more cheaply from Java than from Taiwan. For example, in 1935 the CIF unit value of sugar imported by Japan from Java was 5.41 yen per 60 kg and the unit production cost of sugar in modern Taiwanese sugar refineries was 6.24 yen per 60 kg. Taiwan produced and sold as much sugar as it did only because the island operated within Japan's highly protective tariff wall.

12. A transfer of 126,682 spindles was planned, but only 28,964 spindles arrived in Taiwan before World War II disrupted further shipments. See Tung-tze Huang, "Taiwan's Textile Industry," *Taiwan's Textile Industry* (Taipei: BOT, 1956), p. 8.

13. *Taiwan Province: Statistical Summary*, pp. 773 and 780.

14. Ibid., pp. 773 and 778.

Company in 1935. By 1940 its plants in Kaohsiung and Hualien were producing one-sixth of Japan's aluminum. The rapid expansion of the metal and industrial chemical industries, however, was not sufficient to offset the declining growth of the food processing industry, so that the growth of factory manufacturing as a whole in the 1930s, at 6.4 percent per year, was less than that in the 1920s.[15] The last minute efforts at diversification also achieved little in the way of changing Taiwan's industrial structure.

Because Taiwan's factories reported both their output and employment data, labor productivity can be easily calculated.[16] Table 5.2 presents these productivity measurements for private manufacturing and mining from 1920 to 1939, which are suggestive as to the sources of industrial growth. Mining employment increased rapidly in the colonial period, and judging from the labor productivity measurement, it was the increase in labor that was largely responsible for the increase in mining output. Labor productivity in mining not only showed very little increase but also declined dramatically in the late 1930s, when large numbers of workers were added to the mines. This poor performance is but another reflection of the meagerness and inaccessibility of mineral resources in Taiwan.

Two labor indexes for private factory manufacturing are presented in table 5.2. L is an index of all factory employment in manufacturing, and L_{adj} is an index of factory employment in those manufacturing industries whose outputs are also included in the production index. Because of its greater similarity in coverage to the production index, it is believed that L_{adj} is the more appropriate labor index to use to calculate labor productivity. Regardless of which labor index is used, the labor productivity index derived from it suggests that before the mid-1930s labor productivity was a major source of growth in factory manufacturing. In the late 1930s however, factory output increased primarily because of growth in factory employment.

When the labor productivity of the three major manufacturing industries (food, ceramics, and chemicals) is examined, it is apparent

15. However, it should be noted that for lack of data some of the fastest growing outputs of the heavy chemical and metal industries were not included in our production index. In other words, our production index tends to understate the rate of industrialization in the 1930s.

16. The employment statistics are year-end figures. Because of seasonal variation an annual average would have been preferred; even better, of course, would have been a man-day measurement.

Table 5.2. Index of Labor Productivity in Manufacturing and Mining, 1920–39 (Five-year averages)

	Mining			Private manufacturing					Food			Ceramics			Chemical		
	L	Q	Q/L	L	L_{adj}	Q	Q/L	Q/L_{adj}	L	Q	Q/L	L	Q	Q/L	L	Q	Q/L
1920–24	100	100	100	100	100	100	100	100	100	100	100	100	100	100	100	100	100
1925–29	138	150	109	127	120	165	130	137	118	163	138	119	130	109	130	166	128
1930–34	155	161	104	140	132	211	151	160	139	226	162	139	144	104	95	151	159
1935–39	281	211	75	202	184	306	151	166	198	308	156	164	192	117	130	261	201

Notes and Sources: Factory employment statistics are available from 1914, but the early data are believed to be defective because of under-coverage. Consequently labor productivity is computed only from 1920. L_{adj} is obtained by subtracting the employment in those manufacturing sectors whose outputs are not included in the manufacturing output index, e.g., machinery and wood and wood products. In other words the coverage of the input and output indexes is more comparable when L_{adj} is used than when total manufacturing factory employment (L) is used. The labor indexes are calculated from table A23, and the output indexes are from table A49.

that the rapid rise in labor productivity in manufacturing before the mid-1930s and the decline thereafter are largely reflections of changes in labor productivity in the food processing industry. The accumulation of capital and the improvement of labor skills in the food, but particularly in the sugar, industry prior to the 1930s explain the rapid rise in labor productivity in manufacturing.[17] But in the 1930s, when Japan's need and interest shifted from the food to the nonfood industries, less capital was channeled to the food industry, and accordingly its labor productivity suffered. At the same time, resources were channeled to nonfood industries such as metal products and chemicals, causing their labor productivity to rise rapidly.[18] But because of the prominent position enjoyed by the food processing industry, the decline of its labor productivity more than offset the rise in labor productivity elsewhere so that labor productivity for factory manufacturing as a whole showed only a slight increase in the late 1930s.

The factory enclave, whose growth we have traced, was composed of a handful of very large companies and innumerable small establishments. In 1936, the six largest industrial firms accounted for nearly 80 percent of the paid-up corporate capital in the factory enclave, and of the six, five were sugar companies.[19] The average Taiwanese factory employed only a small number of workers; in 1933 the average was 10.[20] Of the 6,596 factories surveyed in 1933, only 5 percent employed more than 30 workers and nearly 57 percent employed fewer than 5 workers.[21] The larger establishments were mostly in food processing. Eighty-five of the 107 factories that employed more than 100 workers were in food processing, of which 37 were sugar refineries. Food processing establishments also accounted for 62 percent of those factories that employed between 50 and 100 workers. Interestingly enough, the very small manufacturing establishments were also mainly in food processing. Of the 3,751 establishments that employed fewer than 5 workers but used power, 90.1 percent

17. From 1905 to 1920, 58 percent of the total value of machinery imported by Taiwan was for the sugar industry. In the 1930s the share of sugar refining machinery in total machinery imported was only about 10 percent.

18. From 1930–34 to 1935–39 the number of horsepower per factory worker in the metal product industry rose from 1.17 to 6.27.

19. Taiwan Government-General, *Taiwan Commercial and Industrial Statistics*, 1936, pp. 122–23.

20. *Taiwan Province: Statistical Summary*, pp. 763–66.

21. Table A56.

were in food processing. In fact, 78 percent of all food processing establishments, most of which were rice milling shops, were in this category. The lack of any significant economy of scale in rice milling and the increased output of rice made it possible for many small rice milling shops to exist simultaneously.

Handicraft

The factory enclave existed side by side with handicraft shops, of which we know little. Nevertheless it is possible to estimate for several years in the colonial period the number of workers engaged in handicrafts. Five of the seven population censuses conducted during the colonial period (1905, 1915, 1920, 1930, and 1940) reported the total number of persons engaged in manufacturing. These included both factory workers and those handicraft workers who considered their crafts to be their principal occupation. Because, after 1914, the government also collected factory employment statistics, handicraft employment for 1915, 1920, 1930, and 1940 can be derived by subtracting factory employment from the total employment in manufacturing. This is calculated and the results are shown in table 5.3.[22] Before discussing these figures, it should be noted that because handicraft techniques are very labor intensive, a comparison of handicraft employment and factory employment tends to exaggerate the relative importance of handicraft in manufacturing.[23]

Our estimates indicate that in 1915 more workers were engaged in handicraft than in factory production. In fact, handicraft employment was more than three times that of factory employment. Although the size of the difference may be somewhat exaggerated because the 1915 factory employment figure, collected only a few years after the establishment of the factory reporting system, is likely to be understated, the prominence of the handicraft sector cannot be disputed. It is recalled that in 1915 sugar refining, at that time the only modern industry, was still in its infancy. Apparently handicraft was most

22. Because the census and the factory employment data were collected at different times in the year, part of the difference between the census and the factory employment figures may reflect merely the seasonal changes in employment. For this and other reasons, our estimates are far from precise and should be taken to represent only the order of magnitude of handicraft employment.

23. One estimate put the gross value of handicraft production in 1937 at 21.5 million yen, or about 5.5 percent of factory manufacturing. The share of handicraft production in total manufacturing was undoubtedly higher in earlier years. See DGBAS, *Taiwan's National Income and Product*, p. 142.

Table 5.3. Estimated Handicraft Employment: 1915, 1920, 1930, 1940

	A Total persons engaged in manufacturing according to census	B Factory employment in manufacturing	C Estimated handicraft employment (A − B)	C/A (%)
1915	119,142	29,298	89,844	75.4
1920	130,825	51,521	79,304	60.6
1930 A	124,712	60,979	63,733	51.1
1930 B	121,627	60,979	60,648	49.9
1940	172,121	128,505	43,616	25.3

Notes and Sources: Factory employment is the sum of workers engaged by private manufacturing establishments that employed at least five workers or used power and workers employed by factories operated by the Monopoly Bureau. The 1915, 1920, and the 1930A census figures and the 1930B and the 1940 census figures do not represent precisely the same kind of information. The former group represents the distribution of occupied persons by their occupations and the latter group by the industries in which they worked. The category *manufacturing*, however, remains approximately the same for all five observations, as the 1930 figures show. The number of workers employed by the Monopoly Bureau for 1915 and 1940 are the author's estimates and are based on the number employed by the Monopoly Bureau in 1916 and 1938. For the sources of the census figures, see tables A21 and A22. The factory employment of private manufacturing establishments is from table A23 and the employment of the Monopoly Bureau is from Taiwan Government-General, *Monopoly Bureau Annual Business Report*, various issues.

prevalent in the apparel, textile, and wood and bamboo product industries. At least 50 percent of the discrepancy between the census figures and the factory employment statistics in 1920, 1930, and 1940 can be traced to discrepancies in these three industries. This is not surprising, in view of the fact that establishments in these industries are well suited for handicraft: they require little capital, consume little or no nonhuman power, use mostly indigenous raw materials, and cater to traditional tastes not easily satisfied by factory products.

As expected, the size of the handicraft sector declined as the island industrialized and modern means of production were introduced that required larger shops and a more concentrated labor force. Our estimates show that the share of handicraft workers in the total number of persons engaged in manufacturing declined from 75 percent in 1915 to 60 percent in 1920, 50 percent in 1930, and 25 percent in 1940. It is interesting that the period 1930–40, during which the relative size of the handicraft sector in terms of employment declined most drastically, is precisely the same period the Japanese were most actively engaged in broadening Taiwan's industrial base.

The relative position of handicraft deteriorated rapidly in the 1930s, not because of an accelerated decline in handicraft employment, but because of a rapid increase in factory employment. Between 1930 and 1940 handicraft employment decreased by about 20,000, approximately the same number by which it fell in the previous decade, but factory employment increased by more than 60,000, thus doubling its size in a decade. This pattern of growth, i.e., rapid increase in factory employment but not more than usual at the expense of handicraft employment, is supported by the known pattern of industrialization in the 1930s. The factories established or expanded in the 1930s produced goods that did not compete directly with the handicraft shops. Rather they supplied Japan with industrial raw materials or replaced Japanese imports.

SOURCES OF INDUSTRIAL LABOR AND CAPITAL

Labor

From 1905 to 1940, male occupied persons in agriculture increased by 26 percent, in manufacturing (factory and handicraft) by 120 percent, and in mining by 505 percent.[24] That employment in industry expanded more rapidly than in agriculture suggests a movement of workers from agriculture to nonagriculture. However, the indigenous population experienced less of a social change than the increase in industrial employment seems to indicate. The reason is that throughout the colonial period there was a steady migration of Japanese to Taiwan. The colonial government encouraged this migration not only because it thought a growing Japanese population would give greater stability and security to the island but also because it correctly realized that the migration eased the problem of staffing both the political and the corporate establishments in Taiwan without at the same time diluting Japanese control of these organizations. As incentives, favorable treatment was accorded to the Japanese by both the colonial

---

24. These numbers are based on census figures (see tables A21 and A22). The comparison is made in terms of male rather than total employed persons because in an oriental society there is great uncertainty as to how people respond to questions concerning the occupation of women. It is generally thought that in working with census data a more accurate picture is obtained of the employment structure when women are excluded.

government and the Japanese enterprises in Taiwan. Consequently, even unskilled Japanese found it to their advantage to come to Taiwan, where they could sustain a standard of living and reach a status in society not easily achieved at home.[25] The precise number of Japanese who immigrated to Taiwan each year is not known but was on the order of tens of thousands, mostly males of working age.[26] By 1925, 183,722 Japanese resided in Taiwan and by 1940 the number had increased to 312,386.

Significantly, an overwhelming proportion of the Japanese immigrants were skilled in activities other than farming, and even the Japanese farmers who moved to Taiwan found it easier to switch occupations and remain in the cities among their own than to adapt to a totally strange and often hostile rural environment. The Japanese were concentrated in five lines of economic activities: manufacturing, communication and transport, trade, government, and professional service. In 1930 Japanese working males in these five sectors accounted for 80 percent of the total Japanese working males in Taiwan.[27] Similar distributions are found in other census years.

Since the Japanese workers were generally better trained than the Taiwanese, their participation helped to raise the quality of Taiwan's industrial labor force.[28] But at the same time the influx of Japanese reduced the pressure on government and business to train Taiwanese and upgrade their skills. A survey of male workers employed by large (more than 30 workers) industrial establishments in 1943 clearly shows that it was the Japanese who provided the skills and know-how that operated most of Taiwan's large industrial and business enterprises.[29] Japanese accounted for 80 percent of the total technicians employed by the large industrial enterprises and similarly high percentages were found in fields such as trade (74 percent), transportation (80 percent),

---

25. Not only were the more coveted positions reserved for the Japanese, but even for similar work the Japanese workers were given a wage that was generally twice that given to the Taiwanese. Only after 1935, when the demand for industrial workers was greatly intensified by war preparation, did this wage gap narrow somewhat.

26. *Taiwan Province: Statistical Summary*, pp. 322–23.

27. Table A21.

28. Whereas 33.2 percent of the Taiwanese laborers employed by large (more than 30 workers) industrial enterprises in 1943 had no education, fewer than 1 percent of the Japanese laborers fell into this category. In fact nearly 70 percent of the Japanese laborers employed by large industrial establishments had more than a primary school education. For details see Taiwan Government-General, *The Results of the Survey on Labor Skills*, 1943, vol. 1, pp. 266–69 and 734–41.

29. *Taiwan Province: Statistical Summary*, pp. 829–38.

Table 5.4. Occupational Composition (Percentage of occupied males reported in each
occupation: 1905, 1915, 1920, 1930, and 1940)

	1905	1915	1920	1930a	1930b	1940
Agriculture	69.9	71.0	68.9	68.0	69.2	61.5
Fishing	2.8	2.4	2.2	2.0	2.2	1.7
Mining	0.5	0.8	1.4	1.3	1.7	2.5
Manufacturing	5.0	5.8	6.8	5.8	5.9	7.4
Construction	0.6	0.8	1.0	1.7	1.8	2.4
Electricity, gas, and water	—	—	0.1	0.1	0.1	0.2
Communication and transport	2.2	2.7	3.2	3.8	3.2	3.1
Trade	6.7	6.7	6.7	9.5	11.1	9.9
Banking and insurance	—	—	0.2	—	0.1	0.2
Government	0.8	0.6	0.9	0.7	1.7	1.6
Professional service	0.7	0.8	1.3	2.0	1.9	2.5
Other	10.7	8.3	7.3	4.9	1.3	7.2
Total	100.0	100.0	100.0	100.0	100.0	100.0

Notes and Sources: The 1905, 1915, 1920, and 1930a distributions of employed workers
are by occupation grouped along certain economic lines. The 1930b and 1940 distributions are by industry. The Japanese scheme of occupational classification prior to 1940
is not the conventional one in use today and is quite close, as the two sets of figures
for 1930 indicate, to the industrial classification of workers. These figures are from
tables A21 and A22.

and communication (92 percent). Whereas a smaller percentage of the
laborers employed by these enterprises were Japanese, it is interesting
to observe that a higher rate of Japanese participation is found in
those industries that have a greater need for skilled laborers, e.g.,
communication (32 percent), electrical power generation (25 percent),
chemical (11 percent), and machinery (11 percent).

Once the movement of Japanese into Taiwan is taken into account,
it becomes apparent that the growth in industrial employment was
not caused by a redeployment of Taiwanese workers alone. When the
Japanese are excluded from the population data, the impact of industrialization on the Taiwanese becomes clearer. Table 5.4 presents
the distribution of Taiwanese working males by economic sectors for
five census years. Until 1930 there was little change in the occupational
structure of the Taiwanese. Apparently only a relatively small number
of Taiwanese moved out of agriculture and changed their occupation.
Only in the 1930s, when industrialization occurred across a broader
front, did the share of Taiwanese males engaged in agriculture decline
and a larger number of Taiwanese become actively involved in
industrial activities.

The census data, however, tend to underplay the extent to which Taiwanese moved between the agricultural and industrial sectors. The dominant position of agriculture and the fact that in table 5.4 changes in occupation were compared with total occupied persons make marginal shifts between lines of economic activity very much less noticeable. A more sensitive device to observe the movement of Taiwanese is provided by Barclay in his careful analysis of the disposition of manpower in colonial Taiwan. Briefly, Barclay measured the proportion of persons in a particular occupation and age group that remains in the same occupation at a later date. His findings, based on the 1920 and 1930 censuses, reveal that "even though the permanent result of the movement (in terms of changing the age-specific occupational structure of the population) was very small. . . changes in occupation were actually more numerous and followed well-defined patterns. In particular agriculture had a double role. It was the outstanding source of supply of young men in other occupations; and it was a pursuit to which many men returned when they were no longer youthful."[30] In other words, rural Taiwan lends workers to the nonagricultural sector when they are young and takes them back after they become old. The same pattern was observed in the 1930s, i.e., agriculture suffered heavy losses of workers, about 11 percent of survivors, between the ages 25 and 34 while absorbing older workers from other sectors.[31]

Capital

Capital for Taiwan's industry came initially from Japan; later, as the economy developed, it was financed increasingly from within the island.[32] The flow of capital from Japan to Taiwan's nonagricultural sector was most important in the decade immediately after Japan took control of the island. It is uncertain how much capital moved

30. George W. Barclay, *Colonial Development and Population in Taiwan*, pp. 97–98.
31. Paul K. C. Liu, "Population Redistribution and Development in Taiwan, 1951–1965," pp. 29–30.
32. Investment by countries other than Japan was negligible during the colonial period. Two American firms maintained offices in Taiwan for the purpose of buying tea, and the Standard-Vacuum Oil Company had a branch office in Taihoku (Taipei). In industry, the only non-Japanese foreign interest was Tokki Gomei Kaisha, a sulfur mine owned by a British national. Aside from these minor direct investments, Taiwan also borrowed US$ 22.8 million (45.7 million yen) from a New York banking syndicate in 1931 to help construct a power plant on Lake Jitsugetsutan (Sun-Moon Lake). This is the only known non-Japanese foreign loan received by Taiwan before World War II.

from Japan to Taiwan in this early period, but the balance on merchandise trade is suggestive of the magnitude. Except in 1913 Taiwan
did not have a trade deficit after 1908. But between 1897 and 1908,
Taiwan incurred a total deficit of 34.5 million yen.[33] Shipping and
insurance in these years as in later years were services provided largely
by Japan. Thus, when the invisible items are taken into account, the
deficit on current account must have been substantially higher than
the trade deficit. To offset its deficit balance on current account, since
Taiwan did not have foreign reserves to deplete, there must have been
a significant inflow of capital, much of which was used to provide the
island with its industrial superstructure.

That a substantial amount of Japanese industrial capital moved
into Taiwan before 1910 is also suggested by other evidence. The
colonial government, between 1900 and 1906, issued 25 million yen
of par value bonds, nearly all of which were absorbed by Japan. More
than half the receipts from the government bond sales were used to
construct the railroad network in Taiwan.[34] Japanese were attracted
to invest in Taiwan's sugar industry initially by the government
promise of a guaranteed dividend of 6 percent on their investments.
Subsequently, high profits in the sugar industry attracted more investments, so that by 1910 five of the six major sugar companies that
were to dominate Taiwan's manufacturing sector were established. It
is not known how much Japanese capital went into these private
ventures, but it was probably on the order of 20–30 million yen. The
first fully modern sugar refinery was constructed and equipped in
1901 at a total cost of 850,000 yen.[35] By 1910 there were fifteen of
these modern refineries. Altogether, from 1896 to 1910 perhaps
around 80 million yen of Japanese capital flowed into Taiwan.

Although profitable opportunities continued to attract Japanese
investments to Taiwan, industrial investments in the 1920s and 1930s
were probably financed primarily by savings generated in Taiwan. To
finance industrial investments there were two internal sources: agricultural savings and industrial profits. One consequence of rising

33. Computed from Taiwan Government-General, *The Annual Taiwan Trade Statistics,* various issues.
34. The remaining portions of the receipts from the bond sales went to finance the
construction of harbors and government buildings (cf. Tung Huang, Tsung-han Chang,
and Chang-chin Lee, *Government Financing in Taiwan Under the Japanese Regime,*
table 20).
35. James W. Davidson, *The Island of Formosa, Past and Present,* p. 453.

Table 5.5. Share of Dividends in Net Profit in Joint Stock Companies

	All joint stock companies	All industrical joint stock companies	Joint stock companies in food processing
1932	n.a.	62.4	59.1
1933	47.5	46.1	44.7
1934	48.6	45.9	45.1
1935	47.0	43.1	41.2
1936	45.5	44.6	36.4
1937	45.5	42.7	40.7
1938	47.4	42.9	46.5
1939	44.4	45.1	41.5
1940	45.8	44.4	41.7

Sources: Taiwan Government-General, *Taiwan Commercial and Industrial Statistics*, 1932, p. 112; 1939, p. 98; 1940, p. 98; and *Taiwan Commercial Statistics*, 1941, p. 8.

agricultural productivity was the appearance of a substantial surplus, much of which was channeled out of agriculture. Although the amount of agricultural savings that was actually invested in industry is not known, its volume was probably not insignificant and undoubtedly helped finance the large number of small industrial establishments that appeared in the colonial period.

More is known about the second source of industrial capital, the retained profits of industrial enterprises. Table 5.5 presents dividends as a share of net profits for joint stock companies in Taiwan. The evidence suggests that at least in the 1930s a large share of net profits was retained by the companies and presumably reinvested either in Taiwan or elsewhere in the empire. This was the pattern for all joint stock companies as well as for those in industry. Except for 1932, a depression year in Taiwan, retained earnings of the industrial joint stock companies exceeded 50 percent of net profits, and those of the food processing companies were even higher. This is significant because food processing was the largest and most developed industry in Taiwan, and its behavior generally reflected that of its most important and heavily capitalized component, the sugar industry.

With its huge monopoly profits, the sugar industry was able to satisfy its stockholders without sacrificing a large share of its net profits to dividend. Thus, in 1939 the six largest sugar companies paid dividends that ranged from 8 to 12 percent of paid-up capital.[36] In the same year,

36. Andrew J. Grajdanzev, *Formosa Today*, p. 100.

Table 5.6.   Distribution of Paid-up Capital of Companies by Type of Organization
and by Nationality of Ownership, 1929

	Total (million yen)	Percentage of total capital owned by each nationality			
		Total	Japanese	Taiwanese	Other
Joint stock companies	287.9	100.0	78.4	19.8	1.8
Manufacturing[a]	198.9	100.0	90.7	8.4	0.8
Mining	17.1	100.0	71.6	20.1	8.3
Agriculture	9.4	100.0	47.2	52.8	b
Commerce	53.2	100.0	43.4	52.7	3.8
Transportation	5.8	100.0	55.1	44.5	0.4
Fishing	3.4	100.0	65.1	34.3	0.6
Limited partnerships	16.6	100.0	68.0	32.0	—
Unlimited companies	7.9	100.0	23.6	76.4	—
Total	312.4	100.0	76.5	21.9	1.6

Sources: The original source of the data is Shintaro Atomiya, "Characteristics of Taiwan's Business World," *Taiwan Keizai Sosho*, vol. 1. They are also cited in Han-yu Chang, "Transformation of Taiwan's Economy During the Period of Japanese Rule," in BOT, *Collection of Writings on Taiwan's Economic History, no. 2*, pp. 96–97.
[a] Includes electric power generation.
[b] Less than 0.05%.

these firms were earning profits of 20–45 percent of paid-up capital. So the ample dividend payments absorbed only from 26 to 45 percent of the profits, leaving substantial retained earnings for reinvestment. That the sugar companies had a high propensity to reinvest their profits is not surprising, since this behavior was much encouraged by the colonial government, an influential force among sugar producers. Because the capacity of each sugar company was carefully controlled by the government, much of the retained earnings was used not to expand refining capacity but to increase its investments in other industries. Indeed, the sugar companies were major investors in such fields as mining, alcohol, pulp and paper, metal products, pharmaceuticals, canning, and commerce.[37]

Japanese control of Taiwan's modern companies, most of which were in manufacturing, was almost complete. Table 5.6 gives the distribution of paid-up capital of companies in Taiwan by nationality of

37. U.S. Navy Department, Office of Naval Operations, *Civil Affairs Handbook, Taiwan—Economic Supplement*, OPNAV 50 E-13 (Washington, D.C., 1944), p. 118, and "The Investment of Japanese *Zaibatsu* in Taiwan," *Collection of Writings on Taiwan's Economic History, No. 2* (Taipei: BOT, 1955), pp. 136–37.

owners for 1929, and it shows that Japanese owned 78.4 percent of the capital organized as joint stock companies, 68.0 percent of the capital organized as limited partnerships, and 23.6 percent of the capital organized as unlimited companies.[38] Taking these three types of firms together, the Japanese share was 76.5 percent. Japanese capital was predominantly invested in manufacturing (including electric power generation) and mining, where its share of capital was 90.7 and 71.6 percent, respectively.

Japanese ownership was most prevalent among the large and the heavily capitalized companies. In 1938–41, of the paid-up capital of joint stock companies that had authorized capital exceeding 5 million yen, nearly 97 percent were owned by Japanese.[39] Of those joint stock companies that had authorized capital between 200,000 and 5 million yen, the Japanese share of paid-up capital was approximately 65 percent. It is unclear what portion of these large Japanese holdings was under the control of *zaibatsu* (family-owned conglomerates with holdings in many economic sectors). The connection between Taiwan's economy and the zaibatsu was complex and not easy to untangle, but undoubtedly an extremely close relationship existed. The zaibatsu seem to have had a hand in nearly all the major industrial and commercial undertakings in Taiwan. The names of the big four zaibatsu— Mitsui, Mitsubishi, Yasuda, and Sumitomo—appear again and again as owners or part-owners of important industrial and commercial firms in Taiwan as well as of lesser known Taiwanese enterprises.[40]

Not all the Japanese capital in Taiwan was connected with the zaibatsu or owned by Japanese residing in Japan. When the ownership of capital is distributed according to Japanese living in Japan, Japanese

38. Although corporations represent only a very small percentage of the total number of industrial and commercial enterprises in colonial Taiwan, they include most of the larger establishments and probably all those that employed more than 50 workers. I have been unable to identify the nationality of capital in Taiwan for a year closer to the end of the colonial period. However, because most new enterprises created during the 1930s were Japanese owned, it is believed that the situation altered little after 1929.

39. Computed from data in Han-yu Chang, "Transformation of Taiwan's Economy During the Period of Japanese Rule," in BOT, *Collection of Writings on Taiwan's Economic History, No. 2* (Taipei: BOT, 1955), p. 97.

40. For example, Mitsui, Mitsubishi, Sumitomo, Yasuda, and Furukawa were major shareholders in important Taiwanese companies such as Taiwan Sugar Co., Japan Sugar Co., Meiji Sugar Co., Ensuiko Sugar Co., Taiwan Power Co., Japan Aluminum Co., Taiwan Development Co., Keelung Coal Mining, and Taiwan Iron. For a fairly comprehensive compilation see "The Investment of Japanese *Zaibatsu* in Taiwan," in BOT, *Collection of Writings on Taiwan's Economic History, No. 2* (1955), pp. 130–39.

living in Taiwan, and Taiwanese, it becomes evident that a substantial share of the industrial and commerical capital was owned by Japanese who lived and worked in Taiwan. In the late 1930s Japanese capitalists living in Taiwan owned slightly less than 20 percent of the paid-up capital of joint stock companies with authorized capital exceeding 5 million yen. [41] For joint stock companies with authorized capital between 200,000 and 5 million yen, the share owned by Japanese capitalists living in Taiwan was higher (more than one-third). It seems that many of the small and medium-sized companies in Taiwan were owned by ordinary Japanese who wanted to invest their limited savings.

Statistical evidence of Taiwanese investment is scantier, but from what has been presented so far it is clear that most Taiwanese invested their capital in the traditional component of the nonagricultural sector, e.g., small industrial establishments, handicraft shops, traditional transportation, and traditional commerce. There was little Taiwanese capital in the modern industrial sector. In 1929 Taiwanese owned less than 10 percent of the paid-up capital of industrial joint stock companies. In later years the situation was not much altered. In the modern sector the impact of Taiwanese capital was most noticeable in commerce. Here, the Taiwanese share of paid-up capital of joint stock companies was about one-half. Because the export and import trade were dominated by the Japanese, owing to their connections in and knowledge of Japan, Taiwanese capital presumably was invested in domestic wholesale and retail trade.

Very few Taiwanese had large amounts of capital to invest and there is little evidence that institutions were developed to help the Taiwanese pool their resources. For instance, banks did little to mobilize Taiwanese savings. In the 1930s more than 70 percent of the total bank deposits in Taiwan were held by Japanese.[42] Consequently, Taiwanese capital, which presumably was agricultural in origin, when channeled to industry, went primarily to finance small establishments. For example, two industrial activities well known for their small-scale operation, rice milling and noodle manufacturing were overwhelmingly Taiwanese. In the early 1930s, 98.9 percent of the rice milling establishments and 98.8 percent of the noodle factories were owned by Taiwanese.[43] Just as Japanese capital dominated the large industrial

41. Chang, "Transformation of Taiwan's Economy," p. 97.
42. Taiwan Government-General, *Taiwan Monetary Yearbook*, various issues.
43. Benji Negishi, "Agricultural Enterprise and the Competitive Relationship of Rice and Sugar in Taiwan During the Period of Japanese Occupation," in BOT, *Collection of Writings on Taiwan's Economic History, No. 7* (1959), p. 59.

enterprises, so did Taiwanese capital dominate the very small industrial establishments.

The evidence offered in this chapter provides the following picture of industrialization in colonial Taiwan. Industry was partitioned into a large, though shrinking, traditional sector and a modern enclave. The enclave (modern transportation and the corporate industrial sector) was in every sense a Japanese sector. The techniques of production and management as well as much of the capital equipment used in the enclave came from Japan. It was owned, managed, and operated by Japanese. Taiwanese participation in the enclave was limited to the contribution of their labor. And even in this area, Japanese participation was signficant. The traditional sector, made up of small manufacturing establishments and handicraft shops, on the other hand, was the domain of the Taiwanese. In sharp contrast with the Japanese-operated enclave, it was undercapitalized and used traditional or slightly modified traditional production techniques. In terms of production the enclave was by far the more important, but in terms of employment the traditional sector was at least equally important.

From Japan's point of view, its domination of the enclave was necessary to ensure Japanese control of the economy and the sizable profits or "export surplus" produced by the economy. Much of this profit was removed from Taiwan. From 1935 to 1939, for example, incomplete records indicate that there was an average net outflow of investment income and capital from Taiwan amounting to nearly 50 million yen per year.[44] Although Japanese labor and capital undoubtedly contributed to Taiwan's industrial growth, Japanese control and domination of the industrial enclave at the same time limited its interaction with agriculture. Taiwanese-owned capital, mainly from agriculture, was largely kept out of the enclave, although some did flow to the traditional industrial establishments. Since the enclave could draw laborers from Japan, fewer Taiwanese workers moved from agriculture to nonagriculture. And of the Taiwanese who were absorbed by the enclave, the benefit of contact was not so great as it could have been, because the knowledge that technicians and skilled laborers could be attracted from Japan lessened the pressure on the colonial government and the Japanese capitalists to provide training, and most remained unskilled. Such is the cost of colonial development.

Much of the industrial growth experienced in the colonial period

44. Table A67.

came from the modern enclave, as it expanded at the expense of the handicraft sector. Efforts to expand the enclave was especially intense in the 1930s, when war preparation induced Japan to expand its industrial base to the colonies. In the late 1930s, before World War II made further industrialization impossible, Japan made a concerted effort to bring new industries to Taiwan. Scores of modern factories in shipbuilding, basic metals, pulp, oil refining, textiles, and fertilizers were opened, most with new capital equipment but in some cases with old equipment dismantled in Japan and shipped to Taiwan. In spite of these last minute efforts, at the end of the colonial period Taiwan was still basically an agrarian economy. But now it also had an industrial superstructure to provide a strong foundation for future industrialization: an extensive transport system, a substantial electric power generation capacity, a growing indigenous and well-disciplined industrial labor force, and a limited number of fairly modern manufacturing enterprises.

6

Colonial Development and the Taiwanese

Taiwan was developed to satisfy Japanese needs and operated to benefit Japanese investors. These were, after all, the objectives of colonialism and of imposing on Taiwan the triangular mode of resource utilization. An interesting and important question is whether economic development under colonialism also brought benefits to the Taiwanese. In other words, did the economic conditions of the average Taiwanese improve in the colonial period? In this chapter, using the bits of data on wages and consumption that exist, we attempt to provide an answer. Briefly, the evidence is that in the colonial period the average Taiwanese improved his general economic conditions moderately and in a few areas, such as education and health, significantly. Economic development required Taiwanese participation, and had the Taiwanese not benefited from development, it is doubtful that development in the colonial period would have been so smooth and successful.

The usual indicators of economic welfare such as personal income and consumption do not exist for the colonial period. Therefore, to document the changing economic conditions of the Taiwanese, we must turn to other and more disaggregated data. In particular, we draw on two sources of information: wages and estimates of per capita consumption of selected goods and services.

REAL WAGE

From 1910, sufficient data exist to construct nominal wage indexes for male Taiwanese workers in five sectors: agriculture, mining, manufacturing, construction, and government. These are then deflated by a common consumer price index to produce real wage indexes. The average real wage earned by male Taiwanese in these sectors is calcu-

Table 6.1. Average Real Wages by Industry, 1910–38 (1910–14 = 100)

	1910–14	*1915–19*	*1920–24*	*1925–29*	*1930–34*	*1935–38*
Agriculture						
(hired labor)	100.0	109.5	136.5	154.0	137.9	116.7
Mining	100.0	113.3	141.8	148.6	97.9	165.6
Manufacturing	100.0	100.3	138.0	145.1	160.6	152.2
Construction	100.0	95.9	154.9	151.1	157.6	146.1
Government	100.0	87.7	176.5	183.7	232.5	198.1

Notes and Sources: Using the wage rates for various occupations collected in the colonial period, nominal wage indexes were constructed for agriculture, mining, manufacturing, construction, and government. In all cases, except for government, the daily rates of male Taiwanese were used. The government wage rate is the average annual salary paid to clerks, most of whom were Taiwanese. For more information on the nominal wage indexes, see table A30. The real wage indexes were derived by deflating the nominal wage indexes by Mizoguchi's consumer price index I (cf. Toshiyuki Mizoguchi, "Consumer Prices and Real Wages in Taiwan and Korea Under Japanese Rule"). Since Mizoguchi's index I is very similar to his index II, our results would not be significantly different had we used his index II as the deflator.

lated and presented in index forms (1910–14 = 100) in table 6.1. For the period 1910–38, workers in all five sectors experienced moderate to rapid increases in their real wage. The most substantial gains were made in the government sector, where the real wage doubled between 1910–14 and 1935–38. The rise in the real wage was much slower in agriculture, where its growth averaged just slightly better than 1 percent a year.[1] Agricultural real wage was only 17 percent higher in 1935–38 than in 1910–14.

There were considerable fluctuations in the real wage. During World War I, wages in most sectors either lagged or just kept pace with prices so that real wages declined or at best showed small gains. The decline in the real wage was most serious in the government sector, where the nominal wage remained constant from 1914 to 1919. In the years immediately after World War I, wages continued to rise while prices declined, and real wages rose sharply. Most dramatic was the rise in the real wage in the government sector, where the nominal wage

1. Mizoguchi reported a significantly higher growth rate in agricultural real wage (see his "Consumer Prices and Real Wages in Taiwan and Korea under Japanese Rule," p. 49). However, he confined his examination to the period 1915–33, thus neglecting the decline in real wage in the mid- and late-1930s. When limited to the period 1915–33, our real wage index shows an annual growth rate of 2.59 percent, very close to the rate reported by Mizoguchi.

doubled between 1919 and 1920. After prices and wages were realigned in the early 1920s, they became more stable. From 1921 to 1929 real wages increased moderately in all sectors. In the early 1930s, as a result of the Great Depression, prices fell sharply in Taiwan. In agriculture and mining, where nominal wages dropped even more sharply than prices, real wages declined. However, the decline in the nominal wage was less pronounced in the other sectors, where the real wage thus increased in the first half of the 1930s. For example, the nominal wage remained constant in the government sector so the decline in prices in the early 1930s resulted in a considerable rise in the real wage earned by government employees. In the second half of the 1930s, when Japan intensified its drive to industrialize Taiwan, prices again climbed faster than wages. In consequence, real wages fell in most sectors. The exception was in mining, where efforts to attract greater numbers of workers to Taiwan's mines kept its nominal wage growing faster than prices.

The wage data suggest that although the economic conditions of Taiwanese improved, the growth in real wage was significantly slower than that of labor productivity. For example, from 1910 to 1939 agricultural labor productivity increased on the average by 3 percent a year while agricultural real wage increased by 1.3 percent a year; in the 1920s and the 1930s labor productivity in manufacturing rose on the average by 3.3 percent a year while the average annual increase in real wage was only about 1.5 percent.[2] Furthermore, the economic conditions of agricultural workers improved less consistently than did those of non-agricultural workers. This is significant since almost 70 percent of the male Taiwanese workers were engaged in agriculture. Nevertheless, one needs to be reminded that wage earners in Taiwanese agriculture, although important, were but a small portion of the rural labor force. Therefore, how real wage moved is only suggestive and not conclusive evidence of how overall economic conditions changed in rural Taiwan. Before we draw conclusions, other information must be considered.

PER CAPITA CONSUMPTION

Food

The second source of evidence is the trends of per capita consumption of selected goods and services. Our examination begins with food, the

2. For sources, see tables 4.3, 5.2, and 6.1.

Table 6.2. Per Capita Food Availability, 1910–44 (Annual averages)

	Annual per capita production of rice (kg)	Annual per capita export of rice (kg)	Annual per capita availability of rice (kg)	Daily calories from rice and sweet potatoes			Daily food availability (calories)
				Rice	Sweet potatoes	Total	
1910–14	188.6	27.2	133.7	1,319	89	1,408	1,760–2,011[a]
1915–19	188.8	27.9	129.2	1,275	141	1,416	1,770–2,023
1920–24	193.4	34.6	131.2	1,295	213	1,507	1,884–2,158
1925–29	217.6	58.3	131.4	1,296	259	1,546	1,932–2,208
1930–34	242.0	100.7	115.3	1,137	303	1,440	1,800–2,057
1935–39	242.1	119.1	91.7	904	327	1,231	1,865
1940–44	179.8	51.5	108.7	1,074	265	1,339	1,693

Notes and Sources: The annual per capita production and export of rice are measured in terms of brown rice. The estimates of availability and caloric intake from rice and sweet potatoes for 1935–44 are from Ralph N. Gleason, *Taiwan Food Balances 1935–1954*, pp. 54–57. The estimates for the other years are that of the author. Availability is defined as production minus net export, waste, seeds, feeds, industrial uses, and extraction losses. Thus, the annual per capita availability of rice is measured in terms of cleaned rice. When reasonable, Gleason's assumptions and procedures are adopted to estimate availability before 1935. To convert food from physical quantities to calories, the conversion ratios suggested by United States, Department of Agriculture, *Composition of Food Used in Far Eastern Countries*, Agricultural Handbook no. 35 (1952), are used.

[a] The lower estimate assumes that calories from rice and sweet potatoes make up 80 percent of total. The upper estimate assumes that calories from rice and sweet potatoes make up 70 percent of total.

dominant consumption item in the Taiwanese family budget.[3] Estimates of food availability on a daily per capita basis are presented in table 6.2. For the years 1935 to 1944 I use Gleason's estimates of food availability. By using procedures generally similar to those used by Gleason, we can estimate the availability of rice and sweet potatoes for domestic consumption for the years before 1935. The outstanding characteristic of the Taiwanese diet is its heavy dependence on cereals and starchy roots. Gleason found that during 1935–54 the Taiwanese derived from 66 to 82 percent of their food calories from rice and sweet potatoes.[4] Consequently, once the availability of rice and sweet potatoes is known, total food availability for the years before 1935 is also roughly suggested.

Before we discuss and interpret the data in table 6.2 it is important to indicate some of its shortcomings. To derive food consumption from production, seeds, feeds, waste, industrial uses, and extraction losses must first be estimated. The end result, therefore, is only as good as the assumptions and the estimating procedures. Because the method used to obtain food consumption is elaborate and indirect, the estimates must be regarded as quite crude. Furthermore, food consumption is calculated on a per capita rather than on a per adult male basis. Because of the changing composition of the Taiwan population, per adult male data would be more suitable for appraising changes in consumption. In the colonial period, Taiwan's rapid rate of population growth altered the age structure of its population and made it more "youthful." With more children in the population, presumably fewer calories are required per person.[5]

3. Small sample surveys of rice farming families in 1931–32, 1936–37, and 1941–42 show that food accounted for about 50 percent of their total expenditures (see Taiwan Government-General, *Economic Survey of Farm Families, Report of Basic Agricultural Survey no. 30,* 1934, p. 25; *Expenditure Survey of Rice Producing Farm Families, Report of Basic Agricultural Survey no. 38,* 1938, pp. 3–5; and *Expenditure Survey of Rice Producing Farm Families, Report of Basic Agricultural Survey no. 44,* 1943, pp. 4–5). The 1937–38 budget survey of 500 Taiwanese urban families shows that 45.3 percent of their expenditures was spent on food (see Taiwan Government-General, *Report of Family Budget Survey, November 1937–October 1938,* p. 244). Because the selected rice farmers and the urban families were among the more affluent Taiwanese, it is believed that the average Taiwanese probably spent more than 50 percent of their total expenditures on food.

4. Ralph N. Gleason, *Taiwan Food Balances, 1935–1954,* p. 7.

5. There is also the question of the accuracy of the production and population data on which the estimates of per capita food availability are based. There is general agreement that during the colonial period Taiwan kept as accurate a record of its population as most other countries in the world. The production data, though probably less reliable,

Our evidence strongly suggests that Taiwan suffered a decline in per capita availability of rice. The decline, even allowing for statistical errors, is a large one, nearly 24 percent from 1910–19 to 1935–44. How is this decline to be explained? From 1910 to 1939 rice production more than doubled. Per capita production rose rapidly after the early 1920s, reaching a peak in the late 1930s, and then declined during the early 1940s. Thus, until World War II the decline in per capita rice availability came about not because production failed to keep pace with population growth but rather because of the large quantity of rice exported to Japan. Rice export (in terms of brown rice) increased from about 100,000 MT in the early 1910s to almost 650,000 MT in the late 1930s. On a per capita basis the export of brown rice in the 1910s was about 28 kg per person; by the end of the 1920s it had doubled, and by the end of the 1930s it had again doubled, reaching a level of nearly 120 kg per person. The export of rice from Taiwan to Japan reduced the annual per capita availability of rice in Taiwan from about 130 kg in the 1910s to 100 kg in the 1930s but helped Japan to maintain its annual per capita availability of rice at approximately 160 kg.[6]

It is reasonable to assume that the decline in per capita availability of rice led to a decline in per capita rice consumption. But how should this decline be interpreted? There are several possibilities.

1. If the consumption of other types of food did not increase, the decline in per capita rice consumption suggests a decline in total food-caloric intake. This would imply a serious deterioration in the living standard of the Taiwanese.

2. If the decline in per capita rice consumption was accompanied

---

are also of reasonably good quality. This judgment, however, is not shared by all who have used Taiwan's production data. For instance, Wickizer and Bennett expressed the opinion that "for the 1930s [the production statistics] clearly stand too high in relation to those for the 1920s" (V. D. Wickizer and M. K. Bennett, *The Rice Economy of Monsoon Asia*, p. 201). The reason for this is that they feel that between these two periods, the "levels of unit yields [of rice] appear to have been shifted upward, in an incredible degree" (ibid., p. 199). Indeed the average yield of rice increased by 20 percent between the 1920s and the 1930s, from 1,594 to 1,935 kg/ha. This change would seem unreasonable had Taiwan's agriculture remained unimproved during these two decades. But once it is realized that in the late 1920s and the 1930s not only were improved rice seeds introduced but irrigation and chemical fertilizers were also applied with greater intensity, then the 20 percent increase in rice yield no longer seems so incredible.

6. Bank of Japan, *Hundred-Year Statistics of the Japanese Economy* (Tokyo, 1966), pp. 354–55.

by increased consumption of a less desirable food, total caloric intake may not have declined. Indeed, the change may have produced improvements in the Taiwanese diet. But because rice was replaced by a less preferred food, the consumer may still be less satisfied.

3. If the decline in per capita rice consumption was compensated by increased consumption of a more desirable food, presumably the consumer's position was improved.

There is no evidence that the Taiwanese population suffered from chronic hunger. Rather the impression is the opposite. Certainly, in the colonial period the conditions in Taiwan were far better than in Korea and most parts of China.[7] Until the late 1930s, when war erupted in Asia, per capita intake of food in Taiwan is estimated to have been approximately 2,000 calories a day, very close to what experts believe the daily minimum caloric requirement for Taiwanese to be, considering the island's climate, the physical size of the Taiwanese, and the age and sex structure of the population.[8] There is no doubt that the Taiwanese were forced to tighten their belts after the late 1930s, but even then there are reasons to believe that the caloric intake was higher than Gleason's estimates.[9] That total food calories consumed per person probably did not decline until about 1940 suggests that the food gap caused by the decline in rice consumption was filled by the increased consumption of other food, the principal substitute being sweet potatoes. From 1910–14 to 1935–39 the per capita daily calories derived from sweet potatoes increased almost fourfold. The consumption of other foods also increased, but not nearly so much as sweet potatoes. The annual average per capita availability of pork, the meat most consumed in Taiwan, increased from 11.2 kg in 1911–15 to 16.2 kg

7. In the first half of the twentieth century, famine occurred rarely, if ever, in Taiwan. But according to Buck, the average number of famines in 146 *hsien* in China, within the memory of informants in these hsien, was three (cf. John L. Buck, *Land Utilization in China*, pp. 125–27). Conditions in Korea were also worse than those in Taiwan (see Wickizer and Bennett, *Rice Economy*, p. 215).

8. Gleason, using the United Nations formula, calculated the average daily per capita calorie requirement to be 2,030 calories (cf. Gleason, *Taiwan Food Balances*, p. 3).

9. During World War II, because labor, fertilizer, and irrigation inputs declined, rice production fell drastically, and so did food caloric intake. However, the decline may have been somewhat exaggerated, as there is reason to believe that the estimates of rice production for these years were biased downward. Beginning in 1940 several stringent controls over rice were introduced. For instance, starting in 1941 farm families were allowed to keep only a predetermined amount of paddy for seed and food and had to sell the remaining portion of the rice harvest to the government at an official price. (Cf. Sing-min Yeh, *Rice Marketing in Taiwan*, p. 8.) These controls must have had the effect of encouraging farmers to underreport production.

in 1931–35, and then declined slightly to 15.7 kg in 1936–40.[10] Annual sugar consumption also increased from about 4.5 kg per person in 1911–15 to over 9 kg per person in the 1930s.[11] Indications are that the consumption of vegetables and fruits also increased.

Until the mid-1930s, rice consumption declined only slightly and the increased consumption of sweet potatoes and other foods no doubt was able to make up the difference, so total intake of food calories probably did not decrease, and indeed it may have increased slightly. Because of the greater diversification of food in the diet, there is the real possibility that nutritional improvement also occurred. But since both more preferred foods (meat and fruit) and less preferred foods (sweet potatoes) were used to substitute for rice, it is impossible to say whether the altered diet represented nutritional as well as psychological improvements. But it is, I believe, fairly safe to conclude that until the late 1930s the Taiwanese consumer did not suffer noticeably from the decline in rice consumption. Thereafter, the problem becomes quite different. Even allowing for possible statistical errors, the decline of rice consumption in the late 1930s was serious. It is doubtful that the increased consumption of sweet potatoes in these years was sufficient to offset the decline in rice consumption. Furthermore, the consumption of the more desirable foods, such as meat, also declined in the late 1930s. The implication is that in the late 1930s and during the war Taiwanese suffered both a quantitative and a qualitative deterioration in their dietary condition.

Other Goods and Services

In terms of what they indicate of the economic conditions of the Taiwanese, the trends in the per capita consumption of articles other than food are much less difficult to interpret. Table 6.3 presents the relevant statistics for three principal articles, two consumer goods and one consumer durable. Except for a temporary interruption during World War I, when Japan exported less to Taiwan, the per capita consumption of cotton cloth and paper increased steadily until the late 1930s. The number of people with bicycles, perhaps one of the most significant indicators of economic status, increased rapidly in Taiwan. Whereas the bicycle was a rarity before 1920, when there was

10. Calculated from the weight of slaughtered hogs in Taiwan Government-General, *Taiwan Agricultural Yearbook*, various issues.
11. Taiwan Sugar Corporation, *Annual Statistical Report of Taiwan Sugar Industry*, p. 135.

Table 6.3. Availability of Selected Consumer Goods (Annual averages)

	Per capita consumption of cotton cloth 1925 yen/person	Per capita consumption of paper 1925 yen/person	No. of persons per bicycle
1907–10	1.88	0.76	—
1911–15	1.63	1.09	698[a]
1916–20	1.29	0.86	274
1921–25	2.22	0.75	108
1926–30	4.18	1.00	46
1931–35	5.15	1.27	26
1936–40	3.20[b]	1.09	17

Notes and Sources: The value of total consumption of cotton cloth and paper is assumed to be production plus imports minus exports. They are converted to constant prices by deflating the value series by the Taipei wholesale prices for plain cotton cloth and paper. The number of bicycles are those registered with the police at the end of each year. All bicycles required annual registration. The data used to construct this table are from PBAS, *Taiwan Province: Statistical Summary of the Past 51 Years*, pp. 789, 798, 902, and 1347, and PBAS, *Taiwan Trade Statistics for the Last Fifty-three Years (1896–1948)*, pp. 80, 90, and my table A11 below.
[a] The average of 1912–15.
[b] The average of 1936, 1939, and 1940.

only one for every 700 people, it became a reasonably common article in the 1930s when one was available to almost every third household.

In the colonial period the Taiwanese also consumed a steadily expanding flow of publicly financed services, among which those related to public health and education were most important and had far-reaching consequences. Sewage construction, sanitation services, and vaccination programs contributed to a healthier environment and were primarily responsible for eliminating infectious diseases and extending the average life span of the Taiwanese.[12] From 1906 to 1936–40, the mean life expectancy of Taiwanese males at birth increased by 13.4 years to 41.1 and that of Taiwanese females by 16.7 years to 45.7.[13] The better public health environment improved not only the quality and productivity of the labor force but also the general quality of life of all Taiwanese.

Despite the fact that the colonial education system discriminated against the Taiwanese, restricting them to certain levels, qualities,

12. Samuel P. S. Ho, "The Development Policy of the Japanese Colonial Government in Taiwan, 1895–1945," in Gustav Ranis, ed., *Government and Economic Development*, pp. 303–08.
13. George W. Barclay, *Colonial Development and Population in Taiwan*, p. 154.

and types of education, it nevertheless provided formal education for the first time to a broad spectrum of Taiwanese youth. Enrollment in primary schools increased from 13,000 students in 1900–01 to 175,000 in 1920–21 and 671,000 in 1940–41.[14] By 1930–31, 33 percent of the school age (6–14) Taiwanese children were in schools, and this percentage climbed to 71 percent in 1943–44.[15] The gains from education cannot easily be quantified, but they were certainly among the most significant benefits received by the Taiwanese in the colonial period. And since education was partly an investment good, it continued to bring benefits to the Taiwanese far into the postcolonial period.

Both the wage and the per capita consumption data point to the same conclusion: in the colonial period the economic status or the material welfare of the average Taiwanese improved, at least until the late 1930s. Thereafter, but definitely during the war, the economic conditions of Taiwanese deteriorated.

Besides material benefits, economic development also brought to the Taiwanese other subtle but nevertheless important changes. From the development viewpoint, the most vital was perhaps the exposure of the Taiwanese to scientific techniques, machine technology, and modern business practices. The effect of this exposure on the Taiwanese went far beyond improving their living standards. As a result of such exposure in agriculture, the average Taiwanese farmer in the 1930s was quite a different person in terms of his skills and knowledge than his counterpart at the beginning of the century. There were also changes in attitude and behavior, probably the most outstanding being the greater willingness of farmers to listen to and to seek help from agronomists and extension workers.

No doubt the Taiwanese benefited much from the Japanese presence, but had the relationship been on a more equitable basis, the benefit would have been so much greater. The Japanese restricted their contact with the Taiwanese to a minimum, and when contacts were necessary they were conducted on a ruler–subject basis. Whenever possible, the Japanese lived apart from the Taiwanese, resulting in separate residential districts for the two populations in most cities.[16] Even more unfortunate was the attempt by the Japanese to keep some of their knowledge and innovations to themselves. This was parti-

14. PBAS, *Taiwan Province: Statistical Summary of the Past 51 Years*, pp. 1211–13.
15. Ibid., pp. 1241–42.
16. Barclay, *Colonial Development and Population in Taiwan*, pp. 161–62.

cularly true in the nonagricultural sector. Taiwanese were used at menial tasks, and only a small, limited number of them were introduced to more responsible positions. After forty-five years of occupation, only 31 percent of the technicians and 27 percent of the government employees were Taiwanese, and of the Taiwanese technicians, more than one-third were physicians or pharmacists. Thus the extent of Taiwanese participation in running and managing the island's industries was even more limited than the aggregate data indicate.[17]

Under colonial rule, Taiwan developed an effective administrative system, an extensive infrastructure, a productive agriculture, the beginning of an industrial sector, and some modern commercial institutions. The productivity gains that resulted brought not only many benefits to Japan but also improvements in the economic conditions of the Taiwanese. It is doubtful that Taiwan could have done as well economically had it remained a province of China without access to Japan's material resources, administrative and technical know-how, and entrepreneurship.[18] By becoming a colony Taiwan traded political independence for stability and economic progress. But colonialism had other effects as well, which we have not considered. It burdened the Taiwanese with many important but intangible costs: e.g., the humiliation of being ruled by foreigners, the loss of political and often personal freedom, and the lost opportunity to develop its own type of society.

From the economic viewpoint, colonialism also had its intangible costs. To cite but a few examples: Under colonial management Taiwan allocated more resources to the production of sugar than could be justified on grounds of comparative advantage. But perhaps the most serious of these intangible costs was that the colonial conditions prevented the emergence of a dynamic Taiwanese entrepreneur–capitalist class. Thus, an element crucial to sustained economic

17. For example, of the 167 government officials of the *chokunin* class, only 1 was Taiwanese; of the 2,120 officials of the *sonin* class, only 29 were Taiwanese; and of the 21,798 officials of the *hanin* class, only 3,726 were Taiwanese. For other examples, see George W. Barclay, *A Report on Taiwan's Population to the Joint Committee on Rural Reconstruction*, tables 19 and 20.

18. Perhaps some Japanese investments would have come to Taiwan even in the absence of Japanese political control. But Taiwan was able to attract Japanese capital and entrepreneurs on the scale that it did only because the island was under complete Japanese control. But more significant is the likelihood that had Taiwan remained part of China, it would have been drawn into the political and social turmoil on the mainland that brought economic progress in China nearly to a standstill during much of the first half of the twenieth century.

growth was absent in the Taiwanese population. If Japan suddenly decided to withdraw from Taiwan, economic growth would have been retarded and the economy seriously dislocated. Indeed, this was the result when Japanese entrepreneurs and capitalists were hastily repatriated from Taiwan after Japan's defeat in 1945.

7

Postwar Development: Problems, Strategies, and the Role of Foreign Aid

At the conclusion of World War II, Taiwan was returned to Chinese rule and became a province of the Republic of China. Allied bombing and general neglect during the war left much of Taiwan's economy in ruin. But in 1945 the Nationalist government, preoccupied with its struggle against the communists, could provide little assistance or attention to the new province. Thus, for several years after the war Taiwan drifted aimlessly. When the communists gained control of the mainland in 1949, the Nationalist government retreated to Taiwan. Only then did the reconstruction of Taiwan begin in earnest. Since then, Taiwan has consolidated the gains it made in the colonial period and has made impressive advances toward industrialization. The purposes of this chapter are to examine the development strategies that gradually emerged after 1949 to help shape Taiwan's postwar development, and to stress the crucial role played by foreign aid in the successful implementation of these policies. The achievements since 1949 are reviewed in chapter 8, where the overall economic performance and structural changes since the early 1950s are examined. Thus, this and the next chapter provide the background and serve as an introduction to the more detailed sectoral analyses that are to follow in subsequent chapters.

In 1945 the conditions for economic development were far from favorable. War-related damage to industrial capitals and infrastructure had significantly reduced the island's capital stock. The repatriation of Japanese administrators, managers, technicians, and skilled laborers at the end of the war intensified postwar dislocation because their talents and skills could not be replaced quickly. Initial political mismanagement also cost the Nationalist government much goodwill among the Taiwanese.[1] Production in 1945–46 was below one-half the peak reached in the colonial period. But most damaging to the confidence and morale of the people was the accelerating inflation that gripped Taiwan. Despite efforts to isolate Taiwan from the deteriorating conditions on the mainland,[2] the Taipei wholesale price index increased 260 percent in 1946, 360 percent in 1947, 520 percent in 1948, and 3,500 percent in 1949.[3]

However, to bring order and progress to the economy, Taiwan could count on a number of vital assets. Notwithstanding wartime destruction, the island's infrastructure was still sufficiently extensive in 1945 to rank Taiwan as one of the most developed areas in China. Its agriculture, although weaker as a result of the war, was still, after Japan, the most advanced in the Far East. The colonial education system left Taiwan with one of the most literate populations in Asia— a great advantage to any developing country. Institutions favorable to development created during the colonial period, such as the farmers' association, credit cooperative, agricultural experiment station, and various banking facilities, could be quickly revived to again prove their immeasurable usefulness. Most significant, because of the sta- bility it enjoyed during the colonial period, Taiwan at the time of World War II, unlike other parts of China, had an extremely well- ordered society; this enabled it to survive the war in relatively better shape. In fact, in 1945 Taiwan was probably a better-organized society with fewer signs of social disintegration than any other of the political units then governed by the Chinese Nationalist govern- ment.

Besides the favorable inheritance from its colonial past, several critical developments in 1949–50 made postwar recovery and devel- opment less difficult. In the late 1940s, when it became apparent that the Nationalist government's position on the mainland was untenable,

---

1. A highly critical account of the early activities of the Nationalist government in Taiwan is provided by George H. Kerr, who was in Taiwan during 1945–47, first as a member of the U.S. Army Liaison Group and later as a member of the American Con- sultate, in his *Formosa Betrayed*.

2. The government attempted to isolate Taiwan economically by adjusting the rate of exchange between the Taiwan currency (*taipi*) and the mainland currency (*fapi*) and by regulating the flow of funds from the mainland to Taiwan. For more details, see Shun-hsin Chou, *The Chinese Inflation: 1937–1949*, pp. 31–38.

3. The Taipei wholesale price index is a simple geometric average of the wholesale prices of 50 domestically produced and imported commodities (see PBAS, *Taiwan Monthly Commodity-Price Statistics*, Jan. 1960, p. 36).

a large number of mainlanders took refuge in Taiwan. Among the last wave of mainland refugees that reached Taiwan in 1949–50 was a small group of managers, technicians, and entrepreneurs. Their arrival enabled Taiwan to partially bridge the human resource gap that developed after the Japanese departed in 1946. But perhaps most critical to Taiwan's recovery and subsequent development was the United States decision in 1950, after the outbreak of the Korean War, to patrol the Taiwan Strait and to assist Taiwan with economic and military aid. The commitment of United States forces not only made the island militarily more secure, but equally important it gave the Taiwan population a significant and much-needed psychological lift. United States aid, as we shall see, was critically important to Taiwan's development. Indeed, without U.S. aid, recovery would have been more difficult and economic development delayed.

PROBLEMS AND STRATEGIES

From 1946 to 1950, more than 1 million mainland refugees (military and civilian) arrived in Taiwan. With this sudden increase in population, the need for rapid economic development was obvious and urgent. The end of colonial rule and the loss of the protected Japanese market meant that the triangular pattern of resource use based on food export practiced during the colonial period required modification. A different approach was needed.

Taiwan's immediate requirements were obvious: the army and the civilian population had to be fed and clothed and industrialization must begin. To meet these demands, it was also clear that Taiwan must rely upon its agriculture, then the largest and strongest sector in the economy. The role of agriculture was crucial. It not only must feed a much enlarged population but also must supply much of the labor, foreign exchange, and savings required by the emerging industries. Chastised by the consequences of its neglect of agriculture on the mainland, the Nationalist government, rather than only extracting from agriculture, adopted a balanced strategy of joint agricultural and industrial growth. This approach is probably best described by the government's own slogan: "Developing agriculture by virtue of industry and fostering industry by virtue of agriculture."

With the aid of the Sino–American Joint Commission on Rural Reconstruction (JCRR), the government implemented a comprehensive program to reconstruct and develop Taiwan's agriculture. Chapter

9 shall show that by repairing war-torn rural infrastructure and by reintroducing to agriculture industrial inputs and better production techniques, agriculture was made increasingly more productive. The successful implementation of an extensive rent reduction and land redistribution program allocated the gains from agricultural development more equally and ensured the enthusiastic participation of the peasantry in the economic development of the island. In this manner Taiwan's agriculture was strengthened as a base for industrialization. Rising productivity enabled it to become the source of rapid labor transfers to, and a source of savings for, the industrial sector. Furthermore, agricultural and processed agricultural goods were the principal earners of foreign exchange in the 1950s and helped to finance the initial capital and raw material imports required by the growing industrial sector.

To shift its economic center of gravity from agriculture to industry, Taiwan adopted policies that were to a large extent dictated by circumstances. In the early 1950s inflation kept the NT$ (New Taiwan dollar) overvalued, and imports exceeded exports by growing margins. Thus, besieged by inflation and a balance-of-payments crisis, the government imposed strict controls on foreign exchange and imports. In this crisis environment it was relatively easy, if not inevitable, for the government to slip into an import substitution approach to industrialization. In any case the decision was made to encourage the domestic production of consumer and some intermediate goods that heretofore had been imported. Chapter 10 discusses in some detail the instruments used to implement the program as well as the consequences of the import substitution strategy. For now, it is sufficient to note that for a while the strategy appeared to be effective and Taiwan's industrial sector expanded rapidly. But by the mid-1950s, the easy phase of import substitution had ended and the economy turned sluggish. The government was again forced to rethink and to modify its industrialization strategy.

In the early 1960s the new strategy took shape and is aptly described by the government's new slogan "Developing agriculture by virtue of industry, and fostering industry by virtue of foreign trade." Basically, the strategy called for the industrial sector to turn increasingly toward the world market. By removing controls to allow prices to more accurately reflect Taiwan's factor endowments and the world market conditions, the government encouraged Taiwan's industries to shift toward labor-intensive production. In other words both industrial output and exports were increasingly composed of labor-intensive manufacturers in which Taiwan enjoyed comparative advantage. This outward-looking strategy represented a major departure from the previous inward-looking policies and signaled a new phase in Taiwan's development, one in which the industrial sector had become the primary source of growth. By the mid-1960s it also became apparent that agriculture had lost its position as the prime supporter of development. Agricultural growth became sluggish, and to prevent a bottleneck from developing, investments in agriculture had to be increased. Agriculture is now the sector that required support.

The postwar development strategy was developed and implemented not without its share of problems and strains. Economic growth is difficult even when it is the sole objective. However, seldom does a country have the luxury of pursuing a single objective. More often, if not always, a country must simultaneously pursue a number of conflicting objectives. From the moment it retreated to Taiwan in 1949, and continuously thereafter, the Nationalist government pursued three major objectives—rapid economic growth, stable prices, and a strong military presence—that at times have been in sharp conflict with one another. Because of Taiwan's great needs and its limited resources, the strains created by conflicting objectives were intense. Without foreign aid to relax binding constraints on the economy, it is unlikely that these objectives could have been achieved.

Since 1949 Taiwan has had to support, on a per capita basis, one of the world's largest armies. Although the Nationalist government has never officially announced the size of its army, independent estimates have consistently placed Taiwan's military strength at about 550,000–600,000 men.[4] At this level, the armed forces absorbed approximately 14 percent of Taiwan's male population in 1952, 9 percent in 1962, and 7 percent in 1972. The government justifies this unusually large military presence on the grounds that it is engaged in a civil war and a large army is needed not only to protect the island from communist attacks but also to fulfill its foremost political goal: eventual reoccupation of the Chinese mainland. Realizing that success depends on more than military might alone, the Nationalist government, as we have already noted, espoused an active program to

4. The London Institute for Strategic Studies, *The Boei Nenkan* (Defense Yearbook) published in Japan, as well as various U.S. sources, estimates Taiwan's military strength in the 1950s and 1960s at around 550,000–600,000 men.

stabilize and develop the economy. Given its limited resources, serious internal conflicts unavoidably have emerged in the pursuit of these objectives. Most obviously, its large military expenditures not only have diverted resources from economic development but also have made price stability more difficult to attain.

Although details of Taiwan's military budget are not public information, a reasonably accurate estimate of the military's direct claim on output can be made from published government sources, and it indicates that the military has had an immense impact on Taiwan. In the 1950s and most years in the 1960s Taiwan's military establishment consistently absorbed about 12 percent of its GNP. In terms of government outlays, the military claimed from 80 to 90 percent of the current expenditures of the central government, or about 65 percent of government current expenditures at all levels.

Table 7.1 compares Taiwan's defense burden with that of other less developed countries. In terms of the share of GNP allocated to the military in the 1950s and the 1960s, few countries were Taiwan's equal. Of the countries surveyed, only South Vietnam and Jordan were in the same category as Taiwan, and both were involved in a shooting war. Furthermore, the figures for Taiwan understate the actual costs of maintaining the military establishment. For example, they do not include the value of military hardware that the United States has given to Taiwan. From 1946 to 1967 the United States gave Taiwan a total of $2.7 billion in military assistance.[5] The military in Taiwan also enjoys a number of subsidies that are not included in the military budget. For example, rice, transportation services, power, and other goods and services are provided to the military at less than market prices.[6] Given Taiwan's heavy military burden, a serious conflict between defense and stable development was inevitable. Only with massive U.S. aid was this conflict reduced to manageable proportions.

5. The extent of U.S. military assistance to Taiwan may be somewhat overstated since the value of the military hardware given to Taiwan is calculated at the procurement cost to the U.S. Department of Defense rather than the lower market prices.

6. The Taiwan Provincial Food Bureau sells rice to the military at below cost. Military freight is transported by Taiwan's rail system at lower preferential rates, and military personnel pay only half price for use of the public transport system and some other services.

Table 7.1. Burden of National Defense, Selected Less Developed Countries

Defense expenditure as a percentage of

	1955		1960		1965	
	General government current expenditures	*GNP*	*General government current expenditures*	*GNP*	*General government current expenditures*	*GNP*
Asia						
Taiwan (ROC)	65.8	12.9	65.0	12.8	62.3	11.4
Republic of Korea	48.1	4.8	37.0	5.8	35.2	3.7
Philippines	20.5	1.8	15.7	1.6	8.3	0.9
India	22.0	1.9	17.5	1.8	24.0	3.3
Malaysia	n.a.	n.a.	15.1	2.3	19.4	4.3
South Vietnam	n.a.	n.a.	37.7	6.7	57.9	13.7
Middle East						
Israel	8.5	2.1	19.0	5.1	22.9	6.4
Jordan	n.a.	n.a.	59.7	16.5	52.5	11.0
South America						
Colombia	24.5	2.0	15.8	1.4	23.8	2.0
Ecuador	17.5	2.7	14.1	2.3	10.5	1.9
Peru	24.7	2.6	17.1	2.1	17.3	2.7
Chile	20.0	3.3	11.8	2.6	9.4	2.2
Guatemala	13.5	0.9	10.6	0.9	11.7	1.0
Honduras	14.1	1.1	10.3	1.0	10.6	1.1
Venezuela	13.7	n.a.	13.7	2.3	13.7	2.1
Africa						
Nigeria	2.4	0.2	3.9	0.4	15.1	1.1
Ghana	4.1	0.3	9.6[a]	0.9[a]	10.3	1.2

Sources: In most cases, defense expenditures as a percentage of GNP were obtained as $(\frac{\text{defence expenditures}}{\text{government current expenditures}}) \times (\frac{\text{government current expenditures}}{\text{GNP}}) \times 100$. The major sources consulted were United Nations, *Yearbook of National Accounts*, various issues, and IBRD, Economic Department, Comparative Data Unit, *Government Revenue and Expenditure*, Dec. 1968, world table 6.

[a] Defense spending as a percentage of the current expenditures of the central government.

Table 7.2. United States Economic and Military Assistance to Taiwan, Net Obligation and Loan Authorizations (U.S. fiscal years, millions U.S. dollars)

		1949–52	1953–57	1958–62	1963–67	Total 1949–67
I.	Total economic	467.8[a]	529.5	502.3	268.9	1,768.5
	Loans	—	60.0	161.0	168.0	389.0
	Grants	467.8	469.5	341.3	101.0	1,379.5
	A. AID and predecessor agencies	467.4	501.9	383.3	16.6	1,369.2
	Loans	—	60.0	139.3	15.0	214.4
	Grants	467.4	441.9	244.0	1.6	1,154.8
	B. Food for freedom	0.4	27.6	119.0	188.8	335.9
	C. Export–Import Bank long-term loans	—	—	—	63.5	63.5
II.	Military assistance program[b]	48.0	1,178.9	720.4	436.9	2,384.2
	Credit assistance	—	—	—	0.9	0.9
	Grants	48.0	1,178.9	720.4	436.0	2,383.3
III.	Total economic and military	515.8	1,708.4	1,222.7	705.8	4,152.7
	Loans	—	60.0	161.0	168.9	389.9
	Grants	515.8	1,648.4	1,061.7	536.9	3,762.8
IV.	Assistance received per capita (US$ per person)	66.7	188.3	113.4	56.4	424.8
	Economic	60.5	58.4	46.6	21.5	187.0
	Military	6.2	130.0	66.8	34.9	237.9

Notes and Sources: To obtain U.S. assistance per capita, the total net obligation and loan authorization is divided by the average civilian population in Taiwan. The above figures are based on *U.S. Overseas Loans and Grants and Assistance, from International Organizations, Obligations and Loan Authorization, July 1, 1945–June 30, 1967,* Special Report Prepared for the House Foreign Affairs Committee, p. 63, and my table A11 below.
[a] Includes an estimated US$ 192.1 million in economic grant aid to mainland China in FY 1949–50.
[b] Represents deliveries but excludes additional grants from excess stocks totaling, for the period 1949–67, US$ 422.6 million.

FOREIGN AID AND DEVELOPMENT

Beginning in 1950 huge amounts of United States aid flowed into Taiwan, and the flow continued until the late 1960s.[7] Except for a limited amount of surplus agricultural commodities, no U.S. economic aid has been committed to Taiwan after June 30, 1965. Table 7.2, which summarizes the trend and composition of U.S. aid to Taiwan, shows that from 1949 to 1967 Taiwan received over US$ 4.1 billion in U.S. aid, of which US$ 2.4 billion was U.S. military assistance. To appreciate the magnitude of U.S. aid to Taiwan, it is best to put it on a per capita basis. During 1949–67 Taiwan received US$ 425 for every member of its civilian population. In this same period, excluding military assistance, economic aid received per capita was US$ 187. In 1960 Taiwan's per capita income was estimated at around US$ 110. United States economic aid to Taiwan averaged about US$ 110 million a year in the 1950s but declined steadily in the 1960s. Furthermore, since the mid-1950s, an increasing proportion of U.S. economic aid to Taiwan has been in the form of loans rather than of grants. Military assistance, on the other hand, has been provided nearly exclusively in the form of grants. But like economic aid, the size of military assistance also declined in the 1960s, though much less sharply.

Foreign aid increased the resources available to Taiwan and thus enabled it to better meet its economic and military needs. In other words, aid permitted Taiwan to grow and to remain relatively stable while maintaining an unusually large military establishment. It is in this sense that United States aid helped to lessen the conflicts that existed between Taiwan's economic and military objectives. In Taiwan, foreign aid facilitated economic development in several related ways:[8] it helped to control inflation, relaxed a binding foreign exchange constraint, and permitted a higher level of capital formation.

7. An extensive study of U.S. aid to Taiwan is found in Neil H. Jacoby, *U.S. Aid to Taiwan*. It provides a detailed description of the character of the U.S. aid program in Taiwan as well as a general evaluation of its effectiveness in promoting economic and social development.

8. The relationship of foreign aid to economic development has been studied extensively in the literature. For example, see Hollis B. Chenery and Michael Bruno, "Development Alternatives in an Open Economy: The Case of Israel;" Hollis B. Chenery and Alan M. Strout, "Foreign Assistance and Economic Development;" Gustav Ranis, ed., *The U.S. and the Developing Economies*; and Jagdish Bhagwati and Richard S. Eckaus, eds., *Foreign Aid*.

Stabilization

United States aid, in the early 1950s, played a critically important stabilizing role and helped the battered and confused Taiwan economy to recover. In 1950, when the United States resumed aid to the Republic of China, Taiwan was near collapse. With much of its industrial capital destroyed and with widespread shortages of raw materials, food and daily necessities were in short supply. The economy was further strained by the large and sudden inflow of mainland refugees in 1949–50 and by huge government deficits brought about by heavy military expenditures. To help industries recover from the war, the government followed an easy money policy. Bank credit expanded rapidly and the money supply doubled in 1950. Under this intense inflationary pressure, prices soared.

The inflation was quite obviously demand pulled, caused by the sudden increase in population and in military expenditures. Unwilling to reduce its military budget, which accounted for over 90 percent of the central government's expenditures, and unable to substantially increase its taxes, the government resorted to less effective instruments to combat inflation. To increase public confidence in the newly introduced NT$, the government directed the Bank of Taiwan to redeem short-term time deposits in gold. The one noticeable consequence of this action was a large net outflow of nonmonetary gold from Taiwan, valued at US$ 50.8 million in 1950.[9] This wasteful use of government gold at a time when Taiwan was in desperate need of foreign exchange was wisely halted in December 1950.[10] A more effective anti-inflationary policy was the government's attempt to absorb the excessive liquidity in the economy by offering realistic interest rates to bank depositors.[11] With rates of 9 percent a month, which compounded monthly comes to over 180 percent a year, people were diverted from the pursuit of goods to financial assets, and time deposits in the banking system increased dramatically, rising from

9. Table A68, item A3. Instead of redeeming time deposits with gold, a better scheme would have been to tie the capital value of time deposits, as well as interest payments, to a suitable price index so that the effective real interest rate would never become negative.

10. However, the Bank of Taiwan continued to use the gold saving deposit to induce the public to buy government bonds. Until July 1952, by purchasing a certain amount of government bonds, one could buy gold with the gold saving deposit.

11. An interesting discussion of the high interest rate policy is found in Reed J. Irvine and Robert I. Emery, "Interest Rates as an Anti-Inflationary Instrument in Taiwan."

NT$ 2.3 million in March 1950 to NT$ 33.3 million in June 1950.[12] But more than anything else, the government depended on its elaborate system of price–cost controls to combat inflation. The market ceased to function as an allocative agent and rationing became widespread.

However, the main reason why inflation was kept within controllable limits was the resumption of U.S. aid in the latter part of 1950. United States military assistance made it less necessary to divert scarce domestic resources and hard-earned foreign exchange from economic to military uses. United States economic aid provided Taiwan with large amounts of chemical fertilizers, wheat, and cotton, the daily necessities and raw materials needed to stablilize and rehabilitate the economy. Had U.S. aid not arrived in 1950, it is difficult to imagine how Taiwan could have escaped a serious runaway inflation with all its accompanying social and political turmoil.

Although after 1952 Taiwan no longer faced economic chaos, it was far from stable and U.S. aid continued to be the prime stabilizer in the economy. From 1953 to 1960 the implicit GNP deflator increased on the average by 10 percent a year.[13] Thus, even with U.S. military and economic assistance of over US$ 2.5 billion, the economy was stable only relative to the preceding five years, and what little price stability that existed was extremely precarious. The major causes of instability in this period were government expenditures and the weather. Because Taiwan in the 1950s was primarily agrarian, its economic health depended to an unusual extent on the weather. Agriculture was not only the source of food and raw materials for the industrial sector, it was also Taiwan's export sector. During 1953–59, nearly 90 percent of Taiwan's export was composed of agricultural and agricultural processed goods. Because the government was without an adequate reserve of either food or foreign exchange, it was unable to stabilize the market for any extended period of time, and thus any weather condition that adversely affected agricultural production had far-reaching economic effects and inevitably caused prices to rise.

A second source of instability was the military budget. In the 1950s Taiwan's military budget was not only large relative to the size of the economy and kept aggregate demand consistently high and close to

12. BOT, *The Republic of China, Taiwan Financial Statistics Monthly*, Dec. 1954, p. 17.
13. DGBAS, *National Income of the Republic of China*, 1968, pp. 118–19.

being inflationary, but its size, which tended to be extremely sensitive to communist China's activities in the Taiwan Strait, was often unpredictable. After any increase in the tempo of military activity in the Taiwan Strait, the size of the defense budget inevitably increased. These sudden increases in government expenditure, in an already strained economy, tended to upset the delicate balance between supply and demand and caused prices to move upward. Thus, the inability of the government to predict accurately its military needs made the government sector an additional source of economic instability.

The economy was strongly inflationary in 1955–56 and again in 1959–60. In both cases the causes for the instability were poor weather and increased military expenditures. Defense spending increased sharply after communist forces attacked Quemoy in the latter part of 1954. Economic conditions were further aggravated by two successive poor harvests in 1955–56. The 1959–60 inflation followed almost exactly the same pattern: government expenditures increased after a second communist assault on Quemoy in the fall of 1958, which in turn was followed by two consecutive poor harvests. Without U.S. aid, price increases during these two periods could have easily gone out of control.

Gap Filler

The gap analysis advanced by Chenery and his various associates provides a useful framework to examine the relationship of foreign aid to economic development.[14] In this approach, aid is seen primarily as a gap filler. Specifically it could be used to fill either a saving or a foreign exchange gap. It is generally believed that in the 1950s Taiwan was constrained by the lack of foreign exchange, and U.S. aid, by filling the foreign exchange gap, permitted a higher rate of economic growth and a fuller utilization of the other factors in the economy.[15]

---

14. The main ideas of the gap analysis were first set out in Chenery and Bruno, "Development Alternatives in an Open Economy." Perhaps the most systematic presentation of the analysis is in Chenery and Strout, "Foreign Assistance and Economic Development." A lucid and somewhat different presentation of the gap analysis is Ronald I. McKinnon, "Foreign Exchange Constraints in Economic Development and Efficient Aid Allocation." The existence of several gaps or constraints, not all of which are binding on the economy at any one time, is traced to the fact that the gap analysis assumes that underdeveloped countries are considerably less flexible than developed countries so that they cannot adjust quickly to disequilibrium. For critiques of the gap analysis, see John C. H. Fei and Gustav Ranis, "Foreign Assistance and Economic Development: Comment;" and Henry J. Bruton, "The Two Gap Approach to Aid and Development: Comment."

15. For example, see Jacoby, *U.S. Aid to Taiwan*, p. 124.

Empirical studies, using short-term planning models similar to those developed by Chenery et al., have yielded results that are in support of this assessment.[16]

The following statistics suggest the extent to which foreign aid helped to relax the foreign exchange constraint on growth. In the 1950s imports exceeded exports by more than 60 percent, although the gap was smaller in the 1960s. As a share of GNP, Taiwan's import surplus averaged 5.7 percent in 1951–56, 7.1 percent in 1956–60, 3.4 percent in 1961–64, and 2.1 percent in 1965–68.[17] Actually, the import surplus in the 1950s and the 1960s was substantially greater than indicated by these figures because goods imported under the United States military assistance program were not included in the official estimates of imports.[18] From 1951 to the termination of economic aid in 1965, U.S. economic aid financed nearly 80 percent of Taiwan's import surplus. For the critical years 1951–56, when Taiwan was especially vulnerable to economic instability, U.S. economic aid financed 90 percent of the import surplus. To put it another way, during 1951–55 over 40 percent of Taiwan's imports was aid financed. For the longer period (1951–68), almost 30 percent of Taiwan's imports was aid financed.

The contribution of foreign aid to investments in Taiwan was also substantial.[19] In the 1950s nearly 40 percent of the gross domestic capital formation was financed by foreign savings; almost all of it came in the form of U.S. aid.[20] Thus, in the absence of U.S. aid the investment level would have been considerably lower. Because the

16. A short-term planning model for Taiwan that utilizes the gap analysis is in Samuel P. S. Ho, "Development Alternatives—The Case of Taiwan." Kuo-shu Liang has also applied the McKinnon model to Taiwanese data (see his "Foreign Trade and Economic Development in Taiwan: 1952–67," pp. 36–44, and Kuo-shu Liang and Teng-hui Lee, "Process and Pattern of Economic Development in Taiwan," JCRR Rural Economic Division, 1972, mimeo, pp. 27–35).

17. These ratios are calculated from data in table A7. They are somewhat smaller than the earlier estimates made by Jacoby (see his *U.S. Aid to Taiwan*, p. 274). This is because they are based on revised estimates of GNP that were not available to Jacoby.

18. If imports under the military assistance program were included, the excess of gross national expenditures over GNP, or the import surplus, would average about 20 percent of GNP in the 1950s.

19. According to the two-gap analysis, foreign assistance has a greater effect on economic growth when the binding constraint is the foreign exchange constraint and not the saving constraint. Intuitively, given the two-gap framework, this makes sense since the availability of foreign assistance not only increases foreign savings but also makes possible the fuller utilization of domestic savings. See McKinnon, "Foreign Exchange Constraints in Economic Development."

20. DGBAS, *National Income of the Republic of China*, 1970, pp. 136–37, 142–43, 146–47, and 150–51.

level of domestic saving is not unrelated to the level of foreign assistance, it would be simplistic to assume that smaller amounts of foreign aid would have led to a proportionate decline in investment levels. Taiwan's domestic production and U.S. aid formed a fungible pool of resources that was used to support private and government consumption and investment. But keeping in mind Taiwan's low level of per capita private consumption and the preferences of its political leaders, the level of domestic savings probably would not have increased sufficiently to balance any substantial decline in foreign aid. In fact, because the government assigned the highest priority to national defense in the 1950s, it is likely that domestic savings would have been reduced via larger government deficits if had foreign assistance been smaller. Naturally, had this occurred, Taiwan's growth rate in the 1950s and 1960s would have been lower.[21]

Policy Formulation

Since it was a government-to-government program, U.S. economic aid had considerable impact on the government's economic policies and how these policies were implemented. Because the Chinese Nationalist government was preoccupied with its security and the eventual recovery of the mainland, much of its energy and resources was directed at military problems. Without foreign aid to augment its resources, the government would have been less able to formulate and conduct an effective development program. In the 1950s, because of large military expenditures, the government's domestic revenues were not sufficient to cover its current expenditures, not to mention its total expenditures. Until the mid-1960s, domestic revenues financed less than 75 percent of the consolidated expenditures of the central and provincial governments, with the deficits financed primarily by U.S. aid.[22] Since military expenditures had first claim on government

21. Using a simple Harrod–Domar model, Neil Jacoby estimated that without U.S. aid the annual growth rate of Taiwan's GNP during 1951–64 would have been less than one half the rate actually achieved. Among a number of simplifying assumptions he made is the one that Taiwan could have avoided unnecessary price inflation without foreign assistance. Jacoby admits, however, that this is clearly unrealistic. Jacoby's no-aid-growth model is also restrictive in other ways. Among other things, it ignores such important sources of economic growth as technological change, population growth, and economics of scale. So, even if the assumption of no price inflation is acceptable, one must not consider Jacoby's results as precise findings. See Jacoby, *U.S. Aid to Taiwan*, chap. 11 and Appendix E. Similar calculations have also been made by Liang and Lee, "Process and Pattern of Economic Development in Taiwan," p. 33.
22. Jacoby, *U.S. Aid to Taiwan*, table C.12.

revenue, developmental and capital programs would have been hard squeezed had there been less or no foreign assistance.

Because it would have been consistent with government ideology and because it would have strengthened its control of the island, one suspects that the Nationalist government would have preferred the public sector to spearhead Taiwan's economic development.[23] However, for several reasons a different approach was followed. In the 1950s and most of the 1960s the government, as we remarked above, was unable to allocate a large share of the domestic resources it controlled to economic development. Consequently, its economic projects were limited chiefly to those financed by U.S. aid. AID, on the other hand, was strongly committed to the growth of the private sector and used its influences and resources to improve the climate for private enterprises. Without AID's influence and active intervention, the private sector would not have become Taiwan's foremost source of economic growth. AID helped to create a more conducive atmosphere for economic growth, particularly for the expansion of private industries, by (1) financing government projects with strong external economies, (2) inducing the government to liberalize its economic policies, and (3) laying a constraining hand on military expenditures.

From 1951 to 1965, when U.S. economic aid ended, 67 percent of all aid was allocated to public enterprises or agencies, 27 percent to mixed public and private enterprises, and only 6 percent to purely private enterprises.[24] As these figures show, AID provided little direct assistance to the private sector but nevertheless favored its expansion. Table 7.3, which summarizes the distribution of U.S. economic aid by major sectors of the economy, shows that a preponderant share of U.S. aid and capital assistance was allocated to infrastructure and human resources, areas in which substantial external economies existed. Together, infrastructure and human resources absorbed 63 percent of all U.S. economic aid and 57 percent of all

23. The economic ideology of the Chinese Nationalist government is quite vague and includes features of socialism as well as capitalism. It advocates a more balanced ownership of land, a more equitable distribution of wealth and income, state enterprises in certain industries, and state control of private industries. But it also believes in private property, profit incentive, and competition. Its behavior, when it governed the mainland, suggests that the Nationalist government was not strongly predisposed to develop the private sector and indeed on numerous occasions, when it was on the mainland, established public enterprises in competition with the private sector.

24. Jacoby, *U.S. Aid to Taiwan*, p. 51.

Table 7.3. Allocation of United States Economic Aid to Taiwan, by Sector of the
           Economy (Percentage of total)

	All aid[a]	Capital assistance[b]
Infrastructure	37.3	44.0
Agriculture	21.5	23.8
Human resources	25.9	12.8
Industry	15.3	19.4
Total	100.0	100.0

Source: These figures were compiled by Neil Jacoby. For his sources and methods see
Neil H. Jacoby, *U.S. Aid to Taiwan*, tables IV-3 and IV-4, and Appendix B.
[a]The figures are for 1951–65 and include both the allocation of U.S. dollars and aid-
generated NT dollars.
[b]For 1951–63.

U.S. capital assistance. Between 1951 and 1963, U.S. capital assistance
accounted for 75 percent of Taiwan's net domestic investment in
infrastructure but only 13 percent of the net domestic investment in
industry.[25] In other words U.S. aid to public enterprises was used
primarily to increase the productivity of private industrial investments,
and in this manner it helped to ensure the expansion of the private
sector.

To produce a more favorable atmosphere for development, AID
also exerted pressure on the Nationalist government to liberalize its
economic controls and to limit its military expenditures. To stimulate
the desired response from the Chinese government, the level of aid
was used as an instrument of pressure. On a number of occasions
AID offered to increase the level of aid if proper government actions
were taken and threatened to reduce it if the government failed to
act.[26] However, AID's efforts to influence Chinese government policy
were not always successful. Throughout the 1950s and the 1960s AID
brought intense pressure to bear upon the Nationalist government to
exercise fiscal restraint and hold down its military spending. Despite
these pressures the Chinese government adhered to its preference for
the military and continued to enlarge its military budget. But had
AID not exerted pressure, the size of the military budget conceivably
could have increased at a still more rapid rate. Thus, in a negative
sense, AID may have helped to restrain military spending.

    25. Ibid., p. 52.
    26. The most notable example of this was AID's attempt in 1959–60 to induce the
Chinese government to adopt the 19-Point Program of Economic and Financial Reform.
For a discussion of this, see Jacoby, ibid., pp. 134–35.

AID was much more successful in helping the Chinese government to develop economic policies that were more developmental and less control-oriented. In the late 1940s and the early 1950s, when Taiwan was threatened by war and inflation, the government imposed on the economy a large number of temporary regulations and controls. They included a multiple exchange rate system, import and foreign exchange controls, hidden subsidies, and rationing and administrative pricing of certain goods and services, in addition to various bureaucratic obstacles to private business. Once they were introduced, inertia, vested interests of various government agencies, and a genuine fear of economic disorder among high government officials combined to preserve these regulations long after the economy had stabilized. Because these controls created distortions and caused inefficiencies in the economy, their presence reduced the productivity of investment and thus inhibited economic development.

After the Chinese Nationalists successfully repulsed a communist attack on Quemoy in 1958, AID urged the government to be more development oriented. It argued for a relaxation of economic controls and an improvement in the climate for private investment. The government responded constructively and in 1959 took the first step to rationalize its economic regulations and liberalize economic policies. In that year the regulations on foreign investment and overseas Chinese investment were eased and the multiple exchange rate system was simplified. In the subsequent four years (1960–63) the government introduced other and equally important reforms: among others, a statute for the encouragement of investment, the conversion of the multiple exchange rate system to a single rate, the relaxation of trade and exchange controls, and the simplification of business laws and regulations. In general, government red tapes were reduced. Together these actions permitted the economy to pursue an outward-looking growth strategy more in line with its true comparative advantage, one that has been given much of the credit for Taiwan's growth in the 1960s and the early 1970s.

In 1964 AID announced that no economic aid would be committed to the Republic of China after June 30, 1965. This further stimulated the Chinese government to enlarge and intensify its efforts at economic development. Government trade missions were dispatched to developed as well as underdeveloped countries, trade and exchange controls were further relaxed, the government became more receptive to Japanese investments, industrial sites and export-processing zones were created, positive measures to promote export were adopted, and official red tape was further reduced. Chapter 10 shall examine these developments and evaluate the effects they had on Taiwan's industrialization.

In summary, the problem Taiwan faced in 1949 was how to transform the remains of a colonial economy that was heavily dependent on primary exports into an industrialized and more diversified economy. The strategy chosen was to develop agriculture by injecting it with large doses of industrial inputs and at the same time to industrialize through import substitution. Subsequently, the economy continued its transition by turning toward the world market and looking to exports as its primary source of growth. Given Taiwan's heavy military burden, economic development was a formidable task, made manageable only by a large infusion of United States aid.

There is no question that U.S. aid had an immense impact on Taiwan. Yet it is difficult, if not impossible, to precisely measure or quantify its effects. Undoubtedly, U.S. aid permitted a higher rate of growth; but beyond its effects on growth, aid also influenced the type of economy and society that developed in Taiwan. Politically, it made possible the survival of the Nationalist government and allowed it to remain in power in Taiwan. Economically and socially, it was helpful to restore stability and facilitated the development of a viable private sector and a growing middle class. Indeed, in the 1950s and the 1960s there was hardly an aspect of Taiwan's political, economic, and social life that was not in some way influenced by the presence of U.S. economic and military aid, albeit not always beneficially.

8

Economic Growth and Structural Changes, 1952–1972: A Quantitative Record

Nineteen fifty-two was a benchmark year for Taiwan, marking its economic recovery from a decade of war and political and economic disorder. Although many difficult problems remained unsolved, the worst was over. Inflation, although still a problem, had nevertheless slowed down, and the production of most commodities reached or surpassed prewar peaks. The two decades after recovery were for Taiwan a period of unprecedented economic growth. One purpose of this chapter is to measure the growth in output and in aggregate productivity achieved in the 1950s and 1960s. Economic growth was accompanied by structural and demographic changes, and the second purpose of this chapter is to examine some of the more important ones. Of these, three deserve special attention: (1) a shift in industrial structure that saw a dramatic rise in the relative significance of the nonagricultural sector, particularly manufacturing; (2) a demographic transition from high to low fertility that significantly reduced Taiwan's population growth; and (3) a shift in income distribution toward greater equality.

OUTPUT AND AGGREGATE PRODUCTIVITY

Table 8.1 brings together for the two decades since recovery the usual aggregate economic indicators, which show Taiwan to have experienced an impressive rate of economic growth. For the period 1953–73, the annual overall growth rate of the economy was 8.6 percent. During this period, population grew at an average rate of 2.8 percent per annum. Thus real per capita GNP increased at an

121

Table 8.1. Economic Indicators, 1951–73

	Midyear Population (1,000)	GNP (million NT$)		Real per Capita GNP 1971 NT$/ person	Index of agricultural production 1971 = 100	Index of industrial production 1971 = 100
		Current prices	1971 prices			
1951	8,263	12,315	52,121	6,308	38.0	5.8
1952	8,600	17,247	57,795	6,720	41.3	7.3
1953	8,885	22,988	62,582	7,043	45.3	9.1
1954	9,195	25,225	68,022	7,398	46.3	9.7
1955	9,523	30,088	73,270	7,694	46.5	10.9
1956	9,847	34,543	77,149	7,835	50.2	11.3
1957	10,153	40,291	82,461	8,122	53.6	12.7
1958	10,476	44,752	87,184	8,322	57.7	13.8
1959	10,840	51,727	93,278	8,605	58.3	15.5
1960	11,211	62,561	98,523	8,788	59.1	17.7
1961	11,571	69,792	104,974	9,072	64.2	20.4
1962	11,935	76,882	112,622	9,436	65.5	22.1
1963	12,253	87,134	122,262	9,978	65.2	24.0
1964	12,601	102,209	136,197	10,808	73.5	29.1
1965	12,992	112,867	150,342	11,572	79.0	33.9
1966	13,360	125,554	162,058	12,130	83.1	39.2
1967	13,694	145,878	178,790	13,056	87.9	45.7
1968	14,023	170,834	194,648	13,881	93.3	55.9
1969	14,267	195,572	211,341	14,813	92.3	67.0
1970	14,505	226,368	234,161	16,143	97.9	80.6
1971	14,836	261,436	261,436	17,621	100.0	100.0
1972	15,142	307,361	292,693	19,330	101.9	121.0
1973	15,427	388,583	327,588	21,235	105.6	144.2
(Average annual rate of growth)						
1953–73	2.82	—	8.63	5.65	4.63	15.42
1953–63	3.27	—	7.05	3.65	4.32	11.55
1964–73	2.32	—	10.37	7.84	4.99	19.67

Notes and Sources: Except for population, all figures are official estimates. The official population estimates have been adjusted to include military personnel. The midyear population figures are simple interpolations of year-end figures. Agricultural production includes, besides crop and livestock production, forestry and fishery production, and is from PDAF, *Taiwan Agricultural Yearbook*, 1974. The industrial production index is from MOEA, *The Republic of China Taiwan Industrial Production Statistics Monthly*, June 1975, p. 9. The other figures are from DGBAS, *Statistical Abstract of the Republic of China*, Dec. 1974, pp. 72–73, 256–59, and 280–83.

impressive rate of 5.7 percent per year, an enviable performance by any reasonable standard.

The strong growth in GNP is confirmed by the performances of other, less aggregated time series. From 1953 to 1973 agricultural production, as measured by the official agricultural production index, increased at an annual rate of 4.6 percent. In the same period, industrial production increased at an impressive rate of over 15 percent a year, and the rate of increase accelerated in the second half of the period. Industrial output grew at an average annual rate of 11.5 percent from 1953 to 1963 and an astonishing 19.7 percent from 1964 to 1973.

Growth, of course, was not uniform. The largest gains in real GNP were in 1964–65 and 1971–73, when growth exceeded 10 percent each year. The year with the lowest rate of increase was 1956, when real GNP increased by only 5.3 percent. But on the whole, growth was quite steady with only minor fluctuations. During 1953–73, the average rate of growth of real GNP was 4.1 times larger than its standard deviation.

Taiwan's economic performance can perhaps be better appreciated if it is compared with that of other countries. Table 8.2 brings together the average growth rates of real GDP and per capita real GDP for a group of selected developing and developed countries. For the period 1950–71, Taiwan's real GDP grew at rates substantially higher than that attained either by the average less developed country or the average developed country. In Asia, during the 1950s and the 1960s, only Japan, which grew at an average annual rate of 8.4 percent from 1952 to 1960 and 10.7 percent from 1960 to 1971, outperformed Taiwan. Of the non-Asian countries, a search of United Nations sources revealed only Trinidad and Tobago and Israel to have experienced growth exceeding that of Taiwan, and since the mid-1960s Israel's growth rate has fallen below that of Taiwan. Taiwan's postwar economic performance was therefore unique.

Population during the 1950s and the early 1960s grew faster in Taiwan than in most other developing countries. Indeed, in the 1950s few countries had a more rapid rate of population expansion than Taiwan. Despite this, because of the rapid growth of its total product, per capita real GDP increased faster in Taiwan than in any other Asian country except Japan. Rising at 3.8 percent a year from 1951 to 1960, the growth of Taiwan's per capita real GDP exceeded by a substantial margin the average rates achieved by either the developing

Table 8.2. Average Rate of Growth of GDP for Taiwan, Other Developing Countries, and Developed Countries (Percent)

	Taiwan	East and Southeast Asia (exc. Japan)[a]	Developing countries[b]	Developed countries[c]
1950–60				
Real GDP at factor cost	7.4[d]	4.0	4.6	3.7
Per capita GDP at factor cost	3.8[d]	1.8	2.4	2.4
1960–71				
Real GDP	10.1	4.7	5.3	5.0
Per capita GDP	7.3	2.3	2.7	3.9

Sources: Except for Taiwan, all other figures are from United Nations, Department of Economic and Social Affairs, *Yearbook of National Accounts Statistics*, 1968, vol. 2, table 5B, and 1972, vol. 3, table 4B. Taiwan's GDP figures are from DGBAS, *National Income of the Republic of China*, various issues. Taiwan's population figures are those in table 8.1 and include military personnel.

[a] All countries and territories in East and Southeast Asia except the Chinese mainland, Mongolia, and North Korea.

[b] The figures are for 1950–60 and include all countries in Africa (except South Africa), Caribbean and Latin America, East and Southeast Asia (except Japan), and the Middle East (except Cyprus, Israel, and Turkey). For 1960–71, they include the same countries as in 1950–60 plus Cyprus and Turkey.

[c] Countries in Western Europe, North America, and Oceania, together with Israel, Japan, and South Africa.

[d] 1951–60.

or the developed countries. In the 1960s, with its output growth accelerating and its population growth declining, the growth of Taiwan's per capita real GDP increased to 7.3 percent per year, further widening the gap between it and the per capita income growth of the average less developed country.

Taiwan's extraordinary rate of output growth was made possible in part by the growth of factor inputs (table 8.3). Rapid population growth provided Taiwan with an expanding source of labor supply. From 1952 to 1973 employment expanded at an average annual rate of 2.6 percent. Fixed capital stock grew even more rapidly. Helped by United States economic aid, Taiwan maintained a rate of capital accumulation much higher than what its domestic savings alone would have allowed. The average annual rate of increase of real fixed capital stock was 3.3 percent from 1952 to 1963 and 9.5 percent from 1964 to 1973. Clearly, much of Taiwan's growth can be traced to the rapid

Table 8.3. Indexes of Real GDP and Factor Inputs, 1952–72

	Real GDP	*Employment*	*Fixed capital stock*
1952	100.0	100.0	100.0
1953	108.3	100.6	102.7
1954	117.7	102.1	105.0
1955	126.8	103.1	107.5
1956	133.5	102.7	110.2
1957	142.8	105.9	112.6
1958	150.9	108.2	116.1
1959	161.4	111.4	120.5
1960	170.4	113.9	125.5
1961	181.7	116.8	131.2
1962	195.0	119.3	136.6
1963	211.7	123.2	142.9
1964	235.9	123.2	149.2
1965	260.6	123.7	158.4
1966	280.9	124.2	170.0
1967	309.6	135.3	185.9
1968	337.5	141.6	205.6
1969	366.0	151.0	226.9
1970	405.8	154.8	251.0
1971	452.4	161.4	279.6
1972	506.2	165.0	313.7

Notes and Sources: The GDP data are from DGBAS, *National Income of the Republic of China*, various issues. Household registration data on occupied persons over the age of 12 are used to represent employment for 1951–63. After 1963, employment is based on labor survey data. In all cases, employment includes unpaid family workers. The primary sources of labor data are PDCA, *Household Registration Statistics of Taiwan Province*, various issues, and Taiwan Provincial Labor Force Survey and Research Institute, *Report of the Labor Force Survey in Taiwan*, various issues. The fixed capital stock series is derived from benchmark estimates of capital stock and annual net investment in fixed capital by the perpetual inventory method. For details of benchmark estimates, see Shirley W. Kuo, "The Economic Development of Taiwan—An Overall Analysis," in Kowie Chang, ed., *Economic Development in Taiwan*, pp. 88–90.

expansion of its stock of reproducible capital. However, table 8.3 also suggests that factor inputs could not have been the sole source of growth. Output per capita and output per unit of total input also increased. In other words, the economy was using its resources increasingly more efficiently.

If the Taiwan economy is represented by a Cobb–Douglas production function, then

$$\dot{Q} = \alpha_1 \dot{L} + \alpha_2 \dot{K} + \dot{A}, \qquad \alpha_1 + \alpha_2 = 1, \tag{8.1}$$

Table 8.4. Sources of Output Growth

	Total growth in GDP (%)	Percentage of growth in GDP attributed to		
		Labor	*Capital*	*Unexplained*
1953–72	100	17.7	27.6	54.8
1953–62	100	15.2	19.8	65.0
1963–73	100	20.2	35.4	44.4

Notes and Sources: These figures were obtained with the assumption that

$$\dot{Q} = \alpha_1 \dot{L} + \alpha_2 \dot{K} + \dot{A}, \quad \alpha_1 + \alpha_2 = 1,$$

where $\dot{Q}$ is the growth rate of GDP, $\dot{L}$ is the growth rate of labor, $\dot{K}$ is the growth rate of capital, $\dot{A}$ is unexplained output growth, and the α's are factor shares. The input and output data are from table 8.3 and the factor shares for each year were estimated from DGBAS, *National Income of the Republic of China*, 1973, pp. 106–09. Mixed income was distributed equally to labor and capital.

where $\dot{Q}$ is the growth rate of GDP, $\dot{L}$ is the growth rate of labor, $\dot{K}$ is the growth rate of capital, $\dot{A}$ is unexplained output growth, and the α's are factor shares. When the α's, calculated from Taiwan's national income statistics, are applied to the data in table 8.3, $\dot{A}$ is estimated to equal 4.56 percent per year for the period 1953–72. In other words a substantial share of Taiwan's postwar economic growth is not explained by the growth in inputs but by the increases in their productivity. Table 8.4 distributes the growth of output by source. For the period 1953–72, on the average, less than half the total output growth can be attributed to the growth in labor and capital. Unexplained output growth played an especially prominent role from 1953 to 1962, when it accounted for 65 percent of the total growth in GDP. From 1963 to 1972, when growth was extremely rapid, increases in labor and capital inputs accounted for 56 percent of the output growth, with the remaining share unexplained.

That a significant portion of Taiwan's postwar growth in output is not explained by the growth of labor and capital is not surprising, because studies of other rapidly growing economies give similar results.[1] Unexplained growth represents, of course, a composite of factors. In the 1950s, a period of recovery, a major contributory factor was the fuller utilization of resources. For the period 1952–72 as a whole, new technology embodied in the capital equipment imported

1. For two recent studies, see Kazushi Ohkawa and Henry Rosovsky, *Japanese Economic Growth*, and Howard Pack, *Structural Change and Economic Policy in Israel*.

from the United States and Japan undoubtedly improved the quality of the capital stock. Improved public health and expanded education opportunities also helped to raise the quality of the labor force. These two factors surely must account for a large share of the residual in Taiwan's growth. It is also likely that Taiwan's rapidly expanding exports in the 1960s enabled some of its industries to expand sufficiently beyond the limited confines of the domestic market to benefit from economies of scale, which would show up in the above growth accounting analysis as unexplained growth.

CHANGES IN ECONOMIC STRUCTURE

Output

Differences in income elasticities of demand and in the rate of technological change among the industries caused Taiwan's industries to expand at vastly different rates. Table 8.5 compares the apparent differences in the growth rates of Taiwan's major industrial sectors. I use "apparent" because official estimates of real output by industrial origin are available only after 1967, and the pre-1967 estimates were obtained by very crude approximations.

Table 8.5 shows that economic growth in the 1950s and 1960s was not isolated to a few modern sectors but was experienced on a broad front. Most significantly, agricultural growth was vigorous throughout most of the postrecovery period and did not slow down until the late 1960s, when industrialization was already well under way. Manufacturing, growing at about 14 percent a year from 1951 to 1973, emerged in this period as the leading growth sector. Indeed, few countries in the world can match its growth rate of nearly 20 percent a year from 1967 to 1973. Following manufacturing, and growing only slightly slower, were the utilities, transportation, and financial sectors. In the 1950s, construction expanded slowly, for relatively little housing construction occurred in this period. The extensive infrastructure inherited from the colonial period also allowed the economy to postpone for a time the construction of some social capital without doing serious damage to economic development. After the late 1950s, however, as the need for infrastructure and housing became more urgent, the growth of construction accelerated.

The private trade sector grew only modestly in the first part of the postrecovery period, but after the late 1950s its growth also accelerated.

Table 8.5. Annual Growth of Real GDP by Industrial Origin[a] (Percent)

	1951–53 to 1958–60	1958–60 to 1965–67	1967–73
Agriculture[b]	3.1	4.9	1.0
Mining	11.1	3.8	1.2
Manufacturing	11.9	11.2	19.8
Construction	3.8	10.3	6.4
Utility	11.0	13.6	14.5
Transportation, storage, and communication	11.9	13.4	11.1
Trade	4.9	11.1	9.6
Financial services	15.2	6.8	13.6
Housing services	5.6	9.1	8.5
Government services	4.7	2.7	4.7
Other services	2.7	2.7	6.2

Notes and Sources: The 1967–73 figures are based on official estimates from DGBAS, *National Income of the Republic of China*, 1973, pp. 198–99. The other figures are the annual compound rates of growth implied by the average real GDP by industrial origin in 1951–53, 1958–60, and 1965–67. To obtain GDP by industrial origin in constant prices, the sectoral value added in current prices was deflated by the following official price indexes: agriculture, the index of prices received by farmers; mining, the mining component of the index of prices of industrial products; manufacturing, the manufacturing component of the index of prices of industrial products; construction, the construction price index; utility, the fuel and power component of the urban consumers' price index; transport and communication, the transport and communication component of the urban consumers' price index; trade, the Taipei wholesale price index; financial services, government services, and other services, the index of compensations of government employees; and housing services, the rent component of the urban consumers' price index. GDP at factor cost in current prices is from DGBAS, *National Income of the Republic of China*, 1970, pp. 126–29. For the sources of the price data, see the Statistical Appendix.

[a] Except for the period 1967–73, the figures are the annual growth rates of real GDP at factor cost by industrial origin.
[b] Includes forestry, hunting, and fishing.

The 1950s was not a period particularly favorable to the expansion of private trade activities. External trade was controlled and largely managed by government agencies. Government enterprises, then the most important manufacturers in Taiwan, distributed their products for export through government channels rather than through private traders. United States aid imports, about 40 percent of total import in the 1950s, were channeled through and partly distributed by the government. The distribution of key raw materials was also controlled

Table 8.6. Industrial Structure, Selected Years (Percentage of total)

	Real GDP at factor cost			Real GDP	
	1952	1960	1967	1967	1973
Total[a]	100.0	100.0	100.0	100.0	100.0
Agriculture[b]	35.3	28.9	25.3	21.3	11.4
Mining	1.9	2.4	1.7	1.8	1.0
Manufacturing	9.8	17.2	21.4	27.6	43.5
Construction	3.7	3.3	3.8	4.0	3.2
Utilities	0.9	1.7	2.1	2.2	3.0
Transporation, storage and communication	3.0	4.4	6.1	5.7	6.7
Trade	14.9	13.8	16.9	14.4	13.1
Financial services	1.2	2.0	2.1	2.3	2.5
Housing services	6.3	6.1	6.7	5.9	5.1
Government services	14.9	13.9	10.2	9.6	6.5
Other services	8.1	6.2	3.7	5.2	3.9

Sources: See table 8.5.
[a] GDP or GDP at factor cost before adjustments for imputed bank interest and statistical discrepancy.
[b] Includes forestry, hunting, and fishery.

and operated by the government. Even a considerable share of each year's rice harvest was collected and distributed by the government, operating outside the market. Only in the late 1950s, after the private manufacturing sector had become stronger and the government had relinquished some of its controls, was the private trade sector given the opportunity to expand.

The consequence of such vastly differing sectoral growth rates was a dramatic alteration of Taiwan's economic structure. Like so many other countries before it, as per capita income increased, Taiwan saw the share of agriculture in its national output decline and that of industry rise.[2] In table 8.6 Taiwan's industrial structure in 1952, 1960, 1967, and 1973 is presented. When the data for these years are compared, one is immediately impressed by the increasing importance of manufacturing in Taiwan's economy. In 1952, less than 10 percent of Taiwan's real GDP at factor cost originated in manufacturing. However, from 1952 to 1967 it accounted for 27 percent of the total net

2. Simon Kuznets, "Quantitative Aspects of the Economic Growth of Nations II. Industrial Distribution of National Product and Labor Force," *Economic Development and Cultural Change* 5, suppl. (July 1957): pp. 3–111.

increase in GDP, and from 1967 to 1973, over 60 percent. By the mid-1960s, manufacturing accounted for over 20 percent of Taiwan's real GDP, and in 1973, 43 percent. The share of agriculture in GDP, on the other hand, declined sharply. Agriculture, which contributed 35 percent of the real GDP in 1952, accounted for only 11 percent of the real GDP in 1973. By the early 1970s Taiwan was no longer an agrarian economy, although agriculture still played a vital role.

The different sectoral growth rates, the emergence of new industries, and changes in technology also combined to alter the relationship between agriculture and industry in decisive ways. A comparison of input–output coefficient matrices over the years suggests that agriculture, with its rising demand for industrial chemicals and power machineries, became an increasingly important market for Taiwan's industry.[3] On the other hand, through diversification manufacturing became less dependent on agriculture. New industries such as synthetic textile, petrochemical, and metal products increased the demand for industrial raw materials, and consequently intramanufacturing sales.[4] Thus, in the postwar period a significant deepening of production within manufacturing occurred.

Like manufacturing, services that directly support the production of goods (utilities, transport, communication, trade, banking, and insurance) also increased their shares in GDP. In 1973 about one-quarter of Taiwan's real GDP came from this sector as compared to 20 percent in 1952. Finally, the share of housing services, government services, and other services declined, falling from about 29 percent in 1952 to about 15 percent in 1973. Since the contributions to GDP of government and other services are essentially measurements of labor inputs, it should be noted that in the early 1950s, government and other services were inflated by the transfer of government personnel and professional people from the mainland, many of whom were kept on payrolls without contributing much to output. Thus it is likely that the contribution of government and other services to GDP was over-estimated in the early 1950s.

3. For example, a comparison of the 1954 and 1964 input–output coefficients shows that manufacturing inputs to agriculture for every dollar of agricultural output produced increased by about 40 percent.

4. A comparison of the 1954 and 1964 input–output coefficients reveals that the consumption of manufacturing goods by the manufacturing sector for every dollar it produces increased by about 70 percent.

Employment

Taiwan's changing industrial structure is also reflected in the deployment of its labor force. Table 8.7 brings together census and survey data on the distribution of employed persons by industry for 1940, 1956, 1966, and 1974. Although the industrial categories used by the three censuses and the 1974 survey are generally comparable, they are not precisely equal. However, the differences are relatively minor, so the data in table 8.7 provide a useful comparison of how labor deployment changed from 1940 to 1974. Not surprisingly, the

Table 8.7. Labor Deployment, 1940–74 (Percentage of total)

	Distribution of employment				Allocation of increase in employment		
	1940	1956	1966	1974	1940–74	1940–66	1966–74
Total	100.0	100.0	100.0	100.0	100.0	100.0	100.0
Agriculture, forestry, and fishery	64.0	55.4	42.8	31.0	6.8	10.6	−3.6
Mining	2.0	1.4	1.6	1.2	0.7	1.0	0.6
Manufacturing	7.7	12.4	14.4	26.8	40.8	24.6	50.5
Construction	2.0	2.3	2.6	5.8	8.6	3.6	11.8
Utilities	0.2	0.6	0.7	0.6	0.9	1.5	0.3
Transportation and communications	2.8	3.9	4.4	5.3	7.2	6.8	7.3
Trade	8.2	6.9	8.2	13.7	17.7	8.0	19.1
Other services and not classified[a]	13.1	16.9	25.3	15.5	17.3	43.7	14.0

Notes and Sources: The 1940, 1956, and 1966 figures are based on population census data. The 1974 figures are based on the 1974 quarterly labor force surveys. The 1940 figures include all employed persons regardless of age. The 1956 and 1966 figures include only those over the age of 12, and the 1974 survey includes only those 15 and over. In all cases military personnel living on military bases are excluded. (Unlike the other two censuses, the coverage of the 1966 census includes military personnel living on military bases, who are classified in the government sector. To make the 1966 figures comparable to those from the other years, I have assumed the number of military personnel living on military bases in Taiwan in 1966 to be 450,000 and have deducted this from the original census figures.) The data in this table are compiled from PBAS, *Results of the Seventh Population Census of Taiwan, 1940*, 1953, p. 60; *Report of the 1956 Population Census, Republic of China*, table 10, pp. 58–61; *The Report of the 1966 Census of Population and Housing of Taiwan–Fukien Area, Republic of China*, pt. 2, vol. 5a, table 2, pp. 9–12; and Taiwan Provincial Labor Force Survey and Research Institute, *Report of the Labor Force Survey in Taiwan*, no. 46, 1975, tables 9, 10.
[a] Including professional services and government.

redeployment of employment since the end of the colonial period has occurred in a manner very similar to the changes in output structure outlined above.

One-quarter of the increase in employment between 1940 and 1966 and one-half of the increase between 1966 and 1974 were absorbed by the manufacturing sector, raising its share in total employment from less than 8 percent in 1940 to 14 percent in 1966, and 27 percent in 1974. On the other hand, the agricultural labor force, as a share of the total, declined from 64 percent in 1940 to 43 percent in 1966 and 31 percent in 1974. Between 1966 and 1974, agricultural employment declined not only relatively but for the first time also absolutely, falling from 1.67 million to 1.64 million. Because World War II kept economic changes to a minimum in the 1940s, we believe that most of the dramatic shift in labor deployment since 1940 occurred after rather than before 1950. In any case the data suggest in the 25 years since the end of World War II, Taiwan's labor distribution experienced a greater degree of reallocation than it did in the previous half-century.

Besides manufacturing, the service sectors also made impressive gains in employment, together absorbing over 50 percent of the total increase in employment between 1940 and 1966 and about 25 percent between 1966 and 1974. However, the growth of employment in government and in trade was somewhat erratic. Between 1940 and 1956, hampered by war and postwar adjustments, employment in trade showed little increase, with the result that its share in total employment declined from more than 8 to less than 7 percent. But after 1956, trade was one of the faster growing sectors in terms of employment. By 1966 its share of total employment was back to what it was in 1940, and by 1974 it accounted for nearly 14 percent of Taiwan's total employment. The growth of employment in the trade sector confirms what we already observed about its contribution to GDP: the trade sector experienced limited growth in the 1950s and accelerated growth thereafter. The growth of government employment showed an opposite trend. Between 1940 and 1956 the government sector absorbed 20 percent of the total increase in employment. This rapid increase was, of course, a direct consequence of the government's decision to retain in its organization a large number of the mainland refugees who arrived in Taiwan in the late 1940s and early 1950s. After 1956 the government sector was a less important source of employment. Between 1956 and 1966 the census data show that government absorbed just over 1 percent of the total increase in employment.

Trade

Finally, in the postwar period both the level and composition of Taiwan's external trade altered in significant ways. It is a well-established fact that foreign trade is far more crucial for a small economy such as that of Taiwan's than for a large one.[5] Indeed, except for the immediate postwar years Taiwan's foreign trade as a share of its GNP has always been large. In 1951–53 the ratio of foreign trade (exports plus imports) to GNP was 23 percent. In subsequent years, as Taiwan developed, foreign trade grew faster than total product and the ratio of foreign trade to GNP rose steadily until it was 81 percent in 1971–73. This trend is not surprising. Short of resources and with a limited domestic market, Taiwan, to maintain a rapid rate of growth, had to rely heavily on foreign trade. The world market provided Taiwan not only with the capital goods and raw materials for industrialization but also with a much needed outlet for its outputs.

Economic growth was accompanied not only by an increase in the volume of foreign trade but also by an alteration in its structure (table 8.8). In 1952, finished consumer goods accounted for 13 percent, raw materials 74 percent, and capital goods 13 percent of all merchandise imports. Of the consumer imports, textile products, wheat flour, milk and milk products, edible oil, and beans were among the most significant. Strict government controls limited the import of luxury and high quality consumer goods to a minimum. Of the raw material imports, the two most significant were raw cotton and chemical fertilizers. The cotton was raw material for the infant textile industry and the fertilizers were used to revitalize a weakened agricultural sector. The relative low share of capital imports reflected the fact that rapid industrialization was still some years away.

As Taiwan industrialized, its import structure altered considerably. The share of consumer imports as well as that of raw materials declined steadily; from 1952 to 1972, the former declined from 13 to 6 percent and the latter from 74 to 57 percent. The share of capital goods, on the other hand, increased from 13 percent in 1952 to 37 percent in 1972. The development of industries such as textile and chemical fertilizer substituted domestic production for imports and explains in part the relative decline of consumer goods and raw materials in total

5. See Simon Kuznets, "Quantitative Aspects of the Economic Growth of Nations: IX. Level and Structure of Foreign Trade: Comparisons for Recent Years," *Economic Development and Cultural Changes* 13, pt. 2 (Oct. 1964): 1–106.

Table 8.8. Composition of Exports and Imports, Selected Years

	1952	1958	1965	1972
Imports				
Value (US$ million)	207.0	232.8	555.3	2,843.3
Percentage distribution				
Total	100.0	100.0	100.0	100.0
Capital goods	13.1	25.9	29.3	37.3
Raw materials	74.2	62.9	62.9	56.7
Consumption goods	12.7	11.2	7.8	6.0
Exports				
Value (US$ million)	119.5	165.5	495.8	3,114.1
Percentage distribution				
Total	100.0	100.0	100.0	100.0
Agricultural products	26.9	23.6	23.4	7.2
Processed agricultural products	68.3	62.7	30.7	9.9
Industrial products	4.8	13.7	45.9	82.9

Notes and Sources: These figures are based on the import–export exchange settlement statistics compiled by the Foreign Exchange and Trade Commission. They differ slightly from the trade data compiled by the Inspectorate General of Customs. The above figures are from CIECD, *Taiwan Statistical Data Book*, 1973, pp. 167–68.

import. But to implement the import substitution strategy, Taiwan required additional capital equipment, and, as a result, the share of capital goods in total imports rose from 13 percent in 1952 to 26 percent in 1958. Since 1960 Taiwan has pursued an export-oriented industrialization strategy, and the continued high share of capital goods in total import is a reflection of the rapid industrialization that has resulted from this policy. We shall return in chapter 10 to examine Taiwan's industrialization and trade policies in greater detail.

The change in export structure was even more dramatic. In the early 1950s most of Taiwan's exports were agricultural in origin. Two commodities, rice and sugar, accounted for 78 percent of Taiwan's total exports in 1952, and agricultural and processed agricultural products accounted for 95 percent. Since then, the export picture has been extremely dynamic, not only because export has grown rapidly but also because pivotal structural changes have occurred. Of these, the most significant is the decline of natural-resource-intensive exports and the rise of labor- and skill-intensive industrial exports. In absolute terms, industrial exports increased from below US $6 million in 1952 to US $2.58 billion in 1972. Relatively, industrial exports accounted for 5 percent of total merchandise exports in 1952, 46 percent in 1965, and 83 percent in 1972. By the early 1970s textiles, metals, and machinery were as critical to Taiwan's export as sugar and rice were in the early 1950s.

DEMOGRAPHIC CHANGES

Fertility

Rapid economic growth and industrialization were accompanied by important demographic changes. By the early 1970s Taiwan was midway through its demographic transition from high to low fertility. Strict enforcement of public health measures was largely responsible for the sharp decline in mortality in the colonial period, when the crude death rate dropped from over 30 per 1,000 to about 20 per 1,000. With crude birth rate remaining at 40 per 1,000 the annual rate of natural increase rose from 8 per 1,000 in 1906–10 to about 25 in the 1930s. Fertility in the 1950s remained at the high prewar levels but the systematic application of modern public health measures and newly developed pesticides brought about further declines in mortality, and Taiwan's crude death rate dropped from 20 per 1,000 in the mid-1940s to about 7 per 1,000 in the late 1950s.[6] As a consequence, the annual rate of natural increase was in excess of 35 per 1,000 throughout most of the 1950s.

In the late 1950s fertility began to diminish and the downward trend continued throughout the 1960s and the early 1970s. There is speculation that the initial decline in fertility in 1957 was mostly statistical, but even when the 1957 decline is discounted, the downward trend is clear.[7] From 1958 to 1972 the crude birth rate declined by 42 percent, falling from 41.6 to 24.2 per 1,000. With the decline in mortality already near an end, the drop in fertility brought the annual rate of natural

6. Although the death rate has undoubtedly declined, the recorded death rate may be spuriously low. The major source of error is probably the underregistration of infant deaths. Field surveys in three townships in the early 1960s suggest that up to one-third of the infant deaths might not have been registered. In which case, the corrected crude death rate would be about 10–15 percent higher than the official one, but still a very low figure.

7. The crude birth rate declined suddenly in 1957, dropping from 44.8 to 41.6 per 1,000. Andrew Collver et al. have suggested that part of the observed decline in fertility in 1957 may be the result of changes in the registration system after the 1956 census. However, they have been unable to demonstrate that such an error exists in the official data. See Andrew Collver, Alden Speare, Jr., and Paul K. C. Liu, "Local Variations of Fertility in Taiwan," *Population Studies* 20 (March 1967): p. 329.

increase to below 20 per 1,000 in 1972. Although the decline in fertility began in the cities, by the mid-1960s it was observed throughout the island, even in remote areas. Collver, Speare, and Liu found that in 1961–64, total fertility fell in 270 of the 292 administrative units they studied.[8] Their study also indicates that, whereas in 1958–61 the annual rate of decline in fertility was almost three times greater in cities than in rural districts, after 1963–64 the largest rate of decline was in rural townships. The magnitude and the general prevalence of fertility decline in Taiwan strongly suggest that its period of rapid population growth is at an end.

The decline in fertility in the 1960s was largely the consequence of later marriages and decreasing age-specific fertility rates above age 30. From 1960 to 1970 there was a 35 percent decline in the proportion of women married at ages 15–19 and a 19 percent decline in the proportion married at ages 20–24.[9] The trend toward later marriages most probably was influenced by the rapid industrialization and increases in women's education that occurred in Taiwan in the 1950s and the 1960s.[10] While fertility for all women declined in every age group (table 8.9), the most spectacular decline was among older women. Indeed, more than 80 percent of the 1960–70 decline in fertility is attributed to women over age 30. Interestingly, the age-specific fertility rates for married women under 24 rose steadily throughout the 1960s (table 8.9).[11] However, the proportion of women married at ages 15–24 declined sufficiently to compensate for the rise in marital fertility rates at these ages. Freedman et al. found that between 1961 and 1970,

8. Administratively, in the 1950s and 1960s Taiwan was divided into 5 municipalities, 7 cities, 78 urban townships, and 234 rural townships. Thirty-two rural townships were excluded from the study conducted by Collver et al. The excluded areas were primarily inhabited by aborigines and contain less than 2 percent of Taiwan's population. See ibid.

9. PDCA, *Taiwan Demographic Fact Book*, 1971, pt. A, table 8. The significant decline in the proportions of women married at age 15–19 was in part due to a shift in the age distribution within the 15–19 age bracket. Between 1959 and 1965 the proportion of the women aged 15–19 who were under 17 increased from 41 to 47 percent. This reflects the coming of age of the relatively large cohort born during 1950–52, when mortality was lower than the 1940s.

10. By the mid-1950s, nearly all school age (6–12) children in Taiwan were in school, and in the 1960s free education was extended through the ninth grade. In the late 1960s and early 1970s approximately two-thirds of the girls that graduated from the ninth grade continued to the tenth grade.

11. Freedman et al. have suggested that the increasing proportion of young brides (18 or under) with older husbands (35 or over) may be the reason for the increase in the marital fertility rates for ages 15–24 (see Ronald Freedman, Albert I. Hermalin, and Te-hsiung Sun, "Fertility Trends in Taiwan," pp. 141–42).

Table 8.9. Changes in Fertility Rates: Selected Years, 1960–72

	1960	1965	1970	1972	Percentage change			
					1960–65	1965–70	1970–72	1960–72
Crude birth rate	39.5	32.1	27.2	24.2	−18.7	−15.3	−11.0	−38.7
General fertility rate	180	152	120	104	−15.5	−21.0	−13.3	−42.2
Age-specific fertility rates								
15–19	49	36	40	35	−26.5	+11.1	−12.5	−28.6
20–24	254	261	238	208	+ 2.8	− 8.8	−12.6	−18.1
25–29	334	326	293	257	− 2.4	−10.1	−12.3	−23.0
30–34	256	195	147	117	−23.8	−24.6	−20.4	−54.3
35–39	170	100	59	41	−41.2	−41.0	−30.5	−75.9
40–44	79	41	20	13	−48.1	−51.2	−35.0	−83.5
45–49	13	6	3	2	−53.8	−50.0	−33.3	−84.6
General fertility rate for married women	264	225	192	170	−14.8	−14.7	−11.5	−35.6
Age-specific fertility rates for married women								
15–19	300	390	502	522	+30.0	+28.7	+ 4.0	+74.0
20–24	407	447	473	448	+ 9.8	+ 5.8	− 5.3	+10.1
25–29	373	368	332	297	− 1.3	− 9.8	−10.6	−20.4
30–34	279	210	158	126	−24.7	−24.8	−20.3	−54.8
35–39	189	109	64	44	−42.3	−41.3	−31.2	−76.7
40–44	92	47	22	14	−48.9	−53.2	−36.4	−84.8
45–49	16	8	4	3	−50.0	−50.0	−25.0	−81.2

Sources: PDCA, *Taiwan Demographic Fact Book*, 1961, 1965, 1970, 1972.

21 percent of the decrease in the crude birth rate can be attributed to later marriages, 12.4 percent to changes in age structure favorable to a fertility decline, 60.8 percent to a decline in marital fertility, especially among older women, and 5.8 percent to interaction.[12]

Organized family planning activities began in the 1950s as part of a maternal and child care program and intensified in 1963, when a large-scale program to introduce the IUD was launched on an experimental basis in Taichung, the provincial capital. Encouraged by the reception in Taichung, the IUD program was extended to other parts

12. Ibid., table 3.

of the island.[13] Facilitated by Taiwan's limited area, good transportation and mass communication system, and high literacy rate, the family planning program has had considerable impact on the demographic development in Taiwan. From 1964 to 1972 about 860,000 women (about 45 percent of all married women aged 20–44 during the period) had a first IUD insertion and a smaller number also received the pill or condoms through the family planning program. Schultz, using regression analyses, found family planning to be significantly associated with lower birth rates, with the association particularly strong among the older (over 30) age groups.[14]

Both the records of the family planning program and surveys have shown that the practice of contraception was concentrated principally among women over 30 and those with large number of living children.[15] This fact, when combined with the survey finding that the desired family size remained large in the 1960s,[16] suggests that the early phase of fertility decline in Taiwan was mainly the result of efforts by couples to reduce the number of undesired births. In other words, with mortality declining, many families found the number of surviving children exceeding their desired number and adopted birth control to bring actual fertility in line with desired fertility.

In the early 1970s the pattern of fertility decline altered in important ways. First, the decline accelerated. Second, marital fertility for ages 20–24 declined for the first time since 1960 (table 8.9). For the 15–19 age group, martial fertility continued to rise but at a substantially lower rate. Surveys conducted in 1970 and 1973 also indicate a significant decrease in the number of children desired by younger couples.

13. For a description of this program, see Bernard Berelson and Ronald Freedman, "A Study in Fertility," and Lien-ping Chow, "A Programme to Control Fertility in Taiwan."

14. T. Paul Schultz, "The Effectiveness of Family Planning in Taiwan: A Proposal for a New Evaluation Methodology." Rand Corporation, Apr. 1969; "Evaluation of Population Policies: A Framework for Analysis and Its Application to Taiwan's Family Planning Program," Rand Corporation, 1970; and "Explanation of Birth Rate Changes Over Space and Time: A Study of Taiwan," *Journal of Political Economy.*

15. For example, in 1967, a representative year, 62 percent of all IUD acceptors were women age 30 or over and 80 percent had at least three living children. For more supporting data see Freedman et al., "Fertility Trends in Taiwan," and Ronald Freedman, Lolagene C. Coombs, Ming-cheng Chang, and Te-hsiung Sun, "Trends in Fertility, Family Size Preferences, and Practice of Family Planning: Taiwan, 1965–1973."

16. For example, surveys conducted by the Population Studies Center and the Institute for Family Planning of Taiwan in the 1960s show that fewer than 3 percent of married couples wanted fewer than three children.

For example, the percentage of married women aged 22–29 interviewed who preferred two children increased from 8 in 1970 to 25 in 1973.[17] Apparently, industrialization, rising income, the increased availability of consumer durables, and the expanding opportunity and cost of education were beginning to have an effect on the behavior of Taiwanese couples, lowering their demand for children.[18]

Urbanization

Employment tends to be location specific, so economic growth with its accompanying structural shifts is bound to induce significant population movements. In postwar Taiwan, economic development brought about a rapid rate of urbanization. From 1951 to 1972 the population of Taiwan's five largest cities expanded from 1.5 to 4.1 million.[19] In 1951 these five cities contained 18 percent of Taiwan's population; in 1972 they contained 27 percent. Not only did the largest municipalities grow but so did the smaller cities and towns. The census counted 40 communities with population over 30,000 in 1940 and 179 in 1966.

One of the many factors that contributed to Taiwan's unrbanization was the great influx of mainland refugees in the late 1940s. Since most of the mainlanders were originally urban dwellers, a large proportion of them resettled in cities, where they could more easily eke out an existence.[20] In consequence, urban growth was most rapid in the late 1940s and early 1950s. However, thereafter urbanization was primarily the result of a high rate of natural increase in the cities and migration from rural areas.

Although urban Taiwan had a rate of natural increase that was appreciably lower than that of rural Taiwan, it was still high, averaging over 30 per 1,000 in the 1950s and about 23 per 1,000 in the 1960s.[21] Thus, even without migration to the cities, urban population would

17. Freedman et al., "Trends in Fertility," table 6.
18. Numerous models using microeconomic analysis to study fertility behavior have been advanced. In particular, see Harvey Leibenstein, *A Theory of Economic-Demographic Development*; T. Paul Schultz, "A Preliminary Survey of Economic Analyses of Fertility;" Robert J. Willis, "A New Approach to the Economic Theory of Fertility Behavior;" and Richard A. Easterlin, "An Economic Framework for Fertility Analysis," *Studies in Family Planning* 6 (March 1975): pp. 54–63.
19. The five cities are Taipei, Taichung, Keelung, Tainan, and Kaohsiung.
20. At the end of 1951, of the registered mainland civilians in Taiwan, 60 percent lived in the five largest cities. (see PDCA, *Household Registration Statistics of Taiwan Province*, 1959, p. 88).
21. Ibid., various issues.

have increased rapidly. Nevertheless, throughout the postwar period large numbers of Taiwanese moved each year, and the net flow was toward the cities, especially those with a population greater than 250,000. Speare has shown that the large cities received a net flow from both rural areas and the smaller urban towns. Furthermore, the net flow from the smaller urban towns to the large cities was compensated by a net flow from rural areas. His calculation shows that in 1968 the major cities received a net flow of more than 60,000 and the smaller towns almost 17,000. In the late 1960s and the early 1970s the net migration rate for the major cities was close to 20 per 1,000.[22]

The continual movement of people from rural to urban Taiwan was, of course, a reflection of the shift in labor from agriculture to nonagricultural activities. Theory tells us that such movements are closely related to the difference between the workers' expected real income in agriculture and that in the nonagricultural sector.[23] In the early 1950s the per capita real income originating in Taiwan's nonagricultural sector was twice that in agriculture. Despite a steady rise in agricultural productivity, rapid industrialization after the mid-1950s widened this differential considerably so that in 1966–70 the average per capita real income in the nonagricultural sector, at NT$ 11,791 in 1966 prices was more than three times that in agriculture.[24] In this same period, with the average rate of natural increase in rural Taiwan in excess of 30 per 1,000, the pressure of population on land intensified. Thus, there were powerful economic incentives for people to move off their farms and into the cities.

INCOME DISTRIBUTION

Economic development in the postwar period benefited all income groups in Taiwan—the rich and the middle class as well as the poor. Furthermore, the available evidence strongly suggests that the economic position of the poor in Taiwan improved not only absolutely but also relatively. However, the extent of relative improvement is

22. The net migration rate was calculated using the vital statistics residual method based on population, birth, and death data from PDCA, *Taiwan Demographic Fact Book*, various years.

23. For example, see Michael P. Todaro, "A Model of Labor Migration and Urban Unemployment in Less Developed Countries."

24. Paul K. C. Liu, "Economic Development and Population in Taiwan Since 1895: An Over-View," in *Essays on the Population of Taiwan* (Taipei: Institute of Economics, Academia Sinica, 1973), table 22.

Table 8.10. Size Distribution of Personal Income, and Gini Ratios, Selected Years

Income shares received by percentage of households

	0–20	20–40	40–60	60–80	80–90	90–95	Top 5	Gini ratio
1953	1.7	7.9	10.5	18.3	15.8	13.1	32.7	0.56
1964	7.7	12.1	17.0	22.0	14.4	10.4	16.3	0.33–0.36
1966	6.5	13.8	16.3	21.9	15.4	9.9	16.2	0.33–0.36
1968	7.8	12.2	16.3	22.3	14.7	9.4	17.3	0.33–0.36
1972[a]	8.9	13.6	17.4	22.7	14.7	9.7	13.0	0.28

Notes and Sources: The 1953 figures are based on data collected by Kowei Chang and reproduced in Shirly W. Kuo, "The Economic Development of Taiwan—An Overall Analysis," in Kowei Chang, ed., *Economic Development in Taiwan*, p. 135. The 1964 figures are based on data in Chung-li Chang and A. F. Hinrichs, "Personal Income Distribution and Consumption Pattern in Taiwan—1964," *Industry of Free China* 28 (Nov. 1967): 34. The 1966 data are based on PBAS, *Report of the Survey of Family Income and Expenditure in Taiwan, 1966*, June 1968, pp. lxxv–xc. The 1968 data are based on PBAS, *Report of the Survey of Family Income and Expenditure in Taiwan, 1968*, June 1970, pp. 31–35. To interpolate between observed points, we assume the log cumulated income to vary linearly with the log cumulated number of families. The 1953 Gini ratio is calculated by the author. The lower Gini ratios for 1964, 1966, and 1968 and that of 1972 are from John Fei, Gustav Ranis, and Shirley Kuo, "Growth and the Family Distribution of Income by Factor Components: The Case of Taiwan," Economic Growth Center Discussion Paper no. 223, March 1975, table 1a. The higher Gini ratios for 1964, 1966, and 1968 were calculated by the PBAS.
[a] Excludes Taipei.

uncertain because the income distribution data for the early years are very weak.

Table 8.10 presents the available statistics on the size distribution of personal income in Taiwan. If we accept the 1953 income distribution as accurate, then from 1953 to the mid-1960s there apparently was a dramatic shift in income distribution toward greater equality. During this period the top 10 percent, and particularly the top 5 percent, suffered a significant decline in its income share, while the bottom 80 percent gained. That the relative share of the lower income group improved means that in the postwar period the absolute income of the poor (say the lowest 40 percent) increased considerably faster than for the economy as a whole. Given the fact that Taiwan's real GNP increased at a rate of over 7 percent a year from 1953 to 1964, the shift in income distribution in this period implies that the absolute income of the lowest 40 percent increased at an average annual rate that was in excess of 14 percent.

However, simple calculations to test the reasonableness of the 1953 distribution call its reliability into question.[25] For example, by aggregating the product of the average family income and the number of households in each income group, the value of total personal income can be estimated from the income distribution data and compared with the estimate from the national accounts data. By this procedure we obtained a personal income estimate from the 1953 income distribution data that is 20 percent lower than the estimate derived from the national accounts data. But the basic objection to the 1953 distribution is that it was based on a small and unrepresentative sample of households. The 1953 survey sampled a total of 300 households, of which 58 percent were drawn from four major Taiwanese cities that contained only 15 percent of Taiwan's population.[26] Another 26 percent of the sample households came from two of the more urban prefectures, Taipei and Tainan. Thus 84 percent of the sample households came from the more urbanized and industrialized areas in Taiwan. If in 1953 Taiwan's urban income was less equally distributed than rural income, as I believe it was, then the actual distribution of income in the population was likely to be more equally distributed than the observed distribution in the sample survey. Therefore, given the small size and unrepresentativeness of the 1953 sample, estimates based on this survey are likely both to be biased and to have a large variance. Consequently, the 1953 distribution as well as the change in income distribution from 1953 to the mid-1960s must be viewed with considerable caution.

Although the magnitude of change in income distribution from 1953 to 1964 is not certain, we suspect, for reasons we shall shortly elaborate, that the direction of change in this period was toward greater equality.

25. Beginning in 1964, the income distribution data are derived from government surveys of about 3,600 households, or between 1.3 and 1.9 percent of the population, selected on a stratified sampling basis. There are some deficiencies with these data, such as the exclusion of all income of unincorporated enterprises from personal income whenever the enterprise employed more than five workers and operated at a site separate from the family dwelling, that tend to underestimate the high incomes and thus understate the concentration of income. However, the overall quality of the data since 1964 compares favorably with that of 1953 and probably also with that of other LDCs. For more on the surveys, see Chung-li Chang and A. F. Hinrichs, "Personal Income Distribution and Consumption Pattern in Taiwan—1964," pp. 30–33, and PBAS, *Report on the Survey of Family Income and Expenditure in Taiwan, 1966*, June 1968, chap. 2.

26. The four cities are Keelung, Taipei, Kaohsiung, and Taichung. The 1953 survey was conducted privately on a very limited budget using student interviewers. For more information see Kowei Chang, "An Estimate of Taiwan's Personal Income Distribution in 1953."

Taiwan's income distribution showed almost no change from 1964 to
1968, but from 1968 to 1972 it apparently became slightly more equal.
However, the comparison of the 1972 income distribution with those
in the 1960s is somewhat misleading because the 1972 data exclude the
municipality of Taipei, where income distribution was probably less
equal than in the rest of Taiwan.

When Taiwan's income distribution in the 1960s is compared with
those of other countries, its high degree of overall equality becomes
very apparent. In Taiwan the lowest 40 percent received about 20
percent of the income. In comparison, the average income share of
the lowest 40 percent in all less developed countries in Ahluwalia's
study was 12.5 percent, and in half of these LDCs the income share of
the lowest 40 percent was only 9 percent.[27] In fact, Taiwan's income
distribution in the 1960s was among the most equal in the world,
comparable to that in the United States, the United Kingdom, and
socialist countries such as Yugoslavia and Poland.[28]

Part of the reason that Taiwan's income distribution was so equal in
the 1960s is that extensive redistribution of assets occurred in the
postwar period. When Taiwan was a colony, its wealth was concentrated in the hands of the Japanese and a small number of Taiwanese.
The end of colonialism in 1945 brought about a significant leveling of
inequalities in the ownership of physical capital when all Japanese
assets in Taiwan were confiscated by the Nationalist government and,
with some minor exceptions, retained as government property.[29] Thus,
in the early 1950s, with most major industrial enterprises in government
hands and with few mainlanders able to transfer their industrial capital
to Taiwan, privately held industrial assets were limited and fairly
widely dispersed.[30]

Because Taiwanese owned a large proportion of the farmland, asset
distribution in agriculture was less affected by independence. But,
between 1949 and 1953, an extensive land reform program was implemented, so that a wholesale redistribution of rural wealth also occurred.
The land reform placed a ceiling on rent, sold government land to

27. Montek S. Ahluwalia, "Income Inequality: Some Dimensions of the Problem,"
in Hollis Chenery et al., *Redistribution With Growth*, table I.1.
28. Ibid.
29. Some real estate and minor enterprises were sold.
30. In 1952 public enterprises produced 56 percent of the value-added originating in
mining, manufacturing, and utilities (see CIECD, *Taiwan Statistical Data Book*, 1973,
p. 73).

tenants at prices below market values, and finally in 1953 redistributed private holdings of Taiwanese landlords, with partial compensation.[31] In all, one-quarter of Taiwan's farmland changed hands. Before the land reform, nearly 40 percent of all farm households owned no land while the top 30 percent owned 75 percent of the privately held farmland.[32] By 1955 the share of landless farmers in Taiwan had declined to 17 percent.

Not only was Taiwan's physical capital fairly equally distributed, but so was its human capital. At the end of the colonial period Taiwan already possessed a reasonably high literacy rate, at least for a less developed country. In the postwar period the government's continued attention to primary education, the extension of compulsory education to the ninth grade, and the increased opportunities for higher education combined to further equalize the distribution of human capital. At the end of World War II perhaps 30 percent of Taiwan's population was literate.[33] In 1956 the literacy rate was 57 percent, and by the early 1970s it had reached almost 80 percent. Thus, in the postwar period the opportunity for wealth accumulation was not limited to a few, as it was in the colonial period.

Although not selected for equity considerations, the development policies adopted in the postwar period were nevertheless partly responsible for the relatively equal distribution of income observed in the 1960s. Of the various aspects of Taiwan's development strategy that have been favorable to egalitarian growth, two deserve special mention: the emphasis given to agricultural development in the 1950s and the adoption of an outward-looking development strategy in the 1960s. The steady growth of agricultural labor productivity and farm income in the postwar period kept the average family income in Taiwan's agricultural sector from falling too far behind the national average and thus helped to maintain a more equally distributed income for the island as a whole. Oshima, in his study of income distribution of Asian countries, attributes much of the greater inequality in the Southeast Asian countries (the Philippines, Thailand, Malaya, and Sri Lanka) relative to the East Asian countries (Taiwan, Korea, and Japan) to the

31. For more details, see chap. 9.
32. PDCA, Land Bureau, *Statistics on Land-ownership Classification in Taiwan, China,* 1952, tables IV-1 and VII-I, and PDAF, *Taiwan Agricultural Yearbook,* 1956.
33. The 1940 population census found 26.5 percent of the Taiwanese population able to read and write Japanese.

larger difference between the average per family income in the agricultural sector and that in the nonagricultural sector in Southeast Asia.[34]

The shift in development strategy from import substitution to export promotion that began in the late 1950s also helped to produce redistribution with growth. In brief, the new strategy enabled the market to operate more freely and thus permitted the economy to grow more according to its true comparative advantage. The results were spectacular rises in exports and GNP in the 1960s as well as a number of favorable equity consequences. First of all, rapid industrialization increased employment and reduced both unemployment and underemployment in the 1960s.[35] Secondly, industrialization also reduced the importance of agriculture, where average income is lower, and thus improved equity for the economy as a whole. Finally, because the economy expanded along lines closer to its true comparative advantage, the growth path of Taiwan's industries in the 1960s was labor intensive. Consequently, wages, which are distributed more equally, expanded rapidly as a share of national income from about 45 percent in 1960 to nearly 55 percent in 1972.[36]

We conclude this chapter by restating the major economic trends and structural changes Taiwan experienced after its economic recovery in 1952. Between 1953 and 1973 Taiwan experienced rapid economic expansion: its real GNP grew at an average rate of 8.6 percent a year and its real per capita GNP at 5.7 percent a year. About one-half of the output growth can be explained by the increased in primary inputs, labor and capital, and much of the unexplained growth may be attributed to quality changes in labor and capital and the fuller utilization of resources after the mid-1950s. Growth was accompanied by significant shifts in industrial structure. In the early 1950s, although a fragile industrial base existed, Taiwan was essentially an agrarian economy.

34. Harry T. Oshima, "Income Inequality and Economic Growth the Postwar Experience of Asian Countries," pp. 17–25.

35. The rate of unemployment declined from 5.2 percent in October 1963 to 1.1 percent in October 1973, and the rate of underemployment declined from 3 percent in 1965 to 0.7 percent in 1973. See Taiwan Provincial Labor Force Survey and Research Institute, *Report of the Labor Force Survey in Taiwan* no. 46, 1975, table A-1. Unemployment and underemployment statistics in developing countries must be approached with considerable caution. Although most observers consider Taiwan's unemployment and underemployment data to be better than most, skepticism regarding the official estimates still exists.

36. DGBAS, *Statistical Abstract of the Republic of China*, 1974, table 71.

Industrial growth in the next two decades reduced the importance of agriculture, and by the early 1970s it produced only 15 percent of Taiwan's GDP (in current prices) at factor cost and employed one-third of its labor force. Meanwhile, manufacturing emerged as Taiwan's leading economic sector. Industrialization and rapid population growth also helped to change Taiwan's comparative advantage. Increasingly in the 1960s, Taiwan's exports shifted from land-intensive agricultural goods to labor-intensive industrial products.

One of the foremost developments in the postwar period was the dramatic decline in fertility rate, falling from 180 in 1960 to 104 in 1972. By the early 1970s population growth, which averaged over 3 percent in the 1950s, was below 2 percent a year. Many factors contributed to the decline in birth rate. After years of falling mortality, many families adopted birth control to bring actual fertility in line with desired fertility. There are also signs that the number of children desired declined in the early 1970s. If this continues, Taiwan will be one of the first less developed countries to complete the important demographic transition from high to low fertility.

Finally, postwar economic growth was unusually egalitarian. The evidence argues that economic development in Taiwan benefited the poor as much if not more than the rich. A major redistribution of assets at the end of World War II and land reform in the early 1950s explain in part the relative improvement in the economic position of the poor. A strategy of development that stressed agriculture and labor-intensive industries also allowed Taiwan to develop along a more egalitarian growth path.

9

Postwar Growth and Structural Changes
in Agriculture

When Taiwan emerged from the war in 1945, its agricultural production was reduced to the level of 1920. Not until 1952 did agricultural production regain its prewar peak. Between 1952 and 1968 agricultural production grew vigorously at an annual rate in excess of 5 percent, but thereafter agricultural growth became sluggish. Growth was accompanied by important institutional and structural changes, of which the most dramatic was the 1952 land reform. No less important were the changes caused by population growth. By the 1940s, nearly all the available land economically suitable for farming was being cultivated. Thus the steady expansion of farm population in the postwar period led to, among other consequences, a continuous decline in farm size. These developments are the primary topics discussed in this chapter. We begin with an analysis of agricultural growth and examine the sources of this growth. Next, we examine how and to what extent the changes in farm size and in the land tenure system affected the rural sector. Finally, we assess the government's agricultural policy and how it affected agricultural development.

TRENDS IN OUTPUT, INPUT, AND PRODUCTIVITY

Table 9.1 presents the average annual growth rates of the four main components of the official agricultural production index.[1] The general

---

1. Besides this official index, there are several unofficial agricultural production indexes. All the unofficial indexes, however, use the same production statistics as the official indexes. Consequently, there is very little difference between the official and the unofficial indexes.

Table 9.1. Average Annual Rates of Growth in Agricultural Production by Major
Components (Percent)

	General	Crops	Livestock	Forestry	Fishery
1946–52	12.8	11.7	18.4	26.5	16.4
1953–73	4.6	3.6	7.8	4.8	9.0
1953–68	5.3	4.6	7.4	6.4	9.3
1969–73	2.5	0.3	8.9	−0.2	8.3

Sources: PDAF, *Taiwan Agricultural Yearbook*, 1973, pp. 22–23, and DGBAS, *Statistical Abstract of the Republic of China*, 1974, pp. 72–73.

pattern of agricultural growth is clear. Every component of the agricultural sector (here defined broadly to include forestry and fishery) recovered quickly from the war and by 1952 each had equaled or exceeded its prewar peak level of production. The swift recovery was made possible by the return to agriculture of inputs (particularly labor and fertilizer) removed during the war.[2] During most of the post-recovery period, agriculture continued to grow steadily. From 1953 to 1968 agricultural production grew at an average rate in excess of 5 percent per year. Thereafter, crop and forestry production stagnated, and agricultural growth became sluggish. Between 1969 and 1973, crop production increased by only 0.3 percent per year and forestry production declined.

Although forestry and fishery have expanded substantially in the last several decades, they are still secondary to crop and livestock production. They are also organized differently from the rest of agriculture. Whereas crops and livestock are produced primarily by small peasant households, forestry and fishery production are concentrated in relatively large commercial firms. Because our principal interest in this chapter is the peasant economy, we shall exclude forestry and fishery from further discussion and restrict agriculture to the more conventional definition of crop and livestock production.

In the colonial period Taiwan's agriculture was a three-crop industry, with rice, sweet potatoes, and sugar cane accounting for about 85 percent of the value of agricultural production. Although Taiwan's agriculture is still dominated by these traditional crops, their significance has waned. In the 1960s rice, sweet potatoes, and sugar cane accounted for only about 65 percent of agricultural production. Altered

2. During the war, peasants were inducted into the army and construction gangs. Some peasants were also attracted to the nonagricultural sector by its very high wages.

trade opportunities and changed domestic needs in the postwar period have resulted in differences in the composition of demand, and the product mix supplied by agriculture has responded accordingly.

Because it was primarily exported, sugar cane, much more than the other two traditional crops, was profoundly affected by the end of colonialism and the termination of special relationship between Taiwan and Japan. In the colonial· period, when Taiwan's sugar received preferential treatment in Japan, more than 90 percent of Taiwan's annual sugar output was exported to Japan. The collapse of the Japanese Empire was a first order catastrophe for the sugar industry. Furthermore, the hope to replace the protected Japanese market by a protected mainland market quickly faded when the Nationalist government was defeated on the mainland. As a consequence of losing both the Japanese and the mainland sugar markets, sugar cane production was curtailed and resources were reallocated within agriculture. Land was shifted from cane production to the production of a wide variety of minor crops, the foremost being corn, wheat, fruits, and vegetables.[3] Since the early 1950s Taiwan has produced between 6 and 9 million MT of sugar cane a year, with no perceptible upward trend. Thus little of the postwar agricultural growth can be attributed to the growth of sugar cane production.

The domestic demand for rice and sweet potatoes increased steadily in the postwar period. The rapid expansion of population and the continuous rise in per capita income were the major reasons behind the increase in the domestic demand for rice. Indeed, because of Taiwan's greater need for food, its grain export declined despite a sustained increase in rice production. In the postwar period sweet potatoes were used chiefly as an animal feed,[4] and steady growth in production during the 1950s and 1960s was a reflection of the increased demand for livestock products. From 1952 to 1973 livestock production increased more than fourfold, and its share in total agricultural production increased from 15 to 25 percent.

Changing domestic needs and the appearance of new export opportunities also stimulated the production of a number of important minor crops. The arrival of large numbers of mainland Chinese, with noticeably different taste, created in Taiwan a new spectrum of food

3. Land under sugar cane declined from a peak of 169,000 hectares in 1940 to about 96,000 hectares in the 1950s and 1960s.
4. In the 1930s, only 35 percent of the sweet potatoes produced were used as animal feed. In the 1960s this had increased to over 50 percent.

demand. Attempts to satisfy this demand and to develop new agricultural exports stimulated the promotion of new crops. Of the new developments, the most successful was the introduction of new varieties of vegetables and fruits and the improvement of existing varieties. Since the mid-1950s the export of vegetables and fruits has increased by leaps and bounds.[5] In 1951–53 sugar and rice accounted for 82 percent and fresh and canned vegetables and fruits for 6.7 percent of Taiwan's total export of agricultural and agricultural processed products. By 1965–67 the combined share of sugar and rice exports was 34 percent while that of fresh and canned vegetables and fruits was 50 percent.[6]

What makes Taiwan's postwar agricultural growth particularly impressive is that it was accomplished with little or no expansion in cultivated area. By 1940 land that could be economically farmed was already under cultivation. True, since 1952 tidal land has been reclaimed from the sea and marginal upland has been developed into farms, but the land area added in this fashion was limited. From 1952 to 1973 cultivated land area increased by less than 3 percent. What made growth possible in the postwar period was the more intensive use of arable land. The adoption of new cropping patterns and intercropping (the practice of planting a second crop between rows of the first crop before the latter is harvested) have allowed more crops to be grown in a single year. While cultivated areas have remained nearly constant since 1940, crop area has increased about 40 percent, from 1.2 million hectares in 1940 to 1.7 million hectares in the late 1960s.[7] In the late 1960s the multiple cropping index, which measures the frequency with which cultivated land is used, was over 180.[8] In other words, on the average almost every piece of farmland in Taiwan produced two crops a year.

Farm population, estimated by the Provincial Department of Agriculture and Forestry, increased from about 3.5 million in 1946 to a peak of 6.15 million in 1969 before it declined to 5.95 million in 1972. The agricultural labor force increased at a slower pace, rising from

5. Since the mid-1950s Taiwan has emerged as the world's largest exporter of canned mushrooms and canned asparagus and one of the world's largest exporters of banana and canned pineapple.

6. Foreign Exchange and Trade Commission, *The Republic of China Taiwan Export and Import Exchange Settlement Statistics*, Taipei, July 1968, pp. 34–35.

7. PDAF, *Taiwan Agricultural Yearbook*, 1973, p. 21.

8. Ibid.

1.8 million in 1952 to slightly more than 2 million in the late 1960s, or less than 1 percent a year.[9] Because of seasonal variation in labor demand and underemployment, the agricultural labor force and agricultural employment may be very different. Various estimates of the number of man-days used each year in agriculture show that labor input into agriculture grew considerably faster than did the agricultural labor force (table 9.2). This suggests that in the 1950s and 1960s the average number of days worked per agricultural laborer per year increased. Thus if underemployment existed in agriculture in the early 1950s, it was reduced. By the early 1970s, labor input to agriculture began to decline as rapid industrialization accelerated the shift of labor from agriculture to other activities.

Agricultural fixed capital increased steadily in the postwar period. Additions and improvements to farm buildings and structure are readily apparent throughout the countryside. A shift away from animal to mechanical power began in the early 1960s and still continues. The water buffalo population, after recovering from the war, declined regularly after the late 1950s, dropping from 327,000 head in 1959 to 150,000 in 1972.[10] As replacement, Taiwan began to import, and since the mid-1960s to produce domestically, power tillers. From a total number of under 100 in the mid-1950s, the stock of power tillers increased to 3,239 in 1960 and 24,400 in 1972.[11] The greater capacity of the power tiller to clear and prepare land quickly, a valuable and desirable feature when more than one crop is to be planted, and the declining importance of animal manure as a source of fertilizer made this switch from animal to mechanical power profitable.

Of all the inputs into agriculture, the one that registered the most dramatic increase in the postwar period was working capital or nonfarm current inputs, the most significant being chemicals and commercial feeds. Between 1951 and 1970 working capital increased at an average rate of 10.6 percent per year. The growth of imported commercial feeds is another reflection of the rising importance of livestock production in Taiwan. The regular introduction of seeds that are responsive to intensive fertilizer application and the gradual decline in fertilizer prices together explain the increased application

9. CIECD, *Taiwan Statistical Data Book*, 1973, pp. 8–9.
10. PDAF, *Taiwan Agricultural Yearbook*, various issues.
11. Ibid.

Table 9.2. Indexes of Agricultural Outputs and Inputs (1951 = 100)

	Outputs	Inputs			
	Crops and livestock	Crop area	Labor (man-days)	Working capital	Fixed capital
1951	100.0	100.0	100.0	100.0	100.0
1952	108.4	101.6	105.6	120.3	103.6
1953	121.1	101.5	107.7	138.4	104.1
1954	122.7	102.4	107.5	168.9	106.8
1955	120.7	100.8	106.0	163.7	108.7
1956	131.6	103.6	109.9	182.3	111.4
1957	140.6	105.4	117.2	188.8	115.3
1958	149.2	107.2	120.3	207.3	116.8
1959	150.0	107.5	119.9	204.8	119.4
1960	150.8	107.6	117.7	204.1	120.8
1961	162.7	109.2	117.9	228.9	124.5
1962	164.9	108.8	116.9	243.6	126.4
1963	165.7	108.7	120.0	263.1	132.6
1964	182.7	111.8	123.5	289.0	138.4
1965	199.1	113.6	131.2	301.7	147.1
1966	204.6	114.8	134.2	326.6	155.7
1967	213.4	114.0	132.5	372.8	163.1
1968	226.2	114.2	132.9	480.3	171.0
1969	222.3	113.6	130.2	509.1	179.8
1970	234.8	111.4	128.8	550.3	188.5
Annual average rate of growth					
1951–70	4.5	0.6	1.4	9.2	3.5
1951–60	4.4	0.7	1.8	7.8	2.5
1961–70	4.6	0.4	0.9	10.6	4.6

Notes and Sources: Output is agricultural production minus intermediate goods produced on farm (e.g., seeds and some feeds). Working capital represents nonfarm current inputs. Using the data in PDAF, *Taiwan Agricultural Yearbook*, various estimates of inputs to agriculture have been calculated. For example, see You-tsao Wang, "Agricultural Development," in Kowie Chang, ed., *Economic Development in Taiwan*, pp. 143–238; S. C. Hsieh and Teng-hui Lee, *An Analytical Review of Agricultural Development*, and *Agricultural Development and Its Contributions to Economic Growth in Taiwan*; Yhi-min Ho, *Agricultural Development of Taiwan, 1903–1960*; and Teng-hui Lee and Y. E. Chen, "Appendix to Growth Rates of Taiwan's Agriculture, *1911–1970*." Because the underlying data are the same, these estimates are quite similar. The estimates by Lee and Chen are reproduced here because they are most up-to-date and have the widest coverage.

of chemical fertilizers. For example, the fertilizer/rice barter ratio for ammonium sulfate, the most widely used fertilizer in Taiwan, fell from 1.5 kg of rice per kg of ammonium sulfate in 1949 to 0.9 kg in 1960 and 0.53 in 1972.[12] Per hectare consumption of fertilizer in nutrient weight in 1965–67 was double that attained in the prewar peak years of 1935–39 (table 9.3). Taiwan's consumption of chemical fertilizer per hectare of cultivated area is also high in comparison with other countries. In Asia, only Japan exceeds Taiwan in chemical fertilizer consumed per unit area of arable land.[13] In terms of the rate of increase in chemical fertilizer consumed per unit area of arable land, Taiwan also ranks high, again exceeded in Asia only by Japan.

Unlike chemical fertilizer, which has been in use in Taiwan since the 1910s, chemicals such as insecticides and fungicides did not become a significant input to agriculture until the 1950s. Their adoption in Taiwan was therefore a major postwar innovation. Crop losses due to damage caused by insects and diseases have always been serious in Taiwan. A 1952 estimate put the damage from insects and diseases at 15 percent for rice, 25 percent for sugar cane, 20 percent for sweet potatoes, 45 percent for vegetables, 30 percent for bananas, and 50 percent for citrus fruit.[14] After a program was introduced in the early 1950s to teach the Taiwanese farmers the proper usage of chemicals against insects and diseases, the use of insecticides and fungicides became widespread.[15]

Using the estimates of agricultural outputs and inputs in table 9.2 and the annual estimates of the factor shares in the cost of agricultural production, we made an attempt to account for the sources of agri-

12. PFB, *Food Production and Activities of the Taiwan Food Bureau*, 1973, p. 37. In the 1950s and 1960s chemical fertilizers were also used to substitute for farm-produced fertilizers. After a period of continuous increase that goes back to the colonial period, the consumption of farm-produced fertilizer per unit of cultivated area began to fall in the mid-1960s. The gradual decline in the cost of chemical fertilizer and the rising opportunity cost of labor and land in the production and collection of organic fertilizer have combined to bring about this change. With land area increasingly needed to produce food crops, the area planted with green manure crops has declined from over 300,000 hectares (single sowing and mixed sowing) in 1952 to 74,000 hectares in 1967.

13. U.S. Department of Agriculture, *Changes in Agriculture in 26 Developing Nations, 1948 to 1963*, p. 47.

14. JCRR, *General Report of the Joint Commission on Rural Reconstruction*, 1952, p. 25.

15. Between 1951 and 1965 the application of insecticides and fungicides increased 16-fold. See You-tsao Wang, "Technological Changes and Agricultural Development of Taiwan, 1946–1965," paper presented to the Conference on Economic Development of Taiwan, p. E62.

Table 9.3. Estimated Consumption of Fertilizer Nutrients per Unit of Cultivated Area (Annual averages)

| | Consumption of farm-produced (organic) fertilizer | | | | | Consumption of chemical fertilizer nutrients (kg/ha) | | | |
| | Gross weight (MT/ha) | Nutrients (kg/ha) | | | | | | | |
		Total	Nitrogen	Phosphate	Potash	Total	Nitrogen	Phosphate	Potash
1935–39	10.5	95.3	43.6	19.3	32.4	121.7	78.2	28.7	10.8
1955–59	16.5	156.2	67.5	36.4	52.3	166.3	103.8	36.2	26.3
1965–67	16.3	150.6	65.1	35.2	50.3	260.0	178.0	36.7	45.3

	N	P_2O_5	K_2O
Green manure	.0050	.0010	.0050
Animal	.0030	.0015	.0010
Night soil	.0050	.0025	.0050
Compost	.0042	.0021	.0015
Straw	.0057	.0023	.0105
Ash	—	.0167	.0338

Notes and Sources: Farm-produced (organic) fertilizer includes green manure, animal manure, night soil, compost, rice hull, ash, and straw. The annual application of each type of organic fertilizer in gross weight is estimated by the Provincial Department of Agriculture and Forestry and is published in its *Taiwan Agricultural Yearbook*, various issues. To convert gross weight to nutrient weight, the following conversion ratios used by T. H. Shen (see his *Agricultural Development on Taiwan Since World War II*, p. 141) are assumed:

The annual consumption of chemical fertilizers by nutrients per unit area of cultivated area for 1935–64 is estimated by the Plant Industry Division, JCRR (see table A46). For 1965–67 the estimates are the author's. They are obtained by converting the official estimates of chemical fertilizer consumption in gross weight to nutrient weight. The data on cultivated area are from table A39.

Table 9.4. Sources of Agricultural Output Growth, 1951–70 (Percent)

	Total growth in output	Average percentage contribution from				
		Increases in crop area	*Increases in man-days*	*Increases in working capital*	*Increases in fixed capital*	*Residue (changes in productivity)*
1951–70	100.0	5.9	15.1	59.3	9.9	9.8
1951–60	100.0	10.3	−0.6	34.7	10.6	44.9
1961–70	100.0	1.4	30.8	83.9	9.2	−25.4

Notes and Sources: These figures were calculated on the assumption that $\dot{Q} = \dot{A} + \alpha_1\dot{N} + \alpha_2\dot{L} + \alpha_3\dot{K}_1 + \alpha_4\dot{K}_2$, where Q is agricultural output, N is crop area, L is man-day input, K_1 is working capital, K_2 is fixed capital, and A is the residue. The dotted terms are rates of growth and the α's are the cost shares of the inputs. The input and output data are those in table 9.2, and the cost shares are from Teng-hui Lee and Y. E. Chen, "Appendix to Growth Rates of Taiwan's Agriculture, 1911–1970."

cultural growth. The results are summarized in table 9.4. For the postrecovery period as a whole, about 90 percent of Taiwan's agricultural growth can be attributed to the increases in identified inputs: 6 percent to crop area, 15 percent to labor, 59 percent to' working capital, and 10 percent to fixed capital. Thus the principal source of agricultural growth since 1951 was the more intensive use of nonfarm current inputs, especially chemicals and imported feeds. Increased input productivity accounted for 10 percent of the growth in agricultural output. However, when the postrecovery period is divided into two subperiods (1951–60 and 1961–70), productivity is found to be an important source of growth only in the 1950s. Indeed, productivity growth was negative in the 1960s. It seems that agricultural Taiwan is finding it increasingly more difficult to offset the effects of limited arable land and, more recently, labor shortage.

POPULATION GROWTH, FARM SIZE, AND RURAL UNDEREMPLOYMENT

Up to this point, Taiwan's agriculture has been discussed largely in terms of an input–output process by which homogeneous inputs are turned into outputs. But to adequately understand agriculture, there is a need to know not only the input–output relationships but also the environment and the institutions within which these relationships are defined. In this and the following sections we examine some of the more salient environmental and institutional factors and study their effects on agriculture.

During the colonial period, despite a rapidly growing agricultural population, the size of the average Taiwanese farm remained relatively stable. Since the end of World War II rural population has continued to grow. In the 1950s the rate of natural increase in rural Taiwan averaged 3.4 percent per annum. In the 1960s, although the rate of natural increase in rural areas fell, it was still above 2.5 percent per year. But because nearly all the economically cultivable land had already been put to use, the continuous rise in population in the postwar period has put considerable pressure on Taiwan's land resources. One manifestation of this is the decline in farm size. Since the colonial period the size of the average farm has more than halved, decreasing from about 2 hectares to less than 1 hectare of land. In 1939 about 25 percent of the Taiwanese farms had less than 0.5 hectare of land but by 1960 the farms in this category had climbed to 37 percent.[16]

The decline in farm size required adjustments from the Taiwanese farmers. The fact is that small farms are often not viable units in terms of the income they generate. Obviously, the smaller the farm the less able it is by itself to support a farm family of a given size. The *1963 Report of Farm Record Keeping Families* found that as farm size decreases, a larger share of the farmer's income is derived from off-farm economic activities, so that farm families with less than one-half chia (0.48 hectare) of land derived nearly 35 percent of their total income from off-farm sources. Closely related is the fact that as farm size decreases, a smaller share of the available family labor can be productively occupied by on-farm activities. The agricultural census for 1960 found that less than 50 percent of all cultivating farm households in Taiwan were fully engaged in the operation of their farms (table 9.5). But of the cultivating farm families with less than 0.5 hectare of land, only 30 percent were fully engaged in the operation of their farms. Indeed, more than 40 percent of the cultivating farm families with less than 0.5 hectare of land considered farming a side-line. That a small farm cannot fully utilize its farm labor does not of course mean that at all times its family labor exceeds its labor requirement. Agriculture is a highly seasonal activity so that even the smallest farms may find their family labor insufficient during the busy season. In 1960, for instance, 72 percent of the farms with less than 0.5 hectare

16. The 1939 figure is from Taiwan Government-General, *Survey of Conditions of Farmland Ownership and Management, Report of Basic Agricultural Survey no. 41,* pp. 2–7, and the 1960 figures are from the *General Report on the 1961 Census of Agriculture: Taiwan, Republic of China,* pp. 26–27.

Table 9.5. Extent of Off-Farm Economic Activity by Farm Size, 1960

Percentage of farm households

| Farm size (ha) | Total | Full-time farming | Part-time farming | | | Percentage of farm workers with sideline |
			Total	Agriculture as main occupation	Agriculture as sideline	
Under 0.5	100.0	30.1	69.9	26.7	43.2	34.8
0.5–1.0	100.0	55.6	44.4	35.4	9.0	17.9
1.0–2.0	100.0	65.2	34.8	31.7	3.1	11.9
2.0–3.0	100.0	67.3	32.7	30.8	1.9	9.3
3.0–5.0	100.0	66.5	33.5	31.5	2.0	8.5
Over 5.0	100.0	61.4	38.6	35.9	2.7	8.6
Total cultivating farm household	100.0	49.3	50.7	30.9	19.8	20.0

Note and Sources: Farm households are considered part-time if any member of the household has a sideline or participates full time in an off-farm activity. Farm worker includes, of course, only those members of the households that are engaged in farm work, whether as a main operator or as a helper. These figures are calculated from data in *General Report on the 1961 Census of Agriculture: Taiwan, Republic of China*, pp. 15 and 44.

of land used some hired labor. But it is nevertheless evident that in the 1950s and 1960s, as rural population increased and the size of farms diminished, an increasing number of farmers were seeking off-farm economic opportunities, and for them farming had become by necessity a part-time occupation.

Another consequence of rapid population growth was the presence of surplus labor in the agricultural sector.[17] Using farm record-

17. The literature on underemployment or disguised unemployment in agriculture is extensive. For a review see Morton Paglin, "Surplus Agricultural Labor and Development: Facts and Theories," and Charles C. H. Kao, Kurt R. Anschel, and Carl K. Eicher, "Disguised Unemployment in Agriculture: A Survey," in Carl K. Eicher and Lawrence W. Witt, eds., *Agriculture in Economic Development*. Much of the discussion has centered on the definition of *surplus labor*, particularly the use of zero marginal product to define disguised unemployment. In the case of Taiwan, various estimates have found the marginal value product (MVP) of agricultural labor, at least in the 1960s, to be positive and significantly greater than zero (see Su-fen Liu, "Disguised Unemployment in Taiwan Agriculture," tables 4.4 and 4.8). However, surplus labor may exist in other forms such as work sharing and seasonal unemployment. In our discussion we assume surplus labor to exist when the availability of full-time equivalent agricultural workers exceeds the requirement.

keeping data, Liu found that the annual rate of underemployment per farm household was substantial in the early 1960s, averaging about 40 percent of total farm labor available for work.[18] However, the picture changes significantly when the rate of underemployment is computed on a monthly basis. In almost all the regions examined there was at least one month during the year when the estimated number of family labor days available was fewer than the family labor days required. Obviously, surplus labor in Taiwan, at least during the 1950s and 1960s, was primarily a seasonal phenomenon, reflecting the seasonal characteristic of agricultural activity. Furthermore, surplus labor was not concentrated in a small well-defined category but was spread among many people. In consequence, it could not be shifted to other activities even for part of a year without affecting agricultural production, unless its removal was accompanied by extensive reorganization and changes in the agricultural sector.

Because both the economy and the farmers themselves adjusted quickly to the growing population pressure, rural unemployment and underemployment did not develop into a serious problem. Migration to the cities was one and perhaps the most radical adjustment the Taiwanese farmers made. Crude estimates suggest that large numbers of people moved out of agricultural Taiwan. By comparing the rate of natural increase and the actual rate of population growth, the average annual net migration rate out of the agricultural sector was estimated to be −0.8 percent of the agricultural population from 1956 to 1960, −0.4 percent from 1961 to 1965, and −1.6 percent from 1966 to 1970.[19]

Farmers also adjusted to the increased population pressure by adopting more labor-intensive production techniques. Increasingly, farms produced several crops rather than a single crop a year. Multicropping and other changes in production methods such as intensive weeding and the increased application of pesticide and fertilizer all have increased the need for labor per unit of land. Finally, because many industries were developed in the countryside,[20] some farmers

18. The rate of underemployment is defined as $(L - L^*)/L$, where L is the estimated full-time family labor days available for farm work and L^* is the actual number of family labor days used in farm work. Quite clearly, in estimating L, arbitrary assumptions had to be made (see ibid., tables 5.7–5.10).

19. Paul K. C. Liu, "Economic Development and Population in Taiwan Since 1895: An Overview," in *Essays on the Population of Taiwan*, table 16.

20. According to Taiwan's household registration data, about 45 percent of all men employed in manufacturing lived outside the ten largest cities in 1965 (see PDCA, *Taiwan Demographic Fact Book*, 1965, table 4).

were able to change occupation or work in industry in the off-season without moving from the rural areas.

By the mid-1960s, as an increasing number of farm workers moved to other occupations or were finding it profitable to take short-term jobs in cities or in factories, the difficulty of finding laborers in the peak season became intense. The uncertainty of labor supply during the very crucial planting and harvesting months of course impeded the extension of multiple cropping. With agricultural population declining since 1969, some farmers found it more profitable, given the seasonal labor problems, to give up the winter crop altogether and to take temporary off-farm jobs themselves.[21] After reaching a peak of 190 in 1966, the multiple-cropping index fell to 175 in 1972. Thus, by the late 1960s, migration and part-time off-farm jobs had pretty much depleted the pool of surplus labor in rural Taiwan. The need for labor-saving equipment became obvious, and in 1970 the government drafted a program to promote the adoption of farm machinery (garden tractors, rice transplanters, and harvesters).[22] Thus, the 1970s marked the beginning of a new phase in Taiwan's agricultural development, one without an abundance of labor.

LAND REFORM AND AGRICULTURAL DEVELOPMENT

Environmental and institutional changes usually occur slowly in agriculture and therefore are not easily perceived. However, one institutional change in the postwar period occurred abruptly and was obvious to all. An extensive land reform program, involving changes in land distribution, conditions of tenancy, and rent, was carried out between 1949 and 1953.[23] The reform was carried out in three stages: compulsory rent reduction, the sale of public land to actual tillers, and the compulsory sale of private land to actual tillers. The details of the reform and how it was implemented have been

21. *New York Times*, Apr. 6, 1970, p. 11.

22. *Central Daily News*, international ed., March 17, 1970, p. 3; Apr. 1, 1970, p. 3; Apr. 7, 1970, p. 3; Apr. 19, 1970, p. 3; and May 8, 1970, p. 3.

23. The program consisted of the following laws and regulations: "Regulations Governing the Lease of Private Farm Lands in Taiwan Province" (promulgated by the Taiwan Provincial Government, Apr. 14, 1949), "The Farm Rent Reduction to 37.5 Percent Act" (passed by the Legislative Yuan, May 25, 1951), "The Land-to-the-Tiller Act" (passed by the Legislative Yuan, Jan. 20, 1953), and "Regulations Governing the Implementation of the Land-to-the-Tiller Act in Taiwan" (promulgated by the Taiwan Provincial Government, Apr. 23, 1953). All the relevant laws and regulations have been translated into English and can be found in Hui-sun Tang, *Land Reform in Free China*, and Cheng Chen, *Land Reform in Taiwan*.

thoroughly discussed by others, so we shall only sketch the main elements.[24]

Although it is true that large landed estates in the Western sense were not common in Taiwan, a problem of unequal land distribution nevertheless existed. In 1939, 56 percent of the cultivated land in Taiwan was farmed by tenants. Perhaps one-half of Taiwan's farm workers in the 1940s were tenants. The traditional tenure arrangement was sharecropping. Rent varied according to the quality of land, ranging from 40 to 60 percent of output. Soon after the Nationalist government moved to Taiwan in 1949, a program to reduce rent was initiated and was completed in three months.[25] Rent was compulsorily reduced to 37.5 percent of the annual production of main crops, defined to be "the standard amount of the total annual yield [of the crop customarily accepted as payment for rent as] appraised with reference to relevant data and in the light of actual local conditions by the *Hsien* or Municipal 37.5 Percent Rent Campaign Committee."[26] The original intent of the regulation may have been to calculate rent as a share of the standard yield and to appraise the standard yield each year. In actuality, however, rent was changed to a fixed amount, determined as 37.5 percent of the standard yield appraised by the 37.5 Percent Rent Campaign Committee in 1949.[27] The appraisal of

24. See Tang, ibid., and Chen, ibid.

25. Subsequently this program was supplemented and reinforced by the 1951 "Farm Rent Reduction to 37.5 Percent Act," which made more explicit the relationship between tenants and landlords.

26. Paragraph 2, Article 2 of the "Regulation Governing the Lease of Private Farm Land in Taiwan Province" (Tang, *Land Reform*, p. 221).

27. Steven N. S. Cheung argues that rental restriction in Taiwan was not a fixed but a percentage restriction, i.e., the rent share was reduced to 37.5 percent of the actual yield and not of a standard yield. See Steven N. S. Cheung, "The Theory of Share Tenancy—With Special Application to the First Phase of Taiwan Land Reform" (Ph.D. thesis, Department of Economics, UCLA, 1967), pp. 90–98. This difference in interpretation may be due to the ambiguous wording of the 1949 regulations. The relevant part of Article 2 of the 1949 "Regulations Governing the Lease of Private Farm Land in Taiwan Province" reads as follows:

Farm rent shall not exceed 37.5 percent of the total annual yield of the main crops. If the rent originally agreed upon exceeds 37.5 percent, it shall be reduced to 37.5 percent; and if it is less than 37.5 percent, it shall remain unchanged.

The "main crops" referred to in the preceding paragraph shall be chiefly the crop customarily accepted as payment for rent. The *standard* amount of the total annual yield of the main crop shall be appraised with reference to relevant data in the light of actual local conditions by the Hsien or Municipal 37.5% Rent Campaign Committee [done in May 1949] and the results of the appraisal shall be submitted to the Provincial Government for approval (Tang, *Land Reform*, p. 221).

standard yield was carried out separately in each administrative district. Every plot of land was graded (26 grades for paddy land and 26 grades for dry land) and a standard yield was fixed for each grade.[28] There were also provisions for the temporary reduction of rent in times of crop failures, for written contracts, and for the establishment of procedures to settle disputes between tenant and landlord.[29]

In 1951 the government took the first step to transfer ownership of land to actual tillers when it began to sell public land to tenants.[30] More than one-half the farmland owned by the central and provincial government was eventually affected by this policy.[31] This represents a substantial amount of land since over 176,000 hectares of farmland that was originally owned by Japanese citizens, or about 20 percent of the total cultivated area, was transferred to the Chinese government (96 percent to the central and provincial government and 5 percent to the hsien, city, township, or village government) at the end of World War II. Cultivators of public land and other tenant farmers were given first and second priority to purchase public land. The amount of farmland each buyer can purchase was limited according to the quality of land, e.g., the maximum medium quality (9th–18th grade) paddy field that can be purchased was 1 chia (0.9699 ha). However, cultivators of public land can purchase as much of the land they originally leased from the government as they wished. The price of the public land was set at 2.5 times the annual yield of principal crops[32] and was to be paid in twenty installments over a period of ten years. In all, six batches of public farmland, totaling more than 71,000 hectares, were sold between 1948 and 1958.

The most dramatic feature of Taiwan's land reform was the land-to-the-tiller program. That a farmer should own the land he tills is an old political objective of the Nationalist government. Much lip

---

While the first part of Article 2 seems to suggest that the actual yield was to be used in determining rent, the last part of Article 2 makes it quite explicit that a standard yield was to be used. Also see Tang, ibid., pp. 33 and 40–44.

28. Tang, ibid., pp. 40–42.

29. Articles 8, 9, 12, 13, and 15 of the "Regulations Governing the Lease of Private Farm Land in Taiwan Province" (see ibid., pp. 221–23).

30. Detailed descriptions of these regulations and how they were implemented can be found in ibid., chap. 3 and pp. 215–20.

31. Most of the land retained by the government is land operated by the government-owned Taiwan Sugar Corporation.

32. The yield used to determine land price was not the actual yield but the standard yield assigned by the local government to that grade of land for tax purposes. In most instances the standard yield is lower than the actual yield.

service was paid to this idea in the 1920s and 1930s but little resulted from the rhetoric until the land reform program was successfully executed in Taiwan in 1953. The government was able to turn its rhetoric into action because in Taiwan it did not depend on the landlord class for support. The Nationalist government arrived in Taiwan as an "outsider" with no tie or commitment to the established local elites. Thus, on the question of land reform it enjoyed greater political flexibility than do most governments. Besides, sobered by its defeat on the mainland, the Nationalist government felt a strong need to establish a solid political base among the Taiwanese peasants. An obvious policy to adopt, under these circumstances, was the redistribution of land. The Nationalist government therefore was not only politically able but felt an urgent need to carry out a land redistribution program, urgent not only for what it might do for the economy and social justice but also for what it might do for its own political survival.

The legal base for the land-to-the-tiller program was the 1953 Land-to-the-Tiller Act. Under this new law, land owned by landlords in excess of three chia (2.9 hectares) of medium quality (7th–12th grade) paddy field or its equivalent was to be compulsorily purchased by the government and redistributed.[33] The price paid for the land was 2.5 times its annual yield and was to be paid 70 percent in commodity bonds and 30 percent in shares of stock in four government enterprises.[34] Two types of commodity bonds—rice and sweet potatoes— were issued. The rice bond was used to pay for paddy land and the sweet potatoes bond for dry land. The bond paid a 4 percent annual interest, and the principal of the bond together with the interest were to be amortized in 20 equal semiannual installments. Each landlord also received shares of stock in each of the four government enterprises designated for transfer to private ownership. Because they are hedges against inflation, the use of commodity bonds and stocks of government enterprises as payment made the compulsory purchase of land a bit more palatable to the landlord. The land purchased from the

33. Articles 8, 10, and 11 of the Land-to-the-Tiller Act. However, if the landlord cultivates as well as leases his land, he may retain all the land he cultivates (i.e., land operated with no more than the normal seasonal hired help) even if it exceeds the retention limit.

34. The four enterprises are the Taiwan Cement Corporation, Taiwan Pulp and Paper Corporation, Taiwan Industrial and Mining Corporation, and Taiwan Agricultural and Forestry Development Corporation.

Table 9.6. Extent of Land Reform

	Redistribution of land			
	Public land sale 1948–58	*Land-to-the-tiller program 1953*	*Total redistribution*	*Rent control 1952*
Area affected (*chia*)[a]				
Total	71,663	143,568	215,231	256,948
Paddy land	34,089	121,535	155,624	220,029
Dry land	37,524	22,033	59,557	35,305
Other[b]	50	—	50	1,614
Number of farm households affected	139,688	194,823	334,511	302,277
Number of landlords affected	—	106,049	106,049	—
Cultivated area affected as percentage of total cultivated area[c]	8.1%	16.4%	24.6%	29.2%
Farm household affected as percentage of total farm household[d]	20.0%	27.9%	47.9%	43.3%

Sources: Calculated from Hui-sun Tang, *Land Reform in Free China*, pp. 289, 292, and 293; and Cheng Chen, *Land Reform in Taiwan*, p. 311.

[a] 1 *chia* = 0.9699 hectare.

[b] Includes farmhouse sites, ditches, ponds, and other areas.

[c] Total cultivated area used in this calculation is the average of 1951–55.

[d] Total number of farm households used in this calculation is the average of 1951–55.

landlords was resold by the government to the tenants at the same price—2.5 times the annual yield. The tenants paid the land price and a 4 percent annual interest in rice for paddy land and in sweet potatoes (converted to cash) for dry land. The compulsory purchase of farmland and its resale to tenants began in May 1953 and was completed in December of that year. In toto nearly 144,000 hectares of land changed hands.

Table 9.6 summarizes the immediate consequences of Taiwan's land reform. More than 40 percent of Taiwan's farm households, or more than 70 percent of the tenant and part-tenant farm households, had their rent reduced to 37.5 percent of a standard yield by the rent reduction program. Together the sale of public land and the land-to-the-tiller program created more than 215,000 hectares (about 25 percent of the total cultivated area) of owner-cultivated land. In 1948 tenants farmed 44 percent of the total cultivated area; by 1953 the percentage of tenant cultivated land had decreased to 17 percent.[35] Almost 50 percent of Taiwan's farm households, or about 75 percent of tenant and part-tenant farm households, were able to purchase some land as a consequence of land reform. Tenant farm households as a share of total farm households were 41 percent in 1947, 21 percent in 1953, and 10 percent in 1970. Owner-cultivator households as a percentage of total farm households were 32 percent in 1947, 55 percent in 1953, and 78 percent in 1970.[36]

Whereas the direct and immediate effect of land reform on land distribution is easily observable, its effects on agricultural production, savings, and income distribution are very much more difficult to perceive. Yet these other effects are of great interest to us. Specifically we would like to know, and measure if possible, the impact that land reform had on agricultural production and growth, agricultural savings, income distribution, social attitudes, and the rural power structure.[37] But Taiwan's land reform (rent control and land redistribution) did not occur in isolation while other economic, social, and political factors remained constant. As a result, it is extremely difficult to separate the effects of land reform from those caused by other factors.

Taiwan's land reform brought about two basic changes in agriculture: (1) a sizable number of sharecroppers became owner-cultivators, and (2) a ceiling was placed on rent. One important effect of these changes was the elimination of sharecropping. Many have argued that sharecropping leads to the inefficient combination of resources.[38] Therefore it appears that the elimination of cropsharing in Taiwan

---

35. Chen, *Land Reform*, p. 312.

36. PDAF, *Taiwan Agricultural Yearbook*, various issues.

37. Economists usually assume institutional factors to be given. Consequently, we have not given such issues as land reform the attention they rightfully deserve. There are several outstanding exceptions, particularly Doreen Warriner, *Land Reform and Economic Development*; Philip Raup, "The Contribution of Land Reform to Agricultural Development: An Analytical Framework;" and Steven N. S. Cheung, *The Theory of Share Tenancy*.

38. See, for example, D. Gale Johnson, "Resource Allocation Under Share Contract;" N. Georgescu-Roegen, "Economic Theory and Agrarian Economics," *Oxford Economic Papers* NS12 (Feb. 1960): 23–26; A. K. Sen, "Peasants and Dualism with or Without Surplus Labor," *Journal of Political Economy* 74 (Oct. 1966): 445–46; and Dale W. Adams and Norman Rask, "Economics of Cost Share Leases in Less-developing Countries," *American Journal of Agricultural Economics* 50 (Nov. 1968): 935–37.

would increase efficiency and thus the rate of agricultural growth. However, recently the conclusion that sharecropping is inefficient has been challenged by a number of authors, notably Cheung.[39] Historically, Taiwan's agricultural growth does not seem to be closely related to the presence or absence of cropsharing. Between 1921 and 1939, during what are called the golden years of the colonial period, crop production increased at an annual average rate of 4.6 percent. This impressive rate of expansion was accomplished under a sharecropping system, and it is comparable to the rate of growth since the elimination of cropsharing in 1951.

Even though Taiwan's land reform may have had little effect on static efficiency, its effect on equity was substantial. The relationship between land tenure and income distribution is an intimate one. In agriculture, whether a farmer has access to land and whether such access is secure determine not only his economic viability but also his political power and social status. Taiwan's land reform successfully made land, and therefore future income streams, more accessible and secure for a larger group of peasants. This was done partly through the compulsory rent reduction program, partly through the replacement of short-term and often verbal leases by long-term written ones, and partly through land redistribution. The more equal distribution of wealth, income, and power must be judged the most tangible economic effect of Taiwan's land reform.

Because a large landless peasant class does not exist and because of the way the reform was carried out, the impact of Taiwan's land reform on income distribution can be analyzed in a straightforward manner. Taiwan's reform involved primarily the transfer of land from landowners to tenants and did not significantly alter the operational sizes of Taiwanese farms. Consequently, we do not have to consider how land reform affected farm size, and through it, the demand for agricultural labor, agricultural production, and finally agricultural income.[40] Furthermore, since nearly every peasant in Taiwan is either an owner-cultivator or a tenant (or a combination of the two), there is also no need to study the effect of land reform on the landless peasant class.[41]

39. Cheung, *The Theory of Share Tenancy.*
40. For an interesting discussion of the income distribution effect of land reform when farm size is altered, see R. Albert Berry, "Land Reform and Agricultural Wage Rate," Yale Economic Growth Center Discussion Paper, March 1970.
41. In Taiwan, the landless peasant class, i.e., hired laborers and their families, accounts for at most 4 or 5 percent of all agricultural families (see Chen, *Land Reform,* p. 312).

With the problem thus simplified, we can discuss the impact of Taiwan's land reform on income distribution primarily in terms of the direct gains of tenants and the direct losses of landlords.

The effect of land reform on landlords was a substantial reduction in the size of their wealth and therefore a reduction in their future income. Confiscated land, as we have already noted, was compensated by commodity bonds and stocks of government enterprises. The size of the compensation was 2.5 times the annual land yield,[42] but this was very much below the market value of farmland in Taiwan. A 1937 survey showed that the market value of farmland was between 4.5 and 8 times the annual yield of the land.[43] T. H. Lee and Y. T. Chen have estimated that in the period 1914–43 the average market value of paddy fields was about 4 times the annual yield of the main crop, i.e., rice.[44] If the relationship between the yield and the market value of farmland in the 1950s was similar to that which existed in the prewar years, the compensation paid to the landlords in 1953 fell substantially short of the true value of the land confiscated. Certainly this is the feeling expressed by most landowners, both those affected and those unaffected by land reform. If we assume the ratio between the value and the annual yield of farmland to be 5, the Land-to-the-Tiller Act had a net wealth redistribution effect, measured in 1952 prices, of NT$ 2.2 billion, or approximately 13 percent of Taiwan's gross domestic product in 1952.[45] Needless to say, if the compensation had been made at the market value of the land, the income (or wealth) redistribution effect of the land reform would have been lost because the land reform would then have been no more than a simple real estate transaction. By forcing landlords to accept bonds as payment, there was an additional redistribution effect because they were in effect being forced to lend to the government a sizable sum of money at a real rate

42. The Chinese Association of Land Economics found that the average price of land on the mainland was approximately seven times the annual rent. Because in Taiwan rent was fixed at 37.5 percent of annual yield, the government thought that land price should be approximately 2.5 (.375 × 7 = 2.63) times the annual yield.

43. Taiwan Government-General, *The Economics of Renting Farm Land, a Survey, Report of Basic Agricultural Survey no. 39*, pp. 1–2.

44. Teng-hui Lee and H. T. Chen, "Distribution of Agricultural Income in Taiwan," *Cooperative*, no. 26 (Taipei: Cooperative Bank of Taiwan, 1958), pp. 4–5.

45. The land compulsorily purchased from landowners in 1953, when valued at 2.5 times the annual yield, was worth 1,272,850 MT of unhulled rice and 434,709 MT of sweet potatoes. When converted into monetary units, at 1952 prices, this comes to NT$ 2.2 billion (cf. Tang, *Land Reform*, p. 149). Thus, if the market value is five times the annual yield, there was a net wealth distribution of NT$ 2.2 billion in 1952 prices.

of interest (4 percent in the case of Taiwan) substantially below the real current market rate (in the mid- and late 1950s the real market rate of interest in Taiwan ranged between 30 and 50 percent per annum).

The landowners' behavior after they received their compensation further weakened their economic position. Most landowners who received stocks of government enterprises regarded them as an inferior form of asset. Consequently, many of them quickly liquidated part or all of the shares paid to them at substantial losses. Anthony Koo estimates that, depending on the size of land compulsorily purchased, landowners retained only between 4.5 and 9.3 percent of the shares of the Taiwan Cement Company (the most preferred of the government enterprises turned over to the former landlords) given to them in compensation.[46] That most of the stocks issued to landowners were quickly resold is confirmed also by Yang's survey of former landlords.[47] Ninety-eight percent of the 500 former average landlords and 91 percent of the 75 former large landlords questioned by Yang sold their stocks soon after receiving them. Depending on the stock, the sale price was between 36 and 106 percent of par value.

On the other hand, Taiwan's land reform substantially improved the ease and security of tenants' access to future income as well as increasing the size of that income. Although land was not distributed to tenants at zero cost, the reform did give them the opportunity to purchase land at low prices and on very easy terms. Moreover, the adoption of long-term written leases and rent control gave those tenants unable to purchase land a secure access to a source of income, which became more lucrative each year as land productivity increased. Therefore the net effect of land reform was to significantly improve, both absolutely and relatively, the income position of former tenants.

As an illustration, we measure how Taiwan's land reform affected the real income of an average tenant with 1 chia of leased 9th grade (medium quality) paddy land in Taoyuan Hsien. We start in 1948, the year before the implementation of the rent reduction program, and trace the effect of rent reduction and land redistribution on the real

46. Generally, the larger landowners retained a higher percentage of the stocks they received as compensation for their land (see Anthony Y. C. Koo, *The Role of Land Reform in Economic Development*, pp. 44–48 and 156–57).

47. The survey covered 3,075 rural households: 500 nonfarming households, 1,250 former tenant households, 575 former landlord households, and 250 households not directly affected by the land reform. The detailed results of this survey are included in Martin M. C. Yang, *Socio-Economic Results of the Land Reform in Taiwan*, chap. 4.

income of this farmer through the 1950s. Income is defined as the residue to output after the peasant pays the production expenses, including the cost of using the land. Since we have no evidence that land reform, by itself, increased yield, we shall assume that the actual yield of rice is determined independently of the land reform. This assumption allows us to separate more precisely that share of the increase in income which can be attributed to land reform from the increase that would have occurred in the absence of land reform.

Our calculation, shown in table 9.7, suggests that, in the absence of land reform, the income of the Taoyuan farmer, measured in terms of rice, would have increased by nearly 16 percent between 1948 and 1959. Because the terms of trade between the agricultural and nonagricultural sectors were relatively stable in the 1950s,[48] income measured in terms of rice is essentially real farm income. The 16 percent rise in real income is computed under the assumptions that competition for land maintains the rent share at 50 percent and that landlords do not share in any of the current production costs. If his landlord had shared in the production cost or if rent share had declined, the farmer's real income would have increased at a more rapid rate. For example, if his landlord shared his fertilizer cost at the same rate he shared his output (i.e., 50 percent), his real income would have risen by about 40 percent between 1948 and 1959.

Taiwan's land reform increased the tenant-cultivators' income in two ways: (1) it reduced the rent and (2) it allowed some tenants to purchase land and become owner-cultivators. If our Taoyuan tenant were affected only by the rent reduction, his income (measured in terms of rice) would have increased by over 90 percent, from 2,161 kg in 1948 to 4,136 kg in 1959. But if the land reform allowed our Taoyuan tenant to become an owner-cultivator as well, his income from 1948 to 1959, would have increased by 107 percent, rising from 2,161 kg to 4,492 kg. Furthermore, once he completes paying for his land (for most peasants who purchased land under the Land-to-the-Tiller Act, this would have been 1963), his income thereafter would automatically be raised by an amount equal to the annual amortization and interest charge. To put these results in a slightly different way, the farmer's 1959 income (after paying the annual amortization and interest charge) of 4,492 kg of rice under the land reform (rent reduction and land redistribution) represented an increased of 1,990 kg over the income

48. DGBAS, *Monthly Statistics of the Republic of China*, various issues.

Table 9.7. Effect of Land Reform on the Income of Tenant-Cultivator, 1948–59 (kg/chia)[a]

Rent payment

	Actual rice yield (1)	No land reform[b] (2)	With rent reduction[c] (3)	With both rent reduction and land redistribution[d] (4)	Fertilizer[e] (5)	Seed[f] (6)	Land tax paid in kind (7)
1948	4,649	2,324	2,324	2,324	114	50	0
1949	4,860	2,430	1,995	1,995	376	50	0
1950	5,153	2,577	1,995	1,995	590	50	0
1951	5,320	2,660	1,995	1,995	661	50	0
1952	5,530	2,765	1,995	1,995	777	50	0
1953	5,717	2,859	1,995	0	781	50	256
1954	5,696	2,848	1,995	0	948	50	256
1955	6,283	3,142	1,995	0	980	50	256
1956	6,596	3,298	1,995	0	1,020	50	256
1957	7,015	3,508	1,995	0	1,042	50	256
1958	7,200	3,600	1,995	0	1,078	50	256
1959	7,258	3,629	1,995	0	1,077	50	256

	Repayment of land price and interest (8)	Income of cultivator			Source of additional income	
		No land reform (9)	With rent reduction (10)	With both rent reduction and land redistribution (11)	Rent reduction (12)	Rent reduction and land distribution (13)
1948	0	2,161	2,161	2,161	—	—
1949	0	2,004	2,439	2,439	435	435
1950	0	1,936	2,518	2,518	582	582
1951	0	1,949	2,614	2,614	665	665
1952	0	1,938	2,708	2,708	770	770
1953	1,383	2,027	2,891	3,247	864	1,220
1954	1,383	1,850	2,703	3,059	853	1,209
1955	1,383	2,111	3,258	3,614	1,147	1,503
1956	1,383	2,228	3,531	3,887	1,303	1,659
1957	1,383	2,415	3,928	4,284	1,513	1,869
1958	1,383	2,472	4,077	4,433	1,605	1,961
1959	1,383	2,502	4,136	4,492	1,634	1,990

Notes and Sources: These calculations use the data for ninth grade paddy land in Taoyuan Hsien. Columns 1, 5, 7, and 8 are from Cheng Chen, Land Reform in China, p. 313. All other columns are derived from columns 1, 5, 7, and 8 in the manner indicated in the footnotes.

Table 9.7 (continued)

[a] 1 *chia* = 0.9699 hectare.
[b] Assumed to be 50% of actual yield.
[c] Assumed to be 37.5% of standard yield (5,319 kg/chia) determined in 1948.
[d] Assumed to be 37.5% of standard yield until 1953, when the ownership of land was transferred to the cultivator.
[e] Based on data released by the Taiwan Provincial Food Bureau.
[f] Assumed to be 50 kg per chia.
[g] Actual rice yield minus rent, fertilizer, land tax and repayment of land price, and interest.

he would have received as a tenant in the absence of land reform (2,502 kg). Thus, about 85 percent of the rise in his income from 2,161 kg in 1948 to 4,492 kg in 1959 were income that would normally have accrued to the landlord.[49]

That land reform profoundly altered income distribution in Taiwan's agricultural sector cannot be disputed, but not all tillers benefited equally from the land reform. Although the rent reduction regulation explicitly states that landlords, if they had originally supplied some of the inputs, must continue to supply such inputs after rent reduction, there is evidence that many managed to escape this stipulation.[50] Consequently, some of the benefits from rent reduction were negated by rising production costs. There also have been instances where the combined burden of the mortgage and the land tax was greater than the rent that the farmer (now owner-cultivator) used to pay. This extra burden was of course only temporary, but until it was lifted it was very real to the peasant.

Land reform probably also affected the savings rate in agriculture. Assuming landlords, because of their generally higher income, to have a higher marginal propensity to save than do tenants, a shift in income from landlords to tenants will tend to depress the average savings rate in agriculture.[51] Agricultural savings for 1950, 1955, and 1960 can be calculated from estimates of farm income and consumption. But because we suspect both farm income and consumption to be under-

49. Yang's survey of living conditions of landowners and tenants confirms that since land reform the income of tenants has increased while that of landowners has badly deteriorated (see Yang, *Socio-Economic Results of Land Reform*, chaps. 7 and 8).

50. For example, see Bernard Gallin, *Hsin Hsing, Taiwan*, p. 108, and JCRR, *General Report of the Joint Commission on Rural Reconstruction*, 1953, pp. 147–50.

51. Of course, marginal propensity to save may differ as well by factor shares. Thus, it is possible that rent is spent entirely on consumption. In this extreme case, land reform would tend to increase rather than reduce the savings rate.

estimated, the reliability of the savings estimates is questionable. With this reservation in mind, we present the available evidence. The average agricultural savings rate in Taiwan declined between 1950 and 1955, from about 0.14 to about 0.10.[52] Since 1955 it appears to have increased. In 1960 the savings ratio in Taiwan's agriculture was estimated at 0.16.[53] The apparent decline in the average savings rate between 1950 and 1955 was probably a result of the land reform. However, it is more difficult to explain the rise in the savings ratio between 1955 and 1960 solely in terms of the land reform. In this latter case one suspects that many factors other than land reform, such as improved political and economic stability, were involved.

Up to this point in the discussion, we have viewed the effects of Taiwan's land reform in static terms, with social and economic parameters held constant. But a major change in agrarian institutions, such as land reform, has the necessary force to alter these conditions.[54] Land reform, therefore, has great potential to become a powerful influence in the economic life of the country. For instance, land reform might, among other things, significantly alter economic expectations as well as traditional attitudes and behaviors. To the extent that land reform helps a country change those attitudes and values that inhibit development or establish ones that promote development, it has a positive influence on agricultural and general economic growth. In Taiwan there is some evidence to indicate that land reform may indeed have produced some of these effects.

The farmer's propensity to improve his land and to improve himself are two parameters among many that are likely to be affected by land reform. Using the data from Taiwan's 22 major administrative districts, we performed the following regression analysis:[55]

$$\ln y_1 = -3.382 + 1.279 \ln x_1 + 0.592 \ln x_2 \qquad (9.1)$$
$$ (0.266) \qquad\quad (0.493)$$
$$R^2 = 0.601, F = 14.32$$
$$\ln y_2 = 0.151 + 0.863 \ln x_1 - 0.014 \ln x_2 \qquad (9.2)$$
$$ (0.176) \qquad\quad (0.326)$$
$$R^2 = 0.572, F = 12.65$$

52. Hui-sun Tang and S. C. Hsieh, "Land Reform and Agricultural Development in Taiwan," p. 140.
53. Koo, *Role of Land Reform*, p. 59.
54. Philip Raup argues along this line (see his "Contribution of Land Reform").
55. That x_1 and x_2 might interact linearly and additively was also considered but was found to have very much less explanatory power than the form used here.

where y_1 is the percentage of farm households in each district that engaged in some form of land improvement in 1960, y_2 is the percentage of farm households in each district that attended agricultural training classes in 1960, x_1 is the percentage of total cultivated area in each district redistributed by the 1953 Land-to-the-Tiller Act, and x_2 is the percentage of farm households in each district that was owner-cultivator in 1960.[56] The value of x_1's coefficient can be used to measure the initial impact of land reform on the attitudes or values of peasants in a region: a large value means a major impact and a small value a lesser impact.

In both regressions, x_1's coefficient is found to be relatively large, positive, and significantly different from zero and x_2's coefficient to be relatively small and not significantly different from zero.[57] This implies that regional differences both in the degree of participation in land improvement and in agricultural education are closely related to the impact land reform initially made in the region. Interestingly enough, no strong association emerges between regional variations in y_1 (or y_2) and the regional differences in the share of owner-cultivators in total farm population. Therefore, it appears that the occurrence of land reform and the extent of its initial influence on a region are much more important determinants of how peasants behaved in that region than whether there exist in the region a large group of owner-cultivators. Too much should not be made of these regression findings, for correlation is not after all proof of causation. But the results do reveal that to a marked degree regional differences in peasants' attitudes toward farm improvement can be explained by differences in the impact land reform made on the regions. It is also interesting to note that Yang's survey of peasants' responses to Taiwan's land reform found that peasants who were affected by land reform became more "hopeful" toward life and the future and have been motivated to take a greater interest in and to make greater efforts at farming.[58]

Land reform also can profoundly transform social attitudes and alter the rural power structure. To the extent that agricultural development is hindered by a landed oligarchy, a land reform that substantially weakens this class and promotes new rural leadership helps to stimulate

56. y_1 and y_2 are calculated from *Report on the 1961 Census of Agriculture: Taiwan, ROC—10% Sample Census*, pp. 490–93; x_1 is calculated from Tang, *Land Reform*, p. 293, and x_2 is based on data in PDAF, *Taiwan Agricultural Yearbook*, 1961.

57. The correlation between x_1 and x_2 is quite low ($\rho_{x_1x_2} = .2245$).

58. Yang, *Socio-Economic Results of Land Reform*, chaps. 4 and 5.

agricultural growth. We know also that if the structure of land owner-ship and tenure arrangement does not allow social and economic advancement for a majority of the people, political and social unrest is an inevitable consequence. Since economic development cannot take place in the midst of internal turmoil, a land reform that reduces rural tension and conflicts also helps to promote economic development because it permits the less developed country to focus its energy on solving its many serious and complex economic problems.

To say that land reform maintained internal order in Taiwan is perhaps going too far. But there is little doubt that one reason, if not the principal one, that land reform was implemented in Taiwan was the government's concern about, and its desire to minimize the pos-sibility of, rural unrest.[59] Those familiar with rural Taiwan are also in agreement that land reform profoundly changed the rural social and political structure. Traditionally, landlords were the rural leaders and played a major role in village life. Indeed, in the colonial period the Japanese dealt with the peasant almost exclusively through the landlord class, whose hold on land and whose relationship with the colonial government gave it formidable powers over the ordinary peasants. Although the rural power structure in the colonial period was not an obstacle to agricultural development (primarily because the colonial government, the real power in Taiwan, was interested in agri-cultural growth and sponsored those changes that were conducive to growth), it did prevent the development of leadership and community concern among the peasants. As a result of the land reform, this situation changed.

Bernard Gallin, after an extended stay in rural Taiwan, made the following observation in the late 1950s:

> The post-land reform period in the rural area shows signs of being one of social as well as economic transition. Although the landlords still form a definite and important class, the changes taking place may mark the beginning of a decline in the almost exclusive leader-ship of the landlord or gentry class. There are incipient signs of instability in a traditional social system which had grown out of an unequal distribution of rural wealth and income as a result of the land tenure system. The Land Reform Program which has led many

59. This is generally accepted by all those who have studied the government's land reform policy. For example, see Tang, *Land Reform*, pp. 30–31, and Yang, *Socio-Economic Results of Land Reform*, chap. 1.

landlords to withdraw their interests from the rural villages appears
to be leading to some equalization of social status in rural Taiwan,
which may in turn enable new village leaders to become effective.

In the past and, to a lesser degree, in the present, there have been
capable villagers who had no opportunity to compete with the
landlord class for primary village leadership. Now, perhaps for the
first time, these people will have some opportunity to manifest their
leadership abilities. But many traditional attitudes must be cleared
away before such new leaders can gain widespread acceptance. . . .
There must be a change in the villagers' own attitudes toward
leadership and authority, for they have not yet been emancipated
from their respect for wealth and power and the use to which these
two can be put in the manipulation of people and policies.[60]

Yang's survey of rural Taiwan in the early 1960s confirms Gallin's
impressions.[61] Although developing slowly, new attitudes, new social
relationships, and new leaders are beginning to emerge. The traditional landlord–tenant relationship, where kan-ch'ing, or good personal relationship, played such vital role, has become a largely formal
business arrangement. Indeed, it is now not unusual for a tenant to
show his hostility toward his landlord openly. Socially, the hierarchical
relationships have weakened while equalitarian relationships have
strengthened. The more well-to-do small holders (owner-cultivators)
have taken over some of the local leadership abandoned by landlords.
But in some villages, new leaders are yet to emerge, and the vacuum
has caused a certain amount of social disorganization. In general,
however, peasants have become more interested in local politics and
as a result a wider spectrum of rural interest is now represented at the
local level of government. Traditionally the landlord class was the sole
spokesman for the rural area. But since the early 1950s, it no longer
enjoys this political monopoly. In the late 1950s, only 23 percent of
the township representatives were landlords, while 69 percent were
owner-cultivators (40 percent of whom were new owner-cultivators)
and 7 percent were businessmen. In the long run, the emergence of
new rural leadership and greater political participation may turn out
to be the most important consequences of land reform.

    60. Gallin, *Hsin Hsing*, p. 117.
    61. The rest of this paragraph draws heavily on the survey results in Yang, *Socio-Economic Results of Land Reform*, chaps. 9–11.

GOVERNMENT POLICY AND AGRICULTURAL DEVELOPMENT

Land reform was undoubtedly the most dramatic agrarian program implemented by the government. But other aspects of its agricultural policy also had profound effects on agriculture. Briefly stated, aside from land reform the government's agricultural policy in the postwar period was both developmental and extractive.[62] In 1946, with much of its infrastructure in ruins, Taiwan's agriculture was weak and disorganized, and the need for active government participation in its reconstruction and development was great. The extractive part of the agricultural policy was inevitable, considering that suddenly in the late 1940s Taiwan had to feed more than 1 million mainland refugees, support a huge military establishment, and implement an industrialization program. Despite some inherently conflicting elements, both aspects of this policy were reasonably successful.

Table 9.8 portrays the structure of agricultural financing in 1961, which is representative of the extent of government involvement in developing agriculture in the postwar period. In studying table 9.8, it should be observed that government enterprises and financial institutions are under direct government control and therefore should be thought of as parts of the government. The government's development

62. In this discussion the Sino-American Joint Commission on Rural Reconstruction is included as part of the Chinese government, although it is subordinate to both the Chinese and the United States governments. JCRR was established by the 1948 China Aid Act (Public Law 472, 80th Congress) and is authorized to carry out a coordinated program for rural reconstruction in China. Although it operated for a short time in mainland China, its major programs have been in Taiwan. In the 1950s and most years in the 1960s, the commission was composed of two Americans appointed by the president of the United States and three Chinese appointed by the president of the Republic of China. It was financed by U.S. aid but its staff (243 in 1962) was composed primarily of Chinese (the largest number of U.S. experts on the staff at one time, excluding short-term consultants, was 13). Because of its competence and influence, JCRR operated essentially as Taiwan's chief agricultural policymaker and planner. Indeed, the convenor of the highest agricultural policymaking body in Taiwan, the Agricultural Planning and Coordinating Committee (APCC) of the Ministry of Economic Affairs (after 1963 the Agricultural Production Committee of the Council for International Economic Cooperation and Development), was served by one of the JCRR Chinese commissioners. Other senior positions in APCC were also held by JCRR specialists. For information about JCRR and its activities see JCRR, *General Report*, issued annually; John D. Montgomery, Rufus B. Hughes, and Raymond H. Davis, *Rural Improvement and Political Development: The JCRR Model*; Richard L. Hough, "AID Administration to the Rural Sector—The JCRR Experience in Taiwan and Its Application in Other Countries," AID Discussion Paper no. 17 (Apr. 1968); and Yien-si Tsiang, "A Report on the Joint Commission on Rural Reconstruction."

Table 9.8. Agricultural Financing by Source of Funds, FY 1961 (NT$ million)

	Fixed investment	Developmental expenditures[a]	Agricultural credit
Government	432	201	80
Central[b]	—[c]	—	—
Sino-American Joint Commission on Rural Reconstruction	322	111	80
Provincial	46	58	—
Prefectural–city	46	22	—
Township	18	10	—
Government enterprises[d]	204	42	562
Financial institution[e]	—	—	1,409
Farmers' organizations[f]	255	16	645
Private farms	654	n.a.[g]	n.a.[h]
Total	1,545	259	2,696

Source: JCRR, "Statistical Review of Agricultural Financing in Taiwan and JCRR's Constributions."
[a]Includes expenditures for such items as agricultural research, extension, crop pest and disease control, and livestock disease.
[b]There are two agricultural agencies in the central government, both of which are administrative units. In FY 1961 they had a combined budget of only NT$ 300,000.
[c]Excludes the contribution to the multipurpose Shihmen Dam project.
[d]Taiwan Food Bureau, Taiwan Sugar Corporation, Taiwan Tobacco and Wine Monopoly Bureau, Taiwan Forestry Administration, and Ta-shu-shan Timber Corporation.
[e]Land Bank, Cooperative Bank, commercial banks, cooperative credit societies, and cooperative saving banks.
[f]Farmers' Association, Irrigation Association, market cooperatives, and Fishmen's Association.
[g]Developmental expenditures by private farms are probably negligible.
[h]A 1960 credit survey, conducted by the Provincial Department of Agriculture and Forestry, showed that 33% of the agricultural credit came from the government and the banks, 24% from farmers' organizations, and 43% from traders, landlords, friends, and relatives.

efforts in agriculture fall into two broad categories: the repair and improvement of infrastructure created in the colonial period, and the introduction and supply of current inputs, new crops, and new techniques that are compatible with Taiwan's small and intensively worked farms.

Neglect during the war and the immediate postwar years caused serious damage to the rural infrastructure (irrigation and rural organizations) created in the colonial period. The government correctly saw the crucial role these organizations played in agricultural development

Table 9.9. Composition of Fixed Capital Formation in Agriculture, 1952–59
(NT$ million)

	1952		1953–56 Annual average		1957–58 Annual average		1959	
	NT$	*%*	*NT$*	*%*	*NT$*	*%*	*NT$*	*%*
1. Flood control and irrigation	140.4	36.3	202.9	36.4	263.2	33.6	271.3	30.6
a. U.S. aid financed	46.2	—	49.8	—	109.4	—	101.5	—
b. Non-U.S. aid financed	94.2	—	153.1	—	153.8	—	169.8	—
2. Land reclamation	5.6	1.4	11.5	2.1	23.9	3.0	20.0	2.2
3. Draft animals	13.6	3.5	14.5	2.6	14.6	1.9	24.3	2.7
4. Permanent crops	6.0	1.6	8.4	1.5	25.5	3.2	18.0	2.0
5. Machinery and equipment	—	—	—	—	7.5	1.0	25.8	2.9
6. Capital expenditures of government agricultural enterprises	4.5	1.2	17.6	3.2	29.4	3.8	30.0	3.4
7. Private farm improvement	216.9	56.0	303.0	45.3	418.2	53.4	497.4	56.0
8. Total	387.0	100.0	557.9	100.0	782.3	100.0	886.8	100.0

Source: Compiled by the Agricultural Planning and Coordinating Committee of the Ministry of Economic Affairs and published in Tsung-han Shen, *Agricultural Development on Taiwan Since World War II*, p. 316.

and devoted considerable effort in the 1950s to restoring and improving Taiwan's irrigation facilities and rural organizations. Indeed most of the government's capital expenditures for agriculture in the 1950s was allocated to flood control and irrigation. Reflecting these expenditures, about one-third of the total fixed capital formation in agriculture in 1952–59 was in this area (table 9.9).

Less costly to restore and improve, but no less essential for agricultural development, were the rural organizations. For all practical purposes, the farmers' associations and the credit cooperatives established in the colonial period ceased to operate after the war. Many of their physical facilities, such as warehouses, were destroyed by Allied bombing and their personnel was depleted by the repatriation of Japanese at the end of the war. Thus human as well as material capital had to be recreated. In 1952 the government helped to consolidate the credit cooperatives, farmers' associations and various rural community organizations into a new multipurpose Farmers' Association, which has since served the peasants as an extension agent, a major supplier of current agricultural inputs, a marketing cooperative, and a source of agricultural credit.[63] The new Farmers' Association was organized on three administrative levels. In the 1960s there were 1 provincial association, 22 prefectural associations, and 342 township associations. Under the township associations were more than 5,000 small agricultural units. To develop the personnel needed to staff this system, the government initiated programs to train skilled agricultural personnel. Thousands of group leaders of small agricultural units and staff members of the Farmers' Association participated in short training courses sponsored by the government. To provide more complete training, a permanent training school was also established with JCRR financial assistance in 1952, and since then thousands of staff members of the Farmers' Association have attended this school.[64]

Government agencies also operate or help support scores of agricultural research and experiment institutions. Together they have employed about 4,000 research workers, approximately the same number employed in the colonial period. Even if we discount for the possible quality difference between research workers in less developed and developed countries, the size of Taiwan's agricultural research program is large. In 1960 the number of agricultural research workers per 100,000 people active in agriculture was 79 in Taiwan, 60 in Japan, and only 4.7 in Thailand, 1.6 in the Philippines, and 1.2 in India.[65] The work done at these research institutions has provided Taiwan with an impressive number of agricultural improvements and innovations.[66] JCRR, because of its unusually skilled technical staff, played a particularly significant role in this area. It served as the catalytic agent for important innovations such as the adoption of pesticides and insecticides, the development of artificial cultivation of mushrooms, and the introduction of improved farm tools and machinery.

63. For information about the Farmers' Association and its activities, see Min-hsioh Kwoh, "Farmers' Association and Their Contributions Toward Agricultural and Rural Development in Taiwan;" S. C. Hsieh, "Farmers' Organizations in Taiwan and Their Trends of Development"; and Martin M. C. Yang, "A Study on Impact of Farmers' Association and Extension Program on Development of Agriculture in Taiwan."
64. Tsiang, *Report*, pp. 9–10.
65. U.S. Department of Agriculture, *Changes in Agriculture*, p. 61.
66. For example, a large number of new varieties of rice, wheat, sugar cane, pineapple, sweet potatoes, peanuts, and other foods were developed through hybridization. Seed multiplication and certification programs were also established. See JCRR, *Crop and Seed Improvement in Taiwan, Republic of China: June 1956–April 1959*, and JCRR, *Crop and Seed Improvement in Taiwan, Republic of China: May 1959–January 1961*.

The colonial extension service, deactivated after the war, was revived and reorganized. By the 1960s, about 1,000 (presumably full-time) professional extension workers were in the field. Farmers were encouraged to participate actively in extension work. Many farm discussion groups and 4-H clubs were formed and became vital links in the extension system.[67] Through these organizations the more advanced farmers, with some guidance from the extension worker, taught the less experienced. Several decades of rural education have transformed Taiwan's agricultural population into one of the most literate in Asia. In 1960, according to the agricultural census, 57 percent of the farm workers had some formal education. The high degree of literacy in rural Taiwan and the extensive use of modern means of communication (e.g., newspapers, leaflets, and radio) combined to make the extension service an effective instrument of change.[68]

Often small holders cannot adopt new innovations, use more nonfarm current inputs, or invest in fixed capital without credit that extends at least over a production period. In the late 1930s all types of farm credit from official sources amounted to an equivalent of about NT$ 1 billion of 1950 purchasing power.[69] Of this, 60 percent was available for long-term and 40 percent for short-term loans. When the colonial government departed at the end of the war, the farm credit system it operated also disintegrated. For several years the tightened credit conditions in rural Taiwan seriously threatened agricultural development. To relieve this condition, rural credit institutions were revived and reorganized.[70] When the government reorganized the Farmers' Association in 1952, its credit department was given the task of mobilizing rural savings and providing rural credits. To channel funds into agriculture, two government banks, the Land Bank of Taiwan (totally owned by the government) and the Cooperative Bank of Taiwan (60 percent owned by the government), were reorganized

67. T. H. Shen, *Agricultural Development on Taiwan Since World War II*, pp. 96–98.
68. Two agricultural magazines written for the peasants (*Harvest*, a semimonthly, and *Farmers Friend*, a monthly) are available and enjoy a fairly wide circulation. Numerous agricultural radio programs are also broadcast. Because most farm households have a radio, these programs reach a large audience.
69. W. J. Ladejinsky, "Observations on Rural Conditions in Taiwan," p. 11.
70. Agricultural credit institutions are discussed in great detail in the following publications: Hsing-yiu Chen and R. A. Bailey, "Agricultural Credit in Taiwan"; "Agricultural Credit and Cooperatives in Taiwan, China," Country Report presented by the Delegation of the Republic of China to the Fifth Far East Workshop for Agricultural Credit and Cooperatives; and K. H. King, "Agricultural Finance and Credit in Taiwan, China."

from the assets of defunct Japanese banks. Besides these agricultural credit institutions, a number of government agencies (e.g., the Taiwan Provincial Food Bureau, the Taiwan Tobacco and Wine Monopoly Bureau, the Taiwan Sugar Corporation, and JCRR) also injected credit, mostly short term, into agriculture. As a result of these efforts, credit became more accessible and the organized money market (government, financial institutions, and the Farmers' Association) became the foremost source of rural credit. In 1949 only 17 percent of the total farm loans were provided through the organized money market, but by 1960, 57 percent came from this source.[71]

Besides its efforts to develop agriculture, the government also operated programs that allowed it to control a sizable share of the rice crop produced each year. Because peasants were not fully compensated for the rice collected by the government, these programs were in effect extractive instruments. The main methods used by the government to collect rice are taxation, compulsory purchase of rice at prices substantially below the market price, and the bartering of fertilizers for rice at ratios stipulated by the government.

Of the agricultural taxes, the land tax, composed of the land tax proper and various surtaxes, is by far the most important.[72] After World War II, landowners were required to pay to the government a specified quantity of paddy rice for every yen of land tax they used to pay to the colonial government. To increase the yield of the tax, the yen/rice conversion ratio has been raised periodically. In 1946 landowners paid 11.5 kg of paddy rice for every yen of land tax (including surtaxes) owed to the government. By the late 1960s the rate was 27 kg per yen. Cultivators of paddy fields must also sell to the government at an official purchase price 12 kg of rice for every yen of land tax formerly paid to the colonial government. Although the official purchase price has increased steadily in the 1950s and 1960s, it nevertheless remained consistently 25–30 percent below the wholesale market price of paddy.[73] The difference between the two prices is of course essentially a tax on the cultivators.

Since 1950 the government has been the sole source of chemical fertilizer in Taiwan. It controls all fertilizer production and imports

71. The 1949 figure is from PDAF, *Report on Investigation of Agricultural Finance 1949*, 1950; the 1960 figure is from PDAF, *The Survey of the Supply and Demand of Rural Credit 1960*, 1961.

72. Rural taxation is discussed in detail in Sing-min Yeh and T. S. Kuo, *Rural Land Taxation in Taiwan*, and C. Y. Hsu, "Rural Taxation in Taiwan," JCRR, 1952, mimeo.

73. PFB, *Taiwan Food Statistics Book*, 1965, p. 148.

and distributes its supply according to crops: those for sugar cane are distributed by the government-owned Taiwan Sugar Corporation and those for other crops are distributed by the Farmers' Association acting on behalf of the Taiwan Provincial Food Bureau.[74] The bulk, about 70–80 percent, of the fertilizer is allocated to rice and is distributed to rice farmers through a rice–fertilizer barter system. In the 1950s and 1960s the rice collected through this barter system accounted for over one-half the rice collected by the government. Producers of crops other than rice and sugar cane may purchase fertilizer from the Food Bureau at an official price, which is closely tied to the rice/fertilizer barter ratio.

Until the early 1970s the barter ratio between rice and fertilizer, given the market price of paddy, was set consistently to favor fertilizer. In other words, considering the world price of fertilizer, Taiwanese farmers paid much too high a price for the fertilizers they used. For example, in the 1950s and 1960s, compared to Japanese farmers, Taiwanese farmers paid approximately 50 percent more for ammonium sulfate, the most heavily consumed fertilizer in Taiwan.[75] The farm price of fertilizer was high in Taiwan in comparison not only to Japan but also to other Asian countries. In the 1960s the price of ammonium sulfate in Taiwan was twice that in Thailand and Sri Lanka and more than twice that in Pakistan.[76]

The high price of fertilizer was in part a consequence of the government's policy to subsidize industrialization at the expense of agriculture. Beginning in the mid-1950s, to replace imports, Taiwan began to produce sizable quantities of fertilizers at costs substantially higher than imported fertilizers. In 1961, for example, the government paid NT\$ 1,758 (CIF price) for a metric ton of imported ammonium sulfate but paid NT\$ 4,116 (ex-factory price)[77] for a metric ton of domestically produced ammonium sulfate. In that year, the government exchanged ammonium sulfate for rice at the equivalent price of NT\$ 3,685 per metric ton. The government therefore took a loss on the domestically

74. How the Taiwan Provincial Food Bureau operated is described in Takeharu Sasamoto, "A Salient Feature of Capital Accumulation in Taiwan," *Developing Economics* 6 (March 1968): 30–35. Also see PFB, *Taiwan Province: Sixteen Years of Food Administration*, pp. 19–23, 93–113, 163–81, and 209–23.

75. Andron B. Lewis, "The Rice-Fertilizer Barter Price and the Production of Rice in Taiwan, Republic of China," pp. 135 and 170, and PFB, *Taiwan Province Rural Economic Conditions, Collection 4*, 1963, pp. 1–3.

76. P. C. Lei, "A Study of the Fertilizer Problems of the Taiwanese Peasant Families," *Bank of Taiwan Quarterly* 19 (June 1968): 192.

77. Plant Industry Division, JCRR.

produced fertilizer that was more than offset by the profits on the imported fertilizer. In other words, by manipulating the prices, the government on the one hand taxed the farmers and on the other hand subsidized the fertilizer industry. Fortunately, the fertilizer industry, as its scale of operation expanded and as it gained experience, has been able to cut its production cost so that by the mid-1960s the cost difference between the imported and the domestically produced fertilizers had been substantially reduced. Thus, in 1965 the CIF price of imported ammonium sulfate was NT$ 2,103/MT, and the ex-factory price of the domestically produced ammonium sulfate was NT$ 2,700/MT.[78] However, the farm price of fertilizer declined less rapidly than did production cost, so the fertilizer–rice barter program produced large profits for the government, especially in the first half of the 1960s. For example, during 1960–63 I estimate the average annual "profit" from the fertilizer–rice barter program to equal the equivalent of 83,000 MT of paddy per year, or about 80 percent of the rice collected annually as land tax.[79]

The total volume of rice collected by the government was substantial, in some years exceeding 750,000 MT. During the 1950s and 1960s the average annual collection was around 650,000 MT of paddy, or about 25 percent of Taiwan's annual rice production. If we make the reasonable assumption that farmers consumed one-half the rice they produced, then each year in the 1950s and 1960s the government collected about one-half the rice that left the agricultural sector. Approximately one-third the rice collected was rationed to the armed forces, and another 20–25 percent was distributed to military dependents and civilian employees of the government. The remaining balance was either sold on the free market to stabilize the price of rice or exported, a trade that the government monopolized.[80]

78. Ibid.
79. Profit in terms of rice is calculated as $\Sigma x_i (P_{x_i} - C_{x_i})/P_m$, where x_i's are chemical fertilizers distributed by the Food Bureau, P_{x_i}'s are farm prices of these fertilizers (calculated by multiplying the average market price of paddy and the official rice/fertilizer barter ratio), P_m is the average market price of paddy, and C_{x_i}'s are fertilizer costs to the Food Bureau. The cost of fertilizer includes CIF or ex-factory price, procurement costs (e.g., import duties), distributive costs, business costs, administrative costs, and financial cost (e.g., interest payments). Cost data were provided by the Plant Industry Division of JCRR.
80. In part, as a result of the government's stabilization program, the standard deviation of monthly rice price was seven times smaller in 1955–58 than in 1946–50 (see Wei-fan Chuang and Hsing-yiu Chen, "Agricultural Price Policies and Marketing Programs," p. 46).

Since the amount of rice compulsorily purchased from rice farmers was fixed, the program did not discourage efforts to increase production. However, the fertilizer–rice barter program had serious disincentive effects. By artificially keeping the price of fertilizer high in the postwar period, the government in effect reduced the incentive to farmers to expand production through the application of more fertilizer.[81] Possibly, high fertilizer cost also discouraged the rapid adoption of high yield seeds that required intensive fertilization. Furthermore, the program was operated in a way that produced a number of other undesirable effects.

In the postwar period, farmers were unable to purchase one type of fertilizer without at the same time purchasing specified amounts of other fertilizers. The stated rationale of this requirement was that it would ensure the application of a balanced mix of nitrogen, phosphate, and potash fertilizers. But it also enabled the government to reduce its stock of less desirable domestically produced fertilizers. The major objection to this arrangement was that the government was never able to determine accurately the fertilizer needs at the farm level or even at the village level. Consequently, farmers were often required to purchase fertilizers they did not need. It seems that a better and more efficient way to distribute fertilizer is to allow farmers to decide for themselves what they require.

Because the government was more concerned with rice collection than fertilizer distribution, the allocation of fertilizer for rice bartering was always given priority over other crops. As a result, minor crops suffered. For example, in 1959 the estimated amount of fertilizer applied to rice was only slightly below the recommended rate, but for other crops the recommended rate exceeded the actual applied rate by substantial margins.[82] To be most effective, fertilizer must be applied at the proper time. However, the barter system did not always distribute fertilizer according to the needs of the farmers. Because the government was afraid that fertilizers allocated to minor crops would be used on rice and thus reduce the amount of rice it could collect

81. Hsu found the demand for nitrogen fertilizer in Taiwan to be very sensitive to its relative price (see his "The Demand for Fertilizer in a Developing Country: The Case of Taiwan, 1950–1966").

82. For example, in the case of sweet potatoes the estimated actual rate of fertilizer application was only 2 percent of the recommended rate (see JCRR, Plant Industry Division, "Questions and Answers on the Fertilizer Program of Taiwan," 1961, mimeo, p. 9).

through fertilizer–rice bartering, it withheld the distribution of fertilizer to minor crops until after the fertilizer–rice bartering was under way. Unfortunately, this often meant that fertilizer for the minor crops was available only after the most effective application time had passed.

Although the extractive aspect of the agricultural policy undoubtedly caused some inefficiencies in resource use and reduced the farmers' incentive to increase production, its negative influence on output and productivity was more than offset by the positive impact of the government's development and modernization efforts. Certainly, the record of Taiwan's agricultural growth in the 1950s and 1960s is testimony to this. Thus postwar government policy not only helped agriculture to develop but also enabled the government to extract a large share of the agricultural surplus.

The government has not been unaware that its agricultural policy, which has tried to be both extractive and developmental, has conflicting elements. Despite loud complaints about the undesirable effects of some of its extractive programs, the government, until very recently, has been reluctant to change its policy for fear of losing a lucrative and secure source of revenue. Nevertheless, minor adjustments have been made. For example, since 1960 the barter ratio of rice to fertilizer has been gradually lowered but not sufficiently to reduce the effectiveness of the rice–fertilizer barter system as an extractive mechanism. Without a dramatic cut in the rice/fertilizer barter ratio and with rural wages on the rise, farming became less profitable, and a growing number of farmers left agriculture for more profitable occupations.

Alarmed by agriculture's sluggish performance in the late 1960s, the government in 1970 announced new efforts to reduce agricultural production cost. The government proclaimed that, although it still intends to barter fertilizer for rice, it will now operate the fertilizer program on a nonprofit basis. In that year the rice/fertilizer barter ratio was reduced by a sizable margin: the effective price of ammonium sulfate was reduced by 14 percent, that of urea by 26 percent, that of fused phosphate by 13 percent, and that of potassium chloride and calcium ammonium nitrate by 19 percent.[83] The barter ratios were again lowered substantially in 1971 and 1972. In 1973 the government launched a two-year NT$ 2 billion agricultural reconstruction pro-

83. PFB, *Food Production and Activities of Taiwan Provincial Food Bureau*, table 19.

gram and a NT$ 1.8 billion loan program to improve, among other things, rural transportation, cultivation methods, agricultural research and development, and rural community services. If these new efforts continue, 1970 may have marked the end of the extractive phase and the beginning of a new era in agriculture.

10

Postwar Industrialization: Record and Policy

The spectacular performance of Taiwan's manufacturing sector in the postwar period is the envy of most less developed countries. From 1949 to 1973 manufacturing production increased at an average rate of 17.6 percent per year. As a result of this growth, manufacturing, which at the end of World War II was rudimentary except for a sugar industry, had become in the early 1970s the mainstay of the Taiwan economy. In 1973 it produced 31 percent of Taiwan's GDP (in current prices) at factor cost, accounted for over 90 percent (84 percent if processed agricultural goods are excluded) of the exports, and employed more than one-quarter of the labor force. Although most manufacturing enterprises are still small and unincorporated,[1] the number of large enterprises has increased dramatically. Manufacturing enterprises that employed more than 100 workers numbered 387 in 1961, 771 in 1966, and 1,949 in 1971.[2] In 1971 these large and mostly modern enterprises employed 64 percent of the manufacturing labor force, 82 percent of the total assets used in manufacturing, and produced 78 percent of the manufacturing value-added.[3] The purpose of this chapter is to study the process by which rapid industrialization was brought about.

Government economic policies and how they affected the rate and pattern of industrial growth are discussed first. In the 1950s Taiwan followed an inward-looking development strategy based on import substitution in manufacturing. During the early and easy phase of import substitution, this approach appeared to be effective. But by the

---

1. Sixty-nine percent of the 42,488 manufacturing enterprises surveyed by the 1971 industrial and commercial census employed fewer than 10 workers, and 75 percent were unincorporated.
2. Based on the 1961, 1966, and 1971 industrial and commercial censuses.
3. Based on the 1971 industrial and commercial census.

mid-1950s, when that initial stage ended, the economy grew sluggish. Then in the late 1950s and early 1960s, after protracted debate, the government changed its policy and adopted an industrialization strategy that relied heavily on export. The result was a surge in industrial export and production that began in the mid-1960s and continued into the 1970s. In the second part of the chapter, factor inputs and their productivity are examined. Although a large share of the manufacturing output growth is explained by input growth, there remains a substantial residual component. We make the argument that this residue is in effect a reflection of quality improvements in inputs and changes in the rate at which manufacturing capacity was utilized.

DEVELOPMENT STRATEGY AND INDUSTRIAL GROWTH

The postwar growth performance of two-digit manufacturing industries is summarized in table 10.1. The growth rates are arranged into three subperiods (1949–54, 1955–62, and 1963–73) representing the three phases of Taiwan's postwar industrialization: easy import substitution, difficult import substitution and transition to export promotion, and export diversification.

From 1949 to 1954 manufacturing production increased at an average rate of 22 percent a year. While rehabilitation of war-torn industries, particularly in food production, was partly responsible for the rapid rate of growth, import substitution also exerted considerable influence on the pace of industrialization. In this period, significant capacities to produce textile and chemical products heretofore imported were installed. Following the approach used by Chenery, Lewis, and others,[4] Lin calculated that over 91 percent of the increase in nonfood manufacturing production from 1937 (taken as the prewar peak year) to 1954 can be attributed to import substitution, 22 percent to increases

---

4. The change in domestic production can be written as the sum of three components,

$$Y_1 - Y_0 = u_0(D_1 - D_0) + u_0(X_1 - X_0) + (u_1 - u_0)Z_1,$$

where Y is domestic production, X is exports, Z is total supply (import plus production), D is domestic demand (final and intermediate demand), u is the ratio of production to supply, and the subscripts denote the initial and terminal periods. The first term of the above expression is that portion of the increased production attributable to changes in domestic demand, the second is that portion attributable to changes in exports, and the third is that portion attributable to import substitution. For more details, see Hollis B. Chenery, "Patterns of Industrial Gorwth," pp. 639–41, and S. R. Lewis, Jr., *Economic Policy and Industrial Growth in Pakistan* (London: Allen & Unwin, 1969), pp. 20–21.

Table 10.1. Average Annual Growth Rates of Industrial Production, 1949–73 (Percent)

	1949–73	1949–54	1955–62	1963–73
Total	17.6	22.0	10.8	20.1
Food	11.9	28.5	7.3	6.2
Beverages	11.7	16.7	4.7	14.2
Tobacco	8.1	20.8	3.4	4.5
Textiles	26.0	54.9	9.2	22.4
Apparel	—	—	—	25.8
Wood and wood products	15.9	11.0	14.1	19.9
Paper and paper products	17.2	23.0	15.8	15.2
Printing	—	—	—	8.9
Leather products	15.8	24.4	12.7	13.4
Rubber products	20.7	28.3	10.3	24.1
Chemicals	21.2	16.1	16.8	27.3
Products of petroleum and coal	15.8	21.8	8.4	17.9
Nonmetallic mineral products	13.4	13.2	15.6	11.8
Basic metals	19.5	36.8	13.0	14.8
Metal products	20.6	31.9	12.6	20.1
Machinery except electical	17.3	19.9	11.3	20.3
Electrical machinery and supplies	28.8	49.8	24.1	20.7
Transportion equipment	58.9	154.6	26.4	30.2
Miscellaneous	19.2	12.2	5.5	31.3

Sources: MOEA, *The Republic of China, Taiwan Industrial Production Statistics Monthly* July 1963, pp. 8–11, and July 1975, pp. 11–23.

Table 10.2. Import as a Percentage of Supply, Selected Commodities

Commodity	1948	1950	1952	1954	1958	1964
Cotton yarn	79.1	22.0	4.4	0.4	0.0	0.0
Cotton fabric	71.3	58.6	8.8	2.6	0.0	0.2
Iron and steel sheet, bar, plate, and rod	5.6	58.8	36.9	30.5	25.1	25.2
Bicyles	100.0	100.0	54.8	0.4	0.1	0.2
Ammonium sulfate	100.0	100.0	97.2	98.4	95.0	37.2
Flour	46.4	82.5	72.8	5.3	0.0	0.0
Synthetic yarn	0	100.0	100.0	100.0	1.4	0.8
Electric bulbs	59.0	72.2	59.1	47.8	30.7	10.8

Sources: Inspectorate-General of Customs, *The Trade of China*, various issues, and MOEA, *The Republic of China, Taiwan Industrial Production Statistics Monthly*, various issues.

in domestic demand, and −13 percent to changes in export.[5] After 1954 import substitution apparently was less effective as a source of growth. From 1955 to 1962 the average annual growth of manufacturing production slowed to 10.8 percent. Of the growth in nonfood manufacturing output in this period, 91 percent resulted from increases in domestic demand, and the contribution of import substitution on the aggregate level was a negative 2 percent.[6]

However, when viewed at the industry or commodity level, where its impact can be more accurately gauged, import substitution continued to be significant into the 1960s. Table 10.2 presents the share of imports to total supply for a number of important manufactured commodities. In the late 1940s and early 1950s import substitution was most notably successful in cotton textiles. By 1952 however, cotton textile production had reached the limit of the domestic market, and import substitution shifted to other commodities, e.g., synthetic yarn, bicycles, and flour. Because of the limited domestic market, import substitution, once begun, was achieved quickly in those industries where technology was relatively simple. For example, it took only four years for Taiwan to create the capacity to supply its domestic needs in cotton textiles, bicycles, and flour. In the more sophisticated industries, success took longer. Efforts in the early 1950s to substitute domestic chemical fertilizers for imports did not come to fruition until the early 1960s; in 1958, imports still accounted for 95 percent of Taiwan's supply of ammonium sulfate.

In table 10.3 trade and production of manufactured commodities are aggregated into 15 industries, and the ratio of imports to total supply for each of these industries is presented. These ratios confirm that by 1954 Taiwan had pretty much exhausted its import substitution opportunities in the obvious areas such as textiles. Import substitution, however, continued in a number of other industries. Of the 15 industrial groups in table 10.3, the import coefficient $[M/(M + P)]$ of 10 decreased during 1954–61, but in several (e.g., food and basic metals) the decrease was extremely slight; hence significance should not be attached to them. Although the process was less dramatic than the one that operated earlier in the textile industry, import substitution was nevertheless prominent in several industries, especially rubber products, leather and leather products, petroleum and coal products, and

5. [Ken] Ching-yuan Lin, *Industrialization in Taiwan, 1946–1972*, p. 68.
6. Ibid.

Table 10.3. Import Coefficients by Manufacturing Industry: 1954, 1961, 1966

	Import as percentage of supply [(M/P + M) × 100]			Changes in import coefficients[a]	
	1954	*1961*	*1966*	$m_{1961}-m_{1954}$	$m_{1966}-m_{1961}$
Food, beverages, and tobacco	2.6	2.1	1.7	−.005	−.004
Textiles	3.8	5.8	9.5	.020	.037
Wood and wood products	3.9	0.3	0.5	−.036	.002
Paper, paper products, and printing	12.3	9.9	11.9	−.024	.020
Leather and leather products	44.6	36.9	44.4	−.077	.075
Rubber products	37.6	27.5	22.2	−.101	−.053
Chemicals	38.0	34.1	22.7	−.039	−.114
Petroleum and coal products	16.8	5.5	29.5	−.113	.240
Nonmetallic mineral products	8.9	5.4	7.6	−.035	.022
Basic metals	35.5	35.0	40.5	−.005	.055
Metal products	49.2	31.5	44.5	−.177	.130
Machinery	52.4	69.1	60.0	.297	−.091
Electrical products	53.6	55.8	30.7	.022	−.251
Transport equipment	25.6	48.9	48.4	.233	−.005
Miscellaneous	33.8	45.8	93.1	.120	.473
Total	16.4	18.3	19.1	.019	.008

Sources: Inspectorate-General of Customs, *The Trade of China*, various issues; *General Report on Industry and Commerce Census of Taiwan, 1954*, pp. 38–45; *General Report, 1961 Industry and Commerce Census of Taiwan*, vol. 3, pp. 750–51; and *General Report on The Third Industrial and Commercial Census of Taiwan*, vol. 3, pp. 1–18.
[a] $m = M/(P + M)$, where M is import and P is domestic production.

metal products. But because capital imports increased dramatically (e.g., the import coefficients for machinery and transport equipment increased by .297 and .233, respectively), the import share for all manufactured commodities increased slightly, from 16 percent in 1954 to 18 percent in 1961. After 1961 import substitution was important in only two industries. Previous investments in the chemical fertilizer and other chemical industries finally paid off in the early 1960s, and the import coefficient for chemicals declined by .114 during 1961–66. Electrical products is the other commodity group in which the import coefficient declined significantly, falling from .558 to .307.

To promote import substitution, Taiwan employed the usual policy package of tariffs, import controls, and multiple exchange rates.[7] Between 1948 and 1955 the average nominal tariff rate for all imports more than doubled, rising from 20 to nearly 45 percent.[8] Estimates of effective tariff rates, the more appropriate measure of protection, indicate that they were substantially higher than the nominal rates and that protection was greater for nondurable consumer goods than for either intermediate or capital goods.[9] Import quotas were also used. After 1951 imports were classified into four categories: permissible, controlled, suspended, and prohibited. The permissible category included essential capital equipment, raw materials, and essential consumer goods, all of which were importable within the prescribed quotas. The controlled and suspended lists included commodities that were either altogether banned or could be imported only under special conditions, usually by government agencies. The prohibited category comprised goods considered dangerous or luxury items. Of the approximately 500 groups of commodities classified during the early 1950s, 55 percent were in the permissible category, 40 percent in the suspended and controlled categories, and 5 percent in the prohibited category. In the mid-1950s controls became even tighter as many commodities were switched from the permissible to the suspended and controlled categories.[10] In the 1950s the government also kept the

7. Exchange and trade regulations in Taiwan are regularly reviewed in IMF, *Annual Report of Exchange Restrictions.* The U.S. Department of Commerce has also published periodic surveys of Taiwan's exchange and trade controls, e.g., see "Licensing and Exchange Controls—Taiwan," *World Trade Information Service,* pt. 2, nos. 54-7, 59-12, 62-22, and "Foreign Trade Regulations of Taiwan," *Overseas Business Report,* no. 64-89. A less complete but nonetheless useful survey of Taiwan's exchange and trade regulations is in Lih-yong Chang, "Economic Development under Foreign Aid and Preparation for War," chap. 7. For a summary of the more important changes in Taiwan's exchange rate arranged in tabular form, see table A66.

8. Yu-chi Tao, *The Tariff System of the Republic of China* (Taipei, 1969), pp. 175–78.

9. The most comprehensive studies of effective protection in Taiwan and the ones we rely most heavily on are Fu-chi Liu, "The Effective Protective Rates Under the Existing Tariff Structure in Taiwan," in Executive Yuan Tax Reform Commission, *The Report of the Executive Yuan Tax Reform Commission,* June 1970, pt. 3, pp. 379–466; and Mo-huan Hsing, John H. Power, and Gerardo P. Sicat, *Taiwan and the Philippines: Industrialization and Trade Policies,* pp. 238–66. Besides these sources, also see I-shuan Sun, "Trade Policies and Economic Development in Taiwan," and Teng-hui Lee and Kuo-shu Liang, "The Structure of Protection in Taiwan."

10. Among goods suspended or controlled in the mid-1950s were cotton yarn and fabrics, woolen yarn and fabrics, man-made fibers and yarn, ammonium sulfate and other chemical fertilizers, wheat flour, monosodium glutamate, plywood, leather and leather products, cement, paper, rubber products, aluminum ingots and products thereof, sewing machines, bicycles and bicycle parts, and soap and cleaning compounds.

Table 10.4. Comparison of Domestic Prices and Import Costs of Selected Manufactured
Commodities, 1953

Commodity	Ratio of domestic wholesale price[a] to import cost[b] (1)	Ratio of import cost inclusive of tariff to import cost[c] (2)	(1)–(2) (3)
Wheat	1.68	1.20	0.48
Soybean	2.55	1.14	1.41
Dried cuttlefish	2.71	1.75	0.96
Cotton yarn	1.34	1.08	0.26
Cotton piece goods (gray)	1.78	1.26–1.39	0.52–0.39
Cotton piece goods (poplin)	2.89	1.26–1.32	1.63–1.57
Woolen yarn, B.B.	4.17	1.30	2.87
Gunny bag	2.45	1.33	1.12
Leather	1.47	1.26	0.21
Sheet glass	2.15	1.51	0.64
Sulfur black	2.22	1.75	0.47
Soda ash	4.07	1.33	2.74
Ammonium sulfate	2.10	1.08	1.02

Sources: Based on price data in Chi-yeh Hsia, "Import Prices Under Foreign Exchange
Control," *Financial and Economic Monthly*, Dec. 1954, pp. 24–27; and Ching-yuan
Lin, *Industrialization in Taiwan, 1946–72*, p. 51.
[a] Average monthly wholesale prices from January to June (or July) in Taipei.
[b] Import cost is either CIF cost or CIF cost plus interest and banking charges.
[c] Tariff includes harbor dues and the 20% increase in the CIF tax base. In 1953 there was
no defense surtax on imports.

NT$ overvalued and maintained a multiple exchange rate system that
applied lower rates to exports than to imports, and within imports,
lower rates to capital equipment and raw materials (when purchased
by end users) than to other goods.[11]

These exchange and trade controls promoted import substitution by
effectively sealing off many of Taiwan's consumer goods markets from
foreign competition and by conserving foreign exchange for capital
and raw material imports. Consider, first, the protection these controls
provided to Taiwan's manufacturing industries in the 1950s. Table
10.4 compares the domestic wholesale prices with world prices of a
group of fairly important manufactured commodities, mostly nondurable consumer goods, that were on the controlled or suspended
lists in the 1950s. Because the world and domestic prices were some-

11. For annual changes, see IMF, *Annual Report on Exchange Restrictions*.

times not for products of the same quality, the comparison is not precise. With this in mind, let us examine the estimated effects of tariffs and controls. Column (1) in the table gives the ratio of wholesale price to import cost (CIF cost or CIF cost plus interests and banking charges) for each of the selected items. For our purpose, import cost may be considered the world price. In effect, column 1 is a measure of the protection given to these commodities by the entire protective structure of tariffs and controls. Column 2 shows the ratio of import cost inclusive of tariff to import cost and is essentially a measure of the protection provided by tariffs alone. The difference between columns 1 and 2 is an estimate of the extent to which domestic prices were affected by factors other than tariff, the chief one being import controls. In all cases domestic prices were higher than import costs inclusive of tariffs by substantial margins, indicating that during the early 1950s direct licensing or quota was the effective constraint on imports.

By prohibiting the importation of luxury goods and controlling the imports of other consumer goods, the government hoped to conserve foreign exchange for capital and raw material imports. To this end, the exchange and trade controls were largely successful. During 1952–60, as a share of total imports, capital imports accounted for 23 percent, raw material imports 67 percent, and consumer good imports only 10 percent.[12] Industrial production and investment were encouraged by another aspect of the system. The multiple exchange rate system applied an appreciably lower rate to imported capital equipment and raw materials during a period when even the higher rates applied to other imports overvalued the NT$. The exchange rate applied to essential raw materials and capital equipment imported by end users was NT$ 15.65 per US$ in 1953, NT$ 18.78 per US$ in 1954, NT$ 24.78 per US$ in 1955–57, and NT$ 36.38 per US$ in 1958. During this period the average market rate per US$ was NT$ 26.49 in 1953, NT$ 30.31 in 1954, NT$ 39.84 in 1955, NT$ 38.53 in 1956, NT$ 38.40 in 1957, and NT$ 46.58 in 1958.

Although Taiwan's import substitution policy encouraged industrialization, it did not solve, as the government had hoped, the balance-of-payments problem. By decreasing the import of consumer goods and stimulating the import of intermediate and capital goods, import substitution altered the import structure but did not reduce the total

12. CIECD, *Taiwan Statistical Data Book*, 1973, p. 168.

demand for imports. Indeed, during the 1950s imports increased at a faster rate than national income, so the share of imports in total supply (GDP plus imports) increased slightly, rising from less than 14 percent in 1951 to over 15 percent in 1961.[13] Therefore, a large deficit on goods and services, amounting to almost 40 percent of total imports, persisted throughout the 1950s, with the deficit financed primarily by U.S. aid.[14]

The overvalued NT$ also proved to be detrimental to efficient economic growth and aggravated the balance-of-payments problem. By lowering the effective price of capital imports to Taiwan's industrialists, overvaluation encouraged a higher capital intensity in production than would have been the case had foreign exchange been priced at its equilibrium level. Since the larger government enterprises and private corporations had easier access to foreign exchange, the overvalued NT$ may be one reason that large-scale enterprises were significantly more capital intensive than the smaller firms.[15] The overvalued NT$ may have also increased the need to import because the undervalued foreign exchange encouraged local industrialists not only to import capital equipment but also to develop industries that were dependent on imports for raw materials, e.g., flour and vegetable oil. Although the government, through its licensing power, was able to regulate the establishment of new factories, it could not easily control the attempts of existing firms to buy materials from the cheapest source, which, with an overvalued NT$, often meant importing them. The net effect, of course, was to increase the need to import.

The major difficulty and the most damaging effect of the overvalued NT$ was that it penalized exports and discouraged development of export-competing industries. Traditional export industries, such as sugar, which expanded so rapidly during the colonial period, became sluggish. From 1953 to 1960 food constituted from 70 to 90 percent of Taiwan's total exports by value.[16] During this period the food component of Taiwan's export volume index grew at a rate of only 2 percent a year.[17] Because, during the 1950s, Taiwan exported pri-

13. DGBAS, *National Income of the Republic of China*, 1970, pp. 156–57.

14. IMF, *Balance of Payments Yearbook*, various years.

15. For example, in 1966 the average total asset in operation per worker was NT$ 53,000 for enterprises employing fewer than 50 workers but over NT$ 216,000 for enterprises employing 100 or more workers (see *General Report on the Third Industrial and Commercial Census of Taiwan*, vol. 3, pp. 579–620).

16. Inspectorate-General of Customs, *The Trade of China*, various issues.

17. DGBAS, *Statistical Abstract of the Republic of China*, 1963, p. 132.

marily agricultural and processed agricultural commodities, the combined effect of a depressed export market and high prices for imports
and import substitutes was to alter the internal terms of trade between
agriculture and industry in favor of industry. The ratio of the index
of prices paid by farmers to that received by farmers (with 1935–37 = 1)
was 1.06 in 1937, 1.11 in 1950, and 1.41 in 1954.[18] Although the overvalued NT$, by transferring income from the export sector to the
import substitute sector, or from agriculture to industry, supported
industrialization, it also made entrance into the export market difficult
for new industries that had completed their import substitution phase
of development. The export of manufactured goods showed almost no
advance from 1953 to 1956. Most seriously affected was the textile
industry, whose index of production (with 1954 = 100), after rising
rapidly and steadily from 3 in 1946 to 100 in 1954, was 105 in 1955,
99 in 1956, 109 in 1957, and 106 in 1958.[19]

Thus, in the mid-1950s, with the easy phase of import substitution
completed and the export sector depressed, it became increasingly
more difficult to maintain a rapid rate of industrialization. For growth
to continue, either the manufacturing sector had to move into intermediate and capital goods production or the recently established
import substitution activities, primarily in nondurable consumer
goods, had to penetrate the world market. But given the existing
controls and the prevailing industrial environment, neither alternative
seemed likely to succeed. Faced with increasing economic difficulties,
and with encouragement from the local U.S. AID Mission, the government began in 1958 to rationalize the existing import substitution policy
package and to reduce, if not remove, some of its more blatant dis-
criminatory features against the export sector.

Between 1958 and 1963 the government initiated numerous reforms
and new programs to stimulate industrialization and export.[20] Grad-

18. Teng-hui Lee, "Interesectoral Capital Flows in the Economic Development of
Taiwan, 1895–1960," pp. 363–64.
19. MOEA, *The Republic of China, Taiwan Industrial Production Statistics Monthly,*
Dec. 1962, pp. 4–7.
20. One of the most significant developments in this period was the adoption, after
protracted dialogue among policymakers, of the 19-point economic reform program by
the Executive Yuan in January 1960. This program committed the government to, among
other things, encourage savings and investments, remove controls and hidden subsidies,
strengthen tax administration, improve its budget system, develop money and capital
markets, establish a unitary foreign exchange rate, liberalize trade control, and promote
the development of trade. Major changes in regulations are contained in "Regulations
Governing Sale and Purchase of Foreign Exchange Certificates" (promulgated on Apr.

ually, over a period of several years, the NT$ was devalued and the multiple exchange rate system dismantled to end one of the most discriminatory features of Taiwan's import substitution policy.[21] The allocation of foreign exchange for permissible imports was simplified and rationalized. Some goods on the controlled and suspended lists were decontrolled, and more stringent criteria were established to screen products for the controlled list. By these actions the government reduced the level of protection on a large number of nondurable consumer goods and relied increasingly on tariffs rather than quotas to restrict imports.[22] Existing export promotion schemes were expanded and strengthened and new ones introduced. Loans to exporters were provided at low preferential rates. A tax incentive that permitted the rebate of custom duties paid on raw material imports used in the manufacturing of handicraft exports, first introduced in the early 1950s, was expanded to all exports with the remission broadened to include, besides custom duties, commodity tax, defense surtax, harbor dues, salt tax, and slaughter tax.[23] To regulate production and to promote the orderly expansion of export industries, the government approved and supported the formation of export cartels,[24] and on occasion it also restricted investments in overexpanded industries.[25]

14, 1958, and revised on Dec. 12, 1958, and Aug. 8, 1959), "Regulations Governing the Application for Import Exchange by Private Traders" (promulgated on Apr. 13, 1958, and revised on Sept. 12, 1959), "Criteria Governing the Control of Imports" (promulgated on July 27, 1960), "Regulations for Promoting Exports of Products Processed with Imported Raw Materials" (promulgated on Sept. 12, 1959), and "Regulations for Refund of Taxes and Duties on Export Products" (promulgated on Dec. 26, 1958). For discussions of these reforms, see Sze-song Sun, "Export Credit and Export Promotion in the Republic of China," *Foreign Trade Quarterly* (Board of Foreign Trade, MOEA), June 1969, pp. 26–38; Shun-hsin Chou, "The Impact of Fiscal Incentives on the Development of Manufacturing Industries in Taiwan," U.N. Center for Industrial Development, Feb. 1966, mimeo; Hsien-ding Fong, "Taiwan's Industrialization, with Special Reference to Policies and Controls;" and Lin, *Industrialization in Taiwan*.

21. From the beginning of 1958 to the middle of 1959, the NT$ was devalued, depending on the type of transaction, by 50–80 percent.

22. The level of protection for most intermediate and capital goods remained high (see Hsing et al., *Industrialization and Trade Policies*, pp. 242–43).

23. From NT$ 39 million in 1956, remission of taxes on raw materials used in producing industrial exports climbed rapidly to NT$ 303 million in 1960, NT$ 1,496 million in 1964, and NT$ 2,320 million in 1967.

24. In 1972 industries with cartel arrangements included cotton and woolen textiles, paper, steel products, rubber products, monosodium glutamate, cement, canned mushrooms and asparagus, and citronella oil. Production is regulated by the allocation of export quotas.

25. For details on the changing regulations governing the establishment of new factories in manufacturing industries, see Hsing et al., *Industrialization and Trade Policies*, table 5.1, and Lin, *Industrialization in Taiwan*, appendix table A-26.

At first, administrative complexities and continued government control over foreign exchange and imports reduced the effectiveness of these export incentives.[26] However, since 1962 additional reforms and further relaxation of controls have made the export incentives progressively more effective. But some administrative difficulties have persisted. To bypass these difficulties and to make Taiwan more attractive to foreign investors, the government in 1965 enacted the Statute for the Establishment and Management of Export Processing Zones. In 1966 the first export processing zone was established in the southern port city of Kaohsiung.

The export processing zone combines the advantages of an industrial estate with those of a free port. Firms in the zones enjoy all privileges and tax incentives provided to export producers in Taiwan, but without the red tape. Official transactions, from investment application to foreign exchange settlement, are handled by one agency. Furthermore, customs duties, commodity tax, and sales tax are not levied, thus bypassing the bureaucratic procedures of tax rebate. However, only firms in approved industries and those willing to meet certain other conditions are allowed to operate in these zones.[27] For example, excluded are export industries already established in Taiwan. In the late 1960s and early 1970s, precision, labor-using, and relatively high value-added industries (e.g., precision machinery, electronics, optical equipment, and plastic products) were given priority for admission to the zones.

Notwithstanding its slow start, the export processing zones have become a major force in the economy. In 1975, three zones (in Kaohsiung, Nantze, and Taichung) were in operation with a fourth in the planning stage. At the end of 1973, 290 factories were located in the three zones, of which 222 were in operation.[28] The combined investments of these firms exceeded US$ 148 million. In 1973 the three export-processing zones employed 78,000 workers (55,000 in Kaohsiung, 15,000 in Nantze, and 8,000 in Taichung). Exports from the

26. For example, in the early 1960s the average time required to obtain the remission of tax paid on exported goods was two months. Given the high cost of money, the delay was expensive and tended to discourage production for export. For other examples, see Fong, "Taiwan's Industrialization,"pp. 378–90.

27. For details of the regulations, see Export Processing Zone Administration, *Laws and Regulations Concerning Export Processing Zones in the Republic of China*, Aug. 1965. Useful information is also found in *KEPZ Answers*, May 1970, and *NEPZ Answers*, Jan. 1971.

28. This and the other figures in this paragraph are from the *Free China Weekly*, Feb. 3, 1974, p. 1.

zones increased from US$ 8 million in 1967 to US$ 405 million, or about 9 percent of Taiwan's total export in 1973.

The main impact of the post-1958 liberalization reforms was on exports. The substantial devaluation of the NT$ that resulted from elimination of the multiple exchange rate system, and the strengthening of export incentives such as the tax rebate system introduced powerful new forces into the economy to stimulate exports. By changing critical price relationships, the post-1958 reforms made it more profitable for domestic producers to export. For example, in 1953 Lin calculated that for every US$ a Taiwan producer of cotton yarn saved by import substitution, he received NT$ 22.13.[29] However, for every US$ he earned by exporting cotton yarn, he received only NT$ 15.55. But in 1966, partly as the result of devaluation and the extension of export incentives to the textile industry, the producer received NT$ 46.41 for every US$ he saved by import substitution but NT$ 60.35 for every US$ he earned by exporting. In other words, in the eyes of cotton yarn producers, the price relationships have reversed and producing for export has become substantially more profitable than producing for the domestic market. Similar changes in price relationships undoubtedly occurred in many other industries, although perhaps not so dramatic as those in the cotton textile industry.

In the wake of the post-1958 reforms, exports surged ahead. Exports, as a share of GDP (both in 1966 NT$), were 10 percent in 1952, 12 percent in 1962, and 39 percent in 1972.[30] Other measures of export performance are presented in table 10.5. Between 1952 and 1962, before the reforms were fully implemented, the value of Taiwan's exports in US$ increased at an average rate of 8.8 percent a year. After the reforms (1962–72) the average rate of increase of exports more than tripled to nearly 30 percent a year. The export quantum index displayed a similar pattern of growth as export value, increasing at 8.7 percent a year from 1952 to 1962 and at nearly 26 percent since 1962. Although Taiwan's export boom was brought about by many factors, not the least being the Vietnam War, the most significant was the new economic environment created by the post-1958 reforms.[31]

Almost all categories of exports have been affected by the boom.

29. This figure and the other examples in this paragraph were derived by Lin in his *Industrialization in Taiwan*, pp. 111–15.

30. CIECD, *Data Book*, p. 27.

31. Because the United States did not classify Taiwan as one of the 19 financially strong nations, South Vietnam was allowed to procure U.S.-aid-financed imports from Taiwan.

Table 10.5. Export Performance, 1952–72

	1952	1957	1962	1967	1972	Growth rate 1952–62	Growth rate 1962–72
Value of exports (US$ million)							
Total	119.5	168.5	244.4	675.1	3,114.1	8.8	29.7
Agricultural products	32.2	28.1	31.0	118.0	226.0	15.6	24.2
Processed agricultural products	81.6	125.8	89.3	159.4	307.2	2.6	15.5
Industrial products	5.7	14.6	124.1	397.7	2,580.8	40.1	36.0
Export quantum index (1966 = 100)							
General index	23.4	33.9	44.8	116.1	436.8	8.7	25.8
Agricultural and fishery products	—	—	30.0	101.5	154.3	—	22.5
Minerals	—	—	169.7	109.1	35.1	—	−27.9
Food, beverages, and tobacco	—	—	56.6	98.1	123.3	—	8.7
Textile, leather, and wood products	—	—	46.5	132.7	693.4	—	31.5
Nonmetallic mineral prods.	—	—	62.0	118.5	209.9	—	15.8
Chemicals and chemical products	—	—	79.4	120.9	187.2	—	9.8
Basic metals	—	—	46.5	108.8	416.4	—	27.7
Metal products	—	—	35.7	129.7	1,211.7	—	44.2
Miscellaneous manufacturing products	—	—	9.2	146.5	2,145.7	—	76.7

Sources: The value figures are based on exchange settlement data collected by the Bank of Taiwan and the Central Bank of China and reproduced in CIECD, *Taiwan Statistical Data Book*, 1973, pp. 167–68. The export quantum index is based on customs statistics and is published in DGBAS, *Statistical Abstract of the Republic of China*, 1973, pp. 268–71.

The exports of agricultural products and processed agricultural products, which moved sluggishly in the 1950s, showed marked improvements in the 1960s. For example, the export of processed agricultural goods, by far the most important export category in the 1950s, increased at an average annual rate of 2.6 percent in 1952–62 but at 15.5 in 1962–72.[32] More important was the development of the new industrial exports. In the 1950s the export of industrial products

32. Several new processed agricultural goods became important export items in the 1960s. In 1958 canned asparagus and mushrooms were not produced in Taiwan. By the late 1960s the annual rates of production averaged 5 and 3 million boxes, respectively, much of it exported.

indeed grew very rapidly, but because they started from a very small base, their high growth rate is somewhat misleading. The growth of industrial exports in the 1960s, now measured from a much enlarged base, continued to be impressive, averaging 36 percent a year. Particularly strong growth was registered in three major export categories: textile, leather, and wood products at an average annual rate of 31.5 percent, basic metals at 27.7, and metal products at 44.2. The increased diversification in export and the regular appearance of new export goods suggest that Taiwan has acquired the valuable ability to export substitute.

The strong export performance in the 1960s and early 1970s also brought about a significant improvement in Taiwan's balance of payment. Although in the 1960s Taiwan showed a trade deficit in every year except 1964, the deficit as a share of import declined steadily. Import surplus was 40 percent of imports in 1961, 14 percent in 1965, and less than 2 percent in 1969. In the first three years of the 1970s Taiwan had trade surpluses of US$ 89, 291, and 648 million, respectively.[33] Thus, despite the cessation of United States economic aid in 1965, Taiwan's improved trade position, plus the influx of foreign investments attracted by the new economic environment, enabled it to noticeably strengthen its international reserve position in the late 1960s and early 1970s.[34]

Primarily because of the export boom, industrial growth accelerated in the 1960s. From 1963 to 1973 manufacturing production increased at an average rate of over 20 percent a year (table 10.1). Lin estimates that export accounted for one-quarter of the growth in Taiwan's non-food manufacturing output in the 1960s.[35] Table 10.6, which lists the export shares of major manufacturing industries, provides additional evidence of export's contribution to Taiwan's industrialization. With the notable exception of food, a traditional export industry, the export share of nearly all other industries increased dramatically in the 1960s. In 1961 no manufacturing industry exported more than one-quarter of its production. In 1969 industries that exported at least one-quarter of their production included textiles and apparel (38.9 percent), wood products (49.5), leather and leather products (35.2), rubber products

33. CIECD, *Data Book*, p. 159.
34. Foreign asset holdings of Taiwan's banking system increased from NT$ 17 billion in 1968 to NT$ 36 billion in 1971 and NT$ 75 billion in 1974 (see CBC, *The Republic of China, Taiwan Financial Statistics Monthly*, Aug. 1975, pp. 9–12).
35. Lin, *Industrialization in Taiwan*, table 4–3.

Table 10.6. Export as a Percentage of Production, by Industry

	1961	1966	1969
Food	20.8	24.7	23.6
Textiles and apparel	19.6	25.6	38.9
Wood products and furniture	22.7	44.7	49.5
Paper and pulp	5.7	12.7	7.1
Leather and leather products	2.3	16.9	35.2
Rubber products	16.9	20.8	36.9
Chemical fertilizers	4.7	5.5	8.9
Pharmaceuticals	3.1	3.1	7.6
Plastics and plastics products	12.0	26.9	44.2
Other chemicals	14.7	8.3	5.6
Petroleum products	5.0	4.4	11.5
Nonmetallic mineral products	8.7	19.4	14.6
Products of iron and steel	10.6	16.1	16.4
Aluminum and aluminum products	11.9	14.1	18.4
Other metals and metal products	5.3	33.7	24.5
Machinery (not electrical)	3.4	15.4	27.8
Electrical machinery, appliances, and supplies	10.2	19.5	36.3
Transport equipment	0.7	7.1	10.1
Miscellaneous manufacturing products	4.8	15.4	34.2

Sources: Based on input–output tables compiled by CIECD. Production is priced at factor cost.

(36.9), plastic products (44.2), machinery (27.8), and electrical machinery, appliances, and supplies (36.3). Quite clearly, by the end of the 1960s the growth of Taiwan's manufacturing sector was fueled by export expansion.

Import substitution in the 1950s and the development of export industries in the 1960s combined to alter the structure of Taiwan's manufacturing sector. Table 10.7 compares the distribution of real GDP at factor costs originating in the manufacturing sector by major industries. As a share of value-added originating in manufacturing, food processing, traditionally the most important manufacturing industry in Taiwan, accounted for about 25 percent in 1952–54, 29 percent in 1959–61, but only 10 percent in 1967–69. Besides food, the shares of other traditional industries, e.g., beverage, tobacco, wood products, and leather products, also declined. By 1952–54 import substitution had already established textiles as the leading nonfood manufacturing industry in Taiwan. In the 1950s, because of textile's sluggish growth, its relative position in manufacturing value-added declined, falling from 24.1 percent in 1952–54 to 16.6 percent in 1959–61.

Table 10.7. Composition of Manufacturing Sector and Allocation of Change
(Percentage of total)

	Distribution of real GDP at factor cost by industry			Allocation of net increase by industry	
	1952–54	*1959–61*	*1967–69*	*52–54/59–61*	*59–61/67–69*
Total	100.0	100.0	100.0	100.0	100.0
Food	24.5	29.0	10.2	32.5	0.8
Beverage	0.3	0.5	0.4	0.6	0.4
Tobacco	6.5	3.2	2.6	0.5	2.2
Textile and apparel	24.1	16.6	19.8	10.3	21.4
Wood and wood products	6.3	5.3	3.7	4.4	2.9
Paper and paper products	7.0	9.9	8.2	12.3	7.4
Leather and leather products	0.5	0.2	0.1	−0.1	a
Rubber products	1.2	1.3	1.2	1.4	1.2
Chemical and chemical products	11.0	8.7	14.4	6.7	17.4
Products of petroleum and coal	3.7	3.2	4.6	2.7	5.4
Nonmetallic mineral products	4.2	6.6	6.2	8.4	6.1
Basic metals	1.2	3.4	1.8	5.2	1.0
Metal products	1.3	2.4	3.1	3.3	3.5
Machinery	1.7	2.5	4.2	3.1	5.1
Electrical machinery, appliances, supplies	1.1	2.1	10.2	3.1	14.3
Transport equipment	1.4	3.6	6.7	5.4	8.3
Miscellaneous	3.0	1.4	2.2	0.1	2.6

Notes and Sources: Value-added (GDP at factor cost) figures at current prices are from
DGBAS, *National Income of the Republic of China*, 1970, pp. 126–27. They are then
deflated by the appropriate price indexes of industrial products presented in table A52.
ᵃ Less than 0.05%.

However, in the 1960s Taiwan's outward-looking strategy revived the
floundering textile industry, whose growth accounted for nearly one-
quarter of the net increase in manufacturing value-added. By the late
1960s textiles was Taiwan's most important manufacturing industry,
accounting for about 20 percent of the value-added originating in
manufacturing and almost 30 percent of Taiwan's total export.

   Nearly all other branches of manufacturing listed in table 10.7 not
already mentioned are new industries, developed in the postwar period.
Except for chemical and chemical products none of them exerted
much influence in the early 1950s. Together they (all industries from

chemical to transport equipment in table 10.7) accounted for about 25 percent of the manufacturing value-added in 1952–54, of which nearly half was from the chemical industry. It is the growth of this group of new industries that has been steadiest and most vigorous. They accounted for 38 percent of the net increase in manufacturing value-added between 1952–54 and 1959–61 and for 61 percent of the increase between 1959–61 and 1967–69. By 1967–69 their relative share in the value-added originating in the manufacturing sector exceeded 50 percent. Clearly, in the future the performance of these new industries will have a profound effect on how well Taiwan's economy as a whole will perform.

Except for a number of understandable differences, the structural changes in Taiwan's manufacturing sector conform fairly closely to what Chenery and Taylor determined as the normal pattern of change in a period of rising income for small, resource-poor, trade-oriented economies.[36] In table 10.8 Taiwan's manufacturing industries are grouped, according to the classification used by Chenery and Taylor, into early, middle, and late industries, and their contributions to real GDP at factor cost are presented for three periods: 1952–54, 1959–61, and 1967–69. In the 1950s the structure of Taiwan's manufacturing sector differed in two major respects from the norm: (1) In the early 1950s, given Taiwan's income level, the share of early industries was significantly below the norm,[37] and (2) from 1952–54 to 1959–61, when per capita income increased in Taiwan, the share of early industries in GDP, contrary to the normal pattern, increased rather than decreased. The first discrepancy is attributable to the fact that in 1952 Taiwan's food industry (the most important of the early industries) was in a state of disequilibrium, still not fully adjusted to the loss of the Japanese market. The second discrepancy can be interpreted as a movement by the food industry toward its equilibrium position, i.e., toward the norm observed by Chenery and Taylor. Significantly, after 1959–61, consistent with the normal pattern, the share of early industries in GDP declined as Taiwan's per capita income increased.

Aside from the behavior of the early industries in the 1950s, the changing patterns of Taiwan's industries were roughly consistent with

36. Hollis B. Chenery and Lance Taylor, "Development Patterns: Among Countries and Over Time."

37. Given Taiwan's per capita GNP in 1952–54 (about US$ 150), the normal share of early industries should be over 8 percent. The actual share found in Taiwan was 6.5 percent.

Table 10.8. Contribution to Real GDP by Early, Middle, and Late Industries

	Percentage of real GDP at factor cost			Percentage allocation of increase in manufacturing value-added in constant NT$		
	1952–54	1959–61	1967–69	52–54/59–61	59–61/67–69	52–54/67–69
I. *Early industries*	6.5	7.7	7.0	40.1	20.6	24.8
Food, beverages, and tobacco	3.8	5.5	3.2			
Leather	0.1	a	a			
Textiles	2.6	2.2	3.8			
II. *Middle industries*	3.2	4.2	7.3	23.7	32.9	31.0
Nonmetallic mineral products	0.5	1.1	1.5			
Rubber products	0.1	0.2	0.3			
Wood and wood products	0.8	0.9	0.9			
Chemicals and products of petroleum and coal	1.8	2.0	4.6			
III. *Late industries*	2.0	4.7	9.3	36.0	44.2	42.5
Apparel	0.4	0.6	1.0			
Paper and paper products	0.8	1.7	2.0			
Basic metals	0.1	0.6	0.4			
Metal products, machinery (including electrical machinery), and transport equipment	0.7	1.8	5.9			
IV. *I + II + III*	11.7	16.6	23.6	99.8	97.7	98.3

Note and Source: Miscellaneous manufacturing industries are not included. For source, see table 10.7.
a Less than 0.05%.

the norm, although as to be expected the actual rates of change differed somewhat. In Taiwan, as elsewhere, the growth of the middle industries centered on two major sectors: chemicals and products of petroleum and coal and nonmetallic mineral products. Whereas growth of the chemical, petroleum, and coal industries was largely a matter of import substitution, that of the nonmetallic mineral industry was also strongly stimulated by export demand. By 1963–64, about 40 percent of Taiwan's cement production was exported. As predicted by the normal pattern, Taiwan's late industries have grown fastest of all, exceeding the growth of GDP by a substantial margin throughout the 1950s and 1960s. By the late 1960s the contribution of Taiwan's late industries to GNP was about 9 percent, higher than the norm. Because several of Taiwan's late industries, e.g., metal products and machinery, are strongly export oriented, one suspects that their above-norm performance is mostly a consequence of Taiwan's much-above-average export performance in the 1960s.

INPUTS AND INDUSTRIAL GROWTH

In this section the growth of labor and that of capital are examined. Industrial growth in Taiwan was brought about in part by the rapid increase in primary inputs. Indeed, an elastic supply of labor and continual large industrial investments are two of the principal reasons that Taiwan was able to industrialize at such a rapid pace. The reform in economic policy also helped because it permitted Taiwan to use its resources more efficiently.

Labor

For various reasons that are elaborated in the statistical appendix, the annual employment statistics derived from the Household Registration Records and those collected by the Provincial Department of Reconstruction are believed to be unreliable. Therefore, for the purpose of analyzing the growth trend and structural changes of Taiwan's manufacturing employment, we rely primarily on the industrial and commercial censuses conducted in 1954, 1961, 1966, and 1971 and the labor force surveys conducted quarterly since 1964.[38]

38. Besides the commercial and industrial censuses, employment information can also be obtained from the 1956 and 1966 population censuses and from the numerous mining and manufacturing surveys conducted in the 1960s. However, the employment figures provided by the last mentioned are very confusing, unreasonably low in the

Table 10.9 gives the growth and distribution of manufacturing employment by major industries for the census years. From 1954 to 1966, according to the censuses, employment in manufacturing increased by 90 percent (or less than 6 percent a year), from 310,000 to 590,000. However, the 1966 census excluded some small processing and repair establishments that were included in the earlier censuses, so the census figures understate the increase in employment.[39] The quarterly labor force surveys found manufacturing employment in 1966 to be 629,000, or 6.6 percent higher than the 1966 census figure. Thus, between 1954 and 1966 manufacturing employment probably doubled. The labor force surveys show that after 1966 the growth of manufacturing employment accelerated. From 1966 to 1974 manufacturing employment increased at an annual rate of 12.8 percent, indicating a significant rise in the tempo of industrialization.[40] This is, of course, consistent with the growth pattern of manufacturing output.

Within manufacturing, much of the increase in employment was in three industries: food, textiles, and chemicals and chemical products. From 1954 to 1966 they absorbed 55 percent of the total increase in manufacturing employment. After 1966 employment in the food industry advanced only slightly but employment in the textile and chemical industries continued to rise rapidly. From 1966 to 1971 the food industry absorbed 1.3 percent of the total increase in manufacturing employment, while the textile and the chemical industries between them absorbed 35.5 percent. Besides these major industries several minor industries have become important employers. Three relatively new industries, metal products, machinery, and electrical

---

early years, and register large and unexplainable fluctuations from year to year, suggesting changing coverages and definition of employment. Employment figures from the population censuses are reasonably close although somewhat smaller than those from the commercial and industrial censuses. This discrepancy can probably be explained by differences in definition and seasonal variations.

39. Unlike the other industrial and commercial censuses, which covered all profit-making small processing establishments and repair shops, the 1966 census included only those establishments that qualified for factory or small-scale industry registration. The difference in coverage can be seen in the fact that the number of establishments surveyed in 1954 was 40,713; in 1961, 52,152; and in 1966, 28,771. Nevertheless, because all the excluded establishments were extremely small, aggregate statistics such as total employment and hp in operation are still reasonably meaningful.

40. The growth rate is calculated on the basis of the annual average employment figures, i.e., the simple averages of employment figures from the quarterly labor force survey conducted in January, April, July, and October of each year. For the quarterly figures see Taiwan Provincial Labor Force Survey and Research Institute, *Report of the Labor Force Survey in Taiwan*, various issues.

Table 10.9. Employment in Manufacturing Industries according to the First, Second, Third, and Fourth Commercial and Industrial Censuses (Number of persons at end of year)

	1954	1961	1966	1971	Allocation of net increase		
					1954–61	1961–66	1966–71
Manufacturing	309,887	445,667	589,660	1,201,539	135,780	143,993	611,879
Percentage distribution (total mfg.)	100.0	100.0	100.0	100.0	100.0	100.0	100.0
Food	19.4	19.9	20.9	10.9	21.0	24.2	1.3
Beverages	1.2	2.0	0.5	0.3	3.7	-4.1	0.2
Tobacco	1.6	1.2	1.9	0.8	0.4	4.2	-0.2
Textiles	16.9	15.8	17.4	18.8	13.5	22.3	20.1
Apparel	5.0	5.1	2.3	6.4	5.1	-6.3	10.3
Wood and wood products	5.8	5.9	5.4	6.1	6.3	3.9	6.7
Furniture	2.0	2.6	0.8	0.8	4.0	-5.0	0.8
Paper and paper products	2.1	3.0	3.0	2.8	5.1	2.7	2.7
Printing and publishing	3.4	2.9	2.2	1.5	1.9	-0.1	0.8
Leather products	0.5	0.3	0.2	0.6	0.0	-0.2	1.1
Rubber products	1.7	1.5	1.7	1.8	1.0	2.4	1.8
Chemicals and chemical products	7.0	7.0	10.3	12.9	6.8	20.5	15.4
Products of petroleum and coal	1.1	1.2	1.9	1.3	1.6	3.9	0.8
Nonmetallic mineral products	9.6	8.8	7.8	5.3	6.9	4.8	2.8
Basic metals	2.0	2.4	2.9	2.5	3.3	4.5	2.1
Metal products	4.6	4.5	3.8	4.2	4.3	1.7	4.5
Machinery	4.2	3.7	5.2	5.1	2.6	10.1	4.9
Electrical equipment	1.7	2.9	5.5	10.6	5.8	13.5	15.5
Transport equipment	5.9	6.3	4.0	2.9	7.2	-3.1	1.9
Miscellaneous	4.1	2.7	2.1	4.4	-0.5	0.3	6.6

Sources: General Report on Industry and Commerce Census of Taiwan, 1954, pp. 30, 62, 582, 604, 608, 612; General Report, 1961 Industry and Commerce Census of Taiwan, vol. 3, pp. 1–9; General Report on the Third Industrial and Commercial Census of Taiwan, vol. 3, pp. 1–18; and The Report of the 1971 Industrial and Commercial Censuses of Taiwan and Fukien Area, Republic of China, vol. 3, pp. 2–11.

equipment, absorbed 13 percent of the increase in manufacturing employment between 1954 and 1961, 22 percent between 1961 and 1966, and 25 percent between 1966 and 1971. By the end of 1971 they accounted for 20 percent of the total employment in manufacturing.

In Taiwan, the growth of industrial employment lagged behind that of industrial output. Between 1954 and 1961 manufacturing output rose at about 11 percent a year and employment slightly over 5 percent a year.[41] In the 1960s, both output and employment growth accelerated. From 1961 to 1973 the average annual growth rate of manufacturing output was 20 percent and that of employment slightly above 10 percent. During 1955–65 manufacturing employment for all LDCs taken together increased at only 4 percent a year.[42] Thus, in comparison with other LDCs, Taiwan's manufacturing sector has been extremely successful in creating employment opportunities for its workers.

Rapid industrialization explains in part the growth in manufacturing employment. But equally significant is that the liberalization policies adopted in the 1960s, by reducing distortions in relative prices and by making industrialists more conscious of factor endowment, permitted Taiwan to industrialize in a manner more consistent with its comparative advantage, i.e., along a labor-intensive expansion path.

In table 10.10 Taiwan's two-digit manufacturing industries are ranked in order of increasing labor intensity by two criteria: value-added per employee and total asset in operation per employee. Except for a few explainable exceptions, the most important being textiles, beverages, and nonmetallic mineral products, the two rankings produce generally similar results.[43] The petroleum and coal products, chemical,

41. The 5 percent growth rate is based on the industrial and commercial censuses. The household registration data show a lower rate of growth (about 4 percent).

42. David Turnham, *The Employment Problem in Less Developed Countries*, chap. 5, table 1.

43. The textile industry is found to be relatively labor intensive by the value-added per employee measurement (ranking 14 out of 20) but relatively capital intensive by the total asset per employee measurement (ranking 5 out of 20). On the other hand, the beverage and nonmetallic mineral product industries are found to be relatively capital intensive by the value-added per employee criterion (ranking 4 and 5 out of 20, respectively) but relatively labor intensive by the total asset per employee criterion (ranking 14 and 9, respectively). The discrepancies in ranking are explained by the fact that total asset includes both fixed and working capital, and where rankings are significantly dissimilar the industries involved had either unusually high or unusually low working capital. For example, in 1966 the ratio of year-end inventory to revenue was 0.27 for the manufacturing sector as a whole but 0.37 for the textile industry, 0.15 for the nonmetallic mineral product industry, and 0.11 for the beverage industry. The

Table 10.10. Census Value-Added per Employee and Total Asset in Operation per Employee by Industry, 1966

	Ranking by census value-added per employee	Ratio of census value-added per employee of two-digit industry to that of total mfg. sector	Ranking by total asset in operation per employee	Ratio of total asset in operation per employee of two-digit industry to that of total manufacturing sector
Petroleum and coal products	1	5.34	1	3.51
Chemicals	2	1.53	3	1.76
Tobacco	3	1.50	2	2.27
Beverages	4	1.32	14	0.46
Nonmetallic mineral products	5	1.13	9	0.87
Basic metals	6	1.10	4	1.64
Paper and paper products	7	1.07	7	0.94
Wood products (except furniture)	8	1.00	6	0.95
Food	9	0.93	8	0.90
Electrical machinery, appliances, and supplies	10	0.92	10	0.81
Transport equipment	11	0.84	12	0.66
Rubber products	12	0.74	13	0.60
Machinery	13	0.68	15	0.35
Textiles	14	0.66	5	1.08
Metal products	15	0.56	16	0.33
Printing and publishing	16	0.53	18	0.30
Footwear and wearing apparel	17	0.51	19	0.27
Leather and leather products	18	0.44	11	0.73
Furniture	19	0.43	20	0.20
Miscellaneous manufacturing industries	20	0.37	17	0.30

Source: General Report on the Third Industrial and Commercial Census of Taiwan, vol. 4, pp. 1–18.

Table 10.11. Exports by Major Commodity Groups (Percentage of total)

	1964	1968	1972
Total	100.00	100.00	100.00
Agricultural products	10.86	9.75	4.87
Minerals	1.03	0.56	0.06
Food, beverages, and tobacco	46.70	21.93	10.70
Products of textile, leather, and wood	24.78	38.62	43.66
Textile products	10.01	11.66	10.46
Leather and leather products	a	0.11	0.07
Wood and cork products	8.41	9.94	7.71
Knitted and crocheted articles	0.59	6.40	13.30
Footwear and wearing apparel	3.98	7.60	9.87
Furniture	a	0.28	0.59
Others	1.79	2.69	1.66
Nonmetallic mineral products	4.28	3.71	1.74
Chemicals and chemical products	4.20	3.03	1.57
Basic metals	3.26	2.28	3.38
Metal products	0.86	1.48	1.92
Machinery	1.04	2.77	3.28
Electrical machinery, appliances, and supplies	1.13	9.83	16.74
Transport equipment	0.25	0.71	2.20
Miscellaneous manufacturing products	1.60	5.09	9.76
Others	a	0.23	0.12

Sources: DGBAS, *Statistical Abstract of the Republic of China,* 1965, pp. 212–93; 1969, pp. 290–91; 1973, pp. 278–79.
[a] Less than 0.005%.

and tobacco industries are the least labor intensive, while apparel, machinery, and metal product industries are among the most labor intensive.[44] When Taiwan's industrialization is seen in the light of this ranking, it becomes clear that in the 1960s output and export growth were led by labor-intensive commodities.

In 1964, at the beginning of the outward-looking phase of Taiwan's industrialization, agricultural and processed agricultural products comprised nearly 60 percent of Taiwan's exports (table 10.11). Since

---

unusually large inventory of the textile industry partly explains why it is considered relatively capital intensive when judged in terms of total asset per employee but relatively labor intensive when judged in terms of value-added per employee. Similarly, the below-average inventory of the beverage and nonmetallic mineral product industries explains why they are found to be relatively labor intensive in terms of total asset per employee, even though they are found to be relatively capital intensive in terms of value-added per employee.

44. It is interesting to note that metal products, machinery, and electrical machinery are industries with large wage shares (in excess of 60 percent of gross value-added) whereas the petroleum product and chemical industries have low wage shares (see Hsing et al., *Industrialization and Trade Policies,* p. 301).

1964 the export mix has shifted dramatically toward labor-intensive industrial products. Indeed, according to the ranking in table 10.10, the new export products, e.g., textile goods, electrical machinery and supplies, metal products, and machinery (table 10.11), are produced by some of Taiwan's most labor-intensive industries. They are also among the fastest growing industries and the ones with the highest export shares (tables 10.1 and 10.6). In other words, in the 1960s Taiwan shifted from producing and exporting commodities with high natural resource content to producing and exporting commodities with high labor and skill content. It was this shift in output mix as much as the growth in output that enabled the manufacturing sector to absorb employment in large numbers each year.

One reason that manufacturing employment could expand rapidly in a short period of time was that women entered the industrial labor force in large numbers. According to the 1954 industrial census, the ratio of male to female workers in manufacturing was 2.49. Of course within manufacturing there were wide variations, e.g., 0.53 in textiles and 5.37 in electrical equipment.[45] From 1954 to 1961, 38 percent of the increase in manufacturing employment was female; from 1961 to 1966, 54 percent; and from 1966 to 1971, 57 percent. As a result, the male to female ratio of persons engaged in manufacturing declined to 2.18 in 1961, 1.69 in 1966, and 1.13 in 1971. Eighty-two percent of the increase in women employed in manufacturing from 1954 to 1966 was absorbed by four industries: food (26.2 percent), chemicals and chemical products (11.3), textiles (31.6), and electrical equipment (12.5). Textiles had always employed a high percentage of women, and in the other industries there was a significant reduction in the ratio of male to female workers. From 1966 to 1971, 60 percent of the increase in women employed in manufacturing was absorbed by two industries: textile and apparel (43 percent) and electrical equipment (17).

Besides the changes in sex composition, the manufacturing labor force altered in other ways. Reflecting the declining importance of the small-scale family enterprise, the percentage of unpaid family workers declined steadily during the 1950s and 1960s. In 1954 paid employees were 78 percent of the total labor force in manufacturing; in 1966, 93 percent. From the development viewpoint of course, the decisive change is in the quality of the labor force, a difficult concept to quantify even when data are plentiful. In Taiwan, where the data are sketchy, we

45. These and the other figures in this paragraph are based on data from the industrial and commercial censuses in 1954, 1961, and 1966.

Table 10.12. Composition of Employed Persons in Manufacturing, by Occupation and
            Skill: 1954, 1961, 1971

	1954	*1961*	*1971*
Ratio of total laborer to staff [a]	5.8	4.7	4.6
Ratio of production laborer to staff	5.4	4.3	4.4
Percentage of skilled production laborers	44.2	46.4	35.6
Percentage of skilled female production laborers	23.9	28.9	21.9
Percentage of skilled male production laborers	54.0	56.3	50.5
Percentage of female production laborers	32.4	35.1	52.4

*Sources: General Report on Industry and Commerce Census of Taiwan, 1954, pp. 70–71;
General Report, 1961 Industry and Commerce Census of Taiwan, pp. 518–19; The Report
of the 1971 Industrial and Commercial Censuses of Taiwan and Fukien Area, Republic of
China, vol. 3, table 13.*
[a] Staff includes technicians and administrative personnel.

can provide only a very rough indication of how labor quality has
changed. On the whole the data seem to suggest that labor quality
improved during the postwar period.

Although data on the composition of employed persons by occupation and skill were collected by the industrial and commercial censuses,
they do not, unfortunately, provide a reliable measure of labor quality.
Nevertheless, the census data are summarized in table 10.12. Among
other things, the table indicates that an increasing share of those
employed in manufacturing are staff workers, i.e., technicians and
administrative personnel. The ratio of laborer to staff declined from
5.8 in 1954 to 4.6 in 1971. However, the percentage of skilled production
laborers declined significantly, from 44 percent in 1954 to 36 percent
in 1971. But what these figures mean is unclear. Besides stating that
apprentices are included as unskilled workers, the censuses do not in
other ways define the distinction between skilled and unskilled.
However, until 1961 the percentage of production workers described
as skilled increased, and only thereafter did it decline. And, as we noted
earlier, it was in the 1960s that a large number of women entered the
industrial labor force for the first time, most probably as apprentices.
From 1961 to 1971 the percentage of female production laborers (see
table 10.12) increased from 35 to 52 percent. In this period, the percentage of skilled female production laborers declined from 29 to 22
percent. It seems, therefore, that the change in the skill composition
of the labor force is but a reflection of the change in its sex composition.

A better and more precise measure of labor quality, the percentage
distribution of industrial labor force by the level of education attained,
is presented in table 10.13. The 1943 figures are based on an extensive

Table 10.13. Persons Engaged in Industry, by Education, 1943 and 1966

Percentage distribution

	No.	Total	No formal education			Formal education (attendance or graduation)			
			Total	Illiterate	Self-educated	Total	Primary school	Secondary school or equiv.	Higher education inst.
1943									
Industry[a]									
Technicians and workers	105,331	100.0	35.0	—	—	65.0	50.8	12.1	2.0
Workers	101,293	100.0	36.4	—	—	63.6	52.5	10.1	1.0
1966									
Industry	651,727	100.0	11.2	8.1	3.1	88.8	61.7	23.8	3.8
Manufacturing	527,450	100.0	9.9	7.1	2.8	90.1	62.5	23.9	3.7
Construction	97,006	100.0	17.2	12.9	4.3	82.8	65.4	15.0	2.3
Utility	27,271	100.0	13.5	10.2	3.3	86.4	32.4	43.3	10.7

Notes and Sources: The 1943 figures are from Taiwan Government-General, *The Results of the Survey on Labor Skills,* 1943, vol. 1, pp. 266–69 and 734–41. The coverage is all factories and enterprises that employed 30 or more workers. The 1966 figures are from *The Report of the 1966 Census of Population and Housing of Taiwan–Fukien Area, Republic of China,* pt. 2, vol. 3-A, pp. 197–204. The coverage is all employed persons over 12 years of age. Primary school includes grades one to six. Higher education includes advanced vocational schools; in the case of the 1943 survey, it also includes miscellaneous.

[a] Includes manufacturing, construction, and utility.

labor force survey conducted by the colonial government, and the 1966 figures are from the 1966 population census. The two sets of data are not strictly comparable in coverage, because the 1943 survey included only enterprises with 30 or more workers, while the 1966 population census included all employed persons 12 years of age or older. Since it is likely that the workers employed by the larger enterprises were also better educated, the 1943 distribution probably shows a higher percentage of workers with education than that which existed in the total industrial labor force. Consequently, the observed change between the 1943 and 1966 distributions is a conservative estimate of the true change in labor quality.

If the level of education attained is a good indicator of labor quality, the data in table 10.13 demonstrate not only that the quality of Taiwan's industrial labor force was already quite good in the 1940s but also that it improved significantly during the postwar period. In 1943 about 35 percent of Taiwan's industrial workers and technicians had no formal education, 51 percent had attended or graduated from primary school, and only 14 percent attended school beyond the sixth grade. In 1966, only 11 percent of the industrial labor force had no formal education (some of them, however, were literate), 62 percent had attended or graduated from primary school, and more than 27 percent had more than a sixth-grade education. When industry is disaggregated into its major components of manufacturing, construction, and utility, it becomes evident that the labor force in manufacturing is the best educated, with only 7 percent illiterate compared to 10 percent in utility and nearly 13 percent in construction. That the quality of the industrial labor force improved in the postwar years is also confirmed by comparing slightly different data from the 1956 and 1966 population censuses. In 1956, of the 459,000 craftsmen and production workers, almost 29 percent had no formal education (although only 23 percent were illiterate), and 71 percent had attended or graduated from primary school.[46] In 1966, of the 867,000 craftsmen and production workers, 18 percent had no formal education (14 percent illiterate) and 81 percent attended or graduated from primary school.[47]

Capital

Like employment, industrial investments increased steadily in the postwar period and rapidly since 1960. In 1964 prices, gross capital

46. *A Report on the 1956 Census*, pt. 2, vol. 3, pp. 337–48.
47. *A Report on the 1966 Population Census, Taiwan Province*, vol. 2, pt. 3a, pp. 381–88.

formation in manufacturing averaged NT$ 1.58 billion in 1952–54, NT$ 3.50 billion in 1959–61, and NT$ 12.16 billion in 1966–68.[48] Thus, in a period when total investment was increasing very rapidly, investment in manufacturing claimed a growing share, rising from 25 percent in 1952–53 to 35 percent in 1966–68. As a result the fixed capital stock in the manufacturing sector is estimated to have increased more than threefold from 1952 to 1966.[49] Power equipment in the manufacturing sector increased from a reported 429,000 hp in operation in 1954 to 863,000 hp in 1961, 1.30 million hp in 1966, and 2.87 million hp in 1971. In 1954, 66 percent of Taiwan's manufacturing establishments did not use power. This was reduced to 56 percent in 1961, and 9 percent in 1966.[50]

Not all manufacturing industries experienced the same rate of capital accumulation. Table 10.14 presents the distribution of gross fixed capital formation in 1964 prices by major manufacturing industries. In the early 1950s about 60 percent of the total gross fixed capital formation was allocated to the food and textile industries. The chemical industry, which after the food and the textile industries received the greatest share of the total gross fixed capital formation in manufacturing, absorbed only 12 percent of the total. By the late 1950s the distribution pattern had changed drastically. In 1957–59, fewer than 30 percent of the gross fixed investments in manufacturing went to the food and textile industries. On the other hand, the chemical industry by itself absorbed nearly 30 percent of the total gross fixed investment in manufacturing. An increasing share was also allocated to

48. Hsing et al., *Industrialization and Trade Policies*, p. 277.
49. Yuëh Fu, "Estimates of Technological Progress in Taiwan's Manufacturing Sector, 1951–66," p. 22.
50. These figures are from the industrial and commercial censuses in 1954, 1961, 1966, and 1971. The distribution of manufacturing establishments by hp is as follows:

	1954	1961	1966	1971
Total	100.0%	100.0%	100.0%	100.0%
No power	66.0	55.7	8.5 ⎫	
Less than 5 hp	17.0	23.8	37.8 ⎭	45.5
5–19 hp	13.7	16.0	39.9 ⎫	
20–49 hp	1.8	2.4	7.0 ⎭	44.6
50–99 hp	0.5	0.9	2.8	3.9
100–499 hp	0.6	0.9	2.9	4.4
500 hp and over	0.3	0.3	1.1	1.6

However, we should note again that the coverage of the 1966 census is narrower than the other censuses because it does not include all small processing firms and repair shops. Thus the decline in the number of establishments with no power from 1961 to 1966 may be exaggerated.

Table 10.14. Gross Fixed Capital Formation in Manufacturing (Annual averages)

	1952–53	*1957–59*	*1961–64*	*1965–68*
Gross fixed capital formation in manufacturing (in 1964 NT$ million)	1,078	1,731	3,101	8,331
Percentage distribution				
Total	100.0	100.0	100.0	100.0
Food	25.6	16.5	14.6	8.9
Textiles	35.8	12.1	17.7	20.0
Wood and wood products	1.2	2.5	4.2	4.4
Paper and paper products	5.6	6.6	5.5	3.6
Chemical and chemical products	11.7	29.5	20.1	19.2
Petroleum and coal products	2.4	6.8	9.6	10.5
Nonmetallic mineral products	1.8	4.5	7.3	8.8
Metals and metal products	4.1	11.3	9.4	10.5
Electrical products	1.0	1.5	3.9	6.2
Others	10.8	8.7	7.7	7.7

Source: Mo-huan Hsing, John H. Power, and Gerardo P. Sicat, *Taiwan and the Philippines: Industrialization and Trade Policies*, p. 300.

the newer industries, e.g., petroleum and coal products, metals and metal products, and nonmetallic mineral products. In the 1960s this trend away from the traditional, or early, industries continued. About 20 percent of the gross fixed investment in manufacturing was absorbed by the chemical industry. Another 30–35 percent of the total was in four relatively new industries: petroleum and coal products, metals and metal products, nonmetallic mineral products, and electrical products. On the other hand, by 1965–68 the share of fixed investments in the food industry dropped to less than 9 percent of the total. However, the share of fixed investment in the textile industry reversed its declining trend, rising from 12 percent in 1957–59 to 20 percent in 1965–68. In other words, since the mid-1950s but particularly in the 1960s investments have gone increasingly to the newer industries, allowing capital in them to accumulate at a faster than average rate. Consequently, the distribution of capital stock by industry shifted away from the traditional, or early, industries toward the middle and late industries.

This shift in the distribution of capital stock in favor of the middle and the late industries helps to explain the dramatic change in the relative position of labor productivity of individual manufacturing industries. Table 10.15 presents the distribution of product and employment by manufacturing industries for the census years 1954,

Table 10.15. Distribution of Product and Employment in the Manufacturing Sector: 1954, 1961, 1966 (Percentage of total manufacturing)

	1954			1961			1966		
	Value-added (1)	Employment (2)	(1)/(2) (3)	Value-added (4)	Employment (5)	(4)/(5) (6)	Value-added (7)	Employment (8)	(7)/(8) (9)
Total manufacturing	100.0	100.0	100.0	100.0	100.0	100.0	100.0	100.0	100.0
Early industries	61.0	44.6	1.37	45.4	44.3	1.02	33.0	43.2	0.76
Food	27.3	19.4	1.41	25.6	19.9	1.29	11.3	20.9	0.54
Beverage	0.3	1.2	0.25	0.4	2.0	0.20	0.5	0.5	1.00
Tobacco	6.2	1.6	3.87	2.9	1.2	2.42	2.9	1.9	1.53
Textile and apparel	27.1	21.9	1.24	16.3	20.9	0.78	18.2	19.7	0.92
Leather	0.2	0.5	0.40	0.2	0.3	0.67	0.1	0.2	0.50
Middle industries	24.0	27.2	0.88	29.7	27.0	1.10	31.9	27.9	1.14
Wood and wood products	4.6	7.8	0.59	6.8	8.5	0.80	4.2	6.2	0.68
Rubber products	0.9	1.7	0.53	1.3	1.5	0.87	1.3	1.7	0.76
Chemicals and chem. prod.	10.5	7.0	1.50	10.4	7.0	1.48	14.6	10.3	1.42
Products of petroleum and coal	3.6	11.1	3.27	3.4	1.2	2.83	4.1	1.9	2.16
Nonmetallic mineral prod.	4.4	9.6	0.46	7.8	8.8	0.89	7.7	7.8	0.99
Late industries	12.7	23.9	0.53	23.6	25.7	0.92	32.8	26.6	1.23
Paper and printing	5.9	5.5	1.07	9.2	5.9	1.56	9.4	5.2	1.81
Basic metals	1.8	2.0	0.90	3.4	2.4	1.42	2.2	2.9	0.76
Metal products	1.0	4.6	0.22	2.8	4.5	0.62	4.0	3.8	1.05
Machinery	1.2	4.2	0.28	2.9	3.7	0.78	5.0	5.2	0.96
Electrical machinery and supplies	1.2	1.7	0.70	2.2	2.9	0.81	6.1	5.5	1.11
Transport equipment	1.6	5.9	0.27	3.1	6.3	0.49	6.1	4.0	1.52
Miscellaneous	2.3	4.1	0.56	1.3	2.7	0.48	2.3	2.1	1.09

Sources: For the source of the value-added data, see table 10.7. The employment data are from table 10.9.

1961, and 1966. It can be easily shown that the ratio of the *i*th industry's share in total manufacturing product to its share in total manufacturing employment is also the ratio of the *i*th industry's labor productivity to the labor productivity of the manufacturing sector as a whole. Thus, when this ratio rises, it implies that labor productivity in the *i*th industry has increased relative to that of the manufacturing sector.

Table 10.15 shows that the early industries had by far the highest productivity in 1954, followed in descending order by the middle and late industries. In 1954, relative to the average for the manufacturing sector, labor productivity was 1.37 in the early industries, 0.88 in the middle industries, and only 0.53 in the late industries. Thus, average labor productivity in the early industries was more than twice that of the late industries. However, since 1954, partly because of the shift in the allocation of industrial investment, labor productivity increased more rapidly in the middle and late industries than in the early industries. By 1961 the differentials in labor productivity among these industries had substantially narrowed. In that year, relative to the average for the manufacturing sector, labor productivity was 1.02 in the early industries, 1.10 in the middle industries, and 0.92 in the late industries. From 1961 to 1966 growth in labor productivity in the late industries continued at a rate significantly higher than the average for the manufacturing sector, while that of the early industries lagged behind the average. Growth in labor productivity in the middle industries was about average. Consequently, by 1966 differentials in labor productivity among manufacturing industries had again widened, but this time it was the late industries that had the highest average productivity in the manufacturing sector while the early industries had the lowest. Relative to the average for the manufacturing sector, labor productivity in 1966 was 0.76 in the early industries, 1.14 in the middle industries, and 1.23 in the late industries.

Since investment is a major conduit of technological change, the rapid rate of investment in the postwar period undoubtedly improved the quality of Taiwan's industrial capital stock. Unfortunately, information on such matters is very sketchy. Table 10.16 summarizes what is known about the age structure of principal machinery in selected industries in 1961. Lack of data for other years precludes comparison over time. Nevertheless, the information in table 10.16 is of some interest. For example, it shows that the age of machinery in a declining industry, such as sugar refining, where the rate of investment was relatively low, was great in comparison with the other

Table 10.16. Selected Principal Machinery and Equipment by Industry and by Years of Use, 1961

	Total quantity	Percentage distribution by years of use			
		Total	Less than 5 years	5–10 Years	Over 10 years
Food					
Sugar cane roller	142 sets	100.0	13.4	31.7	54.9
Crusher	1,006	100.0	40.2	45.6	14.2
Oil press	1,557	100.0	28.5	37.0	34.5
Milling machine	9,518	100.0	35.5	54.6	9.9
Tobacco					
Cigarette-making machine	109	100.0	0.9	33.9	65.2
Textile and apparel					
Spinning machine	152,799	100.0	38.3	47.5	14.2
Automatic loom	16,654	100.0	23.2	41.9	34.9
Sewing machine	4,744	100.0	31.9	40.8	27.3
Wood and wood products					
Band saw	2,661	100.0	58.3	31.2	10.3
Circular saw	2,039	100.0	67.8	26.3	5.9
Paper and paper products					
Pulp maker	548	100.0	56.0	29.6	14.4
Paper-manufacturing machine	175	100.0	38.8	38.8	22.4
Printing and publishing					
Printing press	1,058	100.0	29.9	50.3	19.8
Chemical and chemical products					
Electrolyzer	2,017 units	100.0	75.8	9.4	14.8
Equipment for the production of hydrochloride acid	134	100.0	46.3	3.0	50.7
Petroleum and coal products					
refining equipment	2	100.0	0	100.0	0
Nonmetallic mineral products					
(kilns of all kinds)	1,351	100.0	67.6	26.1	6.3
Metals and metal products					
(blast furnace)	104	100.0	63.5	28.8	7.7
Machinery found in more than one industry					
Lathe	5,305 sets	100.0	28.9	53.5	17.6
Drill press	2,432	100.0	37.7	47.8	14.5
Punching machine	2,424	100.0	34.4	43.6	22.0

Notes and Source: The coverage includes only manufacturing establishments that employed more than 10 persons or 5 hp of power equipment. The figures are from *General Report, 1961 Industry and Commerce Census of Taiwan*, vol. 3, pp. 620–23.

industries. In 1961 more than half the rollers used in the sugar industry had been in operation for more than 10 years, i.e., they were part of the prewar capital stock. The tobacco industry, which had a relatively low priority in Taiwan's investment plan, also had an older capital stock. On the other hand, industries in which the rates of investment were high employed machinery that was relatively young. For example, in 1961 about two-thirds of the blast furnaces in the metal industry, more than two-thirds of the kilns of the nonmetallic mineral industry, more than 60 percent of the saws in the wood and wood products industry, and more than three-fourths of the electrolyzers in the chemical industry had been in use for less than five years. If we assume that new and better technology is embodied in the more current vintage capital, the rapid rate of investments in Taiwan's manufacturing sector in the 1950s and 1960s not only had the effect of reducing the age of its capital equipment but also improved its quality.

Sources of Growth

The sources of Taiwan's manufacturing output growth have been examined by several studies and their findings are basically similar:[51] a substantial portion of the output growth was unaccounted for by the increase in labor and capital. Furthermore, it seems that the unexplained portion as a share of total output growth was quite large in the 1950s but declined dramatically in the 1960s, particularly after the mid-1960s. For example, Chang's findings show that from 1951 to 1968, on the average about 47 percent of the manufacturing output growth was unexplained by the growth of labor and capital, and that the average annual unexplained portion (the residue) decreased from 63 percent in 1951–56 to about 54 percent in 1956–64 and 15 percent in 1964–68.[52]

---

51. The more important studies are Fu, "Estimates of Technological Progress"; Hung-chang Chang, "The Contribution of Technological Progress and Factor Inputs to the Growth of Manufacturing Industries"; Mo-huan Hsing, Chen-nan Chiang, and Kuo-shu Hwang, "An Analysis of Residual Productivities of the Manufacturing Industries in Taiwan, 1953–71"; and Shirley Kuo, "The Economic Structure of Taiwan." Except for the last item, all these studies focus on Taiwan's manufacturing sector. Kuo's study is focused on the nonagricultural sector, especially the secondary industries (mining, manufacturing, construction, and public services). The procedure used is by now well known. Output growth ($\dot{Y}$), labor growth ($\dot{L}$), capital growth ($\dot{K}$), labor share (α), and capital share (β) are estimated. That portion of output growth attributable to labor is αL and that portion attributable to capital is βK. The residue, r, is simply $r = \dot{Y} - (\alpha \dot{L} + \beta \dot{K})$.

52. Chang, "Contribution of Technological Progress and Factor Inputs," table 2.

Since homogeneous inputs are assumed in all the growth accounting analyses applied to Taiwan's manufacturing sector, it is clear that at least part of the residue reflects the changing quality of inputs. In our discussion of factor inputs we have already taken note of the fact that in the postwar period the quality of both labor and capital improved. An increasing share of the industrial labor force graduated from grade schools or attended secondary (including vocational) schools. Although direct evidence is less plentiful in the case of capital, one suspects that the rapid rate of investment in industrial capital in the postwar period was accompanied by a similar improvement in the quality of capital. Because these quality changes could not be quantified in a meaningful way, their effect on growth was not measured. Therefore one suspects they are responsible for a substantial portion of the unexplained output growth.

If the residue is partly a measure of quality improvements in inputs, should we interpret the decline in the residue in the 1960s as a decline in the rate of quality improvement in industrial labor and capital? The evidence seems to suggest otherwise. Industrial investment was at a higher rate in the 1960s than in the 1950s, and the literacy rate of Taiwan's labor force continued to rise rapidly in the 1960s. However, there is evidence that the rate at which capacity was used was higher in the 1960s than in the 1950s, and this difference may provide part of the explanation for the decline in the residue.

In the growth accounting studies cited above, inputs were not adjusted for their rates of utilization. Thus, in a period when the utilization rate is increasing, the estimated rate of input growth would be lower than the actual rate of growth, causing a large residual component to emerge. In the 1950s, partly as a result of the controls and regulations used to implement import substitution, the capacity of Taiwan's manufacturing sector was persistently underutilized.[53] Although precise utilization rates are not available, we do know from industry studies that in the mid-1950s excess capacity, often higher than 50 percent, was prevalent among manufacturing industries.[54]

53. For example, plant size was one of the factors considered in determining the amount of foreign exchange allocated to private industrial enterprises. This undoubtedly encouraged industrialists to build ahead of demand.

54. For example, a 1961 report by the Office of Economic Policy, USICA Mission to China, that reviewed the conditions in the wheat flour industry in the 1950s states that "the growth of the flour milling industry has resulted in a large excess of milling capacity relative to current and prospective domestic demand." During the mid-1950s, annual production as a percentage of capacity in the wheat flour industry was probably

Table 10.17. Production as a Percentage of Productive Capacity for Selected
              Manufactured Products

Industry	Product	1961	1966	1966/1961
Food	Canned pineapple	47	76	1.62
	Refined sugar	21	96	4.57
Textiles	Cotton yarn	44	85	1.93
	Synthetic yarn	35	48	1.37
Rubber and rubber	Bicycle tires and tubes	73	78	1.07
products	Rubber shoes and boots	59	64	1.08
Chemicals and chemical	Ammonium sulfate	29	87	3.00
products	PVC	57	58	1.02
	Plastic products	48	79	1.64
Metals and metal	Rod, bar, and slab	43	77	1.79
products	Aluminum ingot	45	86	1.91
Machinery	Prime mover	49	53	1.08
	Pumps for liquid	38	56	1.47
	Sewing machine	62	79	1.27
	Electric fan	42	69	1.64
Electrical products	Fluorescent lamp	48	94	1.96
	Dry battery	62	69	1.11

Sources: General Report, 1961 Industry and Commerce Census of Taiwan, pp. 708–23,
and *General Report on the Third Industrial and Commercial Census of Taiwan*, pp. 479–90.

The liberalization policy that began in 1958 increased the tempo of industrialization and enabled many manufacturing industries to operate closer to full capacity. In other words, in the late 1950s and the early 1960s excess capacity in manufacturing declined. We are unable to document the decrease in the late 1950s but table 10.17 shows a significant drop in excess capacity in the first half of the 1960s. This suggests that in the 1950s and early 1960s, because of increases in utilization rate, the growth of capital stock in manufacturing underestimated the actual increase of capital in production. Consequently, for these years a large residual component appeared in the growth accounting analyses. In the latter half of the 1960s, when the economy was operating near capacity, the growth of capital stock was a more accurate measurement of the increase of capital in production.

---

between 30 and 40 percent (wheat milled was around 200,000 MT and capacity was reported to be about 540,000 MT). Similar conditions existed in other industries (cf. the reports on various manufacturing industries prepared by the Office of Economic Policy, USICA Mission to China). A 1959 industrial survey of 2,593 large manufacturing enterprises found that of the 120 items produced, 54 were produced in plants operating at less than 50 percent capacity.

Consequently, after the mid-1960s a significantly larger share of the output growth was explained by the growth in primary inputs.

To summarize, like most developing countries, Taiwan began to industrialize with an import substitution strategy, accompanied by its usual package of policies—exchange and import controls, low interest rates with credit rationing, and often direct controls on industries. For a while the industrial sector expanded rapidly, and the strategy appeared to be effective. But its positive effects were soon overwhelmed by other consequences, i.e., relative price distortions, excess capacity, and sluggish exports. Reacting to this situation, the Taiwan government began in 1958 to slowly liberalize controls, a process that continued into the 1960s. At the same time the government became substantially more trade oriented and introduced numerous export incentives, mostly to redress the existing biases against exports. The policy changes and the greater attention paid to trade after 1958 helped to bring about a remarkable surge in industrial growth.

By turning to export and allowing market forces to play a greater role in the allocation of resources, Taiwan was able to develop its economy more in tune with its comparative advantage, i.e., along a labor-intensive growth path. Thus, unlike many other LDCs, Taiwan enjoyed fast growth in both output and employment. No longer constrained to its limited domestic market, Taiwan's manufacturing production expanded rapidly and as a consequence its industries operated closer to full capacity. In other words, in the 1960s industrial growth was not only more rapid, it was also more efficient.

If the Taiwan government is to be faulted for anything, it is for the caution that characterized its liberalization process. Had it acted with greater speed, the impact of liberalization and decontrol would have been felt substantially sooner, and had it dismantled the controls and limited the distortions more effectively the results of liberalization could have been achieved more efficiently. The caution is understandable because in the late 1950s the new policy package was untested and not at all fashionable. Indeed, that the government acted at all is worthy of praise.

11

Consumption and Investment in Postwar Taiwan

Economic development cannot be sustained if suitable levels of savings and investments are not generated. This chapter examines the allocation of national expenditure by final use and finds that resource allocation altered substantially in the postwar period. Some of the changes, such as the rise in nonfood consumption, are directly related to the rise in income. Others are the results of structural changes associated with economic growth. Significantly, in the postwar period Taiwan allocated an increasing share of its national expenditure to investment. However, at the same time rapid output growth enabled per capita consumption to more than double in two decades. Perhaps the most important development was that, increasingly, Taiwan was able to finance its investments with its own savings, thus enabling growth to continue regardless of the availability of foreign savings.

In the 1950s, because of Taiwan's low per capita income and huge military expenditures, most of its income was consumed. In 1951–55 the average share of total (private and government) consumption in GNP was 95 percent. Nevertheless, in this same period, because of the large inflow of U.S. aid, Taiwan also allocated a creditable share—nearly 14 percent—of its GNP to gross capital formation. Net imports bridged the wide gap between national product and expenditure. In 1951–55 it was 8.2 percent of GNP; in 1956–60, 7.3 percent.[1]

Rapid economic growth after the early 1950s was accompanied by fundamental changes in the relative uses of gross national product. The distribution of both GNP and total available resources for the period 1951–73 is shown in table 11.1. At the aggregate level two important trends are immediately apparent. In the 1950s and 1960s, (1)

1. In the 1950s the NT$ was substantially overvalued. Revaluation of imports at a more realistic exchange rate would increase the import surplus.

Table 11.1. Distribution of GNP by Final Use, 1951–73 (Annual averages, million NT$, 1966 prices)

	1951–55	*1956–60*	*1961–65*	*1966–70*	*1971–73*
GNP	45,784	64,701	94,949	152,610	228,871
Minus					
Net export surplus of goods and services	−3,733	−4,737	−4,133	−3,696	12,974
Net factor income from abroad	−13	−36	−136	−298	−168
Statistical discrepancy	−81	−249	−42	−138	153
Total resources available for domestic use (GDE)	49,611	69,723	99,260	156,742	215,912
Percentage of GNP					
Private consumption	70.0	67.5	64.9	59.0	51.8
Government consumption	24.5	25.4	20.1	16.8	14.1
Gross domestic investment	13.8	14.7	19.6	26.9	28.4
Net exports	−8.2	−7.3	−4.4	−2.4	5.7
Percentage of total resource available for domestic use					
Private consumption	64.6	62.7	62.0	57.4	54.9
Government consumption	22.6	23.6	19.3	16.4	15.0
Gross domestic investment	12.7	13.7	18.7	26.2	30.1

Source: DGBAS, *National Income of the Republic of China*, 1973, supporting tables 13 and 15.

the share of consumption (private and public) declined dramatically, and (2) net imports, or the gap between national product and expenditure, became increasingly smaller and finally turned negative.

Although the share of private consumption in GNP dropped in the 1950s, that of public consumption rose, so that before 1960 the share of total consumption in GNP was only marginally reduced. Needless to say, the investment share also did not improve noticeably before 1960. The allocation of resources by final use was, however, significantly altered in the 1960s. The share of both private and public consumption in GNP declined steadily after the late 1950s: private consumption from 67 percent in 1956–60 to 52 percent in 1970–73, and public consumption from 25 percent in 1956–60 to 14 percent in 1970–73. Because it was able to keep consumption from rising as fast as income, Taiwan was able to allocate a greater share of its GNP to investment. In 1970–73 the share of gross domestic capital formation in GNP was 28 percent, double the 1951–55 level. Taiwan's increasing ability to export also reduced its import surplus, and in 1970–73 it enjoyed substantial export surpluses.

We now examine in detail the behavior and composition of the two major components of domestic expenditure: consumption (private and government) and investment.

CONSUMPTION AND LIVING STANDARDS

Table 11.2 gives per capita consumption and other standard-of-living indicators for Taiwan for selected years. The growth of real private consumption in Taiwan, compared with that of other developing countries, has been rapid, exceeding the growth rate of population by a significant margin. Taiwan's real per capita consumption (in 1966 prices) more than doubled between 1951 and 1973, rising from NT$ 3,097 to NT$ 8,310, an achievement matched by few less developed countries. About three-quarters of the growth in per capita consumption came after 1960.

Theoretical considerations suggest that household consumption pattern alters in important ways when income rises, the chief being the decline in food expenditure as a share of total outlay predicted by Engle's law. The income elasticity of food for Taiwan, estimated from cross-sectional data for 1964, is 0.66.[2] Estimates of income elasticities for other major consumption categories show the following to be also income inelastic: tobacco, fuel and lighting, beverages, and personal care and health. Among categories with high income elasticities are transportation and communication, household furnishing, and recreation.

Structural changes in the economy that are associated with development also worked to change Taiwan's private consumption pattern. For example, the consumption pattern of rural population is quite different from that of urban population. Consumption patterns also differ by occupational group. Thus shifts in occupation and rapid urbanization in the postwar period must have had considerable impact on aggregate consumption. The surveys of family incomes and expenditures conducted in the 1960s found that food absorbed a higher percentage of the family budget of farmers than that of non-farmers.[3] On the other hand, because of the tighter housing market in

2. Chung-li Chang and A. F. Hinrichs, "Personal Income Distribution and Consumption Pattern in Taiwan—1964," *Industry of Free China* 29 (Dec. 1967): 39.

3. Consumption by farmers and nonfarmers and by occupation of head of household can be found in ibid., table 11; PBAS, *Report on the Survey of Family Income and Expenditure in Taiwan, 1966*, June 1968, table 11; and *Report on the Survey of Family Income and Expenditure in Taiwan, 1968*, June 1970, table 8.

Table 11.2. Per Capita Consumption and Other Standard-of-Living Indicators

| | Real consumption per capita (1966 NT$) | Food nutrient available per day | | Consumer durables[a] (sets per 1,000 families) | | No. of persons per registered medical personnel[b] | Percentage of school-age children attending school[c] | Percentage of elementary school graduates progressing to junior middle school |
		Energy (cal.)	Protein (g)	Radios	Bicycles			
1951	3,097	2,069	47.1	33	322	740[d]	81.5	36.6
1955	3,956	2,218	53.2	76	524	686	92.3	43.0
1960	4,313	2,361	57.1	350	759	666	95.6	51.2
1965	5,633	2,381	61.2	579	—	565	97.1	57.4
1970	7,070	—	—	—	—	445	98.0	79.8

Sources: Real consumption: DGBAS, *National Income of the Republic of China*, 1973, pp. 152–53. Food nutrient available per capita per day: JCRR, *Taiwan Food Balance Sheet*, various years. Consumer durables: Neil H. Jacoby, *U.S. Aid to Taiwan*, pp. 304 and 307; U.N., *Statistical Yearbook For Asia and the Far East*, 1969, p. 106. Registered medical personnel: CIECD, *Taiwan Statistical Data Book*, 1973, p. 229. Education Data: DGBAS, *Statistical Abstract of the Republic of China*, various years. Midyear population: table 8.1.

[a] As registered with the provincial government.

[b] Includes physicians, herb physicians, dentists and assistants, pharmacists and assistants, nurses, and midwives.

[c] School-age children are those between 6 and 12.

[d] 1952.

cities, rent claimed a much greater share of the budget of urban dwellers than that of rural dwellers. In comparison with farm families, nonfarm families also spent more of their income on household operation, recreation, and transportation and communication. Although this difference as well as the others may be explained largely by the higher income enjoyed by the nonfarm urban families, higher income alone is an inadequate explanation. For example, even without differences in income, an urban dweller, to perform his daily activities, is likely to require more transportation services than would a person living in rural Taiwan. Thus, one suspects that structural changes in the economy, the foremost being urbanization and shifts in occupation, are in part responsible for the higher income elasticities found for such consumption categories as rent and transportation and communication when estimated from time series data than from cross-sectional data.[4]

Rising income and structural changes in the economy produced the expected changes in Taiwan's aggregate conumption pattern. In accordance with Engle's law, the expenditure on food as a percentage of total outlay (both expressed in 1966 prices) fell from 58 percent in 1951–55 to 43 percent in 1966–70.[5] With the exception of expenditures on tobacco and fuel and light (9.2 percent of total outlay in 1966–70), expenditures on nonfood items as shares of total outlay displayed a rising trend. In 1966–70 they comprised 47.8 percent of total outlay.

The rapidly rising per capita consumption, the declining share of expenditure on food, and the rising share of expenditure on recreation and other semiluxury items all suggest that the standard of living and the quality of life improved considerably in the postwar period. Although the average Taiwanese undoubtedly lived better in 1970 than he did two decades earlier, we nonetheless should not accept the aggregate consumption data as providing a completely undistorted and fully revealing picture of living standards.

First of all, estimates of private consumption often rest on a rather shaky statistical foundation. In Taiwan the primary source of data used in estimating private consumption is the household budget survey. But until recently such surveys have been infrequently taken and often improperly designed.[6] Despite efforts to adjust and improve earlier

4. For example, compare the findings of Yung-san Lee in his "An Analysis of Consumers' Demand Functions in Taiwan 1951–1969," and those in Chang and Hinrichs, "Income Distribution and Consumption in Taiwan."

5. This and the following ratios are based on data in DGBAS, *National Income of the Republic of China*, 1973, pp. 142–45.

6. One problem was small sample size.

estimates, it is generally accepted that the reliability of consumption estimates decreases considerably as we move back into the 1950s. Fortunately, several commonly used standard-of-living indicators are not based on survey results (a number are presented in table 11.2). Together they show unequivocally that living conditions improved in the postwar period. For example, not only has per capita caloric intake increased since the early 1950s, but so has the quality of the diet. Radios and bicycles, owned only by the relatively well-to-do families in the 1950s, were owned by even the relatively poor households in the late 1960s.

Secondly, living conditions of individuals are not a function of private consumption alone; they are also affected by government consumption. Government services rendered to households, such as expenditures on health and education, are treated as government consumption for national income accounting purposes but are ultimately consumed by households as final products. Therefore, they should be taken into account when evaluating changes in the standard of living of individuals. Government consumption is to be discussed below; suffice it to say that since the early 1950s an increasing share of government consumption has been spent on public education. The growing importance of this item is reflected in the education indicators in table 11.2.

Third, Kuznets and others have suggested that some of the goods and services normally categorized as consumption probably should not be treated as final products.[7] For instance, we know that in Taiwan an urban family makes greater consumption outlays for transportation than does a rural household, so that with urbanization a greater share of total consumption would be spent on transportation. But the larger outlay is made necessary partly by the need to work in the city and partly because in an urban environment one is often required to travel a greater distance to satisfy the same needs than one living in rural areas. It can therefore be argued that much of the increased use of transportation should be considered not as an increase in final consumption but as an increase in the cost of production. To the extent that these consumption items are intermediate goods, consumption as defined for national income accounting purposes gives a distorted picture of living standards.

Finally, many benefits and costs of economic growth are not reflected in national product and consumption measurements. Examples of

7. Simon Kuznets, *Modern Economic Growth Rate Structure and Spread*, pp. 220–34.

Table 11.3. Distribution of Government Consumption by Purpose (Annual averages, percentages based on totals in current prices)

	1951–55	1956–60	1961–65	1966–70	1971–73
Total government consumption	100.0	100.0	100.0	100.0	100.0
Administration and defense	66.5	67.7	70.3	64.8	60.8
Developmental expenditures	13.5	21.0	20.1	25.1	27.2
Education and research	6.9	13.0	12.3	18.0	18.9
Public health	1.5	2.0	2.2	2.0	2.1
Economic reconstruction	2.8	3.8	2.9	2.8	4.1
Transport and communication	2.3	2.2	2.2	2.3	2.1
Other consumption	20.0	11.2	9.7	10.2	12.0

Source: DGBAS, *National Income of the Republic of China*, 1973, pp. 32–33.

excluded items are readily available, e.g., leisure, pollution, and various other external economies and diseconomies of economic growth, some of which significantly affect the quality of life. In Taipei, for instance, as a result of industrialization and urbanization, air pollution increased by 50 percent between 1959 and 1965; in residential areas it actually doubled.[8] Clearly, for those living in Taipei and its vicinity the quality of life has been adversely affected by this development—a change not taken into account by the per capita consumption indicator.

General government consumption, in 1966 prices, more than tripled between 1951 and 1973, rising from NT$ 9.77 billion to NT$ 34.33 billion. However, in this same period its relative share in GNP declined from 38 to 27 percent. Table 11.3 presents the distribution of government consumption by purpose. In the 1950s and 1960s, about two-thirds of government consumption was spent on administration and defense. Furthermore, despite great increases in total government consumption, the share spent on administration and defense rose steadily until the late 1960s. A big army and the continued maintenance of central and provincial government agencies with more or less the same responsibilities are the major reasons for the large and increasing expenditure on administration and defense. In the late 1960s and early 1970s actions were taken to streamline the armed forces. These efforts and the greater priority given to economic programs helped to bring about a decline in the share of government expenditure spent on administration and defense.

8. Statistics released by the Taiwan Provincial Institute of Environmental Sanitation show that the average fallout in Taipei increased from 39 tons/square mile/month in 1959 to 56 in 1966. In Taipei's residential areas, the increase was from 30 tons/square mile/month in 1959 to 61 in 1965.

The share of government developmental expenditures has grown significantly. Nearly all the increase in the relative share of developmental expenditures is attributable to the rise in government expenditures on education and research. One major cause of this increase was the government's decision to extend free public education from grades six to nine. It is uncertain whether all developmental expenditures should be categorized as consumption. The importance to economic development of education and other forms of human investment has been made abundantly clear in the literature, and a portion of these expenditures probably should be considered as investment. Similarly, expenditures on economic reconstruction, transportation, and communication may also facilitate economic development and therefore should not be considered as solely consumption.

INVESTMENT

Real gross domestic capital formation (in 1966 prices) increased from an annual average of NT$ 6.31 billion in 1951–55 to 9.54 billion in 1956–60, 18.58 billion in 1961–65, 41.05 billion in 1966–70, and 64.91 billion in 1971–73. As a share of real GNP, real gross domestic capital formation was less than 15 percent in the 1950s but increased to 19.6 percent in 1961–65, 26.9 percent in 1966–70, and 28.4 percent in 1971–73. The performance in the 1960s and the early 1970s is impressive and far surpasses that of other less developed countries.

Inventory investment was relatively important until the mid-1960s. When expressed in 1966 prices, it was about 18 percent of gross domestic investment in the 1950s and over 21 percent in 1961–65 (table 11.4). Several plausible explanations for Taiwan's high inventory/investment ratio can be suggested. First, the replenishment of stocks depleted during the war and the immediate postwar years probably explains much of the inventory investment in the early 1950s. Second, with unstable prices in the 1950s there was also a tendency among businessmen to invest in inventory as a hedge against inflation as well as a possible source of speculative profit. Third, since Taiwan depends heavily on imports for its raw materials, the difficulties and the cost of obtaining goods from distant suppliers, as well as problems caused by Taiwan's strict and complicated import and exchange controls, might have influenced Taiwanese firms to hold more inventory than was usually required. Finally, Taiwan's high inventory/investment ratio may be the result of inferior management and an inefficient distribution

Table 11.4. Composition of Gross Domestic Capital Formation (Annual averages, in percent)

	1951–55		1956–60		1961–65		1966–70		1971–73	
	Current Prices	1966 Prices	Current Prices	1966 Prices	Current Prices	1966 Prices	Current Prices	1966 Prices	Current Prices	1966 Prices
Gross domestic capital formation	100.0	100.0	100.0	100.0	100.0	100.0	100.0	100.0	100.0	100.0
Gross fixed capital formation	79.8	81.0	84.4	82.6	79.3	78.2	85.9	85.6	101.2	100.9
Increase in stocks	20.2	19.0	15.6	17.4	20.7	21.8	14.1	14.4	-1.2	-0.9
Gross fixed capital formation	100.0	100.0	100.0	100.0	100.0	100.0	100.0	100.0	100.0	100.0
Construction	54.0	61.4	50.6	54.2	51.3	53.3	43.4	40.4	36.7	30.8
Dwellings	10.7	a	11.6	a	11.1	a	10.2	a	10.9	a
Nonresidential buildings	22.4	a	20.3	a	20.6	a	19.9	a	14.0	a
Other construction	21.0	a	18.7	a	19.7	a	13.3	a	11.8	a
Producer equip.	46.0	38.6	49.4	45.8	48.7	46.6	56.6	59.6	63.3	69.3
Transport equip.	7.6	6.4	8.5	8.1	10.7	9.6	11.7	11.7	14.1	14.1
Machinery and other equip.	38.4	32.2	40.9	37.7	38.0	37.0	44.9	47.9	49.2	55.2

Source: DGBAS, National Income of the Republic of China, 1973, pp. 114–17 and 142–45.
aData not available.

and transportation system. In the mid-1960s, as prices stabilized, as import controls were relaxed, and as management improved, the inventory/investment ratio declined. Inventory investment was less than 15 percent of total investment in 1966–70, and it was negative in 1971–73.

Table 11.4 also gives the structure of gross fixed capital formation. In real terms, construction accounted for 61 percent of total fixed investment in 1951–55, 54 percent in 1956–65, 40 percent in 1966–70, and 31 percent in 1971–73.[9] When construction is divided into dwellings, nonresidential buildings, and other construction, we see that other construction, consisting primarily of investment in irrigation and flood control facilities, showed the slowest increase and is the main reason for the relative decline of construction in total fixed investment. Judging by its stable share in total fixed investment, residential construction occurred at a rate exceeding that of population growth. However, its share in total construction was small (about 20–25 percent), so that most of Taiwan's construction was in areas more directly related to production. Because advanced technology is often embodied in new machinery, it is significant that investment in equipment accounted for an increasing share of Taiwan's total fixed investment. Investment in equipment, in 1966 prices, was 60 percent of total fixed investment in 1966–70 and almost 70 percent in 1971–73. Its growth in the 1960s and early 1970s reflects the government's decision to modernize Taiwan's transportation system and, more generally, Taiwan's rapid rate of industrialization.

Table 11.5 shows the distribution of total gross fixed capital formation by economic sectors. The share received by agriculture in 1951–55 was nearly 25 percent, greater than that received by any other sector in the economy. Much of this early investment went to repair and improve irrigation and flood control facilities neglected during the war and the immediate postwar period. Thereafter, reflecting the decreasing importance of agriculture in the economy and the higher priority assigned to industrialization, agriculture's share in total investment steadily declined. Investment in industrial (mining, manufacturing, and construction) fixed capital was 24 percent of total fixed investment in 1951–55. With government promoting industrialization

9. Because much of Taiwan's capital equipment was imported and because the NT$ was substantially overvalued in the 1950s, the share of producer equipment in gross fixed investment is probably understated and that of construction overstated.

Table 11.5. Distribution of Gross Fixed Capital Formation by Economic Sector
(Annual averages, percentages based on totals in current prices)

	1951–55	*1956–60*	*1961–65*	*1966–70*	*1971–73*
Classification I					
Total	*100.0*	*100.0*	*100.0*	*100.0*	*100.0*
Agriculture	*24.9*	*19.7*	*18.0*	*12.0*	*8.3*
Industry	*23.6*	*26.1*	*27.4*	*34.7*	*34.9*
Mining	1.1	1.6	1.4	0.9	1.0
Manufacturing	22.1	23.8	25.5	33.1	32.7
Construction	0.4	0.7	0.5	0.7	1.2
Services	*51.5*	*54.3*	*54.5*	*53.2*	*56.7*
Electricity, gas, & water	10.3	14.3	11.2	11.0	14.1
Transportation, storage, & communication	11.2	13.8	16.4	17.6	18.3
Wholesale & retail trade	9.9	4.6	5.0	5.1	3.1
Banking, insurance, & real estate	1.3	0.7	1.0	0.9	0.9
Ownership of dwellings	10.7	11.6	11.1	10.2	10.9
Public administration	6.0	7.8	6.4	5.1	4.7
Other services	2.1	1.5	3.4	3.3	4.7
Classification II					
Total	*100.0*	*100.0*	*100.0*	*100.0*	*100.0*
Agriculture	24.9	19.7	18.0	12.0	8.3
Industry +[a]	45.1	54.1	55.1	63.3	67.3
Service —[b]	30.0	26.2	26.9	24.6	24.3

Source: DGBAS, *National Income of the Republic of China,* 1973, pp. 114–17.
[a] Mining, manufacturing, construction, electricity, gas and water, and transportation, storage, and communication.
[b] Wholesale and retail trade, banking, insurance and real estate, ownership of dwellings, public administration, and other services.

and with the generally high profitability of this sector,[10] industrial investment increased rapidly and its share in total fixed investment increased. After 1966, 35 percent of total fixed investment was in industry, almost all of it allocated to manufacturing. Investment in all service sectors as a share of total fixed investment has held steady at about 53 percent. But when this figure is disaggregated we find that,

10. In 1961–64, according to the results of surveys conducted by the Bank of Taiwan and the Taiwan Provincial Department of Reconstruction, the average earnings on net worth of private industrial firms with assets over 1 million NT$ (US$ 25,000) was about 17 percent. However, this must be considered the lower limit since the reporting firms, if anything, would have tended to underreport profits. See BOT and PDOR, *Report of Survey on the Financial Status of Industrial and Mining Enterprises in Taiwan,* various years.

except for transportation and utility, every service sector suffered a decline in its relative investment share. Because transportation and utility tend to be modern and are closely connected with manufacturing, they are often included as part of the industrial sector. When this is done for Taiwan (table 11.5, classification II), industrial investment becomes by far the largest component of total fixed investment, rising from 45 percent in 1951–55 to 67 percent in 1970–73.

Government played a vital role in the investment process. Indirectly, as we shall soon see, it introduced incentives to influence both the size and direction of investment. Directly, general government and government enterprises together accounted for 54 percent of the total fixed investment in 1955–60 and 40 percent in 1961–73.[11] In the 1950s private investors were uncertain of Taiwan's political and economic future. After the Chinese communist army attacked Quemoy in late 1954, private investment plunged. As a share of total fixed investment, it declined from 63 percent in 1954 to 46 percent in 1955, in a period when total investment (in 1966 prices) declined from 6.2 to 5.4 billion NT$. Private investors did not regain confidence in Taiwan until after the Nationalist army decisively repulsed a second major communist assault on Quemoy in 1959. Thereafter, total real investment increased rapidly as also did the share of private investment in total investment. In 1970–73 the private sector made 59 percent of total fixed investment, government enterprises 30 percent, and general government 10 percent.

THE FINANCING OF INVESTMENTS

The sources of finance for gross domestic capital formation are shown in table 11.6. In the 1950s capital consumption allowances provided about one-third of the financing needed for domestic investment. However, its share decreased in the 1960s, and in 1966–70 capital consumption allowances accounted for only one-quarter of gross domestic investment. The other major source of finance was domestic savings, composed of savings of general government, public corporations, government enterprises, and the private sector. Government savings financed one-third of gross domestic investment in 1951–55 and one-fifth in 1956–60, but only 10 percent in the 1960s. On the other hand, the contribution of private domestic savings has increased from about one-fourth of gross domestic savings in the 1950s to almost

11. DGBAS, *National Income of the Republic of China*, 1973, p. 210.

Table 11.6. National Savings and the Financing of Gross Domestic Capital Formation
(Annual averages, percentages based on totals in current prices)

	1951–55	1956–60	1961–65	1966–70
Classification I				
GDCF	100.0	100.0	100.0	100.0
Capital consumption	33.8	33.4	31.3	24.5
Savings	64.8	51.0	63.1	70.5
General government	33.4	20.4	9.5	12.4
Public corporation & government				
enterprises	4.0	7.1	7.5	9.1
Private sector	27.4	23.5	46.1	49.0
Deficit of nation on current acct.	0.4	13.3	5.5	3.6
Statistical discrepancy	1.1	2.2	0.1	1.4
Classification II				
GDCF	100.0	100.0	100.0	100.0
Foreign savings[a]	39.6	40.4	15.1	5.4
Gross national savings	59.4	57.3	84.7	93.2
Capital consumption	33.8	33.4	31.3	24.5
Net national savings	25.6	23.9	53.4	68.7
General government	− 5.2	− 4.4	1.9	12.2
Public corporation & government				
enterprises	4.0	7.1	7.5	9.1
Private savings	26.8	21.2	44.0	47.4
Statistical discrepancy	1.1	2.2	0.1	1.4

Source: **DGBAS**, *National Income of the Republic of China*, 1973, pp. 110–13, 124–25, 130–33, and 140–41.

[a]Estimates of undistributed earnings of foreign companies in Taiwan are not available. Thus foreign savings are underestimated and national savings overestimated. It is believed that reinvestment of earnings by foreign companies did not become significant until the late 1960s.

one-half in 1966–70. In comparison with the general government and the private sector, the savings of government enterprises have been much less important, accounting for less than 10 percent of gross domestic savings. Finally, the deficit of the nation on current account— the last source of finance of gross domestic capital formation—played a relatively minor role except in 1956–60, when it accounted for over 13 percent of Taiwan's gross domestic savings; but this soon fell to around 5 percent in the 1960s.

In the preceding paragraph the sources of funds for gross domestic capital formation were presented strictly in the national income accounting framework. Thus international transfer payments are recorded in the government and household accounts, so what are really

Table 11.7. Structure of National and Foreign Savings (Annual averages, percentages based on data in current prices)

	1951–55	1956–60	1961–65	1966–70
Share in national income				
Gross national savings	10.3	12.8	20.8	29.0
Net national savings	4.4	5.3	13.1	21.4
Net private national savings	4.6	4.7	10.8	14.8
Contribution of public sector				
(Including public corporations and government enterprises)				
To net national savings	−4.7	11.3	17.6	30.9
To gross national savings	16.5	24.4	23.4	31.0
(Excluding public corporations and government enterprises)				
To net national savings	−20.3	−18.4	3.6	17.7
To gross national savings	−8.8	−7.7	2.2	13.1
Contribution of unrequited international transfers				
To foreign savings	99.3	67.6	69.9	33.3
To gross domestic capital fromation	39.4	27.3	10.6	1.8

Source: Underlying data are from DGBAS, *National Income of the Republic of China*, 1973, pp. 110–13, 124–25, 130–33, and 140–41.

foreign savings appear as government or private savings. This is unfortunate because international transfers played a significant role in Taiwan's development. To more clearly identify the original sources of savings, we make a distinction between national savings (what Taiwan saves out of income produced domestically) and foreign savings (net borrowing from the rest of the world plus net transfers from the rest of the world). The sum of national and foreign savings of course equals gross domestic capital formation. When such a distinction is made (see table 11.6 (classification II) and table 11.7), the importance of foreign savings in financing Taiwan's investment becomes evident. In the 1950s foreign savings was about 40 percent of gross domestic capital formation. Nearly all foreign savings in this early period were U.S. aid. Unrequited transfers from abroad accounted for 99 percent of total foreign savings in 1951–55 and almost 70 percent in 1956–65. In the 1960s, with Taiwan's economic conditions much improved, the size of foreign aid diminished. However, foreign loans and investments became more significant.

Table 11.8 shows that in the 1960s, although the United States government was an important source of loans for Taiwan, it was not

Table 11.8. Long-term Foreign Credits and Loans Received, by Major Source (US$ million)

	1960	1961	1962	1963	1964	1965	1966	1967	1968	1969	1970	1971
Received by private sector[a]	18.6	24.7	11.0	13.8	12.3	28.2	48.1	115.3	73.8	144.5	117.7	111.7
Asian Dev. Bank	—	—	—	—	—	—	7.7	30.5	15.4	10.1	13.7	10.4
Export-Import Bank of Japan	—	—	—	—	—	9.6	17.9	3.3	8.2	18.3	28.8	7.3
IBRD	—	—	0.2	1.2	2.5	1.4	—	—	—	—	—	45.0
IDA	—	—	—	—	—	—	—	—	—	—	—	—
U.S. government	0.9	1.5	2.4	3.0	2.1	2.7	2.0	29.7	19.4	19.7	3.9	10.8
Suppliers' credit[b]	17.7	23.5	8.4	9.6	7.7	14.5	20.5	51.8	30.8	96.4	71.3	38.2
Received by local government	1.9	8.8	6.3	3.5	2.3	0.9	0.2	21.8	6.2	9.3	5.6	3.3
Japanese Overseas Econ. Coop. fund	—	—	—	—	—	—	0.2	0.6	3.3	8.7	5.6	3.3
IDA	—	—	2.6	2.8	1.9	0.6	—	—	—	0.5	—	—
Export-Import Bank of Japan	—	—	3.7	0.7	0.4	0.3	—	—	2.9	—	—	—
U.S. government	1.9	8.8	—	—	—	—	—	18.1	—	—	—	—
IBRD	—	—	—	—	—	—	—	3.1	—	—	—	—
Asian Dev. Bank	—	—	—	—	—	—	—	—	—	0.1	—	—
Received by central government	9.6	14.9	16.1	32.6	25.1	43.0	25.9	8.8	—	—	0.4	3.4
U.S. government	9.6	14.9	14.8	16.3	11.7	27.4	15.6	8.4	—	—	—	0.1
U.S. private sector	—	—	1.3	16.3	13.4	15.6	10.3	0.4	—	—	—	—
Others	—	—	—	—	—	—	—	—	—	—	0.4	3.3

Source: IMF, Balance of Payments Yearbook, various issues.

[a] Includes government enterprises.

[b] Largely advanced by Japanese and U.S. companies. In 1967–71, U.S. and Japanese companies accounted for 82% of the credit listed in this category.

the only source. Increasingly, Taiwan was able to borrow from international lending agencies and from Japan. Efforts to increase foreign investment and to direct such investment toward preferred industries, primarily those in manufacturing, also intensified in the 1960s. In 1959–60 Taiwan amended its investment laws for foreign nationals. Among other features, the amended statutes provided attractive tax concessions, including a five-year holiday from the business income tax, allowed repatriation of profits and interest two years after the completion of the approved investment (annual repatriation not to exceed 15 percent of invested principle), and gave extensive protection against expropriation. Average annual foreign investment approved by the Ministry of Economic Affairs was US$ 20 million in 1961–65, US$ 85 million in 1966–70, and US$ 145 million in 1971–72.[12] About one-third of the approved investment was from overseas Chinese, and the rest from Americans and Japanese. In 1968–72 direct investment arrived at an average rate of US$ 44 million a year.

Although tax incentives undoubtedly helped to create a more favorable investment climate in Taiwan, other factors, particularly political stability, were more important to foreign investors. In the late 1960s the government interviewed foreign investors and asked their reasons for investing in Taiwan. When their answers were compiled into a weighted index of importance, political stability (measured at 1,201) was first, followed by low wage rates (849), attractive domestic market (701), well-educated and dependable laborers (625), low cost of energy fuel (577), assurance of a five-year tax holiday (551), and other tax incentives (202).[13] Given the fact that tax savings in Taiwan were often partially negated by increases in tax paid to the foreign investor's own country and that tax exemption occurred during the initial period of operation, when profits tend to be low, it is not surprising that foreign investors attached relatively little importance to tax incentives.

The value of foreign aid and foreign investment notwithstanding, the bulk of Taiwan's investment was still financed by its own savings. Gross national savings was 60 percent of gross domestic capital formation in the 1950s, 85 percent in 1961–65, and 93 percent in 1966–

12. Based on data in CIECD, *Taiwan Statistical Data Book*, 1973, p. 210.
13. Executive Yuan Tax Reform Commission, *The Report of the Executive Yuan Tax Reform Commission, Part III, Special Research Topics*, vol. 1, June 1970, p. 100. The results of Schreiber's study of U.S. investors in Taiwan are generally consistent with these findings (see Jordan C. Schreiber, *U.S. Corporate Investment in Taiwan*).

70 (table 11.6). As a share of national income, gross national savings increased from 10 percent in 1951–55 to 29 percent in 1966–70 (table 11.7), providing impressive evidence of Taiwan's willingness and increasing ability to save.

In the 1950s, hampered by a relatively inefficient tax system and a large military budget, the government (when net foreign transfers are excluded from its revenue) was a dissaver. Only in the second half of the 1960s did government savings become significant. In 1966–70 it was 13 percent of Taiwan's gross national savings. A government's ability to save is determined, to a great extent, by its ability to generate tax revenue. In Taiwan, government taxes as a share of GNP hovered around 14 percent (table 11.9), substantially below that found in many less developed countries. Furthermore, Taiwan's income elasticity of tax revenue, at unity, was one of the lowest among the 28 estimated for less developed countries by UNCTAD.[14]

To see why Taiwan's tax revenue was relatively income inelastic, we need only to examine its tax structure (table 11.9). As in many other less developed countries, Taiwan's tax system is characterized by an excessive dependence on indirect taxes, which on the whole are not only regressive but also inelastic in yield as income rises. The yields from Taiwan's income taxes were disappointing. Given the exemptions provided by the law and Taiwan's low per capita income,[15] even if everyone had complied strictly with the law, which certainly was not the case, personal income tax would not have yielded large amounts of revenue in the 1960s. Ambiguity and obvious inequities in the tax law also encouraged many business enterprises to evade the business income tax and thus kept its yield low.[16] With income taxes relatively unproductive, indirect taxes produced nearly 80 percent of Taiwan's total tax revenue in the 1950s and 1960s. UNCTAD found

14. UNCTAD Secretariat, *The Mobilization of Internal Resources by the Developing Countries.*

15. In the 1960s a family of five with an income of NT$ 35,000 paid no income tax (see Executive Yuan Tax Reform Comission, *The Report of the Executive Yuan Tax Reform Commission, Part I, Consolidated Report*, June 1970, p. 56). In 1964, three-quarters of the families in Taiwan earned less than NT$ 35,000. Fewer than 0.5 percent of the families in Taiwan earned income in the 3.5 percent or higher income tax brackets.

16. For example, unlike the treatment accorded corporations, the undistributed profits of unincorporated enterprises were considered personal income and therefore were subject to the personal income tax as well. Since those in this category cannot pay the business income tax without also being liable for the personal income tax, there exists a built-in incentive for unincorporated enterprises to avoid paying either of these taxes.

Table 11.9. Structure of Taxes, Selected Years (Percentage of total)

	Direct taxes			Indirect taxes				Total taxes as percentage of GNP
	Total	Income	Property	Total	Monopoly revenue	Domestic products	Imports[a]	
Total taxes								
1952	100	27.8	13.5	14.3	72.2	17.8	30.0	24.3	13.7
1956	100	24.9	10.5	14.4	75.1	20.5	31.4	23.1	15.9
1961	100	22.2	10.3	11.9	77.8	22.7	34.0	21.0	13.2
1966	100	20.0	8.1	11.8	80.0	21.4	32.4	26.2	13.0
1971	100	22.7	10.3	12.4	77.3	16.1	35.0	26.2	15.5

Source: CIECD, Taiwan Statistical Data Book, 1973, pp. 18, 143, and 144.
[a] Includes harbor dues.

Taiwan's tax system to be the most dependent on indirect taxes of the 32 less developed countries it investigated.[17]

In the late 1960s the government became convinced that if it were to play a more active role in the economy, especially if it is to affect savings, the revenue system had to be improved and made more dependent on direct taxes. In early 1969 the income tax law was revised and a new rate structure promulgated.[18] In effect, the tax reform reduced the tax burden on small businesses and individuals with relatively low income and increased the income tax on larger firms and persons with high income.[19] More important, to reduce tax evasion, the government also introduced a computerized system to process and scrutinize tax returns. As a result the revenues from income taxes as a share of total revenue, after declining steadily for two decades, increased in the early 1970s. Partly because of the improved income tax system, but mainly because of the rapid expansion of manufacturing output and trade that increased the revenues from custom duties and commodity taxes, tax revenue increased rapidly in the late 1960s and early 1970s. The rise in revenue in turn enabled the Taiwan government to increase its savings, and in 1966–70, 18 percent of Taiwan's net national savings was generated by the government (table 11.7). When the savings of government enterprises are added to those of general government, the public sector accounted for 31 percent of Taiwan's net national savings in 1966–70 (table 11.7).

Households and private enterprises were responsible for a preponderant share of gross national savings, accounting for 84 percent in 1951–55, 75 percent in 1956–65, and 70 percent in 1966–70. Net private national savings as a share of national income rose dramatically in the 1960s, jumping from 4.7 percent in 1956–60 to 14.8 percent in 1966–70. Unfortunately, a breakdown of private national savings between private enterprises and households cannot be made from the national income data.[20] Most likely, both households and the private business sector contributed to this desirable development.

17. UNCTAD, *Mobilization of Internal Resources.*
18. For a more detailed discussion of the adopted revisions, see Executive Yuan Tax Reform Commission, *The Report of the Executive Yuan Tax Reform Commission, Part I, Consolidated Report*, pp. 45–104.
19. Under the new tax law, a family of five earning less than NT$ 45,454 (US$ 1,364) would pay no income tax.
20. A survey of national savings in 1958–59 found net household savings to be 74 percent of total net private national savings (see BOT, *Survey of National Savings, Taiwan, Republic of China, 1958–59*, pp. 5–10). However, savings of private enterprises were estimated from tax returns and may be biased downward. Flow-of-fund data

Many factors contributed to bring about the increase in private savings. Political stability and the realization that Taiwan was not likely to fall to communist China helped. Rising income also played its part. From cross-sectional studies, we know that Taiwan's marginal propensity to consume is smaller than the average propensity and that both decline as income rises.[21] Moreover, this relationship remained stable over time. Thus, with the rapid rise in real income in the 1960s it is not surprising that the average rate of saving of the household sector increased.

Government economic policy and incentives also encouraged accumulation. To entice more saving in the private sector and to influence the asset choice of individual savers toward holdings of debt instruments, the government enacted the Statute for Encouragement of Investment in 1960.[22] The incentives included the exclusion from taxable income capital gains on securities held for more than one year and interest earned on fixed-term savings deposits of more than two years. The statute also gave a five-year income-tax holiday to qualified newly established enterprises and enterprises that expanded capacity by 30 percent. Furthermore, for all enterprises, reinvested profits, up to 25 percent of total income, were exempt from the business income tax. Unquestionably, these incentives helped to create an environment more conducive to accumulation. But perhaps even more important to the saving–investment process were changes that occurred in the Taiwan money market.

In the 1950s the monetary authority imposed on banks ceilings on lending and deposit rates that were considerably below the market rates.[23] In effect the government removed interest rate as an allocative instrument and banks turned to rationing their credits. Not sur-

---

show that in the late 1960s private enterprises accounted for 30–40 percent of gross private national savings (see CBC, *The Republic of China, Taiwan Financial Statistics Monthly*, Aug. 1975, pp. 96–102).

21. For example, see Chang and Hinrichs, "Income Distribution and Consumption in Taiwan," pp. 41–44, and PBAS, *Report on the Survey of Family Income and Expenditure in Taiwan, 1966*, June 1968, attached table 24.

22. Besides the tax concessions, the statute also removed several serious obstacles imposed by the existing land reform legislation on the acquisition of land for industrial use. The Statute for Encouragement of Investment was amended in 1965 and again in 1970. Among other changes the 1970 regulation allowed qualified productive enterprises to select either a five-year holiday from the income tax or to depreciate fixed assets on the basis of an accelerated service life. But once a selection is made, no change is allowed. For details, see CIECD, *Statute for Encouragement of Investment*, Apr. 1971.

23. The government gave two main reasons for maintaining low interest rates: (1) to induce investment and encourage economic growth and (2) to lower the cost of production and thereby help to stabilize prices. However, the effect was just the opposite.

prisingly, in this period more than 80 percent of the business loans and discounts granted by the Bank of Taiwan (the island's most important lending institution) were to government enterprises.[24] Private firms, shut out of the banking system, turned to the unorganized money market and often had to accept short-term credits to finance long-term investments. Low interest rates (in real terms) in the banks and price instability also drove savings to the riskier and highly imperfect unorganized money market[25] or to unproductive uses, e.g., hoarding of foreign exchange. In other words the government's interest rate policy discouraged both saving and investment.

In the 1960s the government continued to lower the nominal deposit and lending rates. The interest rate on three-month time deposits fell from 9 percent in 1959 to 6.2 percent in 1971. Interest rates on deposits of longer maturities, which were kept above the three-month rate, also declined. The interest on secured bank loans fell from over 17 percent in 1961 to 12 percent in 1971. However, with inflation receding in the 1960s (from 1961 to 1971 the implicit GNP deflator increased at an average annual rate of only 3.3 percent), the real rate of interest increased even as the nominal rate declined. In the 1960s, after accounting for inflation, the real rate of interest on one-year deposits fluctuated between 7 and 10 percent. Price stability and the greater availability of foreign exchange also made the hoarding of U.S. dollars, as well as other unproductive forms of saving, less profitable. Furthermore, the 1960 bankruptcy of Tang Eng Iron Works, once the largest private enterprise in Taiwan and a heavy borrower on the unorganized money market, made the risk of lending outside the banking system abundantly clear, particularly to small individual savers.

These developments not only helped to attract an increasing share of the savings into the financial sytem but also increased the total amount saved. Bank deposits soared. Table 11.10 shows that between 1961 and 1971 deposits increased more than sixfold. Also significant was the fact that time and saving deposits accounted for an increasingly

---

24. CBC, *Taiwan Financial Statistics Monthly*, Apr. 1970, pp. 15–16.

25. In the mid- and late-1950s, banks were offering interest rates of 9–10 percent a year on three-month time deposits. From 1954 to 1960 the implicit GNP deflator increased at an annual rate of 8 percent. Because of the low interest rate (in real terms) offered by the banks, a substantial amount of loanable funds, perhaps in the range of 25–50 percent of the financial system credit volume (see R. F. Leonard, F. L. Deming, and Chester Morrill, *Comments and Recommendations on Central Banking in the Republic of China*, p. 83), was attracted to the unorganized money market by its much higher interest rate.

Table 11.10. Deposits of all Banks by Type, and Time and Saving Deposits by
Maturity

		December 1953	December 1961	December 1971
I.	Total deposits (NT$ million)	2,550	16,722	105,015
II.	Percentage of total deposits:			
	1. Demand and call deposits	76.2	59.5	41.2
	(a) Private	27.6	24.6	23.8
	(b) Government	23.6	14.5	16.3
	(c) U.S. AID/Sino-Am. Dev. Fund	25.0	20.4	1.1
	2. Private foreign currency deposits	0.9	1.6	1.1
	3. Time and saving deposits	22.9	38.8	57.7
III.	Percentage of total time and saving deposits			
	1. Deposits of 3 mo. or less	50.2	5.6	3.1
	2. Deposits or 6 mo. to 1 year	49.8	70.5	50.6
	3. Deposits of 2 yrs. or more	—	23.8	46.2

Sources: BOT, *The Republic of China, Taiwan Financial Statistics Monthly*, Dec. 1954, pp. 23–24; CBC, *The Republic of China, Taiwan Financial Statistics Monthly*, March 1962, pp. 31–34, and Apr. 1972, p. 38.

higher share of total deposits, rising from 23 percent in 1953 to 39 percent in 1961 and 58 percent in 1971. Furthermore, depositors were willing to leave their savings in fixed term deposits of larger maturity. Largely because of the rise in deposits, the ratio of money supply and quasimoney to GNP rose from .28 in 1961 to .49 in 1971.[26] With prices increasing slower in the 1960s, the increase in the real lending capacity of the organized financial sector was even more pronounced.[27] Probably more than anything else, price stability (with the accompanying

26. DGBAS, *Statistical Abstract of the Republic of China*, 1973 p. 347.
27. Perhaps because the banking system became increasingly more important, the antiquated banking law as well as the banks was under much criticism in the 1960s for being too cautious and conservative. For example, the law limited the maximum amount of unsecured loans that can be granted by commercial banks to 25 percent of its deposits. Banks also could not extend unsecured loans for periods longer than six months and secured loans for terms longer than one year. These requirements are difficult to understand when in the 1960s a major share of total deposits was made up of fixed-time and saving deposits of long maturity. With the capital market undeveloped in the 1960s, the inability of banks to provide long-term loans and capital, especially without collateral, made it difficult for investors to raise capital. Indeed, it forced many borrowers to use short-term bank credits to meet long-term needs. There were also many complaints of poor service and inefficient operation. The government owned a majority interest in most banks, so there was little competition in the banking sector. With the government so involved in the banking sector, accusations that banking decisions were made for political reasons were common and perhaps justified.

rise in real interest rates) and the development of the financial sector were responsible for the increase in private savings.

To summarize, this chapter has shown that the distribution of resources among final uses altered substantially in Taiwan, particularly after 1960. Although the share of consumption in GNP fell, its absolute size increased, and all indicators suggest that living conditions improved significantly in Taiwan. Investment grew rapidly both in absolute size and relative to GNP. Fixed investment as a share of total investment also rose and increasingly is composed of producers' goods instead of construction. Not surprisingly, investment in manufacturing and transportation grew more than in any other sector. Investment and output are of course closely related, and the dramatic rise in investment after 1959 was accompanied by an acceleration in the growth of real output.

Because of U.S. aid, foreign savings was important in Taiwan, more so than in most other less developed countries. This was especially the case during the 1950s, when U.S. aid was about one-third of Taiwan's gross domestic investment. Thereafter, investments in Taiwan were increasingly financed by its own savings. With an inelastic revenue system the government was a relatively unimportant saver until the late 1960s. Thus, savings were generated mostly in the private sector. At times in the 1950s the government, perhaps because it failed to understand the role that interest rate plays in the saving–investment process, kept the real rate of interest low and prevented the organized banking sector from performing its proper intermediary function. As a consequence, private saving and investment suffered. However, in the 1960s, with prices stabilized, the real rate of interest rose and increasing amounts of savings flowed into the organized financial sector. This, as much as any other factor, was responsible for Taiwan's growing ability to save and invest.

12

Lessons and Prospects

Viewed from a historical perspective, Taiwan's growth in the twentieth century represents a transition, linking the long epoch of traditional economy with the epoch of modern growth. In the first half of the twentieth century, Taiwan began the transition by developing its agriculture and infrastructure. In the postwar period, with Taiwan building on its strength in agriculture, the transition continued, and gradually the economic center of gravity shifted from agriculture to industry. At first, Taiwan relied on an import substitution strategy to promote development. When this failed to produce the desired result, it switched to a more outward-looking strategy. By relaxing its controls on the economy and allowing prices to play a more prominent role in resource allocation, the government made it possible for Taiwan to develop more in line with its true comparative advantage. The result was a surge in labor-intensive industrial exports and an acceleration in the pace of industrialization. By the early 1970s agriculture, once the mainstay of the economy, produced only 15 percent of the net domestic product and absorbed only one-third of the labor force. At the end of the colonial period manufacturing was rudimentary; in 1973 it produced 30 percent of the net domestic product, accounted for more than 90 percent of the exports, and employed one-quarter of the labor force. It seems that the period of transition growth is near an end, and Taiwan should shortly enter the long epoch of modern growth.

LESSONS FROM THE PAST

In reviewing the Taiwan experience, several lessons stand out. Rapid changes in recent years tend to cloud the fact that modernization in Taiwan occurred not suddenly but gradually over many generations.

Economic development is a cumulative process—today's achievements
are built on past accomplishments. The changes in Taiwanese agriculture that occurred half a century or more ago are as significant to
development as the more visible and spectacular growth of its industry
since 1960. In Taiwan economic transition began with the development
of agriculture and was able to continue because agriculture remained
strong. Rising productivity in agriculture contributed to development
not only because it increased output but also because it facilitated the
transfer of resources from agriculture to the nonagricultural sector.
With a less progressive agriculture, industrialization would have been
more difficult, and certainly delayed. Perhaps the most obvious lesson
we can learn from the Taiwan experience is that agricultural development, although difficult and perhaps less glamorous than industrialization, must be accorded a high priority when planning for development.

Since the end of the nineteenth century, with only a relatively short
interruption, Taiwan has had an open economy, and, through trade
and factor movements, its development has benefited from this
openness. Furthermore, Taiwan also demonstrates the advantage of
pursuing economic development along lines consistent with one's
comparative advantage. Except during 1940–60 a period that includes
a major war and a series of internal crises, exports have been a leading
stimulus to Taiwan's development. The opening-up process that accompanied colonization brought about a widening of the market and
provided the initial stimulus to an export-led growth that lasted four
decades. The end of the colonial period saw Taiwan turn inward, a
reversal brought about largely by necessity. With the protected
Japanese market destroyed, the triangular mode of operation could no
longer continue, and Taiwan sought self-sufficiency and industrialization in import substitution. However, a limited domestic market and a
growing need to import capital goods and raw materials soon pressured
Taiwan to adopt a more outward-oriented approach to development.
As a result, since the early 1960s exports have once again become an
important factor in Taiwan's economic development.

Given its dependence on export, Taiwan's development in the
twentieth century may be usefully viewed as a series of gradual adjustments to changes in its comparative advantages. First it developed its
natural-resource-based industries—agriculture and food processing.
When land became relatively scarce, the economy gradually adjusted
and became increasingly dependent on labor-based industries. At
least for a small trade-oriented economy, the Taiwan experience

suggests that whether transition growth continues depends to a great extent on how well the economy export-substitutes, i.e., adjusts to its changing comparative advantage.

Trade was not the only channel through which contacts with the outside world have facilitated growth in Taiwan. In the twentieth century large amounts of capital, including human capital, have flowed into Taiwan. Of equal, if not greater, significance has been the almost continuous diffusion of advanced technology from the more developed countries to Taiwan. Indeed, this was a principal source of growth even in the eighteenth and nineteenth centuries, a period that saw the gradual filtering of traditional but sophisticated agricultural practices from south China into Taiwan. However, with large inflows of capital in the twentieth century the influx of advanced technology into Taiwan accelerated. In the first quarter of the twentieth century, colonization brought to Taiwan scientific agriculture, along with Japanese capital and know-how. As was observed earlier, these early investments were primarily responsible for the agricultural transformation that occurred during the colonial period. In the postwar period United States economic aid and private U.S. and Japanese investments not only augmented domestic savings but also served as important conduits for advanced technology. The impact of foreign capital, initially on Taiwan's postwar economic stability and later on its growth, has been immense. It appears that one of the strategic reasons for Taiwan's success is its unique relationship with two of the world's most dynamic economies.

External relationship, be it in trade or aid, provides but a partial explanation of Taiwan's success because economic development ultimately depends on internal conditions. In this regard Taiwan's experience is also illuminating. Since the turn of the century, except for brief periods in the 1940s, Taiwan has had an unusually stable and orderly society, which has made the island an attractive place to invest.[1] But because economic stagnation is not unknown in societies that are politically and socially stable, stability, although it may facilitate economic development, is clearly not a sufficient condition for growth.

More fundamental to Taiwan's economic development is that, unlike in many other less developed countries, it has had governments that have given economic development the highest priority. The Taiwan

---

1. This stability, however, was at times maintained at considerable cost to individual freedom.

experience strongly reinforces the view that government often plays the crucial role in development. The colonial government's primary objective was to develop Taiwan into an economic asset, and it acted accordingly. Since retrocession, economic development has retained its priority. When driven from the mainland, the Nationalist government finally realized that its survival and the attainment of its other political aims depended on more than military might. Once it recognized the importance of economic development and the need for economic benefits to touch a broad spectrum of the population, the government moved energetically to transform Taiwan into a showcase. Motive aside, the end result was strong government leadership in pursuit of economic development during both the colonial and postwar periods.

On the whole, Taiwan's government has taken a fairly sensible, practicable approach to development. Grandiose schemes and prestigious but capital-intensive projects have generally been avoided. Because during the colonial period the government's emphasis was on agriculture, development was not confined to a small enclave as it was in many other colonies. Agricultural development not only meant a wider distribution of the benefits of growth, but also, since agriculture was the largest sector, it greatly enhanced the economy's ability to save and invest. In the postwar period, even when the industrial sector moved to center stage, agriculture continued to receive its share of governmental attention, and land reform in the early 1950s ensured a more equitable distribution of the fruits of development. By taking a balanced growth approach and paying some attention to equity issues, the government averted serious bottlenecks and conflicts.

All this is not to imply that mistakes were not made or improper policies ever adopted. In the colonial period Japanese policies led to the overexpansion, from an efficiency viewpoint, of the sugar industry. Discrimination against Taiwanese in the colonial period was also costly to efficiency and growth. More recently, the use of artificially low interest rates to discount future benefits and costs introduced a bias in favor of capital-intensive projects. The usual criticism can also be levied against the import substitution strategy followed in the 1950s. The policy package of exchange control, import licensing, and low real rates of interest used to implement the strategy had the usual consequences: serious market distortions, inefficient growth, sluggish exports. The Taiwan experience once again confirms that administrative controls and other forms of interference with the market can seriously distort the economy, and, when maintained for prolonged periods, inhibit growth. Fortunately, Taiwan's policymakers have been adaptable, and, when made to recognize their errors, they have usually made corrections, although the adjustments were often unnecessarily delayed and sometimes not in the most desirable form.

Economic policies have implications for growth as well as for distribution, and the policy that prevails is often dictated by the interest groups represented by government. In Taiwan's case, one strongly suspects that a number of important economic policies that have had favorable effects on development but adverse effects on the economic position of the elites were successfully implemented only because at the time they were adopted the government was not strongly tied to the elites. For instance, the change in the land tenure system in 1905 would probably not have occurred had the government not been Japanese. The far-reaching 1949–53 land reform program would not have been implemented except for the fact that, unlike when it was on the mainland, the Nationalist government in Taiwan did not depend on the land owning class for support. Perhaps one reason the government has been adaptable and reasonably open-minded about economic policy is that, since retrocession, it has been dominated by mainland Chinese while economic wealth has remained mostly in Taiwanese hands. Thus, the government is relatively neutral to sectoral or regional interests and therefore can take a more balanced view of development.

This is not to suggest that interest groups have not been an influential factor. Far from it. The strongest support for the government has come from both the mainland Chinese and the military establishment. To retain the support of the military, their wishes have had to be satisfied and the economic welfare of mainland Chinese has had to be looked after. These political facts of life explain, at least partly, Taiwan's large military budget, its massive bureaucracy, and the government's reluctance to sell the industrial and commercial enterprises it inherited from the Japanese. Although conflicts existed, they were not allowed to get out of hand, as was the case in some other countries. Foreign aid helped by increasing the size of the economic pie, but more significant was the fact that economic development brought benefits to Taiwanese and mainland Chinese alike, and thus was supported by both.

In the final analysis, the rate at which a country develops is determined by the ability of its population to exploit opportunities. The quality of the human resources available to a country is therefore of

vital importance. The Chinese are an extraordinarily industrious people. But, aside from this, Taiwan, compared with other less developed
countries, has had unique access to special skills, and its population
attained a high average educational level fairly early in its development.
As a colony in the first four decades of this century, Taiwan was able
to draw on Japan for administrative and technical skills. A sizable and
selective group of Japanese migrated to Taiwan in the colonial period,
providing a stock of specialized human capital that otherwise would
have taken several decades and substantial resources to develop. The
migration of mainland Chinese during 1945–50 brought an even larger
number of skilled and highly trained people. Probably more effective
as explanations for Taiwan's high average educational level are the
traditional Chinese respect for learning and the continual attention
paid to education by its governments since the 1920s. In the early
1970s more than 85 percent of the population over the age of six was
literate.[2] These investments in human capital paid rich dividends
because presumably education augmented the productivity of workers.
Undoubtedly, the differential investments in human capital and the
educational levels attained explain a significant part of the difference
in growth between Taiwan and other less developed countries.

PROSPECTS FOR THE FUTURE

The beginning of the 1970s was for Taiwan a period of tremendous
uncertainty, and the consequences of the political and economic events
of these years have not as yet been fully unraveled. Politically, after
1970 Taiwan's position in the international community began to de-
teriorate rapidly. On 13 October 1970, Canada severed diplomatic
relations with Taiwan by recognizing the People's Republic of China.
In the fall of 1971 the Nationalist government was compelled to give
up its seat in the United Nations and subsequently also withdrew from
several other international organizations.[3] Then, in February 1972
came the now-famous Nixon visit to Peking. This resulted in the
historic Shanghai Communiqué, which, among other things, included
the United States declaration that it does not challenge the position

2. CIECD, *Taiwan Statistical Data Book*, 1973, table 2–4a.
3. However, Taiwan continued to hold membership in the more important international financial organizations, such as the International Monetary Fund, the International Bank for Reconstruction and Development, and the Asian Development
Bank.

held by both Chinese governments that Taiwan is part of China, as well as the U.S. promise to progressively reduce its forces and military installations in Taiwan as tension in the area subsides.[4] The "Nixon shock" accelerated the rapprochement between Japan and the People's Republic of China. On 7 July 1972, Japan's new prime minister, Kakuei Tanaka, expressed his desire for an early normalization of relations between the People's Republic of China and Japan. China responded by inviting Tanaka to visit Peking, an invitation that was quickly accepted and fulfilled in September 1972. Upon conclusion of the Tanaka visit, Japan formally recognized the People's Republic of China as the sole legal government of China. Although formal diplomatic relations between Japan and Taiwan ended with Tanaka's Peking visit, economic and cultural relations continued between the two countries on an unofficial basis. Nevertheless, Taiwan's relations with its two most important international partners were drastically and irreparably altered.

It is unclear how the politics of détente will affect Taiwan economically in the long run. In the short term, except for some initial moments of anxiety, political changes in the 1970s have not had much economic impact on Taiwan. Since Canada and Taiwan severed diplomatic relations, trade between the two countries has more than doubled.[5] Despite cooler political relations, Taiwan's trade with the United States and Japan has continued to expand rapidly. Initially, the impact of détente on foreign investments was a bit more noticeable, but after an initial decline they returned to the previous, higher levels.[6] Even if this trend reverses, the economic consequences may not be severe

4. For more details on the Nixon visit, see Richard Wilson, ed., *The President's Visit to China* (New York: Bantam, 1972). Many still consider the status of Taiwan an unsettled legal question (see Lung-chu Chen and Harold D. Lasswell, *Formosa, China, and the United Nations,* and *United States Relations With the People's Republic of China: Hearings Before the Committee on Foreign Relations, United States Senate,* 92d Congress [Washington, D.C.: Government Printing Office, 1972]).

5. In 1970 total trade between the two countries was US$ 70.5 million; in 1973 it was US$ 161.9 million.

6. The total amount of direct private foreign and overseas Chinese investments approved was US$ 138.9 million in 1970, 162.9 million in 1971, 126.6 million in 1972, and 248.8 million in 1973. The 1971 figure, however, includes US$ 65 million for a proposed new steel mill, of which US$ 50 million was to be a loan. In both 1971 and 1972 the decline was most severe among Japanese investors, but in 1973 Japanese investments came back strongly. In 1972 approved Japanese investments amounted to US$ 7.7 million; in 1973, they increased to US$ 44.6 million. It seems that Japanese investors delayed their commitments a year or two to measure the opportunity costs of maintaining economic ties with Taiwan.

Table 12.1. Annual Growth Rate of Prices (Percent)

	1962–69	*1970*	*1971*	*1972*	*1973*	*1974*
Index of wholesale prices	1.63	2.72	0.02	4.65	22.85	40.57
Index of consumer prices	2.61	3.58	2.56	4.85	13.05	47.47
Index of unit value of imports	0.86	3.57	4.56	12.10	23.14	46.51
Implicit GNP deflator	4.42	4.46	3.44	5.01	12.96	37.22

Sources: CIECD, *Taiwan Statistical Data Book*, 1973, table 9.1; DGBAS, *Statistical Abstract of the Republic of China*, 1973, table 78; CBC, *The Republic of China, Taiwan Financial Statistics Monthly*, Aug. 1975, pp. 85–87; MOF, *Monthly Statistics of Exports and Imports, The Republic of China*, May 1975, pp. 5–6, and *Industry of Free China*, July 1975, pp. 50 and 53.

unless a reduction of foreign investments brings about a reduced inflow of foreign technology, since at present domestic investments are sufficiently high to maintain a high rate of growth. The economic repercussions, of course, have not ended. The most recent was the suspension of air services between Taipei and Tokyo by Chinese and Japanese airlines from April 1974 to August 1975, after Japan refused to recognize the flag of the Republic of China as that of a sovereign nation. Taiwan is also finding it more difficult to obtain Japanese credits and is attempting to diversify its market to become less dependent on Japan. Since September 1972 Taiwanese importers are encouraged and in some cases required to import industrial inputs, plants, and equipment from other than Japanese sources. Given the proximity and familiarity of Japan to Taiwan, these developments, if continued, could prove costly to Taiwan. But in the near future, except in symbolic ways, politics is unlikely to take command of Taiwan's external economic relations.

More threatening to Taiwan's economic prosperity is the reappearance of inflation. Table 12.1 summarizes the price trends in Taiwan during the past decade. Until 1972, prices in Taiwan remained relatively stable and were a major factor in Taiwan's international competitiveness. Beginning in 1972, however, prices began to climb rapidly, and the rate accelerated in 1973. In contrast to the price rises of the 1950s, when inflationary sources were internal, the recent surge in prices was caused largely by external forces. Taiwan imports 65 percent of its primary commercial energy and also relies heavily on imports for capital goods, raw materials, and feed grains. Thus, soaring world prices of oil, feeds, and other goods in the early 1970s had the inevitable consequence of pushing up prices in Taiwan. The rise in import prices led all others in 1972 and 1973. Despite a price freeze on key commodities (including textiles, household gas, fertilizers, and several food items), consumer prices rose 13 percent and wholesale prices 23 percent in 1973. Because of black markets and other distortions of price control, the government lifted the freeze in January 1974, and prices rose sharply. In 1974 consumer prices increased 47 percent and wholesale prices 40 percent.

In 1974, with its two major trading partners, the United States and Japan, in a deep recession, Taiwan experienced a sharp drop in the demand for its export. For the first time in the postwar period Taiwan's industrial production declined, and there was no growth in its real GNP. Thus, in 1974 Taiwan suffered from both inflation and recession. Declining exports, tighter money,[7] and greater stability in import prices seem to have brought inflation under control. In the first six months of 1975 prices showed almost no increase. With economic activity picking up in the developed countries, the demand for Taiwan's exports also grew in early 1975. Thus, it seems that Taiwan's economy is now on its way to recovery. However, the events of the early 1970s clearly indicate that, with its economy now closely tied to the world market, Taiwan in the future will need to give considerably more attention to short-run stability problems if economic growth is to proceed smoothly.

Leaving political and short-run economic problems aside, what is Taiwan's future? Like most less developed countries, Taiwan has been hurt by the higher oil prices. But in the long run Taiwan is in a better position than most other LDCs to adjust to the higher oil prices. An expanding hydroelectric system and rapidly increasing production of oil substitutes (e.g., natural gas) will tend to reduce Taiwan's dependence on oil. More important, Taiwan is currently investing heavily in nuclear power plants. The first reactor is expected to be operational in October 1976. By the mid-1980s nuclear energy is expected to supply Taiwan with half its electric power.[8]

With the crude birth rate now at 24 per 1,000 and the crude death rate at 5 per 1,000, the target of reducing the rate of natural increase to below 2 percent, set in the early 1960s, has now been achieved. However, newborns of earlier periods of rapid population growth are now reaching marriageable age. From 1968 to 1973 the number of

7. In contrast with 1971–73, when it expanded at an average annual rate of 33 percent, Taiwan's money supply increased only 7 percent in 1974.
8. *Free China Weekly*, May 26, 1974, p. 4.

females aged 20–24 increased by more than 60 percent, rising to 750,000.[9] This trend will continue in the next decade. Although the marriage age is rising, the expected huge increase in the number of marriageable-age women will make further decline in the population growth rate more difficult. Whether the population growth rate will continue to fall depends on whether the increase in the number of marriageable-age women will be offset by (1) further increases in the proportion of Taiwanese couples using birth control to reduce the number of undesired births, and (2) decreases in the number of children desired. Evidence from the early 1970s suggests that the practice of both contraception and abortion has continued to increase and that an increasing number of young Taiwanese couples want small families.[10] Thus, there is a good chance that marital fertility will decline. Whether the reduction in marital fertility will be sufficient to offset the larger number of marriageable-age women is less certain.

As yet, the government has not announced a definite population policy for the 1970s and 1980s. Many, both within and outside the government, still view population policy as primarily a question of family planning and public health. If the decline in population growth is to continue, this attitude has to change. Agencies other than those related to public health have to become more involved in population control, and measures other than medical ones need to be considered. The recent movement to liberalize abortion (so far unsuccessful) and the government decision to "cut the subsistence allowance paid all government employees for dependants after the third,"[11] are in the right direction, but more active government participation is required.

On the assumption that population in the next decade will increase at an annual rate of 1.8 percent, that per capita income will rise at a rate of 5 percent, and that the income elasticity of demand for food is 0.6,[12] food demand will increase annually by about 4.8 percent.

9. C. H. Yen, C. M. Wang, and Y. T. Wang, "Taiwan," p. 165.

10. However, there is still a strong preference for sons. See Ronald Freedman, Lolagene C. Coombs, Ming-cheng Chang, and Te-hsiung Sun, "Trends in Fertility, Family Size Preferences, and Practice of Family Planning: Taiwan, 1965–1973," pp. 274–83.

11. Yen et al., "Taiwan," p. 166. Those already receiving allowance for more than three dependents are unaffected.

12. An income elasticity of 0.6 for food is close to that estimated for Taiwan using data from its national income accounts for 1951–69. It is also similar in magnitude to the elasticity used by the Food and Agriculture Organization (FAO) of the United Nations in its projection of food demand. Cf. Yung-san Lee, "An Analysis of Consumers' Demand Function in Taiwan, 1951–1969," pp. 108–11, and FAO, *Agricultural Commodities, Projections for 1970*.

Crop production rose at an average rate of 2 percent a year from 1971 to 1974, and it is likely that in the future growth in food production will continue to lag behind that of demand. To rejuvenate the sagging agricultural sector the government has launched several reconstruction programs, but it is becoming increasingly clear that agricultural growth cannot be easily accelerated.[13] With peasants leaving agriculture to work in industries and with farmland converting to factory sites, both land and labor inputs to agriculture have been declining.[14] Mechanization will eventually relieve the labor shortages, especially during peak seasons, in rural Taiwan, but in the short term the higher oil price will tend to slow the adoption of mechanical power. In the future Taiwan will become more dependent on import for its food. Self-sufficiency in food is no longer possible or indeed desirable. The apparent movement of resources away from the staple crops to such highly income-elastic food as vegetables, fruits, and dairy products needs to be encouraged with financial, organizational, and technical assistance. Agriculture is ripe for yet another structural transformation.

For Taiwan the future is clearly in industrialization based on trade. Although the pace of industrialization in the next decade may be slower than that achieved in 1964–73, industrial growth will surely continue. Whether future development will proceed smoothly depends largely on Taiwan's ability to adapt to external changes and to remain competitive. One basic current threat to the island's competitiveness is the developing bottleneck in its infrastructure. In the 1950s and 1960s, apart from improvements, major investments in social overhead capital were postponed. Although the transport system inherited from the colonial period performed satisfactorily in the 1950s, it proved woefully inadequate in the 1960s, when industrialization and trade accelerated. Crowded roads and railways and congested harbors have plagued Taiwan since the late 1960s. Ships are often compelled to wait days before cargo can be discharged or loaded. In 1973 several international shipping conferences threatened to impose a surcharge of 10 percent on all cargo handled by the conference lines using

13. For example, in 1973 the government launched a two-year agricultural reconstruction program costing NT$ 2 billion, and a NT$ 1.8 billion loan program to improve, among other things, rural transportation, cultivation methods, agricultural research and development, and rural community services.

14. The multiple-cropping index has declined since 1967, and cultivated area and agricultural population have declined since 1969. In 1968, at its peak, 790,000 ha of rice were planted; in 1972, only 742,000 were planted.

Keelung, Taiwan's most important northern port.[15] Because a cost increase of even a few percent could force many Taiwanese goods out of world competition, the infrastructure bottleneck poses a major threat to Taiwan's prosperity.

The government has taken steps to alleviate the worst problems. Outdated security precautions, which kept Keelung harbor closed at night, were partially relaxed in 1973 so that the port could be operated for longer hours each day. In addition, existing harbor facilities at Keelung, Hualien, and Kaohsiung are being expanded, and the construction of a fourth major international port near Taichung is under way. Electrification of Taiwan's west coast railroad, begun in 1975, will increase its carrying capacity by one-third and substantially reduce travel time. When this project and the construction of the north–south superhighway are completed, Taiwan will have the more efficient internal transport system its industrialization requires. However, with infrastructure receiving an increasing share of its investments, Taiwan's incremental output/capital ratio will undoubtedly decline in the future.

The basis of Taiwan's export boom has been the competitiveness of its labor-intensive industries. Given its relatively abundant labor supply, and with the real wage rising at rates slower than labor productivity, the island's comparative advantage in labor-intensive goods should run into the next decade. Ultimately, its export strength will depend on its ability to export substitute. As unskilled and semi-skilled labor become relatively cheaper elsewhere, Taiwan's export growth can continue only if it can successfully and economically shift its production to industries that are more technologically sophisticated (skill intensive) and perhaps also more capital intensive.

In adjusting to market changes, Taiwan is already finding skilled workers in short supply. To coordinate the demand and the supply of skilled manpower, sound educational planning is needed, now more than ever. In the future, resources probably should be diverted from general education to·vocational training. With the economy becoming more technologically oriented, it would also help if the migration of some of the country's best manpower to the developed nations could be reduced, if not halted. From 1956 to 1973 more than 32,000 college graduates have gone abroad, but only 3,000 have returned.[16] Nearly

15. *Far Eastern Economic Review*, Apr. 15, 1974, pp. 45–47.
16. DGBAS, *Statistical Abstract of the Republic of China*, 1974, table 178.

60 percent of those leaving are trained in engineering and science, precisely the skills that are now in demand in Taiwan. Because those leaving are among the top 15–20 percent of each year's graduating classes, the exodus is more injurious than the mere number might suggest. Although Taiwan's relatively low standard of living is a major reason that so many Chinese students have remained abroad, lack of political freedom and limited opportunity for quick advancement in a society that still clings to traditional and particularistic social values are also contributory factors.[17] Continued economic development will reduce the income differential between Taiwan and the developed countries, but to retain the best of its youth, Taiwan will need to alter its political and social climate as well.

Finally, Taiwan's economic prospects also depend on whether the government maintains its present policy of economic liberalization. Success of the export-processing zones should indicate to the policy-makers what is possible under even more liberalized conditions. The government is eager for economic development to continue, and therefore its policy will likely remain on its present course. Government officials predict that Taiwan will soon join the ranks of developed countries. Certainly, Taiwan has a better chance of reaching this status in the twentieth century than most other developing nations.

17. For an analysis of Taiwan's brain drain to the United States, see Charles H. C. Kao, "A Preliminary Analysis of the Republic of China's 'Brain Drain' into the United States," and Charles H. C. Kao and Jae Won Lee, "An Empirical Analysis of China's Brain Drain into the United States."

Statistical Appendix

This appendix has two purposes. First, it assesses in greater detail the reliability of the basic statistics used in this study. Second, it is designed to be a source of economic data for those interested in Taiwan's economic development or in economic development generally. With this latter purpose in mind, the range of data included in the appendix is somewhat broader than is required for the text. (A more comprehensive collection of statistics on Taiwan is available in mimeograph form. [Samuel P. S. Ho, "Taiwan Statistical Appendix," Yale Economic Growth Center].) As much as possible, the data in the appendix are presented according to the format suggested in *A System of National Economic Accounts and Historical Data* (New Haven: Economic Growth Center at Yale University, 1964).

My comments on Taiwan's statistics are organized into two main sections. The first part examines the national accounts, and the second part examines a wide variety of historical statistics. In these comments my focus is on data availability and quality. Specific information on sources and methods is appended to each table.

NATIONAL INCOME STATISTICS

History

The earliest attempt at national income estimation in Taiwan was undertaken by the Japanese in the 1930s.[1] However, before these estimates could be fully developed, the process was interrupted by the Sino–Japanese War in 1936. The first postwar attempt to estimate Taiwan's national income was made by PBAS in 1949. Using data collected by the Japanese, it estimated, by the value-added approach,

---

1. U.S. AID/China, Office of Economic Analysis, "National Income Estimates for Taiwan," p. 1.

Taiwan's NDP in 1937 at 842 million T¥ (or Old Taiwan dollars, OT$).[2] Adjusting the NDP estimate for net factor income from abroad resulted in a national income estimate of 724 million T¥. However, this estimate does not include the services provided by owner-occupied dwellings. In the early 1960s Professor M. H. Hsing of the Academia Sinica and Dr. T. H. Lee of JCRR independently constructed estimates of national income in constant prices for the prewar period. Both series were constructed by the value-added approach. Table A1 presents these two series and the deflators used. Because the two series are based more or less on the same body of primary data, they are reasonably consistent with each other and with the less aggregated but probably more reliable agricultural and industrial production indexes (tables A33 and A49).

More recently, T. Mizoguchi has estimated Taiwan's gross national expenditure (GNE) from 1903 to 1938 (table A2). Given the abundance and high quality of Taiwan's trade and government expenditure statistics, his estimates of exports, imports, and government consumption are probably quite reliable. However, the margins of error are considerably larger for his estimates of private consumption and investment. Private consumption is not estimated directly but is based on a real wage index. Investment is estimated by the commodity flow method using Taiwanese production and import data. However, postwar Japanese data were used for markups, undercoverage, and the distribution of goods by end use. The components of GNE are deflated by appropriate price indexes to obtain estimates of real GNE. A comparison of Lee's NDP and Mizoguchi's GNE shows considerable differences in their absolute magnitude and year-to-year movements. However, they both suggest broadly similar growth trends. From 1911 to 1938 Mizoguchi's GNE increases annually at 3.79 percent and Lee's NDP at 3.83 percent.

From 1949 to 1952, annual estimates of national income were prepared on an ad hoc basis by PBAS. In 1953 the National Income Division (NID), a newly created branch of DGBAS, took over the task of making annual estimates of national income. Since then, its annual estimates are published in a pamphlet entitled *National Income of the Republic of China*.

The GNP estimates produced by NID during 1953–64 have been

2. The 1937 estimates were later published by DGBAS as an appendix in its *Taiwan's National Income and Product*, 1955.

severely criticized.[3] Among other deficiencies, these early estimates neglected owner-occupied dwellings, gave incomplete coverage to industrial production, and under-estimated consumption. Dissatisfaction with these early estimates led to the formation of a working group in 1961 to improve the basic data used in national income statistics. At about the same time CIECD, the government organ responsible for economic planning, began to compile its own unofficial estimates of national income. Finally, in April 1965 the Commission on National Income Statistics was organized to act as a consultant body to DGBAS. Its functions, among others, were to appraise the basic data used in national income statistics, to review and improve the existing estimating procedures, to evaluate the annual estimates, and to introduce new techniques and methods of estimation. On the advice of the commission, DGBAS adopted new estimating methods and used improved data beginning with the 1964 estimates. Subsequently, so as to have a more consistent series, estimates for 1951–63 were revised. It is these revised estimates that are reproduced in the appendix (tables A3–A9).

The changes brought about by this major revision were both conceptual and statistical.[4] The most important conceptual change was the inclusion of the housing sector in the estimates of GNP by the value-added approach and the addition to consumption of the imputed rent of owner-occupied dwellings and of free housing provided by employers. Other changes and improvements included: (1) a more complete coverage of agricultural production and agricultural by-products, (2) an improved procedure to adjust industrial production for undercoverage, (3) the inclusion of household handicraft production, (4) the elimination of double counting of some minor activities previously included in more than one sector, (5) a more accurate distribution of GNP by industry, and (6) a slightly different allocation of GNP between consumption and capital formation. Finally, more and better deflators were used to reduce the expenditure components of GDP from current to constant prices.

Current Methods of Estimation

Currently, NID estimates national product and expenditure independently and arranges the results into six accounts and twelve

3. Mo-huan Hsing, "An Appraisal of the Growth Rates of the Taiwan Economy as Revealed in Official National Income Statistics."
4. A relatively detailed discussion of this revision can be found in DGBAS, *National Income of the Republic of China*, 1967, chap. 3.

supporting tables.[5] The structure, terms, and classifications used in these accounts and tables generally correspond with the U.N. system. However, the estimating methods and sources of basic data are not always those suggested by the United Nations. Because NID does not describe its estimating procedures and the source materials used in detail, our knowledge of its estimating procedures is still vague. Probably the best published official description of NID's methods and data sources is DGBAS, *National Income of the Republic of China,* Dec. 1967, chap. 2. The following summary of methods and data sources currently in use to compile national income statistics is based on this publication and some unpublished materials.[6]

GNP by valued-added is estimated from the following sources:

Sector/item	Source of production data	Source of cost data
Govt. enterprises in all industries	Profit and loss statements of govt. enterprises	Statements of cost and detail accounts provided by govt. enterprises
Private enterprises in:		
1. Agriculture	*Agricultural Yearbook* (PDAF)	*Farm Economic Survey* (PDAF)
2. Forestry	Provincial Bureau of Forestry	*Survey of Production Cost of Private Forestry Enterprises* (DGBAS)
3. Fishery	Provincial Bureau of Fishery	*Survey of Production Cost of Private Fishery Enterprises (DGBAS)*
4. Mining	*Industry of Free China* (CIECD). Minor products estimated by PDOR	Tax returns provided by PDOF
5. Manufacturing	*Industry of Free China* (CIECD). Minor products estimated by PDOR	Tax returns provided by PDOF
6. Construction	Estimated by the commodity flow method using data provided by MOEA and MOF	*Survey of Construction Enterprises* (PDOR)
7. Communication & transportation	Final accounts of large enterprises and statistics provided by the Provincial Highway Bureau	Final accounts of large enterprises and cost surveys conducted by the Provincial Highway Bureau

5. NID estimates factor payments from the same cost structure data used in estimating national income by the value-added approach. Consequently, NID's estimate of national income by factor payments is not an independent estimate.

6. The most important unpublished source is the materials prepared by the staff of the Commission on National Income Statistics (評審會資料, mimeo).

Sector/item	Source of production data	Source of cost data
7. Communication & transportation (continued)	The contribution of miscellaneous transportation is estimated by multiplying the number of persons employed and the average income per person. Data are provided by various labor unions and associations.	
8. Wholesale & retail trade	In noncensus years this is based on PDOF surveys of commerce and sales of profit-making enterprises.	Tax returns provided by PDOF
9. Banks, insurance & real estate	Final accounts of financial institutions	
10. Ownership of dwellings	Actual rent payments and imputed rent for owner-occupied dwellings are obtained directly from the *Survey of Family Income and Expenditure* in survey years. In other years it is estimated by extrapolation using a quantity index of private dwellings compiled annually by PDOF.	
11. Other services	Sales statistics of profit-making enterprises (PDOF) and the accounts of private schools, cultural institutions, and civic organizations	Tax returns provided by PDOF
Public administration & defense	Estimated to be the salaries and wages (including payments in kind) of employees in all government institutions and agencies except the public enterprises. The data are from government budgets.	

GNP by expenditure is estimated as follows: The main source of data for estimating private consumption is PBAS, *Report on the Survey of Family Income and Expenditure in Taiwan.* In survey years the consumption of a given item is the product of the per capita consumption of that item as found in that year's survey and population. In nonsurvey years, consumption of a given item is obtained by extrapolation, using estimates of changes in per capita income and estimates of income elasticity.

Gross domestic capital formation is obtained by summing the capital expenditures of public enterprises, private enterprises, government, and households. The estimate of capital expenditures of public enterprises is based on the information provided by the annual questionnaire sent to all public enterprises and is probably the most reliable component. The methods used to estimate the investments of private enterprises differ slightly from industry to industry, but in most cases investments are estimated by multiplying output estimates and investment/output ratios (obtained from sample surveys). Capital formation in agriculture is estimated by JCRR and PDAF. Government capital formation is derived directly from budget data and final accounts. Capital formation by households is limited to the new construction of buildings and is estimated from construction permits and population data.

General government expenditure is estimated from the final accounts of all governments, adjusted according to the ratio of budgeted expenditure and actual expenditure of the preceding year. The estimate is on an accrual basis with intragovernment transfers deleted. The fiscal year used by the government is from July 1 to June 30. Calendar year estimate is derived by averaging two fiscal year figures.

Estimates of exports and imports of goods and services are based on the balance of payment statistics published each year by the Central Bank of China. The original data are in US$ and are converted to NT$ at the official exchange rate.

Without more information it is difficult to assess the quality of Taiwan's national income statistics in greater detail. The general impression I have, after working with the data, is that in terms of reliability and completeness Taiwan national income estimates compare favorably with those of other less developed countries. On the whole they are useful indicators of the level of aggregate economic activity and the structure of the economy. Some components and accounts are clearly more reliable than others. The value-added estimates of the manufacturing industries are more accurate than those of the service industries, and the value-added estimates of public enterprises are definitely more accurate than those of private enterprises. Of the individual expenditure accounts, external transactions and government are more reliable than consumption and gross domestic capital formation.

HISTORICAL AND BENCHMARK DATA

Among less developed countries Taiwan must rank as having one of the most complete and reliable body of economic statistics. To help formulate economic policies and assess economic achievements, the Japanese colonial government, from the beginning of its administration, sought to develop a statistical system in Taiwan. Consequently, the collection and processing of data have gone on for a long time. Indeed, by the 1920s the surveying of economic conditions and the gathering of statistics had become reasonably routine. Because of the administrative efficiency of the colonial government, the quality of data gathered was on the whole high. Most of the statistics collected regularly in the colonial period have continued to be gathered in the postwar period. Further, in the postwar period, to facilitate economic planning, new information about the economy (e.g., input–output tables) have been developed and comprehensive censuses of various sectors are periodically conducted. Subsequent sections provide general information on the following categories of data: population, employment, agriculture, industry, international transactions, money, government finances, and prices.

Population

Population data are probably the most complete and reliable economic statistics available for Taiwan. Information about Taiwan's population can be obtained from two primary sources: the censuses and the household registration records.

Censuses. Population censuses were conducted in 1905, 1915, 1920, 1925, 1930, 1935, 1940, 1956, and 1966. A sample population census was also conducted in 1970. The coverage and characteristics of the population investigated are not identical for all censuses. For example, the 1966 census and the 1970 sample census cover not only the islands of Taiwan and Penghu but also the offshore islands (the Fukien area). However, in this appendix the data from the offshore islands have been excluded. Also, the first four censuses exclude aborigines living in the mountain region. But, on the whole, these differences in coverage are not major problems.

More troublesome are the different ways the censuses treated military personnel. In the first two censuses only those military personnel and their dependents not living in military establishments were enumerated. In the third through the sixth censuses, all army and naval units stationed in Taiwan were enumerated. In the seventh census, the enumerating procedure was again changed to the system of reporting the Japanese military personnel by their legal domicile. The three censuses since the end of World War II also treated military personnel differently: the 1956 census excluded military personnel living in barracks, while the 1966 and the 1970 censuses included them. Because military personnel in the colonial period were almost exclusively Japanese, their exclusion in the prewar censuses does not create a serious problem, for it still leaves the Taiwanese population intact for analysis. The exclusion of military personnel in the 1956 census is, however, a more serious shortcoming because in this case the Taiwanese population is directly disturbed. One manifestation of this is the extremely low sex ratio for the population in the 20–24 age group (table A13).

Of the censuses, the 1925 and 1935 censuses are less comprehensive in design in the sense that fewer characteristics of the population were investigated. All censuses provide certain basic characteristics of the population, among which are sex, date of birth, legal domicile, and customary place of residence. The more comprehensive censuses also classify the population by occupation, by industry, and by proficiency in the use of the Japanese language (in the case of the postwar censuses, the Chinese language). The quality of the seven censuses taken before the war is good. Of these censuses Barclay writes, "They comprise one of the most ample and creditable records for a population of this size that has ever been at the disposal of demographers."[7] The compilation of the 1940 census was interrupted by the war and only a portion of the results was compiled and published. Some experts feel that insufficient time was given to planning the 1956 census and that too few enumerators were used.[8] These facts, combined with the knowledge that the Chinese administrators were inexperienced in census taking, tend to weaken our confidence in the 1956 census. The quality of the 1966 census and the 1970 sample census seems good.

Household registration records.[9] Household registration as a scheme of recording population statistics had its origin in ancient China. It is also a system long practiced in Japan. Consequently, household registration has had a long tradition in Taiwan. Basically, the system requires the household to register a number of important personal events (birth, death, marriage, divorce, change of residence, and change of occupation), and from these data a number of key population statistics can be obtained.

Under the Japanese administration the household registration records were operated by the police and made effective by strict enforcement of the registration regulations through the pao-chia

---

7. George W. Barclay, *Colonial Development and Population in Taiwan*, p. viii.

8. See Taiwan Provincial Government, Manpower Advisor Office, "Proposed Working Paper for the Manpower Resource Committee, Statistics for Manpower Planning," 1965, mimeo. Some evidence suggests that either the 1956 census or the 1956 Household Registration Record has been altered so comparison of the two is not a reliable indication of the accuracy of either set of figures. See U.S. AID/China, "Population Growth in Taiwan."

9. This section draws heavily on George W. Barclay, *A Report on Taiwan's Population to the Joint Commission on Rural Reconstruction*, and PDCA, *A Synopsis of the Taiwan Household Registration System* (Taipei, 1966).

system. Although the records of household registration were kept by the local district government, beginning in 1905 the Government-General's Central Statistical Office established a permanent and competent staff to supervise the collection and tabulation of the population data from these records. From the assembled data, vital statistics were computed, compiled into tables, and published annually. The published statistics for 1905–43 are of first-order quality.

After Taiwan returned to Chinese administration, the responsibility of maintaining the household registration records went to the Taiwan Provincial Department of Civil Affairs. The work of tabulating and compiling the published population statistics from the household registration records, however, was decentralized to the local township offices. I suspect that the more relaxed enforcement of the registration regulations and the decentralization of the statistical work have weakened the accuracy of household registration. Since the mid-1960s, attempts have been made to improve the quality of the household registration statistics by processing some of the data at the provincial level.

A number of weaknesses of the household registration statistics are of sufficient importance that a brief summary is in order. The most serious deficiency is the incomplete coverage of the registration system. The coverage problem is particularly troublesome in the years immediately after the transfer of authority from the Japanese to the Chinese (1945–52), when the administration was least effective. For these years it is also not certain which part of the population went unregistered. There were large increases in population in the late 1940s, caused in part by the enlarged scope and improved enforcement of the registration system. Even though the coverage had been extended and stabilized since the early 1950s, two groups of people, besides aliens, nevertheless remained outside the household registration system: persons in prisons or in detention houses and military personnel living in barracks. Because of its size the exclusion of the latter group creates some problems. Unregistered military personnel are of two types: (1) the remaining members of the army who migrated to Taiwan from the mainland, are still on active duty, and never participated in the household registration scheme; and (2) those who joined the military service in Taiwan and were once registered as civilians but whose registration cards have been temporarily removed from the household registration records for the duration they are in military service. Because Taiwan enforces compulsory military service for all males and because larger portions of the army are made up of these new conscripts, the latter category of unregistered military personnel has assumed greater significance. The systematic removal of males in their twenties from the household registration records not only makes it difficult to estimate the true size of the population but also makes the sex ratio of the population in the age group 20–24 artificially low. Since 1959 the Taiwan Population Center has attempted to take into account the male youth removed by military service in compiling the statistics on population by age from the household registration records.

We now turn to an evaluation of the population information that can be obtained from the household registration records, especially the statistics used in this study or contained in this appendix. Although the coverage of the registration system is no longer complete, birth and death rates may nevertheless still be accurate as far as the registered population is concerned. This is because the registration scheme is a perpetual inventory of events occurring only in those households that are properly registered. The present law requires a newborn to be registered within 15 days of birth. Since proof of registration is required for almost everything in Taiwan, the baby will be eventually registered, but there is usually a delay between birth and registration. This delay is not unique to the system in Taiwan; the Japanese must surely have had similar experiences when they administered the registration system. However, the more relaxed enforcement of the present system has led to longer delays and thus has made the problem more serious. A study conducted by the Provincial Department of Civil Affairs reveals that of those births registered, only 78 percent were recorded by the fifteenth day after delivery. Because vital statistics are based on the date of registration rather than the date of delivery, the delay in registering births introduces errors into the birth statistics. However, because an unregistered child is faced with serious handicaps in Taiwan, large errors of omission in the birth statistics are not suspected.

The reliability of the death statistics is more doubtful. The registered deaths, when converted into crude death rates, produce results (6 to 9 per 1,000 in the 1950s and 1960s) that seem low even after accounting for the dramatic improvements in public health in the postwar period. The low death rates suggest that there may be errors of omission in the death statistics. The law requires the registration of death within five days of the event; cremation or burial is not permitted until registration is completed. With newer methods of protecting health available, sanitation measures such as the above are not nearly so strictly enforced as they were previously. The violation of the law is probably most widespread in cases of infant deaths. Deaths of children, especially those whose births were never registered or whose births were unattended by a doctor or midwife, are often not reported. In a yearlong survey of three Taiwan townships in 1962–63, PDCA discovered that a high percentage of infant deaths went unreported (in one township one-third of the infant deaths were unreported). Because infant deaths in a country such as Taiwan may comprise as many as one-fourth to one-third of total deaths, their omission reduces the reliability of the death statistics as a whole.

Assuming that the coverage of the registration system is unchanging, the registered population is affected only by birth, death, and migration. Here we consider internal migration only. Since the early 1950s the movement of population in and out of the island has been limited. When a person moves from one township to another permanently, he is required to do the following: (1) he must register for out-migration at his original place of residence, and (2) he must register for in-migration at his new place of residence. However, his old registration is not canceled until notification arrives from his new residence stating that he is duly registered. At several points, therefore, errors may be introduced: the migrant may delay his registration, he may decide not to change his registration, his arrival and registration at his new place of residence may not be reported to his old place of residence, and his arrival may be reported but his old registration may not be canceled, through carelessness of the township office. It is quite possible therefore for a person to be registered twice, thus inflating the total population figure. Migration figures are also sometimes used as a means to cover up unregistered deaths. Recently, using survey data, Alden Speare assessed the accuracy of migration registration in Taiwan. He found that although large numbers of errors exist in the data, the "net effect of these errors tend[s] to cancel out so that the total count of registered migrants is approximately equal to the total count of actual migrants."[10] However, the classification of migrants by age and by other characteristics is not as accurate.

The system is improving. Proof of proper registration is necessary for so many crucial activities that almost the total civilian population is registered. Sizable underreporting probably occurs only in the age

10. Alden Speare, Jr., "An Assessment of the Quality of Taiwan Migration Registration Data," p. 24.

group 0–6, where the necessity to register so as to be able to carry out normal daily activities has not as yet become crucial. The size of the staff in local registration offices has been enlarged. Beginning in 1966 certain population statistics (birth, death, and marital status) are being processed directly by PDCA, mainly on a sampling basis, to produce a check on the accuracy of the data compiled by the township offices. One result is the construction of life tables adjusted for underreporting of infant deaths by using the U.N. model life tables. This limited return to centralization will help to eliminate some of the classification errors and to improve the general standard of the population statistics.

Employment

Statistics on employment may be obtained from a number of sources, among which are the population censuses, annual estimates of various government agencies, special labor surveys, and industrial and commercial censuses. They vary widely in definition of employment, coverage, classification, and quality.

Employment estimates of various government agencies. Employment in manufacturing, fishing, and mining was recorded by the Government-General during the colonial period. It is difficult to evaluate these data because very little is known about them. The mining and manufacturing data were compiled from periodic reports made by individual establishments to the Government-General, and the fishing data were based on records maintained by the Fishery Bureau.

In the postwar years, employment statistics are produced by a number of agencies of the Provincial Government using different sources. PDCA bases its estimates on household registration records; PDOR bases its estimates on periodic reports from individual establishments. Both estimates have serious shortcomings.

The Household Registration System maintains a record of the occupation of all persons over the age of 12 living in a registered household. A person who changes his occupational status is required to report the change; thus a current record is maintained at all times. On the basis of this record, PDCA compiles at the end of each year its statistics on employment by industry. Theoretically the system should provide reliable data, but for a variety of reasons the PDCA data are likely to be inaccurate. Besides the shortcomings of the Household Registration System already discussed, the following may be added. Very few people, when they change occupations, report the change. This is recognized by PDCA. Before the PDCA's employment data are released, they are adjusted to account for unreported changes in occupation status. A major source of error is students who have terminated their education but still retain their student status in the registration record. Presumably age would provide a criterion for moving people out of the student category, but there still remains the problem of reclassifying them. It is also doubtful that housewives, who are entering the labor force in greater numbers each year, change their occupational status when they move in and out of the labor force. This would affect both the size and composition of employment. Thus the PDCA's estimates of gainfully occupied persons by industry is at best an educated guess.

Until the mid-1960s PDOR had the primary responsibility for collecting labor statistics. The sources of its data are the monthly reports obtained from commercial and industrial establishments. All public enterprises are required to make monthly reports. Thus the coverage of government-operated establishments is complete except for manufacturing establishments under military command (which include some food, wearing apparel, transport equipment, and ammunition factories). The statistics on the private sector are based on reports mailed in by a small group of private establishments. In 1961, 3,113 manufacturing establishments and 1,997 commercial establishments with a total employment of 227,031 reported. If these establishments are selected scientifically, the results may have validity. However, the selection is not based on random sampling, and there is no way to judge the representativeness of the establishments that reported. It is also not certain how these establishment reports are used to arrive at the final employment figure. For those industries, especially the service industry, where a reporting system does not exist, employment data are estimated on the basis of "whatever appropriate information is available."

Among other weaknesses in the PDOR statistics the following are particularly important. First is the lack of clear, precise, and uniform definition and classification standards. This makes it uncertain that the reports filed periodically by the establishments are consistent with one another. Second is the lack of uniform coverage. The methods of reporting employment data vary from industry to industry, each of which has different coverage. One especially noticeable shortcoming in coverage is the agricultural employment data, which exclude self-employed and unpaid family workers. Third, many establishments still do not keep accurate records, so the reliability of the basic data is questionable. For the above reasons the PDOR data as a whole cannot be accepted as reliable.

Surveys and censuses. The most reliable labor statistics are those provided by censuses and special surveys. Since October 1963 the Taiwan Provincial Labor Force Survey and Research Institute has conducted a labor force survey every three months to obtain current employment data (tables A24 and A25). The population of the survey is those over 12 years of age living in registered households. A two-stage stratified cluster sampling method is used, and the size of the sample is 0.5 percent of the total population for the first survey of each year and 0.1 percent for the remaining three surveys conducted during the year (although on occasions the sample size has been smaller). These surveys represent the most systematic effort on the part of the government to obtain reliable employment statistics. Qualified statistical experts say that the sampling techniques are good. Substantial efforts have been made to keep definitions consistent and usable. The enumerators are mainly teachers and college students, and since the number of enumerators needed is small (approximately 300–320 enumerators are used for the first survey of each year and 100 enumerators for each of the other three surveys), they are probably carefully selected and trained. It is generally recognized that the labor force survey supplies the most reliable current employment information. Unfortunately, data from this source are available only after October 1963.

The most reliable labor statistics before 1964 are those provided by the censuses (tables A21, A22, A26, and A27). In eight of the ten population censuses conducted in the twentieth century, occupation information was collected, and in the 1930, 1940, 1956, 1966, and 1970 censuses information of employed persons by industry was collected as well. Industrial and occupational data do not, of course, offer the same information; the former describes people according to the economic sector in which they work and the latter according to the type of work they perform. Until the 1940 census, however, the occupational data gathered were organized by grouping people with different occupational functions according to economic sector. In fact, the broad categories used to present the occupational data in all the censuses conducted before 1940 were very similar to the ones used to present the industrial data in the later censuses, i.e., agriculture, fishing, manufacturing, and so on. Thus in the 1930 census, which shows both the industrial and occupational distributions, the total number of people classified in each of these broad categories is very nearly equal despite the differences in the type of information that are involved. Since 1940 the occupational data have been classified according to a completely new scheme, by function performed (e.g., managers, technicians, and laborers) rather than by industry (e.g., agriculture, manufacturing, and mining). Because of this change and the inavailability of industrial classification before 1930, there is no common ground for comparison between the post-1930 and the pre-1930 censuses. But because of the similarity between the occupational classification used in the pre-1940 censuses and the industrial classification used in the later censuses, cautious comparisons of people engaged in the major types of industrial activity over time may be made.

Finally, Taiwan has conducted four censuses of industry and commerce, in 1954, 1961, 1966, and 1971. They provide another reliable source of information on industrial and commercial employment (table A28).

Agriculture

To administer and control the island effectively, the colonial government began to collect agricultural data soon after Japan acquired Taiwan in 1895. Consequently, production statistics for a number of the more important crops can be traced back to 1897. The quality of the production data, of course, varies with the crop and with the period. Crop production was estimated as the product of crop area and estimated crop yield. For some crops, such as sugar cane and pineapple, which were purchased in large quantities for processing, the government may have had alternative and independent sources of information to check its field estimates. For instance, the sugar cane transported to factories for processing was weighed and recorded, and the data were made available to the government. But for the majority of the crops, including two of the three most important crops, rice and sweet potatoes, the government had no way to check its production estimates. But, for reasons we shall give below, by the late 1900s, crop estimates were sufficiently reliable to be useful.

In 1904 the colonial government completed the carefully conducted cadastral survey initiated in 1898. Prior to the completion of this survey there was extensive underreporting of cultivated land.[11] With the

---

11. After the survey was completed, registered land more than doubled, increasing from 361,417 to 777,850 chia. See Sing-min Yeh and T. S. Kuo, *Rural Land Taxation in Taiwan*, p. 3.

completion of the survey the government knew for the first time the size of the cultivated area, the owner of the land, the cultivator of the land, and the quality or productivity of the cultivated land.[12] The cadastral survey provided the means to check the reliability of the acreage estimates obtained by the crop reporters. As the results of the cadastral survey became known between 1903 and 1906, sharp rises occurred in the reported cultivated area and in the acreage planted with rice, the most important crop produced in Taiwan. We may therefore tentatively conclude that the acreage data after the completion of the cadastral survey and certainly by the late 1900s are reliable.

During the colonial period, crop yields and crop area were estimated by the district crop reporter using maps derived from the cadastral survey and with the assistance of experienced farmers in his district. Although this method is relatively crude, it is normally employed in most underdeveloped countries. The confidence the government had in this method is probably best exemplified by the fact that although in the 1930s the Japanese conducted sample cutting surveys to determine the yield of rice, rice production statistics were nevertheless still based upon the yield estimates of the crop reporters.[13] Evidently the information from the two sources was sufficiently in agreement to make a change in the method of estimation unnecessary.

The acceptance of crop statistics collected after the late 1900s as usable does not imply that all data after this date are equally reliable. The Japanese statisticians, at times, have voiced dissatisfaction with the crop statistics[14] and have suggested ways to improve them. Because at least some of these suggestions must have been adopted, the quality of the crop statistics must have improved over the years. Although we suspect the data collected in the early period (say, from 1906 to the late 1920s) to be less reliable than those collected later, the available evidence does not indicate the earlier data to be biased in a systematic manner or to be so seriously deficient as to be useless.

12. Land was classified into five categories. Category A included paddy fields, dry fields, and piscicultural ponds. For tax purposes, paddy fields and dry fields were graded according to quality, proximity to water and roads, and other factors. Originally, there were 10 grades; this system was revised and expanded until by 1944 there were 26 grades. For a more detailed description, see Yeh and Kuo, *Rural Land Taxation in Taiwan*, and Tung Huang, Tsong-han Chang, and Chang-chin Lee, *Government Financing in Taiwan under the Japanese Regime*.

13. This information was provided to the author by an agricultural statistician who had participated in the crop reporting system during the colonial period.

14. For example, see Taiwan Government-General, *A Simple Explanation of the Present Agricultural Statistics in Taiwan*, 1924.

The collection of land and agricultural production statistics has continued after World War II as part of the islandwide agricultural statistics reporting system. The procedures followed are generally similar to those developed during the colonial period. In 1953 the government with the financial assistance of JCRR duplicated and distributed to each township detailed cadastral maps as well as the land registration records for the area. Armed with these maps, the crop reporter surveys his district and records changes in land use and cropping pattern. In this manner, data on land use, cultivated area, and crop area are obtained. With the principal exception of rice, crop yields are estimated by crop reporter observation. Rice yield is estimated in the postwar period by the sample cutting method.[15] With the exception of a few industrial crops for which direct evidence of the amount harvested is available, crop production is estimated by multiplying crop acreage and yield. Because of tight budget, the number of crop reporters assigned to each township in the postwar period has been reduced, in some cases significantly. The reduction undoubtedly has affected the quality of the information gathered.[16]

Besides the data collected periodically by crop reporters, a considerable amount of useful information is gathered in the numerous surveys conducted by the government since the 1920s, the 1956 sample (5

15. In the 1960s, approximately 4,000–4,500 sample plots were selected by PFB for sample cutting. On each plot, four cuttings of 2.5 m² were taken, with rice actually havested and measured. If these plots were randomly selected, the sample size was sufficiently large to give an accurate estimate of the average rice yield for the island. However, because PFB wished to estimate production for each township, it adopted a complicated procedure that reduced the reliability of its estimates. On the average, 12 sample plots were allocated to each township. Although the chosen plots in each township were supposed to be randomly selected, crop reporters often replaced randomly selected plots by what they believed to be more "average" plots. In each township, yields from sample cuttings were grouped by quality of land (top, medium, and low grades), and where more than one main variety of rice was included in the sample, they were also separately distinguished. PFB then estimated for each township the acreage of land planted with the main varieties of rice and the quality of land. The production of a given variety of rice planted on a given grade of land is the product of the estimated yield and acreage for that variety and for that grade of land. By adding the production of the different types of rice, a total figure is obtained for each township, and the sum of the township figures is the total production figure for the province. Because of the small number of sample cuttings used to estimate the production of each variety of rice in each township, the reliability of the total production figure, determined in the manner just described, is uncertain.

16. For example, in 1962–63 JCRR conducted a sample survey of rice production in Kaohsiung Hsien and found its estimate of crop area to be significantly lower than that of the crop reporting system. See I-gok Chen, "Report on the Test Survey on Rice Production Estimate in Kaohsiung Hsien" (JCRR, 1963), mimeo.

percent) census of agriculture, and the 1961 and 1970 agricultural censuses. Of the prewar surveys, the most important are the 45 reported in the *Report of Basic Agricultural Survey* (農業基本調查書) series. These reports, issued in the 1920s and 1930s, cover a wide range of topics including cost of production, farm management, farm labor, and rural credit. Of the postwar surveys deserving special attention are those conducted by PDAF and reported in its *Report of Farm Record-keeping Families in Taiwan* (台灣農家記賬報告) series, and its *Report on Agricultural Basic Survey in Taiwan* (台灣農業基本調查報告) series. The first group of surveys deals primarily with farm receipts and expenditures, and the second group with the cost of production of major crops.

Industry

In the colonial period, industrial data were collected chiefly by two government agencies, the Monopoly Bureau and the Bureau of Productives Industries. The Monopoly Bureau was responsible for keeping records of its production of tobacco, alcoholic beverages, crude camphor, and salt. The Bureau of Productive Industries collected production and other data from mines and private manufacturing enterprises that employed five or more workers or used power. Of these two sources the Monopoly Bureau, for obvious reasons, kept the more complete and reliable record. The Bureau of Productive Industries published its statistics without explanation of coverage, terms, or procedures. My belief is that the data were obtained through questionnaires. Although it is difficult to give an accurate assessment of the data collected by the Bureau of Productive Industries, I suspect they suffer from a number of defects. In the early years, coverage was probably incomplete and enterprises did not respond regularly. Over the years the data undoubtedly improved as the statistical system expanded and reporting became more regular. Consequently, growth rates calculated from these data tend to be upward biased. Mining data are available from 1897 and are quite good. Of the other data, those on industries dominated by a few large enterprises (e.g., sugar and electric power) are probably more reliable than those on industries composed of many small enterprises. Even if we assume that the small enterprises wished to cooperate with the government's request for data, it is uncertain that they kept sufficiently reliable records of their activities to make the information they provided meaningful. Because the colonial government paid more attention to industrialization toward the end of its administration, more industrial data were collected after 1930. Presumably the quality also improved.

In the postwar period the foremost source of industrial data is the Industrial and Mining Reporting System. Since 1953 public enterprises are required to report monthly to the Ministry of Economic Affairs their production, sales, wages and employment, consumption of raw materials and fuels, and other pertinent economic information. PDOC also canvasses several thousand large private enterprises each month and collects from them production and other economic statistics. Over the years the Industrial and Mining Reporting System has been strengthened by better supervision, periodic on-the-spot surveys to check for accuracy, and improved methods of data processing. Although the reporting system does not cover all enterprises, the data provided by it, when properly adjusted using information from the censuses, are fairly reliable.

The colonial government did not survey the industrial sector so intensively as it did agriculture. However, useful information such as the consumption of fuel and raw materials by large manufacturing establishments and the size distribution of the larger manufacturing establishments can be found in the *Collection of Factory Related Materials Based on Resource Investigation Statute* (資源調査令二基ク工場関係資料集) published by the Government-General in the 1930s. Another group of interesting prewar surveys is that on labor skills (労働技術統計調査結果表) conducted in 1941, 1942, and 1943.

In the postwar years considerably more attention has been paid to industrial surveys and censuses. Industrial and commercial censuses were conducted in 1954, 1961, 1966, and 1971, and they contain the most reliable information on Taiwan's industries. The 1954 census covered all active public and private industrial (mining, manufacturing, utilities, and construction) establishments. The 1961, 1966, and 1971 censuses, besides industrial establishments, also covered public and private commercial and service establishments. Mobile peddlers and part-time home industries were excluded from all four censuses, and certain small processing establishments and repair shops were also excluded from the manufacturing sector in the 1966 and 1971 censuses.

Since 1959 the Bank of Taiwan in cooperation with PDOR distributed annual questionnaires to large mining and manufacturing enterprises to collect financial information. The results are published annually as *Report of Survey on the Financial Position of Industrial and Mining Enterprises in Taiwan* (台灣工礦企業資金調查報告). The Ministry of Economic Affairs has also on occasion surveyed the larger industrial enterprises, and the results are published as *Report on Industrial and Mining Survey in Taiwan* (台灣省工礦業調查報告). However, these surveys are in general less complete and contain less information than the industrial and commercial censuses.

International Transactions

Raw data on international merchandise trade are abundant and quite reliable. The Chinese Imperial Maritime Customs was established soon after Taiwan was opened to foreign merchants in 1858, and fairly complete trade statistics have been collected since 1864. Although the trade data from the Ch'ing period are far less reliable than those gathered in the twentieth century, they provide the most detailed quantitative information of nineteenth century Taiwan. The Ch'ing custom data need to be used with care. Trade, as reported by the Chinese Imperial Maritime Customs, does not represent the total movement of goods in and out of Taiwan. Excluded are the junk trade (much of which went through nontreaty ports) and smuggling.

The most serious defect is, of course, the exclusion of the junk trade, which was probably sizable. The only reliable evidence I have uncovered on the size of the junk trade is the report in 1897 (the year after the junk trade was included by the customs in Taiwan) of 1,692 junks entering the ports of Tamsui and Keelung and carrying approximately one-fourth the total imports of these two ports.[17] The exclusion of the junk trade, however, does not eliminate the usefulness of the customs data as an indicator of the volume and trend of trade in the last half of the nineteenth century. For one thing, the majority of goods traded was carried by clippers and steamers. Secondly, it seems that the fluctuations of trade as recorded in the customs records usually reflect real movements of trade and not just a switch in carriers, from steamers and clippers to junks or vice versa. The British Consulate in Taiwan studied this problem in 1886, when there was a substantial drop in trade according to the customs data. It found the drop to be real and not caused by a switch in carriers, in this case from steamers to junks.[18] In any case, the limited capacity of junks would prevent any substantial

17. U.K. Foreign Office, *Diplomatic and Consular Reports on Trade and Finance, China: Report for the Year 1897 on the Trade of Tamsui* (London, 1898), p. 8.
18. U.K. Foreign Office, *Diplomatic and Consular Reports on Trade and Finance, China: Report for the Year 1886 on the Trade of Taiwan* [present day Tainan] (London, 1887), p. 3.

switching in the short run between the two major forms of carriers. Using the raw data provided by the Chinese Imperial Maritime Customs, I have constructed export and import quantum indexes from 1868 to 1894 (table A58).

The trade data collected by the Japanese colonial government are quite complete and reliable. I have used these data to construct export and import quantum indexes for the period 1900–42 (table A59). Also, for ease of comparison the trade data for the colonial period have been rearranged (table A63) according to the Standard International Trade Classification (SITC). For the postwar period there are two sources of trade statistics: the customs records and the exchange settlement records. The data from these two sources are slightly different for the following reasons: (1) In the custom records, trade is recorded when cleared by the customs but in the settlement records it is recorded at the time of foreign exchange settlement. (2) The custom records exports on an FOB basis and imports on a CIF basis while the settlement records report exports and imports on whatever terms are used in the exchange settlement (3) The custom data include imports and exports exempted from exchange settlement requirements as well as confiscated contraband imports. (4) The import of military goods involving foreign exchange settlements is included in the settlement records but only appears in the custom data when the goods are shipped by commercial vessels. In general, I have used the custom records because exports and imports are already arranged according to the Standard International Trade Classification and because they are used to construct the official trade indexes (tables A60 and A61).

Official balance-of-payments estimates are available since 1950. In general they are quite reliable although some minor problems do exist and are discussed in table A68. No official balance-of-payments estimates exist for the colonial period. Using the merchandise trade data and scattered bits of data on other types of transactions, I constructed balance of payments estimates for the years 1924 through 1939 (table A67). The merchandise trade estimates are, of course, quite reliable. The estimates of most of the nonmerchandise trade items in the current account, although less reliable, are probably usable. However, the capital account is very weak. Very little is known of private capital movements except that they were very important. The Taiwan Government-General did compile statistics on capital flows, but since most foreign companies in Taiwan were branches of Japanese firms, financial transactions were often of an intracompany nature and many were not recorded by the government. The very large error and omission term in table A67 reflects the weaknesses in the capital account.

Money, Government Finances, and Prices

Estimates of money supply and near money have been extended back to 1900 (table A69). Nevertheless, because interbank deposits and government deposits are included in gross demand deposits, the estimates of money supply for the colonial period are biased slightly upward. For the postwar years official estimates of money supply and near money are available (table A70). Commercial bank balance sheets are also available for both the colonial period and the postwar years.

Statistics on government revenues and expenditures go back to the nineteenth century. However, the earliest data (those on the activities of local government before 1895) are scattered and incomplete and are not presented in the appendix. For the colonial period, detailed statistics on the activities of the Taiwan Government-General and summary data on the activities of the local governments are available. I have arranged the revenue and expenditure data of the Government-General by capital and current transactions and by functions. These accounts can be obtained on request from the Yale Economic Growth Center. In the postwar years detailed government expenditure statistics are not public information. What we know about postwar government activities is summarized in tables A5 and A72.

In the colonial period, prices were collected from selected wholesale firms in major cities and towns by government investigators. Using the prices from five major cities in Taiwan, I have constructed a wholesale price index for the period 1910–41 (table A74). For the period 1930–42 the Bureau of Finance of the Taiwan Government-General published a Taipei City Retail Price Index that is the simple arithmetic average of the prices of 39 commodities (table A75). Recently, Toshiyuki Mizoguchi, using wholesale prices (before 1928) and retail prices (after 1928) collected by the Government-General, has constructed consumer price indexes for the period 1903–38 (table A76).

Price data for the postwar period are more abundant. Since 1961 agricultural prices are reported regularly every ten days by agricultural associations in selected townships. Retail and wholesale prices in Taipei and other major cities, prices of industrial raw materials, and prices received and paid by farmers are also collected, processed, and constructed into price indexes (tables A77–A79). Over the years the formula and weights used in constructing price indexes have changed and they are discussed at the end of each table. Finally, the implicit GDP deflators are available and are reproduced in table A73.

Table A1. National Income Estimates, 1911–44 (Million OT$)[a]

	Lee's estimates of NDP in 1937 prices				Hsing's estimates of national income in 1935–37 prices	Price deflator used by	
	Total	Primary sector	Secondary sector	Tertiary sector		Lee 1937 = 100	Hsing 1935–37 = 100
1911	298.3	143.4	78.8	76.1	—[b]	50.38	—
1912	317.0	173.2	73.6	70.2	—	58.38	—
1913	281.0	158.7	52.5	69.8	—	59.51	—
1914	280.5	120.9	82.2	77.4	—	52.99	—
1915	291.5	106.7	104.0	80.7	—	56.00	—
1916	330.9	104.1	143.0	83.9	—	65.60	—
1917	357.1	120.0	148.7	88.5	—	80.75	—
1918	298.9	129.1	94.4	75.4	—	103.76	—
1919	368.8	151.0	132.9	85.0	—	117.97	—
1920	326.9	111.3	115.8	99.8	—	136.41	—
1921	338.9	139.6	77.9	121.4	—	105.87	—
1922	324.9	127.3	84.4	113.1	—	106.15	—
1923	380.8	137.4	119.6	123.8	—	102.39	—
1924	453.4	176.5	139.7	137.2	—	103.78	—
1925	497.8	215.8	126.0	155.9	—	103.39	—
1926	496.0	207.0	124.0	165.0	—	98.35	—
1927	495.0	193.3	125.9	175.8	—	95.86	—
1928	562.4	223.0	147.4	191.9	—	92.85	—
1929	611.9	237.0	166.4	208.5	534.9	90.08	100.20
1930	635.5	229.6	182.5	223.4	566.8	80.32	89.40
1931	612.3	205.7	176.8	229.8	550.0	72.19	80.20
1932	717.7	277.9	191.4	248.4	614.0	73.65	81.90
1933	657.6	205.4	214.7	237.5	603.2	78.81	87.60
1934	717.8	249.7	215.3	257.8	623.2	82.02	91.20

Table A1 (continued)

	Lee's estimates of NDP in 1937 prices				Hsing's estimates of national income in 1935–37 prices	Price deflator used by	
	Total	Primary sector	Secondary sector	Tertiary sector		Lee 1937 = 100	Hsing 1935–37 = 100
1935	825.7	304.4	248.3	273.0	735.1	83.44	92.70
1936	858.2	308.9	265.9	283.3	768.7	86.31	96.00
1937	805.7	280.7	269.1	256.0	720.2	100.00	111.30
1938	755.1	273.2	249.1	232.8	674.2	119.21	127.10
1939	816.1	287.9	288.9	239.3	737.8	136.84	137.80
1940	748.6	251.1	275.9	221.6	735.2	154.72	152.20
1941	—	—	—	—	808.8	—	168.10
1942	—	—	—	—	868.4	—	179.20
1943	—	—	—	—	592.0	—	302.00
1944	—	—	—	—	406.4	—	506.90

Sources: Lee's estimates are from his "Intersectoral Capital Flows in the Economic Development of Taiwan, 1895–1960," pp. 366–69; Hsing's estimates and the deflators are from Fu-chi Liu, *Essays on Monetary Development in Taiwan*.
[a] These series may be converted to NT$ by dividing them by 40,000.
[b] In this and all subsequent tables, dashes mean data not available.

Table A2. Gross National Expenditure in Constant 1934–36 Prices (Million OT$)

	GNE	Private consumption	Investment Machinery & equip.	Construc-tion	Government consumption	Net export
1903	399.7	386.9	1.9	7.8	10.2	−7.2
1904	348.5	334.5	1.8	8.2	10.0	−6.0
1905	320.0	305.7	2.6	7.0	6.8	−2.1
1906	351.4	334.1	1.8	9.0	7.4	−0.9
1907	395.3	376.4	5.3	14.8	8.0	−9.2
1908	389.8	371.1	13.0	15.6	9.0	−18.9
1909	401.0	363.9	6.8	17.1	9.5	3.7
1910	454.5	387.4	13.0	15.2	23.5	15.3
1911	459.8	369.2	14.1	21.4	33.8	21.3
1912	418.8	363.2	6.6	27.1	28.8	−6.9
1913	431.0	383.8	3.6	23.4	28.5	−8.2
1914	458.3	395.0	3.0	19.4	35.4	4.6
1915	478.3	417.4	3.0	15.6	20.7	21.5
1916	525.3	397.8	2.9	15.8	19.5	89.1
1917	547.8	388.2	4.3	28.7	18.5	108.2
1918	494.8	367.4	6.2	21.5	21.2	78.4
1919	574.7	448.0	9.3	32.6	27.9	57.0
1920	750.5	636.4	11.3	50.8	21.8	30.2
1921	750.7	645.2	11.3	46.4	32.6	15.2
1922	762.4	627.0	6.6	39.1	34.4	55.3
1923	778.4	613.4	8.0	38.5	35.6	82.8
1924	783.4	586.7	5.9	31.7	37.3	121.7
1925	775.9	595.6	7.1	44.4	35.6	93.1
1926	827.4	659.4	9.3	43.7	38.6	76.5
1927	915.5	742.8	10.8	51.9	41.1	68.9
1928	1,008.8	773.4	14.2	62.1	41.4	117.7
1929	940.6	710.9	14.5	66.0	46.9	102.2
1930	944.1	730.4	16.6	57.5	47.3	92.2
1931	1,022.9	775.1	13.3	56.8	48.5	129.2
1932	1,031.0	793.7	11.5	71.9	48.4	105.6
1933	968.8	770.6	12.9	79.4	48.5	57.3
1934	1,003.4	758.7	18.7	85.7	53.3	87.1
1935	1,173.2	755.2	24.7	109.6	66.0	217.8
1936	1,033.3	750.4	23.2	120.0	63.2	76.5
1937	1,051.2	741.2	22.3	91.9	67.3	128.5
1938	1,047.9	735.1	28.6	97.8	76.8	109.5

Source: Toshiyuki Mizoguchi, *The Economic Growth of Taiwan and Korea,* p. 150.

Table A3. Gross National Income and Product Account, 1951–72 (Million NT$ in current prices)

	1951	1952	1953	1954	1955	1956	1957	1958
Expenditures on gross national product								
A. Private consumption expenditures	8,976	12,774	17,457	18,603	21,757	24,312	28,123	31,408
1. Food	5,561	7,912	10,521	11,208	12,984	14,528	16,611	18,453
2. Clothing	485	696	1,054	1,202	1,404	1,461	1,627	1,778
3. Rent	809	1,185	1,714	1,833	2,087	2,437	2,971	3,296
4. Durables	90	132	191	204	233	272	331	366
5. Other	2,031	2,849	3,977	4,156	5,049	5,614	6,583	7,515
B. Government current expenditures	2,189	2,938	3,576	4,615	5,709	7,026	8,137	9,069
1. General expenditures	1,922	2,547	3,065	3,929	4,790	5,447	6,150	6,975
2. Developmental expenditures	267	391	511	686	919	1,579	1,987	2,094
C. Gross fixed capital formation	1,328	1,940	2,678	3,337	3,401	4,591	5,283	6,765
D. Change in stocks	451	703	546	704	597	933	1,072	1,133
E. Exports of goods and services	1,255	1,385	1,977	1,631	2,409	3,097	3,823	5,185
F. Less imports of goods and services	1,834	2,438	3,163	3,738	3,764	5,456	5,879	8,646
G. Statistical discrepancy	−43	−51	−79	77	−78	47	−213	−136
H. Gross domestic product	12,322	17,251	22,992	25,229	30,091	34,550	40,346	44,778
I. Net factor income from abroad	−7	−4	−4	−4	−3	−7	−55	−26
J. Gross national product	12,315	17,247	22,988	25,225	30,088	34,543	40,291	44,752
Distribution of gross national income								
K. Payments by producers to individuals	9,903	13,928	18,797	20,011	23,499	26,296	30,350	33,551
1. Compensation of employees	4,275	6,232	7,878	9,562	11,259	13,131	14,839	16,550
2. Entrepreneurial and property income	5,628	7,696	10,919	10,449	12,240	13,165	15,511	17,001
L. Income retained by producers	700	891	1,207	1,391	1,728	2,172	2,754	3,115
1. Capital consumption allowances	641	827	1,063	1,259	1,504	1,835	2,346	2,622
2. Retained earnings of corporations	59	64	144	132	224	337	408	493
M. Payments by producers to government	1,734	2,569	3,026	3,974	4,970	6,146	7,256	8,139
N. Less adjustment	22	141	42	151	109	71	69	53
1. Subsidies	12	130	13	108	55	22	26	39
2. Interest on public debt	10	11	29	43	54	49	43	14
O. Gross national income	12,315	17,247	22,988	25,225	30,098	34,543	40,291	44,752

Table A3 (continued)

	1959	1960	1961	1962	1963	1964	1965	1966
Expenditures on gross national product								
A. Private consumption expenditures	36,207	43,267	47,886	52,093	56,854	65,683	71,738	76,788
1. Food	21,256	26,230	27,904	29,655	31,861	36,822	39,701	41,744
2. Clothing	2,160	2,289	2,477	2,672	2,976	3,659	4,009	4,130
3. Rent	3,759	4,227	4,841	5,373	6,550	7,329	7,792	8,387
4. Durables	419	471	540	471	588	687	950	1,256
5. Other	8,613	10,050	12,124	13,922	14,870	17,186	19,286	21,271
B. Government current expenditures	10,516	11,758	12,874	14,778	15,877	16,919	18,980	21,602
1. General expenditures	8,174	8,890	10,007	11,692	12,464	13,257	14,577	16,452
2. Developmental expenditures	2,342	2,868	2,867	3,086	3,413	3,662	4,403	5,150
C. Gross fixed capital formation	8,595	10,361	11,349	11,623	13,335	14,872	19,000	23,974
D. Change in stocks	1,173	2,226	2,582	3,000	2,056	4,770	7,006	5,181
E. Exports of goods and services	6,429	7,033	8,991	10,064	15,444	19,202	20,806	26,065
F. Less imports of goods and services	10,880	11,726	13,868	14,990	15,919	18,812	24,493	27,035
G. Statistical discrepancy	−291	−353	53	436	−367	−268	69	−692
H. Gross domestic product	51,749	62,566	69,867	77,004	87,280	102,366	113,196	125,883
I. Net factor income from abroad	−22	−5	−75	−122	−146	−157	−329	−329
J. Gross national product	51,727	62,561	69,792	76,882	87,134	102,209	112,867	125,554
Distribution of gross national income								
K. Payments by producers to individuals	38,713	47,159	53,328	58,052	65,634	77,438	84,230	94,084
1. Compensation of employees	18,736	23,060	26,022	29,094	32,811	38,988	43,895	49,491
2. Entrepreneurial and property income	19,977	24,099	27,306	28,958	32,823	38,450	40,335	44,593
L. Income retained by producers	3,895	5,136	5,405	5,355	6,745	8,416	8,899	9,346
1. Capital consumption allowances	3,239	4,037	4,380	4,846	5,422	6,417	7,049	7,797
2. Retained earnings of corporations	656	1,099	1,025	509	1,323	1,999	1,850	1,549
M. Payments by producers to government	9,224	10,409	11,224	13,677	14,983	16,621	20,131	22,592
N. Less adjustment	105	143	165	202	228	266	360	468
1. Subsidies	44	50	60	64	56	59	93	90
2. Interest on public debt	61	93	105	138	172	207	267	378
O. Gross national income	51,727	62,561	69,792	76,882	87,134	102,209	112,867	125,554

Table A3 (continued)

	1967	1968	1969	1970	1971	1972
Expenditures on gross national product						
A. Private consumption expenditures	86,110	99,986	110,045	122,240	134,471	151,940
1. Food	46,150	51,580	55,157	60,777	65,256	72,721
2. Clothing	4,692	5,424	5,822	6,773	7,405	8,530
3. Rent	9,499	11,343	12,879	13,980	16,460	18,656
4. Durables	1,308	2,658	3,587	3,029	3,394	3,924
5. Other	24,461	28,981	32,600	37,681	41,956	48,109
B. Government current expenditures	24,680	29,817	35,014	40,048	43,868	48,427
1. General expenditures	18,648	21,665	24,365	27,646	30,245	33,783
2. Developmental expenditures	6,032	8,152	10,649	12,402	13,623	14,644
C. Gross fixed capital formation	30,185	37,130	43,107	49,381	60,132	75,275
D. Change in stocks	5,867	6,018	5,138	8,035	5,027	-3,098
E. Exports of goods and services	31,507	41,134	51,477	66,864	91,898	131,293
F. Less imports of goods and services	34,132	45,650	53,248	67,067	83,388	111,550
G. Statistical discrepancy	-959	-2	-514	-794	-610	0
H. Gross domestic product	143,258	168,433	191,019	218,707	249,398	292,287
I. Net factor income from abroad	-213	-458	-213	-279	-123	68
J. Gross national product	143,045	167,975	190,806	218,428	249,275	292,355
Distribution of gross national income						
K. Payments by producers to individuals	106,082	121,491	133,665	154,730	178,860	206,633
1. Compensation of employees	56,504	66,155	75,856	87,587	104,346	122,249
2. Entrepreneurial and property income	49,578	55,336	57,809	67,143	74,514	84,384
L. Income retained by producers	11,160	14,355	17,621	19,483	22,011	25,665
1. Capital consumption allowances	8,789	10,290	11,789	13,894	16,792	19,918
2. Retained earnings of corporations	2,371	4,065	5,832	5,589	5,219	5,747
M. Payments by producers to government	26,410	32,905	40,450	45,184	49,565	61,385
N. Less adjustment	607	776	930	969	1,161	1,328
1. Subsidies	87	94	81	125	106	208
2. Interest on public debt	520	682	849	844	1,055	1,120
O. Gross national income	143,045	167,975	190,806	218,428	249,275	292,355

Note: Notes and sources for tables A3–A9 appear at end of table A9.

Table A4. Personal Income Account, 1951–72 (Million NT$ in current prices)

	1951	1952	1953	1954	1955	1956	1957	1958
Receipts								
A. Payments by producers to individuals	9,903	13,928	18,797	20,011	23,499	26,296	30,350	33,551
1. Compensation of employees	4,275	6,232	7,878	9,562	11,259	13,131	14,839	16,550
2. Entrepreneurial and property income	5,628	7,696	10,919	10,449	12,240	13,165	15,511	17,001
a. Farm income	2,980	4,208	6,096	5,171	6,374	6,961	7,957	8,585
b. Unincorporated nonfarm income	181	216	271	298	338	406	462	586
c. Rental income	1,182	1,560	2,169	2,216	2,563	2,933	3,472	4,054
d. Interest and dividends	1,285	1,712	2,383	2,764	2,965	2,865	3,620	3,776
3. Business transfer payments	—	—	—	—	—	—	—	—
B. Transfer payments from government	18	64	72	137	116	122	172	428
C. Transfer payments from abroad	55	38	38	14	43	16	18	510
D. Personal income	9,976	14,030	18,907	20,162	23,658	26,434	30,540	34,489
Outlays and saving								
E. Private consumption expenditures	8,976	12,774	17,457	18,603	21,757	24,312	28,123	31,408
1. Food	5,561	7,912	10,521	11,208	12,984	14,528	16,611	18,453
2. Clothing	485	696	1,054	1,202	1,404	1,461	1,627	1,778
3. Rent	809	1,185	1,714	1,833	2,087	2,437	2,971	3,296
4. Durables	90	132	191	204	233	272	331	366
5. Other	2,031	2,849	3,977	4,156	5,049	5,614	6,583	7,515
F. Payments to government	251	487	552	672	839	716	904	1,129
1. Social security contributions ⎫ 2. Personal taxes ⎭	81	199	298	327	374	392	407	474
3. Other	170	288	254	345	465	324	497	655
G. Transfer payments to abroad	19	11	2	15	19	24	15	16
H. Personal saving	730	758	896	872	1,043	1,382	1,498	1,936
I. Personal outlays and saving	9,976	14,030	18,907	20,162	23,658	26,434	30,540	34,489

Table A4 (continued)

	1959	1960	1961	1962	1963	1964	1965	1966
Receipts								
A. Payment by producers to individuals	38,713	47,159	53,328	58,052	65,634	77,438	84,230	94,084
1. Compensation of employees	18,736	23,060	26,022	29,096	32,811	38,988	43,895	49,491
2. Entrepreneurial and property income	19,977	24,099	27,306	28,958	32,823	38,450	40,335	44,593
a. Farm income	9,684	12,969	14,061	14,114	14,688	18,550	19,385	20,373
b. Unincorporated nonfarm income	655	681	758	880	887	1,179	1,311	1,980
c. Rental income	4,188	4,675	5,065	5,918	6,432	7,226	7,429	8,102
d. Interest and dividends	5,450	5,774	7,422	8,046	10,816	11,495	12,210	14,138
3. Business transfer payments	—	—	—	—	—	—	—	—
B. Transfer payments from government	408	465	647	651	649	786	1,161	1,148
C. Transfer payments from abroad	386	233	497	635	600	525	650	827
D. Personal income	39,507	47,857	54,472	59,338	66,883	78,749	86,041	96,059
Outlays and saving								
E. Private consumption expenditures	36,207	43,267	47,886	52,093	56,854	65,683	71,738	76,788
1. Food	21,256	26,230	27,904	29,655	31,861	36,822	39,701	41,744
2. Clothing	2,160	2,289	2,477	2,672	2,976	3,659	4,009	4,130
3. Rent	3,759	4,227	4,841	5,373	6,559	7,329	7,792	8,387
4. Durables	419	471	540	471	588	687	950	1,256
5. Other	8,613	10,050	12,124	13,922	14,870	17,186	19,286	21,271
F. Payments to government	1,320	1,439	1,505	1,522	1,747	2,303	2,586	3,259
1. Social security contributions } 2. Personal taxes	559	675	768	799	944	1,026	1,030	1,441
3. Other	761	764	737	723	803	1,277	1,556	1,818
G. Transfer payments to abroad	32	32	28	50	37	42	49	101
H. Personal saving	1,948	3,119	5,053	5,673	8,245	10,721	11,668	15,911
I. Personal outlays and saving	39,507	47,857	54,472	59,338	66,883	78,749	86,041	96,059

Table A4 (continued)

	1967	1968	1969	1970	1971	1972
Receipts						
A. Payment by producers to individuals	106,082	121,491	133,665	154,730	178,860	206,633
1. Compensation of employees	56,504	66,155	75,856	87,587	104,346	122,249
2. Entrepreneurial and property income	49,578	55,336	57,809	67,143	74,514	84,384
a. Farm income	21,688	23,448	22,406	24,079	24,247	27,028
b. Unincorporated nonfarm income	2,030	2,135	2,345	2,668	3,660	3,981
c. Rental income	9,340	10,649	11,536	12,608	14,447	16,131
d. Interest and dividends	16,520	19,104	21,522	27,788	32,160	37,244
3. Business transfer payments	—	—	—	—	—	—
B. Transfer payments from government	1,412	1,866	2,038	3,095	4,520	4,703
C. Transfer payments from abroad	1,123	678	376	648	668	722
D. Personal income	108,617	124,035	136,079	158,473	184,048	212,058
Outlays and saving						
E. Private consumption expenditures	86,110	99,986	110,045	122,240	134,471	151,940
1. Food	46,150	51,580	55,157	60,777	65,256	72,721
2. Clothing	4,692	5,424	5,822	6,773	7,405	8,530
3. Rent	9,499	11,343	12,879	13,980	16,460	18,656
4. Durables	1,308	2,658	3,587	3,029	3,394	3,924
5. Other	24,461	28,981	32,600	37,681	41,956	48,109
F. Payments to government	3,590	4,659	5,259	6,240	7,931	9,439
1. Social security contributions }	1,274	2,252	2,577	3,339	4,315	5,373
2. Personal taxes						
3. Other	2,316	2,407	2,682	2,901	3,616	4,066
G. Transfer payments to abroad	75	66	25	36	145	122
H. Personal saving	18,842	19,324	20,750	29,957	41,501	50,557
I. Personal outlays and saving	108,617	124,035	136,079	158,473	184,048	212,058

Table A3. Government Revenue and Current Expenditure Account, 1951–72 (Million NT$ in current prices)

	1951	1952	1953	1954	1955	1956	1957	1958
A. Payments by producers	1,734	2,569	3,026	3,974	4,970	6,146	7,256	8,139
1. Corporate profit taxes	180	269	233	273	400	456	479	579
2. Property, commodity, & other taxes	1,159	1,897	2,396	3,313	3,955	4,651	5,562	6,248
a. Farm land tax	87	118	210	147	225	230	251	270
b. Wine & tobacco monopoly revenues	273	421	590	846	926	1,144	1,386	1,553
c. Others	799	1,358	1,596	2,320	2,804	3,277	3,925	4,425
3. Property income paid to government	395	403	397	388	615	1,039	1,215	1,312
B. Payments by individuals	251	487	552	672	839	716	904	1,129
1. Social security contributions }	81	199	298	327	374	392	407	474
2. Personal taxes								
3. Other	170	288	254	345	465	324	497	655
C. Transfer from abroad	702	1,026	1,246	1,442	1,640	1,433	1,282	2,289
D. Total receipts	2,687	4,082	4,824	6,088	7,449	8,295	9,442	11,557
Current expenditures								
E. Government current expenditures	2,189	2,938	3,576	4,615	5,709	7,026	8,137	9,069
1. General expenditures	1,922	2,547	3,065	3,929	4,790	5,447	6,150	6,975
a. Administration & defense	1,511	1,909	2,305	3,042	3,904	4,571	5,354	6,221
b. Justice & police	100	176	253	298	369	495	480	481
c. Community services	311	462	507	589	517	381	316	273
2. Developmental expenditures	267	391	511	686	919	1,579	1,987	2,094
a. Education	133	189	242	331	457	859	1,187	1,250
b. Health	29	34	54	73	103	156	154	172
c. Other social	15	18	23	40	52	143	162	177
d. Transport & communications	47	69	90	104	121	151	169	178
e. Agriculture & other industries	43	81	102	138	186	270	315	317
F. Subsidies	12	130	13	108	55	22	26	39
G. Interest on public debt	10	11	29	43	54	49	43	14
H. Transfer payments to individuals	18	64	72	137	116	122	172	428
I. Transfer payments to abroad	0	0	0	0	0	0	5	0
J. Surplus on current account	458	939	1,134	1,185	1,515	1,076	1,059	2,007
K. Total current expenditures & surplus	2,687	4,082	4,824	6,088	7,449	8,295	9,442	11,557

Table A5 (continued)

	1959	1960	1961	1962	1963	1964	1965	1966
A. Payments by producers	9,224	10,409	11,224	13,678	14,983	16,621	20,100	22,592
1. Corporate profit taxes	735	835	766	644	714	874	944	961
2. Property, commodity, & other taxes	6,940	7,746	8,460	10,576	11,165	11,286	14,352	15,880
a. Farm land tax	301	343	400	507	569	618	666	636
b. Wine & tobacco monopoly revenues	1,775	2,086	2,514	2,983	2,785	2,509	3,351	3,633
c. Others	4,864	5,317	5,546	7,086	7,811	8,159	10,335	11,611
3. Property income paid to government	1,549	1,828	1,998	2,457	3,104	4,461	4,802	5,751
B. Payments by individuals	1,320	1,439	1,505	1,522	1,747	2,303	2,586	3,259
1. Social security contributions }	559	675	768	799	944	1,026	1,030	1,441
2. Personal taxes	761	764	737	723	803	1,277	1,556	1,818
3. Other								
C. Transfer from abroad	2,473	3,084	3,376	1,713	1,482	706	760	560
D. Total receipts	13,017	14,932	16,105	16,912	18,212	19,630	23,444	26,411
Current expenditures								
E. Government current expenditures	10,516	11,758	12,874	14,778	15,877	16,919	18,980	21,602
1. General expenditures	8,174	8,890	10,007	11,692	12,464	13,257	14,577	16,452
a. Administration & defense	7,414	8,053	9,186	10,811	11,196	11,879	12,571	14,434
b. Justice & police	498	540	650	687	737	832	964	1,083
c. Community services	262	297	171	194	531	546	1,042	935
2. Developmental expenditures	2,342	2,868	2,867	3,086	3,413	3,662	4,403	5,150
a. Education	1,230	1,484	1,661	1,774	1,897	2,128	2,724	3,279
b. Health	192	272	272	294	303	417	362	417
c. Other social	238	361	276	294	294	299	323	336
d. Transport & communications	276	259	337	344	382	300	399	502
e. Agriculture & other industries	406	492	321	380	537	518	595	616
F. Subsidies	44	50	60	64	56	59	93	90
G. Interest on public debt	61	93	105	138	172	207	267	378
H. Transfer payments to individuals	408	465	647	651	649	786	1,161	1,148
I. Transfer payments to abroad	0	87	102	102	271	342	437	257
J. Surplus on current account	1,988	2,479	2,317	1,179	1,187	1,317	2,506	2,936
K. Total current expenditures & surplus	13,017	14,932	16,105	16,912	18,212	19,630	23,444	26,411

Table A5 (continued)

	1967	1968	1969	1970	1971	1972
A. Payments by producers	26,410	32,906	40,450	45,184	49,565	61,385
1. Corporate profit taxes	963	1,276	1,651	2,206	2,915	3,771
2. Property, commodity, & other taxes	19,124	24,543	30,051	33,574	36,132	44,239
a. Farm land tax	913	1,091	888	1,159	1,327	1,148
b. Wine & tobacco monopoly revenues	4,493	4,674	5,624	6,840	5,931	7,992
c. Others	13,718	18,778	23,539	25,575	28,874	35,099
3. Property income paid to government	6,323	7,086	8,748	9,404	10,518	13,375
B. Payments by individuals	3,590	4,658	5,259	6,240	7,931	9,439
1. Social security contributions }	1,274	2,252	2,577	3,339	4,315	5,373
2. Personal taxes						
3. Other	2,316	2,406	2,682	2,901	3,616	4,066
C. Transfer from abroad	420	300	302	361	292	345
D. Total receipts	30,420	37,864	46,011	51,785	57,788	71,169
Current expenditures						
E. Government current expenditures	24,680	29,817	35,014	40,048	43,868	48,427
1. General expenditures	18,648	21,665	24,365	27,646	30,245	33,783
a. Administration & defense	16,693	19,328	21,611	25,160	27,235	30,079
b. Justice & police	1,282	1,467	1,674	2,214	2,420	2,414
c. Community services	673	870	1,080	272	590	1,290
2. Developmental expenditures	6,032	8,152	10,649	12,402	13,623	14,644
a. Education	3,926	5,416	7,220	7,994	8,541	9,195
b. Health	487	574	724	770	917	994
c. Other social	421	640	1,060	1,400	1,625	1,686
d. Transport & communications	562	776	716	948	1,004	956
e. Agriculture & other industries	636	746	929	1,290	1,536	1,813
F. Subsidies	87	94	81	125	106	208
G. Interest on public debt	520	682	849	844	1,055	1,120
H. Transfer payments to individuals	1,412	1,866	2,038	3,095	4,520	4,703
I. Transfer payments to abroad	238	181	343	416	379	230
J. Surplus on current account	3,483	5,224	7,686	7,257	7,860	16,481
K. Total current expenditures & surplus	30,420	37,864	46,011	51,785	57,788	71,169

Table A6. Gross Domestic Capital Formation Account, 1951–72 (Million NT$ in current prices)

	1951	1952	1953	1954	1955	1956	1957	1958
Gross domestic capital formation								
A. Gross fixed capital formation	1,328	1,940	2,678	3,337	3,401	4,591	5,283	6,765
1. Residential construction	121	178	251	439	430	500	617	685
2. Other construction	610	854	1,148	1,426	1,399	1,826	1,964	2,725
3. Transport equipment	126	198	253	155	144	349	444	643
4. Machinery and other equipment	471	710	1,026	1,317	1,428	1,916	2,258	2,712
B. Change in stocks	451	703	546	704	597	933	1,072	1,133
C. Gross domestic capital formation	1,779	2,643	3,224	4,041	3,998	5,524	6,355	7,898
Gross domestic saving								
D. Income retained by producers	700	891	1,207	1,391	1,728	2,172	2,754	3,115
1. Capital consumption allowances	641	827	1,063	1,259	1,504	1,835	2,346	2,622
a. Private enterprises	405	535	758	820	1,057	1,231	1,525	1,757
b. Public corporations } c. Government enterprises }	236	292	305	439	447	604	821	865
d. General government	—	—	—	—	—	—	—	—
2. Retained earnings of corporations	59	64	144	132	224	337	408	493
a. Private enterprises	—	—	—	—	—	—	—	—
b. Public corporations } c. Government enterprises }	59	64	144	132	224	337	408	493
E. Personal saving	730	758	896	872	1,043	1,382	1,498	1,936
F. Government surplus on current account	458	939	1,134	1,185	1,515	1,076	1,059	2,007
G. Surplus of nation on current account	−152	4	−92	670	−366	941	831	704
H. Statistical discrepancy	43	51	79	−77	78	−47	213	136
I. Gross domestic saving	1,779	2,643	3,224	4,041	3,998	5,524	6,355	7,898

Table A6 (continued)

	1959	1960	1961	1962	1963	1964	1965	1966
Gross domestic capital formation								
A. Gross fixed capital formation	8,595	10,361	11,349	11,623	13,335	14,872	19,090	23,974
1. Residential construction	1,003	1,414	1,269	1,250	1,887	1,424	1,861	2,313
2. Other construction	3,261	4,135	4,312	4,919	5,455	6,507	6,906	8,474
3. Transport equipment	624	1,020	1,423	1,199	1,228	1,505	2,167	2,563
4. Machinery and other equipment	3,707	3,792	4,345	4,255	4,765	5,436	8,156	10,624
B. Change in stocks	1,173	2,226	2,582	3,000	2,056	4,770	7,006	5,181
C. Gross domestic capital formation	9,768	12,587	13,931	14,623	15,391	19,642	26,096	29,155
Gross domestic saving								
D. Income retained by producers	3,895	5,136	5,405	5,355	6,745	8,416	8,899	9,346
1. Capital consumption allowances	3,239	4,037	4,380	4,846	5,422	6,417	7,049	7,797
a. Private enterprises	2,146	2,658	2,954	3,223	3,495	4,242	4,831	5,433
b. Public corporations } c. Government enterprises }	1,093	1,379	1,426	1,623	1,927	2,175	2,218	2,364
d. General government	—	—	—	—	—	—	—	—
2. Retained earnings of corporations	656	1,099	1,025	509	1,323	1,999	1,850	1,549
a. Private enterprises	—	—	—	—	—	—	—	—
b. Public corporations } c. Government enterprises }	656	1,099	1,025	509	1,323	1,999	1,850	1,549
E. Personal saving	1,948	3,119	5,053	5,673	8,245	10,721	11,668	15,911
F. Government surplus on current account	1,988	2,479	2,317	1,179	1,187	1,317	2,506	2,936
G. Surplus of nation on current account	1,646	1,500	1,209	2,852	-1,153	-1,080	3,092	270
H. Statistical discrepancy	291	353	-53	-436	367	-268	-69	692
I. Gross domestic saving	9,768	12,587	13,931	14,623	15,391	19,642	26,096	29,155

Table A6 (continued)

	1967	1968	1969	1970	1971	1972
Gross domestic capital formation						
A. Gross fixed capital formation	30,185	37,130	43,107	49,381	60,132	75,275
1. Residential construction	3,316	4,561	3,947	4,549	6,100	8,214
2. Other construction	10,308	12,748	15,538	14,060	16,892	18,760
3. Transport equipment	3,378	3,647	5,096	6,785	8,346	11,031
4. Machinery and other equipment	13,183	16,174	18,526	23,987	28,794	37,270
B. Change in stocks	5,867	6,018	5,138	8,035	5,027	−3,098
C. Gross domestic capital formation	36,052	43,148	48,245	57,416	65,159	72,177
Gross domestic saving						
D. Income retained by producers	11,160	14,355	17,621	19,483	22,011	25,665
1. Capital consumption allowances	8,789	10,290	11,789	13,894	16,792	19,918
a. Private enterprises	6,040	7,259	8,010	9,384	11,332	13,429
b. Public corporations } c. Government enterprises }	2,749	3,031	3,779	4,510	5,460	6,269
d. General government	—	—	—	—	—	220
2. Retained earnings of corporations	2,371	4,065	5,832	5,589	5,219	5,747
a. Private enterprises	—	—	—	—	—	—
b. Public corporations } c. Government enterprises }	2,371	4,065	5,832	5,589	5,219	5,747
E. Personal saving	18,842	19,324	20,750	29,957	41,501	50,557
F. Government surplus on current account	3,483	5,224	7,686	7,257	7,860	16,481
G. Surplus of nation on current account	1,608	4,243	1,674	−75	−6,823	−20,526
H. Statistical discrepancy	959	2	514	794	610	0
I. Gross domestic saving	36,052	43,148	48,245	57,416	65,159	72,177

Table A7. External Transactions Account, 1951–72 (Million NT$ in current prices)

	1951	1952	1953	1954	1955	1956	1957	1958
Receipts from abroad								
A. Exports of goods and services	1,255	1,385	1,977	1,631	2,469	3,097	3,823	5,185
1. Merchandise	1,170	1,345	1,928	1,587	2,357	2,886	3,462	4,549
2. Other	85	40	49	44	112	211	361	636
B. Factor income from abroad	0	0	0	0	0	0	0	0
C. Transfer payments to individuals	55	38	38	14	43	16	18	510
D. Transfer payments to government	702	1,026	1,246	1,442	1,640	1,433	1,282	2,289
E. Current receipts from abroad	2,012	2,449	3,261	3,087	4,152	4,546	5,123	7,984
Payments to abroad								
F. Imports of goods and services	1,834	2,438	3,163	3,738	3,764	5,456	5,879	8,646
1. Merchandise	1,696	2,278	2,869	3,263	3,393	4,901	5,375	7,633
2. Other	138	160	294	475	371	555	504	1,013
G. Factor income paid abroad	7	4	4	4	3	7	55	26
H. Transfer payments from individuals	19	11	2	15	19	24	15	16
I. Transfer payments from government	0	0	0	0	0	0	5	0
J. Surplus of nation on external account	152	−4	92	−670	366	−941	−831	−704
K. Current payments to abroad and surplus	2,012	2,449	3,261	3,087	4,152	4,546	5,123	7,984

Table A7 (continued)

	1959	1960	1961	1962	1963	1964	1965	1966
Receipts from abroad								
A. Exports of goods and services	6,429	7,033	8,991	10,064	15,444	19,202	20,806	26,065
1. Merchandise	5,957	6,288	7,976	9,140	13,870	17,879	18,401	22,158
2. Other	472	745	1,015	924	1,574	1,323	2,405	3,907
B. Factor income from abroad	18	73	54	51	50	68	106	85
C. Transfer payments to individuals	386	233	497	635	600	525	650	827
D. Transfer payments to government	2,473	3,084	3,376	1,713	1,482	706	760	560
E. Current receipts from abroad	9,306	10,423	12,918	12,463	17,576	20,501	22,322	27,537
Payments to abroad								
F. Imports of goods and services	10,880	11,726	13,868	14,990	15,919	18,812	24,493	27,035
1. Merchandise	9,619	10,424	12,678	13,662	14,418	16,936	22,115	24,801
2. Other	1,261	1,302	1,190	1,328	1,501	1,876	2,378	2,234
G. Factor income paid abroad	40	78	129	173	196	225	435	414
H. Transfer payments from individuals	32	32	28	50	37	42	49	101
I. Transfer payments from government	0	87	102	102	271	342	437	257
J. Surplus of nation on external account	−1,646	−1,500	−1,209	−2,852	1,153	1,080	−3,092	−270
K. Current payments to abroad and surplus	9,306	10,423	12,918	12,463	17,576	20,501	22,322	27,537

Table A7 (continued)

	1967	1968	1969	1970	1971	1972
Receipts from abroad						
A. Exports of goods and services	31,507	41,134	51,477	66,864	91,898	131,293
1. Merchandise	27,445	33,963	44,043	59,537	82,994	120,330
2. Other	4,062	7,171	7,434	7,327	8,904	10,963
B. Factor income from abroad	444	906	1,521	2,354	3,632	4,218
C. Transfer payments to individuals	1,123	678	376	648	668	722
D. Transfer payments to government	420	300	302	361	292	345
E. Current receipts from abroad	33,494	43,018	53,676	70,227	96,490	136,578
Payments to abroad						
F. Imports of goods and services	34,132	45,650	53,248	67,067	85,388	111,550
1. Merchandise	30,993	39,201	47,518	59,480	75,537	98,502
2. Other	2,139	6,449	5,730	7,587	9,851	13,048
G. Factor income paid abroad	657	1,364	1,734	2,633	3,755	4,150
H. Transfer payments from individuals	75	66	25	36	145	122
I. Transfer payments from government	238	181	343	416	379	230
J. Surplus of nation on external account	−1,608	−4,243	−1,674	75	6,823	20,526
K. Current payments to abroad and surplus	33,494	43,018	53,676	70,227	96,490	136,578

Table A8. Industrial Origin of Gross Domestic Product at Factor Cost, 1951–72 (Million NT$ in current prices)

	1951	1952	1953	1954	1955	1956	1957	1958
1. Agriculture, forestry, hunting, and fishing	3,863	5,403	7,661	6,760	8,309	9,081	10,536	11,549
2. Mining and quarrying	143	317	345	393	438	639	866	1,108
3. Manufacturing	1,512	1,731	2,385	3,297	3,735	4,506	5,692	6,197
4. Construction	457	648	774	1,101	1,206	1,360	1,480	1,572
5. Electricity, gas, water, and sanitary services	143	144	204	220	278	357	478	600
6. Transportation, storage, and communication	512	689	842	921	1,231	1,389	1,872	1,967
7. Wholesale and retail trade	1,543	2,796	3,653	3,716	4,221	4,876	5,031	5,689
8. Banking, insurance, and real estate	116	130	192	209	353	432	576	744
9. Ownership of dwellings	966	1,238	1,637	1,810	2,021	2,341	2,867	3,114
10. Public administration and defense	1,269	1,577	1,937	2,483	3,162	3,498	3,727	4,230
11. Other services	681	852	1,041	1,182	1,359	1,601	1,882	2,071
Less imputed interest	30	41	62	68	122	159	197	272
Gross domestic product at factor cost	11,175	15,484	20,609	22,024	26,191	29,921	34,810	38,569

Table A8 (continued)

	1959	1960	1961	1962	1963	1964	1965	1966
1. Agriculture, forestry, hunting, and fishing	13,116	17,206	18,580	18,596	19,640	24,464	25,825	27,403
2. Mining and quarrying	1,113	1,237	1,267	1,653	1,572	1,600	1,878	2,210
3. Manufacturing	8,144	9,496	10,728	11,635	15,412	19,273	20,568	23,052
4. Construction	1,847	2,299	2,549	2,841	3,320	3,660	4,278	4,916
5. Electricity, gas, water, and sanitary services	695	991	1,225	1,475	1,589	1,936	2,168	2,362
6. Transportation, storage, and communication	2,164	2,744	3,492	3,800	3,962	4,779	5,575	6,886
7. Wholesale and retail trade	6,370	7,807	8,471	9,324	10,896	13,116	14,155	15,220
8. Banking, insurance, and real estate	833	862	946	1,128	1,344	1,748	2,175	2,463
9. Ownership of dwellings	3,393	3,737	4,296	5,011	5,716	6,231	6,613	7,238
10. Public administration and defense	5,017	6,071	7,050	7,645	8,562	9,649	10,377	12,466
11. Other services	2,422	2,720	3,071	3,567	4,369	4,920	5,679	6,287
Less imputed interest	261	300	178	183	211	237	357	410
Gross domestic product at factor cost	44,853	54,870	61,467	66,492	76,171	91,139	98,937	110,093

Table A8 (continued)

	1967	1968	1969	1970	1971	1972
1. Agriculture, forestry, hunting, and fishing	29,562	33,173	31,882	34,651	35,782	40,555
2. Mining and quarrying	2,465	2,377	2,299	2,568	2,692	2,921
3. Manufacturing	26,980	32,795	38,680	45,772	57,273	69,840
4. Construction	5,668	6,837	7,921	8,640	10,410	12,021
5. Electricity, gas, water, and sanitary services	2,574	3,049	3,849	5,096	5,713	6,577
6. Transportation, storage, and communication	7,474	8,977	10,318	12,123	14,167	16,732
7. Wholesale and retail trade	17,345	19,257	22,296	25,190	29,054	33,788
8. Banking, insurance, and real estate	2,962	3,716	5,035	6,432	7,030	8,120
9. Ownership of dwellings	8,193	9,757	10,910	11,973	14,124	15,531
10. Public administration and defense	14,457	16,955	19,159	22,457	24,962	27,987
11. Other services	6,914	7,668	9,394	11,182	13,004	15,279
Less imputed interest	373	577	694	825	839	1,094
Gross domestic product at factor cost	124,221	143,984	161,049	185,259	213,372	248,257

Expenditure on Gross Domestic Product, 1951–72 (Million NT$ in 1966 prices)

	1951	1952	1953	1954	1955	1956	1957	1958
1. Private consumption expenditures	25,593	29,658	32,196	35,159	37,670	38,185	41,093	44,306
A. Food	15,117	17,298	18,602	20,182	21,369	21,522	22,933	24,542
B. Beverages	759	899	988	1,086	1,178	1,206	1,311	1,422
C. Tobacco	1,450	1,672	1,808	1,971	2,098	2,123	2,274	2,439
D. Clothing and other personal effects	1,103	1,316	1,453	1,607	1,762	1,809	1,979	2,160
E. Fuel and light	1,296	1,450	1,592	1,724	1,824	1,834	1,953	2,089
F. Rent and water charges G. Furniture, furnishing, and household equipment H. Household operation	2,765	3,259	3,565	3,918	4,251	4,335	4,706	5,115
I. Personal care and health expenses	1,014	1,169	1,261	1,374	1,461	1,474	1,579	1,693
J. Recreation and entertainment	486	601	675	760	854	886	992	1,102
K. Transportation and communication	267	333	377	426	482	503	566	628
L. Miscellaneous	1,336	1,661	1,875	2,111	2,391	2,493	2,800	3,116
2. Government consumption expenditures	9,770	10,417	10,749	12,261	12,984	15,098	16,295	16,273
A. Compensation of employees	7,677	7,648	7,687	8,463	9,001	10,020	10,576	10,079
B. Purchases from enterprise and abroad	2,093	2,769	3,062	3,798	3,983	5,078	5,719	6,194
3. Fixed capital formation	3,504	4,570	5,814	6,255	5,409	6,240	6,184	7,521
A. Construction	2,206	2,641	3,512	3,954	3,386	3,478	3,257	4,244
B. Transport equipment	283	438	458	244	202	438	489	633
C. Machinery and equipment	1,015	1,491	1,844	2,057	1,821	2,324	2,438	2,644
4. Increase in stocks	1,152	1,604	1,021	1,297	907	1,249	1,450	1,510
A. Raw materials	561	518	156	459	533	466	741	1,327
B. Work in process	75	87	61	–36	–15	94	70	33
C. Finished goods	516	999	804	874	389	689	639	150
5. Exports of goods and services	3,923	4,311	5,179	3,891	4,815	5,220	5,943	7,249
A. Merchandise, freight, and insurance	3,624	4,167	5,046	3,778	4,567	4,836	5,285	6,338
B. Services	299	144	133	113	248	384	658	911
6. Less imports of goods and services	6,281	8,358	8,914	9,345	7,887	9,806	10,239	12,267
A. Merchandise, freight, and insurance	5,796	7,780	8,118	8,123	7,066	8,797	9,320	10,815
B. Services	485	578	796	1,222	821	1,009	919	1,452
Plus statistical discrepancy	–131	–125	–158	151	–140	76	–319	–197
7. Expenditure on gross domestic product	37,530	42,077	45,887	49,669	53,758	56,262	60,407	64,395

Table A9 (continued)

	1959	1960	1961	1962	1963	1964	1965	1966
1. Private consumption expenditures	46,516	48,350	51,519	55,659	59,583	67,977	73,182	76,788
A. Food	25,479	25,628	26,057	28,317	29,907	34,039	35,701	35,891
B. Beverages	1,511	1,525	1,540	1,503	1,513	1,721	1,952	2,257
C. Tobacco	2,542	2,579	2,773	2,677	2,715	2,886	3,278	3,596
D. Clothing and other personal effects	2,308	2,377	2,593	2,761	3,012	3,657	3,999	4,130
E. Fuel and light	2,164	2,259	2,677	2,621	2,709	2,844	2,939	3,256
F. Rent and water charges				5,747	6,783	7,495	7,848	8,387
G. Furniture, furnishing, and household equipment	5,418	5,980	6,682	470	584	686	947	1,256
H. Household operation				857	965	1,284	1,423	1,544
I. Personal care and health expenses	1,764	2,258	2,954	3,586	3,936	4,361	4,642	4,791
J. Recreation and entertainment	1,208	1,223	1,210	1,385	1,537	1,727	2,014	2,230
K. Transportation and communication	696	617	645	679	758	1,220	1,554	1,604
L. Miscellaneous	3,426	3,904	4,388	5,056	5,164	6,057	6,885	7,846
2. Government consumption expenditures	17,322	17,290	17,569	19,040	19,282	19,190	20,562	21,602
A. Compensation of employees	10,713	10,882	11,059	11,286	11,443	11,490	11,928	12,466
B. Purchases from enterprise and abroad	6,609	6,408	6,510	7,754	7,839	7,700	8,634	9,136
3. Fixed capital formation	9,109	10,352	11,726	12,239	14,297	15,227	19,132	23,974
A. Construction	4,790	5,608	6,110	6,967	8,306	8,425	8,920	10,787
B. Transport equipment	600	1,015	1,353	990	1,192	1,429	2,038	2,564
C. Machinery and equipment	3,719	3,729	4,263	4,282	4,799	5,373	8,174	10,623
4. Increase in stocks	1,562	2,533	2,784	3,325	2,126	4,792	7,242	5,181
A. Raw materials	921	1,573	346	291	1,076	1,176	2,456	1,840
B. Work in process	96	8	157	51	148	322	895	547
C. Finished goods	545	952	2,281	2,983	902	3,294	3,891	2,794
5. Exports of goods and services	7,531	8,685	9,935	10,726	14,297	17,380	21,834	26,065
A. Merchandise, freight, and insurance	7,012	7,875	8,921	9,803	12,724	16,057	19,429	22,158
B. Services	519	810	1,014	923	1,573	1,323	2,405	3,907
6. Less imports of goods and services	12,560	13,443	14,879	16,494	17,008	20,495	25,962	27,035
A. Merchandise, freight, and insurance	11,174	12,027	13,690	15,167	15,508	18,619	23,584	24,801
B. Services	1,386	1,416	1,189	1,327	1,500	1,876	2,378	2,234
Plus statistical discrepancy	−390	−416	60	0	0	−272	0	−692
7. Expenditure on gross domestic product	69,090	73,351	78,714	84,495	92,577	103,799	115,990	125,883

Table A9 (continued)

	1967	1968	1969	1970	1971	1972
1. Private consumption expenditures	83,287	90,958	96,678	102,551	109,809	117,880
A. Food	37,107	38,344	39,442	41,679	43,443	44,773
B. Beverages	3,073	3,724	3,993	4,557	4,963	5,737
C. Tobacco	4,192	4,673	5,051	5,449	5,427	5,948
D. Clothing and other personal effects	4,683	5,324	5,721	6,597	7,139	7,886
E. Fuel and light	3,441	3,508	3,686	4,438	5,044	5,734
F. Rent and water charges	8,883	9,740	10,462	11,183	13,150	14,208
G. Furniture, furnishing, and household equipment	1,319	2,567	3,375	2,809	3,227	3,715
H. Household operation	1,765	1,888	1,884	1,868	1,939	2,070
I. Personal care and health expenses	5,090	5,593	5,867	5,823	5,576	6,066
J. Recreation and entertainment	2,602	2,852	2,935	3,227	3,667	3,955
K. Transportation and communication	2,073	2,424	2,782	3,057	3,014	3,412
L. Miscellaneous	9,059	10,321	11,480	11,864	13,220	14,376
2. Government consumption expenditures	23,274	25,567	27,942	29,809	30,795	32,000
A. Compensation of employees	13,302	14,082	14,762	15,771	16,097	16,435
B. Purchases from enterprise and abroad	9,972	11,485	13,180	14,038	14,698	15,565
3. Fixed capital formation	29,902	35,576	39,426	46,833	55,993	66,724
A. Construction	12,846	15,456	16,186	15,629	17,876	20,202
B. Transport equipment	3,403	3,554	4,762	6,340	7,874	9,752
C. Machinery and equipment	13,653	16,566	18,478	24,864	30,243	36,770
4. Increase in stocks	5,759	5,878	4,989	7,740	4,862	−2,946
A. Raw materials	2,675	1,792	524	2,843	1,607	−2,893
B. Work in process	489	882	1,057	1,111	1,199	1,935
C. Finished goods	2,595	3,204	3,408	3,786	2,056	−1,988
5. Exports of goods and services	30,350	39,178	47,885	59,686	80,217	107,606
A. Merchandise, freight, and insurance	26,288	32,007	40,451	52,359	71,313	96,643
B. Services	4,062	7,171	7,434	7,327	8,904	10,963
6. Less imports of goods and services	33,837	45,316	52,107	63,348	77,579	94,013
A. Merchandise, freight, and insurance	30,698	38,867	46,377	55,761	67,728	80,965
B. Services	3,139	6,449	5,730	7,587	9,851	13,048
Plus statistical discrepancy	0	0	0	0	0	0
7. Expenditure on gross domestic product	138,735	151,841	164,813	183,271	204,097	227,251

Table A9 (continued)

Notes and Sources: All references, unless stated otherwise, are to DGBAS, *National Income of the Republic of China*, 1973.

Table A3. Gross National Income and Product Account

A.1. Chap. 4, table 9. Includes food (line 1), beverages (line 2), and tobacco (line 3).

A.2. Chap. 4, table 9, line 4. According to DGBAS, this item includes some durable goods such as jewelry and watches. No attempt is made to separate these durable goods from the nondurables.

A.3. Chap. 4, table 9, line 6. Before 1962, rent is presented with furniture, furnishing and household equipment, and household operating expenses. For these early years we separate rent from total expenses for rent, furniture, furnishing, household equipment, and household operation by multiplying the total expenses by the average ratio of rent to total expenses for 1962–66.

A.4. Chap. 4, table 9, line 7. Includes expenditures for furniture, house furnishings, and household equipment. Before 1962, expenditures for durables are included in rent and household operation expenses. We estimate the expenditure for durables in the same way we estimate rent in A.3.

A.5. Chap. 4, table 9, line 13 minus (A.1 + A.2 + A.3 + A.4).

B.1. Table A5, this appendix.

B.2. Table A5, this appendix.

C. Table A6, this appendix.

D. Chap. 4, table 7, line 3B.

E. Chap. 4, table 12, line 1.

F. Chap. 4, table 12, line 4.

G. Chap. 4, table 1, line 10.

I. Chap. 4, table 1, line 11.

K.1. Chap. 4, table 5, line 1.

K.2. Chap. 4, table 5, sum of lines 2 and 3.

L.1. Chap. 4, table 6, line 1.

L.2. Chap. 4, table 6, line 28. This includes only the retained earnings of public enterprises. Consequently items L2 and L are understated and items K2 and K are overstated.

M. Chap. 4, table 10, sum of lines 1, 2, and 3.

N.1. Chap. 4, table 10, line 8.

N.2. Chap. 4, table 10, line 10.

Table A9 (continued)

Table A4. Personal Income Account

A.1. Chap. 4, table 5, line 1.
A.2.a. Chap. 4, table 5, line 2A.
A.2.b. Chap. 4, table 5, sum of lines 2B and 2C.
A.2.c. Chap. 4, table 5, line 3A.
A.2.d. Chap. 4, table 5, sum of lines 3B and 3C. This is grossly overstated because it includes the retained earnings of private enterprises.
B. Chap. 4, table 10, line 8.
C. Chap. 4, table 12, line 3A.
E.1–E.5. Table A3, this appendix.
F.1, F.2. Chap. 4, table 10, line 4.
F.3. Chap. 4, table 10, line 5.
G. Chap. 4, table 12, line 6A.
H. Chap. 4, table 8, line 9. This is grossly overstated because it includes the undistributed profits of private enterprises.

Table A5. Government Revenue and Current Expenditure Account

A.1. Chap. 4, table 10, line 3.
A.2.a. Chap. 4, table 10, line 2b.
A.2.b. Chap. 4, table 10, line 2a.
A.2.c. Chap. 4, table 10, line 2c.
A.3. Chap. 4, table 10, line 1.
B.1, B.2. Chap. 4, table 10, line 4.
B.3. Chap. 4, table 10, line 5.
C. Chap. 4, table 10, line 6.
E.1.a. Chap. 4, table 11, line 2A.
E.1.b. Chap. 4, table 11, line 2B.
E.1.c. Chap. 4, table 11, line 2H. This is a miscellaneous item with an uncertain composition. However, it is believed that expenditures for community services are included here.
E.2.a. Chap. 4, table 11, line 2C.
E.2.b. Chap. 4, table 11, line 2D.

Table A9 (continued)

E.2.c. Chap. 4, table 11, line 2E.
E.2.d. Chap. 4, table 11, line 2G.
E.2.e. Chap. 4, table 11, line 2F.
F. Chap. 4, table 10, line 8.
G. Chap. 4, table 10, line 10.
H. Chap. 4, table 10, line 9.
I. Chap. 4, table 10, line 11.
J. Chap. 4, table 10, line 12.

Table A6. Gross Domestic Capital Formation Account

A.1. Chap. 4, table 7, line 1Aa.
A.2. Chap. 4, table 7, lines 1Ab and 1Ac.
A.3. Chap. 4, table 7, line 1Ad.
A.4. Chap. 4, table 7, line 1Ae.
B. Chap. 4, table 7, line 1B.
D.1.a. Chap. 4, table 6, line 1A.
D.1.b, D.1.c. Chap. 4, table 6, line 1B.
D.2.a. Included in personal savings (E).
D.2.b, D.2.c. Chap. 4, Table 6, line 2B.
E. Chap. 4., table 6, lines 2C and 2D.
F. Chap. 4, table 6, line 2A.
G. Chap. 4, table 6, line 3.

Beginning in 1965, the distribution of gross fixed capital formation can also be arranged as follows:

	1965	1968	1972
A. Gross fixed capital formation (million NT$)	19,090	37,130	75,274
1. Government fixed capital formation	2,401	3,963	7,372
a. Construction	2,138	3,471	5,632
b. Equipment	263	492	1,840

Table A9 (continued)

	1965	1968	1972
2. Residential construction	1,861	4,561	8,214
a. Public	102	174	486
b. Private	1,759	4,387	7,727
3. Enterprise fixed capital formation	14,827	28,606	59,687
a. Public enterprises	3,892	10,435	23,070
1. Construction	936	2,261	3,440
2. Equipment	2,956	8,174	19,630
b. Private enterprises	10,935	18,171	36,617
1. Construction	3,831	7,016	9,786
2. Equipment	7,104	11,155	26,831

Table A7. External Transactions Account

A.1. Chap. 4, table 12, line 1A.
A.2. Chap. 4, table 12, sum of lines 1B–1E.
B. Chap. 4, table 12, line 2.
C. Chap. 4, table 12, line 3A.
D. Chap. 4, table 12, line 3B.
F.1. Chap. 4, table 12, line 4A.
F.2. Chap. 4, table 12, sum of lines 4B–4E.
G. Chap. 4, table 12, line 5.
H. Chap. 4, table 12, line 6.
I. Chap. 4, table 12, line 6B.
J. Chap. 4, table 12, line 7.

Table A8. Industrial Origin of Gross Domestic Product at Factor Cost

Chap. 4, table 2.

Table A9. Real Expenditure on Gross Domestic Product

Chap. 4, table 13.

Table A10. Population at Census Dates by Nationality

	Total	Taiwanese	Other Chinese	Japanese	Others
1905	3,039,751	2,973,280	8,973	57,335	163
1915	3,479,922	3,325,755	18,525	135,402	241
1920	3,655,308	3,466,507	23,467	164,266	1,068
1925	3,993,408	3,775,288	33,814	183,722	584
1930	4,592,537	4,313,681	49,456	228,281	1,119
1935	5,212,426	4,882,945	57,218	270,584	1,679
1940	5,872,084	5,510,259	46,944	312,386	2,495
1956	9,311,312	8,379,920	928,279	526	2,587
1966	13,348,096	11,390,512	1,949,786	7,798	

Notes and Sources: For a description of the coverage of each census, see the introduction to the Statistical Appendix. During the colonial period, Taiwanese were Chinese who considered themselves "islanders" and aborigines living outside the aboriginal territory. For 1956 and 1966 the Chinese population is divided between Taiwanese and other Chinese by place of permanent registry. The sources for these figures are: *Census of 1905, Statistical Tables*, p. 8; *Census of 1915, Statistical Tables*, p. 8; *Census of 1920, Descriptive Report with Appendix of Statistical Tables*, p. 8; *Census of 1925: Statistical Tables*, pp. 2–3; *Census of 1930, Statistical Tables, Total Island*, pp. 6–7; *Census of 1935, Statistical Tables*, pp. 2–3; PBAS, *Results of The Seventh Population Census of Taiwan, 1940*, pp. 2–3; *A Summary Report on the 1956 Census*, pp. 24–25; and DGBAS, *Statistical Abstract of the Republic of China*, 1969, table 24.

Table A11. Total Year-end Population and Vital Rates, 1905–73

	Year-end population	Crude birth rate per 1,000	Crude death rate per 1,000	Rate of natural increase per 1,000
1905	3,123,302	—	—	—
1906	3,156,706	38.6	33.4	5.2
1907	3,186,373	39.1	32.4	6.7
1908	3,213,996	38.2	31.9	6.3
1909	3,249,795	40.2	31.1	9.1
1910	3,299,493	41.3	27.5	13.8
1911	3,369,270	41.8	26.2	15.6
1912	3,435,170	41.3	25.0	16.3
1913	3,502,173	40.8	25.0	15.8
1914	3,554,353	41.4	27.6	13.8
1915	3,569,842	40.0	31.5	8.5
1916	3,596,109	37.3	28.6	8.7
1917	3,646,529	40.9	27.0	13.9
1918	3,669,687	39.7	34.1	5.6
1919	3,714,899	38.5	26.8	11.7
1920	3,757,838	39.5	32.1	7.4
1921	3,835,811	42.8	24.2	18.6
1922	3,904,692	41.8	24.6	17.2
1923	3,976,098	39.1	21.3	17.8
1924	4,041,702	41.4	24.5	16.9
1925	4,147,462	40.8	23.9	16.9
1926	4,241,759	43.7	22.4	21.3
1927	4,337,000	43.2	22.1	21.1
1928	4,438,084	43.7	22.0	21.7
1929	4,548,750	44.0	21.6	22.4
1930	4,679,066	44.8	19.4	25.4
1931	4,803,976	45.8	21.3	24.5
1932	4,929,962	44.0	20.4	23.6
1933	5,060,507	44.3	19.7	24.6
1934	5,194,980	44.6	20.5	24.1
1935	5,315,642	44.9	20.3	24.6
1936	5,451,863	43.5	19.8	23.7
1937	5,609,042	44.8	19.7	25.1
1938	5,746,959	43.1	19.7	23.4
1939	5,895,864	43.7	19.8	23.9
1940	6,077,478	43.0	19.4	23.6
1941	6,249,468	41.1	16.2	24.9
1942	6,427,932	40.3	17.7	22.6
1943	6,585,841	40.0	18.8	21.2
1944	—	—	—	—
1945	6,940,071	—	—	—
1946	6,151,117	—	—	—

Table A11 (continued)

	Year-end population	Crude birth rate per 1,000	Crude death rate per 1,000	Rate of natural increase per 1,000
1947	6,541,734	38.3	18.1	20.2
1948	6,852,601	39.7	14.3	25.4
1949	7,708,200	42.4	13.1	29.3
1950	8,055,588	43.8	11.5	31.8
1951	8,470,612	50.0	11.6	38.4
1952	8,730,256	46.6	9.9	36.7
1953	9,040,783	45.2	9.4	35.8
1954	9,349,574	44.6	8.2	36.4
1955	9,690,643	45.3	8.6	36.7
1956	10,003,381	44.8	8.0	36.8
1957	10,303,250	41.4	8.5	32.9
1958	10,649,435	41.6	7.6	34.0
1959	11,031,341	41.2	7.2	34.0
1960	11,392,202	39.5	6.9	32.6
1961	11,749,139	38.3	6.7	31.6
1962	12,111,728	37.4	6.4	31.0
1963	12,483,523	36.3	6.1	30.2
1964	12,856,682	34.5	5.7	28.8
1965	13,178,348	32.7	5.5	27.2
1966	13,542,763	32.4	5.5	26.9
1967	13,846,571	28.5	5.5	23.0
1968	14,200,370	29.3	5.5	23.8
1969	14,334,862	28.0	5.1	22.9
1970	14,675,964	27.2	4.9	22.3
1971	14,994,823	25.6	4.8	20.8
1972	15,289,048	24.1	4.7	19.4
1973	15,564,830	23.8	4.8	19.0

Notes and Sources: The pre-1945 population figures are from PBAS, *Taiwan Province: Statistical Summary of the Past 51 Years*, pp. 76–77. In the postwar period the population figures include military personnel living in barracks but exclude foreigners. The population figures for 1945–61 are estimated by JCRR by adding "generally accepted estimates" of military personnel to year-end population figures from the household registration records (see JCRR, "Taiwan Food Balance Sheet," various years). The 1962–64 figures are the sum of year-end civilian population according to the household registration records and 600,000. The 1965–68 population figures are the sum of year-end civilian population according to the household registration records and 550,000. The population figures after 1968 are official estimates. Midyear population figures are used to calculate the vital rates. The post-1945 year-end civilian population figures and the vital rates are from Taiwan Population Studies Center, *Demographic Reference: Taiwan, Republic of China*, 1965, vols. 1 and 2; DGBAS, *Statistical Abstract of the Republic of China*, various issues; and CIECD/CUSA, *Taiwan Statistical Data Book*, various issues.

Table A12. Age-Specific Mortality Rate: 1955, 1960, 1965 (Per 1,000)

	1955			1960			1965		
Age	*Total*	*Male*	*Female*	*Total*	*Male*	*Female*	*Total*	*Male*	*Female*
0	48.8	50.5	47.0	37.2	38.6	35.7	27.7	29.1	26.3
1	10.5	9.6	11.5	6.5	6.2	6.8	4.2	4.0	4.4
5	1.6	1.6	1.5	1.1	1.2	0.9	0.7	0.8	0.7
10	1.0	1.1	1.0	0.8	0.9	0.7	0.6	0.7	0.5
15	1.4	1.5	1.2	1.4	1.5	1.3	1.1	1.2	1.0
20	2.0	2.1	1.9	1.8	1.8	1.7	1.6	1.8	1.4
25	2.5	2.7	2.4	2.1	2.3	1.9	1.8	2.0	1.6
30	3.3	3.4	3.1	2.7	3.0	2.5	2.3	2.5	1.9
35	4.2	4.4	4.0	3.5	3.7	3.2	3.1	3.5	2.6
40	6.2	7.1	5.2	5.0	5.6	4.2	4.3	4.9	3.5
45	8.5	10.0	6.7	7.1	8.2	5.7	6.4	7.4	5.1
50	12.2	14.9	9.2	10.8	13.0	8.2	9.8	11.8	7.3
55	18.6	23.1	14.0	16.8	20.6	12.6	14.7	17.9	11.0
60	28.7	35.5	22.3	25.6	30.8	20.5	24.3	29.4	19.0
65	43.5	53.7	35.2	40.0	50.4	31.9	37.4	45.9	29.8
70				62.8	75.3	53.9	58.0	70.5	48.6
75	99.1	116.4	89.1	98.2	115.4	88.4	89.3	104.2	80.2
80+				171.7	203.3	158.7	161.8	182.2	153.1

Notes and Sources: The number of deaths used in the above calculation is that reported by the Taiwan Provincial Department of Health. The data differ from the figures released by the Department of Civil Affairs (based on Household Registration Records) in that it is tabulated according to the date of occurrence rather than the date of registration. The midyear populations were used to calculate age-specific death rates. Population data from the household registration reports usually exclude persons who are in military service or imprisoned, but to calculate the above motality rates these persons were estimated and included in the denominators for 1960 and 1965. These figures are from Taiwan Population Studies Center, *Demographic Reference: Taiwan Republic of China— 1965*, vol. 2, pp. 254–60.

Table A13. Total Population at Census Dates by Age and Sex, 1905, 1915, 1920, 1925,
1930, 1935, 1956, 1966, 1970

		1905			*1915*	
Age	*Total*	*Male*	*Female*	*Total*	*Male*	*Female*
0–4	430,769	224,368	206,401	534,706	272,160	262,546
5–9	355,411	190,458	164,953	446,285	232,203	214,082
10–14	306,502	168,261	138,241	378,916	200,811	178,105
15–19	305,068	169,629	135,439	336,988	180,302	156,686
20–24	322,584	177,634	144,950	295,196	161,165	134,031
25–29	286,315	158,458	127,857	285,666	159,530	126,136
30–34	248,886	137,774	111,112	284,486	156,464	128,022
35–39	190,703	104,752	85,951	237,960	128,593	109,367
40–44	144,937	78,032	66,905	196,257	103,949	92,308
45–49	133,502	67,384	66,118	143,438	73,264	70,174
50–54	106,330	50,819	55,511	102,962	50,184	52,778
55–59	80,254	35,675	44,579	88,163	39,286	48,877
60–64	56,753	23,233	33,520	63,693	26,320	37,573
65–69	37,606	13,659	23,947	42,532	15,742	26,790
70+	34,124	10,678	23,446	42,474	13,080	29,394
Total	3,479,922	1,813,053	1,666,869	3,039,751	1,610,816	1,428,935
		1920			*1925*	
Age	*Total*	*Male*	*Female*	*Total*	*Male*	*Female*
0–4	519,923	264,550	255,373	602,532	304,808	297,724
5–9	489,620	252,764	236,856	493,133	252,829	240,304
10–14	429,949	224,817	205,132	477,502	247,019	230,483
15–19	370,725	196,023	174,702	422,470	220,178	202,292
20–24	327,988	177,762	150,226	366,064	195,234	170,830
25–29	276,353	151,594	124,759	311,661	167,019	144,642
30–34	256,776	142,186	114,590	258,930	141,199	117,731
35–39	251,597	136,240	115,357	235,716	129,256	106,460
40–44	206,400	108,679	97,721	227,151	120,719	106,432
45–49	167,943	85,521	82,422	184,182	94,004	90,178
50–54	119,289	57,737	61,552	145,977	71,280	74,697
55–59	82,047	37,586	44,461	100,332	46,131	54,201
60–64	66,823	27,490	39,333	63,395	27,876	37,519
65–69	44,358	16,623	27,735	49,672	18,844	30,828
70+	45,517	13,969	31,548	52,691	16,273	36,418
Total	3,655,308	1,893,541	1,761,767	3,993,408	2,052,669	1,940,739

Table A13 (continued)

	1930			1935		
Age	Total	Male	Female	Total	Male	Female
0–4	778,067	394,739	383,328	908,055	460,674	447,381
5–9	589,954	300,249	289,705	713,045	363,369	349,676
10–14	491,834	252,738	239,096	578,477	294,365	284,112
15–19	488,030	251,808	236,222	486,269	248,574	237,695
20–24	425,904	225,812	200,092	488,313	254,245	234,068
25–29	358,119	190,266	167,853	413,639	217,471	196,168
30–34	301,039	161,515	139,524	343,262	181,820	161,442
35–39	245,148	133,249	111,899	284,224	151,929	132,295
40–44	222,606	120,262	102,344	227,585	122,625	104,960
45–49	208,803	108,470	100,333	203,083	107,584	95,499
50–54	164,766	81,316	83,450	187,423	94,679	92,744
55–59	126,855	59,183	67,672	144,264	68,694	75,570
60–64	81,597	35,345	46,252	105,328	46,655	58,673
65–69	49,312	19,437	29,875	63,321	25,571	37,750
70+	60,503	18,899	41,604	91,708	47,134	44,574
Total	4,592,537	2,353,288	2,239,249	5,212,426	2,659,819	2,552,607

	1956			1966		
Age	Total	Male	Female	Total	Male	Female
0–4	1,849,933	948,402	901,531	2,016,048	1,038,561	977,487
5–9	1,341,985	689,805	652,180	1,953,025	1,003,739	949,286
10–14	923,794	477,408	446,386	1,806,121	926,662	879,459
15–19	945,995	485,206	460,789	1,376,229	707,409	668,820
20–24	707,754	306,004	401,750	893,933	448,686	445,247
25–29	721,160	366,337	354,823	933,963	476,075	457,888
30–34	621,630	326,845	294,785	843,956	445,561	398,395
35–39	510,066	279,844	236,222	851,460	500,737	350,723
40–44	454,622	254,490	200,132	723,049	432,744	290,305
45–49	371,517	198,555	172,962	563,453	330,851	232,602
50–54	279,416	147,821	131,595	463,837	271,561	192,276
55–59	207,469	104,540	102,929	337,784	177,907	159,877
60–64	141,694	68,165	73,529	239,153	122,393	116,760
65–69	101,520	44,723	56,797	161,589	76,410	85,179
70+	126,757	45,136	81,351	184,496	72,348	112,148
Total	9,311,312	4,743,551	4,567,761	13,348,096	7,031,644	6,316,452

Table A13 (continued)

	1970		
Age	*Total*	*Male*	*Female*
0–4	1,907,350	981,623	925,727
5–9	2,086,905	1,067,865	1,019,040
10–14	1,993,264	1,022,048	971,216
15–19	1,799,803	925,426	874,377
20–24	1,184,874	604,556	580,318
25–29	904,360	456,703	447,657
30–34	894,566	446,731	447,835
35–39	849,850	452,028	397,822
40–44	841,170	496,983	344,187
45–49	692,957	410,172	282,785
50–54	500,018	289,530	210,488
55–59	408,732	230,136	178,596
60–64	288,278	151,618	136,660
65–69	189,118	93,664	95,454
70+	151,768	54,961	96,807
Total	14,693,013	7,684,044	7,008,969

Sources: Census of 1905, Statistical Tables, pp. 26–27; *Census of 1915, Statistical Tables*, pp. 42–43; *Census of 1920, Descriptive Report with Appendix of Statistical Tables*, p. 20; *Census of 1925, Statistical Tables*, pp. 1150–52; *Census of 1930, Statistical Tables, Total Island*, pp. 46–53; *Census of 1935, Statistical Tables*, p. 386; *Report of the 1956 Population Census, Republic of China*, vol. 2, pt. 2, table 13; *The Report of the 1966 Census of Population and Housing of Taiwan–Fukien Area, Republic of China*, vol. 2, pt. 1, table 9; and *The Report of the 1970 Sample Census of Population and Housing of Taiwan–Fukien Area, Republic of China*, vol. 2, table 1.

Table A14. Year-end Population of Five Major Municipalities, 1925–70

City	1925	1930	1935	1940	1943	1950	1955	1960	1965	1970
Taipei	201,374	240,435	287,846	353,744	397,113	503,086	704,124	898,655	1,135,500	1,769,568
Keelung	65,327	78,214	87,400	105,084	107,819	145,405	187,468	234,442	278,320	324,040
Taichung	42,387	55,347	71,742	87,119	103,386	199,519	239,490	298,119	364,262	448,140
Tainan	86,726	98,114	112,142	149,969	162,916	221,088	275,004	337,602	399,820	474,835
Kaohsiung	44,035	62,633	86,848	161,418	218,700	267,515	352,201	467,931	596,092	828,191
Total	439,849	534,743	645,978	857,334	989,934	1,336,613	1,758,287	2,236,749	2,773,994	3,844,774
As % of total year-end population	10.6	11.4	12.2	14.1	15.0	17.7	19.4	20.7	22.0	26.2

Sources: PBAS, *Taiwan Province: Statistical Summary of the Past 51 Years*, pp. 82–85; PDCA, *Household Registration Statistics of Taiwan Province*, 1959, p. 72; Taiwan Population Studies Center, *Demographic Reference: Taiwan, Republic of China*, 1965, pp. 21–34, and DGBAS, *Statistical Abstract of the Republic of China*, 1966, p. 96; 1971, p. 38.

Table A15. Registered Medical Personnel, Selected Years

End of year	Doctor	Herb doctor	Dentist & assistant	Pharmacist & assistant	Midwife	Nurse
1897	259	—	—	30	9	—
1902	250	1,903	—	25	37	—
1907	331	1,458	—	11	163	—
1912	423	1,161	9	46	191	—
1917	610	887	21	49	345	—
1922	821	632	86	66	421	—
1927	1,112	456	117	105	1,071	—
1932	1,403	305	263	123	1,524	91
1937	1,845	181	402	190	1,747	127
1942	2,441	97	567	355	2,159	569
1952	5,049	1,655	956	1,168	2,044	741
1954	5,658	1,861	1,059	1,301	2,429	968
1959	6,659	2,127	1,197	1,491	2,959	1,715
1965	8,416	2,458	1,364	2,151	4,473	4,144
1970	10,716	2,707	1,876	3,510	6,158	7,624

Note and Sources: It is believed that the data before World War II do not include dental assistants or pharmacist assistants. These figures are from PBAS, *Taiwan Province: Statistical Summary of the Past 51 Years*, pp. 1249–50, and CIECD, *Taiwan Statistical Data Book*, 1973, p. 229.

Table A16. Daily Per Capita Nutrient Availability, 1935–64 (Annual averages)

	1935–39	1940–44	1945–49	1950–54	1955–59	1960–64
Calories (cal)	1,865.3	1,692.9	1,751.5	2,132.8	2,285.6	2,344.7
Protein (g)	44.9	35.0	36.7	49.4	55.5	58.8
Vegetable	29.5	27.4	30.3	38.1	41.5	42.8
Animal	15.4	7.6	6.4	11.3	14.0	16.0
Fat (g)	35.5	19.4	19.9	33.9	38.9	42.4
Carbohydrate (g)	339.3	340.5	352.2	402.1	422.5	426.4

Notes and Sources: Food available for human consumption is estimated by adjusting crop, livestock, and fish output for changes in stock, foreign trade, animal feed, seed, raw material for industries, waste, and extraction loss. Food production in private gardens and losses in preparation and cooking are not taken into account. These figures are from Ralph N. Gleason, *Taiwan Food Balances, 1935–54*, and JCRR, "Taiwan Food Balance Sheet," 1955, 1956, 1957, 1958, 1959, 1960, 1961, 1962, 1963, and 1964.

Table A17. School and University Enrollment by Type of Academic Institution, Selected Years

Selected school years	Preschool education	Primary education	Secondary Education					Higher education
			Total	Middle and senior high school	Vocational school	Private school[a]	Normal school	
1900	—	13,272	1,018	—	—	823	195	89
1905	86	31,221	672	136	—	294	242	140
1910	195	49,556	1,451	266	—	742	443	194
1915	203	81,879	3,263	1,357	168	974	764	205
1920	1,279	175,596	6,768	2,279	857	2,444	1,188	508
1925	2,056	244,902	14,003	7,569	2,246	2,489	1,699	723
1930	3,669	282,641	18,892	10,507	4,323	2,872	1,190	1,011
1935	4,255	407,449	23,347	12,241	5,552	4,175	1,379	1,090
1940	7,442	671,059	42,004	20,466	16,240	3,296	2,002	1,400
1946	5,634	823,400	67,036	39,338	24,703		2,995	2,983
1950	17,111	906,950	120,036	79,021	35,364		5,651	6,360
1956	54,239	1,344,432	243,826	170,940	65,903		6,983	22,606
1960	79,702	1,888,783	355,274	263,365	84,337		7,572	35,060
1965	78,878	2,257,720	663,753	543,019	117,575		3,159	85,346
1970	91,984	2,445,405	1,154,589	977,760	175,905		924	203,473

Notes and Sources: Total enrollment does not include private Chinese tutorials, which were popular in the early years. Primary education includes grammar schools and schools for the aborigines. Higher education includes colleges, universities, and their equivalent. These figures are from PBAS, *Taiwan Province: Statistical Summary of the Past 51 Years*, pp. 1211–13 and 1239, and DGBAS, *Statistical Abstract of the Republic of China*, 1973, pp. 516–17 and 522–27.

[a] Private school is equivalent to senior high school or vocational school. In the postwar period the enrollment in private schools is included in the other categories.

Table A18. Number of Teachers by Type of Academic Institution, Selected Years

Secondary school

	Pre school	_Primary school_	_Total_	_Middle and senior high school_	_Voca- tional school_	_Normal school_	_College and university_
1946	95[a]	15,356[a]	3,379	1,883	1,302	194	616
1950	144[a]	20,878[a]	6,562	3,761	2,385	416	948
1956	1,220	29,504	11,673	7,362	3,827	484	1,910
1960	2,020	41,397	16,712	11,288	4,929	495	3,149
1965	2,023	53,522	26,378	19,941	6,212	255	5,622
1970	2,293	59,489	44,283	36,777	7,500	6	10,377

Sources: **DGBAS**, _Statistical Abstract of the Republic of China_, 1956, pp. 320 and 326; 1973, pp. 518–29.
[a] Includes nonteaching staff.

Table A19. Ability of Taiwanese to Speak, Read, and Write Japanese[a] : Census Years, 1905–40

		_1905_	_1915_	_1920_	_1930_	_1940_
(1)	Total Taiwanese population	2,973,280	3,325,755	3,466,507	4,313,681	5,510,259
(2)	Able to read only	3,453	5,272	19,651	69,873	180,716
(3)	Able to read and write	27,202	71,579	115,305	430,825	1,279,077
(4)	(2) + (3)	30,655	76,851	134,956	500,698	1,459,793
(5)	(4) as % of (1)	1.03	2.31	3.89	11.61	26.49
(6)	Able to speak	11,270	54,337	99,065	365,427	1,463,369
(7)	(6) as % of (1)	0.38	1.63	2.86	8.47	26.56

Sources: Census of 1930, Statistical Tables, Total Island, p. 513, and **PBAS**, _Result of the Seventh Population Census of Taiwan, 1940_, pp. 136–37.
[a] The test of the ability to read or write is the knowledge of either Hirokana (plain Kana) or Katakana (curt Kana). The data presented understate the extent of literacy of the Taiwanese Population because those Taiwanese who can read and/or write Chinese but do not know Kana are excluded. However, those who were literate in Chinese were limited; thus the data in this table are a good proxy for the extent of literacy in Taiwan during the Japanese period.

Table A20. Literacy of the Population, Age 12 and Over

	1956	*1966*	*1970*
Total population age 12 and over	5,779,400	8,619,952	9,906,091
Illiterate	2,480,012	2,126,098	1,912,105
Total literate	3,299,151	6,493,854	7,993,986
Self-educated	255,924	339,454	357,785
Elem. school	2,153,294	3,827,370	4,215,351
Jr. high school	467,822	1,206,158	1,673,331
Sr. high school	284,710	790,922	1,305,995
College, univ.	133,766	329,950	441,524
Passed civil service examination	3,635	—	—
Not stated	273	—	—

Note and Sources: A literate person is one who is able to read and write simple Chinese messages. These census data are from *A Summary Report on the 1956 Census*, pp. 34–35; *The Report of the 1966 Census of Population and Housing of Taiwan–Fukien Area, Republic of China*, vol. 2, pt. 3a, table 1, and *The Report of the 1970 Sample Census of Population and Housing of Taiwan–Fukien Area, Republic of China*, vol. 2, table 9.

Table A21. Occupied Males Distributed by Occupation at Census Dates: 1905, 1915, 1920, 1930

Total males

	1905		1915		1920		1930	
Agriculture	731,473	67.6%	776,181	67.2%	761,047	64.5%	864,884	63.2%
Fishing	29,465	2.7	26,911	2.3	25,858	2.2	27,709	2.0
Mining	6,843	0.6	9,741	0.8	17,240	1.5	18,345	1.3
Manufacturing	57,855	5.3	79,170	6.8	94,211	8.0	93,217	6.8
Construction	9,671	0.9	15,168	1.3	16,212	1.4	26,241	1.9
Electricity, gas, & water	—		—		1,640	0.1	2,608	0.2
Communications & transport	29,138	2.7	38,901	3.4	45,645	3.9	61,323	4.5
Trade	74,832	6.9	82,285	7.1	83,189	7.0	135,021	9.8
Banking & insurance	629	0.1	1,238	0.1	3,225	0.3	726	0.1
Government	18,304	1.7	18,884	1.6	29,059	2.5	32,233	2.4
Professional serivce	8,863	0.8	11,965	1.0	18,959	1.6	37,411	2.7
Other occupation	114,594	10.6	95,342	8.2	84,557	7.2	71,794	5.2
Total	1,081,667	100.0	1,155,777	100.0	1,180,842	100.0	1,371,512	100.0

Taiwanese males

	1905		1915		1920		1930	
Agriculture	731,102	69.9	772,437	71.0	757,917	68.9	860,613	68.0
Fishing	29,260	2.8	26,150	2.4	24,261	2.2	25,916	2.0
Mining	5,203	0.5	8,319	0.8	15,629	1.4	16,970	1.3
Manufacturing	52,135	5.0	63,599	5.8	75,188	6.8	73,604	5.8
Construction	6,698	0.6	8,845	0.8	11,397	1.0	21,047	1.7
Electricity, gas, & water	—		—		729	0.1	1,181	0.1
Communication & transport	23,186	2.2	29,505	2.7	35,428	3.2	48,677	3.8
Trade	70,120	6.7	73,140	6.7	74,059	6.7	120,284	9.5
Banking & insurance	286	0.0	396	0.0	1,755	0.2	281	0.0
Government	8,296	0.8	6,883	0.6	9,461	0.9	8,655	0.7
Professional service	7,442	0.7	8,887	0.8	14,350	1.3	25,605	2.0
Other occupation	111,939	10.7	90,038	8.3	80,123	7.3	63,878	5.0
Total	1,045,667	100.0	1,088,199	100.0	1,100,297	100.0	1,266,711	100.0

Table A21 (continued)

Notes and Sources: For comparative purposes the following adjustments are made to the census classification: (a) Salt workers are transferred from fishing to manufacturing in 1905, 1915, and 1920. (b) Ceramics workers and quarry workers are grouped together in 1905 and 1915 and are assigned to manufacturing. (c) The category "industry" used in the censuses is now divided into three categories: manufacturing; construction; and electricity, gas, and water. (d) The category "commerce" used in the censuses is removed. Its components are separated into three subcategories: trade; banking and insurance; and other occupations. Trade includes wholesale and retail traders; commodity brokers and commission merchants; and traders not included elsewhere. Bankers and insurance men are now in a separate category. The remaining components of "commerce" (entertainers and restaurant and hotel workers) are assigned to "other occupations." (e) Government includes military personnel, government officials, and civil servants. (f) Professional service includes lawyers, teachers, clergy, doctors, public health workers, veterinarians, authors, artists, and other professional workers. (g) Other occupation includes entertainers, restaurant and hotel workers, and people with occupations not listed elsewhere. (h) People living on property income were classified as having an occupation in the 1905 and 1915 censuses. This group is eliminated for these years and is not presented in the table. The data are taken from: *Census of 1905, Statistical Tables,* pp. 42–43, 68; *Census of 1915, Statistical Tables,* pp. 78–92; *Census of 1920, Descriptive Report with Appendix of Statistical Tables,* pp. 82–94; and *Census of 1930, Statistical Tables, Total Island,* pp. 56, 114–15.

Table A22. Occupied Persons by Industry, Census Years (Thousands)

Total	1930	1940	1956[c]	1966[c]	1970[d]
Agriculture	1,212	1,400	1,422	1,501	1,741
Fishing	31	34	70	90	112
Mining	24	44	39	58	58
Manufacturing	122	172	332	534	720
Construction	27	44	62	97	200
Elec., gas, & water	3	5	15	27	24
Comm. & transp.	53	63	107	163	237
Trade	174	185	185	289	413
Banking, insurance, & brokerage	2	5	14	45	66
Government	50	58[b]	150[b]	608	675
Professional service	37	59	114	263	266
Other industries[a]	55	174	175	489	318
Total	1,790	2,244	2,684	4,164	4,830
Male					
Agriculture	878	921	1,115	1,129	1,189
Fishing	30	32	62	79	95
Mining	23	41	36	55	51
Manufacturing	93	127	276	404	501
Construction	27	42	61	95	194
Elec., gas, & water	3	5	15	25	22
Comm. & transp.	52	60	·101	149	214
Trade	152	162	161	232	370
Banking, insurance, & brokerage	2	4	11	35	49
Government	48	49[b]	141[b]	589	648
Professional service	31	50	86	196	177
Other industries[a]	33	111	128	347	144
Total	1,372	1,606	2,194	3,335	3,654

Sources: Census of 1930, Statistical Tables, Taotal Island, pp. 232–33; *Result of the Seventh Population Census of Taiwan, 1940,* pp. 60–61; *Report of the 1956 Population Census,* vol. 2, pt. 4, table 30; *The Report of the 1966 Census of Population and Housing of Taiwan–Fukien Area Republic of China,* vol. 2, pt. 5a, table 2; and *The Report of the 1970 Sample Census of Population and Housing of Taiwan–Fukien Area, Republic of China,* vol. 3b, table 4.

[a] Includes the service industries (hotel, restaurant, entertaining, personal service) and industries not classified elsewhere.

[b] Excludes military personnel living on military bases.

[c] Includes only those 12 years of age and over.

[d] Includes only those 15 years of age and over.

Table A23. Employment in Manufacturing and Utilities, 1914–41

	1914		1915		1916		1917		1918	
	Male	Female	Male	Female	Male	Female	Male	Female	Male	Female
Textiles	—	—	—	—	—	—	—	—	—	—
Metal	—	—	—	—	—	—	—	—	—	—
Machinery and tools	—	—	—	—	—	—	—	—	—	—
Ceramics	—	—	—	—	—	—	—	—	—	—
Chemicals	—	—	—	—	—	—	—	—	—	—
Wood and wood products	—	—	—	—	—	—	—	—	—	—
Printing and publishing	—	—	—	—	—	—	—	—	—	—
Food	—	—	—	—	—	—	—	—	—	—
Other manufacturing	—	—	—	—	—	—	—	—	—	—
Total manufacturing	15,616	6,243	21,536	7,012	16,032	8,014	19,857	8,370	31,266	8,739
Utilities	—	—	—	—	—	—	—	—	—	—
Total	15,616	6,243	21,536	7,012	16,032	8,014	19,857	8,370	31,266	8,739

	1919		1920		1921		1922		1923	
	Male	Female	Male	Female	Male	Female	Male	Female	Male	Female
Textiles	—	—	441	414	525	536	640	983	777	1,169
Metal	—	—	805	45	588	48	543	51	717	52
Machinery and tools	—	—	1,676	11	1,308	10	1,188	1	1,104	2
Ceramics	—	—	6,483	631	6,319	568	5,548	499	5,083	543
Chemicals	—	—	3,937	1,153	3,297	986	3,102	747	2,698	697
Wood and wood products	—	—	1,068	13	1,030	15	942	43	1,171	60
Printing and publishing	—	—	956	169	1,061	161	1,228	203	1,183	170
Food	—	—	21,224	6,855	17,786	8,358	16,372	6,091	16,804	6,311
Other manufacturing	—	—	1,010	1,335	940	1,316	993	1,173	987	1,531
Total manufacturing	30,773	9,954	37,601	10,626	32,854	11,998	30,556	9,791	30,524	10,535
Utilities	—	—	233	0	190	0	178	0	188	0
Total	30,773	9,954	37,834	10,626	33,044	11,998	30,734	9,791	30,712	10,535

Statistical Appendix

Table A23 (continued)

	1924 Male	1924 Female	1925 Male	1925 Female	1926 Male	1926 Female	1927 Male	1927 Female	1928 Male	1928 Female
Textiles	793	1,334	781	1,694	400	1,558	666	1,808	562	3,156
Metal	522	71	498	67	749	82	684	104	832	102
Machinery and tools	1,321	9	1,530	18	1,746	21	1,866	15	2,123	2
Ceramics	4,783	542	5,232	576	6,148	718	6,607	866	6,870	1,035
Chemicals	3,460	1,010	3,524	1,076	3,741	1,081	3,885	1,462	3,928	1,885
Wood and wood products	1,185	72	1,297	74	984	128	1,417	185	1,612	98
Printing and publishing	1,198	193	1,207	163	1,408	222	1,377	278	1,501	284
Food	17,283	6,417	19,134	6,875	21,116	7,588	20,639	7,298	21,836	7,673
Other manufacturing	1,218	2,054	1,346	3,178	1,619	2,851	1,368	2,972	1,448	3,593
Total manufacturing	31,763	11,702	34,549	13,721	37,911	14,249	38,559	14,988	40,712	17,828
Utilities	167	1	194	0	181	0	202	0	239	0
Total	31,930	11,703	34,743	13,721	38,092	14,249	38,761	14,988	40,951	17,828

	1929 Male	1929 Female	1930 Male	1930 Female	1931 Male	1931 Female	1932 Male	1932 Female	1933 Male	1933 Female
Textiles	451	1,789	408	1,501	421	1,465	444	1,512	413	1,717
Metal	1,000	49	930	67	977	83	824	117	1,042	100
Machinery and tools	2,208	11	1,895	10	1,696	9	2,037	10	2,199	21
Ceramics	8,377	1,072	7,598	1,070	6,523	941	7,332	1,284	7,580	1,201
Chemicals	3,620	1,281	3,031	1,000	2,660	720	2,790	834	3,120	953
Wood and wood products	1,939	96	1,698	52	1,601	88	1,671	79	1,942	116
Printing and publishing	1,792	294	1,784	276	1,891	266	1,837	258	1,811	259
Food	22,566	10,124	23,194	9,569	22,626	10,605	22,598	10,688	23,921	12,480
Other manufacturing	1,717	4,271	1,537	3,167	1,684	3,140	1,718	3,312	1,919	3,713
Total manufacturing	43,670	18,987	42,075	16,712	40,079	17,317	41,251	18,094	43,947	20,560
Utilities	220	0	227	0	235	0	235	0	251	0
Total	43,890	18,987	42,302	16,712	40,314	17,317	41,486	18,094	44,198	29,560

Table A23 (continued)

	1934		1935		1936		1937		1938	
	Male	*Female*	*Male*	*Female*	*Male*	*Female*	*Male*	*Female*	*Male*	*Female*
Textiles	468	2,084	547	2,105	979	2,709	1,126	2,825	1,117	2,310
Metal	1,258	207	1,772	209	2,370	282	2,613	262	2,504	198
Machinery and tools	2,543	24	2,741	21	3,493	42	4,369	70	4,778	30
Ceramics	7,529	1,233	7,811	1,401	8,761	2,001	8,326	2,249	7,766	2,264
Chemicals	3,425	1,000	3,638	1,113	3,617	1,299	3,675	1,339	4,034	1,052
Wood and wood products	1,988	124	2,323	163	2,610	160	2,534	136	2,694	244
Printing and publishing	1,871	245	2,117	266	2,380	335	2,652	374	2,682	397
Food	24,559	12,028	25,162	11,588	28,586	15,293	30,776	17,893	32,146	22,950
Other manufacturing	1,865	3,955	1,741	3,798	2,105	4,440	2,081	4,733	2,042	6,433
Total manufacturing	45,506	20,900	47,852	20,674	54,901	26,561	58,152	29,881	59,763	35,878
Utilities	153	0	152	0	176	0	—	—	—	—
Total	45,659	20,900	48,004	20,674	55,077	26,561	58,152	29,881	59,763	35,878

	1939		1940		1941	
	Male	*Female*	*Male*	*Female*	*Male*	*Female*
Textiles	1,592	4,358	1,338	3,880	1,577	3,770
Metal	4,138	489	2,682	1,311	9,154	575
Machinery and tools	6,296	60	6,902	86	7,503	227
Ceramics	8,387	2,398	8,877	2,734	8,812	2,837
Chemicals	4,435	1,359	5,619	1,676	6,538	2,267
Wood and wood products	3,108	292	3,797	890	4,794	743
Printing and publishing	2,758	501	2,732	582	3,024	728
Food	35,126	23,576	41,441	29,126	36,079	30,941
Other manufacturing	1,848	6,752	2,751	9,529	3,812	14,245
Total manufacturing	67,688	39,785	76,139	49,814	81,293	56,333
Utilities	34	0	52	0	74	0
Total	67,722	39,785	76,191	49,814	81,367	56,333

Table A23. (continued)

Notes and Sources: It is difficult to evalue the reliability of the statistics in this table because relatively little is known about them. From studying the statistics, it seems that prior to the early 1920s employment is underreported. The data for 1914 to 1929 are from the Taiwan Government-General, *Taiwan Commercial and Industrial Statistics*, various issues. The exact coverage of these data is not clear, although it is believed that only workers in establishment using five or more workers or using power are included. Evidence indicates that the data were gathered from questionnaires sent to the selected establishments. Not all establishments answered all the questions or returned the questionnaires. From detailed tables it can be seen that many establishments reported production but left out the employment information. As the reporting system improved, the coverage became more complete so the increases shown by the figures in the table are the results of better coverage as well as actual increases in employment. The data for 1930–41 are from Taiwan Government-General, *Collection of Factory Related Materials based on the Resource Investigation Statue*, and they represent probably the most reliable prewar statistics on industrial employment. The coverage for this 10-year period is consistent. The coverage includes all industrial establishments that (1) used power, (2) employed five or more workers, or (3) had a production capacity of five or more workers. Employment statistics for the utilities (electricity, gas, and water) are from Taiwan Government-General, *Taiwan Commercial and Industrial Statistics*, various years. It is believed that all figures represent year-end employment.

Table A24. Labor Force, Employment according to the Labor Force Surveys, 1963–75
(Thousands)

	Total population age 15 and over	Labor force			
		Total	Fully employed	Under-employed	Unemployed
1964	6,451	3,782	3,617		165
1965	6,654	3,760	3,518	115	127
1966	6,888	3,764	3,557	90	117
1967	7,166	4,067	3,890	83	94
1968	7,410	4,232	4,108	51	72
1969	7,838	4,517	4,336	98	85
1970	8,125	4,625	4,476	70	79
1971	8,516	4,820	4,684	55	80
1972	8,712	4,947	4,819	54	74
1973	8,935	5,288	5,182	40	67
1974	9,114	5,383	5,257	44	82
1975 (Jan.)	9,206	5,330	5,091	87	152

Notes and Sources: An underemployed person is one who is engaged in part-time work but who is able and willing to do more work. Unemployed persons are those who were available for work during the survey week but did not do more than 15 hours of unpaid family work or did not do any remunerative work. It also includes those who were waiting to be called back shortly to jobs from which they had been laid off or were waiting to report to new jobs. Population figures are from the Household Registration Records. The annual figures are the simple averages of results from the quarterly surveys conducted in January, April, July, and October. These figures are from Taiwan Provincial Labor Force Survey and Research Institute, *Report of the Labor Force Survey in Taiwan*, no. 46, table A-1.

Table A25. Employed Persons by Industry according to the Labor Force Surveys, 1964–74 (Thousands)

	Total	Agric., forestry, fishery	Mining	Mfg.	Constr.	Utilities	Commerce	Transp.	Serv.	Other
1964	3,846	1,922	57	610	114	31	391	161	494	64
1965	3,845	1,831	60	665	128	29	405	178	502	45
1966	3,647	1,586	57	629	134	30	437	175	556	42
1967	3,973	1,705	67	744	154	32	497	191	563	20
1968	4,159	1,652	74	736	182	41	606	210	645	15
1969	4,434	1,728	87	834	215	34	628	209	679	19
1970	4,546	1,672	96	928	227	34	667	245	669	10
1971	4,739	1,667	94	1,026	278	36	685	248	702	4
1972	4,873	1,609	83	1,179	269	34	653	250	799	—
1973	5,222	1,593	65	1,386	288	34	723	288	846	—
1974	5,301	1,641	66	1,422	308	34	728	282	824	—

Notes and Sources: The annual figures are simple averages of results from the quarterly surveys conducted in January, April, July, and October. Since January 1972, the "Revised Standard Industrial and Occupational Classification" has been followed. These figures are from Taiwan Provincial Labor Force Survey and Research Institute, *Report of the Labor Force Survey in Taiwan*, no. 10, p. 8; no. 46, p. 10. It is unclear why the total in this table does not equal the sum of fully employed and underemployed (table A24).

Table A26. Occupation of Employed Persons, Census Years

Occupation	1940[a]	1956[b]	1966[b]	1970[c]
Professional and technical workers	24,707	93,592	229,006	227,274
Manager, administrators, and executive officials	9,891	53,563	74,563	56,744
Clerical workers	42,023	163,149	316,053	399,731
Sales workers	134,351	207,685	335,602	427,983
Farmers, fishermen, lumbermen, and hunters	1,409,663	1,476,953	1,577,810	1,847,373
Miners, quarrymen, and kindred workers	28,141	33,367	53,502	
Workers in transportation and communication	50,976	59,454	176,726	1,098,144
Craftsmen, production workers, and manual laborers	360,426	404,311	866,882	
Service workers	36,526	137,196	529,430	772,132
Others	1,776	54,765	4,302	767
Total	2,099,480	2,684,035	4,163,876	4,830,148

Sources: Results of the Seventh Population Census of Taiwan, 1940, pp. 72–73; A Summary Report on the 1956 Census, pp. 78–81; The Report of the 1966 Census of Population and Housing of Taiwan–Fukien Area, Republic of China, vol. 2, pt. 6a, table 1; and The Report of the 1970 Sample Census of Population and Housing of Taiwan–Fukien Area, Republic of China, vol. 3a, table 1.
[a]Taiwanese only. The number of Japanese in Taiwan in 1940 was sizable. Very few of them were farmers, miners, unskilled production workers, or manual laborers.
[b]Includes only employed persons 12 years and over. The 1956 figures also exclude military personnel living in barracks.
[c]Includes only employed persons 15 years and over.

Table A27. Employed Persons by Employment Status: Census Years 1956, 1966, 1970
(1,000 Persons)

	Total	Employers with paid employees	Self-employed workers	Unpaid family workers	Employees Subtotal	Priv.	Govt.
1956	2,684	87	953	655	988	572	416
1966	4,164	117	1,111	753	2,183	1,200	983
1970	4,830	166	1,244	829	2,590	1,447	1,143

Notes and Sources: The 1956 and 1966 figures include only persons 12 years of age or older. The 1970 figures include only persons 15 years of age or older. The 1956 figures exclude military personnel living in barracks. See *A Summary Report on the 1956 Census,* pp. 58–60; *The Report of the 1966 Census of Population and Housing of Taiwan–Fukien Area, Republic of China,* vol. 2, pt. 6a, table 1; and *The Report of the 1970 Sample Census of Population and Housing of Taiwan–Fukien Area, Republic of China,* vol. 3b, table 4.

Table A28. Industrial Employment according to Industrial Censuses

	1954	1961	1966	1971
Manufacturing	309,887	445,667	589,660	1,201,539
Food	59,997	88,498	123,310	131,279
Beverage	3,882	8,879	3,001	3,971
Tobacco	4,888	5,381	11,456	10,326
Textile	52,321	70,612	102,768	225,959
Apparel	15,612	22,587	13,464	76,335
Wood & wood prods.	17,827	26,353	32,013	72,834
Furniture	6,228	11,700	4,499	9,232
Paper	6,551	13,533	17,439	33,952
Printing	10,514	13,105	12,973	17,868
Leather	1,462	1,462	1,162	7,785
Rubber products	5,382	6,722	10,137	21,440
Chem. & chem. prods.	21,799	31,084	60,598	154,867
Petroleum & coal prods.	3,408	5,538	11,119	15,812
Nonmetal products	29,890	39,312	46,196	63,238
Basic metals	6,375	10,899	17,342	30,135
Metal products	14,328	20,167	22,630	50,101
Machinery, exc. elec.	13,060	16,528	30,864	60,898
Elec. equipment	5,171	13,039	32,523	127,447
Transp. equip.	18,333	28,042	23,558	35,121
Misc.	12,859	12,226	12,608	52,936
Mining	55,416	83,924	78,242	56,152
Construction	9,132[a]	140,074	182,838	188,773
Utilities	7,906	14,675	18,934	19,477

Sources: General Report on Industry and Commerce Census of Taiwan, 1954, pp. 32–33, 62–77, 592–99, 604–05, 608–09, 612–13; General Report, 1961 Industry and Commerce Census of Taiwan, vol. 3, pp. 492–543; vol. 2, pp. 66–71, 156–57, 290–91; General Report on the Third Industrial and Commercial Census of Taiwan, vol. 2, pp. 29–32; vol. 3, pp. 183–220; vol. 4, pp. 5–8; vol. 5, pp. 15–16; and The Report of the 1971 Industrial and Commercial Censuses of Taiwan and Fukien Area, Republic of China, vol. 2, p. 2; vol. 3, pp. 2–11; vol. 4, p. 2; and vol. 5, p. 2.
[a] Includes only staff and office laborers.

Table A29. Male Laborers by Level of Skill and by Nationality, 1943

	Number of establishments	Laborers			Technicians		
		Total	Taiwanese	Japanese	Total	Taiwanese	Japanese
Mining	167	30,027	29,342	685	572	367	205
Industries (total)	790	76,727	69,953	6,774	3,939	774	3,165
Metal	28	5,952	5,447	505	265	51	214
Machinery	80	9,596	8,592	1,004	452	128	324
Chemical	64	7,386	6,589	797	516	99	417
Gas, electricity, and water	20	2,641	1,982	659	557	67	490
Ceramics	58	3,760	3,583	177	98	10	88
Textile	80	2,240	2,226	14	66	21	45
Wood products	60	3,575	3,480	95	49	23	26
Food processing	128	15,776	14,008	1,768	1,337	188	1,149
Printing and publishing	21	1,465	1,343	122	6	1	5
Construction	124	22,646	21,047	1,599	564	175	389
Other	127	1,690	1,656	34	29	11	18
Trade	322	7,576	6,686	890	1,219	313	906
Transportation	207	29,194	26,178	3,016	474	97	377
Communication	45	3,372	2,303	1,069	553	46	507

Notes and Sources: Except for communication, the figures are for those establishments that had more than 30 employees. All communication establishments are included regardless of their size. Included among the Taiwanese laborers are small numbers of foreigners (mostly Koreans) other than Japanese. Trade includes warehouse establishments. Technicians include those who were employed at the time of the survey as technicians, those who were once employed as technicians, and those with the ability of technicians but who were not employed as technicians at the time of survey. The figures are compiled from Taiwan Government-General, *The Results of the Survey on Labor Skills*, 1943, vol. 1, pp. 32–37; and vol. 2, pp. 4, 286–89, 604, 609, and 800.

Table A30. Indexes of Money Wages, 1910–42 (1930 = 100)

	1910	1911	1912	1913	1914	1915	1916
Skilled construction worker	51.4	55.7	54.8	52.9	48.5	49.3	47.1
Govt. employee	34.1	34.8	36.3	38.2	37.7	39.0	38.7
Agricultural hired laborer	51.2	54.9	64.6	57.3	58.5	58.5	58.5
Coal miner	51.3	57.3	60.7	59.0	56.4	60.7	62.4
Manufacturing	44.7	47.9	50.0	50.3	47.5	44.5	42.6
Wood & bamboo prods.	44.5	47.6	48.2	48.5	45.1	43.8	40.6
Metal work	47.6	50.0	53.5	54.3	53.3	48.5	49.4
Apparel	41.8	46.7	54.1	54.1	51.6	42.6	43.4
Food	—	—	—	—	—	—	—
Ceramic	—	—	—	—	—	—	—

	1917	1918	1919	1920	1921	1922	1923
Skilled construction worker	60.8	70.7	118.8	137.0	123.5	121.3	117.6
Govt. employee	39.3	41.0	44.3	96.8	100.3	100.8	93.8
Agricultural hired laborer	61.0	85.4	176.8	139.0	106.1	84.1	86.6
Coal miner	88.0	102.6	119.7	149.6	117.1	118.8	115.4
Manufacturing	61.4	67.5	117.6	120.6	99.5	98.3	90.5
Wood & bamboo prods.	58.2	67.2	114.4	120.0	99.7	102.0	92.9
Metal work	66.8	73.1	138.7	140.4	120.5	105.7	105.9
Apparel	69.7	61.5	105.7	97.5	71.3	71.3	59.0
Food	—	—	—	—	—	—	—
Ceramic	—	—	—	—	—	—	—

	1924	1925	1926	1927	1928	1929	1930
Skilled construction worker	119.2	119.5	116.7	116.7	111.2	125.2	100.0
Govt. employee	92.1	96.3	97.8	99.3	99.3	100.3	100.0
Agricultural hired laborer	86.6	95.1	98.8	109.8	113.4	118.3	100.0
Coal miner	112.8	123.9	123.9	145.3	120.5	112.0	100.0
Manufacturing	95.6	99.7	103.0	100.0	102.5	110.9	100.0
Wood & bamboo prods.	96.8	99.2	100.5	100.6	100.3	117.8	100.0
Metal work	118.1	124.6	125.3	107.0	121.9	119.6	100.0
Apparel	60.7	69.8	86.1	87.7	87.7	96.4	100.0
Food	—	—	—	—	—	104.4	100.0
Ceramic	—	—	—	—	—	113.1	100.0

Table A30 (continued)

	1931	1932	1933	1934	1935	1936	1937
Skilled construction worker	103.6	93.2	100.2	99.9	104.5	117.8	107.4
Govt. employee	100.5	101.0	101.1	101.9	103.4	104.3	100.9
Agricultural hired laborer	—	92.7	92.7	96.3	106.1	90.2	90.2
Coal miner	81.2	89.7	95.7	130.8	116.2	123.9	126.5
Manufacturing	89.5	91.9	94.8	85.8	99.2	94.5	103.9
Wood & bamboo prods.	88.9	86.0	92.8	83.4	97.6	100.3	115.2
Metal work	103.5	100.4	101.1	99.0	105.1	112.6	107.4
Apparel	—	73.2	75.3	78.9	82.0	77.2	65.1
Food	79.6	93.1	94.2	82.0	100.7	83.9	98.6
Ceramic	109.9	107.9	108.2	97.2	104.2	106.5	107.3

	1938	1939	1940	1941	1942
Skilled construction laborer	108.6	121.5	190.1	135.4	146.1
Govt. employee	99.9	103.1	104.6	—	—
Agricultural hired laborer	92.7	98.8	117.1	175.6	175.6
Coal miner	175.2	274.4	279.5	269.2	—
Manufacturing	121.0	117.9	133.2	144.9	141.0
Wood & bamboo prods.	122.5	126.8	157.7	138.4	129.3
Metal work	118.8	125.6	146.8	163.5	165.0
Apparel	95.1	77.7	96.6	124.1	121.7
Food	126.1	109.2	112.0	137.8	138.0
Ceramic	118.3	136.3	140.7	180.7	173.7

Notes and Sources: Except for government, the wage rates used to compile these indexes are those for Taiwanese. The daily wage rates for agricultural, manufacturing, and construction workers were collected in 17 administrative districts during the colonial period. Before 1916 they were collected once a year on December 31; thereafter they were collected twice a year on June 31 and December 31. The wage rates are the average of the highest and lowest found by the statistics collector on the date of investigation. In constructing the present set of wage indexes, only the wage rates of three administrative districts are used: the cities of Taipei, Taichung, and Tainan. They are selected for their geographic locations (one is in the north, one in the center, and one in the south of Taiwan) and because they were the most populous districts during the colonial period. For some occupations, the wage rates of both male and female workers were collected and published separately. In these cases we selected the wage rate of male workers for inclusion in the index. Occasionally the worker received, besides his money wage, his board. In these cases, to account for the "free" meal, an arbitrary 10 percent increase is made to the quoted money wage. The wage data are from Taiwan Government-General, *Taiwan Government-General Statistics Book*, various issues.

Table A30 (continued)

Wages for miners and government workers were also collected by the Government-General. In Taiwan, coal mining dominates the mining industry. For example, in 1940 coal mining accounted for 64 percent of the total value of minerals extracted and 71 percent of the total number of workers engaged in the mining industry (see Taiwan Government-General, *Taiwan Mining Statistics*, vol. 31, 1940). For the mining index, therefore, it is felt that an index of the average wage received by male Taiwanese coal miners is sufficiently representative of the industry. The mining wage data were collected by the mining section of the Bureau of Productive Industries and appear in Taiwan Government-General, *Taiwan Mining Statistics*. The published mining wages are the averages of the wage rates reported by the individual mines, which in turn are the averages of the highest and the lowest wage rate paid by each mine for male coal miners.

Each year the Government-General published the total amount of salary paid to each grade of government employees. By dividing the total amount paid to each grade by the number of employees in that grade, an average annual salary for each grade is obtained. The average salaries selected to represent the wages of government employees are those for clerks and government officials with *Hannin* treatment (the lowest rank in the Japanese civil service system). These data are from Taiwan Government-General, *Taiwan Government-General Statistics Book*, various issues.

The construction procedures are as follows. (a) For the wages of agricultural, manufacturing, and construction workers, an aggregate wage rate is formed for each type of work (occupation) from the wage rates reported in Taipei, Taichung, and Tainan, using as weights the number of workers engaged in that type of work in each of the cities as recorded by the 1930 population census. (b) Each wage series is then converted into indexes with 1930 as 100. (c) These indexes are then grouped into categories as follows: (1) agricultural workers (one item), (2) coal miners (one item), (3) workers in the wood product and bamboo product industries (six items), (4) metal workers (seven items), (5) workers in the apparel industry (three items), (6) workers in the food processing industry (six items), (7) workers in the ceramic industry (four items), (8) construction workers (five items), (9) government clerks (one item), and (10) civil servants (one item). When more than one item (i.e., wage rate for one occupation) is allocated to a category, the wage index for that category is the weighted aggregate of the components, using as weights the total number of workers in each of the included occupations in Taipei, Taichung, and Tainan as recorded by the 1930 population census. (d) Finally, the wages in the various manufacturing industries are aggregated to form a general index. The weights used are the total number of workers employed by each of the component industries as recorded by the 1930 population census. The weights are: wood and bamboo, 33.8 percent; metal, 9.1 percent; apparel, 7.1 percent; food processing, 37.1 percent; and ceramics, 12.9 percent. Similarly, the wage indexes of government clerks and civil servants are aggregated to form a general index for government workers with the number of clerks and the number of officials with the rank of Hannin or of Hannin treatment in 1930 as weights.

Table A31. Indexes of Money and Real Wage by Major Economic Sector, 1953–70
(1961 = 100)

	1953	1954	1955	1956	1957	1958
Money wage						
Mining	33.4	35.0	43.6	58.1	75.7	81.2
Manufacturing	39.7	44.2	44.5	56.1	61.5	65.4
Utilities	49.2	52.9	57.8	55.6	58.5	59.2
Transport & commerce	41.4	47.7	54.9	56.4	57.9	58.8
Real wage						
Mining	56.8	62.5	70.6	85.4	104.3	110.1
Manufacturing	67.6	78.9	80.5	82.4	84.8	88.6
Utilities	83.7	94.4	93.5	81.7	80.6	80.2
Transport & commerce	70.4	85.1	88.9	82.9	79.7	79.6

	1959	1960	1961	1962	1963	1964
Money wage						
Mining	82.3	90.4	100.0	106.7	110.3	117.9
Manufacturing	70.3	82.2	100.0	105.2	109.5	111.8
Utilities	60.7	76.9	100.0	103.5	110.6	120.9
Transport & commerce	60.8	79.6	100.0	101.9	107.3	112.1
Real wage						
Mining	102.2	94.2	100.0	108.5	109.2	114.1
Manufacturing	87.2	85.7	100.0	106.9	108.3	108.1
Utilities	75.4	80.1	100.0	105.2	109.5	116.9
Transport & commerce	75.5	83.0	100.0	103.6	106.2	108.4

	1965	1966	1967	1968	1969	1970
Money wage						
Mining	132.6	140.4	152.8	172.5	186.5	211.2
Manufacturing	121.2	128.7	145.9	162.4	166.9	180.9
Utilities	127.0	135.6	164.0	175.5	190.9	197.5
Transport & commerce	126.0	134.3	154.0	167.0	188.4	219.5
Real wage						
Mining	126.7	131.5	131.3	139.1	144.4	154.4
Manufacturing	115.8	120.4	125.4	130.3	129.1	135.7
Utilities	121.4	127.0	140.9	141.9	147.7	148.2
Transport & commerce	120.4	125.7	130.5	134.9	145.7	165.2

Notes and Sources: The indexes of money wage were constructed by dividing the average wage in the current year by that of the base year. The indexes of real wage were obtained by deflating the money wage indexes by the cost of living index for laborers. The figures are from **PDOR**, *Report of Taiwan Labor Statistics*, various issues.

Table A32. Agricultural Production Indexes, 1946–74

	General index	Agricultural crop index	Livestock index	Forestry index	Fishery index
1946	20.3	26.8	10.3	10.6	7.7
1947	25.4	33.5	12.1	16.8	9.3
1948	32.8	38.2	14.7	28.1	13.0
1949	33.5	44.6	15.0	20.7	12.4
1950	37.4	48.7	20.0	25.9	13.2
1951	39.0	48.7	26.2	28.5	15.9
1952	42.3	52.3	27.3	35.3	18.5
1953	46.3	56.7	33.8	36.0	19.0
1954	47.3	57.1	34.4	38.0	22.7
1955	47.6	56.3	35.7	40.0	26.2
1956	51.2	61.1	38.1	37.8	28.1
1957	54.9	64.6	42.6	43.8	31.0
1958	58.6	68.2	47.8	50.1	31.8
1959	59.6	68.0	47.4	64.2	33.9
1960	60.4	69.1	45.8	66.6	35.3
1961	65.7	74.2	50.7	76.0	40.6
1962	67.4	75.2	55.0	77.9	42.2
1963	67.5	74.2	56.4	77.6	45.4
1964	75.6	83.5	59.9	95.9	49.4
1965	80.5	90.2	61.6	97.9	51.4
1966	83.1	91.6	68.3	90.3	59.0
1967	88.3	95.4	78.0	91.9	66.7
1968	94.2	99.3	83.5	96.9	83.5
1969	93.5	95.3	89.5	91.4	91.2
1970	98.7	99.9	98.3	95.7	95.3
1971	100.0	100.0	100.0	100.0	100.0
1972	102.4	101.1	106.7	93.7	107.1
1973	107.4	102.1	124.2	88.5	119.6
1974	108.3	108.0	114.7	81.8	114.0

Source: MOEA, *Taiwan Agricultural Production Statistics,* 1975, pp. 6–7.

Table A33. Indexes of Agricultural Production, 1901–64 (weighted arithmetic averages) (1935–37 = 100)

	General index: crops; meat & dairy products	All crops	Food crops total	Major food crops			Minor food crops				Industrial food crops	Fiber crops	Other crops	Meat & dairy products
				Total	Common foods	Substitute foods	Total	Beans	Vegetables	Fruits				
1901	25	26	27	31	33	16	13	56	14	8	16	18	21	17
1902	25	26	26	30	31	20	13	70	14	8	17	27	32	22
1903	33	33	33	39	40	34	19	133	17	10	16	44	70	29
1904	37	38	38	45	46	43	22	170	20	11	16	49	58	30
1905	39	40	40	47	48	40	21	119	21	12	23	43	71	32
Average	32	33	38	38	40	31	18	110	17	10	18	36	50	26
1906	37	38	38	43	43	44	21	127	20	11	25	52	121	32
1907	41	42	42	48	49	43	23	158	22	12	24	54	113	32
1908	43	44	44	51	51	53	26	196	23	13	25	38	74	35
1909	43	44	44	50	50	46	24	154	23	13	31	42	56	36
1910	42	42	42	45	46	39	27	163	23	19	38	30	71	40
Average	41	42	42	47	48	45	24	160	22	14	29	43	87	35
1911	45	45	46	48	49	41	25	148	25	14	45	30	103	42
1912	40	40	40	44	44	40	22	129	22	12	34	34	93	44
1913	46	46	46	55	56	50	25	200	25	10	25	36	128	46
1914	44	44	44	50	50	49	25	192	24	10	32	38	117	46
1915	48	48	48	52	52	49	28	222	26	12	42	36	108	48
Average	45	45	45	50	50	46	25	178	24	12	36	35	110	45
1916	50	49	49	50	51	43	33	223	26	22	53	37	146	53
1917	54	54	54	52	53	44	33	188	29	22	71	37	188	54
1918	51	51	51	50	50	48	36	210	28	28	61	41	65	53
1919	52	52	52	54	54	59	27	186	25	14	54	40	83	56
1920	48	48	48	52	53	50	29	140	28	21	39	36	99	55
Average	51	51	51	52	52	49	32	189	27	21	56	38	116	54

Table A33 (continued)

	General index: crops; meat & dairy products	All crops	Food crops total	Major food crops			Minor food crops				Industrial food crops	Fiber crops	Other crops	Meat & dairy products
				Total	Common foods	Substitute foods	Total	Beans	Vegetables	Fruits				
1921	51	50	50	54	54	53	34	148	30	28	45	31	88	57
1922	57	57	57	59	59	56	43	148	43	33	56	40	82	57
1923	55	54	54	54	53	58	54	134	49	52	57	45	110	59
1924	64	65	65	66	66	66	61	141	54	60	64	51	94	62
1925	68	69	69	70	70	67	62	134	58	60	69	50	95	62
Average	59	59	59	60	60	60	51	141	47	47	58	43	94	59
1926	69	67	67	68	68	68	64	127	63	60	68	51	114	64
1927	71	71	71	75	75	74	65	132	65	59	61	48	114	70
1928	73	73	73	74	74	76	67	120	68	60	74	54	118	74
1929	74	74	74	70	70	69	69	96	72	64	89	49	119	72
1930	79	80	80	80	80	78	75	106	76	72	85	50	129	73
Average	73	73	73	73	73	73	68	116	69	63	75	50	119	71
1931	81	81	81	82	81	85	80	115	81	75	80	44	124	80
1932	93	94	95	96	97	84	89	109	87	89	94	48	128	81
1933	84	85	85	90	91	83	89	106	90	87	67	52	102	80
1934	91	92	92	98	99	92	95	107	93	96	71	82	110	89
1935	98	98	98	99	99	95	95	102	98	91	98	109	104	98
Average	89	90	90	93	93	88	90	108	90	88	82	67	114	86
1936	101	101	101	102	103	101	105	112	103	106	96	91	103	99
1937	101	101	101	100	99	104	100	87	99	102	106	101	93	103
1938	106	106	106	105	106	101	101	101	96	107	110	119	94	106
1939	107	108	107	96	99	76	96	83	89	104	149	178	716	97
1940	93	94	94	86	85	89	92	90	87	98	121	128	655	84
Average	102	102	102	98	98	94	99	95	95	103	116	123	332	98

Table A33. (continued)

	General index: crops; meat & dairy products	All crops	Food crops total	Major food crops			Minor food crops				Industrial food crops	Fiber crops	Other crops	Meat & dairy products
				Total	Common foods	Substitute foods	Total	Beans	Vegetables	Fruits				
1941	94	97	97	92	90	100	91	99	82	100	106	108	454	70
1942	94	98	97	89	89	92	95	90	90	100	125	142	787	72
1943	90	92	91	85	85	83	77	71	78	76	118	101	633	81
1944	78	84	84	82	81	92	61	117	74	43	98	76	276	43
1945	49	50	50	51	49	69	49	53	70	27	46	33	170	43
Average	81	84	84	80	79	87	75	86	79	69	99	92	464	62
1946	56	58	58	70	68	83	58	99	80	33	20	29	213	42
1947	71	70	70	80	76	108	99	196	116	72	27	42	349	57
1948	77	81	80	86	82	121	98	250	112	70	54	131	518	56
1949	91	96	96	97	93	130	97	208	121	63	90	108	820	57
1950	102	106	106	112	109	132	108	250	137	66	84	85	2,042	76
Average	79	82	82	89	86	115	92	201	113	61	55	79	788	58
1951	104	106	104	115	114	122	108	248	139	65	67	122	4,122	96
1952	113	114	111	121	120	126	111	294	144	65	78	224	4,836	104
1953	126	125	123	127	126	137	111	317	142	62	115	83	4,800	131
1954	126	125	123	133	130	155	115	386	146	60	96	150	3,498	135
1955	125	122	120	126	124	147	126	502	151	67	98	224	2,676	141
Average	119	118	116	124	123	137	114	349	144	64	91	161	3,986	121
1956	136	134	132	140	138	161	127	538	153	63	108	202	4,188	150
1957	144	141	139	144	142	163	141	580	164	78	120	152	4,315	167
1958	154	148	145	150	146	179	158	716	171	94	124	238	4,896	190
1959	154	148	145	148	144	178	162	746	174	86	130	299	4,579	187
1960	154	150	147	152	148	185	177	803	186	110	118	252	4,301	181
Average	148	144	142	145	144	173	153	677	170	88	120	229	4,456	175

Table A33 (continued)

	General index: crops; meat & dairy products	All crops	Food crops total	Food crops								Fiber crops	Other crops	Meat & dairy products
				Major food crops			Minor food crops							
				Total	Common foods	Substituted foods	Total	Beans	Vegetables	Fruits	Industrial food crops			
1961	165	159	157	161	156	203	185	861	189	119	131	176	5,273	200
1962	167	160	158	167	163	199	192	816	195	132	141	145	5,780	210
1963	164	157	154	159	161	143	198	784	212	131	118	142	7,107	211
1964	182	176	172	177	172	216	235	916	263	193	127	182	9,164	224
Average	170	163	160	166	163	190	203	844	215	144	129	161	6,831	211

Notes and Sources: The above indexes are the results of revision and extension of work originally done by the Rural Economic Division of the Joint Commission of Rural Reconstruction. I am grateful to JCRR for making available to me the worksheets of its agricultural production index, which greatly facilitated the revisions. Needless to say, I alone am responsible for any errors in the revised indexes. These indexes use the Laspeyres formula with the 1935–37 average values of production as weights. 1935–37 were selected because they represent a period of normality between the Great Depression and the Sino–Japanese War. The general index includes 70 crop and 9 noncrop items. A detailed breakdown of the composition is provided below for reference.

Crops; meat and dairy products: 79 items.
I. Crops: 70 items including all food crops, fiber crops, and special crops.
    A. Food crops: 64 items.
       1. Major food crops: 9 items.
          a. Common food crops: 3 items: rice, barley, and wheat.
          b. Substitute food crops: 6 items: sweet potatoes, sorghum, millet, barnyard millet, Indian corn, and buckwheat.
       2. Minor food crops: 48 items.
          a. Beans: 2 items: soybean and other beans.
          b. Vegetable: 26 items.
          c. Fruit: 20 items, of which the most important are banana and pineapple.
       3. Food crops to be processed: 7 items: sugar cane, peanut, tea, tobacco, sesame, arrowroot, and coffee.
    B. Fiber crops: 3 items: jute, ramie, and cotton.
    C. Other crops: 3 items: rapeseed, rush, and citronella oil.
II. Meat and dairy products: 9 items: cattle, hogs, goats, chickens, geese, turkeys, ducks, milk, and honey.

Table A33 (continued)

Although the Japanese had collected crop production data since the end of the nineteenth century, some important crops were neglected and their production data were not collected until much later. Among the crops that were probably cultivated but whose production data were not recorded are (the data in parentheses indicate the first years of recording) sugar cane (1902), vegetables (1918), and fruits (1909). For 1901, sugar cane production is assumed to be the average of 1902–06. Total vegetable production for 1901–18 is assumed to be 2.3% (the 1919–23 average) of total crop production in 1935–37 prices. Total fruit production for 1901–09 is assumed to be 1.3% (the 1910–14 average) of total crop production in 1935–37 prices. There are other omissions such as Indian corn (not recorded until 1928), arrowroot (not recorded until 1919), and citronella oil (not recorded until 1939). They are such minor crops, however, that adjustment seems unnecessary.

Livestock production is taken as the weight of slaughtered cattle, hogs, and goats. Because a substantial number of live hogs were imported before the 1950s and exported since the late 1950s, the slaughtered hog figure is adjusted by adding to it the net export of hogs. Since 1910, records of slaughtered cattle, hogs, and goats are available both in metric tons and in heads. Before 1910, only the head measurement is available. Using the animals' respective head/MT ratios in 1910, these early statistics are converted from head to MT. Because livestock became heavier each year, this method imparts an upward bias to the pre-1910 slaughtered figures. The data for milk, honey, and slaughtered poultry are available only from 1910. In the case of poultry the only available data are estimates of year-end population. By assuming a growth period of 4–8 months for poultry, the number of slaughtered poultry is taken as twice the year-end population. No attempt is made to estimate the production of milk, honey, and poultry before 1910, for which we have no data, is assumed to move in a manner similar to that of the production of livestock.

Although the production records of the two most important crops grown in Taiwan, rice and sugar cane, are not kept in terms of calendar year, the indexes of agricultural production are presented as if the production records of all crops are kept in terms of calendar year. From 1901 to 1944 the production record of rice is kept in terms of the Japanese rice year, representing the production from November 1 of the previous year to October 31 of the calendar year in question. Since 1946 it has been kept in terms of the Taiwan rice year, representing the production from July 1 of the calendar year in question to June 30 of the next year. 1945, the transition year, covered the production from November 1, 1944, to June 30, 1946. For long-term analysis, it is the trend of production that is of interest. Consequently, no attempt is made to convert rice year to calendar year. In any case, except for 1945, every rice year includes the harvest of a spring and an autumn crop. The growth period of sugar cane is approximately 15–18 months, so the production of sugar cane is kept in terms of sugar year, which is an 18-month year. No attempt is made to convert sugar year to calendar year. Thus, for example, the production of sugar cane during the crop year of 1953–54 is assumed to be the production of 1954. Doing this has of course no effect on the trend of sugar cane production.

For reference, the weights given to the components of the general index according to their 1935–37 average value of production are presented below.

Table A33 (continued)

Crops; meat and dairy products	100.00%
I. Crops	86.56
A. Food crops	85.90
1. Major food crops	60.04
a. Common food	53.02
(Rice)	(52.98)
b. Substitute food	7.26
2. Minor food crops	7.50
a. Beans	0.33
b. Vegetables	3.59
c. Fruits	3.58
3. Food crops to be processed	18.36
(Sugar cane)	(14.85)
B. Fiber crops	0.62
C. Special crops	0.04
II. Meat and dairy products	13.44

Considering the extensive coverage of these indexes, they may be considered as accurate indicators of production trends in agriculture. The sources of data used in constructing these indexes are:

1. All crops (except rice) and livestock.
   a. 1901–42: Taiwan Government-General, *Taiwan Agricultural Yearbook*, various issues.
   b. 1943–64: PDAF, *Taiwan Agricultural Yearbook*, various issues.

2. Import and export data of live hogs.
   a. 1901–42: Taiwan Government-General, *The Annual Taiwan Trade Statistics*, various issues.
   b. 1943–48: PBAS, *Taiwan Trade Statistics for the Last Fifty-three Years*.
   c. 1949–64: Inspectorate-General of Customs, *The Trade of China*, various issues.

3. Rice: PFB, *Taiwan Food Statistics Book*, various issues. For 1937–44 the *Taiwan Food Statistics Book* and the *Taiwan Agricultural Yearbook* published conflicting production figures. The figures from the *Taiwan Food Statistics Book* are accepted for the following reason. The predecessor of PFB and the PFB are primarily responsible for the collection and compilation of rice production data. Consequently PFB's figures must be considered more reliable. It should be noted, however, that the discrepancies between the two sets of figures are not large. In general the figures from the *Taiwan Food Statistics Book* are approximately 1% higher.

Table A34. Agricultural Price Indexes, 1952–74

	General	Agricultural crops	Livestock	Forestry	Fishery
1952	100.0	100.0	100.0	100.0	100.0
1953	117.4	116.8	113.4	135.0	108.8
1954	123.4	120.8	117.0	148.4	120.1
1955	147.1	146.9	141.2	169.8	133.6
1956	165.7	151.9	158.5	256.5	172.9
1957	172.6	162.5	172.0	265.7	152.4
1958	183.3	179.4	175.7	261.0	149.4
1959	211.0	208.1	211.9	250.9	189.5
1960	241.7	240.0	260.2	264.1	212.9
1961	239.0	248.8	262.6	222.3	191.4
1962	239.3	257.9	269.6	219.6	159.6
1963	254.8	276.7	283.8	227.9	169.5
1964	268.1	291.0	307.0	231.5	180.3
1965	270.5	283.2	306.8	279.0	184.9
1966	280.1	287.1	300.0	337.6	193.6
1967	282.6	287.8	294.9	353.9	198.1
1968	300.0	302.3	309.3	402.9	209.5
1969	297.7	301.7	294.6	397.8	220.2
1970	313.5	320.3	297.1	406.2	230.9
1971	306.4	300.3	327.7	394.4	247.4
1972	309.2	334.1	345.8	436.1	266.4
1973	409.0	392.6	385.5	720.6	309.3
1974	557.6	525.7	561.5	888.5	382.8

Note and Source: These indexes are based on prices collected through Farmers' Associations and local markets in 55 townships. The data are from PDAF, *Taiwan Agricultural Prices Monthly*, June 1975, p. 46.

Table A35. Utilization of Registered Land, Selected Years (Hectares)

	1920	1930	1940	1950	1960
Total land area	3,597,125	3,597,282	3,596,056	3,596,121	3,596,121
Mountain region [a]	1,684,194	1,678,903	1,615,594		
Civil district	1,912,931	1,918,379	1,980,462		
Total registered land	1,024,115	1,228,033	1,269,636	1,367,016	1,345,518
Paddy field	354,878	389,296	526,458	521,692	513,197
Dry land	353,574	389,737	315,288	328,027	323,683
Pisciculture pond	24,709	21,702	13,716	13,222	16,814
Pond	13,838	12,769	12,158		10,700
Pasture	3,567	5,025	2,426	741	441
Salt field	1,385	2,181	3,184	12,877	5,758
Mineral spring	2	2	1	2	3
Forest	121,405	262,554	273,598	337,555	315,518
Wild land (prairie)	97,742	76,070	37,645		
Building site	34,521	36,454	41,176	46,195	49,814
Land for temple and grave	16,059	13,125	12,310	11,811	11,635
Road and highway		767	6,575	8,571	10,121
Railway		930	1,296	1,311	2,051
Ditches and conduits		99	169	231	417
Irrigation channel		11,889	15,584	16,855	18,820
Land for railway admin.	575	800	901	946	921
Miscellaneous [b]	1,861	4,633	7,151	66,980	65,622

Notes and Sources: Since 1945 the data on registered land are compiled by the Land Bureau of the Taiwan Provincial Government based on reports submitted from the various administrative districts. The pre-World War II data are from Taiwan Government General, *Taiwan Agricultural Yearbook*, and the post-World War II data are from PDAF, *Taiwan Agricultural Yearbook*. The nonregistered land is mostly national forest.

[a] Aborigine territory.

[b] Includes land for gun positions, military training fields, target practice, lighthouses, parks, dykes, swamps, and other uses.

Table A36. Number of Owner-Families by Size of Holding: 1920, 1932, 1939, 1952[a]

	Below 0.5	0.5–1	1–2	2–3	3–5	5–7	7–10	10–20	20–30	30–50	Above 50	Total
1920												
Number of families	172,931	86,711	70,739	28,412	23,276	8,989	5,902	5,454	1,353	842	572	405,181
Percentage of total	42.68	21.40	17.46	7.01	5.74	2.22	1.46	1.35	0.33	0.21	0.14	100.00
Cumulative percentage	42.68	64.08	81.54	88.55	94.29	96.51	97.97	99.32	99.65	99.86	100.00	
Area (chia)	40,987	62,513	100,140	69,749	88,672	52,176	48,890	73,722	32,995	31,837	119,569	721,252
Percentage of total	5.68	8.67	13.88	9.67	12.29	7.23	6.78	10.22	4.57	4.41	16.60	100.00
Cumulative percentage	5.68	14.35	28.23	37.90	50.19	57.42	64.20	74.42	78.99	83.40	100.00	
1932												
Number of families	130,732	71,181	63,851	27,673	22,641	9,181	6,143	5,852	1,594	1,051	775	340,674
Percentage of total	38.37	20.89	18.74	8.12	6.65	2.69	1.80	1.72	0.47	0.31	0.23	100.00
1939												
Number of families	186,423	90,024	74,151	32,114	24,238	9,801	6,210	5,416	1,489	845	655	431,366
Percentage of total	43.22	20.87	17.19	7.44	5.62	2.27	1.44	1.26	0.35	0.19	0.15	100.00
1952												
Number of families	288,955	142,659	103,416	34,762	23,762	12,588		3,685	732	372	262	611,193
Percentage of total	47.28	23.34	16.92	5.69	3.89	2.06		0.60	0.12	0.06	0.04	100.00
Cumulative percentage	47.28	70.62	87.54	93.23	97.12	99.18		99.78	99.90	99.96	100.00	
Area (chia)	67,511	102,578	143,895	83,996	90,045	85,020		49,060	17,633	13,848	13,342	681,154
Percentage of total	9.91	15.06	21.12	12.33	13.22	12.49		7.18	2.59	2.03	4.07	100.00
Cumulative percentage	9.91	24.97	46.09	58.42	71.64	84.13		91.31	93.90	95.93	100.00	

Table A36. (continued)

Notes and Sources: These statistics were compiled by the government based on complete surveys of the land registration records. Land not registered and changes in land use not duly registered are therefore not reflected in these statistics. With the exception of the 1920 survey of land records, the surveys seem to be well conducted, and the results obtained should be considered reliable. The results of the 1920 survey were poorly compiled. Taiwan was divided into enumerating districts for the survey. Families that owned or cultivated land bordering on two districts were probably counted twice. Also, the manager of a landlord's land in an enumerating district is considered to be the owner of the land if the landlord resided in another district. These procedures introduced certain defects into the data: (1) the number of families was overstated; (2) more families were classified in the smaller size categories than was justified by actual conditions; and (3) the data underestimate the concentration of landownership. Thus one must be very careful when using the 1920 data.

The 1952 statistics are for privately owned land only. At the end of World War II all land owned by Japanese was confiscated and became government property. This partly accounts for the low percentage of large land owners in the 1952 statistics. Because of the difference in coverage the 1952 data must not be indiscriminately compared with the prewar data. The figures in this table are taken from Taiwan Government-General, *Report of Basic Agricultural Survey No. 2*, 1922, pp. 2–4; *Report of Basic Agricultural Survey No. 31*, 1934, pp. 2–3; *Report of Basic Agricultural Survey No. 41*, 1941, pp. 2–7; and PDCA, *Statistics on Land-ownership Classification in Taiwan, China (1952)*, tables IV-1 and VII-2.

[a]The numbers in the column headings are in chia (1 chia = 0.9699 hectare).

Table A37. Number of Farm Families by Size of Cultivated Land: 1920, 1932, 1939, 1949[a]

	Below 0.5	0.5–1	1–2	2–3	3–5	5–7	7–10	10–20	Above 20	Total number of farm households
1920										
Number of families	127,998	96,933	100,403	45,563	33,342	10,362	5,101	2,997	579	423,278
Percentage of total	30.23	22.87	23.72	10.76	7.84	2.43	1.24	0.78	0.13	100.00
Cumulative percentage	30.23	53.10	76.82	87.58	95.42	97.85	99.09	99.87	100.00	
Area (chia)	33,745	69,667	143,206	110,531	125,574	60,033	41,724	38,477	68,410	691,367
Percentage of total	4.88	10.08	20.70	15.99	18.16	8.68	6.04	5.57	9.90	100.00
Cumulative percentage	4.88	14.96	35.66	51.65	68.81	78.49	84.53	90.10	100.00	
1932/4/1										
Number of families	93,423	77,477	99,129	51,710	40,007	12,652	6,111	3,190	453	384,152
Percentage of total	24.32	20.17	25.81	13.46	10.41	3.29	1.59	0.83	0.12	100.00
1939/4/1										
Number of families	108,754	88,976	112,555	57,404	41,711	13,122	5,935	2,796	531	431,784
Percentage of total	25.19	20.61	26.07	13.29	9.66	3.04	1.37	0.65	0.12	100.00
1949										
Number of families	163,521	158,518	157,446	54,197	25,641	4,657	1,636	561	93	566,270
Percentage of total	28.88	27.99	27.81	9.57	4.53	0.82	0.29	0.09	0.02	100.00

Notes and Sources: See the note in table A36. The sources of the data for 1920, 1932, and 1939 are those cited in table A36. The 1949 data are taken from JCRR, Land Reform Division, *Abstracts of Land Statistics, Taiwan Province*, 1953, table 17.
[a] The numbers in the column headings are in chia (1 chia = 0.9699 hectares).

Table A38. Number and Area of Farm Holdings by Size of Cultivated Land and Mode of Operation, Dec. 31, 1960 (Hectares)

			Mode of operation			
	Holdings		*By the holder (individual farm households)*		*Through a hired manager (public & private commercial farms)*	
Size class	*Number*	*Area*	*Number*	*Area*	*Number*	*Area*
All holdings[a]	808,267	1,029,503.42	807,600	951,806.14	667	77,697.28
Noncultivating Holdings[b]	31,686	6,357.27	31,598	3,067.93	88	3,289.34
Cultivated land[c]						
under 0.5	290,349	121,663.73	290,268	121,611.13	81	52.60
under 0.1	38,994	7,183.41	38,987	7,181.70	7	1.71
0.1–0.3	121,494	41,739.38	121,450	41,717.40	44	21.98
0.3–0.5	129,861	72,740.94	129,831	72,712.03	30	28.91
0.5–1.0	225,596	217,302.28	225,549	216,362.70	47	939.58
1.0–1.5	119,135	182,892.58	119,100	182,787.20	35	105.38
1.5–2.0	64,670	138,098.16	64,651	137,802.83	19	295.33
2.0–3.0	50,579	150,927.32	50,556	150,078.37	23	848.95
3.0–5.0	21,150	97,995.03	21,113	96,713.93	37	1,281.10
5.0–10.0	4,812	44,546.30	4,765	43,382.05	47	1,164.25
10.0–20.0	32	2,728.55			32	2,728.55
20.0–50.0	33	5,803.35			33	5,803.35
50.0–100.0	37	4,167.43			37	4,167.43
100.0–200.0	78	13,900.26			78	13,900.26
200.0–500.0	101	34,730.10			101	34,730.10
500.0–1,000.0	9	8,391.06			9	8,391.06
1,000.0 & over						

Source: Taiwan Provincial Government, Committee on Census of Agriculture, *Statistical Abstract of the 1961 Census of Agriculture, Taiwan, Republic of China,* 1963, p. 2.

[a] "Holdings" indicates farm households and public and private commercial farms.
[b] Noncultivating holdings are those that cultivate less than 0.02 chia (0.0194 ha) of land but qualify as farm holdings by raising livestock, poultry, bees, or silkworms.
[c] Cultivated land includes paddy land, upland, and land classified otherwise but used as paddy land or up land. Area is given in hectares.

Table A39. Cultivated and Irrigated Area and the Multiple Cropping Index, 1901–70
(Annual averages)

	Cultivated area (ha)	Irrigated & drained area (ha)	Multiple cropping index
1901–05	519,466	178,940[a]	—
1906–10	654,833	216,992	—
1911–15	692,272	236,135	115.1
1916–20	731,288	278,733	113.7
1921–25	758,378	327,385	115.9
1926–30	802,222	403,546	117.9
1931–35	820,305	456,806	127.5
1936–40	856,098	517,274	127.5
1941–45	837,015	544,096[b]	125.3
1946–50	852,911	493,373	147.6
1951–55	873,962	483,084	168.3
1956–60	875,897	491,976	176.3
1961–65	877,527	502,717	182.8
1966–70	903,761	526,565	183.1

Notes and Sources: The figures on cultivated area are those reported by field reporters. The statistics on irrigated and drained area are collected by the Commission on Water Conservancy through field surveys. Since 1946, land irrigated by irrigation facilities other than those regulated by the Commission on Water Conservancy is not included. In constructing the above multiple cropping index, I have adjusted the areas under temporary crops with growing periods longer than one year. Thus, the index is a measure of the frequency with which cultivated land is used each year. The basic data behind these data are from Taiwan Government-General, *Taiwan Agricultural Yearbook*, various years; PDAF, *Taiwan Agricultural Yearbook*, various years; and PBAS, *Taiwan Province: Statistical Summary of the Past 51 Years*, table 214.
[a] Average of 1903–05.
[b] Average of 1941–42.

Table A40. Land Cultivated by Owners and Tenants, Survey Years (Hectares)

Date of survey	Total area surveyed	Cultivated by owners			Cultivated by tenants		
		Total	Paddy	Dry	Total	Paddy	Dry
1920–21	670,567[a]	280,614	101,203	179,411	389,953	226,443	163,509
	100%	41.85%	15.09%	26.76%	58.15%	33.77%	24.38%
1927	762,289[b]	333,453	127,499	205,954	428,837	249,540	179,297
	100%	43.75%	16.73%	27.02%	56.26%	32.74%	23.52%
1930	778,920[b]	352,420	132,396	220,023	426,500	257,437	169,063
	100%	45.25%	17.00%	28.25%	54.76%	33.05%	21.71%
1932	756,758[a]	351,501	128,223	223,278	405,257	256,084	149,172
	100%	46.45%	16.94%	29.51%	53.55%	33.84%	19.71%
1939	827,886[a,c]	361,550	201,368	160,182	466,337	318,881	147,456
	100%	43.68%	24.33%	19.35%	56.32%	38.51%	17.81%
1952	681,154[d]	427,197	235,804	191,393	253,957	219,710	34,248
	100%	62.72%	34.62%	28.10%	37.28%	32.25%	5.03%

Sources: Taiwan Government-General, *Report of Basic Agricultural Survey No. 2,* 1922, p. 3; *Survey of Land Cultivated by Tenants and Owners,* 1927, pp. 2–3; *Survey of Land Cultivated by Tenants and Owners,* 1930, pp. 2–3; *Report of Basic Agricultural Survey No. 31,* 1934, pp. 2–3; *Report of Basic Agricultural Survey No. 41,* 1941, pp. 6–7; and PDCA, *Statistics on Land Ownership Classification in Taiwan, China (1952),* table 11.

[a] Excludes cultivated land owned by government and those in the aborigine territory.
[b] Excludes cultivated land in the aborigine territory.
[c] In 1935 the aborigine territory was reduced in size from 1,678,945 to 1,615,623 ha.
[d] Private cultivated land.

Table A41. Number of Farm Households by Tenure System: Selected Years, 1922–70 (Households)

	Total	Owner-cultivator	Part owner	Tenant	Percentage of total Owner-cultivator	Part owner	Tenant
1922	385,277	116,700	111,512	157,065	30.3	28.9	40.8
1925	393,777	114,291	118,488	160,998	29.0	30.1	40.9
1930	411,377	119,545	126,428	165,404	29.1	30.7	40.2
1935	419,865	132,108	128,395	159,362	31.4	30.6	38.0
1940	429,939	137,399	134,355	158,185	32.0	31.2	36.8
1945	500,569	149,400	147,448	203,721	29.8	29.5	40.7
1950	638,062	231,111	162,573	244,378	36.0	26.0	38.0
1955	732,555	433,115	172,115	127,325	59.0	24.0	17.0
1960	785,592	506,286	166,792	112,514	64.0	21.0	15.0
1965	847,242	565,512	174,874	106,856	66.7	20.6	12.6
1970	880,274	676,554	108,026	95,694	76.9	12.3	10.9

Notes and Sources: Owner-cultivator is one who cultivates only his own land, part-owner is one who cultivates his own land and at the same time tenants the land owned by others, and tenant is one who owns no land and cultivates only the land owned by others. The data are taken from PDAF, *Taiwan Agricultural Yearbook*, various years; PBAS, *Taiwan Province: Statistical Summary of the Past 51 Years*, pp. 513–14.

Table A42. Crop Area of Major Crops: Selected Years, 1901–68 (Hectares)

	Rice	Sweet potato	Soybean	Sugar cane	Tea	Tobacco	Peanut	Banana	Pineapple	Total crop area reported
1901 (ha)	353,360	53,094	—	—	25,311	625	12,267	—	—	477,885
% of total	73.9	11.1			5.3	0.1	2.6			100.0
1906 (ha)	458,591	94,125	—	34,101	32,789	152	18,391	—	—	697,838
%	65.6	13.5		4.9	4.7	0.0	2.6			100.0
1911 (ha)	478,780	104,942	—	87,368	32,379	397	18,149	759	849	792,680
%	60.3	13.2		11.0	4.1	0.1	2.3	0.1	0.1	100.0
1916 (ha)	471,677	107,456	17,665	113,760	43,032	1,073	20,880	2,928	876	832,733
%	56.6	12.9	2.1	13.7	5.2	0.1	2.5	0.4	0.1	100.0
1921 (ha)	495,426	120,740	13,136	116,282	38,089	1,328	23,647	5,963	1,268	875,458
%	56.5	13.8	1.5	13.3	4.3	0.2	2.7	0.7	0.1	100.0
1926 (ha)	567,172	124,515	10,292	120,224	45,879	705	26,292	16,761	2,230	977,530
%	57.9	12.7	1.0	12.3	4.7	0.1	2.7	1.7	0.2	100.0
1931 (ha)	633,726	129,233	8,385	96,113	44,567	758	27,243	13,789	4,980	1,028,718
%	61.6	12.6	0.8	9.3	4.3	0.1	2.6	1.3	0.5	100.0
1936 (ha)	681,548	140,110	7,327	124,469	44,683	1,221	30,735	21,850	7,730	1,144,757
%	59.5	12.2	0.6	10.9	3.9	0.1	2.7	1.9	0.7	100.0
1941 (ha)	646,927	142,242	4,544	157,194	44,763	4,391	24,779	21,613	10,173	1,183,197
%	54.6	12.0	0.4	13.3	3.8	0.4	2.1	1.8	0.9	100.0
1946 (ha)	564,016	176,029	8,454	36,205	35,473	1,016	50,797	10,202	3,163	980,726
%	57.0	17.8	0.9	3.7	3.6	0.1	5.1	1.0	0.3	100.0
1951 (ha)	789,075	231,389	23,251	79,249	42,704	7,708	84,889	14,738	5,662	1,483,399
%	53.2	15.6	1.6	5.3	2.9	0.5	5.7	1.0	0.4	100.0
1956 (ha)	783,629	230,236	37,505	90,901	47,638	8,289	98,258	9,573	6,441	1,537,622
%	50.9	15.0	2.4	5.9	3.1	0.5	6.4	0.6	0.4	100.0
1961 (ha)	782,510	235,794	59,582	100,180	47,632	7,704	98,615	14,751	9,737	1,620,604
%	48.0	14.5	3.7	6.2	2.9	0.5	6.1	0.9	0.6	100.0
1964 (ha)	764,935	246,176	50,970	97,386	38,176	8,688	100,877	31,429	14,552	1,658,878
%	46.0	14.8	3.1	5.0	2.3	0.5	6.1	1.9	0.9	100.0
1968 (ha)	789,906	240,437	49,461	96,779	36,113	11,141	95,421	48,953	16,426	1,694,000
%	46.6	14.1	2.9	5.7	2.1	0.6	5.6	2.8	0.9	100.0

Sources: Taiwan Government-General, *The Taiwan Government-General Statistical Book*, various issues, and *Taiwan Agricultural Yearbook*, ... Yearbook, various issues.

Table A43. Production, Acreage, and Yield for Rice, Sweet Potatoes, and Sugar Cane, 1901–70 (Annual averages)

	Rice			Sweet potatoes		
	Planted area (ha)	*Yield*[a] *(kg/ha)*	*Production*[a] *(MT)*	*Planted area (ha)*	*Yield (kg/ha)*	*Production (MT)*
1901–10	432,021	1,324	571,899	90,107	6,837	616,078
1911–20	486,365	1,379	670,531	111,950	7,063	790,741
1921–30	551,622	1,594	879,516	122,765	9,231	1,133,192
1931–40	654,852	1,935	1,266,622	134,277	11,534	1,548,823
1941–50	645,347	1,667	1,080,040	183,805	9,158	1,683,263
1951–60	776,813	2,228	1,729,782	234,531	10,882	2,547,563
1961–70	779,218	2,942	2,292,870	236,092	13,906	3,270,730

	Sugar Cane			
	Harvested area (ha)	*Cane yield (kg/ha)*	*Cane production (MT)*	*Sugar production*[c] *(MT)*
1901–10	30,823[b]	31,134[b]	959,653[b]	82,236[d]
1911–20	100,258	28,149	2,822,156	251,498
1921–30	115,757	43,836	5,074,342	498,353
1931–40	119,740	68,206	8,166,994	948,344
1941–50	112,287	51,949	5,833,181	583,756
1951–60	94,942	68,056	6,495,760	756,705
1961–70	96,488	75,066	7,374,772	832,401

Sources: PFB, *Taiwan Food Statistics Book*, various issues; PDAF, *Taiwan Agricultural Yearbook*, various issues; Taiwan Government-General, *Taiwan Agricultural Yearbook*, various issues; MOEA, *The Republic of China, Taiwan Industrial Production Statistics Monthly*, various issues; and Taiwan Government-General, *Taiwan Sugar Statistics*, various issues.

[a] In terms of brown rice.
[b] Average for 1902–10.
[c] Includes refined and brown sugar.
[d] Average for 1903–10.

Table A44. Estimated Consumption of Farm-Produced Fertilizer by Major Varieties, 1910–64 (1,000 MT)

	Total	Green manure	Animal manure	Night soil	Compost	Others[a]
1910	3,594	1,193	463	560	897	481
1911	3,642	1,183	458	571	949	481
1912	3,763	1,247	446	585	1,004	481
1913	3,845	1,253	450	598	1,063	481
1914	3,898	1,240	444	609	1,124	481
1915	4,020	1,277	444	629	1,189	481
1916	4,093	1,300	435	619	1,258	481
1917	4,179	1,313	427	626	1,332	481
1918	4,271	1,317	430	634	1,409	481
1919	4,479	1,423	444	640	1,491	481
1920	4,385	1,230	448	649	1,577	481
1921	4,467	1,217	440	660	1,669	481
1922	4,758	1,403	434	674	1,766	481
1923	4,959	1,480	442	688	1,868	481
1924	4,797	1,144	457	631	1,976	588
1925	5,036	1,274	476	705	2,101	479
1926	5,279	1,378	536	746	2,168	450
1927	5,552	1,524	521	750	2,337	419
1928	6,036	1,687	491	840	2,385	634
1929	6,015	1,539	510	824	2,687	456
1930	6,348	1,749	646	850	2,613	489
1931	6,857	1,906	659	837	2,808	646
1932	7,182	2,064	717	877	2,980	543
1933	7,259	1,914	783	893	3,185	484
1934	7,584	2,061	811	862	3,352	499
1935	8,188	2,216	865	903	3,622	581
1936	8,675	2,144	1,014	968	3,827	721
1937	9,001	2,146	1,098	1,011	4,046	699
1938	9,027	1,939	1,169	1,053	4,111	754
1939	9,555	2,008	1,129	1,098	4,622	698
1940	10,219	1,872	1,143	1,044	5,488	671
1941	12,012	2,085	963	1,166	7,264	534
1942	13,752	2,800	890	1,071	8,485	505
1943	24,888	3,733	1,614	1,796	16,866	879
1944	10,772	2,055	838	1,270	6,179	429
1945	9,971	1,255	711	1,223	6,154	628
1946	10,348	1,542	829	1,413	5,033	1,530
1947	9,043	2,286	807	1,237	4,020	692
1948	15,477	2,783	2,205	1,703	6,740	2,045
1949	14,118	2,929	2,058	1,378	6,815	937
1950	13,394	2,078	2,195	1,392	6,905	823

Table A44 (continued)

	Total	Green manure	Animal manure	Night soil	Compost	Others[a]
1951	13,376	1,838	2,349	1,448	7,054	687
1952	13,650	1,878	2,344	1,538	7,069	820
1953	13,534	1,862	2,510	1,465	6,857	839
1954	13,231	1,627	2,597	1,596	6,614	797
1955	13,535	1,490	2,531	1,697	6,902	915
1956	14,040	1,545	2,530	1,652	7,327	985
1957	14,700	1,276	2,484	1,773	8,109	1,058
1958	15,004	1,224	2,920	2,000	7,759	1,101
1959	14,947	1,228	2,732	2,201	7,721	1,066
1960	14,135	1,165	2,628	2,085	7,183	1,074
1961	16,428	1,107	2,669	2,227	9,208	1,217
1962	17,400	1,113	3,031	2,551	9,583	1,122
1963	16,766	999	3,077	2,511	9,095	1,084
1964	14,339	928	3,150	2,725	6,538	998

Notes and Sources: The figures after 1924 are official estimates of the government taken from PBAS, *Taiwan Province: Statistical Summary of the Past 51 Years*, pp. 586–87, and PDAF, *Taiwan Agricultural Yearbook*, various issues. The figures before 1924 are the estimates of the author. The procedures of estimation are as follows. (1) Green manure. A linear relationship between green manure consumption and the crop area planted with green manure is estimated using the data after 1924. The equation is then used to predict green manure consumption during 1910–23 from crop area statistics. (2) Animal manure. The consumption of animal manure in agriculture before 1924 is estimated by multiplying the population of farm animals (hogs and cattle) by the 1924–28 average animal manure consumed in agriculture per head of farm animal. (3) Night soil. A linear relationship between night soil consumed in agriculture and total midyear population is estimated using the data after 1924. The equation is then used to predict night soil consumption during 1910–23 from midyear population data. (4) Compost. The consumption of compost in agriculture before 1924 is assumed to have increased annually at the same rate (5.49%) as it did during 1924–34. (5) Other. The consumption of other farm-produced fertilizers before 1924 is assumed to be the average consumption of 1924–34.

[a] Includes burned soil, rice hull, ash, straw, and other substances.

Table A45. Estimated Consumption of Purchased Commercial Fertilizer, 1901–48

	Total commercial		Vegetables		Chemical	
	1935–37 prices (1,000 T¥)	Index 1935–37 = 100	1935–37 prices (1,000 T¥)	Index 1935–37 = 100	1935–37 prices (1,000 T¥)	Index 1935–37 = 100
1901	—	—	—	—	—	—
1902	11	a	—	—	11	a
1903	108	a	41	a	67	a
1904	51	a	46	a	5	a
1905	74	a	41	a	33	a
1906	122	a	51	a	71	a
1907	226	1	82	0.6	144	0.6
1908	419	1	66	0.5	353	1.5
1909	1,877	5	489	3.4	1,388	5.9
1910	2,897	7	1,114	7.8	1,783	7.5
1911	2,445	6	1,501	10.6	944	3.1
1912	4,622	12	3,038	21.4	1,584	6.7
1913	4,484	12	2,356	16.6	2,128	9.0
1914	5,422	14	2,714	19.1	2,708	11.4
1915	9,405	24	4,055	28.5	5,350	22.6
1916	10,896	28	4,983	35.1	5,913	25.0
1917	11,876	31	5,797	40.8	6,079	25.7
1918	10,040	26	5,434	38.2	4,606	19.5
1919	10,818	28	6,767	47.6	4,051	17.1
1920	14,832	38	8,821	62.1	6,011	25.4
1921	14,290	37	7,622	53.7	6,668	28.2
1922	10,358	27	4,912	34.6	5,446	23.0
1923	11,929	31	5,095	35.9	6,834	28.9
1924	14,969	39	6,234	43.9	8,735	36.9
1925	17,025	44	7,995	56.3	9,030	38.2
1926	17,965	46	8,987	63.3	8,978	38.0
1927	19,994	51	9,251	65.1	10,743	45.4
1928	22,686	58	10,159	71.5	12,527	53.0
1929	22,342	58	9,730	68.5	12,612	53.3
1930	23,214	60	10,428	73.4	12,786	54.1
1931	26,900	69	10,741	75.6	16,159	68.3
1932	24,396	63	11,901	83.8	12,495	52.8
1933	28,050	72	12,284	86.5	15,766	66.7
1934	31,681	82	13,631	95.9	18,050	76.3
1935	36,908	95	14,447	101.7	19,461	82.3
1936	38,673	100	14,604	102.8	24,069	101.8
1937	40,979	105	13,567	95.5	27,412	115.9
1938	42,079	108	12,802	90.1	29,277	123.8
1939	43,559	112	11,155	78.5	32,404	137.0
1940	51,676	133	5,302	37.3	46,374	196.1

Table A45 (continued)

	Total commercial		Vegetables		Chemical	
	1935–37 prices (1,000 T¥)	*Index 1935–37 = 100*	*1935–37 prices (1,000 T¥)*	*Index 1935–37 = 100*	*1935–37 prices (1,000 T¥)*	*Index 1935–37 = 100*
1941	41,375	106	4,601	32.4	36,774	155.5
1942	32,252	83	2,338	16.5	29,914	126.5
1943	17,821	46	4,208	29.6	13,613	57.6
1944	6,430	17	—	—	6,430	27.2
1945	1,377	4	154	1.1	1,223	5.2
1946	4,223	11	1,393	9.8	2,830	1.2
1947	20,202	52	7,799	54.9	12,403	52.4
1948	22,076	57	9,142	64.4	12,934	54.5

Notes and Sources: Vegetable fertilizers include soybean oil cakes, sesame oil cakes, peanut oil cakes, and other vegetable oil cakes. Statistics on the consumption of various types of fertilizer in physical units and in value are available from government sources for 1919–48. Before 1918 they are estimated by the author as production plus net import. In the case of soybean oil cakes, the availability estimates are further divided between usage as fertilizer and usage as feed. The fertilizers are aggregated, using their respective average unit value in 1935–37 as weights. The basic data used to compile this table are taken from Taiwan Government-General, *Taiwan Commercial and Industrial Statistics*, various issues, and *Taiwan Agricultural Yearbook*, various issues; PBAS, *Taiwan Trade Statistics for the Last 53 Years*; and PDAF, *Taiwan Agricultural Yearbook*, 1948, table 6-C.

[a] Less than $\frac{1}{2}$ the unit.

Table A46. Chemical Fertilizer Distributed, by Nutrients, 1932–64

	Index	Total Fertilizer Distributed (MT)			
	1953 = 100	Total	N	P_2O_5	K_2O
1932	52.3	58,425	36,971	16,154	5,300
1933	55.8	62,330	37,318	18,595	6,417
1934	70.8	79,169	49,852	22,309	7,008
1935	75.6	84,441	53,724	22,507	8,210
1936	92.8	103,660	67,224	28,198	8,238
1937	100.9	112,762	71,333	31,338	10,091
1938	102.4	114,483	77,285	28,120	9,078
1939	91.7	102,449	63,148	29,159	10,142
1940	74.1	82,822	52,195	25,540	5,087
1941	69.0	77,094	52,489	21,481	3,124
1942	56.4	63,007	51,646	9,477	1,884
1943	49.2	54,985	47,720	6,377	888
1944	19.0	21,243	18,650	2,199	394
1945	1.2	1,314	864	331	119
1946	6.5	7,255	6,330	924	1
1947	33.7	37,695	26,610	11,085	0
1948	28.5	31,820	23,734	7,900	186
1949	30.7	34,345	25,942	8,082	321
1950	56.2	62,832	48,708	12,790	1,334
1951	68.0	76,047	56,077	12,233	7,737
1952	90.3	100,938	66,118	22,452	12,368
1953	100.0	111,746	71,414	25,397	14,935
1954	109.3	122,151	81,177	26,343	14,631
1955	114.4	127,824	80,283	29,624	17,917
1956	122.1	136,453	86,830	30,433	19,190
1957	131.8	147,244	93,130	31,582	22,532
1958	141.7	158,408	98,007	33,476	26,925
1959	142.7	159,487	97,303	33,592	28,592
1960	125.3	140,042	86,107	27,703	26,232
1961	153.9	172,038	107,169	33,075	31,794
1962	162.7	181,798	117,324	31,804	32,670
1963	167.6	187,262	118,913	32,539	35,810
1964	198.6	221,979	141,604	37,772	42,603

Source: The data are compiled by the Plant Industry Division of JCRR, using data provided by the Taiwan Fertilizer Co., the Kaohsiung Ammonium Sulphate Factory, the Moa-hua Urea Co., the Taiwan Food Bureau, and the Taiwan Súgar Company.

Table A47. Price of Rice, 1924–72 (OT$/100 kg before 1949; NT$/100 kg since 1949)

	Farm price for paddy rice		Wholesale price of brown rice[a]		Retail price of polished rice[a]		Official purchase price of paddy rice[c]
	Ponlai	Chailai	Ponlai	Chailai	Ponlai	Chailai	
1924	—	—	21.60	15.53	—	18.5	—
1925	—	—	21.72	17.83	—	20.7	—
1926	—	—	18.67	16.52	—	19.8	—
1927	—	—	17.27	13.38	—	17.3	—
1928	—	—	14.48	13.83	—	17.2	—
1929	—	—	15.13	13.38	19.5	18.3	—
1930	—	—	12.93	10.53	17.3	15.3	—
1931	—	—	8.92	7.17	11.7	10.5	—
1932	—	—	12.00	10.88	13.5	13.7	—
1933	—	—	10.17	10.93	13.7	13.0	—
1934	—	—	12.80	11.82	15.3	13.8	—
1935	—	—	15.82	15.58	18.8	17.8	—
1936	—	—	16.58	16.25	19.8	19.0	—
1937	12.99	11.10	17.12	15.23	19.8	18.2	—
1938	—	—	17.37	16.90	20.3	19.7	—
1939	—	—	19.87	18.98	23.0	22.5	—
1940	—	—	20.33	18.18	24.2	21.8	—
1941	—	—	22.12	20.03	25.8	23.5	—
1942	—	—	23.25	21.20	27.2	24.8	—
1943	—	—	23.80	21.83	27.8	25.7	—
1944	—	—	25.08	23.22	29.3	27.3	—
1945	—	—	160.83	157.47	205.0	193.0	—
1946	—	—	2,096.75	2,073.67	2,452.0	2,425.0	—
1947	—	—	6,137.33	6,084.32	7,178.0	7,116.0	3,450.00
1948	—	—	20,757.69	20,627.73	24,278.0	24,126.0	36,700.00
1949	—	—	30.04	29.47	34.0	33.0	26.00
1950	82.53	79.77	110.44	108.05	125.0	121.0	60.00
1951	83.80	80.72	117.51	114.30	133.0	128.0	80.00
1952	139.68	136.43	180.62	174.03	207.0	201.0	105.00
1953	219.44	215.43	285.73	279.11	329.0	323.0	146.00
1954	189.12	182.77	251.05	239.02	292.0	280.0	146.00
1955	200.59	194.04	270.18	258.20	315.0	302.0	156.00
1956	217.94	209.74	291.02	277.38	337.0	324.0	163.00
1957	234.36	227.65	310.45	300.10	564.0	340.0	174.00
1958	244.83	233.76	318.20	302.92	369.0	360.0	183.00
1959	258.28	248.55	365.52	298.57	397.0	378.0	196.00
1960	383.11	375.81	488.25	481.75	550.0	545.0	274.00
1961	409.43	397.96	520.35	518.88	599.0	586.0	286.00
1962	377.44	363.82	496.25	479.02	583.0	573.0	292.00
1963	392.78	378.38	508.97	496.88	592.0	576.0	298.00
1964	408.45	389.79	521.38	504.63	596.0	583.0	306.00
1965	413	389	531.78	513.62	603.0	583.0	312.00

Table A47 (continued)

	Farm price for paddy rice		Wholesale price of brown rice[a]		Retail price of polished rice[a]		Official purchase price of paddy rice[c]
	Ponlai	Chailai	Ponlai	Chailai	Ponlai	Chailai	
1966	415	394	536.83	513.93	612.0	586.0	327.00
1967	439	431	569.37	552.03	641.0	627.0	348.00
1968	463	445	598.78	532.37	685.0	681.0	371.00
1969	453	426	594.03	558.78	705.0	825.0[b]	389.00
1970	472	452	640.02	596.37	733.0	715.0	411.00
1971	465	443	620.51	583.13	761.0	719.0	439.00
1972	493	458	661.88	613.69	812.0	760.0	—

Sources: PFB, *Taiwan Province Rural Economic Conditions, Collection 4*, 1963, pp. 1–3; *Taiwan Food Statistics Book*, 1965, pp. 142–48, and 1973, pp. 142–48; and PDAF, *Taiwan Agricultural Prices Monthly*, June 1975, p. 14.

[a] In Taipei.

[b] An obvious misprint. The average price for second grade polished chailai rice in urban Taiwan was 6.88 NT$ per kg in 1969.

[c] Second crop.

Table A48. Local Wholesale Prices of Selected Agricultural Products, 1960–71 (Annual average in NT$)

	Sweet potatoes (feed) (kg)	Official purchase price, sugar (MT)	Sugar 2nd grade (kg)	Tea leaf (machine picked) (kg)	Banana		Chinese cabbage (kg)
					Domestic (kg)	Export (kg)	
1960	0.87	2,837	7.80	—	1.62	2.34	1.09
1961	0.79	3,035	7.96	—	1.52	2.51	0.92
1962	0.81	3,200	9.96	3.94	1.65	2.43	0.84
1963	0.96	4,397	10.68	3.46	2.02	3.49	0.79
1964	0.69	6,599	12.46	2.91	2.65	4.08	1.02
1965	0.89	3,955	9.59	3.36	1.99	3.79	1.02
1966	0.82	3,831	10.13	3.76	1.42	3.67	1.10
1967	0.91	3,831	10.68	3.85	1.29	3.44	1.11
1968	0.90	3,831	9.99	2.90	1.57	3.39	1.39
1969	0.80	3,831	10.10	3.82	1.24	2.93	1.62
1970	0.90	3,900	10.30	3.02	2.35	3.23	1.59
1971	0.78	4,000	10.74	2.95	1.57	2.39	1.43

Notes and Source: These figures are based on prices collected through Farmers' Associations and local markets in 55 townships. The annual average prices are the weighted averages of monthly prices with the monthly quantities sold as weights. The data are from PDAF, *Taiwan Agricultural Prices Monthly*, Jan. 1972, table 1.

Table A49. Indexes of Industrial Production, 1912–46 (1937 = 100)

	1912	1913	1914	1915	1916	1917	1918	1919	1920	1921	1922	1923
General	24.19	19.78	25.21	30.35	37.75	43.92	36.66	34.92	30.16	31.63	38.91	40.99
Mining	34.13	33.58	39.18	44.82	42.21	44.75	35.05	42.28	40.65	42.32	48.87	47.98
Total manufacturing	24.09	18.64	24.44	29.86	39.65	46.95	39.61	35.88	29.80	31.24	39.07	41.51
Private manufacturing	18.00	11.21	16.62	22.35	31.59	41.38	34.68	30.89	24.33	27.41	36.29	37.80
Total food	20.34	11.24	18.39	23.94	33.86	46.19	36.28	31.24	23.81	26.98	36.45	36.80
Sugar	17.43	7.10	14.97	20.69	31.87	45.47	34.16	28.97	22.16	25.09	35.01	35.28
Other food	43.48	44.21	45.64	49.74	49.68	51.88	53.15	49.29	36.97	42.01	47.88	48.86
Chemicals	9.54	10.76	10.47	19.00	27.57	28.66	33.38	33.81	27.53	30.55	38.96	45.64
Nonmetallic mineral	23.49	26.72	22.13	19.82	21.87	23.23	32.01	34.73	49.54	52.01	54.09	57.60
Textiles	13.16	15.21	14.72	13.23	14.30	14.00	15.89	15.70	12.83	22.79	28.84	31.56
Metal	0.00	0.00	0.00	0.00	0.00	0.00	0.00	0.00	0.00	0.00	0.00	0.00
Monopoly	140.89	161.02	174.24	173.68	194.28	153.61	134.09	131.45	134.54	104.56	92.32	112.60
Electric power	0.00	0.00	0.00	0.00	0.00	0.00	0.00	2.76	8.29	9.67	11.23	15.89

	1924	1925	1926	1927	1928	1929	1930	1931	1932	1933	1934	1935
General	47.46	51.26	54.02	51.94	60.35	73.28	70.15	69.70	80.47	65.52	69.25	87.70
Mining	53.01	57.53	71.43	79.91	66.68	74.02	60.95	71.51	75.45	79.41	88.75	87.15
Total manufacturing	48.63	52.47	53.20	48.81	61.70	76.54	74.84	72.16	84.62	64.66	67.16	89.78
Private manufacturing	46.01	49.75	50.89	44.86	59.77	74.94	73.51	71.49	85.03	63.59	65.54	89.28
Total food	46.15	48.71	50.98	43.56	58.28	77.34	79.21	78.76	95.24	64.93	67.09	95.53
Sugar	44.89	47.60	49.63	40.81	57.58	78.36	80.46	79.15	98.18	62.91	64.23	95.86
Other food	56.14	57.53	61.69	65.43	63.80	69.25	69.28	75.70	71.83	80.98	89.78	92.92
Chemicals	51.41	61.34	56.30	53.97	73.92	75.00	59.00	49.42	53.47	64.72	65.96	74.02
Nonmetallic mineral	54.59	54.75	65.88	71.88	72.64	81.07	75.17	72.78	72.90	81.37	84.20	93.56
Textiles	33.84	41.59	45.00	47.59	52.51	46.80	49.49	53.90	60.69	62.32	62.61	74.03
Metal	0.00	0.00	0.00	0.00	0.00	0.00	0.00	0.00	0.00	0.00	0.00	0.00
Monopoly	98.96	104.62	97.55	124.58	98.63	107.28	100.42	85.22	76.85	85.22	98.38	99.27
Electric power	16.93	18.31	20.55	23.32	25.39	26.25	28.84	30.92	35.92	41.62	48.01	60.28

Table A49 (continued)

	1936	1937	1938	1939	1940	1941	1942	1943	1944	1945	1946
General	88.07	100.00	104.41	134.91	123.30	110.65	121.85	114.40	92.63	35.20	21.07
Mining	97.23	100.00	98.87	109.41	111.91	111.75	87.05	83.43	64.86	29.16	31.62
Total manufacturing	86.47	100.00	104.32	139.20	123.96	105.59	123.37	113.52	91.36	33.16	14.73
Private manufacturing	85.51	100.00	104.41	140.94	124.81	104.72	122.81	112.65	91.49	33.12	12.16
Total food	89.54	100.00	99.79	137.83	112.69	83.89	108.35	99.37	84.00	32.03	11.02
Sugar	89.51	100.00	98.29	140.84	112.45	80.87	109.37	103.38	88.58	32.48	8.71
Other food	89.79	100.00	111.73	113.94	114.64	107.96	100.24	67.46	47.60	28.41	29.44
Chemicals	76.17	100.00	116.68	137.15	150.94	145.07	139.23	127.04	89.25	38.38	13.42
Nonmetallic mineral	102.81	100.00	95.87	121.31	118.49	127.18	138.49	149.57	152.96	47.79	56.36
Textiles	101.27	100.00	106.25	124.70	138.46	132.09	126.94	121.41	63.33	17.45	25.05
Metal	7.73	100.00	169.94	282.16	323.07	449.01	444.41	393.08	293.97	21.78	0.00
Monopoly	104.90	100.00	102.44	105.75	107.60	121.99	133.78	129.93	88.60	33.92	63.99
Electric power	86.53	100.00	120.03	141.45	143.70	178.24	190.67	206.39	181.87	78.93	81.52

Notes and Sources: These indexes are the work of the author. The group classification is according to the official classification used by the Government-General. The sources of the production data are as follows:

(I) Mining: gold, silver, copper, crude petroleum, sulfur, coal, and copper–silver–gold ore from Taiwan Government-General, *Taiwan Mining Statistics*, various issues.

(II) Manufacturing: (1) Food: sugar from Taiwan Government-General, *Taiwan Sugar Statistics*, various issues, and PDAF, *Taiwan Sugar Statistics*, 1948, p. 1. Canned pineapple, soy sauce, rice flour, starch, tea, noodles, and ice from various issues of Taiwan Government-General, *Taiwan Commercial and Industrial Statistics*, and *Taiwan Industrial Statistics*. (2) Textile: Cotton fabrics estimated by deflating the value index of cotton fabric manufactured in Taiwan. The value figures are from various issues of *Taiwan Commercial and Industrial Statistics* and *Taiwan Industrial Statistics*. The price figures are from PBAS, *Taiwan Province: Statistical Summary of the Past 51 Years*, 1946, p. 902. Gunny bags, for 1929–42, from various issues of *Taiwan Commercial and Industrial Statistics* and *Taiwan Industrial Statistics*; for 1912–28, based on jute production. (3) Chemical: Sulfuric acid, vegetable oil, fine camphor, paper, bean cake, calcium superphosphate, and combined fertilizer from various issues of *Taiwan Commercial and Industrial Statistics*, *Taiwan Industrial Statistics*, and USICA, *Taiwan Economic Data Book*, vol. 5, pt. 2, 1957, p. 165. Alcohhol, for 1913–36, from *Taiwan Commercial and Industrial Statistics*; for 1937 from DGBAS,

Table A49 (continued)

Taiwan's National Income and National Product 1955, p. 144; for 1938–46, based on the production figures of Taiwan Sugar Company and Chinese Petroleum Corporation as found in USICA, *Taiwan Economic Data Book*, 1957, p. 165. (4) **Building material:** cement, brick, Taiwanese tile, Japanese tile and lime from *Taiwan Commercial and Industrial Statistics*, *Taiwan Industrial Statistics*, and USICA, *Data Book*, p. 190. (5) **Metal:** aluminum ingot from USICA, *Data Book*, p. 209. (6) **Monopoly products:** Liquor, tobacco products (cigarettes, cigars, and tobacco), and salt from Hsien-wen Chou, *Economic History of Taiwan during the Japanese Period*, vol. 1, pp. 114–15, 121–26. Crude camphor from PBAS, *Taiwan Province: Statistical Summary of the Past 51 Years*, 1946, p. 1027.

(III) Electric power from Chou, *Economic History of Taiwan*, p. 102, and USICA, *Data Book*, p. 253.

The index was calculated in two stages. In the first stage the physical output series was grouped by branch of industry (sugar, other food, chemical, textile, and so on) and weighted by their gross value of production in 1937. In the second stage, to form a general index for manufacturing and a general industrial index (including mining, manufacturing, and power), the indexes for individual branches of industry constructed in the first stage were weighted by the value-added for these branches in 1937. The value-added data are from DGBAS, *Taiwan's National Income and National Product*, pp. 140–55. The weights used in the second stage to construct the general industrial production index are:

General		100.00%
Mining		14.77
Total manufacturing		79.47
Private manufacturing	75.53	
Total food	58.71	
Sugar	52.15	
Other food	6.56	
Chemicals	13.01	
Nonmetallic mineral	1.55	
Textiles	0.37	
Metal and metal products	1.89	
Monopoly	3.94	
Electric power		5.76

Table A50. Indexes of Industrial Production, 1946–62 (1954 = 100)

	1946	1947	1948	1949	1950	1951	1952	1953	1954
General (includes sugar)	17.0	22.2	37.1	46.2	50.6	59.6	75.3	93.5	100.0
(excludes sugar)	17.5	24.0	35.9	39.9	45.5	59.9	72.3	87.5	100.0
Mining	42.6	51.9	74.5	69.2	66.1	77.6	104.7	99.9	100.0
Coal mining	49.5	61.8	77.9	76.2	66.3	78.2	108.0	113.0	100.0
Manufacturing (includes sugar)	12.2	16.6	31.0	42.4	46.1	54.4	70.2	93.6	100.0
(excludes sugar)	12.1	18.3	28.5	33.5	38.7	54.3	65.8	85.4	100.0
Food (includes sugar)	12.1	9.1	32.4	66.1	64.5	50.4	77.2	118.0	100.0
(excludes sugar)	11.6	12.1	16.2	29.1	31.9	44.5	52.8	86.8	100.0
Beverages	25.3	28.7	40.6	46.8	56.1	56.2	76.5	90.2	100.0
Tobacco	28.3	24.4	34.0	35.5	56.4	65.7	79.9	88.2	100.0
Textiles	3.0	4.2	7.9	16.1	23.2	35.0	54.8	85.9	100.0
Wood and wood products	29.3	42.9	54.1	55.5	61.0	75.6	78.9	88.1	100.0
Paper and paper products	9.0	23.5	31.3	29.7	46.7	60.0	75.4	82.1	100.0
Leather	32.9	36.3	41.6	31.0	58.4	101.5	129.1	150.5	100.0
Rubber products	15.4	20.6	23.8	30.8	42.5	69.4	72.8	81.1	100.0
Chemicals and chemical products	16.1	23.5	42.6	41.6	51.3	72.9	80.4	91.9	100.0
Petroleum products	3.3	15.6	54.4	54.8	28.9	68.5	71.3	80.2	100.0
Nonmetallic mineral products	23.3	41.4	48.1	54.6	57.8	73.4	83.7	94.4	100.0
Basic metals	4.0	7.4	17.4	15.5	23.4	27.0	39.5	61.5	100.0
Metal products	13.8	19.9	22.8	33.0	31.0	42.5	37.3	60.2	100.0
Machinery	9.8	26.0	34.6	41.5	60.6	64.9	73.6	85.6	100.0
Electric machinery apparatus	4.5	6.2	8.6	11.7	18.6	28.1	40.4	64.0	100.0
Transport equipment	3.8	3.3	3.1	17.6	11.7	6.4	16.1	62.1	100.0
Miscellaneous	42.8	45.9	50.0	51.8	69.8	88.9	97.0	86.6	100.0
Construction	—	—	—	—	—	—	—	94.7	100.0
Public utilities	24.9	30.8	42.5	49.6	65.1	76.1	81.1	86.9	100.0

Table A50 (continued)

	1955	1956	1957	1958	1959	1960	1961	1962
General (includes sugar)	111.4	117.0	133.0	143.2	161.8	184.1	205.5	229.6
(excludes sugar)	109.7	116.4	131.6	144.1	164.5	190.3	213.9	244.1
Mining	113.5	120.0	133.4	143.5	154.6	174.0	183.3	203.0
Coal mining	111.4	119.4	137.7	150.2	168.3	187.1	200.1	215.0
Manufacturing (includes sugar)	111.9	116.7	133.8	143.2	164.1	187.0	210.7	235.9
(excludes sugar)	109.7	115.9	132.1	144.4	168.2	196.0	223.0	256.8
Food (includes sugar)	119.1	122.3	148.9	143.3	142.2	161.4	177.9	173.1
(excludes sugar)	111.2	123.0	154.6	152.6	145.7	197.4	229.8	252.2
Beverages	111.8	114.0	122.7	134.4	150.0	138.8	146.2	145.8
Tobacco	112.3	116.2	112.5	120.9	128.0	128.1	132.0	129.3
Textiles	104.8	98.8	109.7	106.4	130.6	145.8	171.5	191.2
Wood and wood products	102.1	102.6	111.7	147.4	153.0	170.5	245.7	298.7
Paper and paper products	116.3	141.9	167.7	193.2	242.5	277.9	300.7	324.7
Leather	123.4	154.0	162.8	183.8	145.4	167.0	199.2	189.4
Rubber products	103.4	95.0	116.0	113.1	126.2	156.4	184.0	444.1
Chemicals and chemical products	110.6	123.3	145.1	165.6	201.4	235.0	286.1	361.7
Petroleum products	122.0	123.6	135.8	144.9	165.5	190.1	200.0	216.9
Nonmetallic mineral products	110.6	128.0	128.8	170.8	186.4	234.0	261.9	305.2
Basic metals	97.9	115.9	138.8	148.4	191.5	232.6	244.8	240.9
Metal products	101.4	91.9	119.9	166.2	197.5	230.3	228.4	265.0
Machinery	120.9	114.4	148.5	147.3	181.1	214.6	187.1	207.7
Electric machinery apparatus	144.8	184.8	227.0	230.8	350.2	405.7	518.4	547.7
Transport equipment	122.5	97.3	140.1	274.8	460.5	409.9	253.1	475.9
Miscellaneous	94.8	104.9	91.0	94.2	97.5	98.5	104.8	114.2
Construction	137.0	99.0	111.3	167.2	111.8	127.2	121.0	133.4
Public utilities	107.0	117.6	129.6	141.0	158.2	179.6	199.8	222.1

Table A50 (continued)

Notes and Sources: These are official indexes compiled by the Ministry of Economic Affairs. They are computed on the basis of the Laspeyres formula with the 1954 value-added as weights. Monthly production figures for public enterprises were reported directly by the various enterprises; figures for private enterprises were supplied by the Provincial Department of Reconstruction. The index includes 160 commodities in the following categories: mining, 16; manufacturing, 137; construction, 4; and public utilities, 3. As a share of the gross value of production reported in the *General Report on Industry and Commerce Census of Taiwan, 1954,* the coverage of the index is as follows: mining, 99.9 percent; manufacturing, 75.9 percent; and public utilities, 100.0 percent. Construction data are confined to only the construction of buildings approved, completed, inspected, and accepted by city authorities. The value-added weights are from the *General Report on Industry and Commerce Census of Taiwan, 1954,* and can be found in any issue of *Taiwan Industrial Production Statistics Monthly* published before 1963. The above figures are from MOEA, *The Republic of China, Taiwan Industrial Production Statistics Monthly,* no. 66, Dec. 1962, pp. 4–7.

Table A51. Indexes of Industrial Production, 1961–72 (1966 = 100)

	1961	1962	1963	1964	1965	1966	1967	1968	1969	1970	1971	1972
General	49.9	55.5	60.6	72.5	86.2	100.0	116.8	141.8	167.9	197.4	238.9	301.0
Mining	79.0	85.7	88.5	94.1	97.4	100.0	103.7	103.4	104.3	104.3	111.0	115.9
Coal mining	84.5	90.8	95.9	100.3	100.3	100.0	101.3	100.0	92.7	89.2	81.7	78.0
Manufacturing	48.1	53.5	59.2	71.8	71.8	100.0	117.9	145.4	173.9	205.7	252.4	322.3
Food	64.9	62.2	67.8	85.1	85.1	100.0	104.5	107.1	116.3	123.9	133.8	146.5
Beverages	68.0	71.5	71.8	79.8	79.8	100.0	112.9	136.6	163.2	171.4	194.7	232.2
Tobacco	89.3	86.5	90.2	93.8	99.5	100.0	110.2	119.9	118.4	117.5	120.4	124.3
Textiles	52.4	57.9	59.9	67.9	78.9	100.0	127.2	162.7	210.9	277.4	354.9	412.4
Apparel processing	44.2	53.9	66.0	76.1	86.7	100.0	132.9	211.5	306.4	387.1	557.4	469.6
Wood and wood products	56.8	60.0	70.6	89.2	91.4	100.0	103.4	115.3	129.1	133.1	164.6	233.9
Paper and paper products	50.9	55.6	58.6	72.8	78.0	100.0	115.9	131.2	149.1	179.7	213.9	254.9
Printing	63.6	72.1	72.4	78.3	84.8	100.0	106.2	124.3	137.1	152.7	185.6	194.5
Leather	79.5	70.9	60.5	62.4	87.1	100.0	97.1	100.1	134.8	170.5	155.8	209.5
Rubber products	44.8	58.9	55.8	64.6	72.0	100.0	124.0	197.0	211.3	253.5	336.9	405.9
Chemicals and chemical products	28.7	36.7	44.0	69.1	89.2	100.0	118.7	135.8	149.5	162.1	191.1	239.4
Products of petroleum and coal	55.2	63.8	62.9	66.3	80.1	100.0	110.2	132.7	174.9	211.9	229.3	289.3
Nonmetallic mineral products	49.3	57.5	70.6	68.9	80.6	100.0	119.3	128.1	135.4	149.4	189.0	214.1
Basic metals	53.7	61.1	66.7	78.3	90.1	100.0	110.7	119.0	144.0	167.3	188.9	219.1
Metal products	52.5	56.6	68.2	72.4	83.0	100.0	113.5	109.6	140.6	147.3	131.6	155.4
Machinery	42.2	47.7	59.1	77.6	88.3	100.0	126.4	158.8	166.0	157.0	215.4	295.2
Electric machinery apparatus	19.0	23.4	30.4	54.8	78.2	100.0	144.0	329.2	470.4	610.3	806.4	1,391.7
Transport equipment	21.3	29.1	34.7	49.9	74.8	100.0	138.6	165.5	193.4	224.8	239.1	388.6
Miscellaneous	47.3	51.7	62.1	75.3	88.4	100.0	107.6	116.2	111.0	121.1	125.0	118.8
Construction	10.9	12.9	14.3	17.3	64.3	100.0	121.8	156.0	189.1	198.3	256.4	326.6
Public utilities	56.4	64.1	67.9	80.2	88.0	100.0	114.8	134.6	154.3	184.1	211.6	247.5

Notes and Sources: These indexes are compiled by MOEA using the 1966 value-added as weights. They are constantly under revision. The index includes 273 commodities in the following categories: mining, 15; manufacturing, 250; construction, 4, and public utilities, 4. As a share of the gross value of production reported by the *General Report on the Third Industrial and Commercial Census of Taiwan*, the coverage of the index is as follows: 78.4 percent for all industries, 91.8 percent for mining, 76.8 percent for manufacturing, 82.4 percent for construction, and 100 percent for public utilities. The above figures are from MOEA, *The Republic of China, Taiwan Industrial Production Statistics Monthly*, June 1969, pp. 10–17, and Apr. 1973, pp. 12–15.

Table A52. Index Numbers of Prices of Industrial Products, 1952–69 (1953 = 100)

	General index	Mining and quarrying		Manufacturing		
		Group index	Coal	Group index	Food	Beverages
1952	91.6	99.0	101.0	91.4	110.2	134.3
1953	100.0	100.0	100.0	100.0	100.0	100.0
1954	103.7	100.5	100.0	104.2	101.3	144.0
1955	119.3	110.2	107.3	120.0	128.3	151.2
1956	142.4	154.1	165.2	142.9	141.8	169.7
1957	161.5	193.3	219.7	161.5	175.3	192.9
1958	158.9	195.8	219.7	158.1	170.0	188.5
1959	168.7	197.2	219.7	167.3	161.4	170.2
1960	181.5	197.3	219.7	189.3	173.3	213.4
1961	178.0	198.6	221.3	175.6	180.6	229.7
1962	191.1	237.2	272.9	187.2	204.1	255.5
1963	209.6	248.6	286.2	207.1	272.1	267.6
1964	227.1	250.1	288.0	225.1	353.1	268.9
1965	225.1	279.8	328.3	220.6	295.1	288.9
1966	236.5	319.1	383.4	230.1	319.6	287.1
1967	244.4	361.5	442.5	236.4	336.6	301.0
1968	243.6	364.0	443.6	235.5	319.4	374.7
1969	246.2	379.8	458.0	236.3	324.6	377.2

Manufacturing

	Tobacco	Textiles	Wood products	Paper and paper products	Leather	Rubber products
1952	69.5	101.5	79.1	81.6	87.1	106.6
1953	100.0	100.0	100.0	100.0	100.0	100.0
1954	100.0	91.8	107.0	100.0	123.3	103.8
1955	100.0	121.8	114.6	97.0	107.3	129.4
1956	120.8	130.1	168.1	99.6	182.4	144.5
1957	127.7	127.6	238.0	114.8	175.8	142.9
1958	127.7	128.8	212.8	112.0	182.8	142.7
1959	133.7	164.1	200.5	120.7	205.5	151.0
1960	159.1	166.9	196.9	144.8	268.3	154.5
1961	163.7	159.0	153.8	149.7	278.0	156.8
1962	189.0	169.3	147.2	147.2	299.6	157.6
1963	200.2	180.1	149.2	135.2	248.7	155.2
1964	200.2	185.9	152.4	131.1	288.5	163.7
1965	200.3	183.9	196.9	130.2	310.1	162.8
1966	200.2	174.7	240.1	129.1	311.1	162.8
1967	200.2	172.6	251.0	129.9	311.1	162.8
1968	200.2	171.7	266.9	131.4	315.7	163.2
1969	200.2	169.8	263.2	142.6	342.3	163.0

Table A52 (continued)

	Manufacturing				
	Chemicals and chemical products	*Products of petroleum and coal*	*Nonmetal mineral products*	*Basic metals*	*Metal products*
1952	103.1	89.0	80.6	104.2	112.1
1953	100.0	100.0	100.0	100.0	100.0
1954	107.2	108.5	138.4	112.8	136.9
1955	113.4	151.5	153.5	164.6	188.1
1956	121.9	200.9	218.3	171.8	175.4
1957	126.0	217.3	207.8	196.9	206.2
1958	137.7	237.1	170.5	198.5	202.5
1959	148.7	292.7	199.5	197.0	205.0
1960	150.3	310.6	224.5	217.4	228.0
1961	155.7	310.8	181.6	216.3	193.1
1962	158.3	326.3	173.7	204.0	175.9
1963	155.6	352.1	170.2	205.0	177.3
1964	154.5	354.6	172.0	212.5	181.1
1965	157.3	388.3	185.1	219.7	182.7
1966	158.3	395.9	193.2	214.3	165.2
1967	159.0	398.5	224.6	210.2	178.3
1968	155.5	405.4	225.4	207.6	178.1
1969	154.4	412.6	219.3	209.9	192.3

	Manufacturing			
	Machinery	*Electrical machinery apparatus*	*Misc.*	*Public utilities*
1952	79.1	103.8	95.9	86.8
1953	100.0	100.0	100.0	100.0
1954	111.3	117.0	111.5	100.1
1955	125.8	142.7	111.4	117.1
1956	141.2	166.5	123.4	121.5
1957	149.0	170.1	158.6	125.8
1958	156.7	169.6	180.6	130.8
1959	160.5	170.0	185.7	159.9
1960	161.0	177.6	184.4	183.0
1961	161.1	179.0	184.3	191.0
1962	159.9	177.8	183.7	198.9
1963	158.2	175.6	183.7	214.4
1964	157.9	176.3	182.5	229.9
1965	154.3	190.7	176.0	239.9
1966	153.1	202.4	167.4	245.6
1967	153.1	172.6	168.4	241.4
1968	156.9	162.1	195.3	241.4
1969	160.9	174.3	195.3	245.3

Note and Sources: These official indexes were compiled by MOEA using the 1951 value of production as weights. The price data were gathered by PDOR. The prices of 98 commodities are included in the index: 12 in mining, 83 in manufacturing, and 3 in public utilities. The figures are from *Industry of Free China*, various issues.

Table A53. Availability of Main Building Materials, Selected Years

	Cement (1,000 MT)				Brick production (million pieces)
	Prod.	Import	Export	Avail.	
1906	0	10	0	10	—
1910	0	30	0	30	—
1913	0	62	0	62	76
1915	0	35	0	35	63
1920	48	21	3	67	126
1925	96	18	41	73	105
1929	128	46	17	157	192
1935	144	143	35	252	262
1939	224	122	2	344	309
1946	97	0	2	95	129
1949	291	0	17	274	265
1954	536	30	24	542	466
1959	1,067	8	115	960	567
1964	2,341	0	899	1,442	1,319

Sawn timber (1,000 m³)

	Prod.	Import	Export	Avail.
1906	—	66	0	—
1910	—	125	—	—
1913	—	125	1	—
1915	—	78	5	—
1920	—	137	14	—
1925	188	100	28	260
1929	166	246	25	387
1935	232	379	20	591
1939	321	422	32	711
1946	113	a	a	—
1949	247	a	a	—
1954	477	a	a	—
1959	818	a	a	—
1964	1,070	a	a	—

Sources: Cement: *Bank of Taiwan Quarterly* 9, no. 4 (1958): 20–21; 16, no. 3 (1965): 128. Brick: Taiwan Government-General, *Taiwan Industrial and Commercial Statistics*, various issues, and MOEA, *Republic of China, Taiwan Industrial Production Statistics Monthly*, various issues. Timber: Taiwan Government-General, *Taiwan Forestry Statistics*; PBAS, *Taiwan Province: Statistical Summary of the Past 51 Years*, and Taiwan Provincial Forestry Bureau, *Taiwan Province: Forestry Statistics for the Past 50 Years*. Trade data: PBAS, *Taiwan: Trade Statistics for the Last Fifty-three Years*, and Inspectorate General of Customs, *The Trade of China*, various issues.
a Cannot be separated from other wood products.

Table A54. Power Consumption by Industry (Million kwh)

	Total[a]	Irrigation	Mining	Industry	Residential and commercial customers
1952	1,076	18	65	734	259
1955	1,497	45	78	1,033	341
1960	3,136	64	177	2,304	591
1965	5,672	165	296	4,096	1,115
1970	11,964	231	474	8,537	2,722
1972	16,080	251	475	11,789	3,565

Source: CIECD, *Taiwan Statistical Data Book*, 1973, pp. 89–91.
[a] Excludes the consumption of power by Taipower Co.

Table A55. Overland Transportation: Freight Carried

	Railroad			Push car	Highway
	Freight distance of public railroad (net of mail and luggage) (1,000 MT·km)	Freight distance of other railroad[a] (1,000 MT·km)	Freight carried by all railroad (1,000 MT)[c]	Freight carried (1,000 MT)	Freight distance (1,000 MT·km)[d]
1900	3,785	—	114	—	—
1905	26,503	—	425	—	—
1910	88,026	—	2,591	225	—
1913	101,632	—	2,663	307	—
1915	143,846	—	4,869	563	—
1920	219,869	—	4,515	834	—
1925	386,050	—	7,671	803	—
1929	506,632	—	9,893	—	—
1930	507,627	—	9,339	694	—
1935	638,971	—	11,537	571	—
1939	908,189	—	15,358	470	—
1940	903,978	—	14,762	398	—
1946	334,071	36,995[b]	5,814	—	—
1949	793,066	88,510[b]	13,985	—	20,118
1956	1,647,250	148,896	23,615	—	155,360
1959	1,805,262	159,160	26,487	—	250,593
1964	2,179,452	184,296	29,025	—	520,990
1968	2,544,287	165,334	29,875	—	988,757
1970	2,476,758	153,865	28,419	—	1,363,548
1973	2,779,598	182,529	35,756	—	1,944,060

Sources: PBAS, *Taiwan Province: Statistical Summary of the Past 51 Years,* pp. 1164, 1174–75, 1178, 1180; *Taiwan Statistical Abstract,* no. 23, pp. 242, 244, 250–51; DGBAS, *The Taiwan Economic Indicators,* 1955, no. 2, p. 29; *Monthly Statistics of the Republic of China,* 1966, no. 3, p. 46; *Statistical Abstract of the Republic of China,* 1969, pp. 414, 424, 430; 1974, pp. 435, 445, 450.

[a] Railroads of the sugar companies, Bureau of Forestry, mining companies, and so on.

[b] Excludes military freight.

[c] Prior to 1946, includes baggage and parcel post. This represents the total freight carried by all rail lines in Taiwan.

[d] Freight traffic of private trucking companies only.

Total Manufacturing

... ...ring & ...ments by Size of Work Force

	Fewer than 5 workers but uses power	5–15 workers	15–30 workers	30–50 workers	50–100 workers	100 workers and more	Total
1930	3,261	2,152	380	107	124	85	6,109
1931	3,355	2,052	369	90	122	85	6,073
1932	3,596	1,969	388	95	115	98	6,261
1933	3,751	2,088	428	109	113	107	6,596
1934	3,837	2,122	433	138	111	108	6,749
1935	4,124	2,125	435	125	96	101	7,006
1936	4,740	2,210	520	157	109	110	7,846
Specific industry, 1933							
Textiles	17	16	16	5	1	5	60
Metals	35	48	14	1	2	1	101
Machinery	74	80	21	9	3	2	189
Ceramics	0	450	164	11	9	4	638
Chemicals	79	364	14	9	10	2	478
Wood products	93	157	11	3	2	1	267
Printing	22	81	17	12	3	2	137
Foods	3,378	622	119	34	70	85	4,308
(Sugar)	(0)	(3)	(58)	(11)	(13)	(37)	(122)
Other	53	270	52	25	13	5	418
Specific industry, 1936							
Textiles	33	19	9	11	3	6	81
Metals	44	63	13	6	2	4	132
Machinery	82	108	29	14	6	3	242
Ceramics	26	418	207	24	8	7	690
Chemicals	122	314	20	12	8	3	484
Wood products	161	176	22	5	13	1	366
Printing	28	100	22	8	1	3	169
Foods	4,168	758	154	49	49	77	5,255
Other	76	254	44	28	19	6	427

Source: Taiwan Government-General, *Collection of Factory Related Materials Based on Resource Investigation Statue, 1933*, pp. 22–29, and *1936*, pp. 22–31.

Table A57. Manufacturing Enterprises by Number of Workers Engaged, Census Years

	1961		1966		1971	
	Enter- prise	Worker	Enter- prise	Worker	Enter- prise	Worker
Total	51,567	454,272	27,709	589,660	42,636	1,201,539
1–9 workers	46,145	141,121	19,982	75,621	29,274	113,507
10–29 workers	3,872	63,985	3,726	50,275	10,785	126,429
30–49 workers	737	27,430	2,476	74,805	2,028	77,267
50–99 workers	426	29,052	754	51,176	1,600	110,785
100–499 workers	318	63,723	640	132,764	1,628	339,389
500 workers and over	69	128,961	131	205,019	321	434,162

Notes and Sources: The coverage changes slightly from census to census. See the introduction to this appendix for detail. The above figures are from *General Report, 1961 Industry and Commerce Census of Taiwan*, vol. 3, pp. 124–39; *General Report on the Third Industrial and Commercial Census of Taiwan*, vol. 3, pp. 751–94, and *The Report of the 1971 Industrial and Commercial Censuses of Taiwan and Fukien Area, Republic of China*, vol. 3, p. 428.

Table A58. Export and Import Volume Indexes, 1868–94 (1881 = 100)

	Export				Import				
	Total adjusted	Total unadjusted	Sugar	Tea	Total adjusted	Total unadjusted	Exc. Opium adjusted	Exc. Opium unadjusted	Opium
1868	26	22	38	4	26	33	14	26	35
1869	30	22	36	6	35	43	16	36	44
1870	51	43	82	11	41	49	22	47	49
1871	57	43	78	15	45	56	28	61	56
1872	51	49	82	20	42	53	18	30	57
1873	42	38	66	16	47	59	23	45	61
1874	54	54	88	26	54	69	26	59	71
1875	53	52	62	43	62	72	40	79	71
1876	85	84	115	61	66	76	45	70	77
1877	77	77	81	72	77	87	54	91	86
1878	73	72	55	83	72	79	54	70	80
1879	96	95	105	88	87	96	68	104	94
1880	133	114	143	94	93	99	79	101	99
1881	100	100	100	100	100	100	100	100	100
1882	95	88	83	94	82	79	82	82	78
1883	102	101	103	103	71	73	71	104	68
1884	112	112	131	102	63	64	63	81	61
1885	105	102	78	128	98	71	115	114	64
1886	94	92	53	126	89	81	103	104	77
1887	104	103	74	131	89	77	125	114	72
1888	118	115	88	141	115	85	176	114	82
1889	91	108	75	136	94	82	113	94	80
1890	118	116	97	134	108	92	141	128	88
1891	115	113	75	141	114	97	116	111	95
1892	123	116	82	142	119	88	150	89	87
1893	131	129	68	170	112	82	168	96	80
1894	148	139	101	160	100	70	173	113	64

Notes and Sources: The volume indexes are Laspeyres indexes with 1881 value weights. The unadjusted export volume index includes five export items: camphor, coal, brown sugar, white sugar, and tea. Together these five items accounted for 97% of total export by value in 1881–85. The adjusted export volume index is obtained by multiplying the unadjusted index by V/V', where V is the value index when all export commodities are included and V' is the value index when only the commodities included in the unadjusted volume index are included. This adjustment assumes that the prices of the excluded items move in the same manner as those included in the unadjusted volume index. The export index for sugar includes both brown and white sugar. The unadjusted import index includes nine import items: gray plain shirting, white plain shirting, T cloth, Japanese cotton cloth, English camlets, plain lasting, opium, hemp bags, and tobacco. Together they account for 75% of total import by value in 1881–85. The adjusted import volume index is obtained in the same fashion as the adjusted export volume index, by multiplying it by V/V'. Because the coverage is less complete in the case of the imports, particularly toward the end of the nineteenth century, the import volume index is more affected by the adjustment. The data used in constructing these indexes are from Chinese Imperial Maritime Customs, *Annual Trade Tables for Various Chinese Ports (Taiwan)*, various issues.

Table A59. Import and Export Volume Indexes, 1900–42 (1925 = 100)

	1900	1901	1902	1903	1904	1905	1906	1907	1908
General imports	32.91	34.40	34.77	35.78	31.93	31.21	35.78	32.68	40.82
1. Food and live animals	13.82	12.66	10.96	14.36	13.76	11.26	10.66	12.73	13.06
2. Beverages and tobacco	117.06	147.96	126.90	99.38	80.49	79.50	82.14	59.67	56.57
3. Inedible crude materials	—	—	—	—	37.85	36.50	48.63	36.62	40.81
4. Mineral fuels and lubricants	—	—	—	—	—	—	60.36	52.01	66.31
5. Chemicals	32.10	32.18	28.09	19.35	42.93	32.80	63.25	44.07	47.99
6. Manufactured goods	31.01	36.55	39.68	47.20	39.19	44.71	40.31	41.77	53.15
7. Machinery and transportation equipment	—	—	—	18.30	7.33	18.76	13.13	44.97	136.84
General exports (includes sugar)	13.54	14.46	18.15	18.39	19.65	20.96	24.63	21.94	28.49
General exports (excludes sugar)	19.54	19.25	24.17	28.09	28.45	29.70	32.12	29.09	39.66
1. Food and live animals (includes sugar)	11.70	13.19	16.62	17.14	18.66	20.86	25.17	21.01	29.21
2. Food and live animals (excludes sugar)	18.20	18.55	23.42	29.35	29.82	32.88	36.12	29.98	45.47
3. Inedible crude materials	52.64	50.79	74.18	65.60	68.89	58.46	57.37	62.82	52.27
4. Mineral fuels and lubricants	4.09	4.39	5.64	4.70	1.45	3.24	3.69	2.92	2.52
5. Oil and fat	53.06	67.98	46.14	60.32	75.67	58.24	58.73	91.70	99.89
6. Chemicals	—	—	—	—	—	—	—	0.00	0.61
7. Manufactured goods	0.93	0.76	1.42	2.41	3.69	3.15	2.83	13.15	23.79
8. Miscellaneous manufactured goods	—	—	—	1.48	0.17	1.43	4.63	6.33	3.38

Table A59 (continued)

	1909	1910	1911	1912	1913	1914	1915	1916	1917
General imports	39.06	48.70	57.50	62.08	57.50	53.12	54.24	51.35	54.67
1. Food and live animals	16.16	19.97	25.97	39.59	42.15	36.12	38.01	41.71	50.25
2. Beverages and tobacco	67.29	74.11	81.26	89.72	79.90	89.66	109.01	74.93	68.37
3. Inedible crude materials	40.45	56.86	89.39	85.81	75.09	59.44	58.12	47.57	50.94
4. Mineral fuels and lubricants	63.14	61.17	83.68	93.94	97.15	104.62	86.42	93.79	110.51
5. Chemicals	54.32	54.61	36.18	52.32	64.81	60.38	73.65	72.49	65.07
6. Manufactured goods	48.81	60.56	71.71	77.76	65.82	63.74	55.97	48.73	50.16
7. Machinery and transportation equipment	48.05	181.02	215.84	127.49	56.99	43.62	57.39	41.79	46.04
General exports (includes sugar)	36.10	38.97	43.98	38.61	34.46	36.41	49.03	61.62	72.72
General exports (excludes sugar)	42.65	37.61	36.80	40.59	51.04	41.50	51.22	55.34	58.96
1. Food and live animals (includes sugar)	35.58	38.36	44.22	34.93	30.16	31.72	45.03	57.46	70.89
2. Food and live animals (excludes sugar)	44.07	35.74	34.45	33.81	48.81	33.86	43.92	44.37	49.80
3. Inedible crude materials	96.44	95.36	83.13	125.20	114.29	125.51	129.05	161.71	117.58
4. Mineral fuels and lubricants	2.61	1.94	3.22	6.42	6.54	11.04	8.91	19.84	55.62
5. Oil and fat	81.08	130.13	116.14	75.24	81.02	79.78	91.58	112.72	89.08
6. Chemicals	0.75	1.08	2.60	9.55	7.70	8.87	26.80	47.42	63.02
7. Manufactured goods	29.30	32.19	52.25	68.94	83.31	83.99	105.80	89.37	95.02
8. Miscellaneous manufactured goods	1.03	0.82	0.82	2.74	3.44	3.62	8.71	23.48	26.13

Table A59 (continued)

	1918	1919	1920	1921	1922	1923	1924	1925	1926
General imports	51.95	65.25	67.80	73.63	73.36	68.20	76.44	100.00	109.91
1. Food and live animals	45.62	68.31	57.46	56.28	64.91	54.15	69.05	100.00	99.85
2. Beverages and tobacco	79.35	111.98	101.29	133.61	106.89	77.14	92.41	100.00	106.29
3. Inedible crude materials	58.86	79.00	86.41	94.19	104.90	99.00	91.49	100.00	120.89
4. Mineral fuels and lubricants	82.43	74.13	76.49	105.30	74.61	98.96	114.81	100.00	98.05
5. Chemicals	65.48	53.14	75.21	50.24	54.44	57.37	69.31	100.00	103.54
6. Manufactured goods	45.10	55.07	58.43	86.05	79.27	76.36	80.58	100.00	125.41
7. Machinery and transportation equipment	56.64	84.09	160.47	126.81	93.44	99.49	85.23	100.00	127.16
General exports (includes sugar)	61.80	60.62	43.74	51.43	64.21	73.34	94.27	100.00	105.05
General exports (excludes sugar)	57.70	54.68	38.85	47.24	52.11	65.13	90.46	100.00	107.66
1. Food and live animals (includes sugar)	60.96	60.69	41.93	51.49	61.80	73.09	93.75	100.00	103.77
2. Food and live animals (excludes sugar)	54.37	52.49	33.08	45.66	42.43	61.30	87.83	100.00	106.10
3. Inedible crude materials	84.78	79.65	67.53	30.98	85.32	91.41	106.05	100.00	106.29
4. Mineral fuels and lubricants	35.76	60.89	62.30	56.76	73.20	74.01	99.77	100.00	99.67
5. Oil and fat	65.45	64.67	78.75	142.64	85.82	122.66	103.65	100.00	174.06
6. Chemicals	65.94	50.59	30.44	49.34	66.93	72.09	105.36	100.00	91.88
7. Manufactured goods	90.06	53.11	49.07	53.88	80.56	51.70	81.49	100.00	130.08
8. Miscellaneous manufactured goods	16.36	9.77	7.92	24.93	48.26	34.96	43.60	100.00	103.70

Table A59 (continued)

	1927	1928	1929	1930	1931	1932	1933	1934	1935
General imports	123.38	126.51	139.14	136.08	146.40	151.32	141.30	163.14	179.42
1. Food and live animals	112.73	88.95	103.67	86.69	93.25	99.93	86.07	100.13	99.87
2. Beverages and tobacco	108.38	113.27	113.04	111.50	100.11	97.79	108.91	118.85	98.30
3. Inedible crude materials	118.09	150.26	200.43	166.02	192.59	187.11	171.72	148.66	189.27
4. Mineral fuels and lubricants	123.79	135.10	156.04	162.35	171.40	164.45	204.80	232.10	293.49
5. Chemicals	134.71	158.34	153.56	189.34	194.53	185.40	189.64	225.07	251.62
6. Manufactured goods	137.14	154.29	167.36	161.98	181.02	191.22	170.70	200.92	230.04
7. Machinery and transportation equipment	138.99	182.56	175.13	189.71	146.67	181.71	177.45	249.61	306.98
General exports (includes sugar)	106.14	113.42	129.01	122.43	139.88	155.37	134.37	160.62	180.48
General exports (excludes sugar)	115.36	100.74	102.64	91.34	112.17	126.89	137.43	171.98	165.41
1. Food and live animals (includes sugar)	107.33	115.15	132.27	129.51	149.28	168.20	140.40	169.16	188.16
2. Food and live animals (excludes sugar)	121.39	99.27	98.93	93.51	120.43	141.84	150.71	193.80	175.36
3. Inedible crude materials	113.70	139.52	135.76	112.87	92.88	106.35	148.92	149.34	125.94
4. Mineral fuels and lubricants	88.03	56.67	48.00	48.45	60.32	37.28	39.82	39.41	38.92
5. Oil and fat	130.64	161.80	191.66	145.77	126.15	145.04	90.54	107.52	199.64
6. Chemicals	86.06	101.25	123.90	90.58	81.11	102.53	107.16	95.99	132.34
7. Manufactured goods	103.39	97.06	115.05	72.44	82.66	67.86	73.27	125.68	225.23
8. Miscellaneous manufactured goods	63.99	87.84	112.76	70.23	198.95	152.02	199.14	252.76	160.58

Table A59 (continued)

	1936	1939	1940	1941	1942
General imports	194.02	186.44	171.93	157.18	142.48
1. Food and live animals	102.06	89.37	86.31	66.98	46.58
2. Beverages and tobacco	111.10	216.53	129.89	91.49	66.83
3. Inedible crude materials	221.20	—	236.19	209.89	83.91
4. Mineral fuels and lubricants	329.23	—	257.68	168.61	85.66
5. Chemicals	294.43	352.58	297.43	308.59	330.32
6. Manufactured goods	236.52	—	199.86	182.03	175.34
7. Machinery and transportation equipment	295.96	321.20	214.11	301.61	135.26
General exports (includes sugar)	182.74	243.23	196.59	144.62	147.25
General exports (excludes sugar)	174.69	199.26	173.61	126.34	107.85
1. Food and live animals (includes sugar)	190.53	232.59	176.64	135.79	144.97
2. Food and live animals (excludes sugar)	187.47	174.91	125.82	102.72	89.10
3. Inedible crude materials	179.39	—	239.07	135.65	65.35
4. Mineral fuels and lubricants	31.62	—	82.11	55.86	43.04
5. Oil and fat	110.59	190.79	131.48	87.40	65.58
6. Chemicals	130.45	287.84	331.88	255.94	262.80
7. Manufactured goods	224.03	—	557.17	314.89	311.25
8. Miscellaneous manufactured goods	138.55	196.25	177.31	.156.45	86.94

Notes and Sources: The volume indexes are Laspeyres indexes with 1925 value weights. For various well-known reasons it is usually impossible to include all individual commodities entering into trade in the construction of volume indexes. In compiling the above indexes, 35 export items and 56 import items are included. The included import items represent 41.4% of total import by value in 1910, 59.7% in 1925, and 43% in 1940. The included export items represent 96.2% of total export by value in 1910, 96.9% in 1925, and 77.5% in 1940.

Table A59 (continued)

The indexes were constructed in the following manner. The volume indexes (Q_i) of major commodity classes (i) are first compiled. The major commodity classes are those of the Standard International Trade Classification. Because the Taiwan data are not sufficiently detailed, an individual index was not constructed for each of the major SITC commodity classes. Q'_i, of course, does not include all items classified in the ith class. To bring it to full coverage, the assumption is made that the prices of items belonging in the ith class but not included in the construction of Q'_i move in the same way as the prices of those items included in Q'_i. On this assumption, Q'_i was brought to full coverage as follows:

$$Q_i = \frac{V_i}{V'_i} Q'_i$$

where Q'_i is the adjusted index for the ith commodity class and V_i and V'_i are the value index formed from total coverage of the ith class and the value index formed from partial coverage of the ith class, respectively.

A general volume index, $\overline{Q}'$, was formed by aggregating the separately adjusted group indexes (Q_i) using the value of each class in 1925 as weights. The weights are:

Export (%)	
Food and live animals	84.03
Inedible crude materials	4.40
Mineral fuels and lubricants	3.63
Oil and fat	0.98
Chemicals	2.69
Manufactured goods	3.34
Miscellaneous manufactured goods	0.93

Import (%)	
Food and live animals	40.89
Beverages and tobacco	4.71
Inedible crude materials	7.08
Mineral fuels and lubricants	2.67
Chemicals	13.35
Manufactured goods	26.66
Machinery and transport equipment	4.64

Because a group index was not constructed for each of the SITC groups $\overline{Q}'$ gives only partial coverage to total export or import. To bring $\overline{Q}'$ to full coverage, we again make the assumption that the prices of items in those SITC classes not included in the construction of $\overline{Q}'$ move in the same way as the prices of items covered by $\overline{Q}'$. Thus on this assumption

$$\overline{Q} = \frac{\overline{V}}{V'} \overline{Q}'$$

where $\overline{Q}$ is the adjusted general index, $\overline{V}$ is the value index formed by including all SITC commodity classes, and V' is the value index formed by including only those SITC classes used in constructing $\overline{Q}'$.

In 1937 and 1938, presumably for national security reasons, many import and export items were excluded from the published trade data. Consequently, indexes for these two years are not included in this table.

The data for these indexes are from PBAS, *Taiwan Trade Statistics for the Last Fifty-three Years* and Taiwan Government-General, *The Annual Taiwan Trade Statistics*, various issues.

Table A60. Old Export and Import Volume Indexes, 1952–62

	1952	1953	1954	1955	1956	1957	1958	1959	1960	1961	1962
Export											
General index	59.35	94.88	61.58	76.42	73.87	86.04	104.95	98.94	97.08	100.00	91.51
Food	61.80	95.17	64.25	81.33	83.29	91.16	107.49	102.82	100.48	100.00	88.04
Manufactured articles	36.01	47.61	30.92	30.91	41.90	46.60	94.17	61.47	129.07	100.00	133.99
Raw materials	64.90	77.77	87.63	79.72	70.76	67.00	95.11	101.73	102.75	100.00	98.76
Fuel	5.36	87.44	42.47	19.61	44.32	12.56	12.59	37.74	79.27	100.00	86.23
Import											
General index	53.66	66.27	69.65	64.76	62.31	67.31	75.10	83.04	91.89	100.00	86.52
Food	94.71	106.83	139.69	105.49	112.61	84.53	118.82	91.58	150.18	100.00	143.77
Beverages and tobacco	63.20	38.05	50.78	70.06	87.01	81.48	36.07	111.97	103.49	100.00	119.02
Crude materials	32.52	53.30	57.27	55.14	54.00	65.10	58.86	62.33	91.26	100.00	76.13
Mineral fuels and lubricants	26.04	52.62	31.32	59.71	41.16	72.24	53.72	55.11	81.10	100.00	98.45
Animal and vegetable oils and fats	51.76	45.18	57.87	58.35	59.30	60.57	53.77	92.08	100.83	100.00	88.27
Chemicals	93.41	68.87	99.28	86.96	87.33	70.39	133.81	148.21	112.38	100.00	112.79
Manufactured goods by materials	99.97	109.96	99.40	78.26	69.55	65.17	38.67	77.44	87.92	100.00	98.09
Machinery and transport equipment	37.95	66.37	55.04	54.42	53.46	77.51	80.86	111.47	82.64	100.00	57.01
Miscellaneous manufactured articles	43.96	62.87	64.73	62.95	81.60	70.81	71.01	76.66	76.33	100.00	80.19

Notes and Source: The export index includes 28 export items, and the import index about 100 import items. Both are arranged according to the classification suggested by the United Nations Statistical Commission. The figures are from DGBAS, *Statistical Abstract of the Republic of China,* various issues.

Table A61. New Export and Import Volume Indexes, 1961–73

	1961	1962	1963	1964	1965	1966	1967
Export							
General index	39.39	44.84	55.56	73.03	120.18	100.00	116.09
Agric., forestry, hunting, & fish. products	33.04	30.00	28.64	65.88	91.34	100.00	101.48
Minerals	245.64	169.74	165.18	191.48	126.23	100.00	109.09
Food, bev., & tobacco	56.26	56.65	71.83	88.12	104.21	100.00	98.13
Prods. of textile, leather, & wood	32.18	46.47	58.27	75.08	80.51	100.00	132.69
Nonmetallic products	39.31	62.01	82.19	85.86	64.87	100.00	118.52
Chem. & chem. & pharmaceutical products	58.05	79.35	80.68	97.30	104.71	100.00	120.89
Basic metals	45.70	46.48	70.13	74.08	74.49	100.00	108.85
Metal products	26.62	35.70	46.61	72.89	79.96	100.00	129.66
Misc. mfg. products	3.69	9.17	17.71	47.93	62.01	100.00	146.47
Import							
General index	56.33	56.51	65.28	74.49	94.53	100.00	128.57
Agric., forestry, hunting, & fish. products	64.70	128.90	93.28	84.04	97.33	100.00	145.63
Minerals	51.55	43.73	53.44	54.92	60.26	100.00	72.59
Food, bev., & tobacco	136.61	74.62	57.81	126.64	95.01	100.00	136.18
Prods. of textile, leather, & wood	46.40	45.14	77.65	83.77	85.36	100.00	121.05
Nonmetallic products	46.19	67.01	54.44	73.03	84.42	100.00	182.06
Chem. & chem. & pharmaceutical products	64.66	74.62	64.73	101.60	109.55	100.00	123.81
Basic metals	41.32	44.63	55.02	68.07	98.46	100.00	111.36
Metal products	52.67	50.45	45.99	56.31	98.94	100.00	145.55
Misc. mfg. products	61.01	63.34	59.32	76.23	94.99	100.00	130.03

Table A61 (continued)

	1968	1969	1970	1971	1972	1973
Export						
General index	142.40	181.64	239.32	325.22	436.75	527.77
Agric., forestry, hunting, & fish. products	96.78	112.41	107.06	156.88	154.35	198.40
Minerals	108.79	85.75	50.71	30.92	35.13	105.41
Food, bev., & tobacco	104.00	103.35	96.43	106.86	123.29	148.06
Prods. of textile, leather, & wood	183.16	252.77	381.25	536.47	693.40	685.81
Nonmetallic products	106.98	99.72	117.93	131.31	209.87	237.55
Chem. & chem. & pharmaceutical products	99.65	123.51	145.45	172.61	187.19	186.46
Basic metals	97.43	152.12	273.60	275.07	416.44	536.12
Metal products	216.95	316.29	452.03	613.05	1,211.66	1,900.97
Misc. mfg. products	314.74	597.01	835.38	1,217.95	2,145.72	3,762.80
Import						
General index	144.89	194.44	239.72	273.02	331.98	388.02
Agric., forestry, hunting, & fish. products	188.22	237.65	300.39	296.10	457.10	491.94
Minerals	117.96	132.10	164.80	163.94	393.14	250.72
Food, bev., & tobacco	143.82	188.11	227.30	269.84	276.89	297.93
Prods. of textile, leather, & wood	138.68	185.18	253.80	341.64	298.07	391.26
Nonmetallic products	172.59	213.89	256.62	367.16	463.32	502.53
Chem. & chem. & pharmaceutical products	134.33	199.85	218.45	258.56	408.72	548.96
Basic metals	114.37	138.03	160.61	190.06	227.27	287.43
Metal products	147.19	206.43	234.47	259.20	297.91	349.85
Misc. mfg. products	153.27	183.80	238.10	346.17	428.00	574.31

Notes and Source: The export index includes 108 export items, and the import index 121 import items. Both indexes are arranged into 9 subgroups according to the standard commercial classification in use in the Republic of China. The figures are from DGBAS, *Statistical Abstract of the Republic of China,* 1974, pp. 230–31.

Table A62. General Export and Import Price Indexes, 1952–74

	Export	*Import*
1952	135.72	108.33
1953	120.38	98.04
1954	125.85	105.78
1955	133.00	108.88
1956	126.38	103.82
1957	139.11	107.81
1958	119.81	103.69
1959	108.83	97.05
1960	102.30	97.70
1961	104.13	94.91
1962	100.21	91.83
1963	126.84	96.24
1964	129.69	93.22
1965	101.25	95.13
1966	100.00	100.00
1967	102.92	100.71
1968	103.34	100.17
1969	107.73	100.21
1970	111.86	103.79
1971	114.49	108.52
1972	124.51	121.66
1973	147.85	149.81
1974	204.53	219.49

Notes and Source: These indexes, constructed by the Ministry of Finance, are unit value indexes. The number of items included, the weights, and the grouping of items were altered in 1963. Because of these changes, only the general index can be linked in a meaningful way. For 1952–62 the MOF import price index is a weighted average of about 100 items and the MOF export price index is a weighted average of 28 items. Imports were classified into 9 groups and exports into 4 groups. The old price indexes were obtained by dividing a value index by a volume index. In other words the Paasche formula was used. In 1963 these indexes were revised. The new indexes are still unit value indexes, but the coverage, weights, and formula have been altered. In the new construction, 131 import items and 118 export items are arranged into 9 categories. The formula used is the Laspeyres formula with 1961 as the base year. During 1956–60 the NT$ was devalued in a number of steps. To account for this devaluation MOF adjusted its price indexes by the ratio of the official exchange rate in 1952 to the official exchange rate in the current year. The ratios for the years 1956–60 are:

Table A62 (continued)

	Applied to import price indexes	Applied to export price indexes
1956	.6316	.6275
1957	.6316	.6275
1958	.6316	.6275
1959	.4302	.4274
1960	.4302	.4274

The MOF index attempts to measure the movement of the prices of Taiwan's exports and imports from the point of view of the world market. Thus, the MOF export price index attempts to indicate the changes in the competitiveness of Taiwan's exports in the world market and the MOF import price index attempts to reflect the movement of the prices of Taiwan's imports in the world market. Because Taiwan possessed a multiple exchange system prior to 1961, perhaps the adjustment would have been more accurate had the effective exchange rate been used instead of the official rate in calculating the ratio. The figures are from MOF, *Monthly Statistics of Exports and Imports: The Republic of China*, May 1975, pp. 5–6.

Table A63. Taiwan Export and Import Classified according to SITC, Selected Years (Million T¥ before 1945; million NT$ since 1945)

	1900	1913	1920	1929	1939	1950	1954	1959	1965	1971
Export										
Food & live animals	10	40	173	227	463	525	1,269	4,161	9,322	13,205
Beverages & tobacco	0	0	0	0	1	0	1	5	77	115
Inedible crude materials	3	7	11	13	59[b]	29	58	277	973	2,343
Mineral fuels, lub., & related materials	0	0	11	4	10	3	15	53	76	373
Animal & veg. oils & fats	1	2	2	3	7[c]	0	1	6	28	4
Chemicals	0	2	11	7	23	30	54	186	735	1,464
Mfg. goods	0	3	7	8	15	4	37	897	4,501	20,624
Mach. & transp. equip.	0	0	0	0	2	1	1	25	780	13,803
Misc. mfg. articles	0	0	1	7	10	2	12	97	1,494	27,939
Misc., n.e.c.[a]	1	0	0	0	3	5	1	1	2	37
Total	15	53	214	270	592	599	1,451	5,708	17,987	79,906
Import										
Food & live animals	4	17	52	57	76	145	525	596	1,838	5,466
Beverages & tobacco	2	4	9	9	28	5	21	104	147	529
Inedible crude materials	2	5	14	19	71	77	795	1,669	5,714	15,248
Mineral fuels, lub., & related materials	1	2	5	5	1	22	112	588	1,107	3,580
Animal & veg. oils & fats	0	1	1	1	3	20	57	177	227	489
Chemicals	4	8	24	25	72	116	580	1,747	2,853	7,695
Mfg. goods	5	16	35	55	76	238	570	1,131	3,232	12,521
Mach. & transp. equip.	1	3	20	13	39	139	506	2,080	6,399	25,329
Misc. mfg. articles	0	4	11	18	39	23	117	299	712	2,813
Misc., n.e.c.	3	2	2	1	3	9	20	27	90	273
Total	22	61	172	204	409	794	3,304	8,420	22,296	73,942

Notes and Sources: Sum may not equal total because of rounding. The above figures are based on data in Taiwan Government-General, *The Annual Taiwan Trade Statistics*, various years, and Inspectorate General of Customs, *The Trade of China*, various years.

[a] Not elsewhere classified.
[b] Includes metal.
[c] Includes fuel oil.

Table A64. Distribution of Exports by Country: Selected Years, 1897–1968 (Million TY before 1950 and million NT$ after 1950)

	U.S.A., Hawaii, and Canada	Central and South America	Western Europe	Asia			Rest of the world	Total
				Mainland China	Japan	Others		
1897	1.2	0	a	9.9	2.1	1.7	a	14.8
1900	1.0	0	0	7.8	4.4	1.8	0	14.9
1905	3.4	0	a	5.0	13.7	2.2	0	24.3
1910	5.1	0	2.5	3.7	48.0	.5	.2	60.0
1913	5.7	0	2.7	2.9	40.4	1.5	.1	53.4
1915	6.2	0	1.3	5.0	60.2	2.8	.1	75.6
1919	7.0	0	1.3	12.8	142.2	10.2	4.2	177.8
1920	6.8	0	1.7	11.9	181.1	12.2	2.4	216.3
1925	7.0	0	2.0	27.5	215.2	11.2	.2	263.2
1929	4.1	0	1.0	18.8	238.7	8.6	.7	271.9
1930	2.8	0	1.5	10.7	218.6	7.4	:4	241.4
1935	5.7	0	1.4	17.5	314.2	10.9	1.0	350.7
1939	9.5	0	1.6	70.0	509.7	.6	1.5	592.9
1940	6.7	0	4.3	94.2	459.3	1.1	.5	566.0
1945	0	0	0	9.4	14.3	.3	a	24.1
1950	33.3	12.4	57.3	0	216.5	170.0	109.5	599.0
1954	79.3	20.4	88.1	0	737.5	381.6	143.9	1,450.8
1955	86.0	6.7	104.3	0	1,140.2	386.9	192.9	1,916.9
1959	522.2	4.0	320.0	0	2,369.1	1,614.2	878.7	5,708.2
1960	733.7	2.8	357.9	0	2,247.0	1,817.4	806.8	5,965.7
1965	4,228.2	84.0	1,840.3	0	5,504.6	5,083.8	1,257.3	17,998.2
1968	12,532.7	310.0	2,926.6	0	5,115.5	8,842.9	1,839.6	31,567.3

Sources: PBAS, *Taiwan Trade Statistics for the Last Fifty-three Years (1896–1948)*, pp. 4–11, and Inspectorate General of Customs, *The Trade of China*, various issues.
a Less than 50,000 TY.

Table A65. Distribution of Imports by Country: Selected Years, 1897–1968 (Million T¥ before 1950 and million NT$ after 1950)

	U.S.A., Hawaii, and Canada	Central and South America	Western Europe	Asia			Rest of the world	Total
				Mainland China	Japan	Others		
1897	.8	0	1.8	7.4	3.7	1.1	1.7	16.4
1900	1.5	0	1.5	6.0	8.4	1.2	3.3	22.0
1905	1.2	0	1.9	5.4	13.5	1.5	1.0	24.4
1910	3.1	0	6.5	5.8	29.1	2.1	2.3	48.9
1913	1.3	0	2.4	7.6	42.8	4.7	2.0	60.9
1915	.8	0	.8	8.0	40.6	2.0	1.2	53.4
1919	3.7	0	1.7	32.4	90.6	10.1	16.2	154.7
1920	6.2	0	1.0	33.2	112.1	13.5	6.4	172.4
1925	3.0	0	7.4	32.7	129.9	14.0	14.2	186.4
1929	4.3	0	11.2	31.8	140.4	15.1	2.1	204.9
1930	5.0	0	10.0	23.5	123.1	5.0	1.6	168.2
1935	3.2	0	5.0	30.5	218.1	5.2	1.1	263.1
1939	1.9	0	2.5	36.6	357.6	9.3	.7	408.6
1940	3.4	0	2.5	39.9	425.8	9.3	1.0	481.8
1945	0	0	0	4.8	16.7	.8	a	22.3
1950	170.5	.1	71.5	0	253.2	192.8	105.8	794.0
1954	1,580.0	10.6	280.9	0	1,105.0	189.5	137.6	3,303.7
1955	1,540.2	5.5	218.8	0	958.3	174.1	248.9	3,146.0
1959	3,076.6	8.7	818.3	0	3,396.6	483.4	636.2	8,419.8
1960	4,190.9	13.5	1,219.3	0	3,814.6	572.1	986.5	10,796.9
1965	7,347.5	616.1	1,887.0	0	8,874.9	1,600.1	1,970.5	22,296.0
1968	10,321.0	340.6	3,561.3	0	14,500.6	3,429.7	4,068.3	36,221.5

Sources: **PBAS**, *Taiwan Trade Statistics for the Last Fifty-three Years, (1896–1948),* pp. 4–11, and Inspectorate General of Customs, *The Trade of China,* various issues.
[a] Less than 50,000 T¥.

Table A66. Major Changes in Official Exchange Rates (NT$ per US$)

Effective date of change	Rates for exports				Rates for imports				
	Exports by government enterprises			Exports by private enterprises	Imports by government and government enterprises	U.S. aid imports		Imports by private enterprises	
	Sugar and rice	Salt	Others			Basic raw materials and industrial project imports	Ordinary imports under commercial procurement	Raw materials and equipment for end users	Others
11 April 1951	10.25[a]			14.73[g]	10.30[a]	10.30		15.95[n]	
21 May				14.49[g]				15.69[n]	
1 Sept.	10.25	12.37[d]	10.25						
1 Aug. 1952	14.49						15.65		
4 Jan. 1953	14.49	15.55	15.55	15.55	15.65	15.65		15.65	
16 Sept.	15.55								
4 Jan. 1954									18.78[o]
29 May					18.78			18.78	

Table A66 (continued)

	Rates for exports					Rates for imports			
	Sugar, rice, petroleum, and aluminium	Salt	Others	Bananas	Others	Imports by government and imports by government enterprises whose prices are controlled	Other imports by government enterprises		
24 Aug.								18.78	18.78
1 March 1955	15.55[b]	15.55	20.35[f]	18.60[h]	20.43[j]	18.78[l]	24.78[m]	18.78	24.78
1 May						24.78		24.78	
10 Sept.	20.35[c]	18.55[e]				24.78			
1 July 1956		20.35		23.95					
1 Sept.				25.55[i]					
27 Oct.				26.35	28.99				
1 June 1957									38.58
8 July				26.35	26.35[k]			24.88[p]	32.28[q]

Table A66 (continued)

	Rates for exports			Rates for imports			
	Sugar and rice	Salt	Others	Essential machines,[y] fertilizer, and crude oil for domestic use	Wheat and beans	Raw cotton	Others
14 April 1958	24.58[r]		36.08[s]	24.78[r]			36.38[z]
5 July–20 Nov.			36.28–39.78[t]				36.48–39.98[t]
21 Nov.–31 Dec.	36.08		36.38–37.88[u]	36.38			36.58–38.08[u]
1 Jan.–9 Aug. 1959	36.08	37.08–42.38[v]					37.28–42.58[v]
10 Aug. 1959–29 Feb. 1960		37.70–40.10[w]	37.70–40.10[w]	36.38		40.03[a']	37.70–40.10[w]
1–31 March 1960		39.97–40.07[w]	39.97–40.07[w]				39.97–40.07[w]
1 April–30 June		39.90–40.06[w]	39.90–40.06[w]	36.38	40.03		39.90–40.06[w]
1 July 1960–29 Sept. 1963	40.04	39.60–40.05[w]	39.60–40.05[w]	40.03			39.60–40.05[w]
30 Sept. 1963		40.00[x]			40.10[x]		
16 Feb. 1973		39.90[x]			38.10[x]		
10 Dec. 1974		37.95[x]			38.05[x]		

Source: CBC, *The Republic of China: Taiwan Financial Statistics Monthly*, March 1975, pp. 78–82.

a Official buying or selling exchange rates.
b Official buying basic exchange rate.
c This rate was applied to sugar and rice beginning 10 Sept. 1955, to aluminum beginning 26 Oct. 1955, and to petroleum beginning 4 Jan. 1956.
d 60 per cent × $10.25 + 40 per cent × $15.55.
e $15.55 + 50 per cent × $6.00.
f $15.55 (basic exchange rate) + 80 per cent × $6.00 (official price of certificate).
g 20 per cent × $10.25 + 80 per cent × $15.85 (or 15.55).
h $15.55 + 50 per cent × $6.10–$16.80 (range of the market price of certificate).
i $15.55 + 80 per cent × $12.50–$13.50 (range of the market price of certificate).
j $15.55 + 80 per cent × $6.10–$16.80.
k $15.55 + 80 per cent × $13.50 (price of certificate quoted by commercial banks).
l $15.65 (official selling basic exchange rate) + $3.13.
m $15.65 + $6.00 + $3.13.

n Official buying or selling certificate rates (inclusive of exchange rate).
o $15.65 + $3.13 (defense tax).
p $15.65 + $3.13 + $6.10–$16.80.
q $15.65 + $3.13 + $13.50.
r Official buying or selling exchange rates.
s $24.58 (buying exchange rate) + $11.50 (buying price of certificate).
t $24.58 (or $24.78) + $11.70–$15.20 (range of the market price of certificate).
u $24.58 (or $24.78) + $11.80–$13.30.
v $24.58 (or $24.78) + $12.50–$17.80.
w Range of the market price of certificate (inclusive of basic exchange rate).
x Official buying or selling exchange rates.
y Major machines to be imported for Taiwan Sugar Corporation, Taiwan Power Company, and Taiwan Railway Administration, and machines to be imported under industrial projects specially authorized by government or U.S. aid projects.
z $24.78 (selling exchange rate) + $11.60 (selling price of certificate).
a' $40.03 (Taiwan Sugar Corporation selling price of certificate).

Table A67. Balance of Payments, 1924–39 (Million T¥)

	1924	1925	1926	1927	1928	1929	1930	1931
A. Goods and services	69.0	27.1	10.8	−12.8	3.2	13.7	34.4	39.4
1. Merchandise	120.7	76.8	68.0	59.8	57.8	67.0	73.1	75.4
1.1 Exports (FOB)	253.7	263.2	251.4	246.7	248.4	271.9	241.4	220.9
1.2 Imports (CIF)	−133.0	−186.4	−183.4	−186.9	−190.6	−204.9	−168.3	−145.5
2. Freight and insurance	−2.5	−3.4	−6.4	−5.8	−9.0	−7.4	−6.9	−4.7
2.1 Freight	−1.6	−2.1	−5.5	−4.2	−7.3	−4.8	−4.2	−2.4
2.2 Insurance	−0.9	−1.3	−0.9	−1.6	−1.7	−2.6	−2.7	−2.3
3. Other transportation	−1.1	−1.1	−1.2	−1.2	−1.3	−1.4	−1.4	−1.3
4. Travel	−1.9	−0.4	−1.4	−0.2	−0.5	1.3	1.0	0.6
5. Investment income	−40.0	−32.5	−33.0	−31.5	−25.9	−24.9	−20.6	−16.3
6. Government, n.i.e.[a]	−6.5	−7.5	−7.9	−8.6	−8.2	−9.9	−7.1	−10.4
7. Other services	0.3	−4.8	−7.3	−25.7	−9.7	−11.0	−3.7	−3.9
B. Transfer payments	—	—	—	—	—	—	—	—
8. Private	—	—	—	—	—	—	—	—
9. Government	—	—	—	—	—	—	—	—
C. Capital (except short-term funds)	6.7	34.6	15.6	21.6	39.7	0	0	0
10. Common stocks	3.6	2.2	3.2	19.1	0.4	−4.1	23.2	6.2
11. Loans and other securities	7.8	13.8	3.6	12.3	6.1	0.7	4.2	−20.7
12. Central government bonds	−0.6	1.4	1.9	−9.8	31.0	−11.6	−0.9	43.2
12.1 Japan	−0.6	1.2	1.9	−9.8	31.0	6.4	19.9	−3.9
12.2 Others	0	0.2	0	0	0	6.4	19.9	−3.9
13. Local government bonds	−4.1	17.2	6.9	[b]	0	0	0[b]	0
13.1 Japan	−0.8	17.2	6.9	[b]	2.2	0.4	[b]	−12.4
13.2 Others	−3.3	0	0	0	2.2	0.4	[b]	−12.4
D. Cash	−1.4	7.4	12.6	4.2	26.0	9.2	−16.6	9.3
14. Short-term funds	−1.3	7.8	12.9	4.2	26.0	9.2	−15.2	10.2
14.1 Inflow	10.4	21.5	26.9	34.2	57.2	40.3	29.6	36.3
14.2 Outflow	−11.7	−13.7	−14.0	−30.0	−31.2	−31.1	−44.8	−26.1
15. Monetary metal	−0.1	−0.4	−0.3	[b]	[b]	[b]	−1.4	−0.9
E. Errors and omissions	−74.3	−69.1	−39.0	−13.0	−68.9	−18.8	−41.0	−54.9

Table A67 (continued)

	1932	1933	1934	1935	1936	1937	1938	1939
A. Goods and services	22.7	34.3	56.7	56.0	65.7	80.9	75.0	119.9
1. Merchandise	76.2	63.0	90.7	87.6	95.3	118.1	89.8	184.3
1.1 Exports (FOB)	240.7	248.4	305.7	350.7	388.0	440.2	456.4	592.9
1.2 Imports (CIF)	-164.5	-185.4	-215.0	-263.1	-292.7	-322.1	-366.6	-408.6
2. Freight and insurance	-9.3	-11.0	-14.2	-18.2	-18.2	-25.9	-29.9	-24.3
2.1 Freight	-2.6	-5.5	-8.4	-9.8	-10.1	-17.4	-19.4	-5.0
2.2 Insurance	-6.7	-5.5	-5.8	-8.4	-8.1	-8.5	-10.5	-19.3
3. Other transportation	-1.3	-1.4	-1.4	-1.7	-1.8	-1.8	-2.0	-2.6
4. Travel	0.6	b	7.5	12.1	18.8	21.6	50.4	52.1
5. Investment income	-33.6	-12.3	-18.9	-15.2	-16.3	-15.8	-5.9	-47.2
6. Government, n.i.e.	-7.1	-6.3	-10.9	-12.0	-14.1	-18.0	-22.7	-44.7
7. Other services	-2.8	2.3	3.9	3.4	2.0	2.7	-4.7	2.3
B. Transfer payments	—	—	—	—	—	-6.3	-14.5	-17.6
8. Private	—	—	—	—	—	—	—	—
9. Government	0	0	0	0	-1.9	-6.3	-14.5	-17.6
C. Capital (except short-term funds)	-8.5	-5.9	-13.2	-17.6	-25.3	15.9	-27.9	-92.2
10. Common stocks	2.5	21.3	-2.2	3.5	-2.5	14.7	-6.7	-1.7
11. Loans and other securities	-10.7	-26.2	-4.5	-10.7	-0.7	1.0	-5.2	-9.5
12. Central government bonds	2.7	2.0	-7.0	-9.7	-20.1	0.5	-17.6	-68.9
12.1 Japan	2.7	2.0	-10.8	-9.7	-19.8	0.5	-17.6	-68.9
12.2 Others	0	0	3.8	0	-0.3	0	0	0
13. Local government bonds	-3.0	-3.0	0.5	-0.7	-2.0	-0.3	1.6	-12.1
13.1 Japan	-4.3	-3.0	0.5	-0.7	-2.0	-0.3	1.6	-12.0
13.2 Others	1.3	0	0	0	0	0	0	-0.1
D. Cash	-7.0	-7.3	-2.1	16.6	14.0	25.9	27.9	4.1
14. Short-term funds	-7.0	-7.5	-1.7	25.8	14.5	25.9	27.9	4.1
14.1 Inflow	146.1	153.8	231.2	257.3	231.3	205.9	269.6	330.9
14.2 Outflow	-153.1	-161.3	-232.9	-231.5	-216.8	-180.0	-241.7	-326.8
15. Monetary metal	b	0.2	-0.4	-9.2	-0.5	—	—	—
E. Errors and omissions	-7.2	-21.1	-41.4	-55.0	-52.4	-116.4	-60.5	-14.2

Notes and Sources: The table is based on data collected by the Bureau of Finance of the Taiwan Government-General. Unless stated otherwise, the merchandise data are from *The Annual Taiwan Trade Statistics*, and the nonmerchandise data are from *Taiwan Monetary [...]*. Details of the entries are given in the following notes:

Table A67 (continued)

Item 1.1. Exports include reexports. For 1924 to 1939, reexports are estimated to be:

	Million T¥		Million T¥
1924	1.5	1932	.9
1925	1.8	1933	.5
1926	1.8	1934	1.4
1927	1.9	1935	1.5
1928	2.4	1936	.4
1929	2.4	1937	—
1930	1.8	1938	—
1931	.4	1939	.7

In 1937 and 1938, presumably for security reasons, many export items were excluded from the published data. The export figures for these two years are therefore underestimated.

Item 1.2. Imports include reimports, taxable items accompanied by passengers, goods confiscated by customs, and goods placed in bond. The amounts of each of these items (in 1,000 T¥) for 1924–39 are:

	Reimports	Taxable items	Goods confiscated by customs	Goods placed in bond
1924	59	198	16	0
1925	20	176	11	1
1926	62	207	62	1
1927	819	282	15	7
1928	93	263	34	1
1929	531	248	90	3
1930	110	30	24	2
1931	10	85	1	5
1932	17	90	24	4
1933	43	70	15	2
1934	7	113	22	4
1935	6	125	0	0
1936	173	289	0	0
1937	—	—	—	—
1938	—	—	—	—
1939	133	0	0	0

Table A67 (continued)

In 1937 and 1938, presumably for security reasons, many import items were excluded from the published data. Thus the import figures for these two years are underestimated.

Item 3. Since nearly all overseas passenger lines were owned and operated by Japanese companies, the total outgoing passenger fares are placed in this item. The data are from PBAS, *Taiwan Province: Statistical Summary of the Past 51 Years*, pp. 1202–03.

Item 5. Only the recorded flow of investment income is included in this item. No attempt has been made to impute income reinvested by foreign firms. Furthermore, most, if not all, of the foreign companies in Taiwan were branches and subsidiaries of Japanese firms, their transactions with the home office were of an intracompany nature, and many probably were not included in the government's records. Consequently one suspects that the outflow of investment income is underestimated.

Item 6. The spending of Taiwan government agencies abroad minus that of foreign government agencies in Taiwan. The personal expenditures of Japanese troops stationed in Taiwan are probably excluded.

Item 7. This is an undefined item listed in the records of the Bureau of Finance as "other current non-merchandise flow."

Item 9. No record of government transfer payments has been found for the period 1924–35. The figures for 1936–39 represent funds transferred from the Taiwan colonial government to the "Special Military Account" of the Japanese government.

Items 10–13. Because nearly all the major commercial and industrial enterprises in Taiwan were branches or subsidiaries of Japanese firms, many of the private capital flows were of an intracompany nature and some probably were never recorded by the government. Consequently the capital figures are not nearly so complete or so accurate as the figures for merchandise trade and some of the invisibles. The figures included in these items are only those recorded by the government. The credit entry of item 10 includes the transfer of Taiwanese stocks, the sale of newly issued stocks of Taiwanese companies, the sale of foreign (the term *foreign* as used by the colonial government does not include Japan) stocks and of Japanese stocks held by Taiwanese to nonresidents. The debit entry of item 10 includes the purchase of foreign stocks and of Japanese stocks by Taiwanese residents and the repurchase of foreign stocks by nonresidents. The credit entry of item 11 includes the sale of newly issued bonds of Taiwanese corporations to nonresidents and loans from abroad. The debit entry of item 11 includes the repayment and repurchase of Taiwan corporation bonds from abroad and the repayment of foreign loans and other securities by Taiwanese residents.

Item 14. The inflow consists of the following: inflow of foreign deposits, inflow of working capital, withdrawal of bank deposits, postal deposits, and postal insurance from Japan, return of working capital, and outflow of coins and currencies. The outflow consists of the following: increase of bank deposits, postal deposits, and postal insurance in Japan, outflow of working capital, and inflow of coins and currencies.

Item 15. This item represents the net flow of gold and silver bars.

[a] Not included elsewhere.
[b] Less than 50,000 T¥.

Table A68. Balance of Payments, 1950–68 (Millions of U.S.$)

	1950	1951	1952	1953	1954	1955	1956	1957	1958	1959
A. Goods and services	-89.3	-52.6	-98.9	-78.2	-130.2	-68.4	-104.5	-98.5	-127.2	-121.4
1. Export, FOB	93.1	93.1	119.5	128.6	95.9	127.1	124.1	148.3	155.8	156.9
2. Import	-123.9	-142.5	-208.3	-192.9	-204.9	-184.7	-222.1	-244.7	-273.5	-264.0
2.1 Financed by U.S. aid	-20.5	-56.6	-92.6	-84.0	-87.8	-90.0	-96.5	-98.8	-87.3	-79.7
2.2 Other	-103.4	-85.9	-115.7	-108.9	-117.1	-94.7	-125.6	-145.9	-186.2	-184.3
Trade balance	-30.8	-49.4	-88.8	-64.3	-109.0	-57.6	-98.0	-96.4	-117.7	-107.1
3. Nonmonetary gold	-50.8	0.6	1.9	1.6	1.3	1.1	1.4	0.9	1.3	-2.1
4. Freight and insurance on mechandise	—	1.3	-0.8	-4.9	-4.8	1.1	7.1	9.5	7.2	6.9
4.1 Freight	—	1.3	-0.8	-4.9	-4.8	1.1	7.1	9.3	6.9	6.7
4.2 Insurance								0.2	0.3	0.2
5. Other transportation				-0.5	-1.0	-2.2	-6.8	-3.1	-3.2	-4.2
6. Travel	-2.8	-2.5	-1.7	-1.4	-2.0	-1.0	-0.1	-1.8	-3.7	-0.6
7. Investment income	-1.0	-0.6	-0.3	-0.2	-0.2	-0.1	-0.3	-2.5	-0.9	-1.1
7.1 On direct investment								-2.1		
7.2 Other								-0.4	-0.9	-1.1
8. Government, n.i.e.	-2.9	-2.9	-7.2	-5.6	-12.7	-4.6	-2.9	0.7	-2.6	-8.2
9. Other	-1.0	0.9	-2.0	-2.9	-1.8	-5.1	-4.9	-5.8	-7.6	-5.0
B. Transfer payments	34.2	62.2	95.8	84.4	87.1	89.2	62.5	56.5	97.6	76.2
10. Private	4.0	2.2	1.8	2.4	-0.1	1.3	-0.4	0.1	14.4	9.8
11. Central government	30.2	60.0	94.0	82.0	87.2	87.9	62.9	56.4	83.2	66.4

Table A68 (continued)

	1950	1951	1952	1953	1954	1955	1956	1957	1958	1959
C. Capital and monetary gold	64.0	−11.4	1.0	−4.5	43.5	−23.0	50.1	38.7	19.1	45.3
Nonmonetary sector	3.7	−2.0	2.4	12.1	19.9	1.9	35.3	46.4	38.4	38.3
12. Direct investment	—	3.0	3.3	8.1	6.8	0.8	4.4	2.4	11.7	3.8
13. Other private long term	−4.1	−4.5	−1.2	2.2	−1.5	−0.4	−1.6	−2.9	1.8	1.7
13.1 Loans and credit received	−4.1	−4.5	−1.2	2.2	−1.5	−0.4	−1.6	−2.9	1.8	1.7
13.2 Import prepayments	0	0	0	0	0	0	0	0	0	0
14. Other private short term	0	1.7	0.8	1.8	3.9	1.0	—	9.3	24.2	23.8
14.1 Trade credits	0	0	0	0.6	3.2	0.4	−0.2	8.0	26.0	10.7
14.2 Loans received	0	0	0	0	0	0	0	0	0	0
a. Government enterprises	0	0	0	0	0	0	0	0	0	0
b. Private enterprises	0	0	0	0	0	0	0	0	0	0
14.3 Other assets	—	1.7	0.8	1.2	0.7	0.6	0.2	1.3	−1.8	13.1
15. Local government	—	—	—	—	—	—	—	—	—	—
16. Central government	7.8	−2.2	−0.5	0	10.7	0.5	32.5	37.6	0.7	9.0
Monetary sector	60.3	−9.4	−1.4	−16.6	23.6	−24.9	14.8	−7.7	−19.3	7.0
17. Commercial banks: liabilities	0	0	0	0	0	0	0	0	0	0
18. Commercial banks: assets	0	0	0	0	0	0	0	0	0	0
19. Central bank: liabilities	0	0	0	0	0	0	20.0	21.9	−7.7	10.3
20. Central bank: assets	60.3	−9.4	−1.4	−16.6	23.6	−24.9	−5.2	−29.6	−11.6	−3.3
20.1 Claims	12.1	−8.8	0.5	−15.0	24.9	−23.7	−3.6	−28.7	−10.3	−5.3
20.2 Monetary gold	48.2	−0.6	−1.9	−1.6	−1.3	−1.2	−1.6	−0.9	−1.3	2.0
D. Errors and omissions	−8.9	1.8	2.1	−1.7	−0.4	2.2	8.1	3.3	10.5	0.1

Table A68 (continued)

	1960	1961	1962	1963	1964	1965	1966	1967	1968
A. Goods and services	-129.7	-130.8	-124.0	-12.4	12.1	-91.7	-26.2	-70.9	-133.9
1. Export, FOB	164.0	196.2	218.2	331.7	434.5	450.8	542.7	653.7	825.9
2. Import	-286.5	-330.3	-341.0	-359.8	-407.8	-522.8	-585.6	-716.3	-900.0
2.1 Financed by U.S. aid	-97.1	-120.7	-97.8	-89.6	-53.3	-67.0	-36.3	-30.6	-19.8
2.2 Other	-189.4	-209.6	-243.2	-270.2	-354.5	-455.8	-549.3	-685.7	-880.2
Trade balance	-122.5	-134.1	-122.8	-28.1	26.7	-72.0	-42.9	-61.6	-74.0
3. Nonmonetary gold	-0.7	0.2	-0.3	3.7	0.4	-0.4	0.5	1.0	0.1
4. Freight and insurance on merchandise	8.8	9.8	10.1	10.8	-15.8	-21.5	-23.7	-27.1	-56.9
4.1 Freight	8.5	9.5	9.7	10.4	-12.6	-17.3	-19.1	-19.3	-49.9
4.2 Insurance	0.3	0.3	0.4	0.4	-3.2	-4.2	-4.6	-7.8	-7.0
5. Other transportation	-6.2	-8.0	-10.5	-3.3	-8.0	-6.8	-9.8	-8.0	-9.9
6. Travel	-1.1	1.2	0.7	3.3	7.7	8.8	16.8	26.5	48.8
7. Investment income	-0.5	-2.0	-2.4	-2.6	1.0	-2.6	-2.0	-5.3	-18.0
7.1 On direct investment	1.3	1.3	1.2	1.0	1.0	-2.4	-1.3	-2.7	-11.6
7.2 Other	-1.8	-3.3	-3.6	-3.6	0	-0.2	-0.7	-2.6	-6.4
8. Government, n.i.e.	-8.0	0.7	1.3	3.5	3.0	2.5	32.0	19.7	12.3
9. Other	0.5	1.4	-0.1	0.3	-2.9	0.3	2.9	-15.1	-36.2
B. Transfer payments	88.3	98.4	54.8	44.7	20.2	32.9	23.7	24.4	16.1
10. Private	5.5	14.7	14.6	14.1	12.1	15.2	18.2	26.2	15.3
11. Central government	82.8	83.7	40.2	30.6	8.1	17.7	5.5	-1.8	0.8

Table A68 (continued)

	1960	1961	1962	1963	1964	1965	1966	1967	1968
C. Capital and monetary gold	39.3	33.8	74.4	-35.7	-17.4	67.8	2.3	51.9	144.4
Nonmonetary sector	61.8	52.1	56.7	69.3	48.2	50.9	72.1	111.0	101.4
12. Direct investment	5.8	9.5	9.0	18.3	15.6	10.0	8.4	26.5	27.3
13. Other private long term	10.9	6.2	-4.6	-5.2	-2.9	13.7	34.4	111.4	52.1
13.1 Loans and credit received	10.9	6.2	-4.6	-4.6	-2.0	13.9	34.4	111.4	50.4
13.2 Import prepayments	0	0	0	-0.6	-0.9	-0.2	0	0	1.7
14. Other private short term	26.5	16.9	14.8	20.1	18.9	-4.9	40.7	-41.4	-13.4
14.1 Trade credits	11.8	-0.5	21.9	15.2	11.1	-2.5	19.9	-44.5	-21.6
14.2 Loans received	5.4	7.8	-8.0	1.0	-1.3	-3.2	4.5	-3.5	0.7
a. Government enterprises	0.6	1.7	-0.2	-0.3	-0.8	0	5.6	-4.5	1.6
b. Private enterprises	4.8	6.1	-7.8	1.3	-0.5	-3.2	-1.1	1.0	-0.9
14.3 Other assets	9.3	9.6	0.9	3.9	9.1	0.8	16.3	6.6	7.5
15. Local government	1.7	4.9	6.2	7.1	1.2	-0.7	-1.2	0.9	4.8
16. Central government	16.9	114.6	31.3	29.0	15.4	32.8	-10.2	15.4	30.6
Monetary sector	-22.5	-18.3	17.7	-105.0	-65.6	16.9	-69.8	-59.1	43.0
17. Commercial banks: liabilities	0.6	2.2	-14.3	21.7	21.2	3.0	-0.4	42.9	19.8
18. Commercial banks: assets	-0.5	-77.8	32.6	-75.9	16.3	21.7	-47.2	-53.8	43.9
19. Central bank: liabilities	-22.4	0	0	0	0	0	0	0	0
20. Central bank: assets	-0.2	57.3	-0.6	-50.8	-103.1	-7.8	-22.2	-48.2	-20.7
20.1 Claims	-0.2	59.9	-0.6	-43.3	-98.8	-7.8	-14.7	-29.4	-20.9
20.2 Monetary gold	0	-2.6	0	-7.5	-4.3	0	-7.5	-18.8	0.2
D. Errors and omissions	2.1	-1.4	-5.2	3.4	-14.9	-9.0	0.2	-5.4	-26.6

Table A68 (continued)

Notes and Sources: All figures, unless stated otherwise, are taken directly from *IMF Balance of Payments Yearbook*, various issues. Some points of particular interest concerning some of the items are provided in the following notes:

Item A.2. The valuation of imports has changed from time to time. During 1950–54, imports are recorded largely on a CIF basis. However, imports on which the freight and insurance are paid to residents are recorded FOB. In addition, some other imports are recorded FOB, and the freights and insurance on these imports are included in item A.4 since they are paid to foreigners. In 1955 imports are recorded mainly on a CIF basis, but freight and insurance on import paid to residents during the first half of the year are excluded. From 1956 through 1963, imports are fully adjusted to a CIF basis. Since 1964, imports are recorded on an FOB basis.

Items A.4.1 and A.5. For 1950–56, the item "freight and insurance on merchandise" was not separated from "other transportation." The IMF, through personal correspondance, made available the necessary data for separating "freight and insurance on merchandise" from "other transportation" for 1953–56. Comparable data for 1950–52 are not available, thus arbitrarily both items ("freight and insurance on merchandise" and "other transportation") are allocated to item A.4. It may also be of interest to note that, for 1957–68, "other transportation" can be broken down into greater detail in the following manner:

	1957	1958	1959	1960	1961	1962	1963	1964	1965	1966	1967	1968
Passenger fares	-1.3	0.8	-0.4	-1.3	-1.3	-2.3	-2.4	-4.0	-4.1	-2.1	4.5	2.4
Port disbursement	-1.9	-4.5	-3.0	-4.5	-6.3	-7.3	-1.4	-4.0	-2.2	-5.6	-12.4	-7.0
Others	0.1	0.5	-0.8	-0.4	-0.4	-0.9	0.5	0	-0.5	-2.1	-0.1	-5.3

Item A.6. The IMF figures until 1964 cover only transactions through banks but thereafter they also include tourist expenditures other than those recorded by banks. The Taiwan Provincial Travel Bureau has made estimates of tourist expenditures in Taiwan for 1956–67. With the exception of 1966 and 1967, we believe the TPTB's estimates to be more accurate. Consequently, for 1956–65, we have used TPTB's estimates of tourist expenditures in Taiwan instead of the official credit entries recorded by IMF. Had the original credit entries been used, item A.6. for 1956–65 would be as follows:

	1956	1957	1958	1959	1960	1961	1962	1963	1964	1965
Travel	-0.9	2.3	0.7	-1.2	-1.4	1.1	-0.8	1.3	4.2	4.7

Because Taiwan's tourist trade was not developed until the late 1950s or the early 1960s, no attempt is made to adjust the travel figures recorded by IMF prior to 1956.

Table A68 (continued)

Item A.7. Includes only actual and not imputed income. The most important item excluded is the undistributed earnings of direct investments in Taiwan, which became quite sizable in the 1960s.

Item A.8. Prior to 1957, contributions to international agencies were included in this item. Since 1957 a new methodology was adopted by IMF and such contributions have been entered as debits in "central government transfer payments." For consistency the data prior to 1957 have been adjusted accordingly using information provided by the IMF.

Item B.10. For 1956–65, this item can be disaggregated in the following manner:

	1956	1957	1958	1959	1960	1961	1962	1963	1964	1965
Personal & institutional remittance	−0.6	−0.2	0.5	−0.2	0.2	1.5	0.4	3.5	2.9	3.3
Donation in kind	0.2	0.3	13.9	10.0	5.3	13.2	14.2	10.6	9.2	11.9

Item C.12. This item does not include the undistributed earnings of foreign companies in Taiwan (see A.7).

Item C.13.1. The following breakdown of this item is particularly useful:

	1950	1951	1952	1953	1954	1955	1956	1957	1958	1959	1960
Loans received minus repayment from											
a. IBRD	0	0	0	0	0	0	0	0	0	0	0
b. IDA	0	0	0	0	0	0	0	0	0	0	0
c. U.S. government	−4.1	−4.5	−1.2	−1.4	−0.7	−0.8	−1.1	0	0	1.8	0.4
d. Export–Import Bank of Japan	0	0	0	0	0	0	0	0	0	0	0
e. Others (mainly suppliers' credit)	0	0	0	3.6	−0.8	0.4	−0.5	−2.9	1.8	−0.1	10.5

Table A68 (continued)

Loans received minus repayment from

	1961	1962	1963	1964	1965	1966	1967	1968
a. IBRD	0	0	0	0	9.6	17.6	5.7	7.4
b. IDA	0	0.2	1.2	2.5	1.4	0	0	0
c. U.S. government	0.8	1.6	1.0	-0.2	-0.6	-0.1	41.5	11.4
d. Export–Import Bank of Japan	0	0	0	0	0	7.7	30.5	15.6
e. Others (mainly suppliers' credit)	5.4	-6.4	-6.8	-4.3	3.5	9.2	33.7	16.0

Item C.16. The following breakdown of this item is particularly useful:

	1950	1951	1952	1953	1954	1955	1956	1957	1958	1959
Loans received minus repayments	0	0	0	0	0	0	20.0	37.7	-3.3	1.8
a. From U.S. government	0	0	0	0	0	0	20.0	38.3	0	2.3
b. Other lenders	0	0	0	0	0	0	0	-0.6	-3.3	-0.5
U.S. government holding of NT$	0	0	0	0	0	—	12.1	0.3	6.2	5.0
Accounts with IBRD, IDA, and ADB	0	0	0	0	0	0	0	0	-0.1	0
Import prepayments	7.8	-2.2	-0.5	0	9.7	-3.4	0.2	0	0	0
Other assets	0	0	0	0	1.0	3.9	0.2	-0.4	-2.1	2.2

	1960	1961	1962	1963	1964	1965	1966	1967	1968
Loans received minus repayments	9.6	14.4	15.2	30.7	22.2	40.7	19.9	2.3	-3.7
a. From U.S. government	9.6	14.8	14.4	14.4	8.8	25.1	9.7	1.9	-3.7
b. Other lenders	0	-0.4	0.8	16.3	13.4	15.6	10.2	0.4	0
U.S. government holding of NT$	6.5	11.0	14.4	2.7	-3.1	-13.9	-27.3	14.6	17.1
Accounts with IBRD, IDA, and ADB	0.5	-0.4	-0.4	-0.4	-0.9	-1.5	-1.5	-0.9	-0.8
Import prepayments	0	0	-3.3	-3.0	-2.8	7.5	-1.3	-0.6	18.0
Other assets	0.3	-10.4	5.4	-1.0	0	0	0	0	0

Table A69. Money Supply, 1900–42 (1,000 T¥)

	1900	1901	1902	1903	1904	1905	1906	1907	1908	1909	1910
Money supply	8,730	7,307	8,130	8,294	12,879	13,902	17,694	19,649	19,057	24,886	30,146
Currency in circulation	4,710	4,151	4,846	4,967	6,929	9,482	11,976	13,336	12,063	15,391	18,806
Bank notes	3,691	2,944	3,977	4,161	5,902	7,815	9,888	10,639	9,704	13,007	16,049
Coin	1,019	1,207	869	806	1,027	1,667	2,088	2,697	2,359	2,384	2,757
Demand deposit	4,020[a]	3,156[a]	3,284	3,327	5,950	4,420	5,718	6,313	6,994	9,495	11,340
Near money	4,691	2,708	3,040	3,215	2,931	3,227	4,080	4,588	4,443	10,695	10,622
Time and savings deposit	4,046	2,052	2,276	2,308	2,066	2,118	2,675	2,815	2,641	8,794	8,703
Time	4,046	2,052	2,147	2,183	1,998	2,045	2,537	2,659	2,439	8,554	8,459
Savings	—	—	129	125	68	73	138	156	204	240	244
Urban credit cooperatives											
Rural credit cooperatives											
Postal savings	645	656	764	907	865	1,109	1,405	1,773	1,802	1,901	1,919

Table A69 (continued)

	1911	1912	1913	1914	1915	1916	1917	1918	1919	1920	1921
Money supply	36,646	40,476	41,878	38,115	38,209	50,409	54,398	102,198	120,058	100,327	109,596
Currency in circulation	22,544	23,981	22,448	17,838	21,152	29,355	38,223	48,452	56,645	47,858	48,510
Bank notes	19,382	20,415	18,786	14,248	17,611	25,452	33,513	42,108	49,654	40,249	40,864
Coin	3,162	3,566	3,662	3,590	3,541	3,903	4,710	6,344	6,991	7,609	7,646
Demand deposit	14,102	16,495	19,430	20,277	17,057	21,054	16,175	43,746	63,413	52,469	61,086
Near money	11,378	12,213	11,180	14,393	16,407	21,044	37,099	28,552	35,675	43,678	29,074
Time and savings deposit	9,101	9,812	8,716	11,784	12,845	16,076	29,958	18,323	23,833	31,603	14,802
Time	8,797	9,465	8,254	11,217	12,323	15,041	28,537	16,088	20,745	27,870	10,040
Savings	304	347	462	567	522	1,035	1,421	2,235	3,088	3,733	4,762
Urban credit cooperatives											
Rural credit cooperatives		{—	84 —}	154	385	1,033	2,408	4,711	5,529	4,522	6,738
Postal savings	2,277	2,401	2,380	2,455	3,177	3,935	4,733	5,518	6,313	7,253	7,534

Table A69 (continued)

	1922	1923	1924	1925	1926	1927	1928	1929	1930	1931	1932
Money supply	102,968	115,026	128,469	133,211	126,275	142,581	142,407	128,121	114,082	121,626	144,153
Currency in circulation	41,269	46,829	58,844	61,779	57,426	61,767	63,686	57,050	46,858	50,638	59,053
Bank notes	34,244	39,703	51,260	53,186	48,640	53,602	55,713	49,241	39,904	44,414	52,620
Coin	7,025	7,126	7,584	8,593	8,786	8,165	7,973	7,809	6,954	6,224	6,433
Demand deposit	61,709	68,197	69,625	71,432	68,849	80,814	78,721	71,071	67,224	70,988	85,100
Near money	30,186	35,432	52,286	65,762	70,441	73,971	80,777	85,060	84,428	95,965	113,106
Time and savings deposit	13,673	15,176	23,278	30,657	33,318	30,972	32,523	33,273	33,737	40,092	47,330
Time	10,739	11,564	19,400	25,841	27,357	24,754	25,594	25,531	26,100	32,305	38,656
Savings	2,934	3,612	3,878	4,816	5,961	6,218	6,929	7,742	7,637	7,787	8,674
Urban credit cooperatives	8,342	11,724	6,402	8,423	9,523	9,958	11,207	11,632	11,777	12,759	15,299
Rural credit cooperatives			13,445	17,624	18,455	20,818	23,704	25,091	22,840	25,258	32,379
Postal savings	8,171	8,532	9,161	9,058	9,145	12,223	13,343	15,064	16,074	17,856	18,148

Table A69 (continued)

	1933	1934	1935	1936	1937	1938	1939	1940	1941	1942
Money supply	139,087	161,770	175,470	190,467	231,061	310,667	381,230	449,193	597,216	642,992
Currency in circulation	55,512	69,461	77,355	86,593	120,667	151,751	185,765	217,577	272,522	309,329
Bank notes	48,994	62,654	70,191	79,138	112,033	140,019	171,169	199,685	252,845	289,275
Coin	6,518	6,807	7,164	7,455	8,634	11,732	14,596	17,892	19,677	20,054
Demand deposit	83,575	92,309	98,115	103,874	110,394	158,916	195,465	231,616	324,694	333,663
Near money	119,974	146,024	155,545	190,419	187,800	238,186	326,377	366,723	401,556	505,235
Time and savings deposit	48,693	59,119	73,958	76,491	76,496	90,252	125,728	130,261	139,225	187,539
Time	39,282	48,800	63,164	65,235	64,819	74,187	100,434	96,037	96,030	132,057
Savings	9,411	10,319	10,794	11,256	11,677	16,065	25,294	34,224	43,195	55,482
Urban credit cooperatives	16,633	17,706	19,493	20,712	20,465	25,860	36,052	46,499	49,988	59,155
Rural credit cooperatives	35,441	47,832	38,412	67,291	63,732	87,235	120,382	134,046	140,457	160,959
Postal savings	19,207	21,367	23,682	25,925	27,107	34,839	44,215	55,917	71,886	97,582

Notes and Sources: Because both the Bank of Taiwan and the Huanan Bank had branches outside Taiwan, the data were adjusted so as to include data for only the branches in Taiwan. Further, because it was not possible to separate interbank deposit and government deposit from gross demand deposit, no calculations of net demand deposit could be made. The data are taken from PBAS, *Taiwan Province: Statistical Summary of the Past 51 Years*, pp. 1097 and 1135; Taiwan Government-General, *Taiwan Monetary Yearbook*, various issues; Taiwan Government-General, *Taiwan Government-General Statistical Book*, various issues; and Y. I. Chen, *Taiwan Monetary Statistics* (Taipei: BOT, 1953), pp. 153–59.

[a] Includes savings deposits.

Table A70. Money Supply and Its Components, 1949–74 (Million NT$)

End of Year	Money supply			Near money[a]
	Total	Net currency	Net demand deposits	
1949	293	192	101	—
1950	584	365	219	—
1951	940	559	381	—
1952	1,311	762	549	630
1953	1,654	918	736	822
1954	2,096	1,140	956	1,070
1955	2,523	1,368	1,155	1,290
1956	3,161	1,540	1,621	1,417
1957	3,740	1,896	1,844	1,982
1958	5,041	2,351	2,690	3,332
1959	5,486	2,572	2,914	4,515
1960	6,037	2,666	3,371	5,933
1961	7,231	3,076	4,155	9,501
1962	7,832	3,396	4,436	12,145
1963	10,060	4,127	5,933	15,510
1964	13,259	5,198	8,061	19,702
1965	14,695	5,779	8,916	23,431
1966	17,004	6,584	10,420	29,428
1967	21,875	8,363	13,512	35,512
1968	24,649	9,409	15,240	39,978
1969	28,584	11,015	17,569	48,544
1970	34,508	13,499	21,009	60,755
1971	40,914	16,681	24,233	80,749
1972	55,066	20,340	34,726	105,359
1973	80,938	29,002	51,936	128,199
1974	86,617	32,853	53,764	174,756

Source: BOT/CBC, *The Republic of China, Taiwan Financial Statistics Monthly*, various issues.

[a] Includes time deposits, savings deposits, and foreign currency deposits (excluding the amount held by government) with banks and credit cooperatives as well as all deposits with mutual loans and savings companies, farmers' associations, and the Postal Savings System.

Table A71. Selected Interest Rates, 1949–74

Year end	Demand deposits (%/yr)	Three-month time deposits (%/yr)	Unsecured loans (%/month before 1970) (%/year after 1970)	Secured loans
1949	16.20	54.00	—	—
1950	8.10	27.00	—	—
1951	8.10	27.00	—	—
1952	8.10	21.60	—	—
1953	5.40	16.20	—	—
1954	5.40	10.80	—	—
1955	5.40	—	—	—
1956	3.60	—	1.86	1.80
1957	2.88	10.20	1.86	1.65
1958	2.88	10.20	1.86	1.65
1959	2.88	9.00	1.74	1.50
1960	2.88	9.00	1.74	1.50
1961	1.44	7.20	1.56	1.35
1962	1.44	6.48	1.56	1.32
1963	1.44	6.00	1.38	1.17
1964	1.44	6.00	1.29	1.17
1965	1.44	6.00	1.29	1.17
1966	1.44	6.00	1.23	1.17
1967	1.44	5.40	1.17	1.11
1968	1.44	6.48	1.17	1.11
1969	1.44	6.48	1.17	1.11
1970	1.25	6.24	13.20	12.60
1971	1.25	6.50	12.50	12.00
1972	1.25	6.50	11.75	11.25
1973	1.25	8.00	13.75	13.25
1974	1.25	10.00	15.50	14.75

Source: CBC, *The Republic of China, Taiwan Financial Statistics Monthly,* March 1975, table 24.

Table A72. Net Revenues and Net Expenditures, All Levels of Government: Selected
    Fiscal Years (Million NT$)

	1950	1955	1960	1965	1970
Total revenues	1,683	6,685	12,111	23,384	51,214
Taxes	707	4,174	6,915	11,974	30,656
Revenues from monopolies	164	921	1,886	3,273	6,007
Revenues from public enterprises	89	250	1,144	3,109	4,937
Others	723	1,340	2,166	5,028	9,624
Total expenditures	1,954	6,534	12,193	22,391	49,153
General admin. and defense	1,451	4,154	7,371	12,055	23,977
Education, science, and culture	180	892	1,648	2,794	7,992
Econ. reconstruction and communication	94	556	1,387	1,816	5,619
Others	229	932	1,787	5,726	11,565
Surplus	−271	151	−82	−7	2,061

Notes and Source: These figures include both current and capital expenditures and all
sources of revenues, including receipts from bonds and loans. The figures are from
DGBAS, *Statistical Abstract of the Republic of China*, 1973, tables 83 and 86.

Table A73. GNP Deflator and Its Components, 1951–72

	1951	1952	1953	1954	1955	1956	1957	1958
Gross national product	32.79	40.98	50.09	50.78	55.97	61.40	66.74	69.52
Gross national expenditure	32.51	40.59	49.67	50.62	55.67	61.04	66.02	69.42
Private consumption expenditures	35.07	43.07	54.22	52.91	57.76	63.67	68.44	70.89
Government consumption expenditures	22.41	28.20	33.27	37.64	43.97	46.54	49.94	55.73
Fixed capital formation	37.90	42.45	46.06	53.35	62.84	73.57	85.43	89.95
Increase in stocks	39.15	43.83	53.48	54.28	65.82	74.70	73.93	75.03
Export of goods and services	31.99	32.13	38.17	41.92	51.28	55.33	64.33	71.53
Merchandise, freight, and insurance	32.28	32.28	38.21	42.00	51.61	59.68	65.50	71.77
Others	28.43	27.70	36.95	38.87	45.20	55.00	54.83	69.77
Import of goods and services	29.20	29.17	35.48	40.00	47.72	55.64	57.42	70.48
Merchandise, freight, and insurance	29.26	29.28	35.34	40.17	48.02	55.71	57.67	70.58
Others	28.43	27.70	36.95	38.87	45.20	55.00	54.83	69.77
Expenditures on gross domestic product	32.83	41.00	50.11	50.79	55.97	61.41	66.79	69.54
Net domestic product	32.28	40.59	50.64	50.94	55.62	60.51	65.65	68.59
National income	31.92	40.12	50.11	50.73	55.26	60.06	64.73	68.45

Table A73 (continued)

	1959	1960	1961	1962	1963	1964	1965	1966
Gross national product	74.89	85.30	88.75	91.12	94.27	98.62	97.58	100.00
Gross national expenditure	74.99	86.02	89.10	90.75	92.24	95.48	97.41	100.00
Private consumption expenditures	77.84	89.49	92.95	93.59	95.42	96.63	98.03	100.00
Government consumption expenditures	60.71	68.00	73.28	77.62	82.34	88.17	92.31	100.00
Fixed capital formation	94.36	100.09	96.78	94.97	93.27	97.67	99.78	100.00
Increase in stocks	75.10	87.88	92.74	90.23	96.71	99.54	96.74	100.00
Export of goods and services	85.37	80.98	90.50	93,83	108.02	110.45	95.29	100.00
Merchandise, freight, and insurance	84.95	79.85	89.41	93.24	102.01	111.35	91.71	100.00
Others	90.95	91.95	100.08	100.08	100.08	100.00	100.00	100.00
Import of goods and services	86.62	87.23	93.21	90.88	93.60	91.79	94.34	100.00
Merchandise, freight, and insurance	86.08	86.67	92.61	90.08	92.97	90.96	93.77	100.00
Others	90.95	91.95	100.08	100.08	100.08	100.00	100.00	100.00
Expenditures on gross domestic product	74.90	85.30	88.76	91.13	94.28	98.62	97.59	100.00
Net domestic product	73.56	84.14	88.11	90.68	93.78	98.45	96.51	100.00
National income	73.68	85.01	88.51	90.21	91.30	94.69	96.30	100.00

Table A73 (continued)

	1967	1968	1969	1970	1971	1972
Gross national product	103.27	110.96	115.92	119.36	122.21	129.61
Gross national expenditure	102.60	109.75	114.16	117.15	120.54	127.57
Private consumption expenditures	103.39	109.93	113.83	119.20	122.46	128.89
Government consumption expenditures	106.04	116.62	125.31	134.35	142.45	151.33
Fixed capital formation	100.95	104.37	109.34	105.44	107.39	112.82
Increase in stocks	101.88	102.38	102.99	103.81	103.39	105.16
Export of goods and services	103.81	104.99	107.50	112.03	114.56	122.01
Merchandise, freight, and insurance	104.40	106.11	108.88	113.71	116.38	124.51
Others	100.00	100.00	100.00	100.00	100.00	100.00
Import of goods and services	100.87	100.74	102.19	105.87	110.06	118.65
Merchandise, freight, and insurance	100.96	100.86	102.46	106.67	111.53	121.66
Others	100.00	100.00	100.00	100.00	100.00	100.00
Expenditures on gross domestic product	103.26	110.93	115.90	119.34	122.20	128.62
Net domestic product	103.31	111.44	116.53	120.62	123.66	130.21
National income	102.49	109.95	114.29	117.79	121.52	128.84

Source: DGBAS, *National Income of the Republic of China*, 1973, chap. 4, table 14.

Table A74. Wholesale Price Indexes for Major Cities, 1910–41 (1925 = 100)

	General index	Food			Yarns and textile material	Construction materials	Fertilizer	Fuel
		Total	Basic	Others				
1910	46.99	43.07	40.76	63.46	60.55	79.76	—	50.53
1911	54.50	51.96	50.57	64.25	65.14	79.23	—	53.41
1912	61.53	61.75	60.05	76.80	61.47	77.04	—	53.37
1913	60.07	58.61	56.65	75.94	66.05	82.20	—	56.60
1914	51.94	49.32	46.93	70.42	58.71	79.76	—	57.89
1915	47.09	43.47	39.46	78.83	58.71	78.37	—	52.59
1916	53.14	48.62	44.05	88.98	64.22	97.66	—	59.11
1917	71.57	61.99	58.87	89.56	115.60	125.01	—	75.72
1918	98.36	87.40	86.74	93.28	116.05	139.18	—	90.36
1919	129.86	116.35	112.69	148.59	235.78	140.38	—	118.93
1920	124.42	113.62	105.94	181.37	166.97	205.12	—	131.69
1921	89.11	81.52	76.95	121.82	120.18	134.51	80.55	108.36
1922	82.79	77.47	74.75	101.48	95.41	101.46	89.72	101.10
1923	82.30	78.85	74.13	120.41	88.99	96.09	86.50	96.78
1924	91.13	88.79	86.40	109.82	99.08	103.13	89.29	101.82
1925	100.00	100.00	100.00	100.00	100.00	100.00	100.00	100.00
1926	93.52	94.53	94.75	92.60	83.49	109.39	84.44	106.69
1927	81.49	80.89	78.68	100.36	78.90	95.40	73.42	104.90
1928	83.07	81.20	80.65	86.06	90.83	94.30	77.12	99.57
1929	81.97	80.85	80.13	87.16	81.65	97.97	77.84	93.85
1930	67.76	67.04	65.89	77.13	61.72	94.72	57.89	89.27
1931	50.68	47.69	45.37	68.12	54.04	87.42	40.94	75.25
1932	62.35	62.83	61.43	75.24	58.57	78.76	53.26	67.58
1933	65.16	64.36	62.28	82.73	67.79	76.88	60.26	71.29
1934	67.08	67.59	66.15	80.29	68.85	67.76	58.90	76.78

	General index	Food			Yarns and textile material	Construction materials	Fertilizer	Fuel
		Total	Basic	Others				
1935	80.41	83.78	84.12	80.77	72.48	71.43	71.03	80.33
1936	85.60	88.76	89.16	85.20	76.94	71.67	78.64	91.15
1937	86.76	87.59	86.91	93.56	82.43	82.47	84.07	98.08
1938	98.12	96.13	95.96	97.57	127.37	81.18	86.17	117.74
1939	118.19	115.26	116.71	102.50	152.29	98.54	107.81	141.89
1940	126.95	120.98	122.46	107.89	164.27	108.45	130.25	155.91
1941	137.00	132.64	134.90	112.68	168.67	138.55	129.00	153.14

Notes and Sources: The prices were collected by special collectors who were sent to selected wholesale firms in major cities and towns. The prices from five cities were selected to construct the above indexes. Cities were selected for their geographic importance, size, and availability of data. Yearly prices are averages of the monthly prices.

By using as weights the population of each of these five cities, based on the averages of the censuses of 1920 and 1930, weighted average prices for the island are obtained. The five cities and their weights are: Taipei, 41.71%; Keelung, 13.87%; Taichung, 10.06%; Tainan, 22.54%; and Kaohsiung, 11.82%.

The islandwide prices are then converted to price relatives with 1925 = 100. The price relatives are then made into general and group indexes using the total availability as weights. Total availability is defined as production plus import minus export. The weights of the various groups are: food, 69.66%; yarn and textile materials, 10.06%; construction materials, 5.38%; fertilizer, 11.32%; and fuel, 3.58%.

Prices for the five cities are obtained from Taiwan Government-General, *Taiwan Government-General Statistical Book*, various issues. Availability figures used as weights are estimated from Taiwan Government-General, *Taiwan Agricultural Yearbook*, 1926; PBAS, *Taiwan Province: Statistical Summary of the Past 51 Years*; and Taiwan Government-General, *Taiwan Commercial and Industrial Statistics*, 1929.

Table A75. Taipei City Retail Price Indexes, 1930–42 (1929 = 100)

	Total	Food	Luxury	Clothing	Fuel	Misc.
1930	88.7	84.5	94.6	80.7	96.5	98.0
1931	77.0	72.3	86.0	68.1	87.0	69.3
1932	78.8	78.6	84.4	69.4	78.8	65.9
1933	82.2	83.6	89.4	80.8	72.3	69.9
1934	82.0	83.8	88.4	84.0	74.5	64.7
1935	83.4	94.7	90.5	86.5	76.3	69.0
1936	86.4	102.4	92.1	83.9	78.8	74.8
1937	94.2	104.5	94.8	95.5	89.7	86.5
1938	115.3	100.2	99.8	156.0	120.7	90.9
1939	137.2	133.4	108.1	200.8	153.4	90.2
1940	155.2	160.5	116.8	201.2	165.6	116.7
1941	180.6	178.2	122.1	222.9	177.9	201.8
1942	185.7	197.9	125.3	224.5	210.8	168.4

Notes and Source: These indexes were compiled by the Bureau of Finance of the Taiwan Government-General. They are the simple arithmetic averages of the prices of the following commodities: food, 19 items; luxury goods, 9 items (including tobacco and alcoholic beverages); clothing, 4 items; fuel, 4 items; and miscellaneous, 3 items. The figures are taken from *Bank of Taiwan Quarterly* 5, no. 3 (1957): 238.

Table A76. Mizoguchi's Indexes of Consumer Prices, 1903–38 (1934–36 = 100)

	General	Food	Clothing	Fuel and light	Accommo-dation	Miscel-laneous
1903	49.62	52.18	47.30	60.12	39.69	49.42
1904	54.39	57.82	55.83	51.92	40.13	55.17
1905	57.19	59.51	60.46	49.29	45.60	58.79
1906	57.20	60.77	62.08	49.66	42.65	57.12
1907	57.41	61.20	64.00	54.90	42.27	55.37
1908	60.36	65.97	63.27	58.26	48.18	55.34
1909	64.37	72.63	59.44	56.01	58.76	56.39
1910	69.68	81.24	62.78	52.02	56.15	62.62
1911	75.28	93.17	64.03	53.45	55.63	62.88
1912	81.79	105.82	65.16	55.89	60.22	62.80
1913	79.30	101.49	64.90	57.62	67.47	56.68
1914	77.65	99.40	61.82	57.20	62.85	57.85
1915	72.94	89.33	56.54	48.39	63.16	61.39
1916	78.21	94.83	74.47	59.65	63.44	61.16
1917	96.37	117.64	110.55	70.33	76.97	65.59
1918	119.83	157.12	142.33	87.24	77.95	68.50
1919	148.78	193.21	195.58	136.70	88.18	81.70
1920	133.11	133.40	189.17	163.35	94.30	117.86
1921	117.74	112.38	137.80	148.89	88.49	126.03
1922	109.43	105.48	138.50	131.81	76.97	113.94
1923	107.44	101.78	146.65	125.62	73.32	111.53
1924	114.82	113.44	156.73	131.29	80.08	110.07
1925	119.65	119.99	156.32	137.62	93.63	110.07
1926	116.39	118.61	135.81	136.30	96.15	108.89
1927	109.23	103.36	124.71	136.94	105.47	108.46
1928	111.16	105.18	126.47	136.42	113.67	107.96
1929	111.86	107.20	120.75	131.53	122.95	106.17
1930	97.86	90.66	100.08	126.56	106.38	98.29
1931	88.43	81.29	91.20	119.98	95.07	90.38
1932	87.17	83.13	87.51	103.02	85.53	92.21
1933	91.79	87.55	96.86	98.16	89.60	96.74
1934	94.00	90.94	99.35	95.94	89.70	98.62
1935	99.92	99.89	99.63	100.39	100.96	99.48
1936	106.31	107.06	100.79	103.67	118.89	101.88
1937	112.84	112.14	108.05	103.41	117.97	115.79
1938	119.39	118.80	129.23	115.06	127.34	112.26

Notes and Source: Prior to 1929, wholesale prices were used. The prices were weighted according to the budgets of urban workers as revealed in a 1934–35 budget survey. These figures are from Toshiyuki Mizoguchi, "Consumer Prices and Real Wages in Taiwan and Korea Under Japanese Rule," table A.2.

Table A77. Indexes of Wholesale Prices and Urban Consumer Prices, 1950–74

	Wholesale prices	*Urban consumer prices*
1950	20.54	—
1951	34.09	—
1952	41.97	—
1953	45.65	—
1954	46.73	—
1955	53.31	—
1956	60.08	—
1957	64.42	—
1958	65.32	—
1959	72.03	58.95
1960	82.22	69.81
1961	84.88	75.31
1962	87.46	77.09
1963	93.11	78.77
1964	95.41	78.63
1965	90.98	78.58
1966	92.32	80.16
1967	94.65	89.85
1968	97.46	89.38
1969	97.23	93.91
1970	99.87	97.26
1971	100.00	100.00
1972	104.46	102.99
1973	128.34	111.42
1974	180.41	164.31

Notes and Source: The consumer price index is obtained by joining two indexes. Prior to 1968 the index was weighted according to the budgets of wage earners and salaried employees as revealed in a 1954–55 budget study. The new consumer price index, available since 1968, is weighted according to the budgets of urban consumers as revealed in a 1971 budget study. The wholesale price index is obtained by joining three indexes. Prior to 1958 it is a simple geometric average of wholesale prices in Taipei. From 1958 to 1967 it is a weighted average of wholesale prices in Taipei. After 1967 it is a weighted average of wholesale prices in Taiwan District, with 1971 transaction values as weights. The figures are from DGBAS, *Commodity-Price Statistics Monthly, Taiwan District, The Republic of China,* Oct. 1975, tables 24 and 25.

Table A78. Indexes of Prices of Industrial Raw Materials, 1952–68

	General index	Fuel	Metal	Nonmetallic minerals	Animal and plant	Chemical
1952	94.7	94.0	140.8	130.8	91.3	119.1
1953	100.0	100.0	100.0	100.0	100.0	100.0
1954	99.6	99.9	104.1	104.1	98.5	108.3
1955	115.9	110.7	172.9	119.2	110.2	115.4
1956	137.8	165.4	202.4	136.6	128.8	124.9
1957	162.6	207.5	249.6	166.1	150.5	132.9
1958	163.0	211.8	230.0	148.6	153.1	135.1
1959	191.2	221.8	223.3	166.3	189.0	128.8
1960	197.1	219.2	236.9	162.5	194.9	142.0
1961	186.5	218.6	222.0	172.1	183.0	137.8
1962	186.4	249.1	191.2	185.0	182.7	132.7
1963	189.5	259.3	186.4	182.9	186.4	121.7
1964	189.3	260.3	201.8	197.3	185.1	116.2
1965	193.3	286.3	208.1	189.2	186.5	118.9
1966	204.2	296.9	201.2	197.9	196.8	126.0
1967	205.9	363.1	198.4	198.5	195.3	128.2
1968	203.2	366.9	201.2	200.7	190.6	129.7

Notes and Sources: These are official indexes compiled by the Department of Statistics of the Ministry of Economic Affairs. The prices of 60 items are included: fuel, 4 items; metal, 12 items; nonmetallic minerals, 12 items; animal and plant, 20 items; and chemical, 12 items. They are computed on the basis of the Laspeyres formula with the 1953 supply of raw materials as weights. The above figures are from DGBAS, *The Taiwan Economic Indicators*, no. 38, p. 38, and *Statistical Abstract of the Republic of China*, 1966, p. 456, and 1969, p. 396.

Table A79. Indexes of Prices Received and Paid by Farmers, 1952–72

Old Indexes (1953 = 100)

	1952	1953	1954	1955	1956	1957
Prices received by						
farmers	74.21	100.00	92.08	101.82	109.94	121.81
Agric. products	71.98	100.00	88.86	99.33	105.58	117.75
Livestock	89.97	100.00	114.83	119.41	140.81	150.53
Prices paid by farmers	73.06	100.00	92.60	101.48	110.66	118.20
Intermediate goods	72.94	100.00	93.47	105.66	113.44	119.92
Daily necessities	73.10	100.00	92.23	99.68	109.47	117.46
Terms of trade	101.57	100.00	99.44	100.34	99.35	103.05

	1958	1959	1960	1961	1962	1963
Prices received by						
farmers	122.37	135.78	189.19	195.06	185.07	201.71
Agric. products	119.18	127.63	183.93	189.56	180.84	196.61
Livestock	144.97	193.48	226.34	233.98	214.97	237.80
Prices paid by farmers	119.51	131.66	178.08	186.14	183.37	187.33
Intermediate goods	124.67	135.85	175.94	188.88	189.81	191.34
Daily necessities	117.30	129.86	179.00	184.96	180.60	185.60
Terms of trade	102.39	103.13	106.24	104.79	100.93	107.68

New Indexes (1961–63 = 100)

	1961	1962	1963	1964	1965	1966
Prices received by						
farmers	100.65	95.84	103.07	108.59	107.47	109.79
Agric. products	99.86	96.74	102.76	107.18	104.95	109.45
Livestock	102.20	94.08	103.72	111.35	112.41	110.43
Prices paid by farmers	98.63	99.26	101.65	104.62	105.38	108.11
Intermediate goods	103.21	97.79	99.54	104.24	105.04	105.31
Daily necessities	97.54	99.26	102.31	104.27	104.97	108.71
Financial & other						
expenses	94.30	102.19	102.97	106.90	107.87	111.07
Terms of trade	102.05	96.55	101.40	103.79	102.00	101.55

	1967	1968	1969	1970	1971	1972
Prices received by						
farmers	112.56	118.26	115.19	120.43	123.98	130.83
Agric. products	113.53	115.75	116.01	123.77	122.02	128.69
Livestock	110.65	123.18	113.58	113.89	127.81	135.03
Prices paid by farmers	112.03	117.87	120.27	123.11	124.72	131.95
Intermediate goods	105.96	109.64	107.73	104.02	101.16	104.78
Daily necessities	111.57	117.21	119.63	123.87	127.14	135.28
Financial & other						
expenses	126.09	137.05	147.92	157.67	160.89	171.31
Terms of trade	100.47	100.33	95.78	97.82	99.41	99.15

Table A79 (continued)

Notes and Sources: The old indexes were constructed by PBAS. The prices of 33 items were collected in 18 townships three times a month and are the raw data for these indexes. The 33 items are distributed among the following categories:

Commodities sold by farmers		14
Agricultural products (crops and fruits)	10	
Livestock.	4	
Commodities purchesed by farmers		19
Intermediate goods	7	
Daily necessities	12	

The group indexes of prices received by farmers are weighted averages with the value of the marketed supplies of agricultural products in 1952 as weights. The group indexes of prices paid by farmers are also weighted averages. The value of the supplies of intermediate goods in 1952 are used as weights for the index of prices of intermediate goods, and the weights used in constructing the index of the prices of daily necessities are based on a survey of agricultural family expenditures conducted in 1950. The general index is constructed by weighting the group indexes in percentages as follows:

Prices received by farmers		100
Agricultural products	85	
Livestocks	15	
Prices paid by farmers		100
Intermediate goods	30	
Daily necessities	70	

These weights are determined on the basis of the 1950 survey of agricultural family expenditures and a 1952 survey of marketed supplies of agricultural products.

The new indexes of both prices received and prices paid by farmers are Laspeyres indexes. The weights are based on a 1962 survey of quantity and value of goods purchased and sold by farm households. The prices of 42 crops are included in the price index of agricultural products and the prices of 6 livestock products are included in the price index of livestock products. The prices of 79 commodities are included in the general index of prices paid by farmers: 26 items in intermediate goods, 48 items in daily necessities, and 5 items in financial and other expenses. The weights in percentages used to obtain the general index are as follows:

Prices received by farmers		100
Agricultural products	66.2	
Livestock products	33.8	
Prices paid by farmers		100
Intermediate goods	27.0	
Daily necessities	59.4	
Financial and other expenses	13.6	

The data are from DGBAS, *Monthly Statistics of the Republic of China*, various issues, and PBAS, *Monthly Statistics on Prices Received and Prices Paid by Farmers in Taiwan*, June 1973, tables 3 and 5.

Selected Bibliography

I. *Publications of the Colonial Government (Taiwan Government-General)*

The Annual Taiwan Trade Statistics (台灣貿易年表), annually from 1896 to 1942.

Census of 1915 (Second Provisional Household Census of Taiwan), *Statistical Tables* (大正四年第二次台灣臨時戶口調查結果表), 1918.

Census of 1905 (First Provisional Household Census), *Statistical Tables* (明治38年臨時戶口調查結果表), 1908.

Census of 1930, Statistical Tables: Total Island (昭和五年國勢調查結果表：全島編), 1934.

Census of 1935, Statistical Tables (昭和十年國勢調查結果表), 1937.

Census of 1920—First [Regular] Population Census, Summary Tables (大正九年第一回台灣國勢調查要覽表), 1922.

Census of 1925, Statistical Tables (大正十四年國勢調查結果表), 1927.

Collection of Factory Related Materials Based on the Resource Investigation Statute (資源調查令ニ基ク工場関係資料集), 1931, 1933, 1936.

Collection of Local Laws and Regulations in Taiwan (台灣地方制度法規輯覽), 1938.

Monopoly Bureau Annual Business Report (専売局事業年報), annually from 1908 to 1942.

Okamatsu, Santaro. *Provisional Report on Investigation of Laws and Customs in the Island of Taiwan*, English ed. Kobe, Japan: Provisional Commission for Research on Customs in Formosa, 1902.

An Outline of the Tax System in Taiwan (台湾税制の沿革), 1936.

Report of Basic Agricultural Survey (農業基本調查書), nos. 1–45, issued irregularly from 1920 to 1944.

Report of Family Budget Survey, November 1937–October 1938 (家計調査報告昭和十二年十一月〜十三年十月).

Report on Taiwan Agricultural Affairs (台灣農事報), monthly from 1907 to 1941.

The Results of the Survey on Labor Skills (勞働技術統計調查結果表), 1941, 1942, 1943.

Special Population Census of Formosa, 1905 [English translation of a descriptive report of the 1905 census], 1909.

427

Summary of Accomplishments of Civil Administration (民政事務成績提要), annually (under slightly different titles) from 1895 to 1940.

Summary of Local Public Finance in Taiwan (台灣地方財政概要), annually from 1925 to 1943.

Taiwan Agricultural Yearbook (台灣農業年報), annually (under slightly different titles) from 1905 to 1942.

Taiwan Commercial and Industrial Statistics (台灣商工統計), annually from 1921 to 1940.

Taiwan Commercial Statistics (台灣商業統計), 1941, 1942.

Taiwan Government-General Statistics Book (台灣總督府統計書), annually from 1899 to 1942.

Taiwan Industrial Statistics (台灣工業統計), 1941.

Taiwan Monetary Yearbook (台灣金融年報), annually from 1934 to 1943.

Taiwan Sugar Statistics (台灣糖業統計), annually from 1913 to 1943.

Taiwan Tax Yearbook (台灣稅務年報), annually from 1907 to 1939.

Taiwan Vital Statistics of the Population (台灣人口動態統計), annually from 1906 to 1942.

II. *Publications of the Government of the Republic of China, the Taiwan Provincial Government, and Other Official Agencies in Taiwan*

"Agricultural Credit and Cooperatives in Taiwan, China." Country Report presented by the Delegation of the Republic of China to the Fifth Far East Workshop for Agricultural Credit and Cooperatives, Seoul, Korea, 1965.

BOT. *The Agricultural Economy of Taiwan* (台灣之農業經濟), 1962.

————. *Bank of Taiwan Quarterly* (台銀季刊), quarterly since 1947.

————. *Collection of Writings on Taiwan's Economic History, No. 1* (台灣經濟史初集), 1954.

————. *Collection of Writings on Taiwan's Economic History, No. 2* (台灣經濟史二集), 1955.

————. *Collection of Writings on Taiwan's Economic History, No. 3* (台灣經濟史三集), 1956.

————. *Collection of Writings on Taiwan's Economic History, No. 4* (台灣經濟史四集), 1956.

————. *Collection of Writings on Taiwan's Economic History, No. 5* (台灣經濟史五集), 1957.

————. *Collection of Writings on Taiwan's Economic History, No. 6* (台灣經濟史六集), 1957.

————. *Collection of Writings on Taiwan's Economic History, No. 7* (台灣經濟史七集), 1959.

————. *Collection of Writings on Taiwan's Economic History, No. 8* (台灣經濟史八集), 1959.

————. *Collection of Writings on Taiwan's Economic History, No. 9* (台灣經濟史九集), 1963.

————. *Collection of Writings on Taiwan's Economic History, No. 10* (台灣經濟史十集), 1966.

————. *Collection of Writings on Taiwan's Industry* (台灣工業論集), no. 1 (1958), no. 2 (1958), no. 3 (1965), no. 4 (1968).

————. *Financial History of Taiwan* (台灣之金融史料), 1953.

————. *The Foreign Trade of Taiwan* (台灣之對外貿易), 1964.

————. *Price Indices of Imported and Exportable Commodities in Taiwan* (台灣進出口貨價指數), monthly since 1959.

————. *Research on Taiwan's Economic Development* (台灣經濟發展之研究), 1970.

————. *Special Features of Taiwan's Economy During the Japanese Period* (日據時代台灣經濟之特徵), 1957.

————. *Survey of National Savings, Taiwan, Republic of China, 1958–59*, n.d.

————. *Taiwan's Rice* (台灣之米), 1949.

————. *Taiwan's Sugar* (台灣之糖), 1949.

————. *Taiwan's Textile Industry* (台灣之紡織工業), 1956.

BOT/CBC. *Export and Import Exchange Settlements* (出進口結滙統計), annually since 1952.

————. *The Republic of China, Taiwan Financial Statistics Monthly* (中華民國台灣金融統計月報), monthly since 1951.

BOT/PDOR. *Report of Survey on the Financial Status of Industrial and Mining Enterprises in Taiwan* (台灣工礦企業資金調查報告), annually since 1959.

CBC: See BOT/CBC.

Chang, Chung-li, and Hinrichs, A. F. "Personal Income Distribution and Consumption Pattern in Taiwan—1964." *Industry of Free China* 28 (Nov. 1967): 30–48; 28 (Dec. 1967): 29–44.

Chang, H. T.; Wong, C. M.; and Lee, Sylvia. "Essential Statistics of the Fertilizer Program of Taiwan." JCRR, July 1962. Mimeo.

Chien, C. T. "Export Promotion Efforts in the Republic of China." *Industry of Free China* 25 (August 1963): 2–10.

Chiu, John Shih-yao. "The Taiwan Economy: An Input–Output Study." *Industry of Free China* 30 (November 1968): 2–28.

Chou, Hsien-wen. *Economic History of Taiwan during the Japanese Period* (日據時代台灣經濟史). 2 vols. Taipei: BOT, 1958.

————. *History of Taiwan's Economy during the Ch'ing Dynasty* (清代台灣經濟史). Taipei: BOT, 1957.

Chuang, Wei-fan, and Chen, Hsing-yiu. "Agricultural Price Policies and Marketing Programs." JCRR, February 1963. Mimeo.

CIECD (see also MOEA/CIECD). *Annual Report on Taiwan's Economy*, annually since 1964.

————. *Fifth Four-year Plan for Economic Development*, 1969.

————. *Fourth Four-year Plan for Economic Development*, 1965.

————. *Statute for Encouragement of Investment*, April 1971.

CIECD/CUSA. *Taiwan Statistical Data Book*, annually since 1952.

CUSA (see also CIECD/CUSA). *Selected Laws and Regulations Affecting Industry* (English trans.), 1960.

DGBAS, *Monthly Bulletin of Labor Statistics, Republic of China* (中華民國勞工統計月報), monthly since November 1973.

————. *Monthly Statistics of the Republic of China* (中華民國統計月報), monthly since January 1966.

————. *National Income of the Republic of China* (中華民國國民所得), annually since 1953.

————. *Statistical Abstract of the Republic of China* (中華民國統計提要), annually since 1955.

————. *Statistical System and Operation in the Government of the Republic of
China*, July 1957.

————. *The Taiwan Economic Indicator, Republic of China* (中華民國經濟動向
統計), quarterly from 1955 to 1965.

————. *Taiwan's National Income and Product* (台灣之國民生產與國民所得),
1955.

ESB. *First Four-year Plan for Economic Development*, n.d.

————. *Second Four-year Plan for Economic Development*, 1957.

Executive Yuan Tax Reform Commission. *The Report of the Executive Yuan
Tax Reform Commission* (行政院賦稅改革委員會報告書), 1970.

"Export Promotion in the Republic of China." *Industry of Free China* 29
(January 1968): 34–42.

Foreign Exchange and Trade Commission. *Foreign Trade Quarterly*.

General Report, 1961 Industry and Commerce Census of Taiwan (中華民國
台灣省第二次工商業普查總報告), 1962.

General Report on Industry and Commerce Census of Taiwan, 1954 (中華民國
四十三年台灣省工商業普查總報告), 1956.

General Report on the 1961 Census of Agriculture: Taiwan, Republic of China
(中華民國五十年台灣省農業普查總報告), 1963.

General Report on the Third Industrial and Commercial Census of Taiwan
(中華民國台灣省第三次工商業普查總報告), 1968.

Gleason, Ralph N. *Taiwan Food Balances, 1935–1954*. Taipei: JCRR, 1956.

Ho, Hsien-chung. *Finance and Financial Institutions in Taiwan* (台灣之金融).
Taipei: BOT, 1966.

Hsieh, S. C. "Farmers' Organizations in Taiwan and Their Trends of Development." *Industry of Free China* 24 (December 1963): 23–38.

————, and Lee, Teng-hui. *Agricultural Development and Its Contributions
to Economic Growth in Taiwan*. Taipei: JCRR, 1966.

————. *An Analytical Review of Agricultural Development in Taiwan*. Taipei:
JCRR, 1958.

————; Yeh, S. M.; and Kuo, T. S. *Food Administration in Taiwan*. Taipei:
JCRR, 1953.

Hsing, Mo-huan. *Input–output Relationship for the Economy of Taiwan* (台灣
經濟的投入產出關係). Taipei: CUSA, 1961.

Huang, Tung; Chang, Tsong-han; and Lee, Chang-chin. *Government Financing in Taiwan under the Japanese Regime*. Taipei: JCRR, 1951.

Industry of Free China (自由中國之工業), monthly since 1954.

Inspectorate General of Customs. *The Trade of China* (中國進出口貿易統計年刊),
annually since 1950.

JCRR. *Abstracts of Land Statistics, Taiwan Province*, 1953.

————. *Crop and Seed Improvement in Taiwan, Republic of China: June
1956–April 1959*, 1960.

————. *Crop and Seed Improvement in Taiwan, Republic of China: May 1959
–January 1961*, 1961.

————. *General Report of the Joint Commission on Rural Reconstruction*,
annually since 1949.

————. "Statistical Review of Agricultural Financing in Taiwan and JCRR's

Contribution." December 1961. Mimeo.

———. *Taiwan Agricultural Statistics, 1901–1955*, 1956.

———. *Taiwan Agricultural Statistics, 1901–1965*, 1966.

———. *Taiwan Farm Income Survey of 1967*, 1970.

Kao, Charles H. C. "A Preliminary Analysis of the Republic of China's 'Brain Drain' into the United States." *Industry of Free China* 31 (September 1969): 22–33.

King, K. H. "Agricultural Finance and Credit in Taiwan, China." JCRR, n.d. Mimeo.

Kirby, E. Stuart. *Rural Progress in Taiwan.* Taipei: JCRR, 1960.

Kwoh, Min-hsioh. "Farmer's Associations and Their Contributions Toward Agricultural and Rural Development in Taiwan." JCRR, October 1963. Mimeo.

Ladejinsky, W. I. "Observations on Rural Conditions in Taiwan." A Report to the National Government of China and to the JCRR. June 1951. Mimeo.

Lee, Teng-hui "Government Interference in the Rice Market in Taiwan." JCRR, 1971. Mimeo.

Leonard, R. F.; Deming, F. L.; and Morrill, Chester. *Comments and Recommendations on Central Banking in the Republic of China.* Taipei: CBC, 1961.

Ma, Fengchow C.; Takasaka, T.; and Yang, Ching-wen. *A Preliminary Study of Farm Implements Used in Taiwan Province.* 2d ed. Taipei: JCRR, 1958.

MOEA. *The Republic of China, Taiwan Agricultural Production Statistics* (中華民國台灣農業生產統計), annually since 1953.

———. *The Republic of China, Taiwan Industrial Production Statistics Monthly* (中華民國台灣工業生產統計月報), monthly since June 1957.

———. *Third Four-year Plan for Economic Development*, 1961.

MOEA/CIECD. *Report on Industrial and Mining Survey in Taiwan* (台灣工礦調查報告), annually since 1962.

MOF. *Monthly Statistics of Exports and Imports, The Republic of China* (中華民國進出口貿易統計月報), monthly since 1968.

———. *A Review of Taiwan's Money and Banking for 1949–1958* (十年來台灣金融), June 1959.

National Resource Commission. *Industrial Enterprise of National Resource Commission in Taiwan*, 1951.

PBAS. *Monthly Statistics on Prices Received and Prices Paid by Farmers in Taiwan* (台灣省農民所得所付物價統計月報), monthly since 1967.

———. *Report on Family Living Studies of Wage Earners and Salaried Employees in Taiwan, May 1954 to April 1955* (台灣省薪資階級家計調查報告 中華民國四十三年五月～四十四年四月).

———. *Report on the Survey of Family Income and Expenditure in Taiwan* (中華民國台灣省家庭收支調查報告), 1964, 1966, 1968, annually since 1970.

———. *The Republic of China Taiwan Monthly Commodity-Price Statistics* (中華民國台灣物價統計月報), monthly (under slightly different title) since 1946.

———. *Results of the Seventh Population Census of Taiwan, 1940* (台灣第七次人口普查結果表), March 1953.

———. *Taiwan Province: Statistical Summary of the Past 51 Years* (台灣省五十一年來統計提要), 1946.

———. *Taiwan Statistical Abstract* (台灣省統計要覽), annually since 1946.

————. *Taiwan Trade Statistics for the Last Fifty-three Years (1896–1948)* (台灣貿易五十三年表).

PDAF. *The Reorganization of Farmers' Associations in Taiwan* (台灣省農會之改組), 1950.

————. *Report of Farm Record-Keeping Families in Taiwan* (台灣農家記賬報告), annually.

————. *Report on Agricultural Basic Survey in Taiwan* (台灣農業基本調查報告), annually.

————. *Taiwan Agricultural Prices Monthly* (台灣農產物價統計月報), monthly since 1964.

————. *Taiwan Agricultural Yearbook* (台灣農業年報), annually since 1947.

PDCA. *Household Registration Statistics of Taiwan Province* (台灣省戶籍統計要覽), annually since 1959.

————. *Taiwan Demographic Fact Book* (台灣省人口統計), annually since 1959.

————. *Taiwan Demography Monthly* (台灣人口統計月刊), monthly since January 1966.

PDOR (see also BOT/PDOR). *Report of Taiwan Labor Statistics* (台灣勞工統計報告), annually since 1954.

————. *Taiwan Reconstruction Statistics* (台灣建設統計), 1961, 1962, 1963, 1964, 1965.

PFB. *Food Production and Activities of Taiwan Provincial Food Bureau*, 1973.

————. *Taiwan Food Statistics Book* (台灣糧食統計要覽), annually.

————. *Taiwan Province: Sixteen Years of Food Administration*, 1962.

————. *Taiwan Province Rural Economic Conditions, Collection 4* (台灣省農業經濟概況第四輯), 1963.

Rada, Edward L., and Lee, Teng-hui. *Irrigation Investment in Taiwan*. Taipei: JCRR, 1956.

Raper, Arthur F. *Rural Taiwan—Problems and Promise*. Taipei: JCRR, 1956.

Report of the 1956 Population Census, Republic of China (中華民國戶口普查報告書), 1959.

The Report of the 1970 Agricultural Census of Taiwan–Fukien District, Republic of China (中華民國五十九年台閩地區農業普查報告), 1973.

The Report of the 1970 Sample Census of Population and Housing of Taiwan–Fukien Area, Republic of China (中華民國五十九年台閩地區戶口及住宅普查報告書), 1972.

The Report of the 1971 Industrial and Commercial Censuses of Taiwan and Fukien Area, Republic of China (中華民國六十年台閩地區工商業普查報告), 1973.

The Report of the 1966 Census of Population and Housing of Taiwan–Fukien Area, Republic of China (中華民國五十五年台閩地區戶口及住宅普查報告書), 1969.

Report on the 1956 Sample Census of Agriculture (台灣省農業選樣普查報告), 1959.

Report on the 1961 Census of Agriculture: Taiwan, Republic of China, 10% Sample Census (中華民國五十年台灣農業普查報告百分之十選樣普查), 1963.

A Summary Report on the 1956 Census, 1960.

Sung, Tsay-yan. *Development of Seed Technology in Taiwan*. Taipei: JCRR, 1965.

Taiwan Provincial Department of Communication. *Annual Statistical Report of Taiwan Communication and Transportation* (台灣交通統計彙報), annually since 1947.

Taiwan Provincial Labor Force Survey and Research Institute. *Report of the Labor Force Survey in Taiwan* (台灣省勞動調查報告), quarterly since October 1963.

Taiwan Sugar Corporation. *Annual Statistical Report of Taiwan Sugar Industry* (台灣糖業統計年報), 1948.

Tang, Hui-sun. *Land Reform in Free China*. Taipei: JCRR, 1954.

Tsiang, Yien-si. "A Report on the Joint Commission on Rural Reconstruction." JCRR, June 1964. Mimeo.

Tsui, Young-chi. *A Summary Report on Farm Income of Taiwan in 1957 in Comparison with 1952*. Taipei: JCRR, 1959.

———, and Hsieh, S. C. *Farm Income of Taiwan in 1952*. Taipei: JCRR, 1954.

———, and Lin, Tai-lung. *A Study on Rural Labor Mobility in Relation to Industrialization and Urbanization in Taiwan*. Taipei: JCRR, 1964.

Watkins, Ralph J. "Economic Development Planning in Taiwan." Prepared for U.S. AID and CIECD, ROC. n.d. Mimeo.

Yeh, Sing-min. *Per Capita Consumption Level of Basic Food in Taiwan*. Taipei: JCRR, 1957.

———. *Rice Marketing in Taiwan*. Taipei: JCRR, 1955.

———, and Kuo, T. S. *Rural Land Taxation in Taiwan*. Taipei: JCRR, 1952.

Yeh, Wan-an. *Taiwan's Economy in the Past 20 Years* (二十年來之台灣經濟). Taipei: BOT, 1967.

Yin, K. C. *Economic Development in Taiwan, 1950–1960*. Taipei: CUSA, 1962.

———. *My Views of Taiwan's Economy* (我對台灣經濟看法). Taipei: CUSA. Vol. 1 (1953), vol. 2 (1960), vol. 3 (1962), vol. 4 (1963).

III. Other Publications

Academia Sinica, Institute of Economics. *Taiwan Economic Projection* (台灣經濟預測). Taipei, semiannually since 1969.

Asian Development Bank. *A Comparative Study of National Income Statistics in the Philippines, Malaysia, China, and Thailand*. Occasional Papers no. 1, November 1969.

Baran, Paul. *The Political Economy of Growth*. New York: Monthly Review Press, 1957.

Barclay, George W. *Colonial Development and Population in Taiwan*. Princeton: Princeton University Press, 1954.

———. *A Report on Taiwan's Population to the Joint Commission on Rural Reconstruction*. Princeton: Office of Population Research, Princeton University, 1954.

Berelson, Bernard, and Freedman, Ronald. "A Study in Fertility." *Scientific American* 210 (May 1964): 29–37.

Bhagwati, Jagdish, and Echaus, Richard S., eds. *Foreign Aid*. Baltimore: Penguin, 1970.

Birnberg, Thomas B., and Resnick, Stephen A. "A Model of the Trade and Government Sectors in Colonial Economies." *American Economic Review*

63 (Sept. 1973): 572–97.

Boserup, Ester. *The Conditions of Agricultural Growth*. Chicago: Aldine, 1965.

Bruton, Henry J. "The Two Gap Approach to Aid and Development: Comment." *American Economic Review* 59 (June 1969): 439–46.

Buck, John L. *Land Utilization in China*. Chicago: University of Chicago Press, 1937.

Callis, Helmut G. *Foreign Capital in Southeast Asia*. New York: Institute of Pacific Relations, 1942.

Chang, Han-yu. "A Study of the Living Conditions of Farmers in Taiwan, 1931–1950." *Developing Economics* 7 (March 1969): 35–62.

———, and Myers, Ramon H. "Japanese Colonial Development Policy in Taiwan, 1895–1906." *Journal of Asian Studies* 22 (August 1963): 433–50.

Chang, Hung-chang. "The Contribution of Technological Progress and Factor Inputs to the Growth of Manufacturing Industries (技術進步與生產因素對製造成長的貢獻)." *Academia Economic Papers* (經濟論文). Selected essay no. 20, August 1971.

Chang, Kowei. "An Estimate of Taiwan's Personal Income Distribution in 1953 (民國四十二年台灣個人所得分配之估計)." *Journal of Social Science* (社會科學論叢) 7 (1956).

———. ed. *Economic Development in Taiwan*. Taipei: Cheng Chung, 1968.

Chang, Lih-yong. "Economic Development under Foreign Aid and Preparation for War: A Case Study of Taiwan, 1942–1962." Ph.D. dissertation, Cornell University, 1965.

Chen, Cheng. *Land Reform in Taiwan*. Taipei: China Publishing Co., 1961.

Chen, Cheng-hsiang. *Atlas of Land Utilization in Taiwan* (台灣土地利用圖集). Taipei: National Taiwan University, 1950.

———. *Land Utilization in Taiwan* (台灣土地利用). Taipei: National Taiwan University, 1950.

———. *Taiwan, An Economic and Social Geography*. Taipei: Fu-Min Geographical Institute of Economic Development, 1963.

Chen, Ching-chih. "The Japanese Adaptation of the Pao-chia System in Taiwan, 1895–1945." *Journal of Asian Studies* 34 (February 1975): 391–416.

———. "The Police and Hokō Systems in Taiwan under Japanese Administration." *Harvard East Asian Research Center Paper on Japan* 4 (1967): 147–203.

Chen, Hsing-yiu, and Bailey, R. A. "Agricultural Credit in Taiwan." Ohio State University Agricultural Finance Center Publication 109, Columbus, Ohio, Aug. 1966.

Chen, Lung-chu, and Lasswell, Harold D. *Formosa, China and the United Nations*. New York: St. Martin's Press, 1967.

Chen, Ta. *Chinese Migration with Special Reference to Labor Conditions*. U.S. Bureau of Labor Statistics Bulletin, no. 340. Washington, D.C.: Government Printing Office, 1923.

Chenery, Hollis B. "Patterns of Industrial Growth." *American Economic Review* 50 (September 1960): 624–54.

———; Ahluwalia, Montek S.; Bell, C. L. G.; Duloy, John H.; and Jolly, Richard. *Redistribution with Growth*. London: Oxford University Press, 1974.

————, and Bruno, Michael. "Development Alternatives in an Open Economy: The Case of Israel." *Economic Journal* 72 (March 1962): 79–103.

————, and Strout, Alan M. "Foreign Assistance and Economic Development." *American Economic Review* 56 (September 1966): 679–732.

————, and Syrquin, Moises. *Patterns of Development*. London: Oxford University Press, 1975.

————, and Taylor, Lance. "Development Patterns: Among Countries and Over Time." *Review of Economics and Statistics* 50 (November 1968): 391–416.

Cheung, Steven N. S. *The Theory of Share Tenancy*. Chicago: University of Chicago Press, 1969.

Chinese Imperial Maritime Customs, *Annual Trade Tables for Various Chinese Ports (Taiwan)* (支那各港貿易年表台灣之部), 29 vols. [These are handcopied volumes deposited in the library of the Government-General. Currently, this set is kept at the Taiwan Provincial Library in Taipei.]

Chou, Shun-hsin. *The Chinese Inflation: 1937–1949*. New York: Columbia University Press, 1963.

Chow, Lien-ping. "A Programme to Control Fertility in Taiwan." *Population Studies* 9 (November 1965): 155–66.

Chu, Samuel C. "Liu Ming-ch'uan and Modernization of Taiwan." *Journal of Asian Studies* 23 (November 1963): 37–57.

Davidson, James W. *The Island of Formosa, Past and Present*. New York: Macmillan, 1903.

Essays on the Population of Taiwan. Taipei: Institute of Economics, Academia Sinica, 1973.

Fei, John C. H., and Ranis, Gustav. *Development of the Labor Surplus Economy Theory and Policy*. Homewood, Ill.: Irwin, 1964.

————. "Foreign Assistance and Economic Development: Comment." *American Economic Review* 58 (September 1968): 897–912.

————; and Kuo, Shirley W. "Growth and the Family Distribution of Income by Factor Components: The Case of Taiwan." Yale Economic Growth Center Discussion Paper no. 223, March 1975. Mimeo.

Fong, Hsien-ding. "Taiwan's Industrialization, with Special Reference to Policies and Controls." *Journal of Nanyang University* 2 (1968): 365–425.

Food and Agricultural Organization. *Agricultural Commodities, Projections for 1970*. Rome: FAO, 1963.

Freedman, Ronald; Coombs, Lolagene C.; Chang, Ming-cheng; and Sun, Te-hsiung. "Trends in Fertility, Family Size Preferences, and Practice of Family Planning: Taiwan 1965–1973." *Studies in Family Planning* 5 (September 1974): 270–88.

————; Hermalin, Albert I.; and Sun, Te-hsiung. "Fertility Trends in Taiwan." *Population Index* 38 (April–June 1972): 141–66.

Fu, Yüeh. "Estimates of Technological Progress in Taiwan's Manufacturing Sector, 1951–66 (民國四十年至五十五年台灣製造業部門技術進步之預測)." *Academic Economic Papers* (經濟論文). Selected essay no. 11, October 1970.

Gallin, Bernard. *Hsin Hsing, Taiwan: A Chinese Village in Change*. Berkeley: University of California Press, 1966.

Ginsburg, Norton S. "Taiwan: A Resource Analysis of an Oriental Economy."

Economic Development and Cultural Change 1 (March 1952): 37–56; 1 (June 1952): 110–31.

Glass, Sheppard. "Some Aspects of Formosa's Economic Growth." *China Quarterly*, no. 15, July–September 1963, pp. 12–34.

Grajdanzev, Andrew J. *Formosa Today: An Analysis of the Economic Development and Strategic Importance of Japan's Tropical Colony.* New York: Institute of Pacific Relations, 1942.

Hayami, Yujiro, and Ruttan, Vernon W. *Agricultural Development in International Perspective.* Baltimore: Johns Hopkins Press, 1971.

———. "Korean Rice, Taiwan Rice, and Japanese Agricultural Stagnation: An Economic Consequence of Colonialism." *Quarterly Journal of Economics* 84 (November 1970): 562–89.

Ho, Ping-ti. *Studies on the Population of China, 1368–1953.* Cambridge: Harvard University Press, 1959.

Ho, Samuel P. S. "Agricultural Transformation under Colonialism: Reply and Further Observation." *Journal of Economic History* 31 (September 1971): 682–93.

———. "Agricultural Transformation under Colonialism: The Case of Taiwan." *Journal of Economic History* 28 (September 1968): 313–40.

———. "Development Alternative: The Case of Taiwan." *Yale Economic Essays* 5 (Spring 1965): 63–142.

———. "The Development Policy of the Japanese Colonial Government in Taiwan, 1895–1945." In *Government and Economic Development*, edited by Gustav Ranis, pp. 287–328. New Haven: Yale University Press, 1971.

———. "The Economic Development of Colonial Taiwan: Evidence and Interpretation." *Journal of Asian Studies* 34 (February 1975): 417–39.

———. "Industrialization in Taiwan: Recent Trends and Problems." *Pacific Affairs* 48 (Spring 1975): 27–41.

Ho, Yhi-min. *Agricultural Development of Taiwan, 1903–1960.* Nashville: Vanderbilt University Press, 1966.

———. "Development with Surplus Population—the Case of Taiwan: A Critique of the Classical Two Sector Model, à la Lewis." *Economic Development and Cultural Change* 20 (January 1972): 210–34.

———. "Korean Rice, Taiwan Rice, and Japanese Agricultural Stagnation: An Economic Consequence of Colonialism—A Comment." Rice University Program of Development Studies Paper no. 16, Summer 1971. Mimeo.

———. "Taiwan's Agricultural Transformation under Colonialism: A Critique." *Journal of Economic History* 31 (September 1971): 672–81.

Hsieh, S. C., and Ruttan, Vernon W. "Environmental, Technological and Institutional Factors in the Growth of Rice Production: The Philippines, Thailand, and Taiwan." *Food Research Institute Studies* 6 (August 1967): 307–41.

Hsing, Mo-huan. "An Appraisal of the Growth Rates of the Taiwan Economy as Revealed in Official National Income Statistics." Presented to the Eighth General Conference of the International Association for Research in Income and Wealth, Corfu, Greece, June 24–30, 1963. Mimeo.

———. "Capital Accumulation in Taiwan during 1951–65." Paper presented to the Conference on Economic Development of Taiwan, Taipei, Taiwan,

June 19–28, 1967. Mimeo.

————. "The Development Experiences of Taiwan and South Korea: A Comparison." *Academia Economic Papers* (經濟論文) 3 (March 1975): 1–20.

————; Chiang, Chen-nan; and Hwang, Kuo-shu. "An Analysis of Residual Productivities of the Manufacturing Industries in Taiwan, 1953–71." *Academia Economic Papers* (經濟論文) 1 (March 1973): 75–89.

————; Power, John H.; and Sicat, Gerardo P. *Taiwan and the Philippines: Industrialization and Trade Policies.* London: Oxford University Press, 1970.

Hsu, Robert C. "The Demand for Fertilizer in a Developing Country: The Case of Taiwan, 1950–1966." *Economic Development and Cultural Change* 20 (January 1973): 299–309.

IMF. *Annual Report of Exchange Restrictions*, annually.

————. *Balance of Payments Yearbook*, annually.

Irvine, Reed J., and Emery, Robert I. "Interest Rates as an Anti-Inflationary Instrument in Taiwan." *National Banking Review* 4 (September 1966): 29–39.

Jacoby, Neil H. *U.S. Aid to Taiwan: A Study of Foreign Aid, Self-help and Development.* New York: Praeger, 1966.

Johnson, Bruce F. "Agricultural Development and Economic Transformation: A Comparative Study of the Japanese Experience." *Food Research Institution Studies* 3 (November 1964): 223–76.

————, and Mellor, John W. "The Role of Agriculture in Economic Development." *American Economic Review* 51 (September 1961): 566–91.

Johnson, D. Gale. "Resource Allocation under Share Contract." *Journal of Political Economy* 58 (April 1950): 111–23.

Kao, Charles H. C. "The Factor Contribution of Agriculture to Economic Development: A Study of Taiwan." *Asian Survey* 5 (November 1965): 558–65.

————; Anschel, Kurt R.; and Eicher, Carl K. "Disguised Unemployment in Agriculture: A Survey." In *Agriculture in Economic Development*, edited by Carl K. Eicher and Lawrence W. Witt, pp. 129–44. New York: McGraw-Hill, 1965.

————, and Lee, Jae Won. "An Empirical Analysis of China's Brain Drain into the United States." *Economic Development and Cultural Change* 21 (April 1973): 500–13.

Kawano, Shigato. "The Reasons for Taiwan's High Growth Rates." In *Economic Development Issues: Greece, Israel, Taiwan, and Thailand*, pp. 121–58. New York: Praeger, 1968.

————. *A Study of Taiwan's Rice Economy* (台灣米穀經濟). Tokyo: Yuhikaku, 1941.

Kerr, George H. *Formosa Betrayed.* Boston: Houghton Mifflin, 1965.

Koo, Anthony Y. C. *The Role of Land Reform in Economic Development: A Case Study of Taiwan.* New York: Praeger, 1968.

Kuo, Shirely W. "The Economic Structure of Taiwan (台灣的經濟結構)." *Economic Essays* (經濟論文叢刊) 1 (November 1970): 173–294.

Kuo, T'ing-i. *A Summary Account of the History of Taiwan* (台灣史事概說). Taipei: Cheng Chung, 1954.

Kusui, Ryūzo. *The Economy of Taiwan during the War* (戰時台灣經濟論).

Taipei: Nampō Jimbun Kenkyu Sho, 1944.

Kuznets, Simon. *Modern Economic Growth Rate Structure and Spread.* New Haven: Yale University Press, 1966.

Lee, Teng-hui. "Intersectoral Capital Flows in the Economic Development of Taiwan, 1895–1960." Ph.D. dissertation, Cornell University, 1968.

———. *Intersectoral Capital Flows in the Economic Development of Taiwan, 1895–1960.* Ithaca: Cornell University Press, 1971.

———. "Process and Pattern of Growth in Agricultural Production of Taiwan." *Economic Essays* (經濟論文叢刊) 1 (November 1970): 15–62.

———, and Chen, Y. E. "Appendix to Growth Rates of Taiwan's Agriculture, 1911–1970." September 1972. Mimeo.

———, and Liang, Kuo-shu. "The Structure of Protection in Taiwan." *Economic Essays* (經濟論文叢刊) 2 (November 1971): 69–96.

Lee, Yung-san. "An Analysis of Consumers' Demand Functions in Taiwan, 1951–1969 (民國四十年至五十八年台灣消費者需求函數分析)." *Economic Essays* (經濟論文叢刊) 2 (November 1971): 97–121.

Leibenstein, Harvey. *A Theory of Economic-Demographic Development.* Princeton: Princeton University Press, 1954.

Lewis, Andron B. "The Rice-Fertilizer Barter Price and the Production of Rice in Taiwan, Republic of China." *Journal of Agricultural Economics* (Research Institute of Agricultural Economics, Taiwan Provincial Chung-Hsing University), June 1967, pp. 127–79.

Liang, Kuo-shu. "Foreign Trade and Economic Development in Taiwan, 1952–67." Ph.D. dissertation, Vanderbilt University, 1970.

Lin, Ken Ching-yuan. "Industrial Development and Change in the Structure of Foreign Trade: The Experience of the Republic of China in Taiwan, 1946–1966." *IMF Staff Papers* 25 (July 1968): 290–321.

———. *Industrialization in Taiwan, 1946–72: Trade and Import-Substitution Policies for Developing Countries.* New York: Praeger, 1973.

Little, Ian; Scitovsky, Tibor; and Scott, Maurice. *Industry and Trade in Some Developing Countries: A Comparative Study.* London: Oxford University Press, 1970.

Liu, Fu-chi. *Essays on Monetary Development in Taiwan.* Taipei: China Committee for Publication Aid and Prize Awards, 1970.

Liu, Paul K. C. *Interactions Between Population Growth and Economic Development in Taiwan.* Taipei: Institute of Economics, Academia Sinica, 1973.

———. "Population Redistribution and Development in Taiwan, 1951–1965." Paper presented to the Conference on Economic Development of Taiwan, Taipei, Taiwan, June 19–28, 1967. Mimeo.

———, and Speare, Alden. "Urbanization and Labor Mobility in Taiwan (台灣都市化與勞動流動性的研究)." *Academia Economic Papers* (經濟論文) 2 (September 1973): 71–83.

Liu, Su-feng. "Disguised Unemployment in Taiwan Agriculture." Ph.D. dissertation, University of Illinois, 1966.

Lockwood, William W. *The Economic Development of Japan.* Princeton: Princeton University Press, 1954.

McKinnon, Ronald I. "Foreign Exchange Constraints in Economic Development and Efficient Aid Allocation." *Economic Journal* 74 (June 1964): 388–409.

———. *Money and Capital in Economic Development.* Washington, D.C.: Brookings Institution, 1973.

Meier, Gerald M. *The International Economics of Development Theory and Policy.* New York: Harper & Row, 1968.

Mellor, John W. *The Economics of Agricultural Development.* Ithaca: Cornell University Press, 1966.

Mizoguchi, Toshiyuki. "A Commodity Flow Estimate of Capital Formation in Korea and Taiwan under Japanese Rule." *Economic Journal* (經濟論集) 12 (December 1973): 72–84.

———. "Consumer Prices and Real Wages in Taiwan and Korea under Japanese Rule." *Hitotsubashi Journal of Economics* 13 (June 1972): 40–56.

———. "An Econometric Comparison of Farm Households' Economic Behavior in Japan, Korea and Taiwan." *Developing Economics* 11 (September 1973): 231–43.

———. *The Economic Growth of Taiwan and Korea* (台湾、朝鮮の経済成長). Tokyo: Iwanami Shoten, 1975.

———. "Foreign Trade in Taiwan and Korea under Japanese Rule." *Hitotsubashi Journal of Economics* 14 (February 1974): 37–53.

Montgomery, John D.; Hughs, Rufus B.; and Davis, Raymond H. *Rural Improvement and Political Development—The JCRR Model.* Washington, D.C.: AID, 1964.

Myers, Ramon H. "Agrarian Policy and Agricultural Transformation: Mainland China and Taiwan, 1895–1945." *Journal of the Institute of Chinese Studies of the Chinese University of Hong Kong* 3 (December 1970): 521–42.

———. "Economic Growth and Population Change in Taiwan." *Malayan Economic Review* 8 (October 1963): 104–17.

———. "Land Reform and Agricultural Development in Taiwan." *Malayan Economic Review* 8 (April 1963): 111–14.

———. "Taiwan as an Imperial Colony of Japan: 1895–1945." *Journal of the Institute of Chinese Studies of the Chinese University of Hong Kong* 6 (December 1973): 425–51.

———. "Taiwan under Ch'ing Imperial Rule, 1684–1895: The Traditional Economy." *Journal of the Institute of Chinese Studies of the Chinese University of Hong Kong* 5 (December 1972): 373–409.

———. "Taiwan under Ch'ing Imperial Rule, 1685–1895: The Traditional Order." *Journal of the Institute of Chinese Studies of the Chinese University of Hong Kong* 4 (December 1971): 495–520.

———. "Taiwan under Ch'ing Imperial Rule, 1684–1895: The Traditional Society." *Journal of the Institute of Chinese Studies of the Chinese University of Hong Kong* 5 (December 1972): 414–51.

———, and Ching, Adrienne. "Agricultural Development in Taiwan under Japanese Colonial Rule." *Journal of Asian Studies* 23 (August 1964): 555–70.

Nakamura, James I. "Incentives, Productivity Gaps, and Agricultural Growth Rates in Prewar Japan, Taiwan, and Korea." In *Japan in Crisis*, edited by Bernard S. Silberman and Harry D. Harootunian, pp. 329–73. Princeton:

Princeton University Press, 1974.

Ohkawa, Kazushi, and Rosovsky, Henry. *Japanese Economic Growth*. Stanford: Stanford University Press, 1973.

Oshima, Harry T. "Income Inequality and Economic Growth the Postwar Experience of Asian Countries." *Malayan Economic Review* 15 (October 1970): 7–41.

Paauw, Douglas S., and Fei, John C. H. *The Transition in Open Dualistic Economies*. New Haven: Yale University Press, 1973.

Pack, Howard. *Structural Change and Economic Policy in Israel*. New Haven: Yale University Press, 1971.

Paglin, Morton. "Surplus Agricultural Labor and Development: Facts and Theories." *American Economic Review* 55 (September 1965): 815–34.

Ranis, Gustav. "Industrial Sector Labor Absorption." *Economic Development and Cultural Change* 21 (April 1973): 387–408.

———, ed. *Government and Economic Development*. New Haven: Yale University Press, 1971.

———, ed. *The U.S. and the Developing Economies*. Rev. ed. New York: Norton, 1973.

Raper, Authur F.; Chuan, Han-sheng; and Chen, Shao-hsing. *Urban and Industrial Taiwan—Crowded and Resourceful*. Taipei: U.S. Mutual Security Mission to China and National Taiwan University, 1954.

Raup, Philip. "The Contribution of Land Reform to Agricultural Development: An Analytical Framework." *Economic Development and Cultural Change* 12 (October 1963): 1–21.

Rhodes, Robert I. *Imperialism and Underdevelopment, A Reader*. New York: Monthly Review Press, 1970.

Rhynsburger, Willert. *Area and Resources Survey: Taiwan*. Taipei: International Cooperation Administration Mutual Security Mission to China, 1956.

Sasamota, Takeharu. "A Salient Feature of Capital Accumulation in Taiwan: The System of Rice Collection by the Taiwan Food Bureau." *Developing Economies* 6 (March 1968): 27–39.

Schreiber, Jordan C. *U.S. Corporate Investment in Taiwan*. New York: Dunnellen, 1970.

Schultz, T. Paul. "Explanation of Birth Rate Changes Over Space and Time: A Study of Taiwan." *Journal of Political Economy* 81, pt. 2 (March/April 1973): 238–74.

———. "A Preliminary Survey of Economic Analyses of Fertility." *American Economic Review* 63 (May 1973): 71–77.

Schultz, Theodore W. *Transforming Traditional Agriculture*. New Haven: Yale University Press, 1964.

Shen, Tsung-han. *Agricultural Development on Taiwan Since World War II*. Ithaca: Cornell University Press, Comstock Publishing Associates, 1964.

———. *The Sino-American Joint Commission on Rural Reconstruction*. Ithaca: Cornell University Press, 1970.

Shih, Chien-sheng. "Economic Development in Taiwan After the Second World War." *Weltwirtschaftliches Archiv* 100, no. 1 (1965): 113–34.

Shinohara, Miyohei, and Ishikawa, Shigeru. *Taiwan's Economic Growth* (台湾の経済成長). Tokyo: Ajia Keizai Ken Kyujo, 1972.

Snodgrass, Donald. *Ceylon: An Export Economy in Transition.* Homewood, Ill.: Irwin, 1966.

Speare, Jr., Alden. "An Assessment of the Quality of Taiwan Migration Registration Data." Taiwan Population Studies Working Paper no. 12, Population Studies Center, University of Michigan, 1970. Mimeo.

———. "Urbanization and Migration in Taiwan." *Economic Development and Culture Change* 22 (January 1974): 302–19.

Sun, I-shuan. "Trade Policies and Economic Development in Taiwan." Presented to the Conference on Economic Interdependence in Southeast Asia, University of Wisconsin, October 1966. Mimeo.

Tang, Hui-sun, and Hsieh, S. C. "Land Reform and Agricultural Development in Taiwan." In *Land Tenure, Industrialization and Social Stability*, edited by Walter Froehlick, pp. 114–42. Milwaukee: Marquette University Press, 1961.

Todaro, Michael P. "A Model of Labor Migration and Urban Unemployment in Less Developed Countries." *American Economic Review* 59 (March 1969): 138–48.

Tsurumi, E. Patricia. "Japanese Colonial Education in Taiwan, 1895–1945." Ph.D. dissertation, Harvard University, 1971.

———. "Taiwan under Kodama Gentarō and Gotō Shimpei." *Harvard University East Asian Research Center Papers on Japan* 4 (1967): 95–146.

Turnham, David. *The Employment Problem in Less Developed Countries.* Paris: OECD Development Centre, 1971.

United Kingdom Foreign Office. *Diplomatic and Consular Reports on Trade and Finance, China: Report on the Trade of Taiwan [Tainan].* London, 1887–1895.

———. *Diplomatic and Consular Reports on Trade and Finance, China: Report on the Trade of Tamsui.* London, 1888–1898.

United Nations. "Relationship between Agriculture and Industrial Development: A Case Study in Taiwan, China, 1953–1960." *Economic Bulletin for Asia and the Far East* 14 (June 1963): 29–70.

———. *Yearbook of National Accounts*, annually.

UNCTAD Secretariat. *The Mobilization of Internal Resources by the Developing Countries.* TD/7/Suppl. 2, September 15, 1967.

U.S., AID/China, Office of Economic Analysis. "Estimates of National Income and Capital Formation in Taiwan, Republic of China, 1954–1960." Taipei, April 1962. Mimeo.

———. "National Income Estimates for Taiwan." *Economic Explorations*, no. 3, September 27, 1963.

———. "Population Growth in Taiwan." *Economic Explorations*, no. 4, September 30, 1963.

U.S., Department of Agriculture. *Changes in Agriculture in 26 Developing Nations, 1948 to 1963.* Foreign Agricultural Economic Report no. 27, 1965.

U.S., Department of Commerce. *Investment in Taiwan (Formosa).* (Washington, D.C.: Government Printing Office, 1959).

———. *World Trade Information Service*, pt. 1, no. 60-7; pt. 1, no. 61-67; pt. 1, no. 62-16; pt. 2, no. 61-2; pt. 2, no. 62-22.

U.S., House Foreign Affairs Committee. *U.S. Overseas Loans and Grants and*

Assistance from International Organizations, Obligations and Loan Authorization July 1, 1945–June 30, 1967.

U.S., ICA Mutual Security Mission to China, Office of Assistant Director for Industry. "Taiwan Economic Data Book." Pt. 2, vol. 5. Taipei, December 1957. Mimeo.

U.S., ICA Mutual Security Mission to China, Office of Economic Policy. "Taiwan Economic Data Book." Pt. 2, vol. 8. Taipei, July 1960. Mimeo.

U.S., Office of Naval Operations (OPNAV). *Civil Affairs Handbook, Taiwan (Formosa).* OPNAV 50E-12. Washington, D.C., 1944.

———. *Civil Affairs Handbook, Taiwan (Formosa)—Economic Supplement.* OPNAV 50E-13. Washington, D.C., 1944.

Wang, You-tsao. "Technological Changes and Agricultural Development of Taiwan, 1946–1965." Paper presented to the Conference on Economic Development of Taiwan. Taipei, Taiwan, June 19–28, 1967. Mimeo.

Warriner, Doreen. *Land Reform and Economic Development*, 50th Anniversary Commemorative Lectures. Cairo: National Bank of Egypt, 1955.

Wickberg, Edgar. "Japanese Land Policies in Taiwan, 1895–1945." *Agricultural History* 43 (July 1969): 369–78.

———. "The Tenancy System in Taiwan, 1900–1939." University Seminar on Modern East Asia: China, Columbia University, March 1969. Mimeo.

Wickizer, V. D., and Bennett, M. K. *The Rice Economy of Monsoon Asia.* Stanford: Stanford University Press, 1941.

Willis, Robert J. "A New Approach to the Economic Theory of Fertility Behavior." *Journal of Political Economy* 81, pt. 2 (March/April 1973): 14–64.

Wu, Hwei-ran. "Economic Effects of Rice Control Policy in Postwar Taiwan." *Developing Economies* 8 (March 1970): 52–78.

Yanaihara, Tadao. *Taiwan Under Imperialism* (帝国主義下の台湾). Tokyo: Iwanami Shoten, 1929.

Yang, Martin M. C. *Socio-Economic Results of Land Reform in Taiwan.* Honolulu: East–West Center Press, 1970.

———. "A Study on Impact of Farmers' Association and Extension Program on Development of Agriculture in Taiwan." Study jointly sponsored by ECAFE, National Taiwan University, and JCRR. June 1959. Mimeo.

Yen, C. H.; Wang, C. M.; and Wang, Y. T. "Taiwan." *Studies in Family Planning* 3 (May 1974): 165–69.

Index

Abortion, 256

Administration: colonial period, 101; expenditures of, 230

Age group, and occupation, 83

Agricultural development policy: during colonial period, 35, 250; complimentary inputs in, 64–65; extractive policy in, 175–85; financing by source of funds in, 175–76; income distribution and, 144; industrialization as extension of, 71; Japanese skills in, 65; phases of, 56–57; postwar government policy in, 175–85; postwar infrastructure repair in, 175, 176–77; postwar land reform and, 159–74; technology and, 56–65

Agricultural growth: chemical industry and, 73; during colonial period, 45, 46, 53–56; industrial infrastructures and, 70–71; outputs in, 2; during postrecovery period, 127, 128; sharecropping and, 165; sources of output growth (1951–70) in, 153–55

Agricultural labor, 247; agricultural growth and, 155; during colonial period, 51–52, 93; farm size and, 156; as input, 49, 51–52, 56, 57; labor-intensive techniques and, 158; off-farm economic activity of, 156–57; during postrecovery period, 131, 132, 148; during postwar period, 144, 150–51, 155, 158, 247; postwar surplus of, 157–58, 159; productivity of, 55, 56, 93, 144; research programs and, 178; statistical estimates of, 273; wage indexes for, 336–38

Agricultural Practice Society, 63

Agricultural productivity: during

Ch'ing dynasty, 17; economic development and, 248; estimated annual rates of, 55; indexes of, 54; industrial labor transfers and, 105, 106; land tax and, 45; measures of, 53; postrecovery urbanization and, 140; postwar period and, 155; surplus and, 65–69, 85; technological change and, 56

Agricultural products industry: as export-competing industry, 194–95; export rates for, 199, 210; during postrecovery period, 134; wholesale prices (1960–71) for, 364

Agricultural sector: animal husbandry in, 47; annual net migration in, 158; annual growth rates of main components in, 147–48; assets distribution in, 143–44; capital formation in, 233–35; Cheng administration and, 10; during Ch'ing dynasty, 16–17; during colonial period, 28, 40, 41–69, 91–92, 148; credit cooperatives and, 63–64; cumulative changes in, 248; during Dutch period, 9; early settlements and, 8; economic development and, 248; economic integration and, 29; employment in, 82; fertilizer imports for, 133; foreign aid and, 113, 114; future trends in, 256–57; gross domestic product (1951–72) and, 302–04; growing season in, 1; households distribution in, 42–43; indexes for production (1946–74) in, 262, 340–46; industrial employment and, 80, 83; industrialization and, 145, 181, 195; inputs to, 49–53; insect damage in, 152; land reform and, see Land reform; manufactured consumption goods and, 66; mid-

443

444

Index

Agricultural sector (*continued*)
*1960*s period, 107; occupational distribution in, 324–26; outputs and inputs (*1910–42*) in, 50; outputs and inputs (*1951–70*) in, 152; postrecovery GDP and, 129, 130; postrecovery period and, 122, 123, 133, 140, 147–85; postwar period and, 104, 105–06, 149–53, 187, 188, 233–35, 247; prices indexes (*1952–74*) for, 347; real wage index in, 91–92; relative prices and output in, 49; rural framework for, 42–45; savings in, 84–85; statistical estimates for, 264, 275–78; supply function for, 48–49; technology in, 100; urbanization and, 140; working capital in, 151–53. *See also specific crops*
Agricultural Small Society, 63
Agricultural surplus: annual averages (*1911–40*) for, 67; definition of, 65; industrial development and, 85
Ahluwalia, Montek S., 143
Aid. *See* Foreign aid
Air pollution, 230
Alcohol industry, 30, 73, 86
Aluminum industry, 74–75
Ammonium sulfate fertilizer, 60–61, 153; import substitution policies in, 188, 189; rice barter system and, 181, 182, 184
Amoy (China), 13, 21
Amoy Chamber of Commerce, 21
Animal husbandry, 47
Anping (Taiwan), 13, 24
Apparel industry, 79, 200, 201, 211
Army, 107
Asia: economic growth in, 123; income distribution in, 144–45; Western exports to, 73

Bag manufacturing, 47
Balance of payments: export performance and, 200; import substitution policy and, 193–94; *1924–39* period, 397–400; for *1950–68* period, 401–07; postwar period, 106; statistical estimates of, 281
Bamboo cane, 58
Bamboo products industry, 79
Bananas, 153, 364

Banking institutions: colonial development of, 29; gross domestic product and, 302–04; lending and deposit rate ceilings in, 243–44; occupational distribution in, 324–26; postrecovery GDP and, 129, 130; during postwar period, 104, 112; rural credit and, 64, 179–80; savings and, 88, 244–45; statistical estimates in, 165
Bank of Taiwan, 112, 244, 279
Bankruptcies, 244
Barclay, George W., 83, 268
Bean imports, 133
Beverage industry, 201, 202, 208, 209
Bicycles, 98–99, 188, 189, 227, 229
Birth control programs, 146, 256
Birth rates; during colonial period, 26; family planning and, 138; future trends in, 255; for *1905–73* period, 313–14; population estimates and, 270; postrecovery period and, 135
Black markets, 255
Bonds, 84, 162, 166
Brown rice production, 17, 96
Buck, John L., 68
Building materials, 374
Business income tax, 240

Calcium superphosphate fertilizer, 60–61
Caloric intake: during colonial period, 95, 96–97; daily availability of, 320; during postwar period, 229
Camphor and camphor oil exports, 30
Canada, 252, 253
Canning industry, 86
Capital: during Ch'ing dynasty, 12, 13; during colonial period, 29, 35, 36, 83–89; distribution (*1929*) of, 86–87; Japanese ownership of, 86–88; manufacturing output growth and, 220–21; during postrecovery period, 86–88, 124, 125, 143; during postwar period, 103, 106, 214–20, 221; tea exports and, 21; trade and, 249. *See also* Fixed capital; Working capital
Capital formation: by economic sector, 233–35; foreign aid and, 111, 115; gross national (*1951–72*), 296–98; national differentiated from

Economic Growth Center Book Publications

Werner Baer, *Industrialization and Economic Development in Brazil* (1965).

Werner Baer and Isaac Kerstenetzky, eds., *Inflation and Growth in Latin America* (1964).

Bela A. Balassa, *Trade Prospects for Developing Countries* (1964). Out of print.

Albert Berry and Miguel Urrutia, *Income Distribution in Colombia* (1976).

Thomas B. Birnberg and Stephen A. Resnick, *Colonial Development: An Econometric Study* (1975).

Benjamin I. Cohen, *Multinational Firms and Asian Exports* (1975).

Carlos F. Díaz Alejandro, *Essays on the Economic History of the Argentine Republic* (1970).

Robert Evenson and Yoav Kislev, *Agricultural Research and Productivity* (1975).

John C. H. Fei and Gustav Ranis, *Development of Labor Surplus Economy: Theory and Policy* (1964).

Gerald K. Helleiner, *Peasant Agriculture, Government, and Economic Growth in Nigeria* (1966).

Samuel P. S. Ho, *Economic Development of Taiwan, 1860–1970* (1978).

Lawrence R. Klein and Kazushi Ohkawa, eds., *Economic Growth: The Japanese Experience since the Meiji Era* (1968).

Paul W. Kuznets, *Economic Growth and Structure in the Republic of Korea* (1977).

A. Lamfalussy, *The United Kingdom and the Six* (1963). Out of print.

Markos J. Mamalakis, *The Growth and Structure of the Chilean Economy: From Independence to Allende* (1976).

Markos J. Mamalakis and Clark W. Reynolds, *Essays on the Chilean Economy* (1965).

Donald C. Mead, *Growth and Structural Change in the Egyptian Economy* (1967).

Richard Moorsteen and Raymond P. Powell, *The Soviet Capital Stock* (1966).

Douglas S. Paauw and John C. H. Fei, *The Transition in Open Dualistic Economies: Theory and Southeast Asian Experience* (1973).

Howard Pack, *Structural Change and Economic Policy in Israel* (1971).

Frederick L. Pryor, *Public Expenditures in Communist and Capitalist Nations* (1968).

Gustav Ranis, ed., *Government and Economic Development* (1971).

Clark W. Reynolds, *The Mexican Economy: Twentieth-Century Structure and Growth* (1970).

Lloyd G. Reynolds, *Image and Reality in Economic Development* (1977).

Lloyd G. Reynolds, ed., *Agriculture in Development Theory* (1975).

Lloyd G. Reynolds and Peter Gregory, *Wages, Productivity, and Industrialization in Puerto Rico* (1965).

Donald R. Snodgrass, *Ceylon: An Export Economy in Transition* (1966).